# An Approach to
# Professional Cookery

# An Approach to
# Professional Cookery

## Henry F. Wood MHCI

*Principal Lecturer in Professional Cookery and
Food Administration at Brighton Technical College
and examiner in cookery to the City and Guilds of
London Institute*

**HODDER AND STOUGHTON**
LONDON SYDNEY AUCKLAND TORONTO

# Introduction

ISBN 0 340 14793 8

First published 1972
Reprinted (with revisions) 1976

Printed in Great Britain for
Hodder and Stoughton Educational,
a division of Hodder and Stoughton Ltd, London
by Hazell Watson & Viney Ltd, Aylesbury, Bucks

In compiling this book, I hope to meet the requirements of younger people, particularly students, entering the catering industry. The contents cover all aspects of professional cookery needed for those taking Higher and Ordinary Diploma Courses, and college, City and Guilds and other courses.

While many changes are taking place in patterns of eating, and new food preparation techniques are being employed, the best methods of cookery still require a good basic knowledge of traditional methods of cookery. Information and recipes given here, while generally based on the traditional kitchen, meet the requirements of first class modern trade cookery, although the student should realise that there are other methods in use.

Cookery is not only an art; it forms a part of good living to be appreciated by all. To tempt people to eat, food must not only be correctly prepared, but served with the best presentation. Service and presentation, points so often overlooked, are a particular feature of this book.

In the recipes I have given quantities in British units for eight portions, and in metric units for ten. Sauces are in pints and litres.

Finally, I would like to pay tribute to my colleagues at Brighton for research assistance during the preparation of this book.

H.F.W.

# Contents

# General Section

# General Section

## THE PRINCIPLES OR METHODS OF COOKERY AND RELATED FACTS

Various methods of cookery are used to change raw foods, by physical and chemical processes, into attractive dishes or accompaniments and, further, to ensure that they are made digestible and safe to eat, without danger from bacteria, etc.

The methods selected may be used not only to obtain variety, but also to safeguard the shape or composition of the foods used.

---

### VARIOUS METHODS USED IN COOKERY

| | |
|---|---|
| 1 Poaching | 7 Steaming |
| 2 Boiling | 8 Grilling |
| 3 Stewing | 9 Baking |
| 4 Roasting | 10 Frying (deep) |
| 5 Pot roasting (poêlé) | 11 Frying (shallow) |
| 6 Braising | 12 In a paper casing (en papillote) |

### Poaching

Poaching is generally applied to foods of a delicate texture, fish in particular, in order to retain a desired shape. Most fruits, because they contain a considerable amount of acid, are poached to prevent 'blowing' or loss of shape.

Liquid is generally sparingly used in poaching (except when poaching eggs– see recipe) and it may be water, stock or a syrup. The liquid is gently raised to boiling point if it contains food or, alternatively, it is brought to boiling point and the food then added. In both cases only sufficient heat is then used to maintain a temperature of around 93–97°C (200–206°F) i.e. just below boiling point. Cooking may take place on the stove or in the lower part of an oven, according to the recipe.

### Boiling

The use of this method varies according to the foods to be cooked.

#### VEGETABLES

After preparation, vegetables grown above the ground, i.e. the green varieties, are placed into plenty of boiling salt-water (ratio 8–10 parts water to 1 part food), reboiled rapidly, and then, after all scum has been removed to prevent discolouration, allowed to boil steadily until cooked.

Vegetables grown beneath the ground (i.e. the root varieties) are placed, after preparation, in sufficient cold water to cover them. When boiling point is reached, all scum is removed and the necessary amount of salt is added. They are then allowed to boil steadily until cooked, according to the recipe.

#### MEAT

Salted or pickled meats are placed in cold water and brought to boiling point, then refreshed to extract any excessive salt. They are then reset to boil in clean cold water, and, when boiling, the scum is removed and garnish is added, according to the recipe.

Joints or cuts of meat are placed into boiling water to seal the pores in order to help retain the natural juices; all scum should be removed as it rises. Seasoning, aromats and vegetable garnishes are then added, as per recipe.

In both of the above cases, all fat should be removed from the cooking liquid to prevent any unpleasant flavour.

When boiling, the heat should be reduced to allow the liquid to simmer.

To allow for combination of age, grades, quality, etc. of meat, guides to cooking times are given with the individual recipes.

#### POULTRY

The prepared poultry is covered with cold water then brought to boiling point, all scum being removed as it rises. Seasoning, aromats and vegetable garnishes are then added. Cooking times are quoted in the recipes.

#### FISH

Whole fish are covered with a cold cooking liquor dependent on the type of fish: i.e. salmon in a court-bouillon, large white fish in water, or water and milk, containing aromats, salt and lemon juice. The liquid is raised gently to boiling point, the scum removed and the liquid allowed to simmer for the cooking period.

Cuts of fish are placed into the boiling liquid suitable for the type of fish. This seals the natural juices into the fish and prevents excessive loss of albumen, giving a better presentation when cooked. When reboiling, all scum should be removed from the liquid and the temperature reduced to simmering point.

## Stewing

Stewing is generally applied to the more fibrous types of meat unsuitable for roasting, pot roasting, grilling or braising.

Sufficient liquid, which is sometimes previously thickened, i.e. a sauce, is used to cover the food which is then cooked in a covered pan on the stove or in the lower part of the oven.

In other cases, the meat may first be fried to colour and seal, then, after a thickening agent, e.g. flour, has been added, it is moistened with stock and cooked in the oven.

After boiling, the scum is removed, the utensil is covered and then maintained at simmering temperature.

Nutritionally, this is a good method of cooking since it retains the full flavour of the meat or poultry within the liquid, which is itself served as part of the dish.

This method is also used in certain fish and vegetable dishes but is better described in the individual recipes rather than in general terms.

## Roasting

Originally, roasting was carried out by brushing the seasoned meat or poultry with fat, then rotating it on a revolving spit in front of an open fire. During the cooking process, the article was constantly basted with the dripping from the tray situated beneath and this helped to give a very fine moist flavouring to the food. The modern electric version of the spit is used in some speciality restaurants. However, most roasting today is carried out in the oven. The meat, poultry or game, after seasoning, is placed in a roasting tray and well covered with clean fat. Joints of meat are usually placed on a trivet if small in size, larger pieces being placed on bones from the meat or on thickly sliced carrots and onions. This prevents the meat from becoming immersed in the fat which would cause frying to form a crust around the meat.

When starting to roast, a high temperature is used to set and seal the pores of the meat or poultry to retain the natural juices. After 15–20 minutes, the temperature is lowered for the remainder of the cooking period. During cooking, the meat, poultry or game is turned and basted with the fat in the tray to retain a moist surface and to give flavour.

The reduction of the oven temperature is carried out on the following basis: the larger the article being roasted, the lower the temperature used.

GUIDANCE CHART FOR ROASTING TIMES

| Beef | 15–20 minutes setting time |
| | plus 15 minutes per lb (30 minutes per kg) |
| Lamb | 15–20 minutes setting time |
| | plus 20 minutes per lb (45 minutes per kg) |
| Mutton | 20 minutes setting time |
| | plus 20–25 minutes per lb (45–55 minutes per kg) |
| Veal | 20 minutes setting time |
| | plus 25 minutes per lb (55 minutes per kg) |
| Pork | 25 minutes setting time |
| | plus 30 minutes per lb (65 minutes per kg) |

Due to their considerable fluctuation in size, poultry and game are dealt with under the appropriate recipes.
*Note.* Where certain joints of meat have a stuffing placed in the centre, the cooking time needs to be increased by approximately 5 minutes per lb (10 minutes per kg).

The method of roasting vegetables is described in the appropriate recipes.

## Pot Roasting (poêlé)

This is a very fine method of cooking since it retains all the natural juices of the meat or poultry, which are enhanced by the flavour of the vegetables used. With the condensation produced during the cooking process, the liquor produces a highly flavoured glaze around the meat or poultry. The juices produced during cooking also form part of the gravy or sauce to be served.

A braising pan or casserole with a tight-fitting lid is used for pot roasting. The pan is lined at the bottom with a bed of roots, the seasoned meat or poultry is placed on top, basted with butter, then tightly covered. The pan is heated on top of the stove for a few minutes, then placed in the centre of the oven. During cooking, the meat or poultry should be turned over a few times and well basted. 10–15 minutes before cooking is finished, the cover should be removed to colour the meat very lightly to improve its presentation. Temperatures and approximate cooking times are given in the recipes.

## Braising

Braising is a form of cookery used to cook many foods of a fibrous nature while retaining the natural juices. Very lean meat is sometimes 'larded' for braising, and in some cases marinaded in vegetables and wine.

The meat is fried on top of the stove to seal the pores and to colour it; it is then placed into a braising pan on a fried bed of roots. When other foods, such as sweetbreads, vegetables, fish etc. are braised, neither the bed of roots nor the food to be cooked are coloured. A moistening of stock, thickened gravy or a sauce is then added and a tight-fitting cover is applied. During the latter stages of braising meat, the cover is removed to allow the meat to be basted with the adjusted sauce to form a glazed surface.

Braising is particularly suitable for joints of meat slightly below the quality required for roasting.

## Steaming

Commercially, this form of cookery is carried out in a steaming oven, which is an enclosed space supplied with steam under pressure either directly or by means of a heated water tank below. The pressure is generally from 5 lb per square inch upwards.

A moist form of heat is produced, so such articles as puddings, sponges, etc. need to be well protected from condensation, which would allow moisture to enter the food, by greased greaseproof paper.

Steaming is particularly suitable for the cooking of certain vegetables when they are required whole, e.g. potatoes for sauté.

## Grilling

Grilling is a quick method of cookery widely used in à la carte menus. All meat, poultry and certain types of fish cooked by this method must be of prime quality to allow an acceptable cooked article of food to be produced in a short time.

Many types of grills, using a variety of fuels, are in use today. True grilling is carried out by brushing the prepared and seasoned food with oil. Fish is lightly floured first to give a dry surface which will accept the oil and assist colouring. The food to be grilled is then placed on the hot greased grill bars over a clear charcoal or coke fire. It is then moved about the grill and turned to give the grill markings on both sides and, if necessary, moved to a less hot part of the grill for further cooking.

Some modern grills are heated from underneath by gas or electric elements, which enable a grilling process to be carried out. However, the finished article of food lacks the grilled flavour imparted by charcoal or coke.

A salamander is also used, particularly for grilling prepared foods such as tomatoes, mushrooms, etc. which are cooked on trays. The heat, from gas or electric elements comes from above.

When other foods, i.e. meat, fish, etc., are 'grilled' under a salamander, the grill bar markings are generally simulated by marking with a hot iron bar prior to cooking.

There are a few types of grills in use today which are virtually two serrated metal plates heated by electric elements, for cooking above and beneath at the same time. These are most suitable for limited quantities of catering, as in a snack bar, for example.

## Baking

This process of cooking is generally effected by dry heat within an oven heated by gas, electric elements or oil.

In the oven, various foods or food mixtures produce a certain amount of moisture which is turned to steam by the heat. This steam then moderates the heat and gives certain desired effects. In the baking of bread and roll doughs, additional steam is sometimes injected into the oven for this purpose.

In conventional ovens, the temperature used, together with the position within the oven of the foods being baked, brings about certain effects. For instance, where 'rising', colouring or setting into a required shape are required, the centre to top positions of the oven are used. Where an article needs to be cooked for a reasonable length of time, the lower part of the oven is used to give a gentler heat. In general, the temperature of most conventional ovens will vary 5–10°C (10–18°F) throughout the oven, with the lower temperature towards the bottom. This temperature fluctuation does not take place in a forced-air (convection) oven, however, because of the continuous circulation of the heat around the oven when the fan is in motion.

## Frying (deep)

This method is carried out using either a specially built deep fryer heated by gas or electric elements, or a friture.

Some deep fryers contain a cool zone, where the oil or clarified fat remains at a lower temperature. The advantage of this is that particles of food, especially breadcrumbs, fall to the bottom of the 'cool zone', thus preventing the appearance of the food being deep fried from being spoiled by coming into contact with burned particles.

If a friture is used for frying, it should be adequate in size for the type of food being fried and should never be more than half full as the moisture content of the food causes the level of the frying medium to rise rapidly.

At all times, the articles being fried should be within a frying basket or on a frying grill so that they can be removed temporarily from the fat. Alternatively, a frying-spider may be used in certain instances.

The frying medium may be oil (corn, cotton or tea seed) or a first class clarified fat.

The 'life' of oil or fat used for deep frying is governed by the periods of time it is used at high temperatures, i.e. when it is smoking, particularly when unnecessarily so. The more these high temperatures are used, the quicker the oil or fat becomes darker in colour and thickens by adulteration. It should be strained after use and replaced when the colour has darkened to the point of affecting the desired golden-brown crisp finish on the food.

Deep frying commences at a temperature around 140°C (280°F) at which point the article of food will begin to move in the frying medium without dropping to the bottom.

The temperatures used vary considerably, according to the thickness of food to be fried and whether it is raw or cooked. The following temperatures are given for guidance.

Cooked food preparations, i.e. croquettes, médaillon, etc. are fried at a temperature of 180°C (360°F). Care should be taken never to try to cook too many articles at any one time. Correctly used, this temperature will, where applicable, immediately seal the coating of egg or batter and thus prevent the oil or fat from entering the food. Where too low a temperature is used, or where too many articles of food are cooked together, the reduced temperature allows the oil or fat to enter the food raising the temperature of the moisture contained in the food to boiling point and causing the article being fried to distort from its original shape; the food will then be spoiled.

Raw foods that are not more than 6 mm thick, i.e. fillets of many fish, are fried at 180°C (360°F). A temperature around 160°C (320°F) is used to fry whole fish or thick cuts, which require 7–10 minutes cooking time.

Certain mixtures containing raw and cooked foods, i.e. choux paste, require a temperature of around 160°C (320°F) to allow the mixture to cook through without becoming too dark.

Due to the thickness they are cut, many fried potatoes are fried twice. The first frying, 'blanching', is carried out at 140–150°C (280–300°F) to allow the potato to cook without colouring. When required for service, they are refried at 180°C (360°F) to colour them and give them a crisp finish.

Wet articles of food to be deep fried should always be well drained and dried in a cloth before frying, to prevent the frying medium overflowing and catching fire.

### Frying (shallow-sauté)

Various fats or oil are used in shallow frying and the method employed varies according to the type of dish to be prepared. For example, where the article of food is fried, with garnish placed alongside and possibly surrounded with a sauce or gravy, the presentation side is the first side to be placed into the heated fat or oil, in a sauté or frying pan; the food is then cooked on both sides to the desired colour.

Where various cuts of prime meat or poultry are cooked by this method, only a sauté pan is used. Generally, after cooking, a fluid (wine, stock, sauce) is added to déglacé the pan, i.e. to recover essences or juices left behind from the cooking process and, in many cases, a garnish and sauce is then combined with the food. Only in these cases, not when the food is cooked within a liquid, can the word 'sauté' be used as a prefix to the name of the dish.

In certain vegetable dishes, the fat or oil is heated in the frying or sauté pan and the pan is one-third filled with the food. The food should then be allowed to colour and be tossed over during the cooking process.

When shallow-frying fish, oil used alone or with a little added butter will give the best results. After seasoning, the fish is coated with the minimum of flour to give a dry surface to help colour and to improve presentation. Where fillets or cuts from fillets are used, the 'cut' side, i.e. the side nearest to the bone, is cooked first.

*Note.* Fat or oil should be strained after use and the pan be cleaned before being used again.

### 'En Papillote'

This is a traditional method of cookery where the article of food is placed inside oiled greaseproof paper, constructed according to the shape of the food. It is generally applied to certain fish and cuts of prime quality meat. Meat, when cooked by this process, is set rapidly by shallow frying, without cooking, to seal the natural juices.

Generally a garnish is placed on the oiled greaseproof paper, which is wrapped round the article of food and the edges sealed by folding them over. The bag is then placed on the service dish and cooked in the oven. The steam created within the paper container will make the top surface of the paper rise.

## OVEN TEMPERATURE CHART

| Definition | Degrees Farenheit | Degrees Celsius | Gas regulo 1–9 |
|---|---|---|---|
| Very slow (cool) | 200 | 93–95 | 1 |
| Slow | 250–300 | 120–148 | 2–3 |
| Moderate | 300–350 | 148–180 | 3–3/4 |
| Moderately hot | 350–400 | 180–205 | 3/4–4 |
| Hot | 425–475 | 218–245 | 5–8 |
| Very hot | 475–500 | 245–260 | 8–9 |

## SMALL QUANTITY MEASURES

| Level spoonful | Tea | Dessert | Table |
|---|---|---|---|
| Chopped parsley | 2 g | 3 g | 5 g |
| Baking powder | 3 g | 7 g | 15 g |
| Spices, salt | 3 g | 6 g | 12 g |
| Pepper, dried powders | 3 g | 6 g | 12 g |
| Arrowroot, cornflour | 3 g | 7 g | 13 g |
| Custard powder | 3 g | 7 g | 13 g |
| Olive oil | 3½ g | 8 g | 21 g |
| Tomato purée | 4 g | 11 g | 22 g |
| Tomato ketchup | 4 g | 11 g | 22 g |

9 level teaspoons of salt, pepper, spices, baking powder, cornflour = 1 oz (28 g).

## METRICATION – WORKABLE EQUIVALENTS

| Oz/fl. oz | Grammes/ml | Oz/fl. oz | Grammes/ml |
|---|---|---|---|
| ½ | 15 | 11 | 310 |
| 1 | 30 | (¾ lb) 12 | 340 |
| 2 | 55 | 13 | 370 |
| 3 | 85 | 14 | 395 |
| (¼ lb) 4 | 110 | 15 (¾ pt) | 425 |
| 5 (¼ pt) | 140 | (1 lb) 16 | 450 |
| 6 | 170 | 17 | 480 |
| 7 | 200 | 18 | 510 |
| (½ lb) 8 | 225 | 19 | 540 |
| 9 | 255 | (1¼ lb) 20 (1 pt) | 560 |
| 10 (½ pt) | 280 | | |

*Note (a) In the recipes, where for example 2 oz (70 g) of butter is called for, the imperial quantity refers to the preparation of 8 portions, the metric to 10 couverts.*

*(b) Dimensions of cuts, equipment, etc. are given in mm based on a conversion of 1 inch = 25 mm.*

## CULINARY TERMS

| | |
|---|---|
| Abats | Offal (liver, heart, kidneys, head, feet) |
| Aiguillette | Long thin cuts of meat, game, etc. |
| Aile | Wing portion of chicken or game |
| à la (mode) | In the style of |
| à la carte | Dishes prepared to order |
| à la française | In the French style |
| Aloyau | Sirloin of beef (on the bone) |
| Appareil | A mixture of various commodities |
| Aromates | Herbs, roots, spices to produce flavour |
| Arroser | To baste (applied in roasting) |
| assaisonner | To apply seasoning |
| Assorti | Assortment of |
| au beurre | With butter |
| au four | In the oven (applied to baking) |
| au gratin | Sprinkled with cheese or crumbs and melted butter, and coloured golden brown |
| Bain-marie | (a) A container of boiling water in which to keep foods hot without burning |
| | (b) A container, generally shallow, used in cooking foods to prevent burning or overheating |
| | (c) Various sized deep containers for storing soups, sauces, etc. |
| Beignets | Any type of fritters |
| Beurre fondu | Melted butter |

| | |
|---|---|
| Beurre manié | A mixture of butter and flour used as a thickening |
| Beurre noir | A very dark brown butter (almost black) |
| Beurre noisette | A light nut brown butter |
| Blanc | (a) Applied to the white flesh of poultry |
| | (b) A cooking liquid lightly thickened with liquid flour and water; lemon juice is added to help keep the product white |
| Blanchir | To blanch (used in different ways) |
| | (a) by plunging in boiling water to release the skin (e.g. tomatoes) |
| | (b) by plunging in boiling water to set and retain the colour of vegetables |
| | (c) to remove impurities and to whiten when applied to poultry, meat and bones |
| | (d) to partially cook to an extent to make foods pliable |
| | (e) to cook by deep frying without colouring (e.g. potatoes) |
| Bouchée | A puff pastry case of varying size; when filled, used in hors d'oeuvre or as a course within a menu |
| Bouquet garni | A bundle of herbs, thyme, bay leaves tied within an outer layer of leek and celery |
| Brunoise | A very small dice |

7

| | |
|---|---|
| Canapé | A base of bread or toast, with various hot or cold foods placed on top |
| Carte du jour | Menu of the day |
| Casserole | An earthenware fireproof receptacle with fitted cover |
| Chapelure | Crumbs of dried bread |
| Chauffant | Container of boiling water for reheating foods |
| Chinois | Conical shaped strainer |
| Clarify | To clear, as in rendering of fat or in making of consommé or aspic jelly |
| Clouté | Studded (e.g. cloves inserted in an onion) |
| Cocotte | A fireproof dish of porcelain or earthenware |
| Concasser | To coarsely chop foods |
| Consommé | A clear soup |
| Cordon | A ribbon or thread of sauce |
| Couper | To cut |
| Coupe | An individual stem-type cup |
| Court-bouillon | A prepared cooking liquid used for fish, brains, etc. |
| Crêpe | Pancake |
| Croûton | Various shaped pieces of bread, jelly, etc. |
| Croquette | A cylindrical shape of prepared food. Egg, crumbed and deep fried |
| Cuisse | The leg part of poultry and game |
| Dariole | A tapered sided mould |
| Darne | A slice of fish on the bone (round) |
| Déglacer | To moisten a pan with liquid, to release the sediment from cooking for use within a sauce or gravy |
| Dégraisser | To remove fat from the surface of a liquid |
| Demi-glace | A refined brown sauce |
| Drain | To remove the fluid, generally in a perforated container |
| Dilute | (a) to add liquid to thin<br>(b) To dissolve a powder in liquid |
| Doily | A fancy cut round paper |
| Dish paper | An oval cut paper with decorative edge |
| Duxelle | A cooked mixture of finely chopped shallot and mushroom |
| Egg wash | Beaten egg |

| | |
|---|---|
| Émincer | To cut in small pieces |
| Escalope | A thin slice |
| Espagnole | A basic brown sauce |
| Étuver | To cover and slowly cook in natural juices extracted or with a minimum of moistening (à l'étuvée) |
| Farce | A filling – stuffing – forcemeat |
| Farcir | To insert a filling or stuffing into an article |
| Flake | To break or cut into slivers. In fish, to separate the flesh by using the natural divisions |
| Flan | A shallow pastry case filled with various mixtures of food |
| Fleurons | Puff paste crescents or 'flowers' |
| Friture | A pan used for deep frying |
| Fumé | Smoked |
| Garnir | To add other foods to a prepared dish or in the course of preparation |
| Glace | A frozen sweet mixture of egg or fruit base, i.e. ice cream |
| Glace | A concentrated form of various stocks, i.e. glace de viande (meat glaze) |
| Glace à rafraîchir | Ice used for chilling or freezing |
| Glacer | (a) To freeze<br>(b) To colour the top surface of food, often sauces, under a salamander, e.g. filet de sole Bercy<br>(c) To incorporate the natural juices with other additives around foods to form a shiny flavoured coating<br>(d) By various methods in pastry work, to impart a shiny finish |
| Gratiner | To colour food golden brown under a salamander or in an oven, after sprinkling with cheese or breadcrumbs (see 'au gratin') |
| Haché | Finely chopped |
| Hors d'oeuvre | A single or variety of foods, served at the commencement of a meal to stimulate appetite |

8

| | | | |
|---|---|---|---|
| Jardinière | Vegetables cut into bâtons, forming part of a dish or garnish | Proving | The active expansion of yeast within fermented paste or dough. |
| Julienne | Cut into very fine strips | Pulse | Any vegetable, grown in a pod or casing in the dried preserved form |
| Jus-lié | A thickened gravy | | |
| | | Réchauffer | To reheat |
| Lardons | Small pieces of bacon cut into bâtons | Réduire | To reduce in quantity a liquid of sauce to thicken, concentrate, or improve the flavour |
| Liaison | Used to thicken, bind or enrich | | |
| Macédoine | Vegetables or fruits cut into dice and mixed | Refresh | To make cold under running water |
| Macérer | To soak fruits in liqueur or wine | Rissoler | To toss or move in hot fat to give colour |
| Marinade | A mixture of various seasonings, herbs and spices with vinegar/wine/oil/water used to flavour and tenderise | Roux | A mixture of cooked fat and flour used as a thickening. |
| Marmite, petite – | (a) Stockpot  (b) An earthenware pot used for cooking and serving particular soups | Sabayon | A mixture of yolks of egg and liquid cooked to the smooth texture of cream |
| Menu | A list of dishes offered | Salamander | An appliance heated from above; used for cooking and colouring foods |
| Mignonnette | Coarsely milled pepper | Salpicon | A mixture of diced foods |
| Mirepoix | A roughly diced mixture of carrot, onion, celery, used for flavouring | Sauté | See Principles of cookery for how applied |
| | | Seasoned flour | Flour with the addition of salt |
| Mise en place | Basic preparations made in advance | Shred | To thinly slice |
| Mouiller | To moisten foods to be cooked | Singe | (a) To colour lightly in an oven  (b) To remove the hair from poultry, etc. by the use of a flame |
| Moulin à poivre | A mill for grinding pepper | | |
| Napper | To cover or mask with a sauce, aspic jelly, etc. | Strain | To separate the liquid from food by the use of various equipment |
| | | Suer (sweat) | To place food in a covered pan with fat to reheat or lightly cook or finish cooking |
| Paner | To pass through flour, beaten egg and crumbs prior to shallow or deep frying | Suprême | A choice cut, e.g. Suprême de volaille (wing and breast) |
| Parer | To trim | | |
| Paupiette | A rolled, lightly flattened strip of fish or meat enrobing a forcemeat or stuffing | Table d'hôte | A set menu at a fixed price |
| Paysanne | A thin cut approximately 12 mm in diameter if round or 12 mm × 12 mm across | Timbale | A service dish in two parts, (a) base (b) insert |
| | | Tourner | To prepare food to a defined regular shape (mainly applied to vegetables) |
| Persillé | Finished with or incorporating chopped parsley e.g. Pommes persillées | Tranche | A slice |
| Piquant | An induced, sharp acid flavour | Tronçon | A slice of fish on the bone (flat) |
| Piquer | To insert strips of fat, bacon, ham, truffle, etc. in fish, meat or poultry. | Velouté | A basic sauce or a thick soup of a creamy nature |
| Plat du jour | A dish specially featured on a day | | |
| Printanière | A garnish of spring vegetables | Vol-au-vent | A large pastry case for one or more covers |

# HERBS – SPICES – SEASONINGS

**Allspice**

The fruit of a West Indian tree; about the size of a small pea, gathered when fully grown and nearly ripe, then sun dried. The name is given because of the resemblance in flavour to a mixture of all spices, particularly cinnamon, nutmeg and cloves.

**Angelica – Angélique**

An aromatic plant, native to the Alps and other parts of Europe. Commercially, the young tender leaf stalks are candied. Used mainly for decorating purposes and flavouring.

**Aniseed – Anis**

The small dried seeds of an annual plant. Grown mainly in countries around the Mediterranean, Switzerland and Germany. Used in medicine and as a flavouring in sweets and syrups.

**Basil – Basilic**

A highly aromatic sweet herb, native to India. The flavour somewhat resembles that of the clove. Mountain mint is sometimes called by this name.

**Bay leaves – Laurier**

Are aromatic and come from the sweet bay or laurel tree. The dried leaves are powerful in flavour. Used for flavouring soups, stews, pickles and some fish dishes.

**Borage – Bourrache**

The tender young leaves are used to flavour certain salads and to flavour fruit cups, etc.

**Capers – Câpres**

The picked flower buds of the caper bush. After drying, they are preserved in vinegar or a brine solution. Used mainly in hors d'oeuvre.

**Caraway seeds – Cumin**

Very small dark-brown seeds of an aromatic plant that grows wild in certain European countries and the USA. Used mainly in bakery and confectionery and in flavouring liqueurs.

**Celery seeds**

Seeds of the celery plant, generally used in the form of celery salt.

**Chervil – Cerfeuil**

An aromatic herb cultivated in most temperate climates. The small leaves are used as a garnish in soups and as a flavouring in salads. Used in cold buffet decoration.

**Chilli – Poivrons – Piment**

The small fruit pods of a variety of pungent capsicum plants. Used in the fresh and dried form; in the ground form they are known as cayenne pepper.

**Chives – Ciboulette**

In appearance, like very young spring onions. Used as a flavouring in salads, soups and various dishes.

**Cinnamon – Cannelle**

The inner bark of the young wood of the cinnamon tree, native to most of tropical Asia. Used in stick and ground form, mainly in sweet dishes and cakes.

**Cloves – Clou de Girofle**

The dried flower buds of the clove tree. Native to Zanzibar and the East Indies.

**Coriander – Coriandre**

The seed from the coriander plant. Grown in many countries. Used mainly as one of the chief ingredients of curry powder, and as a flavouring in various dishes.

**Fennel – Fenouil**

In appearance somewhat like a squat bulbous celery with bright green top shoots. Possesses a slight aniseed flavour. Used as a vegetable and in salads.

**Garlic – Ail**

A very pungent bulbous plant divided inside the skin into natural sections. The sections are generally referred to as cloves or pods. Used for flavouring soups, stews, sauces and salads.

**Ginger – Gingembre**

The root of a perrenial reed-type plant, producing leafy stems annually. Grown in many tropical countries. Ground, when dried, to a powder which has a very powerful flavour. The young green roots are preserved in syrup or candied.

**Horseradish – Raifort**

A long stem-type root plant scraped into shreds when peeled, and used as a flavouring. Particularly well-known as a condiment to roast beef.

**Mace – Macis**

These are thin red-coloured strips that adhere to the aromatic kernel below the outer casing of the nutmeg, the fruit of a tree found in many tropical countries. These strips are dried and ground to a powder. Possesses a more temperate flavour than nutmeg. Used to flavour many dishes.

**Marjoram – Marjolaine**

An aromatic sweet herb, grown mainly in southern Europe. Used in flavouring soups, stews and stuffings.

**Mint – Menthe**

Grows in most temperate climates. Used in the fresh form as a flavouring and as a garnish in vegetable dishes. Used in the fresh and preserved form for making sauce.

**Mustard – Moutarde**

The seed of the mustard plant. Dried after removal of the oil content, then ground to a fine powder. Used as a flavouring and, when mixed with water, as a condiment (English mustard).

**French mustard – Moutarde française**

The dry mustard powder mixed with salt, sugar, vinegar or wine, and spices.

**Nutmeg – Noix de Muscade**

The aromatic kernel of the fruit of the nutmeg tree. Ground, then used as a flavouring, mainly in sweet dishes and cakes.

**Parsley – Persil**

A herb easily grown in any temperate moist climate. Used extensively as a flavouring and for garnishing.

**Pepper – Poivre**

The dried berries of the pepper plant. Black pepper is the whole berry, picked and dried just before ripening occurs.

White pepper is the ripe berry with the outer husk removed, then dried. Used in the whole, crushed or powdered form as a seasoning agent.

**Pepper (Cayenne)**
See Chili.

**Pepper (Paprika) – Paprika**

Produced from the large red sweet peppers grown in Hungary and Spain. Dried and ground.

**Poppy seed – Pavot**

Produce of Holland with small deep blue seeds. Used in bread and confectionery production.

**Rosemary – Romarin**

The leaves of an evergreen plant native to Europe and Asia. Used in flavouring meat and poultry.

**Saffron – Safran**

The orange-red stigmas of the purple autumn crocus. Produced mainly in Spain. Used to flavour rice, fish dishes and particularly pastry buns.

**Sage – Sauge**

The silver-white dried leaves of a shrub. Used for flavouring meat and stuffings.

**Sorrel – Oseille**

This leaf is very similar to the young leaves of summer spinach in appearance. Possesses a distinct sharp flavour. Used in soups.

**Tarragon – Estragon**

A perennial aromatic herb. The small thin green leaves are used in cold buffet decoration. Other uses are as a flavouring in sauces, pickles and for tarragon vinegar.

**Thyme – Thym**

A very small-leaved garden herb. Used to flavour sauces, soups and stews.

**Salt – Sel**

Produced from natural brine springs or from deposits of rock salt.

**Saltpetre – Salpêtre**

A coarse acrid type of salt used with common salt for making brine.

**Turmeric – Safrau des Indes**

Part of the pepper plant, dried and ground to a powder. Used in the production of pickles. Used with ground coriander seeds and other spices to make curry powder.

**Vanilla beans – Vanille**

The fruit of a variety of climbing orchid plants; also produced in essence form. Used in pastry work as a flavouring.

# SEASONS OF FRESH FOODS

The seasons of various fresh foods have been considerably extended during the last decade as a result of the following factors:

1. faster modern refrigerated transportation, and air freight,
2. modern production techniques,
3. supplies from new areas, particularly from developing countries.

---

| Butchers' meat | Viande |
|---|---|
| Beef: all the year | Boeuf |
| Lamb: best in spring and summer | Agneau |
| Mutton: all the year | Mouton |
| Pork: September–end of April | Porc |
| Veal: all the year | Veau |

| Poultry | Volaille |
|---|---|
| Chicken: all the year | Poulet |
| Duck: all the year | Canard |
| Duckling: April, May, June | Caneton |
| Goose: autumn–winter | Oie |
| Gosling: September | Oison |
| Guinea-fowl: all the year | Pintade |
| Spring chicken: spring (cheapest) | Poussin |
| Turkey: all the year | Dinde |

| Game (feathered) | Gibier |
|---|---|
| Capercailzie: July–November | Coq des bois |
| Grouse: 12 August–9 December | Grouse |
| Hazel hen: all the year | Gelinotte |
| Partridge: September–1 February | Perdreau |
| Pheasant: October–1 February | Faisan |
| Ptarmigan: August–December | Ptarmigan |
| Quail: all the year (Egypt) | Caille |
| Snipe: October–March | Bécassine |
| Teal: winter–spring | Sarcelle |
| Wild duck: September–March | Canard sauvage |
| Woodcock: September–March | Bécasse |
| Wood-pigeon: August–March | Pigeon des bois |

| Game (ground) | |
|---|---|
| Hare: August–end of February | Lièvre |
| Rabbit: preferably autumn–spring | Lapin de garonne |
| Venison: male best May–September female best September–January | Venaison |

| Fish | Poisson |
|---|---|
| Barbel: June–March | Barbeau |
| Bream (sea): July–end of December | Brème |
| Brill: August–March | Barbue |
| Cod: best May–February | Cabillaud |
| Dab: July–December | Limande |
| Eel: all the year (poor quality in summer) | Anguille |
| Flounder: January–May | Carrelet |
| Haddock: all the year | Aiglefin |
| Hake: September–February | Merluche |
| Halibut: all the year | Flétan |
| Herring: best September–April | Hareng |
| John Dory: January–July | St Pierre |
| Lemon sole: October–March | Limande |
| Mackerel: late February–August | Maquereau |
| Mullet (red): December–May | Rouget |
| Plaice: best May–January | Plie |
| Salmon: February–September | Saumon |
| Salmon trout: March–September | Truite saumonée |
| Skate: September–May | Raie |
| Smelt: October–May | Éperlan |
| Sole: all year (poor quality in spring) | Sole |
| Sturgeon: December–April | Esturgeon |
| Trout (river): March–October | Truite de rivière |
| Turbot: all the year (best October–April) | Turbot |
| Whitebait: February–15 September | Blanchaille |
| Whiting: August–February best | Merlan |

| Shellfish | Crustacés et mollusques |
|---|---|
| Crab: preferably summer | Crabe |
| Crawfish: January–July | Langouste |
| Crayfish: October–March | Écrevisse |
| Lobster: preferably summer | Homard |
| Mussel: September–May | Moule |
| Oyster: 1 September–30 April | Huître |
| Prawn: September–May | Crevette rose |
| Scallop: September–April | Coquille St Jacques |
| Shrimp: all the year | Crevette grise |
| Snail: September–April | Escargot |

## Vegetables / Légumes

| Vegetables | Légumes |
|---|---|
| Artichoke, globe: summer–autumn best | Artichaut |
| Artichoke, Jerusalem: October–March | Topinambour |
| Asparagus: May–July | Asperges |
| Beetroot: all the year | Betterave |
| Broad bean: July–August | Fève |
| Broccoli: October–April | Brocoli |
| Brussels sprout: October–March | Choux de Bruxelles |
| Cabbage: all the year | Chou |
| Carrot: all the year | Carotte |
| Cauliflower: all the year | Chou-fleur |
| Celeriac: November–February | Céleri-rave |
| Celery: August–March | Céleri |
| Chicory (Belgian): best in winter | Endive |
| Cucumber: best in summer | Concombre |
| Egg-plant: summer, autumn best | Aubergine |
| French bean: May–September | Haricot fin |
| Leek: October–March | Poireau |
| Lettuce: best in summer (available all year) | Laitue |
| Mushroom: all the year | Champignon |
| Onion: all the year | Oignon |
| Parsnip: October–March | Panais |
| Pea: June–September | Petit pois |
| Radish: best in summer | Radis |
| Runner bean: July–October | Haricot vert |
| Salsify: October–February | Salsifis |
| Sea kale: January–March | Chou de mer |
| Shallot: September–February | Échalote |
| Spinach: all the year | Épinards |
| Swede: December–March | Rutabaga |
| Sweetcorn: Autumn | Maïs |
| Tomato: all the year (best summer) | Tomate |
| Turnip: October–March | Navet |
| Vegetable marrow: July–October | Courge |
| Baby vegetable marrow: July–October | Courgette |
| Corn salad: autumn–winter | Mâche |

## Fresh Herbs / Herbes

| Fresh Herbs | Herbes |
|---|---|
| Bay leaf: September | Laurier |
| Borage: March | Bourrache |
| Chervil: spring–summer | Cerfeuil |
| Fennel: March | Fenouil |
| Marjoram: March | Marjolaine |
| Mint: spring–summer | Menthe |
| Parsley: all the year | Persil |
| Rosemary: August | Romarin |
| Sage: April–May | Sauge |
| Savory: March–April | Sarriette |
| Tarragon: January–February | Estragon |
| Thyme: September–November | Thym |

## Fruits / Fruits

| Fruits | Fruits |
|---|---|
| Apple: all the year | Pomme |
| Apricot: May–September | Abricot |
| Blackberry: autumn | Mûre |
| Cherry: May–July | Cerise |
| Cranberry: November–January | Airelle rouge |
| Currants (Black and Red): summer | Groseille |
| Damson: September–October | Prune de Damas |
| Gooseberry: summer | Groseille à maquereau |
| Grapes: all the year | Raisin |
| Greengage: August–September | Reine-claude |
| Medlar: November–January | Nèfle |
| Melon (cantaloup): May–October | Melon |
| Nectarine: June–September | Brugnon |
| Peach: all the year (best June–September) | Pêche |
| Pear: all the year (best autumn–winter) | Poire |
| Pineapple: all the year | Ananas |
| Plum: July–October | Prune |
| Quince: winter | Coing |
| Raspberry: summer | Framboise |
| Rhubarb: January–July | Rhubarbe |
| Strawberry: June–September | Fraise |
| Strawberry: February–May (Kenya and America) | Fraise |

### Varieties of Dessert Apples (English)

| | |
|---|---|
| Beauty of Bath | Cox's Orange Pippin |
| Worcester Pearmain | Orleans Reinette |
| King of the Pippins | Charles Ross |
| Blenheim Orange | Allington Pippin |

### Varieties of Cooking Apples (English)

| | |
|---|---|
| Bramley Seedling | Lane's Prince Albert |
| Wellington | Codling |
| Newton Wonder | |

### Varieties of Dessert Pears (English)

| | |
|---|---|
| Doyenne du Comice | Louise Bonne of Jersey |
| Conference | William |
| Pitmaston Duchess | Beurre Hardy |

# Larder Section

16

# Larder Section

The larder can be regarded as one of the most important sections of the kitchen. It is here that the majority of perishable foods are received and checked for quantity and quality before the correct preparation and storage is effected.

The preparation of these perishables is very highly specialised, particularly when it is related to portion control, and all the skills of the various 'chefs de parties' cannot completely correct any deficiencies in the preparation, which then result in the completed dishes being technically incorrect.

Due to the considerable variety of preparations within this section, each is dealt with under subheadings.

## COLD SAUCES

### 1 Mayonnaise sauce — Sauce mayonnaise

| 1 pint | Ingredients | 1 litre |
| --- | --- | --- |
| 1 pint | olive oil | 1 litre |
| 3 tablespoons (1½ fl. oz) | vinegar | 75 ml |
| 1 dessertspoon | boiling water | 10 ml |
| 4 | egg yolks | 7 |
| ¼ level teaspoon | English mustard | 2½ g |
| 1 level teaspoon | salt | 5 g |
| ¼ level teaspoon | ground white pepper | 1 g |

#### Method

1. Place the yolks in a 2-pint basin; whisk in the mustard, salt, pepper and one-third of the vinegar.
2. Add the oil very slowly to one side of the yolks, whisking well to thicken (to form a 'core'). Then work into the other side of the yolks, after approximately each 2 fl. oz of oil has been added. This will correct any curdling tendency.
3. When half the oil has been absorbed, add another one-third of the vinegar.
4. When all the oil has been absorbed, add the remainder of the vinegar and the boiling water. The water takes away the oily appearance.
5. When the sauce needs thinning for any purpose, taste and adjust with a little more vinegar. If the sauce is sharp enough, adjust with boiling water.
6. In cooler temperatures (winter), warm the oil a little to make it flow easily. Cold oil, or oil added too quickly, are the main reasons for curdling.

### 2 Andalusian sauce — Sauce andalouse

| 1 pint | Ingredients | 1 litre |
| --- | --- | --- |
| 1 pint | mayonnaise | 1 litre |
| 3 fl. oz | tomato ketchup | 150 ml |
| 2 oz | red pimento (canned) | 100 g |

#### Method

1. Pass half of the pimento through a hair or fine sieve; whisk into the mayonnaise with the ketchup.
2. Cut the remainder of the pimento into 25 mm julienne and add to the sauce.

### 3 Green sauce — Sauce verte

#### Method

1. Blanch in boiling salt water for 3–4 minutes 2 oz per pint (100 g per litre) of well washed spinach, watercress, tarragon and chervil leaves. Refresh and drain.
2. Squeeze out all water thoroughly. Rub through a hair or fine wire sieve.
3. Whisk the mayonnaise on to the purée.

### 4 Tartar sauce — Sauce tartare

| 1 pint | Ingredients | 1 litre |
| --- | --- | --- |
| 1 pint | mayonnaise | 1 litre |
| 3 oz | gherkins | 150 g |
| 1½ oz | capers | 75 g |
| 1 tablespoon | chopped parsley | 15 g |

#### Method

1. Squeeze the vinegar or brine from the capers. Crush the gherkins and chop both together until fine.
2. Add to the mayonnaise with the parsley and mix.

### 5 Rémoulade sauce — Sauce rémoulade

#### Method

1. Add to prepared Tartar sauce 1 teaspoon (1½) French mustard and 2 teaspoons (3) of anchovy essence. Mix well.

## 6 Tyrolese sauce — Sauce tyrolienne

| 1 pint | Ingredients | 1 litre |
|---|---|---|
| 1 pint | mayonnaise | 1 litre |
| 1 oz | finely chopped shallot | 50 g |
| 1 fl. oz | olive oil | 50 ml |
| 2 tablespoons | tomato ketchup | 50 ml |
| 4 oz | tomatoes | 200 g |
| ¼ pod | garlic | ½ pod |

### Method

1. Sweat the shallot in the oil for 6–7 minutes; do not colour.

2. Blanch and skin the tomatoes, cut in halves, remove the seeds and chop roughly.

3. Add the peeled, crushed garlic to the shallots with the tomatoes and ketchup. Cook together for 5 minutes, then reduce to a thick paste, stirring to prevent burning.

4. Pass through a hair or very fine wire sieve.

5. When cold, whisk into mayonnaise.

## 7 Vinegar and oil sauce — Sauce vinaigrette

| 1 pint | Ingredients | 1 litre |
|---|---|---|
| ¾ pint | olive oil | 750 ml |
| ¼ pint | vinegar | 250 ml |
| 3 teaspoons | French mustard | 15 g |
| 2 teaspoons | salt | 10 g |
| ½ teaspoon | ground white pepper | 2½ g |

### Method

1. Whisk all ingredients together before using.

*Note.* Other cold sauces, such as mint, horseradish, etc., are shown under Garnishes and accompaniments where appropriate.

## HORS D'OEUVRE, SINGLE FOOD TYPE

Many hors d'oeuvre dishes consist of one single food, or one single food predominates; these are classified as 'single food hors d'oeuvre'.

The remainder are generally served within a variety of hors d'oeuvre, and the recipes given for this group (36–110) include certain dishes which may also be served on their own; these are marked with an asterisk.

## 8 Avocado pear, Vinaigrette sauce — Poire d'avocat, sauce vinaigrette

| 8 portions | Ingredients | 10 couverts |
|---|---|---|
| 4 | avocado pears | 5 |
| ½ pint | vinaigrette sauce | 350 ml |
| 1 | lettuce, large | 1 |

### Method

1. Trim away the discoloured leaves of lettuce and cut a little away from the root. Separate the leaves, wash well in cold water, and thoroughly dry by shaking in a cloth. Crisp in the refrigerator for 30 minutes.

2. Wash the avocado pears, wipe, then cut in halves lengthways.

3. Twist slightly to separate the halves and remove the hard kernel.

4. Dress the lettuce leaves on an oval silver dish and arrange the pear halves on the lettuce. Chill for 1 hour.

5. Serve the sauce in a sauceboat on an underdish with dishpaper.

## 9 Avocado pear (dancer style) — Poire d'avocat soubrette

| 8 portions | Ingredients as above, plus | 10 couverts |
|---|---|---|
| 4 oz | peeled shrimps | 140 g |
| 2 oz | peeled walnuts | 70 g |
| 1 oz | red pimento | 35 g |
| 2 | hard boiled eggs | 2 |
| 1 tablespoon | chopped parsley | 5 g |
| ¼ teaspoon | seasoning salt | 1 g |
| 1/16 teaspoon | milled pepper | ¼ g |

### Method

1. Prepare as in previous recipe to 3 in method (inclusive).

2. Wash and drain the shrimps. Select one-quarter of the best shrimps for decoration and set aside.

3. Remove the flesh of the pears with a spoon, retaining the casings. Pass the flesh through a coarse sieve.

4. Finely chop the walnuts and pimento. Add the sieved pear and three-quarters of the shrimps; season with a little salt and milled pepper. Mix well with a little of the vinaigrette and replace the mixture level in the casings.

5. Decorate down the centre, lengthways, with a row of shrimps, then on each side with a thin line of sieved white of egg, chopped parsley, and sieved yolk of egg.

6. Chill in a refrigerator for 30 minutes.

7. Dress on an oval flat dish on a base of the lettuce leaves. Serve the remainder of the vinaigrette in a sauce boat.

## 10 Avocado pear and grapefruit
## Poire d'avocat et pamplemousse

| 8 portions | Ingredients | 10 couverts |
|---|---|---|
| 4 | avocado pears | 5 |
| 4 | grapefruit | 5 |
| 8 | cocktail cherries | 10 |
| ½ pint | fresh cream | 350 ml |
| 1 | juice of lemon | 1 |

### Method

1. Wash the pears and peel with a peeler. Cut in halves lengthways and remove the kernel.

2. Cut the halves in half again, across the pear, then lengthways into 16 (20) sections per pear; place to chill in a basin.

3. Prepare the grapefruit as for cocktail (recipe 20) and chill.

4. Divide the fruits equally into 8 (10) cocktail glasses and mask over with the juice. Place a cherry in the centre.

5. Add the strained lemon juice to the cream with a few grains of cayenne pepper and mix.

6. Serve the glasses on a flat dish on a doily, with the acidulated dressing in a sauceboat.

## 11 Caviar
## Caviar

Caviar is the prepared salted eggs that form the roe in sturgeon. The best types are known as Beluga and Sevruga. The caviar is packed in tins and glass jars, and served on crushed ice in a timbale on an underdish with a doily, or inserted into an ice socle (base).

The following garnishes are served: wedges of lemon; sieved hard-boiled egg; chopped onion in small dishes on a flat dish with a doily; half slices of trimmed hot toast and/or blinis in a serviette on a flat dish.

## 12 Small buckwheat pancakes
## Blinis

| 24 pieces | Ingredients | 30 pieces |
|---|---|---|
| 6 oz | buckwheat | 210 g |
| 2 oz | flour (strong) | 70 g |
| 3 (small) | eggs | 3 |
| ½ oz | yeast | 20 g |
| 12 fl. oz | milk | 420 ml |
| pinch | salt, milled pepper | pinch |

### Method

1. Sieve the buckwheat and flour into a basin and make a bay.

2. Dissolve the yeast in half of the tepid milk; pour into the bay. Incorporate a little of the buckwheat and flour to form a loose batter.

3. Cover with a cloth and prove in a warm temperature at 32°C (90°F) until doubled in size.

4. Separate the eggs, add the yolks to the ferment, then, using a whisk, gradually add the remainder of the milk. Season with a little salt and milled pepper.

5. Allow to stand for 30 minutes, then lightly fold in the stiffly whipped whites of egg.

6. Cook as for pancakes (1394), using special size blinis pans, approximately 85 mm in diameter.

7. Serve on a hot flat dish in a folded serviette.

## 13 Dressed crab
## Crabe garni

Generally, the crabs are purchased already cooked. The weight should be comparable to the size and they should be undamaged, with both claws.

If raw, place into boiling salt water containing a little vinegar (1 part to 20 parts water); this helps to soften the fibre of the flesh. Reboil, simmer for 15 minutes (2 lb, 1 kg crab) to 30 minutes (5 lb, 2½ kg) then allow to cool in the liquor.

| 8 portions | Ingredients | 10 couverts |
|---|---|---|
| 2 × 2 lb | cooked whole crab | 2 × 1 kg |
| 1 | lettuce | 1 |
| 2 | hard boiled eggs | 2 |
| 4 | anchovy fillets | 4 |
| 2 oz | fresh breadcrumbs | 70 g |
| ¼ pint | mayonnaise | 175 m |
| 4 | stuffed olives | 4 |
| 1 oz | capers | 35 g |
| 1 teaspoon | Worcester sauce | 4 g |
| 1 teaspoon | salt | 4 g |
| ¼ teaspoon | milled pepper | 1 g |

### Method

1. Sever the claws from the crab by pulling away from the body.

2. Remove the lower pincer from the claw by opening beyond its full extent.

3. Crack the claws and joints; avoid splintering into the flesh. Remove the flesh with a small knife and the back of a table fork.

4. Remove the soft under shell and honeycomb structure by piercing with a knife where it joins the hard shell and pull away.

5. Remove and discard the gills and sac behind the eyes.

6. With the back of a fork, remove the soft brown-coloured flesh inside the shell. Pass through a sieve.

7. By lightly cracking open and using a fork, remove the

white/pink flesh from the honeycomb structure and place with the flesh from the claws.

8. Trim the shell back to the natural hard casing, scrub and dry thoroughly.

9. Mix the sieved brown-coloured flesh with the mayonnaise, Worcester sauce and white breadcrumbs; season with salt and milled pepper.

10. Place this mixture in the centre of the shell. Shred the white/pink flesh, removing any bone, and arrange this on each side of the brown flesh mixture in the shell.

11. Decorate the centre part with a trellis of thinly cut anchovy fillets, with capers in the apertures. Place lines of sieved hard-boiled yolk of egg, chopped parsley, and sieved white of egg down each side of the mixture.

12. Fill the shell with the other flesh on each side of the centre and decorate with overlapping slices of stuffed olive.

13. Place the dressed crabs on a flat oval dish and surround them with the crisp, cleaned lettuce leaves. Place the legs, brushed with oil to give a shine, around the crab shells for decoration.

Serve Sauce vinaigrette and mayonnaise.

## 14 Foie gras

This is a prepared delicacy of goose livers, mainly from the Alsace-Lorraine region, which is served in the following forms.

### PÂTÉ

Pâté should be served in decorative pastry casings placed on a round silver dish on a doily and garnished with sprigs of fresh parsley.

### BLOC OR ROULEAU

This is available in rectangular or long round tins. Set the bloc in the refrigerator for a few hours, unmould, cut it into slices 10–12 mm in thickness and dress them on crisp prepared overlapping lettuce leaves on a flat dish. Garnish with 6 mm dice of aspic jelly. Alternatively, glaze the bloc with aspic jelly flavoured and coloured with port wine and dress the slices overlapping each other on a flat dish on a 3 mm base of set natural-colour aspic jelly.

The debris remaining after cutting or from cheaper grades is passed through a very fine sieve and mixed with half its quantity of fresh whipped cream to form a Mousse de foie gras.

## 15 Fruit cocktail — Cocktail de fruits

| 8 portions | Ingredients | 10 couverts |
|---|---|---|
| 4 | grapefruit | 5 |
| 4 | oranges | 5 |
| 1 small or ½ large | melon | 1 small or ½ large |
| 8 oz | grapes | 280 g |
| 8 | cocktail cherries | 10 |

### Method

1. Remove the grapes from the stalk, blanch, refresh, skin and remove the seeds. Place into a basin.

2. Prepare the grapefruit and orange as for cocktail (20, 21).

3. Prepare the melon as for cocktail (26).

4. Carefully combine the fruits and juice and chill for 1–2 hours.

5. Divide equally into the cocktail glasses, placing a cherry in the centre of each. Serve on a flat dish on a doily or dishpaper.

## 16 Fruit juice

The most popular types of juice used are orange, grapefruit, pineapple and passion-fruit.

The juice is chilled for 1–2 hours, before serving in a jug on an underdish with a doily.

When served in glasses, an average portion is 4 fl. oz (110 ml).

## 17 Tomato juice — Jus de tomate

When fresh tomatoes are used, the washed tomatoes are cut in halves and pulped through a juice extractor or passed through a sieve; the juice is then strained. In all cases, the juice has one level teaspoon of Worcester sauce with a little salt and pepper added per pint, and is chilled for 1–2 hours. Serve as for fruit juice.

## 18 V8 Juice

This is a juice extracted from high-vitamin root vegetables and other plants. Chill for 1–2 hours and serve as for fruit juice.

## 19 Grapefruit (half) — Demi-pamplemousse (cerisette)

Cut the very minimum from each end of the grapefruit to allow it to stand level, then cut into equal halves across the grapefruit.

With a sharp knife, cut a cone 18 mm in diameter from the centre. Carefully cut around each segment to completely free from the skin. Chill for 1–2 hours.

Serve in a glass or silver cup on an underflat with a doily

and place a maraschino cocktail cherry in the centre of each half.

If desired, the grapefruit may be sprinkled with kirsch.

## 20 Grapefruit cocktail — Cocktail de pamplemousse

| 8 portions | Ingredients | 10 couverts |
|---|---|---|
| 6 | grapefruit | 8 |
| 8 | cocktail cherries | 10 |

### Method
1. Cut away sufficient from each end of the washed grapefruit to expose the fruit.
2. Cut away the skin and pith from top to bottom of the fruit, following the natural curved shape.
3. Over a basin, cut between the skin to free the segments then chill them for 1–2 hours.
4. Divide equally into cocktail glasses and place a cherry in the centre of each. Serve on an underdish on a doily.
*Note.* If desired, the cocktails may be sprinkled with kirsch.

## 21 Grapefruit and orange cocktail — Cocktail Florida

| 8 portions | Ingredients | 10 couverts |
|---|---|---|
| 6 | grapefruit | 8 |
| 4 | oranges | 5 |
| 8 | cocktail cherries | 10 |

### Method
1. Prepare the grapefruit and oranges separately, as in the previous recipe.
2. When chilled, equally divide the grapefruit into cocktail glasses. Attractively arrange the orange on top, with a cherry in the centre.

Serve as in previous recipe.

## 22 Grapefruit and mandarin cocktail
Prepare as for Grapefruit and orange cocktail, replacing the orange with mandarin segments.

## 23 Liver pâté or terrine — Pâté ou terrine de foie
This recipe will produce a 2 pint (1·4 litre) terrine equivalent to 16–20 portions.

| | Ingredients | |
|---|---|---|
| 1½ lb | chicken/pigs Liver | 675 g |
| 12 oz | larding bacon | 340 g |
| 2 oz | finely chopped onion | 55 g |
| ½ pod | finely chopped garlic | Point |
| 1 | egg | 1 |
| 1 oz | butter | 30 ml |
| ¼ pint | cream | 140 ml |
| 2 fl. oz | brandy | 55 ml |
| 1 teaspoon | seasoning and spices | 4 g |

### Method
1. Line the terrine with very thin slices of two-thirds of the larding bacon, allowing enough to overhang the sides of the terrine to cover the top surface later.
2. Roughly dice the remainder of the larding bacon, fry it lightly in the butter with the onion, garlic, seasoning and spices for 8–10 minutes, then cool completely.
3. Finely mince with the liver; pass through a fine sieve.
4. Well mix in the brandy, beaten egg, then the cream, with a spatule.
5. Pour into the prepared terrine and cover the surface completely with the overhanging larding bacon.
6. Cover with foil and a close-fitting piece of wood with a one pound weight on top to press lightly during cooking.
7. Place the terrine in a tray of water to come two-thirds of the way up the sides of the terrine and bring to boiling point.
8. Cook in a slow oven, without boiling, for 2½ hours.
9. When cooked, allow to go cold.
10. For Liver terrine, cover with a thin coating of clarified chicken fat and set or, alternatively, decorate the surface with truffle, pimento, white of egg, etc. and cover thinly with aspic jelly and set.
11. For Liver pâté, unmould by running hot water on the base of the terrine, and turn out. Decorate the upturned base as in 10 and glaze with aspic jelly. Serve on a round flat dish lined with aspic jelly. Alternatively, dip a knife in boiling water and cut into 16–20 wedge-shaped portions and serve these on crisp prepared lettuce leaves on a flat dish.
12. Thick rectangular slices of trimmed toast are served separately inside a serviette on an underdish.

*Note.* When filling the terrine, pieces of truffle, pistachio nuts, strips of ham, tongue and breast of chicken may be added in layers for variation.

## 24 Chilled melon — Melon frappé
The melons generally used are honeydew (6–8 portions) or cantaloup (8–10 portions).
1. Wash the melon, dry and cut a cone-shaped piece 40 mm wide out of the stalk end. Remove all the seeds from inside the melon with a spoon, without damaging the flesh.
2. Chill for 1–2 hours. Serve on crushed ice in a timbale on an underdish with a doily.

For table d'hôte and banquet service, the melon is cut into wedge-shaped portions along the length of the melon and served on crushed ice or a flat dish. When designated 'Oporto' on the menu, a little port wine is poured in the melon and swilled around before chilling.

### 25 Melon and Parma ham      Melon au jambon de Parme

1. Wash the melon, cut in half and remove the seeds.
2. Cut into wedge-shaped portions lengthways and pass a knife close to the skin to remove the flesh.
3. Wrap a slice of Parma ham around the flesh and hold in position with a cocktail stick. Place a maraschino cherry on the stick, level with the ham, and serve on a flat dish after chilling for 1–2 hours.

### 26 Melon cocktail      Cocktail de melon

| 8 portions | Ingredients | 10 couverts |
|---|---|---|
| 2 × 1¼ lb | honeydew or cantaloup melon | 2 × 700 g |
| 2 oz | castor sugar | 70 g |
| ¼ level teaspoon | ground ginger | 1 g |
| 1 small | lemon | 1 large |
| 8 | cocktail cherries | 10 |

**Method**

1. Wash and cut the melons in halves lengthways and remove the seeds with a spoon.
2. Cut each half into 3 wedge-shaped sections; pass a knife close to the skin to remove the flesh.
3. Cut the melon in strips 12 mm wide, then in the opposite direction 12 mm apart to form small pieces.
    The melon may be cut into balls with a ball scoop, the debris being cut into rough 12 mm dice.
4. Sprinkle with the mixed sugar and ginger and the strained lemon juice. Chill for 1–2 hours.
5. Divide equally into the cocktail glasses. When cut into balls, the rough dice are placed in the bottom of the glass first.
6. Place a cherry in the centre. Serve on a flat dish with a doily.
7. When designated 'Oporto', the cocktails are sprinkled with port wine.

### 27 Oysters      Huîtres

The shells of fresh oysters must be firmly closed and the oysters must be discarded if the shells are open, since this indicates they are withered or dead.

To open the shells, carefully insert the point of an oyster knife at the pointed hinged end of the shell and twist it slightly. Run the oyster knife under and close to the flat shell to release the shell.

To be sure of removing any grit or other deposit, flush the oysters quickly through salt water.

Pass the point of the knife under the oyster to free it from the shell, turn it over and straighten the beard if necessary. Serve them on crushed ice in a soup plate or on a flat dish; six oysters is an average portion. Garnish with a wedge of lemon and serve brown bread and butter separately.

### 28 Plovers' eggs      Oeufs de pluvier

These are considered a delicacy and they are usually in short supply. Because of their size, the eggs are hard-boiled for only 5 minutes. The shells are removed in cold water and the eggs drained.

Serve them on crisp prepared lettuce leaves and garnish with washed and drained mustard and cress; 2 eggs are served per portion. Brown bread and butter and Sauce mayonnaise are served separately.

### 29 Potted shrimps      Crevettes au beurre

Purchased in the prepared form, these are small shelled cooked shrimps in butter. They are served alone or with sliced smoked salmon, and brown bread and butter is served separately.

### 30 Shellfish cocktails
#### Lobster cocktail      Cocktail de homard

| 8 portions | Ingredients | 10 couverts |
|---|---|---|
| 1 × 1½ lb | cooked lobster | 840 g |
| ½ pint | mayonnaise | 350 ml |
| 2 tablespoons | tomato ketchup | 80 ml |
| 2 tablespoons | cream | 80 ml |
| 1 teaspoon | Worcester sauce | 5 ml |
| 1 teaspoon | horseradish relish | 5 ml |
| 1 large | lettuce | 1 or 2 small |
| 1 | lemon | 1 |

**Method**

1. Trim, well wash and drain the lettuce. Crisp in the refrigerator.
2. Shred the lettuce finely and half fill into the cocktail glasses.
3. Split the lobster in half lengthways and remove any secretion. Wash and drain. Retain the coral and place it to one side.
4. Crack the claws and joints; remove the flesh.

5. Cut the lobster flesh into thin slices (scallops) and place them on top of the lettuce. Chill for 30 minutes.

6. Lightly whisk the ketchup, Worcester sauce and horse-radish into the mayonnaise, then fold in the softly whipped cream.

7. Mask the lobster with the sauce when required. Decorate by sprinkling the sieved coral on top.

8. Serve on a flat dish on a doily with a slice of lemon on the edge of the glass. Brown bread and butter is served separately.

### 31 Prawn or shrimp cocktail    Cocktail de crevettes roses
Cocktail de crevettes

Prepare as for Lobster cocktail, replacing the lobster with 1½ oz (45 g) of peeled and cooked prawns or shrimps per portion, according to the name of the cocktail. After masking with the sauce, decorate on top with a few of the prawns or shrimps.

### 32 Crab cocktail    Cocktail de crabe

Prepare as for prawn cocktail, replacing the prawns with shredded cooked crabmeat, free from bone. After masking with the sauce, sprinkle the surface with a little sieved hard-boiled egg and chopped parsley.

### 33 Seafood cocktail    Cocktail fruits de mer

Proceed as for Lobster cocktail, replacing the lobster with ¼ oz (15 g) of cooked and flaked white fish, ½ oz (15 g) of diced cooked mussels and ½ oz (15 g) of shrimps or prawns. After masking with the sauce, decorate as for Crab cocktail.

### 34 Smoked salmon    Saumon fumé

Prepare the side of smoked salmon for carving as follows: cut away a very thin layer of the dry surface. Run the fingers along the salmon to feel the small protruding bones and remove them with a pair of small pliers. Brush the surface with olive oil and carve the flesh very thinly on the slant into slices approximately 50 mm wide. Arrange the slices to over-lap each other on a flat oval dish and garnish with wedges of lemon and washed sprigs of parsley. Serve brown bread and butter separately. (1½ oz (45 g) of smoked salmon is a general portion.)

### 35 Smoked trout    Truite fumée

Prepare the trout as follows: remove the skin by cutting just through it down the back of the trout, then from behind the head down to the stomach aperture and pulling it off from the head to the tail.

Brush the trout liberally with olive oil and place it on a flat dish. Place slices of lemon on the trout and garnish around it with small crisp prepared lettuce leaves. Serve brown bread and butter separately.

---

## VARIETY OF HORS D'OEUVRE—HORS D'OEUVRE VARIÉS

*Note.* The quantities given are those required for serving a variety of hors d'oeuvre; the ingredients should be doubled when the hors d'oeuvre are served individually.

---

### 36 Anchovy fillets    Filets d'anchois

Anchovy fillets are purchased canned in olive oil. Arrange them in a ravier, trellis-fashion, or folded in knots, present-ing the side of the fillet taken from the bone. Place capers between them and surround the edges of the dish with thin lines of sieved hard-boiled yolk of egg, chopped parsley and sieved white of egg. Pour a little oil over the fillets.

### 37 Anchovy paupiettes    Paupiettes d'anchois

Roll the fillets around the finger and place them in a ravier; place capers in the centre. Decorate around the dish as for Anchovy fillets.

## 38 à la grecque (Greek style) – cooking liquid

This is the basic cooking liquid for all preparations of this group.

| 8 portions | Ingredients | | 10 couverts |
|---|---|---|---|
| 6 | coriander seeds | tie in muslin for ease of removing | 7 |
| 6 | peppercorns | | 7 |
| ½ | bayleaf | | ½ |
| small sprig | thyme | | small sprig |
| 8 fl. oz | water | | 280 ml |
| 3 fl. oz | olive oil | | 100 ml |
| 1 | lemon (juice) | | 1 |
| ½ pod | garlic (chopped finely) | | ½ pod |
| 1 level teaspoon | salt | | 4 g |

### Method
Boil all the ingredients together.

## 39 Artichoke                    Artichaut à la grecque

| 8 portions | Ingredients | 10 couverts |
|---|---|---|
| 4 | artichokes | 5 |

### Method
1. Remove any discoloured outer leaves, cut off the stalk and trim across the base with a peeler. Cut across the leaves 25 mm from the base.
2. Remove the choke (the centre soft leaves and fur).
3. Cut each artichoke into 8–10 sections.
4. Cook in boiling salt water with a little lemon juice for 10 minutes then refresh.
5. Place them in a suitable sized pan and cover them with the cooking liquid. Boil, remove any scum, simmer for 15–20 minutes then test the artichokes with the point of a knife; it should penetrate without pressure. Allow to cool in the liquid.
6. Remove the muslin bag (see 38). When cold, serve in a ravier, masked over with the cooking liquid to a depth of 5 mm.

## 40 Cauliflower                   Chou-fleur à la grecque

| 8 portions | Ingredients | 10 couverts |
|---|---|---|
| 1 × 1½ lb | cauliflower | 840 g |

### Method
1. Trim away the green leaves from the cauliflower.
2. Cut the white part into buds 20 mm in diameter.
3. Blanch in boiling salt water for 3–4 minutes and refresh.
4. Drain, cover with the cooking liquid, boil and simmer for 10 minutes. Allow to cool in the liquid.
5. Finish as at 6 in method of Artichaut à la grecque. Sprinkle with chopped parsley.

## 41 Celery                        Céleri à la grecque

| 8 portions | Ingredients | 10 couverts |
|---|---|---|
| 1 large head | celery | 1 large head |

### Method
1. Remove any outer discoloured part, peel with a peeler and trim the root clean. Wash well by soaking in water.
2. Blanch for 8–10 minutes in boiling salt water with a little lemon juice. Refresh and rewash to remove any dirt or grit.
3. Cut into 50 mm lengths and divide the root portion into 8–10 sections lengthways.
4. Place in a shallow pan and cover with the prepared liquid. Reboil, cover, then braise for 1 hour until tender. Allow to go cold in the liquid.
5. Finish as for Artichaut à la grecque, 6 in method, and sprinkle with chopped parsley.

## 42 Marrow (baby)               Courgettes à la grecque

| 8 portions | Ingredients | 10 couverts |
|---|---|---|
| 1¼ lb | Baby marrows (courgettes) | 700 g |

### Method
1. Wash, peel and rewash the courgettes. Cut them lengthways into four pieces and remove the seeds.
2. Cut on the slant into 25 mm-long scallops.
3. Blanch in boiling salt water for 2 minutes and refresh.
4. Drain, place in shallow pan and cover with the cooking liquid. Boil, then simmer for 8–10 minutes. Allow to go cold.
5. Finish as at 6 in method for Artichaut à la grecque.

## 43 Leeks                         Poireaux à la grecque

| 8 portions | Ingredients | 10 couverts |
|---|---|---|
| 4 × 4 oz | leeks | 5 × 110 g |

### Method
1. Remove one layer of the outer leaves and any discoloured parts. Trim away the top dark green part to a point. Cut down the centre 10 mm away from the root.
2. Wash well and blanch in boiling water for 4–5 minutes. Refresh and rewash.

3. Split completely in halves and fold each half over so that the white part is showing. Braise in the cooking liquid for 30–35 minutes then allow to go cold.

4. Finish as at 6 in method for Artichaut à la grecque and sprinkle with chopped parsley.

## 44 Onions (button)  Oignons à la grecque

| 8 portions | Ingredients | 10 couverts |
|---|---|---|
| 1 lb | button onions | 560 g |

### Method

1. Place the button onions in warm water and peel.

2. Blanch for 4–5 minutes in boiling salt water; refresh.

3. Place in a shallow pan with the cooking liquid. Boil, cover and braise for 20–25 minutes. Allow to go cold.

4. Finish as at 6 in method for artichaut à la grecque and sprinkle with chopped parsley.

## 45 Soft roes  Laitance à la grecque

| 8 portions | Ingredients | 10 couverts |
|---|---|---|
| 12 oz | soft herring roes | 420 g |

### Method

1. Wash the soft roes in cold salt water and remove any silver-coloured thread.

2. Place in a shallow pan or tray. Cover with the cooking liquid, carefully bring to the boil, cover and poach gently for 2–3 minutes. Allow to go cold.

3. Finish as at 6 in method for Artichaut à la grecque and sprinkle with chopped parsley.

## 46 à la portugaise (Portuguese style) – cooking liquid and garnish.

| 8 portions | Ingredients | 10 couverts |
|---|---|---|
| 8 oz | tomatoes (into concassé) | 280 g |
| 4 fl. oz | olive oil | 140 ml |
| 4 fl. oz | vinegar | 140 ml |
| 8 fl. oz | water | 280 ml |
| 1 oz (tablespoon) | tomato purée | 35 g |
| ½ pod | garlic | ½ pod |
| 4 oz | finely chopped onion | 140 g |
| 1 | bayleaf | 1 |
| 1 level teaspoon | salt | 4 g |
| ¼ level teaspoon | milled pepper | 1 g |

### Method

1. Sweat the onion in half the oil for 5 minutes without colouring.

2. Add the remainder of the ingredients, except the 10 mm-diced tomato, and boil.

3. Sprinkle the diced tomato over the prepared food when cooked.

4. Using the prepared cooking liquid and garnish, the following are prepared and served as for à la grecque:

## 47 Artichoke  Artichaut à la portugaise

## 48 Cauliflower  Chou-fleur à la portugaise

## 49 Marrow (baby)  Courgettes à la portugaise

## 50 Onions (button)  Oignons à la portugaise

*Note.* By adjusting the prepared amounts, recipes 39, 40 and 44 may be blended together after cooking to give further varieties.

## 51 Soft roes  Laitance à la portugaise

## 52 Herring* or mackerel*  Hareng* ou maquereau* à la portugaise

| 8 portions | Ingredients | 10 couverts |
|---|---|---|
| 4 × 5–6 oz | herring or mackerel | 5 × 140–170 g |
|  | cooking liquid and garnish |  |

### Method

1. Scale, wash and fillet the fish. Cut away the dark part of the belly. Cut the fillets into 25 mm-wide strips on the slant.

2. Place the strips of fish in a shallow tray or pan. Sprinkle with the diced tomato and add the cooking liquid.

3. Cover with oiled paper. Carefully bring to the boil then poach in the oven at 148°C (300°F) for 6–7 minutes until the fish will just flake. Remove and allow to go cold.

4. Carefully dress in earthenware dishes and mask over with the sauce. Sprinkle with chopped parsley.

5. Serve on an underdish with dishpaper.

## 53 à la mexicaine (Mexican style) – cooking liquid and garnish

Prepare the cooking liquid and garnish as for à la portugaise and add to the garnish the following:

| 8 portions | Ingredients | 10 couverts |
|---|---|---|
| 3 oz | fresh red pimento or | 100 g |
| 1½ | tinned red pimento | 50 g |

### Method

1. If using fresh pimento, dip in hot, deep fat (180°C, 360°F) for 1 minute. Remove the skin, the top stalk and all the seeds inside.

2. Then for both types cut into 5 mm dice and add to the garnish.

**54 Artichoke** **Artichaut à la mexicaine**

**55 Cauliflower** **Chou-fleur à la mexicaine**

**56 Marrow (baby)** **Courgettes à la mexicaine**

**57 Onions (button)** **Oignons à la mexicaine**

*Note.* Cook and serve as for à la portugaise.

### 58 Bagration salad — Salade Bagration

| 8 portions | Ingredients | 10 couverts |
|---|---|---|
| 3 oz | plain boiled macaroni | 100 g |
| 2 | cooked artichoke bottoms | 2 |
| 2 oz | cooked white fish | 70 g |
| ½ | raw celery heart | ½ |
| 4 oz | tomatoes | 140 g |
| 1 | hard boiled egg | 1 |
| ½ medium | truffle | ½ medium |
| ½ gill (2½ fl. oz) | vinaigrette sauce | 90 ml |
| 1 teaspoon | chopped parsley | 2 g |
| 1 level teaspoon | salt | 4 g |
| ¼ level teaspoon | pepper (milled) | 1 g |

**Method**

1. Cut the cooked macaroni into 10 mm lengths and place them in a basin.
2. Blanch and peel the tomatoes, cut across into halves and remove the seeds.
3. Cut the tomato, artichoke, celery, truffle and white of egg into julienne, and add to the macaroni with the cooked and flaked white fish.
4. Lightly bind with the vinaigrette and season with salt and white pepper.
5. Dress to a dome shape in a ravier and smooth it with a palette knife. Sprinkle with chopped parsley.
6. Pass the cooked yolk of egg through a sieve and fill into a star cutter. Press lightly in the centre of the salad, then remove the cutter.

### 59 Beef salad — Salade de boeuf

| 8 portions | Ingredients | 10 couverts |
|---|---|---|
| 6 oz | cooked beef (braised or boiled) | 210 g |
| 4 oz | tomatoes | 140 g |
| 4 oz | cooked French beans | 140 g |
| 4 oz | boiled potatoes | 140 g |
| ½ oz | finely chopped onion | 20 g |
| 2 oz | gherkins | 70 g |
| ½ | lettuce | ½ |
| 2 oz | cooked beetroot | 70 g |
| ½ gill (2½ fl. oz) | vinaigrette sauce | 90 ml |
| 1 teaspoon | chopped parsley | 2 g |
| 1 teaspoon | salt | 4 g |
| ¼ teaspoon | pepper (milled) | 1 g |

**Method**

1. Blanch and skin the tomatoes then cut them in halves and remove the seeds.
2. Cut the beef, tomato, cooked potato and half the gherkins into 5 mm dice. Place in a basin with the onion.
3. Season with salt and white pepper and lightly bind with the vinaigrette.
4. Place the prepared crisp lettuce leaves around the edge of the ravier. Place the salad in the centre in a loose dome shape.
5. Cut the beetroot into 5 mm dice, moisten with vinaigrette and place it in four bouquets around the dish. Cut the other gherkins in fans and place them between the beetroot. Sprinkle lightly all over with chopped parsley.

*Note.* To make gherkin fans, cut the gherkins in half, well on the slant, and round the uncut ends. Place the flat side on a board, thinly slice the gherkin to within 3 mm of the pointed end and open fanwise.

### 60 Beetroot salad — Salade de betterave

| 8 portions | Ingredients | 10 couverts |
|---|---|---|
| 1 lb | cooked beetroot | 560 g |
| ½ oz | finely chopped onion | 20 g |
| ½ oz | button onions | 20 g |
| ½ gill (2½ fl. oz) | vinaigrette sauce | 90 ml |
| 1 teaspoon | chopped parsley | 2 g |
| 1 level teaspoon | salt | 4 g |
| ¼ level teaspoon | pepper (milled) | 1 g |

**Method**

1. Wash the beetroots carefully before cooking. Place them to steam, or cover them with water and boil steadily until cooked (test by seeing whether the skin will come away easily).
2. When cold, peel, cut into bâtons 25 × 5 × 5 mm and place in a basin. Add the finely chopped onion, then the vinaigrette and season with salt and pepper. Toss over to mix.
3. Dress in a ravier in a loose dome shape and sprinkle with chopped parsley. Decorate with the button onions, peeled and sliced very thin; half overlap the onion rings.

## 61 Beetroot cases      Cassolette de betterave

| 8 portions | Ingredients | 10 couverts |
|---|---|---|
| 1½ lb | cooked beetroots | 840 g |
| 8 oz | vegetable salad (108) | 280 g |
| 1 teaspoon | chopped parsley | 2 g |
| ½ gill (2½ fl. oz) | vinaigrette sauce | 90 ml |

### Method

1. Peel the beetroots and cut across the base to make them 30 mm long. Cut through the centre with a fluted round cutter 35 mm in diameter. Cut off a slice 3 mm thick from each beetroot and set aside for the covers.
2. Using a 30 mm plain cutter, cut through the cases to 5 mm from the base. Pass the point of a small knife through the side of the case 5 mm from the base to release the centre.
3. Marinade the cases and covers with vinaigrette sauce for 10 minutes, then drain well.
4. Fill the cases with the prepared vegetable salad in a dome shape. Place cases in a ravier.
5. Place covers on the cases, slightly sloping to show the salad. Place a pinch of chopped parsley on the centre of each cover.

## 62 Cabbage salad      Salade de choux

| 8 portions | Ingredients | 10 couverts |
|---|---|---|
| 1 lb | hard white cabbage | 560 g |
| ½ gill (2½ fl. oz) | vinaigrette sauce | 90 ml |

### Method

1. Trim away any discoloured leaves from the cabbage, cut into quarters and remove the centre stalk.
2. Wash well in cold salt water and thoroughly drain.
3. Shred very fine; crisp for 1 hour in refrigerator.
4. When required for service, blend with the vinaigrette sauce. Serve in a loose dome shape in a ravier.

## 63 Cole slaw

### Method

1. Prepare as for Cabbage salad. Add 2 oz (70 g) of peeled carrot, shredded on a coarse grater to produce 25–40 mm lengths, and 1 oz (35 g) of very finely shredded peeled onion.
2. When required for service, add a mixture of half olive oil with half mayonnaise sauce (90 ml for 10) to the salad. Serve in a loose dome shape in a ravier.

*Note.* For both these salads, never add the dressing before service or the cabbage will go limp.

## 64 Caroline      Caroline vannoise

| 8 portions | Ingredients | 10 couverts |
|---|---|---|
| ¼ pint | choux paste (343) | 175 ml |
| 4 oz | foie gras or liver pâté mousse | 140 g |
| ½ pint | white chaud-froid sauce | 350 ml |
| ½ pint | aspic jelly | 350 ml |

### Method

1. Using a 5 mm plain tube, pipe the choux paste on to a greased baking tray 40 mm long, either in the shape of the letter C or straight.
2. Egg-wash and bake at 205°C (400°F) at the top of the oven for 8–10 minutes until crisp. Allow to go cold.
3. Split the side and, using a 3 mm plain tube and bag, fill the cases with the foie gras or liver pâté.
4. Glaze by dipping half the top surface in the white chaud-froid sauce at setting point; place on a wire grill.
5. Decorate with a small truffle motif. Glaze with aspic jelly at setting point. Set in the refrigerator.
6. Serve in a ravier with washed sprigs of parsley in each corner.

## 65 Celeriac      Céleri-rave à la moutarde

| 8 portions | Ingredients | 10 couverts |
|---|---|---|
| 1¼ lb | celeriac | 700 g |
| 1 gill (5 fl. oz) | mayonnaise | 175 ml |
| 1 fl. oz | cream | 35 ml |
| 1 teaspoon | English mustard | 4 g |
| 1 | lemon | 1 |
| 1 level teaspoon | salt | 4 g |
| ¼ level teaspoon | pepper (milled) | 1 g |

### Method

1. Wash, peel thickly, then rewash the celeriac.
2. Cut into 40–50 mm lengths. Cut these into thin slices, then into julienne.
3. Whisk the mustard, salt and pepper in a basin with the strained lemon juice; add the mayonnaise, then lightly whisk in the cream.
4. Add the celeriac; mix with a spoon. Serve in a loose dome shape in a ravier. Dust very lightly with paprika pepper.

## 66 Cucumber salad      Salade de concombre

| 8 portions | Ingredients | 10 couverts |
|---|---|---|
| 1 medium | cucumber | 1 large |
| 1 fl. oz | vinaigrette sauce | 35 ml |
| 1 teaspoon | chopped parsley | 2 g |

## Method

1. Wash and peel the cucumber. Slice into 1·5 mm-thick slices.

2. Arrange the slices three-quarter overlapping in a ravier. Sprinkle with the vinaigrette, then the chopped parsley.

### 67 Cucumber cases      Cassolette de concombre

| 8 portions | Ingredients | 10 couverts |
| --- | --- | --- |
| 1 large | cucumber | 1 very large |
| 8 oz | vegetable salad (108) | 280 g |
| ½ gill (2½ fl. oz) | vinaigrette sauce | 90 ml |

## Method

1. Peel the cucumber. Prepare into cases as for beetroot cases (61, 1 and 2 of method).

2. Blanch for 2 minutes in boiling salt water, then refresh and drain.

3. Marinade the cases and covers in the vinaigrette and drain.

4. Fill the cases with the vegetable salad. Place the covers on top at an angle to expose the salad. Dress in a ravier.

### 68 Eels (Russian style)      *Anguilles à la russe

### 69 Herring (Russian style)      *Hareng à la russe

### 70 Mackerel (Russian style)      *Maquereau à la russe

| 8 portions | Ingredients | 10 couverts |
| --- | --- | --- |
| 1¼ lb | eels or | 700 g |
| 4 × 5–6 oz | herring or mackerel | 5 × 140–170 g |
| 2 oz | carrot | 70 g |
| 2 oz | button onions | 70 g |
| 4 oz | tomatoes | 140 g |
| 1½ oz | gherkins | 50 g |
| 1 fl. oz | olive oil | 35 ml |
| 1 fl. oz | white wine (or lemon juice) | 35 ml |
| 1 level teaspoon | salt | 4 g |
| ¼ level teaspoon | pepper (milled) | 1 g |

## Method

1. Prepare the fish as follows: make a shallow incision around the back of the head of the eel, sprinkle the body with salt to grip and, with a cloth, roll off the skin from head to tail. Open the belly and thoroughly clean. Cut off the head and wash well.

2. Remove any scales from the herring. Fillet the mackerel or herring.

3. Cut the eels in 25 mm lengths. Cut the other fish into 25 mm strips on the slant.

4. Cut the carrot into paysanne and peel and thinly slice the button onions. Sweat in the oil gently for 7–8 minutes without colouring.

5. Add the wine and fish stock, boil, then simmer for 15 minutes.

6. Place the prepared fish in a shallow pan and sprinkle with the tomato prepared in concassé. Season with the salt and pepper, add the cooking liquid and garnish.

7. Cover with an oiled paper. Bring gently to the boil and poach the eels for 12 minutes, the other fish for 6–7 minutes. Allow to go cold.

8. Serve in a ravier, sprinkled with the gherkins cut into a fine 40 mm julienne.

### 71 Egg mayonnaise      *Mayonnaise d'oeuf

| 8 portions | Ingredients | 10 couverts |
| --- | --- | --- |
| 8 | hard boiled eggs | 10 |
| 1 | lettuce | 1 large |
| 6 oz | tomatoes | 210 g |
| 4 oz | cooked beetroot | 140 g |
| 4 | anchovy fillets | 5 |
| 4 | stuffed olives | 5 |
| ½ pint (10 fl. oz) | mayonnaise | 350 ml |
| 1 teaspoon | chopped parsley | 2 g |

## Method

1. Trim, wash and drain the lettuce and refrigerate to crisp.

2. Dress the lettuce leaves in a plat en terre, breaking the larger leaves in halves if necessary.

3. Cut the eggs on a slicer or into halves. Dress on the lettuce leaves. If sliced, three-quarter overlap by lightly pressing together after removing the slices from the slicer.

4. Check the consistency of the mayonnaise and mask the eggs to cover them without running.

5. Decorate the eggs with 2–3 thin slices of overlapping olives. Cut the anchovy into thin strips and place 2 strips crosswise on each egg.

6. Garnish around the edge with sections of peeled tomato and bâtons of beetroot 25 × 5 × 5 mm moistened with vinaigrette. Sprinkle the beetroot with chopped parsley.

7. Serve on an underdish with dishpaper.

### Egg mayonnaise (for variety of hors d'oeuvre)

1. Finely shred the prepared lettuce and place it in a ravier.

2. Cut the eggs in quarters, or slice them, and mask with the mayonnaise. Sprinkle very lightly with paprika pepper

*Note.* Variety may be obtained by using half the quantity of egg with an equal quantity of sliced, peeled tomatoes for Mayonnaise d'oeuf et de tomate.

## 72 Eggs (stuffed)                                            *Oeufs farcis

| 8 portions | Ingredients | 10 couverts |
|---|---|---|
| 8 | hard boiled eggs | 10 |
| 1 small | lettuce | 1 medium |
| 2 oz | butter | 70 g |
| ½ gill (2½ fl. oz) | mayonnaise | 90 ml |
| 1 level teaspoon | salt | 4 g |
| ¼ level teaspoon | ground pepper | 1 g |

### Method

1. Remove a thin slice from each end of the egg to allow them to stand straight. Cut the eggs in half and, with the point of a knife, make 5 mm-wide cuts towards the centre of the egg, alternating the direction of the slant of each cut to form serrated edges.
2. Remove the yolks and pass them through a sieve with the butter. Cream them together in a basin and add the seasoning and the mayonnaise gradually to form a medium-soft texture.
3. Using a 5 mm star tube and bag, pipe the mixture to a dome-like shape into the egg cases.
4. Dress in a ravier and garnish with sprigs of washed picked parsley. Place on an underdish with dishpaper.

*Note.* By replacing half the butter with the purée mentioned in the recipes, the following variations can be obtained:

## 73 Ham, purée of (1 oz (35 g))       Oeufs farcis au jambon
When complete (method 4 in previous recipe), decorate in the centre with very small diamond of ham.

## 74 Spinach, purée of (1 oz (35 g))     Oeufs farcis florentine

## 75 Anchovy, purée of (½ oz (20 g))   Oeufs farcis aux anchois

## 76 Tomato, ketchup (1 oz (35 g))     Oeufs farcis aux tomates

## 77 Foie gras, purée of (1 oz (35 g))  Oeufs farcis Strasbourg
Decorate the centres of the eggs with small diamonds of truffle.

## 78 Fécampoise salad                        Salade fécampoise

| 8 portions | Ingredients | 10 couverts |
|---|---|---|
| 4 oz | cooked shrimps | 140 g |
| 2 | hard boiled eggs | 3 |
| 8 oz | boiled potatoes | 280 g |
| 3 oz | smoked herring fillet | 100 g |
| 1 oz | finely chopped onion | 35 g |
| ½ oz | capers | 20 g |
| 4 | gherkins | 5 |
| ¼ gill (1¼ fl. oz) | vinaigrette | 45 ml |
| 3 fl. oz | mayonnaise | 100 ml |
| 1 teaspoon | chopped parsley | 2 g |
| ¼ teaspoon | milled pepper | 1 g |

### Method

1. Cut the boiled potato into 10 mm dice and place in a basin.
2. Add the shrimps, retaining a few for decoration.
3. Cut 16 thin strips of smoked herring for decoration, and the remainder into 5 mm dice.
4. Mix the potato, the chopped onion and the diced herring with the pepper and vinaigrette. Bind with the mayonnaise.
5. Dress to a dome shape in a ravier and sprinkle with chopped parsley.
6. Decorate with thin strips of the herring, trellis-fashion. Place the shrimps in the centre apertures with the capers in the remainder.
7. Cut the eggs in halves, then each half into 4 pieces; place these around the base of the salad.

## 79 Fish salad                              *Salade de poisson
Any poached white fish or salmon is suitable for this salad. The name of the salad should define the fish used, e.g. Salade de turbot (Turbot salad).

| 8 portions | Ingredients | 10 couverts |
|---|---|---|
| 8 oz | poached fish | 280 g |
| 1 | lettuce | 1 large |
| 4 oz | tomato | 140 g |
| 4 oz | beetroot | 140 g |
| 2 | hard boiled eggs | 3 |
| 4 oz | cucumber (with salmon) | 140 g |
| 6 | anchovy fillets | 8 |
| ½ oz | capers | 20 g |
| 3 fl. oz | vinaigrette sauce | 100 ml |
| 1 level teaspoon | salt | 4 g |
| ¼ teaspoon | pepper | 1 g |
| 2 teaspoons | chopped parsley | 5 g |

### Method

1. Remove all skin and bone from the fish, lightly flake, season and marinade with half the vinaigrette.
2. Shred the outer leaves of the cleaned crisp lettuce and place in a ravier, with small heart leaves around the edge.

3. Place the fish on the shredded lettuce in a dome shape. Decorate the surface of the fish with thin strips of anchovy, trellis-fashion with capers in between.

4. Decorate around the outer edge with sections of peeled tomatoes, quarters of hard boiled eggs, 25 × 5 × 5 mm bâtons of beetroot moistened with vinaigrette. When cucumber is served, overlap it around the base of the flaked fish.

5. Sprinkle the remainder of the vinaigrette over the fish and beetroot. Sprinkle both with chopped parsley.

## 80 Fish mayonnaise *Mayonnaise de poisson

The fish used should be named, as in Mayonnaise de saumon (Salmon mayonnaise).

| 8 portions | Ingredients | 10 couverts |
|---|---|---|
| | As for Fish salad, reducing vinaigrette by half | |
| 8 fl. oz | mayonnaise | 280 ml |

### Method

1. Prepare as for Fish salad. After dressing the fish on the lettuce, completely mask with mayonnaise instead of vinaigrette, and decorate in the same manner.

2. Moisten the beetroot with vinaigrette and sprinkle with chopped parsley.

## 81 Shellfish salad: shrimp *Salade de crevettes

Shellfish salad: prawn *Salade de crevettes roses

Shellfish salad: crab *Salade de crabe

Shellfish salad: lobster *Salade de homard

### Method

1. Prepare and serve as for Fish salad, replacing the fish with the shellfish which is prepared as for Shellfish cocktail.

2. When fresh lobster is used, 25 mm of the head and tail are placed at each end of the dish to denote its freshness.

## 82 Shellfish mayonnaise: shrimp *Mayonnaise de crevettes

Shellfish mayonnaise: prawn *Mayonnaise de crevettes roses

Shellfish mayonnaise: crab *Mayonnaise de crabe

Shellfish mayonnaise: lobster *Mayonnaise de homard

### Method

1. Prepare and serve as for Fish mayonnaise, replacing the fish with the shellfish (prepared as for Shellfish cocktail).

2. The head and tail are served with lobster, as mentioned in the previous recipe.

## 83 French bean salad Salade de haricots verts

| 8 portions | Ingredients | 10 couverts |
|---|---|---|
| 1 lb | French beans | 560 g |
| ½ gill (2½ fl. oz) | vinaigrette sauce | 90 ml |
| 1 teaspoon | salt | 4 g |
| ¼ teaspoon | milled pepper | 1 g |

### Method

1. Prepare and cook the beans then refresh and drain (see 1031).

2. If large, cut them into 40 mm lengths.

3. Add seasoning and vinaigrette; mix well. Serve in a loose dome shape in a ravier.

## 84 Italian salad Salade italienne

| 8 portions | Ingredients | 10 couverts |
|---|---|---|
| 8 oz | carrot | 280 g |
| 6 oz | turnip | 210 g |
| 2 oz | gherkins (large) | 70 g |
| 2 oz | sliced cooked ham | 70 g |
| 2 oz | sliced salami | 70 g |
| ½ gill (2½ fl. oz) | vinaigrette sauce | 90 ml |
| 1 level teaspoon | salt | 4 g |
| ¼ level teaspoon | milled pepper | 1 g |

### Method

1. Wash, peel, rewash, then plain boil the carrots and turnip separately.

2. Pass a 10 mm column cutter through the carrots, turnips and gherkins, and cut these rings into thin slices.

3. Cut 10 mm rings of ham and salami.

4. Cut the trimmings of all these into a rough 40 mm julienne. Season, add two-thirds of the vinaigrette and mix well.

5. Dress to a dome shape in a ravier; smooth with a palette knife.

6. Arrange the rings of carrot, half overlapping, around the sides, at the base of the julienne. Then continue up to the top in horizontal rows with rings of the turnip, ham, gherkin

and finally, the salami. Each layer should overlap the lower layer by one-quarter.

7. Sprinkle all over with the remainder of the vinaigrette.

### 85 Half mourning salad         Salade demi-deuil

#### Method

1. Dress on a ravier a prepared Potato salad (see 94) on a bed of small lettuce leaves.
2. Sprinkle the surface with a fine julienne of truffle.

### 86 Haricot bean salad       Salade de haricots blancs

| 8 portions | Ingredients | 10 couverts |
|---|---|---|
| 4 oz | haricot beans | 140 g |
| 2 oz | carrot | 70 g |
| 1 oz. | onion } garnish | 35 g |
| 1 oz | bacon trimmings } | 35 g |
| 1 oz | finely chopped onion | 35 g |
| ¼ gill (2 fl. oz) | vinaigrette | 90 ml |
| 1 level teaspoon | salt | 4 g |
| ¼ level teaspoon | milled pepper | 1 g |
| 1 teaspoon | chopped parsley | 2 g |

#### Method

1. Soak the beans overnight then change the water. Boil, remove the scum, add garnish, and simmer for approximately 1½ hours until tender. Remove the garnish.
2. Drain and marinade with the vinaigrette while hot.
3. When cold, add the onion. Toss to mix.
4. Serve in a dome shape in a ravier; sprinkle with chopped parsley.

### 87 Hussard salad         Salade hussarde

| 8 portions | Ingredients | 10 couverts |
|---|---|---|
| 4 oz | cooked beef (braised or boiled) | 140 g |
| 4 oz | dessert apple | 140 g |
| 4 oz | cooked beetroot | 140 g |
| 4 oz | boiled potato | 140 g |
| 4 | gherkins | 5 |
| 4 oz | cooked french beans | 140 g |
| 1 oz | finely chopped onion | 35 g |
| 1 teaspoon | chopped parsley | 2 g |
| 3 fl. oz | vinaigrette sauce | 100 ml |
| 1 level teaspoon | salt | 4 g |
| ¼ level teaspoon | milled pepper | 1 g |

#### Method

1. Peel the apple and beetroot and cut both into 5 mm dice. Cut the beef, potato and French beans to the same size.
2. Keep each separate. Divide the onion between the potato and beetroot. Season each, except the apple, with salt and pepper.

3. Sprinkle each commodity with vinaigrette, then marinade for 30 minutes.
4. Dress in a ravier in separate bouquets, contrasting the colours.
5. Sprinkle chopped parsley on the beef, beetroot and potato.
6. Decorate around the edges with gherkin fans.

### 88 Mussel salad         Salade de moules

| 8 portions | Ingredients | 10 couverts |
|---|---|---|
| 3 pints | mussels | 2 litres |
| 1 oz | finely chopped onion | 35 g |
| 1 | lemon | 1 |
| 2 fl. oz | white wine | 70 ml |
| 1 tablespoon | olive oil | 25 ml |
| 1 level teaspoon | salt | 4 g |
| ¼ level teaspoon | milled pepper | 1 g |
| 2 teaspoons | chopped parsley | 4 g |

#### Method

1. Wash the mussels well, scrape, and discard any that are open.
2. Place the onion in a shallow pan and add the mussels. Cover, then boil rapidly until the shells open (approximately 4–5 minutes).
3. Remove the mussels. Allow the liquor to stand, then carefully run off the liquid into a clean pan, leaving any sediment behind.
4. Add the strained lemon juice and wine to the liquid and reduce to half a gill. Allow to go cold then mix in the oil.
5. Remove the mussels from the shells and remove the beard (the thin stringy edge). Place into the cooking liquor and marinade for 1 hour.
6. Dress in a ravier, with the liquor, and sprinkle with chopped parsley.

### 89 Mussels (gribiche)         Moules gribiche

| 8 portions | Ingredients | 10 couverts |
|---|---|---|
| | As for Mussel salad, plus | |
| ½ oz | gherkins | 20 g |
| ½ oz | capers | 20 g |
| 2 | hard boiled eggs | 3 |
| ¼ teaspoon | French mustard | 2 g |

#### Method

1. Prepare as for Mussel salad to method 5. When reducing the cooking liquor, etc., reduce it to a tablespoonful. Do not add the oil.

2. Pass the yolks of egg through a fine sieve and place in a basin. Cut the white into a fine julienne.

3. With a spatule, slowly work into the yolks three tablespoons (60 ml) of olive oil, then gradually add the reduced cooking essence, then the French mustard.

4. Finely chop the capers and gherkins and add to the sauce.

5. Add the prepared cooked mussels and mix lightly.

6. Dress in a ravier, sprinkle on top with the julienne of white of egg and chopped parsley.

## 90 Mushrooms in mustard sauce  Champignons à la moutarde

| 8 portions | Ingredients | 10 couverts |
|---|---|---|
| 10 oz | small closed mushrooms | 350 g |
| 1½ teaspoons | French mustard | 6 g |
| 1 tablespoon | olive oil | 25 ml |
| 4 fl. oz | cream | 140 ml |
| ½ | lemon | ½ |
| 1 teaspoon | salt | 4 g |
| ¼ teaspoon | milled pepper | 1 g |

### Method

1. Place 10 mm of water in a small sauteuse and add the strained juice of the ½ lemon, salt, pepper and the oil. Bring to the boil; place aside.

2. Wash the mushrooms, turn or peel and place in the prepared liquid.

3. Boil, then simmer for 6–7 minutes until cooked. Place the mushrooms in a basin.

4. Reduce the liquid to a tablespoonful; allow to go cold. Whisk on to the French mustard, then gradually add the cream. Pour over the mushrooms.

5. Immerse in the sauce for 30 minutes. Serve in a ravier, masked over with the sauce.

## 91 National salad                    Salade nationale

### Method

1. Serve a prepared potato salad on a bed of prepared crisp lettuce leaves, the ends exposed.

2. Garnish around the base with 16–20 quarters of small peeled tomatoes. Sprinkle with chopped parsley.

## 92 Olive salad                    Salade olivette

| 8 portions | Ingredients | 10 couverts |
|---|---|---|
| 8 oz | boiled potatoes | 280 g |
| 4 oz | dessert apples | 140 g |
| 4 oz | tomato | 140 g |
| 4 oz | celery | 140 g |
| 16 | queen olives | 20 |
| ½ gill (2½ fl. oz) | vinaigrette sauce | 90 ml |
| 1 teaspoon | French mustard | 4 g |
| 1 teaspoon | salt | 4 g |
| ¼ teaspoon | milled pepper | 1 g |

### Method

1. Pour the egg whites into a greased pudding mould and place it in a saucepan with water half-way up the mould. Bring almost to boiling point, cover, cook in an oven at 148°C (300°F) until set, then allow to go cold.

2. Blanch the tomatoes, peel, cut in halves and remove seeds.

3. Wash the celery. Peel, quarter and core the apple.

4. Cut all these into a coarse julienne 40 mm in length; place in a basin. Add the vinaigrette mixed with the French mustard and carefully mix together.

5. Dress in a smooth dome shape on a ravier.

6. Stone the olives with a column cutter and cut into thin slices. Arrange half overlapping in lines to three-quarter cover the salad from the base. Sprinkle the top with chopped parsley.

## 93 Pimento salad                    Salade de piments

| 8 portions | Ingredients | 10 couverts |
|---|---|---|
| 4 oz | fresh red pimentoes | 140 g |
| 4 oz | fresh green pimentoes | 140 g |
| 1 oz | finely chopped onion | 35 g |
| ½ gill (2½ fl. oz) | vinaigrette sauce | 90 ml |
| 1 teaspoon | salt | 4 g |
| ¼ teaspoon | milled pepper | 1 g |

### Method

1. Wash the pimentoes, remove the stalk and cut in halves lengthways. Remove all seeds.

2. Cut the halves in two lengthways, then shred across 3 mm thick.

3. Mix with the chopped onion, seasoning and vinaigrette sauce.

*Note.* If only one type of pimento is used, the French name is Salade de piment.

## 94 Potato salad          Salade de pommes de terre

| 8 portions | Ingredients | 10 couverts |
|---|---|---|
| 1¼ lb | potatoes (medium) | 700 g |
| 1 oz | finely chopped onion | 35 g |
| 1 teaspoon | salt | 4 g |
| ¼ teaspoon | milled pepper | 1 g |
| 1 teaspoon | chopped parsley | 2 g |
| ½ gill (2½ fl. oz) | vinaigrette sauce | 90 ml |
| 4 fl. oz | mayonnaise | 140 ml |

### Method

1. Wash the potatoes; plain boil or steam in the skins for approximately 20–25 minutes then cool slightly.
2. Peel with a knife and cut into 10 mm dice. Add the onion and seasoning. Sprinkle with the vinaigrette while still warm.
3. When cold, mix carefully with the mayonnaise.
4. Serve in a loose dome shape in a ravier, sprinkled with chopped parsley.

## 95 Radishes (with butter)        Radis au beurre

| 8 portions | Ingredients | 10 couverts |
|---|---|---|
| 2 × 6 oz bunches | radishes | 420 g |
| 2 oz | butter | 70 g |

### Method

1. Trim the green stalk to 20 mm then wash the radishes well.
2. Make two incisions 10 mm deep across the radishes at the root end. Place into ice water for 15 minutes.
3. Cream the butter and place it in greaseproof piping bag with a 5 mm star tube.
4. Pipe a small star in the split base of each radish.
5. Replace in ice water to set the butter. Drain, then place in a ravier.

## 96 Rice salad          Salade de riz

| 8 portions | Ingredients | 10 couverts |
|---|---|---|
| 6 oz | patna rice | 210 g |
| 8 oz | tomatoes | 280 g |
| 2 oz | shelled or frozen peas | 70 g |
| 1 teaspoon | salt | 4 g |
| ¼ teaspoon | milled pepper | 1 g |
| 3 fl. oz | vinaigrette | 100 ml |

### Method

1. Wash the rice and place into plenty of boiling salt water; stir until reboiling. Simmer for 17–18 minutes. A small 'bite' should remain in the cooked rice.
2. Well wash in cold water to remove all starch and thoroughly drain in a colander. Place in a basin.
3. Blanch and skin the tomatoes, cut in halves across, remove the seeds, and cut them into 5 mm dice.
4. Cook the peas in boiling salt water for 7 minutes if frozen or 12–15 minutes if fresh. Refresh and drain.
5. Add the tomato and peas to the rice, season then add the vinaigrette. Fork over to mix.
6. Dress in a loose dome shape in a ravier.

## 97 Salami          *Salami

### Method

Slice the salami very thin and dress 3 slices per portion on a crisp cleaned lettuce leaf. Place in a ravier.

## 98 Salami cornets          *Cornets de salami

| 8 portions | Ingredients | 10 couverts |
|---|---|---|
| 16 | slices of salami | 20 |
| 4 oz | pâté de foie (23) | 140 g |
| 1 fl. oz | cream | 35 ml |
| 4 | gherkins | 5 |
| ½ | lettuce | 1 small |

### Method

1. Place the point of a cornet mould to one edge of the salami, roll the salami round the mould and press tightly to retain the shape.
2. Pass the pâté de foie through a fine sieve, place in a basin, and gradually stir in the cream. Place the mixture into a piping bag with a 5 mm star tube.
3. Pipe the mixture into the cornets to fill to the top edge.
4. Place the prepared crisp leaves of lettuce in a ravier. Dress the cornets in rows and decorate each with a very small gherkin fan (4 fans per gherkin).

## 99 Sardines          Sardines à l'huile

### Method

1. Invert the opened tin of sardines into a dish to prevent breaking the fish.
2. Dress in line or fanwise in a ravier. Mask over with olive oil, 1 large or 2 small fish is the normal portion.
3. Decorate each sardine with a thin quarter slice of scrolled lemon. Garnish the corners of the dish with washed, picked parsley.

## 100 Smoked herring fillets · Gendarme à l'huile

### Method

1. Remove the fillets from the can carefully. Cut on the slant in 25 mm strips and give 3 pieces per portion.
2. Arrange in rows in a ravier, mask with olive oil and garnish the corners of the dish with picked parsley.

## 101 Sweet corn · Maïs à la crème

| 8 portions | Ingredients | 10 couverts |
|---|---|---|
| 1 × 16 oz can | creamed corn (canned) | 1 × 500–550 g |
| ½ oz | red pimento (canned) | 20 g |
| 2 fl. oz | cream | 70 ml |

### Method

1. Lightly drain the corn in a conical strainer.
2. Dress in a smooth dome shape in a ravier. Mask over with the cream.
3. Decorate with thin strips of the pimento, 20 mm apart, slantwise, along the corn.

## 102 Tomato salad · Salade de tomate

| 8 portions | Ingredients | 10 couverts |
|---|---|---|
| 1 lb (8 × 2 oz) | tomatoes (firm) | 560 g (10) |
| 1 oz | finely chopped onion | 35 g |
| ½ | lettuce | 1 small |
| ½ gill (2½ fl. oz) | vinaigrette sauce | 90 ml |
| 1 teaspoon | chopped parsley | 2 g |

### Method

1. Remove the stalk base from the tomatoes with a small knife. Blanch for 6–7 seconds in boiling water, refresh and peel.
2. Cut into 3 mm-thick slices, down the tomato.
3. Dress in a ravier on the prepared crisp lettuce leaves (optional), three-quarters overlapping the slices.
4. Sprinkle all over with the onion, then the vinaigrette, and sprinkle with chopped parsley.

## 103 Tomato and cucumber salad · Salade de tomate et de concombre

### Method

Using half quantities of tomato and cucumber slices, arrange in rows, half overlapping.

## 104 Tomato and egg mayonnaise · Mayonnaise d'oeuf et de tomate

### Method

Using half quantities of tomato and egg, arrange alternate slices and finish as for Egg mayonnaise (71).

## 105 Tomatoes (Antibe style) · *Tomates antiboise

| 8 portions | Ingredients | 10 couverts |
|---|---|---|
| 12 oz (8 × 1½ oz) | tomatoes (firm) | 420 (10) |
| 4 oz | cooked white fish | 140 g |
| 4 oz | shellfish (shrimps, prawns, crab) | 140 g |
| 1 oz | finely chopped onion | 35 g |
| ½ oz | capers | 20 g |
| 2 teaspoons | chopped parsley | 4 g |
| ½ gill (2½ fl. oz) | vinaigrette sauce | 90 ml |

### Method

1. Remove the stalk base from the tomatoes, blanch, refresh and peel.
2. Cut off one-quarter of the tomato from the opposite end and remove the seeds with a teaspoon.
3. Flake the fish and place in a basin. Add the shellfish (flake the crab and remove bone).
4. Add the remainder of the dry ingredients. With a fork, lightly mix with three-quarters of the vinaigrette, and add a pinch of salt and pepper.
5. Fill the mixture into the tomato cases then replace the tomato 'caps' at an angle to show the filling.
6. Place in a ravier and sprinkle over with the remainder of the vinaigrette.

*Note.* If desired, the 'caps' may be decorated with small crescents or diamonds of hard-boiled white of egg.

## 106 Tomatoes (Monaco style) · *Tomates monégasque

| 8 portions | Ingredients | 10 couverts |
|---|---|---|
| 12 oz (8 × 1½ oz) | tomatoes (firm) | 420 (10) |
| 8 oz | tunny fish | 280 g |
| 2 | hard boiled egg | 3 |
| 1 oz | finely chopped onion | 35 g |
| ½ oz | capers | 20 g |
| 2 teaspoons | chopped parsley | 4 g |
| 1 teaspoon | chopped chervil | 2 g |
| 2 fl. oz | vinaigrette sauce | 70 ml |
| 4 fl. oz | mayonnaise | 140 ml |

### Method

1. Prepare the tomato cases and 'caps' as for Tomates antiboise.
2. Sprinkle the cases with vinaigrette and drain.

3. Flake the tunny, season with a little pepper, and add the remainder of the ingredients. Mix lightly with a fork.

4. Finish and serve as for Tomates antiboise (105).

## 106a Tomatoes (Russian style)   Tomates à la russe

**Method**

1. Prepare the tomatoes and 'caps' as for Tomates antiboise.

2. Fill with Russian salad (see 109).

3. Finish as for Tomates antiboise (105).

## 107 Tunny fish   Thon à l'huile

**Method**

1. Flake 1 oz (30 g) of canned tunny fish per portion and season with a little milled pepper.

2. Dress in a ravier on prepared crisp lettuce leaves. Sprinkle with olive oil, then chopped parsley.

## 108 Vegetable salad   Salade de légumes

| 8 portions | Ingredients | 10 couverts |
| --- | --- | --- |
| 8 oz | carrots | 280 g |
| 4 oz | turnips | 140 g |
| 4 oz | French beans | 140 g |
| 4 oz | shelled or frozen peas | 140 g |
| 1 teaspoon | chopped parsley | 2 g |
| 1½ teaspoons | salt | 6 g |
| ¼ teaspoon | milled pepper | 1 g |
| 2 fl. oz | vinaigrette sauce | 70 ml |
| 4 fl. oz | mayonnaise | 140 ml |

**Method**

1. Wash, peel and rewash the carrots and turnips. Cut them into 5 mm dice or batons 20 × 5 × 5 mm.

2. Cover each separately, boil, skim, then add a pinch of salt. Boil the turnips for 10–12 minutes, the carrots for 20–25 minutes, until tender.

3. Drain in a colander and marinade with the vinaigrette while hot.

4. Prepare and cook the beans as in 1031. Cut into 5 mm dice.

5. Add the peas to boiling salt water, boil for 7 minutes if frozen or 12–15 minutes if fresh; refresh and drain.

6. Combine the vegetables in a basin. Season, then bind with the mayonnaise.

7. Serve in a loose dome shape in a ravier and sprinkle with chopped parsley.

## 109 Vegetable salad (Russian style)   Salade à la russe

**Method**

1. Prepare as for Vegetable salad. When mixed, add 4 oz (140 g) of cooked flaked fish, free of skin and bone.

2. Dress to a dome shape in a ravier and sprinkle with chopped parsley. Decorate with a trellis of anchovy, and small sections of hard-boiled egg to one-eighth of the height from the base.

## 110 Various canapés   Canapés variés
Canapés à la russe

**Method**

1. Canapés consist of a variety of garnished or decorated foods served on a base of bread, toast, biscuit, puff pastry or small barquettes.

2. For toasted types, the bread is cut 5 mm thick, toasted on both sides, lightly pressed, then separated to release any steam. The toast is then well buttered.

3. The finished size, irrespective of the shape, should not be more than 50 mm (finger type), 40 mm (diamond shape) or 30 mm in diameter (circles) and the corresponding size for crescents, etc.

4. Some types are produced in slices and, for a first class finish, these should be cut to the finished size before the jelly is applied.

5. Some of the foods used are caviar, foie gras, salami, liver sausage, Parma ham, York ham, smoked salmon, anchovy, smoked herring fillet, rollmop herring, cheese, creamed cheese, ox-tongue, tomato, egg slices or purée and sardines (skinned).

6. Decoration consists of piped, creamed butter either alone or with other garnishes. The general rule applied should be that the decoration should contrast in colour and blend in flavour, e.g. small gherkin fans on a circle of salami on toast or creamed cheese on biscuit with a small diamond of ham.

7. Before glazing, the canapés should be placed to chill in the refrigerator to set the decoration. This will also assist the acceptance of the jelly and avoid the base becoming soaked with jelly.

8. Lightly stir a little of the aspic jelly in a sauteuse on ice until it begins to lightly thicken to the consistency of olive oil. Mask it over the canapés and set in refrigerator. Repeat the glazing if necessary.

9. Add a little warm jelly to that remaining and use.

10. Serve canapés on flat dishes on doilys, garnished with halves of lemon or tomato cut with a serrated edge, and sprigs of fresh washed parsley. Care should be used when arranging to contrast the colours.

## 111 HOT HORS D'OEUVRE—HORS D'OEUVRE CHAUDS

**Method**

1. These consist of a variety of garnished or decorated foods, mainly savoury in flavour, served on toast, in small bouché cases (30 mm in diameter), small tartlets or barquettes. Other sizes should be as for Canapés variés.
2. The ingredients used are prepared and served in the same manner as for savouries, but the size varies, e.g. Canapé Diane, Bouchée Ivanhoë, Scotch woodcock, etc.
3. These savoury-type foods are supplemented for variety with those such as Goujonnette de sole, Barquette de laitance Mornay, small salmon or deep fried fish cake mixture balls, grilled chipolata sausages, young spinach leaves (3 or 4 together) dipped in curry-flavoured batter and deep fried, etc.
4. They are served on hot, flat dishes and garnished with sprigs of fresh or fried parsley.
5. Those foods not on toast or within a case are impaled on a cocktail stick.

The varieties given here are but a sample of the variations possible, and the savoury fillings used will in many cases be suitable for more than one type, e.g. Barquettes, Beignets, Bouchées, Croustades, Petits pâtés.

**Small skewers**  **Attereaux**

These are made from a variety of pieces of cooked meat, fish or fowl, together with pieces of mushroom, bacon, tongue, ham, truffles, brain, liver, oysters, sweetbread or kidney. The ingredients are cut into 25 mm squares and then the pieces are pierced on a skewer, alternating the basic ingredients with the appropriate variety of garnish. The completed skewers should be approximately 75 mm in length; these are lightly coated with a well reduced sauce while the sauce is warm. When the sauce has set, the skewer is breadcrumbed 'à l'anglaise' and cooked in a friture as required for service.

### Attereaux de cervelle à l'ancienne

Poached brain with slices of mushroom cooked in blanc and slices of truffle; coat with Sauce Villeroi.

### Attereaux de cervelle à l'italienne

Poached brain with slices of cooked ham and slices of grilled mushroom; coat with Sauce italienne.

### Attereaux à l'écarlate

Cooked tongue with slices of grilled mushroom and slices of truffles; coat with a reduced sauce of veal velouté and tomato.

### Attereaux de foies de volaille

Pieces of chicken liver set stiff in butter with grilled mushrooms and streaky bacon; coat with Sauce italienne.

### Attereaux de homard

Lobster slices with slices of mushroom cooked à blanc, and slices of truffle; coat with Sauce Villeroi.

### Barquettes

Barquettes are small pastry cases cooked in boat-shaped barquette moulds. The paste used is generally a short paste but puff paste trimming may be used. The paste in the moulds is well pricked and the cases are cooked blind (i.e. with a filling of beans to keep the shape of the cases during cooking; they are removed when the cases are cooked).

The fillings for the barquettes are savoury mixtures made from purée or diced savoury ingredients and are generally sprinkled with grated cheese or breadcrumbs fried golden in butter. The barquettes are passed through a hot oven when required for service.

### Barquettes à l'américaine

Salpicon of cooked lobster bound in an Américaine sauce, sprinkled with browned crumbs.

### Barquettes aux anchois

Chopped onions cooked without colouring in butter with diced anchovies and diced cooked mushrooms. They are bound together in a thick sauce béchamel and sprinkled with browned crumbs.

### Barquettes Mornay

Small pieces of fish or shellfish bound in a Sauce Mornay, sprinkled with grated cheese.

### Barquette florentine

Place a little purée of spinach in the bottom of the barquette and on top of this place a piece of poached herring roe. Coat with Sauce Mornay, sprinkle with grated cheese and glaze.

### Barquette au parmesan

Fill the barquette cases with a Soufflé au parmesan mixture and cook in a hot oven at 180°C (350°F).

These mixtures can be varied as desired and may also be served in small pastry tartlet cases.

### Fritters                                                  Beignets

These small fritters are made by two methods:

(a) A non-sweetened Pâte à choux mixture with savoury ingredients incorporated and cooked 'à la friture', or the Pâte à choux mixture cooked 'à la friture' and then the beignets stuffed with a suitable savoury mixture.

(b) Small pieces or escalopes of cooked ham, tongue, brains, sweetbreads, meat, fish, mussels, oysters, game or fowl. These are marinaded with salt, pepper, parsley and oil with lemon juice or vinegar for 30 minutes before cooking. The prepared pieces are dipped in Pâte à frire and cooked 'à la friture'.

### Bouchées

These are small puff paste cases either round, oval, square or oblong in shape with a savoury filling and, if desired, a slice of truffle, ham, tongue or other appropriate garnish may be used in place of the pastry lid.

### Bouchées à l'américaine

Salpicon of cooked lobster bound in an Américaine sauce. Other shellfish can be used in a similar manner.

### Bouchées à la reine: Bouchées à l'ancienne

Diced cooked chicken, mushrooms and truffles bound in a Sauce suprême. A round of lean ham or a slice of truffle is used as a lid.

### Bouchées à la bouquetière

Diced cooked vegetables bound in a cream sauce.

### Bouchées aux huîtres

Poached oysters lightly bound with a creamed Sauce vin blanc.

### Bouchées aux moules

Poached mussels lightly bound with a creamed Sauce vin blanc.

### Bouchées à la St Hubert

Salpicon of game with truffles, bound in a Sauce salmis. A turned mushroom head is used for a lid. The cases are oval-shaped.

### Brioches garnies

The small unsweetened brioches have the top removed and the centre emptied. The cases are then dried a little in an oven and used in a similar manner as for Bouchées. The tops are used as lids.

### Brochettes

Small brochettes or skewers of mixed ingredients are served as Hors d'oeuvre chauds. The ingredients are cut into small squares or pieces, tossed in butter to part-cook then placed on a skewer, brushed with melted butter and coated in fresh breadcrumbs, and then gently grilled.

The ingredients that can be used are chicken liver, bacon, sweetbreads, ham, tongue, mushrooms, kidneys, bay leaves, onions, lamb or beef fillet. Pieces of cooked fish, bay leaves and mushrooms make another variety.

### Caissettes or Petites caisses

These are small receptacles of fireproof china, glass, metal or oiled paper which have a mixture placed in them. This is well sprinkled with breadcrumbs or cheese and then gratinated in an oven when reheated. If the gratination is not appropriate to the mixture, a turned mushroom or a slice of ham or truffle can be placed on top at the moment of serving.

The mixtures used are as for Bouchées or Barquettes.

### Cannelons (or: Canneloni)

These are made from puff paste shaped as follows:

(a) A cornet, as for cream horn, filled with a savoury mixture or salpicon of fish.

(b) In small rolls, as for sausage rolls, with a suitable savoury filling.

(c) A small piece of puff paste (40 × 100 × 5 mm) rolled on to a greased rod of 20 mm diameter to form a ring and cooked in this form. When cool, it is stuffed with a suitable mixture and reheated.

(d) Rolled in small rolls as for Jam roll, using a suitable savoury mixture in place of jams.

### Cassolette

(a) Small cases are made by piping Duchess potatoes, which are egg-washed, then baked to dry and colour in the oven. They are then filled with a similar filling as used for Bouchées.

(b) Small balls of Duchess potatoes, flattened a little and then egged and breadcrumbed thoroughly. They are fried 'à la friture' and a small hole is cut with a round cutter in the top of each, so forming a case. Similar filling is used as for Bouchées and the cut out lids replaced.

### Choux garnis (duchesse, éclairs, carolines)

Use an unsweetened Pâte à choux to make small buns, and fill them with savoury fillings. Éclairs are piped in small finger shapes and Carolines in small crescent shapes.

### Chaussons

These are made of chicken, game, meat, fish or shellfish. The main ingredient may have hard-boiled eggs, mushroom or truffles as a garnish. Dice all the ingredients and reduce them together in the appropriate sauce, thickening with yolks of egg. Place the mixture in a flat dish to cool.

When cold, mould into flat galettes and dip in Pâte à frire and fry 'à la friture'. If desired, they may be first wrapped in a thin pancake or in a piece of pig's caul.

### Croquettes

The basic mixture is similar to Cromesquis, but they are moulded into cork shapes, then egg and breadcrumbed and fried 'à la friture'.

### Croustades

These contain fillings similar to those for Bouchées, placed in cases as follows:

(a) A deep tartlet cooked blind; Pâte à brisée is used.

(b) Duchess potatoes, gnocchi romaine, with the gnocchi made with rice in place of semolina.

Mould the Duchess potatoes into balls, flatten them a little and then egg and breadcrumb them twice to give a good coating. Fry 'à la friture' and then cut them with a round cutter and empty the centre, leaving a case; the piece cut out is used as a lid.

The semolina or rice gnocchi mixtures, when cold, are cut into rounds 50 mm in diameter 25 mm thick. These are then egged and breadcrumbed twice, the lid marked with a cutter and they are then cooked 'à la friture'. When fried, the lid can be lifted off and the inside emptied to leave a case.

### Dartois

Prepare two strips of puff paste 4 mm thick × 75 mm wide. Place one on a baking tray, brush with egg wash and place or pipe the required savoury filling along the centre of the strip, leaving 12 mm of edge clear on each side. Cover with the other strip of paste which has been cut with slots or pricked. Notch the edges with the back of a knife to seal them together. Egg wash, and then cook in a hot oven. When cooked, cut in strips 25 mm wide.

### Fondants

These are croquettes made in an egg or pear shape which are egged and breadcrumbed and cooked 'à la friture'. Although similar mixtures can be prepared as those for croquettes, they are different from these because the ingredients of fondants should be a purée, and therefore the more 'fondant', or melting, when eaten.

### Cheese straws          Paillettes au fromage

Use a three-part puff paste, or puff paste trimmings. Roll it out on to a sheet on a slab which has been sprinkled with grated cheese, dust with more grated cheese and give the paste a turn. Then roll the paste out in a strip 200 mm wide × 1·5 mm thick and cut it into fine strips each 200 mm long × 5 mm wide. Twist these strips and place them on a baking sheet in neat rows, pressing the ends to the sheet so that they will remain twisted. Cook in a hot oven and trim to even lengths when removed.

Use 4 oz grated cheese and ¼ teaspoonful of cayenne pepper with each 1 lb of prepared puff paste (250 g and ½ teaspoonful per kg). Parmesan cheese is best for cheese straws, although Cheddar, Chester or Gruyère may be used.

### Small patties          Petits pâtés

These are made from a bottom and top of puff paste cut in the same small shape (round, square, oval or oblong). The bottom is egg washed, a small portion of a suitable savoury filling placed in the centre and then covered with the top. They are then placed on a baking sheet, the top egg washed and pricked, and placed in a hot oven to cook. The fillings are similar to those used for Bouchées.

## Pannequets

To make pannequets, prepare some very thin pancakes from a non-sweetened Pâte à crêpes, spread each with a savoury mixture, and roll as for Swiss roll. Cut into 50 mm lengths, then egg and breadcrumb. Cook 'à la friture'.

## Ramequins

These are small tartlet cases of cheese soufflé mixture cooked in a hot oven.

## Subric

The following are recipes that can be easily adapted if other ingredients are to be used:

### Subric de boeuf

| 8 portions | Ingredients | 10 couverts |
|---|---|---|
| 10 oz | cooked diced braised beef | 350 g |
| 1 oz | finely chopped onion | 35 g |
| ½ oz | butter | 20 g |
| 3 | eggs | 4 |
| ½ oz | flour | 20 g |
| 2 oz | oil | 70 g |
| 3 teaspoons | salt | 12 g |
| ¼ teaspoon | ground white pepper | 2 g |
| Produces 24 50 mm rounds | | |

## Method

Cook the onions in the butter without colouring and allow to cool. Beat the egg thoroughly and beat in the flour, then mix in the other ingredients. To make neat round subrics, heat the oil in a pan and stand 50 mm plain round cutters in it. Place a heaped teaspoon of the appareil in each cutter and shape to the round. When they are set, remove the cutter and allow to cook and colour on both sides.

### Subric de cervelle: de ris de veau: d'amourettes

| 8 portions | Ingredients | 10 couverts |
|---|---|---|
| 8 oz | brain, sweetbread or bone marrow | 280 g |
| ½ pint | sauce béchamel or allemande | 350 ml |
| 2 | eggs | 3 |
| | salt, pepper and nutmeg to flavour | |

## Method

Mix the eggs, sauce and seasoning thoroughly, then fold in the cooked offal which has been cut into 10 mm dice. Cook as before.

Subric florentine has 1 oz (35 g) of grated Parmesan cheese added to the appareil.

---

# SAVOURY BUTTERS

## 112 Anchovy butter      Beurre d'anchois
### Method

1. Pound ½ oz (15 g) of anchovy fillets to a purée.
2. Thoroughly mix in 6 oz (170 g) of firm butter.
3. Add 1 teaspoon (4 g) anchovy essence and rub the mixture through a hair sieve.
4. Roll in greaseproof paper to 25 mm in diameter, twisting the ends of the paper to remove any cavities in the butter.
5. Chill in a refrigerator to set then, when set, cut into 5 mm slices and place into ice water until required. Serve in a sauceboat or place on the article of food served.

## 113 Montpellier butter      Beurre Montpellier
### Method

1. Cook, in boiling salt water for 3 minutes, 2 oz (55 g) of mixed washed spinach, parsley, tarragon and chervil.
2. Refresh, drain and squeeze out all water. Pound to a purée with 4 hard-boiled yolks of egg, 6 fillets of anchovy, 1 oz (30 g) gherkin, ½ oz (15 g) capers and ¼ pod of garlic.
3. Thoroughly mix in 6 oz (170 g) of firm butter then rub it through a hair sieve.
4. Finish and serve as from 4 in Anchovy butter.

## 114 Oriental butter      Beurre orientale
### Method

1. Slowly sweat ½ oz (15 g) of finely chopped shallot in 1 oz (30 g) of butter for 6–7 minutes without colouring.
2. Add 1 teaspoon (3 g) of paprika pepper, sweat for 2–3 minutes, then add 2 oz (55 g) of red pimento, 2 oz (55 g) of skinned and diced tomato, ¼ pod of garlic and 1 tablespoon (15 ml) of vinegar.
3. Boil the mixture and reduce until all the moisture has been evaporated. Allow to go cold. Pound to a purée,

thoroughly mix in 6 oz (170 g) of firm butter then rub through a hair sieve.

4. Finish and serve as from 4 in Anchovy butter.

### 115  Paprika butter                     Beurre de paprika

**Method**

1. Sweat 2 teaspoons (6 g) of paprika pepper in 1 oz (30 g) of butter for 2–3 minutes; do not allow to colour.

2. When cold, thoroughly mix into 6 oz (170 g) of firm butter, then mix in the strained juice of half a lemon, together with 1 or 2 drops of cochineal to give a pink tint.

3. Finish and serve as from 4 in Anchovy butter.

### 116  Parsley butter                   Beurre maître d'hôtel

**Method**

1. Thoroughly mix together 6 oz (170 g) of butter, 6 teaspoons (12 g) of chopped parsley, the strained juice of half a lemon and a few grains of cayenne pepper.

2. Finish and serve as from 4 in Anchovy butter.

### 117  Shrimp butter                     Beurre de crevettes

**Method**

1. Pound 2 oz (55 g) of shrimps to a purée.

2. Thoroughly mix in 6 oz (170 g) of firm butter with a few grains of cayenne pepper and 1 or 2 drops of cochineal to give a pink tint.

3. Pass through a hair sieve.

4. Finish and serve as from 4 in Anchovy butter.

### 118  Tomato butter                      Beurre de tomate

**Method**

1. Sweat ½ oz (15 g) of finely chopped shallot in 1 oz (30 g) of butter for 6–7 minutes; do not allow to colour.

2. Add 1 oz (30 g) of tomato purée; evaporate any moisture.

3. When cold, pound to a purée and thoroughly mix in 6 oz (170 g) of firm butter and 1 or 2 spots of cochineal to give a clear red colour. Pass through a hair sieve.

4. Finish and serve as from 4 in Anchovy butter.

---

## SALAD DRESSINGS

Allow ½ pint (280 ml) for 8–10 portions.

### 119  Acidulated cream                       Crème acidulée

**Method**

1. Whisk into ½ pint (280 ml) of double cream 2 fl. oz (55 ml) of strained lemon juice and a few grains of salt and milled pepper. Serve in a sauceboat, on an underflat with a doily, or combine with the garnish as per recipe.

### 120  Mayonnaise                              Mayonnaise

See Cold sauces (1). Serve in a sauceboat or combine with the garnish as per recipe.

**Mayonnaise with cream**        Mayonnaise à la crème

Combine into ½ pint (280 ml) of mayonnaise 2 fl. oz (55 ml) of double cream.

### 121  Roquefort                   Roquefort à la vinaigrette

**Method**

1. Pass 3 oz (85 g) of Roquefort cheese through a very fine wire sieve then gradually mix in ½ pint (280 ml) of Vinaigrette sauce.

### 122  Thousand island

**Method**

1. Finely chop 1 oz (30 g) each of gherkins and red pimento, and ½ oz (15 g) of chives or onion.

2. Add this to ½ pint (280 ml) of mayonnaise, then add 1 tablespoon of tomato ketchup, 2 teaspoons (4 g) of chopped parsley, and 10 drops of chilli sauce (tabasco). Mix thoroughly.

### 123  Vinegar and oil                          Vinaigrette

See Cold sauces (7).

**Vinegar, oil and lemon**           Vinaigrette au citron

Prepare Sauce vinaigrette, using strained lemon juice in place of vinegar.

## 124 Preparation of lettuce for salads (cabbage type)

**Method**

1. Cut off a slice from the root base. Remove any outside leaves if they are withered, discoloured, or broken with a discoloured edge, and any other parts similarly affected.
2. Separate the leaves and place them in plenty of cold water. If the heart, the centre of the lettuce, is required whole, only remove the outer leaves.
3. Wash thoroughly, drain, then shake out all water by placing in a salad basket or cloth and shaking until dry. Place in a refrigerator for 1 hour to crisp.

*Note.* Hot-house lettuce, when used, should not be cleaned until required, and then washed quickly, as they tend to go limp.

4. For certain salads, such as those prepared to be served individually, the lettuce leaves are prepared as a 'cup'. This is formed by placing 3 or 4 lettuce leaves on top of each other, the smaller ones inside, then crisping in a refrigerator to set the raised edges to form the 'cup'. Quantities expressed are for 8–10 portions.

## 125 Beetroot salad      Salade de betterave

See Hors d'oeuvre (60). Serve in a salad bowl.

## 126 Cole slaw

See Hors d'oeuvre (63). Serve in a salad bowl.

## 127 Cucumber salad      Salade de concombre

See Hors d'oeuvre (66). Serve in a salad bowl.

## 128 Half mourning salad      Salade demi-deuil

See Hors d'oeuvre (85). Dress (a) individually by placing a heaped tablespoon of the potato salad in a cup of lettuce leaves, then sprinkling the top with a fine julienne of truffle. (b) in a salad bowl by placing the potato salad in the centre of the lettuce leaves, then sprinkling the top with a fine julienne of truffle.

## 129 Endive salad      Salade d'endive belge
   (Belgian-type, chicory)

**Method**

1. Take 1 lb (560 g) of Belgian endive and cut off a thin slice from the root end.

2. Remove one layer of the outer leaves and any other damaged or discoloured ones. Wash in cold salt water and drain well.
3. Cut the endive in 25 mm lengths and the root end into 4 or 6 sections lengthwise.
4. To serve, rub a salad bowl with the cut edge of a piece of garlic. Dress the endive in a loose dome shape and sprinkle with chopped parsley. A sauceboat of vinaigrette is served separately.

## 130 Endive salad (curly type)      Salade de chicorée

**Method**

1. Pull away a few of the outer leaves of 2 heads of curly endive. With a small knife, trim off any discoloured parts of leaves, especially around the edges.
2. Release the leaves by cutting away the base of the root stem and separate.
3. Wash well in cold salt water. Drain and thoroughly dry by shaking in a basket or cloth. Crisp the leaves for 1 hour in the refrigerator.
4. Dress the leaves loosely in a salad bowl. Serve a sauceboat of vinaigrette separately.

*Note.* If desired, the salad may be garnished with a little Beetroot salad in the centre with sections of peeled tomatoes around the edge.

## 131 Florida salad      Salade Florida

**Method**

1. Prepare ½ a grapefruit and ½ an orange per portion, as for cocktail.
2. Dress (a) individually by placing cups of lettuce leaves on a flat dish and attractively arranging the segments of grapefruit in a circle with the orange on top, or (b) by dressing the lettuce leaves in a bowl with the grapefruit segments in a circle in the centre and the oranges on top.
3. Serve acidulated cream dressing in a sauceboat.

## 132 French salad      Salade française

**Method**

1. Dress the lettuce leaves in a salad bowl, leaving a bay in the centre. Fill the bay with beetroot salad (1 oz (30 g) per portion) sprinkled with chopped parsley.

2. Garnish around the edges with sections of peeled to-matoes ($\frac{1}{2}$ per portion), quarters of hard boiled egg (2 per portion) and slices of cucumber, if available.

3. Serve vinaigrette separately in a sauceboat.

### 133 Green salad             Salade verte

**Method**

1. Dress loosely in a salad bowl a mixture of any prepared green-type salad available.

2. Serve vinaigrette separately in a sauceboat.

### 134 Italian salad             Salade italienne

See Hors d'oeuvre (84). Dress in the same manner in a salad bowl.

    Serve vinaigrette separately in a sauceboat.

### 135 Japanese salad          Salade japonaise

**Method**

1. Blanch, refresh and skin 1 lb (560 g) tomatoes. Cut across, remove the seeds and cut into 10 mm dice.

2. Blanch, skin and remove the seeds from 8 oz (280 g) of grapes.

3. Peel 8 oz (280 g) dessert apples and cut into 10 mm dice.

4. Prepare 4–5 oranges as for cocktail.

5. Cut 8 oz (280 g) pineapple into 10 mm dice.

6. Combine these ingredients with approximately $\frac{1}{2}$ pint (350 ml) of acidulated cream dressing.

7. Serve (a) by dividing the mixture and placing it in dome shapes, into lettuce cups, or (b) in dome shapes in a salad bowl, surrounded by small sections of lettuce heart. In both methods, dust the surface with a little paprika pepper.

### 136 Jardinière salad         Salade jardinière

**Method**

Prepare as for Vegetable salad (108), cutting the root vege-tables into bâtons 20 × 5 × 5 mm.

    Serve in a salad bowl.

### 137 Lettuce heart salad      Salade cœur de laitue

**Method**

1. Cut the lettuce hearts into 4–6 sections lengthways, according to size. Allow 2 pieces per portion.

2. Dress in a salad bowl with the root ends of the sections to the centre.

3. Serve vinaigrette separately in a sauceboat.

### 138 Corn salad            Salade Lorette

**Method**

1. Take 8 oz (280 g) corn salad (mâche). Remove any of the small discoloured leaves, the root and any violet-coloured ends of the stalks.

2. Thoroughly wash in cold salt water and drain. Dry by shaking in a cloth.

3. Dress loosely piled in a salad bowl, leaving a bay in the centre.

4. Fill the bay with 1 oz (30 g) of beetroot salad per portion.

5. Cut 1 oz (30 g) per portion of prepared celery into 25 mm coarse julienne. Place around the edge of the beetroot.

### 139 Macédoine salad      Salade macédoine

**Method**

Prepare as for Vegetable salad (108), cutting the root vege-tables into 5 mm dice.

    Serve in a salad bowl.

### 140 Mercédès salad       Salade Mercédès

**Method**

1. Prepare 8 oz (280 g) Belgian endive as for Salade d'endive belge (129).

2. Prepare 8 oz (280 g) beetroot as for Salade de betterave (60).

3. Prepare 1 lb (560 g) tomatoes by blanching; peel, re-move the seeds and cut into 10 mm dice.

4. Cut 8 oz (280 g) celery into 25 mm coarse julienne.

5. Serve dressed in bouquets in a salad bowl or on indi-vidual salad dishes and sprinkle lightly with vinaigrette.

6. Pass 2 hard boiled eggs through a coarse wire sieve and sprinkle over the salad.

7. Serve vinaigrette separately in a sauceboat.

### 141 Mimosa salad           Salade mimosa

**Method 1**

1. Blanch, skin and remove the seeds from 1 lb (560 g) of grapes.

2. Prepare 8 medium oranges as for cocktail.

3. Skin three-quarters of a banana per portion and cut it into 5 mm-thick slices; sprinkle with a little lemon juice to prevent discolouring.

4. Mix the fruit with ½ pint (350 ml) of acidulated cream dressing.

5. Serve as for Salade japonaise (135).

**Method 2**

1. Prepare a Salade coeur de laitue (137).

2. Pass 1 hard-boiled yolk of egg per portion through a coarse sieve and sprinkle it over the lettuce.

## 142  Mixed salad                           Salade panachée

**Method**

1. Serve a mixture of any prepared green-type salad. If desired, a little Belgian endive may be added.

2. Garnish with sections of peeled tomato, radishes and slices of peeled cucumber around the edge. Place a little beetroot salad in the centre.

3. Serve vinaigrette separately in a sauceboat.

## 143  Orange salad                            Salade d'orange

**Method**

1. Remove the zest thinly with a peeler from 2 oranges for each portion. Cut the zest into a fine 25 mm julienne. Blanch for 2 minutes, refresh and drain.

2. Prepare the oranges as for cocktail.

3. Serve the orange segments in a loose dome shape in a salad bowl or in individual salad dishes. Sprinkle over with the blanched julienne.

4. Serve acidulated cream dressing in a sauceboat.

## 144  Orange and lettuce salad   Salade d'orange et de laitue

**Method**

1. Prepare a Salade coeur de laitue (137).

2. Prepare half the quantity of Salade d'orange (143).

3. Place the orange segments between the lettuce hearts. Sprinkle over with the blanched julienne.

4. Serve acidulated cream dressing in a sauceboat.

## 145  Potato salad                 Salade de pommes de terre

See Hors d'oeuvre (94).

## 146  Tomato salad                           Salade de tomates

See Hors d'oeuvre (102).

## 147  Waldorf salad                            Salade Waldorf

**Method**

1. Peel 1½ lb (840 g) Russet apples, remove the core and cut into 5 mm dice.

2. Cut into 5 mm dice 8 oz (280 g) of prepared celery.

3. Blanch and skin 4 oz (140 g) walnut halves or pieces.

4. Mix with ½ pint (350 ml) mayonnaise.

5. Dress (a) individually in cups of lettuce leaves, or (b) place the lettuce leaves in a salad bowl with the mixture in the centre. Dust lightly with paprika to decorate.

# SHELLFISH

### Shrimps and prawns

These are sometimes purchased already cooked, in which case they should have been recently boiled. This will show if the shells are shining. In the salted varieties (Norwegian) the shell will be dull and soft but clear in colour. There should be no signs of green colour around the head.

### Lobster

(a) Lobster should be alive when purchased, and this is denoted by the sharp retraction of the tail. Both claws should be attached.
(b) They are brilliant dark bluish-black in colour.
(c) The carcass should not be broken or damaged.

### Crab

(a) Crab should be alive when bought. It is a dark greenish-brown colour.
(b) Both claws should be attached and it should be fairly heavy in weight.

### Oysters

(a) These must be alive when bought and the presence of life is indicated by tightly closed shells.

(b) There should be a fresh smell of the sea with no staleness.

### Mussels

(a) Shells must be tightly closed, not encrusted with barnacles, when they are bought.
(b) They should be large in size.
(c) Damaged shells must be discarded immediately, as the mussel inside will be dead.
(d) A fresh smell of the sea should emanate from the shells.

### Scallops

(a) The shells should be tightly closed; open shells indicate that the scallop inside is dead.
(b) The orange part when opened should be bright in colour and moist.

### Storage of shellfish

All shellfish should be stored for the minimum period possible.

They should be placed into boxes, covered with a wet sack, with a little crushed ice on top and kept in refrigeration at 5°C (40°F).

---

# FISH

**148 The preparation, cutting, storage, portions and factors of quality of fish.**

### Round and flat varieties: quality factors

(a) The eyes should be bright and not sunken.
(b) The gills should be light red in colour.
(c) The flesh should be firm and resilient, not limp.
(d) The scales should be moist, plentiful and lying flat. In salmon they should be silver in colour.
(e) The skin should be moist, with some sea slime.
(f) In best grade plaice, the skin will be brownish in colour, with orange-red spots.
(g) There should be no unpleasant smell.
(h) In flat fish, the white skin side should show tinges of pink at the edges.

(i) In herring, the head, around the mouth and eyes, should be bright red; this also applies to sprats.

### Storage of fish (not shellfish)

(a) Fish is stored in special types of refrigerators which have perforated non-rust trays. Special drainage facilities are fitted to allow easy and frequent washing of the base of the refrigerator.
(b) It should be placed on crushed ice on a wet cloth, covered with another cloth, then more crushed ice.

### Cleaning

1. Scales, where applicable, are removed by a knife which is held at a slight angle from the flesh and moved from the tail to the head of the fish.
2. In small fish, like whiting, the gills located behind the head are removed by breaking them away at each end with

the fingers. In larger fish, like salmon, they are cut free with a knife or scissors and pulled away.

3. The end of the tail is squared off to give a straight end. The fins are cut off with a knife or scissors.

4. The gut is removed as follows.

(a) Insert the point of a knife in the excretia vent and cut up the belly of the fish to a point halfway to the head. Wash thoroughly under running cold water until the cavity is quite clean. In salmon, it is often necessary to run the end of a small ladle handle along the backbone to release congealed blood.

(b) Fish required to be opened but left whole for cooking is cleaned by cutting it down the back from head to tail, along each side of the bone. The bone is then clipped free at the tail and head and the gut removed. The fish is then thoroughly washed.

## Cuts of fish

(a) Darne: a slice of fish cut on the bone from a large round-type fish, e.g. Darne de saumon.

(b) Tronçon: a slice cut on the bone from a large flat fish, e.g. Tronçon de turbot.

(c) Filet: the flesh of the fish removed from the bone, e.g. Filet de sole.

(d) Suprême: prime cuts (on the slant) from fillets of the larger type of fish, e.g. Suprême de turbot.

(e) Goujon: strips of fish 60–75 mm long × 10 × 10 mm, free from skin and bone.

(f) Goujonette: smaller strips of fish cut 50 × 5 × 5 mm.

(g) Paupiette: small fillets, lightly flattened, spread with a fish force-meat, then rolled.

(h) Délice: folded fillets from the smaller types of fish, e.g. Délice de sole. Sometimes a little farce is placed inside.

## Filleting

1. To fillet flat fish, place the dark skin side on the cutting board and, with a sharp knife, cut through the flesh on a straight line down the centre, from the head to the tail, keeping the knife at a shallow angle to the bone. Carefully cut away the fillet. Repeat the operation on the other side of the fish.

2. To fillet round-type fish, place the fish on a board with the head to the left. With a sharp knife, cut the thinner flesh through behind the head, then cut through the thicker flesh behind the head to separate. Carefully pass the blade of the knife, at a shallow angle to the bone, along the bone

## FILLETING OF FLAT FISH

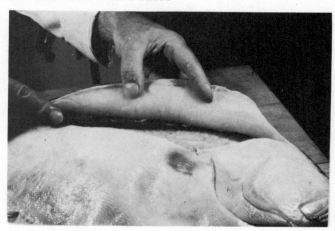

**Large Fillet:**
first stage of removal

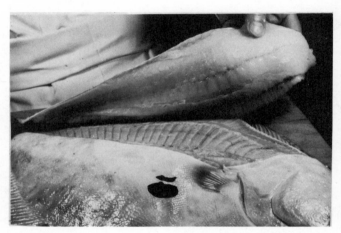

**Large Fillet:**
final stage of removal

**Small Fillet:**
first stage of removal

49

**Small Fillet:**
final stage of removal

Removing of skin from tail to head

from head to tail. To assist in keeping the flesh firmly in position, place the opened hand along the flesh of the fish. Repeat the operation on the other side of the fish.

**Skinning**

1. Dover soles are the only fish that are skinned before filleting. To remove the skin, scrape the squared off end of the tail on both sides with a knife. This will begin to release the skin. Dip the end in salt to grip and then pull the skin off from the tail to head on each side.
2. With other fillets, the dark skin is always removed. Place the skin side of the fillet on the board. With a knife slightly angled towards the board, cut the flesh free from tail to head of the fillet. For certain preparations, the white skin is also removed.

First stage of preparation of Sole Colbert

# PREPARATION OF DOVER SOLE

Scraping skin from squared off tail prior to removal of skin

Second stage with, *right*, a completed sole showing bone cut in 3 places

## PREPARATION OF FILLET SOLE: FOLDED, PAUPIETTE

## PREPARATION OF CURLED WHITING

Cutlet bat in position for flattening. Hand above for even pressure

Removal of skin, after trimming, from head to tail

Knife in position to make shallow incision on skinned side of fillet

Whiting, skinned, ready for curling. Eyes to be removed

*Left:* Paupiette in process of rolling
*Right:* Finished paupiette

Curled whiting complete

51

3. To prepare whiting for curling, trim along the back of the fish rather liberally with a pair of scissors and likewise along the belly. Remove the eyes. Pass a small knife under the skin close to the head and cut through the skin. The skin can now be easily pulled off from head to tail. Pull the skin off the head towards the mouth. Place the tail through the eye sockets.

## Portion control

| | |
|---|---|
| Cod | |
| Fresh haddock | $\frac{3}{4}$ lb (340 g) (unprepared): 1 portion |
| Salmon | 1 lb (455 g) (filleted): 3–4 portions |
| Crab, lobster | $\frac{1}{2}$–$\frac{3}{4}$ lb (225–340 g) (cooked flesh): 1 portion |
| | (*Note.* The best size is $1\frac{1}{4}$–$1\frac{1}{2}$ lb (560–680 g); a 1 lb ($\frac{1}{2}$ kg) lobster yields 5 oz (150 g) of cooked flesh, 2 lb (1 kg) yields 12 oz (350 kg).) |
| Herring, trout (whole) | 6–8 oz (170–225 g): 1 portion |
| Mackerel, whiting (whole) | 8–10 oz (225–280 g): 1 portion |
| Plaice | $1\frac{1}{4}$ lb (560 g): 2 portions (4 fillets) |
| Plaice (whole) | 8–10 oz (225–280 g): 1 portion |
| Slip sole | 6–8 oz (170–225 g): 1 portion |
| Sole for filleting | $1\frac{1}{4}$–$1\frac{1}{2}$ lb (560–680 g): 1 portion |
| Sole (whole) | 10–12 oz (280–350 g): 1 portion |
| Turbot, brill (whole) | 8 lb (3·6 kg): approximately 12 portions |
| Whitebait | 1 lb (455 g): 4–5 portions |

## Fish force-meat      Farce de poisson

Quenelle   ⎱ These are made from a fish force-meat, with
Mousse    ⎰ varying amounts of cream added.

## 149 Fish force-meat      Farce de poisson

| 8 portions | Ingredients | 10 couverts |
|---|---|---|
| 4 oz | fillet of whiting | 140 g |
| 12 oz | fillet of bream, pike, sole, salmon, etc. | 420 g |
| $\frac{1}{2}$ oz (4 level teaspoons) | salt | 20 g |
| $2\frac{1}{2}$ oz | flour panada mixture (361b) | 90 g |
| 2 | whites of egg | 2 |
| 7 fl. oz | double cream | 250 ml |
| $\frac{1}{4}$ teaspoon | ground white pepper | 1 g |

## Method

1. Remove the skin from the fillets.
2. Pound the fish vigorously in a mortar or pass through a very fine blade on a mincing machine.
3. Work in the salt to give body to the mixture. If a mortar is not available, mixing can be effected in a general purpose mixer, but use a low speed to avoid generating heat.
4. Gradually work in the white of egg, then the panada.
5. Rub the mixture through a fine wire sieve then place into a sauteuse on crushed ice in a bowl for 1 hour.
6. Add the pepper, then, with a spatula, gradually work in the cream.
7. Test the mixture by placing a little into boiling salt water, then gently poach at 95°C (200°F) for 4–5 minutes. The texture should be light and spongy, but with sufficient firmness to retain shape.

*Note.* Although the type of fish used may vary according to the fish for which the farce is made, the amount of whiting should always be retained. This particular fish helps to provide body to the mixture. When salmon is used, it may be necessary to add a few drops of cochineal to give a light pink colour.

## 150 Fish quenelles      Quenelles de poisson

### Method

1. The quenelles are generally moulded in two sizes: (a) for garnish, and (b) for a fish course.
2. For garnish, place one dessert spoon in the mixture and one into a bowl of water. Mould the mixture in the spoon up the side of the sauteuse to a smooth dome shape.
3. Using the wet spoon, cut the mixture out of the other spoon and reverse it on to a buttered shallow tray ready for poaching.
4. For a fish course, the quenelles are prepared in the same manner, using tablespoons.
5. The basic farce will produce:
    (a) 28–30 quenelles for garnish, or
    (b) 12 quenelles for a fish course of $2\frac{1}{4}$ oz (65 g) each.
    Use two quenelles when served as a main dish.

## 151 Fish mousse (hot)      Mousse de poisson

### Method

1. Prepare the Farce de poisson (149).
2. Use double the quantity of cream.

3. Using a piping bag with a large plain tube, pipe into well-buttered dariole or charlotte moulds, ready for cooking.

4. Lightly tap the base of the mould on a cloth to remove any pleats in the mixture.

5. The basic mixture will produce 10 portions of 3½ oz (100 g).

---

## MEAT, BACON, POULTRY

### 152 The preparation, dissection, storage, portions and factors of quality of meat, bacon and poultry.

QUALITY, FRESHNESS AND STORAGE

#### Beef

(a) Sides or quarters of first class beef should be compact in formation.

(b) Lean meat should be bright red in colour and marbled with small flecks of white fat.

(c) The fat should be firm, crisp in texture, creamy white in colour, with no unpleasant odours.

(d) The kidney should have a good covering of fat.

(e) Yellow fat is an indication of age, deterioration and low grade meat.

#### Storage

All sides, quarters or whole carcasses in smaller types of meat should be hung in a cold room at 0–2°C (32–35°F) with a space between them to allow a free circulation of air. Drip trays are placed beneath to collect any blood.

The period of hanging will vary from two to ten days, depending on the type of meat. The term 'ageing' is often used; this permits chemical changes to take place, producing a more tender meat.

#### Veal

(a) The flesh is firm and pale pink, not soft or flabby.

(b) Any cut surfaces should be moist, not dry.

(c) Bones should be pink to white in colour and porous, with a small amount of blood in the structure.

(d) The fat should be firm and pinkish white.

(e) The kidney should be firm and well covered with fat.

#### Lamb and mutton

(a) Lamb is under one year of age; after one year it is termed mutton. Various grades are available.

(b) The carcass should be firm and evenly fleshed.

(c) The lean flesh should be of a pleasing dull-red colour and the grain of the meat should be fine in texture.

(d) The fat should be evenly distributed, flaky, crisp and clear white in colour.

(e) The bones in young lamb are porous and pink in colour.

#### Pork

(a) The lean flesh should be pale pink in colour.

(b) The fat should be white, firm, smooth and not excessive.

(c) The bones should be small, fine and pinkish in colour.

(d) The skin or rind should be smooth and moist.

(e) No stickiness or unpleasant smell should be apparent.

#### Bacon

(a) There should be no sign of stickiness, particularly around the exposed ends of bones (curing often causes this to happen).

(b) The skin (rind) should be smooth and free from wrinkles.

(c) The fat should be white and not excessive in proportion to the lean part.

(d) The lean flesh should be firm and deep pink in colour.

(e) There must be no unpleasant smell.

#### Poultry

#### Chicken (roasting)

(a) The breast should be plump with the end of the breast bone pliable.

(b) The flesh should be firm with unbroken skin; the skin should be white with a faint bluish tinge.

(c) There should be no bruising or broken bones, especially at the wing and at the end of the drumstick.

(d) The legs should be smooth, with small scales lying tightly flat. The spurs should be small.

(e) There should be no stickiness or unpleasant smell.

#### (boiling)

(a) The breast should be plump with the end of the breast bone firm but not really hard.

(b) The flesh should be firm with unbroken skin, which should be white with a faint bluish tinge, and not yellow.

(c) The legs should be smooth with medium-tight scales

lying flat. Protruding scales and large spurs indicate age.
(d) There should be no stickiness or unpleasant smell.
(e) The fat at the vent end of the carcass should not be too excessive, and should be creamy white in colour; yellow fat denotes age.

### Duck

(a) The feet and bill should be bright yellow in colour.
(b) The upper part of the bill should break easily.
(c) The flesh covering the breast bone should be level with the top of the bone and in proportion with the size.
(d) The webbing between the feet should easily tear.

### Turkey

(a) The breast should be large and plump, particularly in the hen.
(b) Other factors are as for chicken.

### Storage of all poultry

(a) If undrawn, it should be hung in refrigeration at 0–2°C (32–35°F).
(b) If drawn (eviscerated), they should be placed on shelves, preferably of a slatted type, in refrigeration at 0–2°C (32–35°F).

### 153 HINDQUARTER OF BEEF: average weight 160 lb (73 kg)

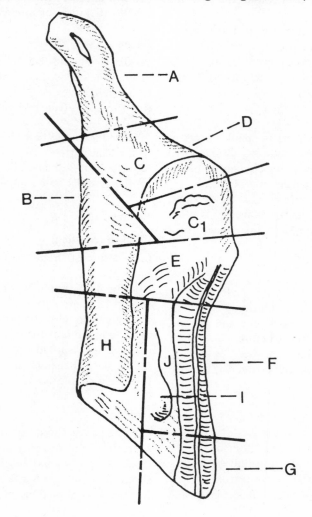

| Key | Name of cuts | Weight | Uses |
|---|---|---|---|
| A | Shank | 12 lb (5·5 kg) | Beef tea, consommé, stews |
| B | Thick flank | 18 lb (8 kg) | Stews, pies, sausages, braise |
| C | Topside and | 18 lb (8 kg) | Braise, braising steaks |
| C1 | Aitchbone | 12 lb (5·5 kg) | Braise, roast (second class) |
| D | Silverside | 22 lb (10 kg) | Salting, braising, braising steaks |
| E | Rump and thick fillet | 22 lb (10 kg) | Roast, steaks, braise Roast, steaks |
| F | Sirloin and fillet | 18 lb (8 kg) | Roast, steaks |
| G | Wing rib | 11 lb (5 kg) | Roast |
| H | Thin flank | 16 lb (7·5 kg) | Stews, pies, sausages |
| I | Suet and kidney | 9 lb (4 kg) | Suet paste, first class dripping, pies and puddings |
| J | Cod (Male) or Doug (Female) fat | 3 lb (1·5 kg) | First class dripping |

## 154 PRODUCTS FROM HINDQUARTER JOINTS

| | | |
|---|---|---|
| C | Topside ⎫ | Braising steaks, carbonnade, paupiettes |
| C1 | Aitchbone ⎭ | Braising and second class roast |
| E | Rump and thick fillet | Rump steaks (Pointe de culotte can be removed) Châteaubriand |
| F | Sirloin and fillet | Entrecôte steaks, minute steaks, porterhouse, T-bone, aloyau, contre-filet, faux-filet. Fillet steak, tournedos, filet de boeuf piqué, tail (mignon) for sauté |

## 155 ORDER OF DISSECTION – HINDQUARTER

1. Cut through and remove shank, A.
2. Saw, then cut through to divide B, C, C1 and D from E, F, G, H, I and J.
3. Saw, then cut through to remove B (thick flank).
4. Cut, saw, then continue to cut to remove aitchbone, C1.
5. Cut between the natural tissue dividing-line to separate D (silverside) from C (topside).
6. Saw, then cut through to remove rump, E.
7. With a knife to release, remove I and J (kidney suet, cod or doug fat).
8. Saw, then cut through to remove thin flank, H.
9. Saw, then cut through to divide F (sirloin) from G (wing rib).
10. If the fillet is required whole to include rump or head fillet, remove the whole fillet before commencing at point 6, i.e. removal of rump.

## 156 PREPARATION OF DISSECTED JOINTS – HINDQUARTER

### 157 Shank (A)

Cut between the natural tissue separating the flesh until the bone is reached. Pass the knife point along and around the bone until the meat is free.

Remove the main sinew by passing the knife carefully underneath it and cutting it free.

The thicker end of the flesh may be cut into 25 mm cubes for stewing. The remainder is minced coarsely for consommé or beef tea.

### 158 Thick flank (B)

The thicker and less fibrous part of thick flank is cut with the grain then trimmed and tied for braising. The remainder, after removing the excess fat, is cut into 25 mm cubes for stewing, or set aside for manufacturing purposes.

### 159 Topside (C)

The better parts of topside are cut lengthways with the grain, then tied for braising if required.

For braising steaks or carbonnade, the topside is cut lengthways with the grain into pieces approximately 100–110 mm thick × 60 mm wide. These pieces are then cut across, against the grain, approximately 10 mm thick. The thinner end pieces need to be cut a little thicker, then flattened with a wet cutlet bat to obtain an overall standard size.

For paupiettes, the topside is cut with the grain into 5 mm-thick slices approximately 125 mm long × 75 mm wide then trimmed to a rectangle, the trimmings being used for the forcemeat; the trimmings should amount to approximately one-quarter of the meat used.

Place the forcemeat on one end of the flattened 75 mm-wide piece of meat, then roll up and tie the paupiette at each end and in the centre.

## 160  Stuffing (farce) for paupiette de boeuf

| 8 portions | Ingredients | 10 couverts |
|---|---|---|
| 8 oz | beef trimmings (from cutting) | 280 g |
| 4 oz | bread | 140 g |
| 1 oz | onions | 35 g |
| 1 oz | dripping | 35 g |
| 2 teaspoons | chopped parsley | 4 g |
| ½ teaspoon | salt | 1½ g |
| ¼ teaspoon | ground white pepper | 1 g |

**Method**

1. Finely chop the peeled onion and sweat gently in the fat for 7–8 minutes, colouring lightly. Allow to go cold.
2. Mince the beef through a fine blade then add the soaked and squeezed bread. Pass again through the mincer.
3. Combine all the ingredients, thoroughly mix and use.

The remaining pieces of topside and aitchbone not used for braising, steaks, etc., may be cut into 25 mm cubes for steak pudding or first class stewing meat.

## 161  Silverside (D)

The name comes from the thick, silver-coloured nerve and tissue found on this joint. This is completely removed by running the knife point along its entire length, just beneath the tissue.

The silverside is then tied into shape for pickling (salting), or cut with the grain into smaller joints then tied in shape for braising. It is also cut as for topside into braising steaks.

## 162  Rump (E)

Rump is usually cut into long 20 mm-thick slices across the grain. The outer edge of fat is trimmed to a depth of 10 mm, then cut into portions of individual rump steaks for grilling by cutting on the slant.

This cut may be prepared into roasting joints if desired.

## 163  Fillet (E and F)

The whole fillet is trimmed by first removing the fillet chain. This is the rough piece, approximately 25 mm in diameter, found loosely fastened to the side of the fillet. Pull it away with the hand, releasing it, if necessary, with a knife. Next remove the shining silver-coloured nerve by carefully pass-ing the knife point just beneath it and taking away thin strips of the nerve at each time.

The prepared fillet can then be larded (piqué) for roasting by inserting 50 × 5 mm strips of larding bacon (salt-preserved bacon fat) into the fillet at a depth of 10 mm in the flesh. The strips are placed 25 mm apart in rows with the intermediate rows between.

The grilling steaks, the head of the fillet (the thick end), can be used for châteaubriand. This is a thick cut steak for 2 or more couverts, varying in weight from 12 oz (350 g) to 2 lb (900 g).

Irrespective of the size, the châteaubriand is flattened with a wet cutlet bat across the grain down to a thickness of 50 mm, for ease of grilling. Two strings are tied around it 10 mm from the top and bottom. Fillet steak is also cut from the head of the fillet, in thickness varying from 20–25 mm and approximately 5–6 oz (140–170 g) in weight.

The centre part of the fillet is cut into tournedos 30–40 mm thick, approximately 4–5 oz (115–140 g) in weight. Two strings are tied around it 10 mm from the top and bottom, ready for grilling or sauté. In American cookery for grilling, 1 or 2 thin slices of streaky bacon are wrapped around the edge of the tournedo before stringing.

The tail end (mignon) of the fillet is cut into 25 mm cubes for general sauté or into strips 40 × 50 mm for Sauté Strogonoff.

## 164  Sirloin (F)

The sirloin with fillet removed is trimmed as follows:

**Aloyau:** pass the point of the boning knife along the back flesh, close to the bone, until the flesh is clear of the bone, and until the part of the vertebrae bone that runs under the lean part is met.

Carefully release the top fat near the back bone in order to fold back and expose the heavy layer of sinew. Remove the sinew by passing the knife point underneath it and completely cutting it away. Reform the fat and smooth it into position with the back of the knife.

Saw through the lower part of the back bone, from where the fillet has been removed, to chine.

Cut off the excess fat from the side opposite the back bone, retaining a width of approximately 60 mm beyond the lean part (eye) of the sirloin. Tie the sirloin firmly with string, 25 mm apart.

**Contre-filet:** prepare as for Aloyau. When the vertebrae bone is met, turn the edge of the knife along the bone. Turn the sirloin over and pass the knife point along each of the

# PREPARATION OF FILLET OF BEEF

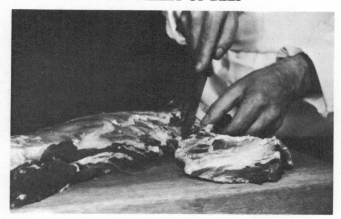

Removal of the 'chain' running along the outer edge of fillet

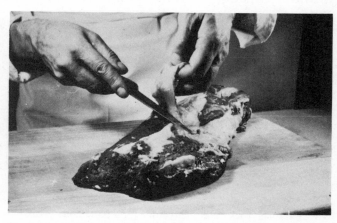

Removal of the sinew, with knife point just below surface of sinew, from head to tail of fillet

Slight flattening of châteaubriand; (approximately 15–16 oz, 425–450 g)

*Left:* Châteaubriand
*Centre:* Tournedos

*Right:* Fillet steak
*Rear right:* Tail (mignon)

Inserting strip of larding bacon into end of larding needle. *Note* basin of ice water

Pulling the larding needle through the fillet. End of bacon held with other hand

57

## SIRLOIN OF BEEF – VARIOUS PREPARATION STAGES

Sawing through back bone after cutting for a porterhouse steak

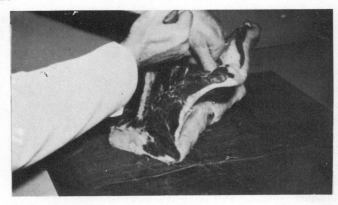

Boning of sirloin

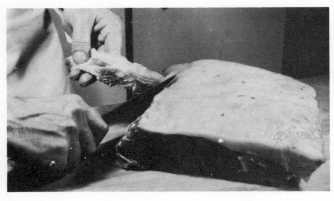

Cutting away the heavy sinew after boning

Removing thinner sinew after lifting back the fat

Prepared contrefilet ready for roasting

Entrecôte minute 6 oz (170 g), Entrecôte 8 oz (225 g), double entrecôte 14–15 oz (395–425 g), remainder of contrefilet

58

bones to free completely from the lean part. Trim the outer edge of the fat to a width of 40 mm. Remove the sinew and tie as for Aloyau.

**Faux-filet:** proceed as for Contre-filet, trimming the outer edge of fat to 20 mm.

**Entrecôte steaks:** cut in a straight line across a prepared Contre-filet approximately 10 mm thick to give a weight of 5½–6 oz (150–170 g).

Entrecôte double are cut similarly but are approximately 25 mm thick, then lightly flattened with a wet cutlet bat to a thickness of 20 mm.

Entrecôte minute is a single entrecôte steak, flattened carefully with a wet cutlet bat to a thickness of 4 mm.

**Porterhouse steak:** the true porterhouse steak is cut from the part of the sirloin which joins the last rib bone of the wing rib. It is cut 40 mm thick and slightly flattened with a wet cutlet bat (2–3 portions). Modern kitchen practice includes cutting this steak from the thin end of the sirloin and sawing through the bone.

**Tee-bone:** T-bone steak is so called as it is cut, then sawed, right through the sirloin, including the fillet and T-shaped piece of back bone. It is cut approximately 10 mm thick to produce an 8 oz (225 g) steak, including bone.

## 165 Wing rib (G)

This joint consists of the last three rib bones. Pass the point of the boning knife along the back bone, proceeding downwards until meeting the rib bones.

Carefully release the top fat near the back bone, then fold back and remove the sinew (nerve). Reform the fat to its original position. Chine by sawing along the inner part of the back bone, where it joins the rib bones. Cut, then saw through the thin end of the ribs to trim off any excess width, retaining 60 mm of fat beyond the lean part (eye) of the ribs.

## 166 Thin flank (H)

Cut away all excess fat and light sinew. Cut the lean parts into 25 mm cubes for stewing, or use them for manufacturing purposes.

## 167 Kidney and suet (I)

Break the suet apart and remove the kidney, cutting through the attachment. Cut away the 'core' of the kidney, i.e., the fat part containing the ventricles. Cut the kidney into pieces of the required size, according to use.

Free the suet from all skin then chop with one-quarter its weight of flour to separate. When stored in refrigeration, the quantity of added flour should be clearly marked.

## 168 Cod or doug fat (J)

Pass the fat through a 10 mm mincer blade, or cut it into rough cubes, then add a little water in a friture. Clarify steadily until the moisture is completely removed, which is indicated by the clearness of the liquid fat and a little blue vapour arising. Allow to cool, pass and use for first class dripping.

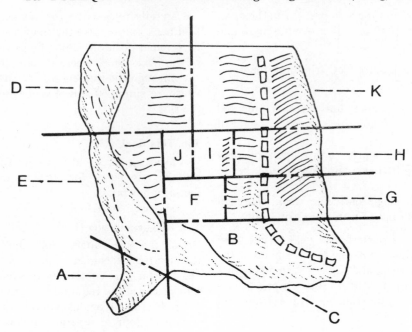

| Key | Name of cuts | | Weight | Uses |
|---|---|---|---|---|
| A | Shin | | 7½ lb (3·5 kg) | Beef tea, consommé, stews |
| B | Clod | | 9 lb (4 kg) | Stews, pies, sausages |
| C | Sticking piece | | 9 lb (4 kg) | Stews, sausages |
| D | Plate | | 18 lb (8 kg) | Salting, stews, pies, sausages |
| E | Brisket | | 31½ lb (14 kg) | Salting, stews, pies, sausages |
| F | Leg of mutton cut | Steak piece | 7½ lb (3·5 kg) | Braising, stews |
| G | Chuck ribs and | | 9lb (4 kg) | Braising, stews |
| | Blade bone | | 7½ lb (3·5 kg) | Braising, stews |
| H | Back ribs | | 11 lb (5 kg) | Roast, braising |
| I | Top ribs | Middle ribs | 7½ lb (3·5 kg) | Braising, boiling, stews |
| J | Flat ribs | | 5½ lb (2·5 kg) | Braising, boiling, stews |
| K | Fore ribs | | 11 lb (5 kg) | Roast |

## 170 ORDER OF DISSECTION – FOREQUARTER
(along lines in illustration)

1. Saw, then cut through the meat to remove cuts D and K, then divide into the two joints, as indicated.
2. Remove cut A (shin).
3. Saw, then cut off brisket, E.
4. Saw, then cut off H, I and J, then divide into back ribs, top ribs and flat ribs.
5. Saw, then cut off F and G, then divide into leg of mutton cut and chuck ribs.
6. Saw, then cut through to divide cuts B and C.

## 171 PREPARATION OF DISSECTED JOINTS – FOREQUARTER

### 172 Shin (A)
Prepare as for Shank in Hindquarter section.

### 173 Clod (B) and Sticking piece (C)
Remove the small amount of bone by passing the knife point around the underside. Cut down into smaller pieces, removing all excess fat in the process. Cut the better or more fleshy parts into 25 mm cubes for stewing and set the remainder aside for manufacturing purposes.

### 174 Plate (D)

Remove the bones by passing the knife point along each side, then underneath until the bones are freed. Cut away the thick gristle and fibre and the excess fat. If required for pickling (salting), roll it with the grain and tie tightly. Otherwise, remove all the fat and cut into 25 mm cubes for stewing. The leaner trimmings are set aside for manufacturing purposes.

### 175 Brisket (E)

Remove the bones as for Plate and cut away all gristle and excess fat (a considerable amount). Roll the trimmed meat with the grain and tie tightly, then divide into joints for pickling (salting) or as second class braising joints. Otherwise, prepare cubed as for Plate.

### 176 Leg of mutton cut (F)
### Chuck ribs and Blade Bone (G)

The leg of mutton cut is so called because the bone formation is similar to that of the pelvic ball and socket bones in a leg of mutton. In all these joints, remove all bones by passing the knife point around the bones then cut through the sinew attachment in the ball and socket joint for easy removal. Trim the thicker parts, cut lengthways with the grain then remove any fibrous sinew and tie tightly into joints if required for braising. Otherwise, remove all fat and cut into 25 mm cubes for stewing.

### 177 Back ribs (H)

Remove the rib bones and the small amount of blade bone by passing the knife point along each side of the bones, then underneath. Cut lengthways with the grain into joints, then tie tightly for roasting or braising (both second class).

### 178 Top ribs (I) Flat ribs (J)

Pass the knife point along and under the ends of the rib bones. Remove any sinew and excess fat. For boiling or braising (second class), roll with the grain then tie tightly into joints. Otherwise, cut into 25 mm cubes for stewing.

### 179 Foreribs (K)

From the thicker back bone part of the ribs, measure approximately 225 mm, mark a line along the rib bones, then remove the thinner remaining part by first sawing and then cutting through the bones. Use these trimmings, in 25 mm cubes, for stewing.

Pass the point of a knife along under the fat which covers the thickest part of the fore ribs to a depth of 40–50 mm. Remove the exposed thick piece of gristle by passing the knife point underneath and pulling the gristle away. Re-form the fat into position. Chine the bottom part of the rib bones, located at the base of the backbone, by sawing through at a point where the flat part of the back bone commences. Turn the joint, with the rib bones facing the board or block. Pass the knife point right along, close to the back bone, down to where the rib bones commence. Press the bone back into position to afford protection to the meat during cooking. Tie tightly across the joint in line with the rib bones.

### 180 BONING AND TYING OF MEAT

The boning of all meat is quite easy provided the following points are carried out:
1. The correct size of sharp knife is used.
2. The point of the knife is used and kept close to the bone at all times.
3. If in doubt, feel the line of the bone before cutting, and remember that most joints are of the ball and socket type in the legs and shoulders.
4. Between cutlet, saddle, sirloin and similar parts of the meat, the knife should be carefully run between the bones just deep enough to ease them so that the knife can easily be operated behind the back of the bones.
5. When tying joints, always remember to set them into shape first so that the meat when cooked, can be cut against the grain.

First tie the meat firmly in the centre, then at each end, and afterwards tie the string at intervals of 25 mm apart.

String should be tied in individual pieces so that in the event of one piece breaking the joint will not lose shape.

Joints incorrectly tied can lead to excessive waste and difficulty in carving.

Joints should not exceed 110 mm in diameter, as this causes difficulties in cooking and excess waste, but they should be the length of the natural cut. This gives a natural size slice when carving.

### 181 PREPARATION OF OFFALS – BEEF

### 182 Heart

With the point of the knife, cut the heart conically, removing all ventricles, and trim off any excess fat. If the hearts are to be stuffed, the stuffing is placed in the cavity to within 25 mm of the top. Using a trussing needle and string, sew across the aperture to close, and knot the string securely.

### 183 Kidney

Cut away the fat part and all ventricles. For soup, cut to the required size, as per recipe. For pies and puddings, cut into slithers approximately 25 × 25 × 5 mm thick for ease in cooking.

### 184 Liver

Cut away all the veins and gristle. Remove the skin by starting with a knife point at the edge, then by forcing the thumb across the liver under the skin. Cut, on the slant, 5 mm thick slices of a reasonable size. Cut lengthwise first if it is necessary to divide the liver.

### 185 Sweetbreads

The sweetbreads from fully-grown beef are inclined to be too coarse in texture and rather strong in flavour to produce a good finished dish. However, those from 'baby beef', killed between 12–15 months, are a reasonably good quality. Even so, these do not compare favourably with those from calves.

Soak the sweetbreads in a solution of 1 part salt to 16 parts of cold water, changing frequently. The salt will remove the congealed blood and lighten the colour of the sweetbreads. Cut away any attached pipe and any fat, if present.

Blanch in cold salt water, removing all scum as it rises. Allow to simmer for 7–8 minutes, then refresh and thoroughly wash off.

Each pair of sweetbreads consist of a 'throat' and 'heart' bread. The 'heart' breads are placed on a shallow tray. Another tray is placed on top and weighted to press the sweetbreads to a depth of 20–25 mm. Place them in refrigeration for a few hours to set. It is now quite easy to cut the pressed sweetbreads into escalopes, on the slant, 10 mm thick. Flatten very lightly with a wet cutlet bat and trim the edges evenly.

### 186 Oxtail

Trim off all the fat from the thick end of the tail, level to the lean part. Cut off the thin end of the tail where it is below 25 mm in diameter. This part is cut through in pieces 10 mm in size for soup garnish. Cut the remainder of the tail through at the natural joints. If necessary, use a chopper and divide the few pieces from the thick end into 2 parts to bring all the parts to a uniform size.

### 187 Ox-tongue

Remove the bones from the base of the tongue with a boning knife. Cut away any gristle and pipe that may be attached and place the tongue into pickling brine for 10–12 days. Ox-tongue is sometimes used fresh.

### 188 Tripe

This is purchased already dressed. Cut away any gristle along the outer edge then wash well. Cut into 50 mm squares or into slices 50 mm long × 5 mm thick, for use according to recipe.

### General notes

### Larding

For larding small pieces of meat, the larding bacon is cut into 50 mm lengths × 5 mm × 5 mm, or thinner if required. Place into ice water to firm. Insert the bacon strip into the split end of a larding needle. Insert into the flesh, secure the loose end between the fingers, and sew until only the last 10 mm remains. Withdraw the needle. For large pieces of lean meat, the pieces of larding bacon are cut 60 × 10 × 10 mm and inserted with a larding pin. Sometimes the pieces of larding bacon are marinaded in brandy and spices.

For pickling brine, marinades, etc. see 195 and 196.

### 189 MANUFACTURED PRODUCTS – BEEF

#### 190 Beef sausage meat

| 8 portions (4 oz) | Ingredients | 10 couverts (110 g) |
|---|---|---|
| 1 lb | lean manufacturing beef | 560 g |
| 8 oz | pork fat | 280 g |
| 8 oz | white bread or rusks | 280 g |
| 1 oz | special seasoning (192) | 35 g |

### Method

1. Soak the bread or rusks in ice-cold water for 2 minutes only.
2. Remove all the water by squeezing.
3. Pass all ingredients first through a 5 mm mincer blade, then through a 3 mm blade. Thoroughly mix together.

*Note.* The use of ice water in soaking helps keep the mixture at a low temperature during mincing.

# 191 Preparation of sausages

## Method

1. The sausage skins (sheaths) are purchased in varying diameters to give a sausage size which allows 8, 10 or 16 sausages to the pound weight of sausage meat.
2. Soak the skins in cold water for a few hours.
3. Place the sausage filling attachment on the mincing machine.
4. Remove the soaked skins from the water. Turn the first 40 mm of the skin back and roll it on the end of the filler. Place the sausage meat in the machine feeder.
5. Start the machine and allow the skins to fill, holding the attached end, or clipping it in position.
6. When the skins are filled, divide off by twisting around and over to form 'links' to the desired size.
7. Hang in refrigeration at 0–2°C (32–35°F) to set and dry the skins.

# 192 Special seasoning for manufactured products

| | | | |
|---|---|---|---|
| 1½ lb (690 g) | salt | 1 oz (30 g) | ground thyme |
| 2 oz (55 g) | ground white pepper | ½ oz (15 g) | ground allspice |
| 2 oz (55 g) | ground black pepper | ½ oz (15 g) | ground ginger |
| 1 oz (30 g) | ground nutmeg | 1 oz (30 g) | ground dried |
| 1 oz (30 g) | ground mace | | parsley |

Thoroughly mix these ingredients together several times then store them in a covered jar with a tight fitting lid; mark the jar.

# 193 Russian minced steak                 Bitok à la russe

| 8 portions | Ingredients | 10 couverts |
|---|---|---|
| 1¼ lb | lean beef (topside, thick flank) | 700 g |
| 2 oz | fat pork | 70 g |
| 5 oz | white breadcrumbs | 175 g |
| 2 oz | finely chopped onion | 70 g |
| 1 oz | butter | 35 g |
| 1 tablespoon | chopped parsley | 5 g |
| 1 | egg | 1½ |
| 2 fl. oz | milk | 70 ml |
| ½ oz (4 level teaspoons) | salt | 15 g |
| ⅛ oz (1 level teaspoon) | ground white pepper | 4 g |

## Method

1. Sweat the finely chopped onion in the butter for 7–8 minutes without colouring then allow to go cold.
2. Pass the beef and fat pork through a 3 mm mincer blade.
3. Soak the breadcrumbs with the milk. Beat the egg.
4. Combine all the ingredients and the seasoning; mix well.
5. Divide equally into eight 4 oz (ten 115 g) pieces.

6. Roll into balls, without any cracks. Flatten with a palette knife into a médaillon approximately 10 mm thick, using a little breadcrumbs or flour.

# 194 German (Austrian) minced steak          Hamburg (Vienna) steak

## Ingredients

Follow the ingredients for Russian minced steak (193), substituting water for milk, ground black pepper for white, and omitting the chopped parsley.

## Method

Prepare in the same manner.

# 195 Brine for pickling                 Saumure liquide

For red meats: ox-tongue, brisket, silverside, pressed beef.

## Method

1. Boil the following ingredients together: 1 gallon (4·5 litres) water, 3 lb (1·35 kg) salt, 1 oz (30 g) saltpetre, 2 bayleaves, 2 oz (55 g) brown sugar, 8 cloves and 20 peppercorns.
2. Remove the scum and simmer for 10 minutes. Allow to go cold. To test it, place an egg in the brine: it should float. Adjust with salt if necessary.
3. Strain into a pickling container of wood or fibre glass, and chill in refrigeration at 2–3°C (35–38°F).

## To pickle meats

Wash the prepared joints well and place them into the chilled brine for 6–10 days, according to thickness and size. Press the meat below the surface of the liquid with a floating wooden cover. A further cover should be placed over the brine to prevent contamination.

# 196 Marinade for meat and poultry (liquid)

## Method

1. Prepare and roughly cut 4 oz (110 g) carrot, 4 oz (110 g) onion, 2 oz (55 g) celery, ½ oz (15 g) parsley stalks, 1 bayleaf, a sprig of thyme, 3 cloves, 10 peppercorns, ¼ oz (7 g) salt, ¼ pint oil (140 ml) and 1 pint of wine (560 ml). Red wine should be used for red meats, and white wine for white meats and poultry. Marinade for 24 hours in refrigerator at 2–3°C (35–38° F).

# LAMB

**197  Carcass of lamb**    **Agneau (up to 1 year of age)**    Pré-salé – grazed on salt earth, near the sea
    **mutton**    **Mouton (beyond 1 year of age)**    de lait – milk fed

**Seasons:** both are available all the year from different sources of supply. Fresh lamb is best during April and May.

**Grading**

English is graded nos. 1 and 2 for quality.

New Zealand is available in several qualities, and is graded for size as follows: D, 28–33 lb (12·5–15 kg) per carcass; 2, 32–34 lb (14·5–15·5 kg); 8, 34–38 lb (15·5–17 kg); and 4, 38–40 lb (17–18 kg).

**Types**

Southdown – Sussex    Canterbury – New Zealand

(see 199 opposite)

**198  Key**

| | English | French | Lamb | Mutton | |
|---|---|---|---|---|---|
| | | CUTS | WEIGHTS | | USES |
| A | Neck | Cou | 2 lb (1 kg) | 4 lb (2 kg) | Boiled, stewed, braised |
| B | Shoulder | Épaule | 6 lb (3 kg) (2) | 8 lb (3·5 kg) | Roast, stewed, stuffed and roasted, braised |
| C | Middle neck | Basseo côtes | 3 lb (1·5 kg) | 4 lb (2 kg) | Stewed |
| D | Best end | Carré | 5 lb (2) (2·5 kg) | 7 lb (3 kg) | Roast, cutlets-fried, grilled |
| E | Breast | Poitrine | 5 lb (2) (2·5 kg) | 8 lb (3·5 kg) | Stewed, braised, boned and stuffed roast, epigrammes |
| F | Saddle | Selle | 7 lb (3 kg) | 11 lb (5 kg) | Roast, poêlé, braised, chops, noisettes, rosettes |
| G | Chump | | 2 lb (1 kg) | 3 lb (1·5 kg) | Chops – grilled, fried, braised |
| H | Leg | Gigot | 7 lb (2) (3 kg) | 9 lb (4 kg) | Roast, braised, boiled |
| I | Kidney | Rognon | 4 oz (2) (110 g) | 6 oz (170 g) | Grilled, fried, sauté – stewed |
| J | Liver | Foie | 1½ lb (675 g) | 2 lb (1 kg) | Grilled, fried, braised |
| K | Tongue | Langue | ½ lb (225 g) | ¾ lb (340 g) | Boiled, braised |
| L | Sweet breads | Ris | ¾ lb (340 g) | 1 lb (450 g) | Braised, fried, grilled |

Whole carcass – lamb 30–40 lb (13–18 kg), mutton 40–50 lb (18–23 kg)

## 200  ORDER OF DISSECTION OF CARCASS OF LAMB OR MUTTON

1. Remove the two shoulders by cutting through the flesh, starting at the top centre of the shoulders, just past the third rib bone from the neck, and approximately 60 mm from the back of the middle neck (C in diagram). Continue in a circular motion, with the point of the knife against the rib bones, then ease the cut flesh with the fingers; this will assist in finding the natural dividing tissue to the base of the shoulder.

In the opposite direction, continue to cut down to the rib bones in a circular motion to the base of the shoulder (B in diagram) to a point 50 mm beyond the end of the front leg (shoulder). Release any part that may be slightly attached by running the point of the knife along the rib bone structure.

2. Turn the carcass on to the back. Cut, then saw through on a straight line across the carcass between the last two rib bones, to divide F, G and H from A, B, C and D.

3. Remove the two legs by cutting in a very slight circular fashion from the base of the tail, across to the area where the flesh becomes thin at the base of the chump (G in diagram).

4. Cut, then saw through the chump end of the saddle at a point where the end of the saddle begins to rise. This point can be located by feeling the end of the saddle, where the pelvic bone starts. Cut and saw straight across when required for short cut saddles.

5. Remove the breast (E in diagram) by sawing on a straight line, then cutting through with a knife. Commence at the base of the best ends (D in diagram), leaving approximately 100 mm of fat beyond the lean part (eye) of the best end, to a point 25 mm below the neck bone on the first rib.

6. Remove the neck (A in diagram) by cutting through the

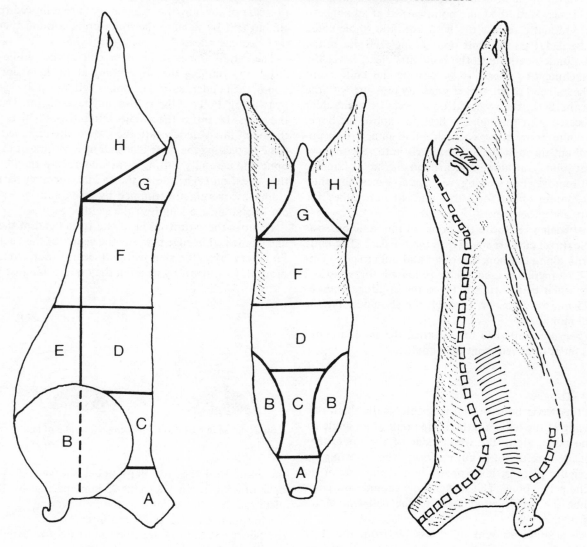

Whole carcass – lamb 30–40 lb (13·5–18 kg), mutton 40–50 lb (18–23 kg)

back of the neck. Then saw through on a straight line against the first rib bone down the carcass.

7. Divide the best end (D in diagram) from the middle neck (C in diagram) by counting the rib bones from the end of the best end, where the saddle was removed. Leaving seven rib bones on the best end, cut through and complete the dissection by sawing. In best ends purchased cut, often eight rib bones will be found. However, the last cutlet when cut will contain too much shoulder blade bone to

hold together when removed.

## 201 PREPARATION OF DISSECTED JOINTS – LAMB OR MUTTON

### 202 Shoulder (B)

This is boned in two ways, according to use:

(a) **Open boning.** Place the skin side of the shoulder on a board or block and make a 50 mm incision in the meat in

65

the centre of the shoulder blade, so that the end of the bone becomes visible. With the knife point turned at an angle to the bone, gradually release the flesh until the whole blade bone is revealed. Pass the knife point along each side of the bone, then underneath, until the bone lifts clear. Sever the gristle attachment to release it by passing the knife point around the ball end of the socket joint. By pressing with the finger on the flesh, the rounded bone across the shoulder can be located. Cut through the flesh to expose the bone. Pass the knife point along each side and under. Pull upwards and cut through the attached gristle to release from the socket joint. Cut along and around the small knuckle bone and remove. For stewing, remove all excess fat, then cut into 25 mm cubes for curry and 40 mm cubes for blanquette and other stews.

(b) **Tunnel boning.** Remove the bones in the same order as for (a). No direct cuts are made through the flesh. The knife point is run along the bones, around and underneath. This method is sometimes used when prepared for roasting, especially when being stuffed. Place the stuffing, approximately 25 mm in diameter, through the shoulder. Tie the strings 25 mm apart.

*Note.* When used unboned for roasting, the small amount of excess fat is removed from the shoulder.

## 203 Legs (H)

Remove the pelvic bone, which is visible in the thick part of the inside of the leg. Pass the knife point at an angle towards the bone, along the whole edge of the bone, then around it. Be careful not to cut too deep when locating the small irregular piece of bone protruding at the rear of the base of the pelvic bone. The socket bone should now come away when the gristle attachment to the ball end of the main leg bone is cut.

Remove a small amount of excess fat from the thick under-edge of the leg.

Cut through the loop at the knuckle end of the leg and saw across squarely at the end of the bone. Clean around the end of the bone to a depth of 25 mm, removing the small amount of meat.

Tie three or four strings 25 mm apart around the thick end of the leg to retain the shape.

## 204 Saddle (F) and chump (G)

These are prepared in the following ways:

(a) For cold buffet use, long cut saddles are normally used, and the saddles, are generally cut to include the chump end. For ease of carving, the pelvic bones are removed from the chump end by passing the knife point around them until they become released.

The two rib bones at the other end of the saddle are removed by running the knife point along each side of the bones, then underneath. The bones will now pull clear easily by twisting. Pull out the kidney and covering fat. Trim away the excess fat inside the saddle. Often the two filets mignon, the small fillets underneath the saddle, are removed; this is done by passing the knife blade along each side of the centre bone and carefully cutting away underneath the fillets. The thin ends, on each side of the saddle, forming part of the stomach covering are trimmed by 50–60 mm in a straight-cut line along the length of the saddle.

Remove the skin from head end to tail end of the saddle and from the thin edge towards the centre of the back. If the fat is very crisp, the skin will pull clear, if not, carefully remove in long strips by running the knife blade just beneath

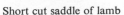

Short cut saddle of lamb          Long cut saddle of lamb

the skin. Roll the side flaps under the saddle. With the back of a knife, mark a trellis 25 mm apart across the complete saddle; do not cut into the fat covering.

Tie across the saddle at 25 mm intervals.

(b) Short cut saddles are normally used for banquet purposes and the saddles are cut lengthwise, French style ('en aiguillette'). The chump is then prepared as explained in the dissection notes and the saddle in the same way as for long cut.

## Chump chops

These are cut across the chump in line with the end that was attached to the legs. They are cut approximately 20 mm thick to produce 4 or 6 chops, according to size, from the chump. The weight should be approximately 6 oz (170 g).

# SADDLE OF LAMB – VARIOUS PREPARATION STAGES

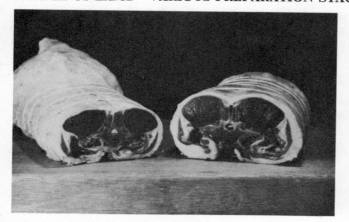

Long and short cut saddles prepared for roasting

Splitting short cut saddle into loins, using needle for guidance

Removing bone from loin, with the filet mignon laid back

Boned, rolled and tied loin, ready for roasting or poêlé

Trimming of loin for noisettes. *Note* In foreground, sinew removed

Cutting of noisettes with knife at an angle. *Right:* Finished noisette

## 205 Loins

The two loins are produced by splitting the saddle lengthways, with a chopper, before or after skinning of the saddle. Until experienced, it is wise to place a trussing needle in the natural small cavity running down the centre of the saddle as a guide and to chop carefully towards the needle.

For roasting, turn the skin side to the board, run the knife point along the side of the fillet (filet mignon) then halfway underneath, along the bone. Fold back the fillet to expose the vertebrae bones. Pass the knife point alongside, then under the bones. Reverse the loin and remove the skin as for saddle. Pass the knife point along against the centre back bone, down to the cross vertebrae bones, which should now lift clear. Trim the outer thin edge by cutting 50–60 mm away in a straight line.

Cut away the back nerve which is located along the thick lean part.

Reform the fillet into position and tightly roll the thin edge of the meat towards the thicker part. Tie at 12 mm intervals.

When required stuffed, place a roll of stuffing 25 mm in diameter along the length of the loin before rolling.

### Loin chops

These are cut straight through the skinned loins and they are between 30–40 mm thick. A quarter of a kidney is placed inside each, the flap end rolled around and secured with a skewer. They are approximately 4½–5 oz (125–140 g) in weight.

### Crown chop

These are a pair of loin chops, 25 mm thick, cut as one piece across the saddle. A piece of kidney is placed in each side and fastened with a skewer. These chops are not often served today.

### Noisette

The fillets (filets mignon) are removed from the skinned short cut saddles or loins and the flesh then boned out. The excess fat is then cut off the boned meat, lengthways, retaining 40 mm beyond the lean (eye) of the boned loins.

The meat is cut on the slant at an angle of 30°, approximately 30 mm thick. Flatten slightly with a wet cutlet bat, then trim the fat to a point to give an inverted pear-shaped piece. The approximate weight is 3–3½ oz (85–100 g).

### Filet mignon

The skin is removed and very lightly trimmed if necessary. Filet mignon may be lightly piqué with larding bacon. It is used grilled, sauté or for kebab.

## 206 Breast (E)

For stewing, cut the thicker part the length of the breast about 50 mm wide, then cut into 50 mm squares (for Irish stew, navarin, hot-pot). For other stews, cut the leaner parts into 25 mm squares.

For roasting, remove all bones by passing the knife point along the sides, then underneath. Pull off or cut away the skin and cut off square the very thin pointed end which is mostly fat.

Remove all the excessive fat, place a roll of stuffing 25 mm in diameter in the centre and roll the breast tightly, against the grain. String at intervals of 25 mm.

### Épigramme

Boil the skinned breasts of lamb in the normal manner. Cook until the breast bones pull clear easily. Remove all the bones, press between two weighted trays to give a thickness of 10 mm. When cool, refrigerate to set.

Cut into triangles with 60 mm sides and lightly flour, egg and breadcrumb. Two triangles are served per portion.

## 207 Neck (A)

Split the neck through the centre of the bone with a chopper and remove the sinew at the back; generally used for flavouring broth.

Otherwise bone out and cut for stewing.

## 208 Middle neck (C)

Using a chopper, split down on each side of the centre bone and cut away the heavy sinew.

Chop away the rib bones at the point where there is no longer a covering of meat.

For stewing (navarin, Irish stew, hot-pot) cut into double cutlets and remove one bone, leaving pieces weighing approximately 2 oz (55 g).

For other types of stews, completely bone out and cut into 25 mm dice or 2 oz (55 g) pieces.

## 209 Best end (D)

Divide the pair of best ends by making two cuts, approximately 5 mm apart, for the length of the best end, along the centre bone, until the rib bones are reached. Care should be taken to keep the knife point close to the bone, as the bone steps out a little, to avoid leaving good meat on the bone.

Chop down inside of the rib bones with the point of the chopper raised to a 45° angle.

Where single best ends are used, saw across the inside rib bones at the base, where it meets the backbone, then cut free, as previously mentioned.

Measure 60 mm from the lean (eye) of the best end, mark with a knife, then chop or saw and cut through. Turn over to the skin side and mark a line down the fat part 25 mm from the end of the bones. Cut down to the bones, turning the knife along to remove the fat.

If crisp and well-set, pull the skin off from the exposed bone side towards the lean part from head end to tail end. Otherwise, cut away the skin carefully in strips the length of the best end, just below the skin surface.

With a small knife, cut away the fat between the bones, and scrape the bones clean. With the end of a chopper, trim the end of the bones across at an angle. Cut away the back nerve which is located on the end of the lean part. Remove the small piece of blade bone from the thicker end. For roasting, mark the fat with the back of a knife in a trellis-fashion; do not cut through the fat.

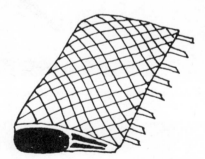

Best end of lamb prepared for roasting

## Cutlets

Single cutlets for grilling are obtained by cutting through between the bones of the prepared best ends to produce 7–8 cutlets. Flatten these slightly and trim the fat if necessary. Two cutlets are normally served per portion and one for mixed grill.

For entrées, cut one large cutlet by removing the odd bone, to obtain five 3½ oz (100 g) pieces from each prepared best end. Flatten these with a wet cutlet bat, then trim them.

## Double cutlets

These are prepared for grilling by cutting behind every second cutlet bone to give two cutlet bones on one piece of meat. Double cutlets should weigh approximately 5 oz (140 g) each.

## 210 PREPARATION OF OFFALS – LAMB

### 211 Heart

Prepare lamb's heart in the same manner as for beef (182).

### 212 Kidney

For grilling, cut three-quarters of the way through the kidneys, lengthways from the oval edge towards the core. Pull off the skin and cut out the core (the small fat piece). Pass a skewer through the cut side across the kidney to keep it open. Two or three kidneys may be placed on one skewer.

For sauté, cut the kidney through lengthways into two complete halves. Remove the skin and core. Cut each half into three or four pieces on the slant.

### 213 Liver

Prepare the liver in same manner as for beef (184).

### 214 Sweetbreads

Soak the sweetbreads in salt water for 2–3 hours to whiten, changing the water often. Blanch for 3–4 minutes, refresh, wash well, then trim if necessary.

If large enough, they are generally used for braising, if not, they are used for bouchée, vol-au-vent, etc.

### 215 Tongue

Wash the tongues and trim the thick end. The bones are left in and removed after cooking and skinning.

### 216 Stuffing for lamb or mutton

|  | Ingredients |  |
|---|---|---|
| 12 oz | white breadcrumbs | 340 g |
| 6 oz | finely chopped suet | 170 g |
| 6 oz | finely chopped onion | 170 g |
| 2 oz | butter or dripping | 55 g |
| 4 teaspoons | chopped parsley | 8 g |
| ½ teaspoon | powdered thyme | 1½ g |
| 2 | eggs | 2 |
| 1 teaspoon | salt | 3 g |
| ¼ teaspoon | ground white pepper | ¾ g |

## PREPARATION OF LAMB

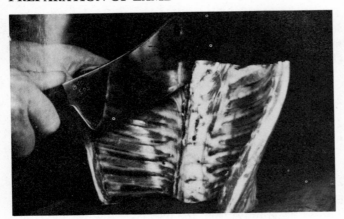

Splitting a pair of best ends

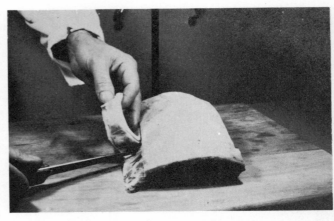

Trimming away excess fat to expose ends of cutlet bones

Trimming between bones in preparation stage

Prepared best end, with bone ends trimmed at an angle

From saddle: *Left:* Loin chop *Right:* Crown chop *Centre:* Filet mignon

## Method

1. Combine all the dry ingredients and mix thoroughly.
2. Add the beaten egg and mix.

*Note.* The quantities given are sufficient to stuff two shoulders, four loins or three breasts.

### 217 Lamb on a skewer (brochette)  Kebab d'agneau

| 8 portions | Ingredients | 10 couverts |
|---|---|---|
| 1 lb | lamb fillets (filet mignon) | 565 g |
| 8 oz | lamb kidney | 280 g |
| 8 oz | small open mushrooms | 280 g |
| 1½ oz | dripping | 55 g |
| 4 oz | sliced streaky bacon | 140 g |
| 4 | bayleaves | 5 |
| 1½ fl. oz | olive oil | 55 ml |
| teaspoon | salt | 4 g |
| ¼ teaspoon | milled white pepper | 1 g |

## Method

1. Melt the dripping in a sauté pan and add the peeled and washed small mushroom heads (caps).

2. Cook slowly for 5–6 minutes without colouring then allow them to go cold.

3. Cut the lamb fillets into slices 5 mm thick, slightly on the slant (escalopes).

4. Cut the kidneys in halves then remove the skin and the fat core. Cut each half kidney into 4 slices, on the slant.

5. Cut the bacon slices into 30 mm pieces.

6. Place the pieces of lamb and kidney on a tray and season with the mixed salt and pepper. Sprinkle over with the oil and allow to marinade for 1 hour.

7. Using 150–175 mm skewers, assemble the kebab, using the lamb, kidney, mushrooms and bacon in alternate order. Place a half bayleaf in the centre of each skewer.

*Note.* The lean prime part of loins or best ends of lamb may be used instead of lamb fillets.

# VEAL—VEAU

| Types | Weights per side |
|---|---|
| Dutch | 90–100 lb (40–50 kg) |
| English | 60–70 lb (27–32 kg) |
| English (bobby calves) | 30–40 lb (13–18 kg) |

The weights vary considerably in veal, because of the following factors:

### (a) Rearing

Dutch and some English veal is produced by intense farming methods which are designed to add weight more rapidly.

### (b) Age when killed

English veal is usually killed between 12–15 weeks from birth. Bobby calves are very young calves, killed earlier than usual because of their inability to make normal growth.

71

**218 OUTER AND INSIDE VIEW–SIDE OF VEAL**

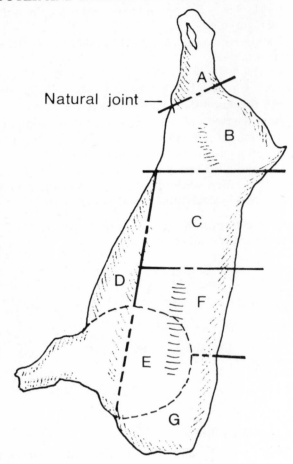

Natural joint —

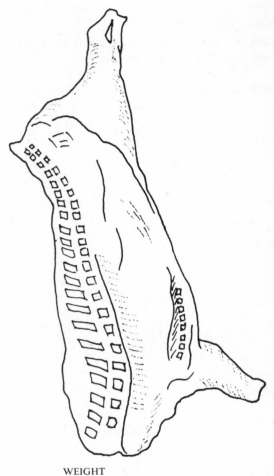

## SIDE OF VEAL

| Key | Name of Cut | French | Bobby | English | Dutch |
|-----|-------------|--------|-------|---------|-------|
| A | Knuckle | Jarret | 1½ lb (675 g) | 3½–4 lb (1·5–2 kg) | 4–5 lb (2–2·5 kg) |
| B | Leg | Cuissot | 7½ lb (3·5 kg) | 13–15 lb (6–7 kg) | 20–25 lb (9–11 kg) |
| C | Loin | Longe | 5 lb (2·5 kg) | 8½–10 lb (4–4·5 kg) | 10–12 lb (4·5–5·5 kg) |
| D | Breast | Poitrine | 3 lb (15 kg) | 4–6 lb (2–3 kg) | 5–7 lb (2·5–3 kg) |
| E | Shoulder | Epaule | 7 lb (3·5 kg) | 12–14 lb (5·5–6·5 kg) | 18–21 lb (8–9·5 kg) |
| F | Best end | Carré | 4 lb (2 kg) | 6½–8 lb (3–3·5 kg) | 8–11 lb (3·5–5 kg) |
| G | Neck end and scrag | Cou | 5 lb (2·5 kg) | 6½–9 lb (3–4 kg) | 8–12 lb (3·5–5·5 kg) |
| | | | 33 lb (15 kg) | 53–66 lb (24–30 kg) | 73–93 lb (33–42 kg) |

**WEIGHT**

**Offals**

| | | | | | |
|-----|-------------|--------|-------|---------|-------|
| | Feet (2) | Pieds | — | 3 lb (1·5 kg) | 3 lb (1·5 kg) |
| | Head | Tête | 6 lb (3 kg) | 9 lb (4 kg) | 12 lb (5·5 kg) |
| | Kidney | Rognon | ½ lb (225 g) | ¾–1 lb (340–450 g) | 1½ lb (675 g) |
| | Liver | Foie | 1½ lb (675 g) | 2 lb (1 kg) | 3 lb (1·5 kg) |
| | Sweetbreads | Ris | ¾ lb (340 g) | 1 lb (450 g) | 1½ lb (675 g) |

## 219 ORDER OF DISSECTION – SIDE OF VEAL

1. In larger veal, remove the fillet first when it is required whole, as for beef.

2. Cut, then saw straight across 50–75 mm behind the base of the tail, towards the loin, to divide A and B (whole leg) from C, D, E, F, and G.

3. Separate the knuckle (A) by cutting it from the natural joint, as indicated on the diagram, to a point across the leg where the flesh begins to thicken.

4. Remove the shoulder (E) in the same manner as for lamb (200).

5. Cut, then saw through the breast (D) to the point where the neck flesh falls away to the place from which the leg has been removed; follow right through in a straight line between these points.

6. Divide the loin (C) from the best end between the last two rib bones.

7. From the point where the loin has been removed, count back eight bones then cut and saw through to divide the best end (F) from the neck end and scrag (G).

### Division of leg

1. Pass the knife around and under the pelvic bone and cut through the sinew attachment between the socket and the ball-shaped leg bone.

2. On the inside centre of the leg, seen through the skin, is the beginning of the natural tissues dividing the quasi (thick flank in beef), from the sous-noix (silverside in beef). Carefully separate these with the knife point, pushing the meat aside with the other hand to ease separation.

3. A further natural tissue will then show at the beginning of the noix (topside in beef).

Continue to separate with the knife point, passing it around the leg bone, to divide the three pieces.

4. Place the skin side flat to the board or block and remove the skin by passing the knife blade, slightly angled to the skin, along the whole length of each piece.

## 220 PREPARATION OF THE DISSECTED JOINTS – VEAL

### 221 Knuckle (A)

Cut the gristle loop free and remove it. If required for Osso bucco, saw off the thin end of the knuckle to clean the end, then cut and saw into slices between approximately 40 mm down to 20 mm thick, as the flesh becomes wider and more plentiful; the approximate weight with the bone is 6 oz (170 g).

If not for Osso bucco, bone out, remove the nerve and cut into 40 mm cubes for stewing, e.g. blanquette.

### 222 Leg (B)

When required whole for roasting or poêlé, the smaller legs are left whole and they include the knuckle end. Prepare them in the same manner as for leg of lamb (203). Cuts from the divided leg are prepared as follows:

### Noix (cushion)

This is used whole for roasting or poêlé. Remove the skin and the nerve on the opposite side; piqué as for fillet of beef (163).

### Escalopes

Escalopes are prepared by cutting the noix into thin slices on the slant to approximately 2½–3 oz (70–85 g) each. Flatten these carefully with a wet cutlet bat and lightly trim the edges even.

### Grenadin

For grenadin, cut the noix into flat pear-shaped pieces 10 mm thick and approximately 2½–3 oz (70–85 g) in weight. Flatten them slightly to 8 mm and lightly trim even. Piqué with four strips of larding bacon in the centre of the wider part to form a star pattern.

### Sous-noix (under cushion)

This is prepared as for noix. The grain of the flesh is not as fine as that of the noix.

### Quasi

Remove the skin and nerve of the quasi and cut into 40 mm cubes for stewing (fricassée, blanquette, etc.). Cut it into small, thin slices for pies.

In larger carcases of veal, it is possible to trim the quasi into a braising joint.

When trimmed, quasi is suitable for pojarski.

### 223 Shoulder (E)

Prepare shoulder of veal in the same manner as for shoulder of lamb (202).

For stewing, cut it into 40 mm cubes. The difference in size for veal is to allow for the heavy shrinkage which occurs in cooking.

The better quality fleshy parts can be used for pies and pojarski.

When the shoulder is required stuffed, use Veal stuffing (241).

### 224 Breasts (D)

For stewing, the breast is boned out as for lamb and cut into 40 mm cubes.

For roasting, it is prepared as for breast of lamb (206), and Veal stuffing (241) is used.

### 225 Loin (C)

For roasting, prepare the loin as for loin of lamb (205). Médaillons are cut from boned, rolled loin into slices 12–18 mm thick and approximately 4 oz (110 g) in weight.

When the fillet is large enough, it can be used for escalopes, or cut into bâtons 40 × 10 mm for sauté.

### Saddle

This is cut from the whole carcass of veal and it is not skinned. Prepare it as for lamb (204).

### 226 Best end (F)

Rarely prepared as a roast, although it can be used as such, best end is usually prepared into cutlets in the same manner as for lamb cutlets (209). Remove the skin when trimming after cutting, not before; the cutlets weigh approximately 4–4½ oz (110–125 g).

### 227 En papillote

For Côte de veau en papillote, prepare as follows: fold the greaseproof paper as illustrated and well cover with oil. Place on the paper a thin pear-shaped slice of ham the same size as the cutlet. Spread the ham lightly with duxelle (338).

Lightly sauté the prepared seasoned veal cutlets for 2 minutes on each side. Place a cutlet on the duxelle, thinly spread with duxelle and place another slice of ham on top.

Seal the paper, starting at point A in the illustration, and fold at 20 mm intervals, flattening each time before the next fold, as far as point B

### 228 Neck piece and scrag (G)

Pass the knife point around and under the bones to remove them. Skin by the same method as is used for the leg. Cut away the sinew, then separate the flesh from the blown tissue. Cut the flesh into 40 mm cubes for stewing; the better parts can be used for pies.

## 229 PREPARATION OF OFFAL – VEAL

### 230 Brain                                              Cervelle

When removed from the skull, carefully break the skin and place the brain into cold salt water. Remove the skin in the water to release the clotted blood. Change the water frequently, gradually removing the blood until the water becomes quite clean.

The brain is then gently poached in a Court-bouillon (see 626) for 6–7 minutes.

### 231 Feet                                              Pieds

Singe off any hair from the feet, scrape, then scrub them under running cold water until thoroughly clean. Soak them for 2–3 hours in salt water to whiten.

From the hoof knuckle joint, cut an incision in the back of the foot up to the direction of the leg end (this allows for easy removal of the bone when cooked) and tie around with two pieces of string.

### 232 Head                                              Tête

Place the head on a board with the under cheek, or jaw, uppermost, i.e. with the eyes to the board.

Make a straight incision from the centre of the lower jaw to the back of the head. Do not cut into the tongue which is located beneath.

With the knife point close to the skull, follow the head formation until the skin and flesh is removed. Avoid leaving any flesh on the bone.

Cut along the sides and the end of the tongue to release it, then soak it to whiten. Blanch, refresh and cut into portions approximately 60 mm square.

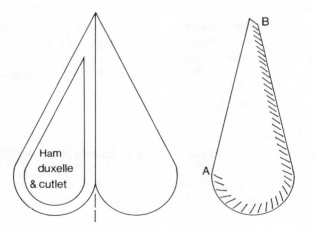

Ham duxelle & cutlet

To remove the brain, saw or chop across the skull just above the eyes, then downwards on an imaginary line on each side of the head 25 mm from the eyes to the rear of the head. Cover the fingers with a cloth and force back the cut portion of skull, easing with the end of a chopper to start. Then carefully remove the brain in one piece.

## 233 Heart                                                   Coeur

Prepare the heart as for beef (182).

## 234 Kidney                                                 Rognon

Remove the skin and cut the kidney in half lengthways. Remove the core, then cut the kidney into small slices 5 mm thick for sauté.

## 235 Liver                                                     Foie

Prepare the liver as for beef (184).

## 236 Sweetbreads                                              Ris

Prepare the sweetbreads as for beef (185).

For escalope or médaillon, use the lightly pressed 'heart' sweetbreads. Cut across or on the slant, according to size, slices 10–12 mm thick, each approximately 3 oz (85 g) in weight, or in smaller sizes of 1½ oz (40 g) to allow two per portion of this size.

Flatten slightly with a wet cutlet bat and lightly trim the edges.

For braising, use either 'heart' breads or the best of the throat breads, cutting into evenly trimmed portions of 3–3½ oz (85–100 g) in weight.

The débris (pieces) are braised for use in bouchée or vol-au-vent.

## 237 Tongue

Prepare the tongue as for beef (187).

The tongue is generally used unsalted, although the larger ones are placed in brine to pickle.

## PREPARATIONS – VEAL

### 238 Paupiettes

Prepare these as for beef paupiettes (159), using veal in place of beef.

### 239 Veal pojarski                          Pojarski de veau

| 8 portions | Ingredients | 10 couverts |
|---|---|---|
| 14 oz | prepared and trimmed veal | 500 g |
| 2½ oz | white bread | 90 g |
| 2½ oz | veal suet or marrow fat | 90 g |
| 3 fl. oz | milk | 110 ml |
| 7 fl. oz | double cream | 250 ml |
| ⅜ oz (3 level teaspoons) | salt | 12 g |
| ¾ level teaspoon | milled white pepper and paprika (mixed) | 3 g |
| 5 oz | breadcrumbs (for moulding) | 175 g |

### Method

1. Finely mince or chop the veal.
2. Soak the bread in the milk then squeeze it dry.
3. Pound the veal, bread and finely chopped suet or fat well together, adding the seasoning.
4. Rub through a fine sieve then place in a basin on ice.
5. When chilled, gradually work in the cream with a spatule.
6. Divide into 8 or 10 equal parts of approximately 3–3½ oz (85–100 g).
7. Roll into balls, then into an oval shape without cracks and coat with the breadcrumbs.
8. Flatten gently with a palette knife into oval shapes approximately 10 mm thick.

### 240 Stuffing for veal

Prepare veal stuffing as for Stuffing for Lamb (216), adding the grated rind of 1 lemon.

### 241 Veal quenelles                        Quenelle de veau

Note. For Veal quenelles, see Chicken quenelles (283) and use veal in place of chicken.

## 242 INSIDE VIEW OF SIDE OF PORK
**Head shown whole**

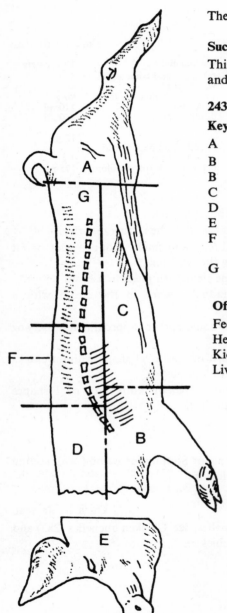

The average weight of a side of pork is 40–50 lb (18–23 kg)

**Suckling pig**

This is a small whole baby pig carcass, approximately 3–5 weeks of age, and 11–14 lb (5–6·5 kg) in weight.

### 243 Side of pork

| Key | Name of cut | French | Weight |
|-----|-------------|--------|--------|
| A | Leg | Cuissot | 10–12 lb (4·5–5·5 kg) |
| B | {Shoulder (cut square)} | Épaule | 6–7 lb (2·5–3·5 kg) |
| B | {Hand and spring} | | |
| C | Belly | Poitrine | 3½–4½ lb (1·5–2 kg) |
| D | Blade bone and spare ribs | Basse–côte | 4–5 lb (2–2·5 kg) |
| E | Head (½) | Tête (demi) | 3½–4 lb (1·5–2 kg) |
| F | Best end | Carré | 6–7 lb (2·5–3·5 kg) |
| | (English cut. Loin cutlet end) | | |
| G | Loin | Longe | 8–10 lb (3·5–4·5 kg) |
| | Whole side | | 41–51½ lb (18·5–23 kg) |

**Offals**

| | | | |
|-----|-------------|--------|--------|
| Feet (4) | Pieds | 2 lb (1 kg) |
| Head (whole) | Tête | 7–8 lb (3–3·5 kg) |
| Kidneys (2) | Rognons | 8–10 oz (3·5–4·5 kg) |
| Liver | Foie | 2½–3 lb (1–1·5 kg) |

**244 ORDER OF DISSECTION**

1. Divide the leg (A) from the side by cutting, then sawing, from a point 50 mm above the tail base to a point where the belly ends.

2. Cut off the half head (E) straight across, just behind the ear.

3. Cut right down the remainder of the side, sawing when necessary. For guidance, mark a line down the centre, then cut along another line drawn 10 mm towards the best end and loin (long loin). This will leave the belly and the hand and spring, the wider part of the carcass.

4. Remove the square-cut shoulder or hand and spring (B) on a straight-cut line 50 mm behind the point where the front leg meets the carcass.

5. Remove the bladebone (D) from the best end (carré) by cutting along a line behind the fourth rib bone, down from the neck.

6. For long loin, leave the best end (F) attached to the loin (G).

To divide into best end (carré) and loin (longe), cut straight across between the last two rib bones.

**245 PREPARATION OF THE DISSECTED JOINTS – PORK**

**246 Leg** (A)

For roasting or boiling, cut off the foot from the leg and remove the pelvic bone as for lamb (203).

For roasting, score the skin across the grain of the meat by just cutting through the skin with the point of a sharp small knife, about 5 mm apart. This allows the skin (crackling) to be cut easily when cooked.

**247 Shoulder** (Hand and Spring) (B)

First cut off the foot from the joint. For roasting or boiling, completely bone out, and score the skin if it is to be roasted. Reform to its long shape and tightly tie with string about 10 mm apart.

For pies, cut away all the skin from the shoulder in thin strips, after it has been boned, then either cut it into thin slices or coarsely mince it.

**248 Belly** (C)

For roasting, remove the ends of the rib bones from the belly by cutting along each side of them to the depth of the bone, then passing the knife underneath.

Score the skin, roll tightly and tie with strings about 25 mm apart. If required stuffed, place stuffing (258) about 25 mm in diameter along the centre of the joint, before rolling.

For boiling, leave the bone in and remove it after cooking. When required salted (for cold meat), place in brine (195) for 5–6 days.

For pies, prepare as for shoulder (247).

**249 Bladebone and spare ribs** (D)

For roasting or braising the bladebone, remove the bones by carefully following the bones with the knife point. Score the skin, reform into shape, then tie with strings about 25 mm apart.

**250 Best end** (top end of long loin (F)

To prepare for roasting, cut along the back bone in the best end down to the base of the rib bones. On the inside, saw across the base of the rib bones, towards the back bone, to chine. Score the skin and tie with string about 25 mm apart. For cutlets for grilling or sauté, chine and completely remove the back bone. Cut off the skin by placing the skin side of the joint on the board and passing the knife point at an angle to the skin along the whole length, then gradually across, to remove it in one piece.

Cut between the bones and trim off any excess fat to produce cutlets of 4–4½ oz (110–125 g) in weight.

**251 Loin** (G)

For roasting, pass the knife point along the back bone down to the cross vertebrae bones and remove the sinew. Remove the bone at the thick end of the loin by passing the knife point around and underneath. Chine, score and tie with string at about 25 mm intervals.

**To bone out**

On the inside of the loin, pass the knife along the edge of the fillet, close to the bone, then turn the knife under to half way along the width of the fillet. Lift the fillet back then pass the knife point along and under the bones to remove them.

Reshape the loin, score, roll and tie at 25 mm intervals; it may be stuffed as for belly (248).

**252 PREPARATION OF OFFALS – PORK**

**253 Feet**

Prepare the feet as for calves feet (230).

After boiling and removing the bones, the feet are floured, egged and crumbed for grilling.

77

## 254 Head

Bone out in the same way as for calves head (231).

Remove the tongue and brain and soak in salt water to whiten and clean. Head is used for brawn (260).

## 255 Heart

Prepare the heart as for beef hearts (182).

## 256 Kidney

The kidney is prepared as for grilling lamb kidney (212).

## 257 Liver

Remove the skin from the liver, if possible, and all the veins, then cut on the slant into 5 mm-thick slices.

## 258 Stuffing for pork joints

### Method

Prepare the stuffing as for stuffing for lamb (216), replacing the suet with finely chopped pork fat. Add ½ teaspoon of powdered or fine sage.

## 259 MANUFACTURED PRODUCTS – PORK

## 260 Brawn – A half head will produce 8–10 portions.

| | Ingredients | |
|---|---|---|
| | ½ pig's head | |
| 4 oz | carrots | 110 g |
| 4 oz | onion | 110 g |
| 2 oz | celery | 55 g |
| 8 | white peppercorns | 8 |
| 1 | bayleaf | 1 |
| 1 | sprig of thyme | 1 |
| ½ teaspoon | allspice | 1½ g |

### Method

1. Place the washed and boned ½ pig's head and tongue into brine (195) for 4 days. Remove and wash off the brine thoroughly.
2. Blanch and refresh. Place to boil in a pan, covered with cold water. Bring to the boil and remove all scum.
3. Add the remainder of the ingredients then simmer gently for 2 hours until tender.
4. Drain in a colander. Remove the flesh and tongue. Remove the skin from the tongue in cold water.
5. Reduce the cooking liquid to ½ pint (280 ml).
6. Cut the pig's head into rough pieces approximately 25 mm in diameter. Cut the tongue lengthways, then into thin slices across. Place them all into a 2 pint bowl or mould.

7. Pass the reduced liquor through a gauze strainer and pour into the bowl until it just covers the meat. Allow to cool.
8. Set in a refrigerator for a few hours until firm.
9. To serve, unmould under hot water tap to release the brawn. Cut across in half, then into thin D-shaped slices and arrange the slices overlapping on a flat dish. Garnish with washed watercress.

## 261 Pork crépinette     Crépinette de porc

| 8 portions | Ingredients | 10 couverts |
|---|---|---|
| 1 lb | lean pork | 560 g |
| ½ lb | fat pork | 280 g |
| 1 oz | finely chopped shallot/onion | 35 g |
| 2 oz | white bread | 70 g |
| 1 oz | butter | 35 g |
| 1 | egg | 1 + 1 yolk |
| 1 tablespoon | chopped parsley | 7 g |
| ¾ oz (6 level teaspoons) | special seasoning (192) | 30 g |

### Method

1. Sweat the finely chopped shallot or onion in the butter for 6–7 minutes without colouring then allow to cool.
2. Soak the bread in ice water and squeeze it dry.
3. Pass the fat and lean pork with the bread through a 3 mm mincer blade.
4. Add the remainder of the ingredients and bind together with the beaten egg. Mix thoroughly.
5. Divide into equal portions of 3½ oz (100 g).
6. Mould to an oval shape, then flatten with a palette knife to 15 mm thick. Wrap with pig's caul (see note) which should be previously soaked in cold water; the dish is now ready for grilling or sauté.

*Note.* Pig's caul is part of the membrane lining in a pig's stomach; it is obtainable from abbatoir wholesalers.

A little chopped truffle and a teaspoon of brandy may be added to the mixture if desired.

## 262 Pork pies     Pâté de porc

See Pies and puddings, 306.

## 263 Pork sausage meat

Prepare this as for Beef sausage meat (190), replacing the lean beef with lean pork. Add ½ teaspoon (2 g) of powdered sage.

## 264 Pork sausages     Saucisses de porc

Using pork sausage meat, prepare into sausages, as in 191.

## 265 SIDE OF BACON – INSIDE VIEW

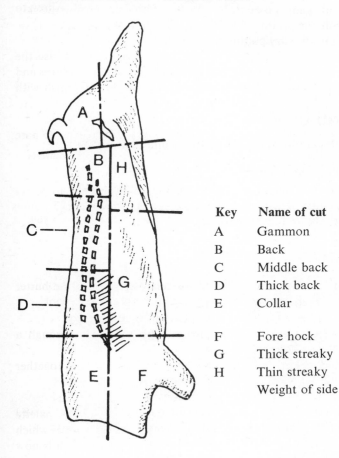

### Order of dissection

1. Cut across on a slight angle from end of belly to 25 mm beyond base of tail where joining back.
2. Cut straight across 50 mm behind front leg, to divide E and F. Divide down centre.
3. Cut, then saw down the centre to divide B, C, D from G and H.
4. Divide B, C, D into approximately equal parts.
5. Divide G ($\frac{2}{3}$) from H ($\frac{1}{3}$).

| Key | Name of cut | Weight | Uses |
|---|---|---|---|
| A | Gammon | 14–15 lb (6·5–7 kg) | Boiled, braised, grilled, fried |
| B | Back | 5–6 lb (2·25–2·7 kg) | Grilled, fried |
| C | Middle back | 6–7 lb (2·7–3·2 kg) | Grilled, fried |
| D | Thick back | 7–8 lb (3·2–3·6 kg) | Grilled, fried |
| E | Collar | 8–9 lb (3·6–4·1 kg) | Boiled, braised (second class), grilled, fried, pies |
| F | Fore hock | 7–9 lb (3·2–4·1 kg) | Boiled, pies |
| G | Thick streaky | 6–7 lb (2·7–3·2 kg) | Grilled, fried, lardons |
| H | Thin streaky | 3–4 lb (1·4–1·8 kg) | Grilled, fried, lardons |
|  | Weight of side | 56–65 lb (25–30 kg) |  |

## 266 PREPARATION OF CUTS AND JOINTS – BACON

### 267 Gammon (A)

For boiling gammon whole, pass the knife point around the pelvic bone; this allows the bone to be easily removed when the joint is cooked.

For grilling, the thick part of the gammon is removed by cutting alongside the whole length of the leg bone. The pelvic bone is removed, then the skin (rind) by carefully passing the knife blade just underneath it. Cut away the skin in 25 mm-wide strips then cut into slices 4–5 mm thick. Make small incisions 5 mm deep along the edge of the fat, 25 mm apart, to prevent curling while the gammon is being grilled.

Gammon is most economically divided by cutting approximately through the centre, as shown on the diagram.

The thicker part is still wide enough for grilling slices, and the other half, when boned and rolled, is of a suitable size slice for boiling or braising.

### 268 Back (B), middle back (C) and thick back (D)

Remove the bones from the joints by passing the knife point along each side of the bone, according to the depth of the bone, then underneath. Remove the skin (rind) in long strips approximately 25 mm wide, just below the skin level. Slice thinly by hand or machine.

### 269 Collar (E)

Remove any small parts of vertebrae bone from the collar, if necessary. For boiling, tie with strings 25 mm apart.

For slicing, first remove the skin as for back.

**270 Fore hock (F)**

Tunnel-bone by passing the knife point along and around the bones, if it is to be used for boiling. Tie with strings 25 mm apart.

For pies, open-bone then slice thinly.

**271 Streaky (G and H)**

This joint is prepared as for back. When removing the skin, roll the width of bacon to eliminate the wrinkles in the skin for easy cutting away.

---

## 272 POULTRY—VOLAILLE

The term poultry is applied to all domestic types of birds, such as chicken, duck, goose, pigeon and turkey. In menu terms, the word 'volaille' is related only to chicken, e.g. Suprême de volaille; in addition, the type of chicken can also be specified, e.g. Poussin en cocotte. All other types of poultry are specified in the name of the dish, even in preparations, e.g. Côtelette de dindonneau.

**Types of poultry**

Due to intensive production methods, the age at which poultry reaches a certain size varies. The guidance figures given are for normal growth.

| English | French | Weight | Approximate age | Portions |
|---|---|---|---|---|
| Baby chicken | Poussin | 12–14 oz (340–390 g) | 4–5 weeks | 1 |
| Double baby chicken | Poussin double | 1¼–1½ lb (565–675) | 5–6 weeks | 2 |
| Roasting chicken (small) | Poulet de grain | 2–2½ lb (1–1·1 kg) | 11–13 weeks | 3–4 |
| Roasting chicken (medium) | Poulet reine | 2½–4½ lb (1·1–2 kg) | 4–6 months | 4–6 |
| Roasting chicken (large) | Poularde | 4½–7 lb (2–3 kg) | 6–8 months | 6–10 |
| Boiling chicken (large) | Poularde | 5–8 lb (2·5–3·5 kg) | 12 months | 7–10 |
| Capon (castrated cock) | Chapon | 5½–8½ lb (2·5–4 kg) | 6–9 months | 7–11 |
| Aged boiling fowl | Poule | 5½–8 lb (2·5–3·5 kg) | 12–18 months | Not served |
| Duckling | Caneton | 3–4 lb (1·5–2 kg) | 10–12 weeks | 3–4 |
| Duck | Canard | 4–6 lb (2–3 kg) | 4–5 months | 5–6 |
| Gosling | Oison | 6–8 lb (3–3·5 kg) | 10–12 weeks | 7–9 |
| Goose | Oie | 8–15 lb (3·5–7 kg) | 4–6 months | 9–18 |
| Pigeon | Pigeon | 14 oz–1¼ lb (390–560 kg) | 7–11 weeks | 2 |
| Young turkey | Dindonneau | 7–10 lb (3–4·5 kg) | 5–6 months | 14–16 |
| Hen turkey | Dinde | 8–30 lb (3·5–13·5 kg) | 5–10 months | 16–60 |
| Cock turkey | Dindon | 8–30 lb (3·5–13·5 kg) | 5–10 months | 16–60 |

Estimated weight per portion (undrawn): chicken, 11–12 oz (310–340 g), turkey: 8 oz (225 g).

## 273 PREPARATION, TRUSSING, DISSECTION – POULTRY

**Plucking**

Most poultry supplied to caterers is already plucked, i.e., it has its feathers removed. However, small stubs are removed by placing the point of a small knife alongside the stub and the thumb, then jerking away.

**Cleaning**

Place the chicken with one side of the breast to the board and draw the skin at the back of the neck taut. Make an incision from the point where the neck joins the carcass to a point behind the head. Cut through the neck, close to the head, to sever, keeping the knife as close as possible to the carcass. Leave the neck skin 75–85 mm long.

# CLEANING OF POULTRY

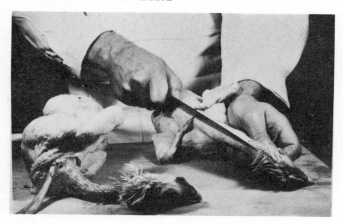

1 Back of neck skin held taut, ready for cutting through

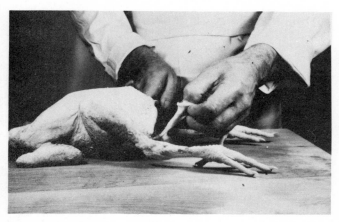

2 Removal of vent

3 Trimming of toes

Pass one finger inside the chicken, through the small hole between the neck and wish-bone, to loosen the inside.

Turn the chicken on the back. Press the vent between the fingers and cut away down to the beginning of the tail (the parson's nose). Place two fingers through the aperture and move in a circle to loosen the intestines. Carefully withdraw the intestines; avoid enlarging the aperture.

After withdrawal is complete, check to see whether the lights have been removed. These are easily distinguished by their bright red colour and they are located halfway along the base of the rib bones, where they join the back bone.

Separate the gizzard, heart and liver from the intestines. When removing the liver, be careful not to break the gall bladder, which should be carefully cut away.

Place the neck, opened gizzard, heart and liver on a plate and discard the head, vent and intestines. Clean the board.

Clean the legs by immersing in boiling water for 2–3 seconds. Firmly wipe with a cloth to remove the scales.

Cut the toes off the feet, retaining only the centre one, which is trimmed to the first joint.

Cut off the first 10 mm from the top of the winglet. Wipe the chicken with a clean cloth.

Singe the chicken by holding the chicken taut between the hands and passing over a naked flame quickly to remove all hair. Wipe thoroughly afterwards to remove any singed hair roots which might adhere to the chicken.

## Trussing

For roasting, turn the wing tips under the wings to bring the second joint of the wing alongside the base of the breast.

With the back of the chicken on the board, span the thumb and fingers across the breast to hold the legs well forward, to force the breast out.

Pass a trussing needle and string through at the joint of the drumstick (base of leg) and upper thigh, then pass right through the chicken, emerging at the same point on the opposite leg. Leave 50 mm of string at the first incision end.

Turn the chicken over on to the breast. Pass the trussing needle through the winglets, fastening the neck skin into position to cover the breast and come between the winglets. Reverse the chicken, pull the two ends of the string tight and double knot.

Pass the trussing needle through the centre of the thigh, halfway along to the tail of the chicken. Pass through the chicken to the same point on the opposite side. Hold the thin end of the breast firmly and pass the needle through the skin 25 mm down. Pull the strings tight and double knot and cut away any excess.

81

## TRUSSING OF POULTRY

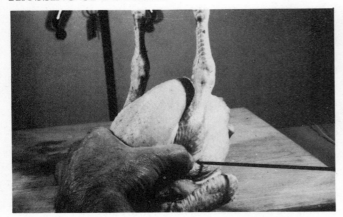

1 Legs held forward to push out breast

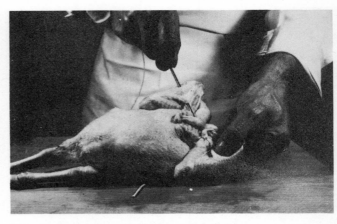

2 Needle passing through winglets and neck skin

3 Entering of leg into cut slit. *Note* sinew cut at base of drumstick

4 Legs entered. First insertion of trussing needle

**For entrées** (poêlé or boiling)

Make an incision half-way through the back of the leg joint, at the base of the drumstick, to sever the ligaments. Hold the thin end of the breast taut and make a 10 mm incision in the skin 25 mm down. Place the end of the drumstick part of the leg, where the first cut was made, into the second incision, to show only part of the end of the leg. Complete trussing in the same manner as for roasting, with two separate strings.

## DISSECTION

### 274 For grilling

Prepare the roasting chicken with the legs 'entered'. Place a large knife inside the vent, along the side of the back bone, and cut through. Part open, then cut along the other side of the back bone. Place the breast to the board, remove the breast bone (wish bone) by passing the knife point along each side of it until it is clear of the wing bone. Turn the breast bone between the fingers to pull clear.

# PREPARATION OF CHICKEN FOR GRILLING

1 Knife passed through chicken, alongside back bone, prior to cutting

2 Cutting through other side of back bone, prior to removal

3 Removal of rib and wish bone. Thigh bones to be removed

The chicken will now open completely flat. Pass the knife point under the rib bones and remove. Begin to release the piece of bone attached to the end of the thigh by passing the knife point underneath, then pulling it clear with the fingers.

Turn the chicken over so that the skin side is now uppermost. With a wet cutlet bat, flatten the thicker part of the legs to the same thickness as the remainder of the chicken; this allows for even cooking.

## 275 For sauté

Place the prepared chicken with one side to the board.

Hold the thick part of the visible leg away from the chicken to tighten the skin, make an incision in the skin then fold back the leg to the rear. Sever the sinew on the ball and socket joint. Hold the carcass with the flat side of the knife, then gently pull away the leg. Remove the other leg in the same manner.

Cut through the legs at the natural joint, separating the thigh from the drumstick. Cut the toe-end of the leg from the drumstick at the joint then trim round the last 10 mm of the drumstick to leave a clean bone.

Cut through the winglet at the first joint from the breast, then cut off the tip of the winglet at the next joint.

Place the chicken on to the back, hold firmly at the top of the breast and cut through the flesh, on a line parallel to the breast bone, halfway between the edge of the wing and the breast bone, to remove the wing.

Remove the other wing in the same manner. Hold the breast in the left hand, in an upright position, with the neck end to the board.

With the end of a large knife blade, chop through just below the point where the breast flesh ends, to separate the breast from the carcass.

Cut the breast into two pieces of equal size. Now cut the back part of the carcass into three pieces.

The dissected chicken will now consist of two drum sticks, two thighs, two wings, two pieces of breast, two winglets for serving, together with three pieces of carcass and the neck, legs, etc., to use for stock for strengthening the sauce flavour.

## CUTTING OF CHICKEN FOR SAUTÉ – FRICASSÉE

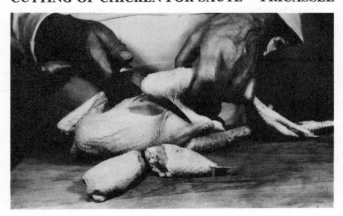

1 *Top:* Removal of leg as in suprême
*Lower:* Leg divided with drumstick end bone trimmed

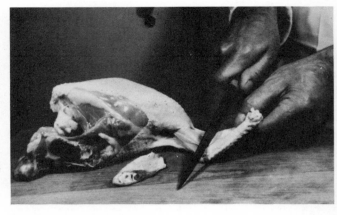

2 *Right:* Removal of winglet
*Front:* Winglet trimmed

3 Removal of wing. Cut through halfway from wing bone and breast bone

4 Dividing breast from back of carcass

5 Cutting through trimmed breast to divide

6 Ten portioned pieces with three pieces of back carcass

### 276 For suprêmes

Take a 2¼–2½ lb (1 kg) prepared roasting chicken and re-move the two legs in the same manner as for sauté (275).

Hold the winglet to extend it, then pass the knife blade 10 mm away from the wing, through the flesh down to and around the bone.

Reverse the knife, tap the winglet bone with the back of the knife to pull the winglet clear, leaving 10 mm of ex-posed bone attached to the wing.

With both hands, pull the skin off the breast part of the carcass from the thick end of the breast to the thinner end.

Pass the knife point down the inside of the wish bone, on each side, towards the board, to free it from the bottom of the breast where the breast joins the wing bone.

Lift the wish bone upwards and twist to pull it clear. Pass the blade of the knife along the breast bone, angled to-wards the bone, and cut the flesh clear in a downward stroke, passing through the natural ball and socket joint at the base of the wing and breast.

If a smaller suprême is required, remove the fillet from the back of the breast, to use for other purposes.

Otherwise, make an incision parallel with the top edge of the fillet about 10 mm in depth (this is halfway through the depth of the flesh). Turn the fillet upwards into the pocket made by the incision. Flatten very gently with a wet cutlet bat to seal into position. Trim the edges of the suprême lightly. Remove the other suprême in the same manner.

### 277 Boning of whole chicken

Whole chickens are usually only boned when they are 4–6 lb (2–2½ kg) in weight.

Place the prepared chicken on a board, breast downwards, and cut through the skin along the whole length of the back, in the centre.

With the point of a boning knife always angled towards the bone, gradually pass the knife point down, along and around the body carcass, until it meets the breast bone.

Carefully run the knife along each side of the breast bone without penetrating the skin. Using the fingers, gently press the breast bone to ease the skin covering free.

Cut the winglets off at the first joint from the wing. Tunnel-bone around the small wing bone with the knife point and scrape with the knife to free it.

Make a shallow incision on the inside of the thigh to re-veal the bone. Pass the knife point underneath the bone to free the end furthest away from the drumstick, then scrape

## PREPARATION OF SUPRÊME DE VOLAILLE

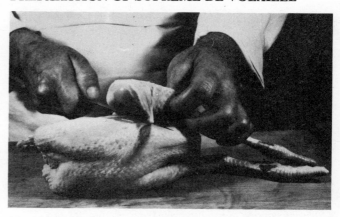

1 Leg held away from breast. First incision through skin

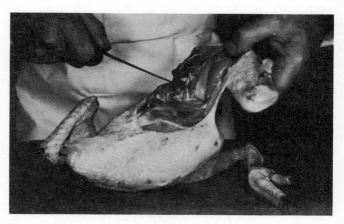

2 Leg folded back. Cutting through sinew prior to final removal

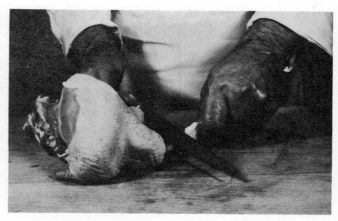

3 Trimming of winglet bone, showing other trimmed bone

# PREPARATION OF SUPRÊME DE VOLAILLE

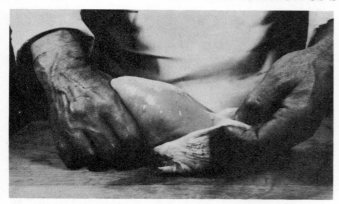

4 Showing position of hand to make the breast firm for easy removal of skin

5 Knife point passing below wish-bone prior to removal

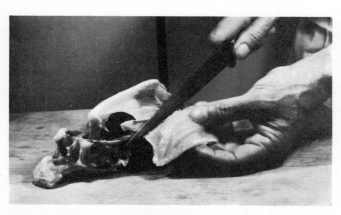

6 Removal of suprême from breast bone

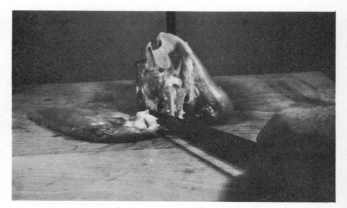

7 Finish of removal of suprême, with knife passing through natural joint

8 *Left:* Suprême with fillet showing *Right:* Suprême with fillet entered

down on each side of the raised bone to the ball and socket joint to free the bone.

Cut the base of the leg off at the bottom of the drumstick and hold the drumstick upright. Carefully cut around the top of the bone, then scrape downwards to free it.

Whole chicken dissected in this manner is generally used for the making of galantine.

## 278 PREPARATIONS – CHICKEN

### 279 Ballotine of chicken — Ballotine de volaille

| 8 portions | Ingredients | 10 couverts |
|---|---|---|
| 8 | legs of chicken | 10 |
| 1 lb | pork sausage meat (263) | 560 g |

#### Method

1. Bone out the chicken legs whole, as mentioned in 277.
2. Equally divide the sausage meat and fill it into the cavity of the legs, where the bone has been removed, pressing it gently.
3. With a trussing needle and string, sew across the leg from the top of the drumstick, upwards across the thigh, to draw the skin together. Turn the skin over at the top of the thigh to seal the filling. Finish by tying the two ends of string together. The chicken is usually braised.

### 280 Brochette of chicken livers — Brochette de foies de volaille

| 8 portions | Ingredients | 10 couverts |
|---|---|---|
| 1¾ lb | chicken livers | 700 g |
| 16 slices | streaky bacon | 20 slices |
| 8 oz | small open mushrooms | 280 g |
| 8 | bayleaves | 10 |
| 1 oz | butter | 35 g |
| 2 teaspoons | salt | 10 g |
| ¼ teaspoon | milled pepper | 3 g |
| 2 fl. oz | oil | 70 ml |

#### Method

1. Carefully cut away the gall bladder from the livers, without breaking, and remove any parts stained by the gall.
2. Place half the oil in a large frying pan over a fierce heat. When smoking, add half the seasoned livers and sauté quickly to just set, then place them on a tray. Repeat to cook the other livers.
3. Wash and peel, then sauté the mushrooms in the butter for 5–6 minutes.
4. Cut each of the slices of bacon across into four pieces.

5. Assemble the livers, mushrooms and pieces of bacon on 150 mm skewers, placing ½ bayleaf one-third and two-thirds along the skewer.

### 281 Galantine of chicken — Galantine de volaille

| 8 portions | Ingredients | 10 couverts |
|---|---|---|
| 1 × 3½–4 lb | boiling chicken | 1 × 2 kg |
| 1 lb | lean veal | 560 g |
| 8 oz | lean pork | 280 g |
| 8 oz | fat pork | 280 g |
| 1 | egg | 1 + 1 yolk |
| ½ oz (4 level teaspoons) | salt | 16 g |
| ¼ oz (2 level teaspoons) | ground white pepper | 10 g |
| 2 oz | lean cooked ham | 70 g |
| 2 oz | cooked ox-tongue | 70 g |
| ½ oz | pistachio nuts | 20 g |
| 1 oz | butter | 35 g |

#### Method

1. Bone the cleaned, prepared chicken whole (277).
2. Remove the fillets from the breast and also cut from the breast a few other similar-sized strips. Shrink these strips in the butter in a sauteuse slowly for 4–5 minutes, without colouring, then allow to cool.
3. Lay the chicken in a cloth, skin side down. Make side incisions in the thicker parts of the flesh and fold over to fill the parts of the skin not covered with flesh to make an even thickness all over.
4. Pass the veal, lean and fat pork through a 3 mm mincer blade and mix with the seasoning and beaten egg.
5. Cut the ham and ox-tongue in 10 mm-thick strips, then add to the shrunken chicken fillets. (Marinade with a little brandy if desired.)
6. Blanch the pistachio nuts; remove the skins.
7. Lay half of the pork mixture evenly across the chicken to within 25 mm of each edge.
8. Place the rows of the ham, tongue and chicken along the length of the chicken 6 mm apart, with the nuts down the centre.
9. Place the remainder of the pork mixture evenly on top.
10. Take the edges of the cloth in the hands and roll the chicken to meet the other side to form the galantine.
11. Move the galantine carefully to the edge of the cloth and completely cover by rolling in the cloth. Tie tightly with treble knots at each end of the galantine. Place one loose string around the centre.
12. Place into boiling chicken or veal stock, reboil and skim. Simmer gently for 1½–1¾ hours.
13. Remove from the stock and allow to set for 5–10 minutes. Cut the string, re-roll tightly in the cloth and tie at the ends only.

14. Place on a tray, with another tray on top, with sufficient weights evenly placed to press lightly to a depth of 50–60 mm Allow to cool.

**Chicken galantine (finish)**      **Galantine de volaille**

**Method**

1. Place the trimmed, cooked galantine on a wire grill.
2. Mask over (nappé) with white chaud-froid as for Poularde Vendôme (319). Decorate as desired and set.
3. Glaze with aspic jelly. Serve on an oval flat dish on a base of 3 mm of set aspic jelly and pipe chopped jelly around the base of the galantine.

**282 Chicken pojarski**      **Pojarski de volaille**

**Method**

1. Prepare this in the same manner as for Pojarski de veau (239), replacing the prepared veal with boned roasting chicken, free of skin.

**283 Chicken quenelles**      **Quenelles de volaille**

**Method**

1. Prepare the mixture as for Farce de poisson (149), replacing the total weight of fish with the same weight of boned chicken, free of skin.
2. Mould in the following manner.

    For serving as entrée, mould, use the same method as for Fish quenelles (150), using tablespoons.

    For entrée garnishes, mould in the same way, using teaspoons.

    For soup garnishes, grease a shallow poaching tray or plat sauté and place the mixture in a piping bag with 3 mm plain tube. Pipe on to the tray in rows, in straight scrolls 20 mm long.
3. The quenelles for garnishes are gently poached in white stock for 6–8 minutes and carefully refreshed. They are then placed in a basin in cold water and refrigerated until required.

*Note.* Veal quenelles are prepared in the same manner, with veal in place of chicken.

**284 Chicken cutlets**      **Côtelette de volaille**
    **Chicken croquettes**      **Croquette de volaille**
    **Chicken médaillon**      **Médaillon de volaille**

| 8 portions | Ingredients | 10 couverts |
|---|---|---|
| 1¼ lb | cooked chicken, free of skin and bone | 700 g |
| ¾ pint | chicken velouté or bechamel | 525 ml |
| 2 | yolks of egg | 3 |
| 2 level teaspoons | salt | 10 g |
| ¼ level teaspoon | ground white pepper | 1 g |

**Method**

1. Cut the chicken into 3 mm dice.
2. Reduce the velouté or béchamel by one-third in a thick plat sauté.
3. Add the chicken and seasoning. Mix with a wooden spatule, stirring continuously until it is reboiling.
4. Cover with a lid and pass through the oven for 10 minutes at 160°C (325°F).
5. Stir in the yolks of egg and mix well.
6. Turn out into a shallow tray and cover with a greased paper. Allow to go cold.
7. Mould into the required shape. (See Moulding of cooked food preparations, 310.)

**285 Chicken and ham cutlets**      **Côtelette de volaille et de jambon**
    **Chicken and ham croquettes**      **Croquette de volaille et de jambon**

**Method**

1. Prepare as for Côtelette de volaille (284), using 25% lean cooked ham in place of the same amount of chicken.

**286 Chicken salad**      **Salade de poulet**

**Method**

1. Prepare as for Fish salad (79), doubling the quantity of all the ingredients. Replace the flaked fish with boiled chicken, free of skin and bone, cut into 10 mm scallops (pieces cut on the slant).

**287 Chicken mayonnaise**      **Mayonnaise de poulet**

**Method**

1. Prepare as for Fish mayonnaise (80), doubling the quantity of all ingredients. Replace the flaked fish with chicken as in 286.

## 288 PREPARATION OF DUCK, GOOSE, PIGEON

Duck, goose and pigeon are all cleaned and trussed as for chicken (273), whether they are for roasting or entrée.

---

## 289 PREPARATION OF TURKEY

Turkey is cleaned and trussed as for chicken (273), according to use.

The wish bone is always removed to assist carving. Remove it by passing the knife point along each side and underneath the bone, passing at the base of the natural joint to the wing. Then turn the bone to remove it cleanly at the opposite end.

Remove the sinews from the legs by making an incision around the skin at the end of the drumstick, where it joins the leg.

Place the end of the leg into a V-shaped hook attached to the wall in the larder for this purpose. Drop the leg until it grips firmly in position. Hold the drumstick with a cloth to grip and give a quick jerk to pull the drumstick away from the base of the leg and sinews.

## 290 STUFFINGS FOR POULTRY – FARCE FOR GAME

### 291 Loose stuffing for chicken    Farce à l'anglaise

| 8 portions | Ingredients | 10 couverts |
|---|---|---|
| 6 oz | fresh breadcrumbs | 210 g |
| 2 oz | chicken fat or butter | 70 g |
| 2 oz | finely chopped onion | 70 g |
| 1 level teaspoon | finely chopped thyme | 4 g |
| 2 dessert spoons | finely chopped parsley | 6 g |
| 2 level teaspoons | salt | 8 g |
| ½ level teaspoon | ground white pepper | 2 g |
| ½ level teaspoon | English mustard | 2 g |

### Method

1. Gently cook the onions in the chicken fat or butter for 7–8 minutes, without colouring. Allow to cool.
2. Add the remainder of the ingredients and mix well.

### 292 American stuffing    Farce à l'américaine

### Method

Cut 2 oz (70 g) of lardons 25 × 5 × 5 mm, blanch, then very lightly fry. Allow to cool, then add to Farce à l'anglaise (291).

### 293 Californian stuffing    Farce à la californienne

1. Prepare the same amount of lardons as in the previous recipe.
2. Finely chop 2 oz (70 g) of chicken livers.
3. Add them together and mix into a Farce à l'anglaise (291).

### 294 Sage and onion stuffing    Farce à la sauge

This is an English stuffing used for duck or goose.

| 8 portions | Ingredients | 10 couverts |
|---|---|---|
| 6 oz | fresh breadcrumbs | 210 g |
| 3 oz | finely chopped onion | 100 g |
| 1 dessertspoon | finely chopped or powdered sage | 7 g |
| 2 dessertspoons | finely chopped parsley | 15 g |
| 2 oz | duck fat or butter | 70 g |
| ½ level teaspoon | powdered thyme | 2 g |
| 2 level teaspoons | salt | 8 g |
| ½ level teaspoon | ground white pepper | 2 g |

### Method

1. Gently cook the onions in the fat for 7–8 minutes, without colouring, then allow to cool.
2. Add the remainder of the ingredients and mix well.
3. Place in small greased tray to a depth of 10 mm; the stuffing is now ready for cooking.

### 295 Apple and prune or raisin stuffing

This is a German stuffing for duck or goose.

| 8 portions | Ingredients | 10 couverts |
|---|---|---|
| 1¼ lb | cooking apples | 700 g |
| 2 oz | prunes or raisins | 70 g |
| 1 | lemon | 1 |
| ½ level teaspoon | cinnamon | 2 g |
| 1 oz | brown sugar | 35 g |
| 1½ oz | butter | 50 g |
| 2 oz | fresh breadcrumbs | 70 g |

### Method

1. Peel and core the apples, and cut them into 8–10 sections.
2. Thickly grease a sauteuse with the butter and add the apples. Cover, sweat gently on a low heat to just cook, and remove from the fire.

3. Grate the rind of the lemon, add to the apple with all the other ingredients and mix gently. Allow to go cold before stuffing the duck.

## 296 Liver farce       Farce au gratin

| 8 portions | Ingredients | 10 couverts |
|---|---|---|
| 6 oz | chicken livers | 210 g |
| 3 oz | fat bacon | 100 g |
| 1½ oz | chopped onion | 50 g |
| ½ | bayleaf | ½ |
| ½ level teaspoon | thyme | 2 g |
| 1 level teaspoon | salt | 4 g |
| ¼ level teaspoon | milled pepper | 1 g |

### Method

1. Heat the fat bacon in a frying pan, add the onion and fry gently for 3–4 minutes.
2. Add the livers and other ingredients. Fry quickly for 2–3 minutes, colouring slightly, but keeping the liver underdone.
3. Pass through a fine mincer blade, then rub through a sieve.

## 297 Game farce       Farce de gibier

### Method

1. Prepare as for Liver farce in previous recipe, replacing the chicken livers with liver from game.

## 298 Chestnut stuffing (for turkey)       Farce aux Marrons

### Method

1. Make a small incision on each side of 1 lb (560 g) of chestnuts. Dip them in smoking fat for 10 seconds.
2. Remove both skins, place in a shallow tray with a bouquet garni and add stock to come three-quarters of the way up the chestnuts.
3. Boil, cover and braise in the oven until tender (approximately 45–60 minutes) then allow to go cold.
4. Mix the drained nuts with 2 lb (1 kg) of Pork sausage meat (263).

## 299 STUFFING OF POULTRY

When stuffing chicken, duck or goose, place the stuffing inside the carcass, leaving a 25 mm space beneath the breast bone. Sometimes, for chicken only, some of the stuffing is also filled through the neck end, the neck skin then being folded over before trussing to hold the stuffing in position. For a turkey of 17–20 lb (7½–9 kg) undrawn weight, place the Chestnut stuffing (296) in the neck end, after removing the wishbone, then place 32 portions of Farce à l'anglaise (291) inside through the vent end. Leave a space of 50 mm beneath the breastbone to allow hot air to penetrate during cooking.

In both cases, turn the tail inwards; truss with two strings, as for roasting.

---

## GAME—GIBIER

## 300 FEATHERED GAME – PREPARATION AND TRUSSING

Feathered game are comprised of the variety of birds that live in freedom. There are many kinds, of which only the types generally used are listed as follows:

| English | French | Weight | Portions |
|---|---|---|---|
| Grouse | Grouse | 10–14 oz (280–390 g) | 1–2 |
| Guinea fowl | Pintade | 1½–2½ lb (675 g–1 kg) | 2–4 |
| Hazel hen | Gelinotte | 1¼–2 lb (565 g–1 kg) | 2–3 |
| Partridge | Perdrix | 10–16 oz (280–450 g) | 2 |
| Partridge (young) | Perdreau | 8–10 oz (225–280 kg) | 1 |
| Pheasant | Faisan | 2½–3½ lb (1–1·5 kg) | 2–5 |
| Plover | Pluvier | 8–9 oz (225–255 g) | 1 |
| Quail | Caille | 6–8 oz (170–225 g) | 1 |
| Snipe | Bécassine | 4–5 oz (110–140 g) | 1 |
| Teal | Sarcelle | 1–1½ lb (450–675g) | 1–2 |
| Wild duck | Canard sauvage | 1½–3 oz (675 g–1.5 kg) | 2–4 |
| Woodcock | Bécasse | 8–12 oz (225–340 g) | 1 |

All feathered game should be hung initially for 3–4 days at 10–15°C (50–60°F) in a good circulation of air. Further storage, if necessary, should be in refrigeration at 3–4°C (38–40°F). This 'ageing' process helps to tenderise the flesh and to improve the flavour.

### Removal of feathers (plucking)

Frequently dip the fingers in cold water and always hold the skin taut with the thumb; remove the tail feathers first.

Next, pluck the legs from the bottom of the drumstick upwards. Pluck the back, then the breast from the tail end towards the neck.

Finally remove the neck feathers towards the head.

When pheasant plumage is required for serving as a decoration, i.e. 'en volière' (in flight), the tail is cut off with the feathers, the head with approximately 40–50 mm of neck, and the wings at the first joint from the wing. Pieces of wire 200 mm in diameter and 50–75 mm in length are then partially inserted into these pieces, the other end being inserted into a flat-sided potato. The potato is then placed in a tray in a hot plate at 65–90°C (150–200°F) for 2–3 hours to sterilize the feathers.

### Cleaning and trussing (all types except snipe and woodcock)

This is carried out in the same manner as for chicken, whether the game is for roasting or entrée.

When used for roasting, a thin slice of fat bacon (bard de lard) is placed over the breast after trussing and tied in position; this protects the delicate skin and imparts some fat to the lean flesh.

### Snipe and woodcock

After plucking, the eyes of snipe and woodcock are removed with a knife point (the head is left on). Except for the gizzard, the entrails are not removed. The gizzard is removed by making a very small incision in the side of the bird behind the raised leg.

To truss, hold the legs well forward to push the breast out. Turn the neck and, instead of using a trussing needle and string, pass the long thin beak through the bird.

## 301 FURRED GAME – PREPARATION

### Venison

Venison is a term which is generally applied to include deer, roebuck and stag.

Due to the fast movement of the animal, the flesh is rather tough. To overcome this toughness, the animal should be hung at 10–15°C (50–60°F) in a good circulation of air for 5–6 days, and afterwards in refrigeration at 3–4°C (38–40°F) for a further 7–10 days to prevent 'sweating', which causes the flesh to be sticky.

If supplied in the whole carcass, the intestines are removed by making an incision down the centre of the breast (belly) from a point half way down the ribs to the start of the legs.

Remove and discard all the intestines except the liver and heart.

To skin, extend the cut already made in the breast up to the neck. Cut the skin around the top of the hind legs, then down the inside of the legs for 300 mm.

Gradually pull the skin down along the carcass towards the back, easing the tissue with a knife point.

Continue from under the neck towards back of the neck. When the shoulder (foreleg) is met, make an incision in the skin on the inside, down the centre of the leg for approximately 200–225 mm. Continue towards the back of the carcass, until the skin is free, then ease the skin down each of the legs to the hoof. Cut around the hoof to free it.

The carcass of venison is then dissected as for lamb (200), the saddle being left long. When the saddle and legs are left together it forms a 'haunch' of venison.

The flesh in the forequarter, except the part that corresponds to the best end, is not suitable for use in dishes.

The prepared joints are placed to marinade (see 303) in a refrigerator for 12–24 hours.

### Hare                                                                 Lièvre

The younger hares of 5–7 lb (2·2–3 kg) in weight are easily recognised by:

(a) the edge of the ear, which should tear easily between the fingers, and (b) the hare-lip, very prominent in older hares, which will only just be visible.

Older hares from 7–12 lb (3–5·5 kg) in weight are only suitable for soup, pâté or terrine.

Hare requires hanging for 5–7 days to tenderise the flesh.

To skin the hare, carefully make an incision in the lower part of the stomach; do not pierce the diaphragm (the tissue at the base of the ribs, dividing the base of the rib cavity from the stomach).

Remove the intestines and retain the liver. Carefully cut away the gall bladder, placing the liver in a basin.

To remove the skin, ease the thumb between the skin and the flesh towards the back, then towards the legs.

Cut off the feet and tail, then ease the legs clear of the skin. Next, pull the skin away from the flesh from the rear end, towards the head.

Place the diaphragm over the basin containing the liver, then make an incision to perforate it and catch all the blood in the basin. Place this in refrigeration at 2–3°C (35–38°F) for use as a liaison.

## Rabbit                                                    Lapin

The intestines and skin of rabbit are removed in the same manner as for hare. There will be no blood, as the throat of the rabbit should be cut, if not already done so, to drain off the blood to whiten the flesh.

### 302 Dissection of hare and rabbit

1. Remove the head, cutting straight across at the beginning of the neck. Then cut the head through lengthways in halves.

2. Remove the front legs by holding the base of the leg to force the shoulder blade outwards. Cut behind the shoulder blade.

3. Remove the hind legs by cutting across the point where they join the thick end of the saddle. Divide the legs by cutting across into 2–3 pieces.

4. Cut through, straight across, at the end of the rib bones to separate the saddle.

5. Chop away the base of the rib bones, then cut across the remainder into 3–4 pieces.

6. The saddle is prepared for roasting, if required, by passing the knife point under the silver-coloured sinew on top of the saddle and carefully cutting away along the whole length. Cut around the pieces of pelvic bone at the thicker end and remove them. Shorten the stomach flap underneath to 25 mm in length on each side. Piqué the flesh of the saddle with larding bacon as for Fillet of beef (163).

7. Hare is then placed to marinade (see 303), for 8–12 hours.

### 303 MARINADE FOR GAME

| 8 portions | Ingredients | 10 couverts |
| --- | --- | --- |
| ½ pint | red wine | 350 ml |
| ¼ pint | olive oil | 175 ml |
| 3 oz | onions | 100 g |
| 4 oz | carrots | 140 g |
| 1 oz | celery | 35 g |
| 1 oz | shallots | 35 g |
| 1 oz | parsley stalks | 35 g |
| small sprig | thyme | small sprig |
| 1 | bayleaf | 1 |
| 1 pod | garlic | 1 pod |
| 2 | cloves | 3 |

### Method

1. Cut the prepared onions, shallots and carrots into thin slices across. Coarsely shred the prepared celery across.

2. Thoroughly mix all the ingredients together.

3. Cover over the game.

---

## 304 PREPARATIONS AND FILLINGS FOR PIES AND PUDDINGS

### 305 Chicken pie

| 8 portions | Ingredients | 10 couverts |
| --- | --- | --- |
| 2 × 3 lb | roasting chicken | 2 × 1·7 kg |
| 8 oz | streaky or collar bacon | 280 g |
| 2 oz | finely chopped onion | 70 g |
| 1 oz | butter | 35 g |
| 2 tablespoons | chopped parsley | 15 g |
| ½ oz | salt | 15 g |
| 1 teaspoon | milled white pepper | 4 g |
| 2 | hard boiled eggs | 3 |

### Method

1. Cut the cleaned chickens (273) as for sauté (275).

2. Prepare 1 to 1½ pints (560–850 ml) chicken stock (347) from the bones and giblets. Allow to go cold.

3. Sweat the onion in the butter for 6–7 minutes without colouring. Allow to go cold.

4. Cut the skin off the bacon and thinly slice; bat out if necessary.

5. Season the chicken and place it into a 2¾ pint pie dish (3½ pint – 2 litres – for 10 portions). Sprinkle with the onion.

6. Cover the chicken with the sliced bacon, then sliced hard-boiled eggs. Sprinkle with chopped parsley.

7. Add sufficient cold, strained chicken stock to come two-thirds of the way up the pie dish. For covering, see Pastry section, or (777).

*Note.* For Chicken and mushroom pie add to the onion 4 oz (140 g) washed, sliced and peeled mushrooms, cooked in 1 oz (35 g) butter for 5 minutes, without colouring.

### 306 Pork pie filling

| 8 portions | Ingredients | 10 couverts |
| --- | --- | --- |
| 1¼ lb | lean pork | 700 g |
| 8 oz | fat pork | 280 g |
| ¾ oz (6 level teaspoons) | special seasoning (192) | 30 g |
| ½ teaspoon | powdered sage | 2 g |

**Method**

1. Cut the lean and fat pork into 5 mm dice or coarsely mince with a 5 mm blade.
2. Mix thoroughly with the seasoning.

For raised pies, see Pastry section.

### 307 Steak and kidney pie

| 8 portions | Ingredients | 10 couverts |
|---|---|---|
| 1¼ lb | prepared beef | 700 g |
| 7 oz | ox kidney | 250 g |
| 3 oz | finely chopped onion | 100 g |
| 3 dessert spoons | chopped parsley | 12 g |
| ½ oz (4 level teaspoons) | salt | 15 g |
| ⅛ oz (1 level teaspoon) | milled white pepper | 4 g |
| 1 teaspoon | Worcester sauce | 5 ml |

**Method**

1. Because the meat takes approximately 2 hours to cook, it is preferable to half-cook the preparation; the cooking is completed when the pie is covered (see Pastry section for the covering) or (777).
2. Cut the prepared beef and kidney into small slices 25 × 25 × 5 mm thick.
3. Place into a stew pan and just cover with cold water. Boil, remove the scum and add all the other ingredients, except the parsley. Simmer, covered, for 1 hour.
4. Cool rapidly in a shallow tray.
5. Place into a 2¾ pint pie dish (3½ pint – 2 litres – for 10 portions).
6. Sprinkle with chopped parsley.
7. For Steak, kidney and mushroom pie, add 4 oz (140 g) of sliced, cooked mushroom.

### 308 Steak and kidney pudding

**Method**

1. Prepare the same ingredients as for Steak and kidney pie (307) and cut as in 2 of Method.
2. Mix all the ingredients in a 2 pint pudding basin, just cover with cold water and allow to marinade for 1–2 hours.
3. To finish, see Pastry section.
4. For variation, the basic pudding may be garnished with 4 oz (140 g) of washed, sliced cooked mushroom.

The meat may be reduced by 25% and substituted by this amount of cooked, boned game, e.g. pheasant, for Steak, kidney and game pudding.

### 309 Veal and ham pie (with gammon)
### Veal and bacon pie (with bacon)

| 8 portions | Ingredients | 10 couverts |
|---|---|---|
| 1¼ lb | lean prepared veal | 700 g |
| 8 oz | gammon, streaky or collar bacon | 280 g |
| 1 oz | finely chopped onion | 35 g |
| 2 dessertspoons | chopped parsley | 8 g |
| ½ teaspoon | milled white pepper | 2 g |
| ⅛ teaspoon | powdered marjoram | ½ g |
| ⅛ teaspoon | powdered thyme | ½ g |
| ¼ lemon | grated lemon rind | ⅓ lemon |
| 2 | hard boiled eggs (6 minutes) | 3 |
| ¾ pint | cold veal stock | 525 ml |
| 6 fl. oz | double strength aspic jelly (for cold) | 210 ml |

**Method**

1. Peel and finely chop the onion and mix it with the parsley, herbs, pepper and grated lemon rind. Sprinkle on the table.
2. Cut the veal in thin slices. Slice the bacon thinly.
3. Dip the veal in the onion mixture, lay on to the bacon slices and roll them together.
4. Pack closely in a 2¾ pint pie dish (3½ pint – 2 litres – for 10 portions), placing the hard boiled eggs in the centre, spaced in line.
5. Add cold stock to fill two-thirds of the pie dish.
6. To finish, see Pastry section or (777).

---

## 310 MOULDING OF COOKED FOOD PREPARATIONS

For preparing these various mixtures, see the appropriate recipe, as, for example, Côtelette de Saumon.

**Method**

1. Using a minimum of flour, roll the mixture into a long cylindrical shape, then divide into the required number of pieces. Where the portion is 4 oz (110 g), for presentation purposes it is preferable to mould each portion into 2 pieces of 2 oz (55 g).
2. Mould in the palm of the hands into a ball, without cracks, irrespective of final shape.
3. Flour, egg and crumb (pané) if required.
4. For médaillons, gently flatten with a palette knife until the ball is 15 mm thick.
5. For croquettes, roll the ball into a cylindrical shape 50–60 mm long × 25 mm in diameter.

6. For cutlets, roll the ball between the palm and fingers to a pear shape, then flatten to 15 mm thick and turn the pointed end slightly to form the cutlet shape. Place a 25 mm piece of raw macaroni in the pointed end to represent a cutlet bone.

## 311 Flour, egg and crumbing      Panée à l'anglaise

The purpose of flour, egg and crumbing is to give a thin coating of crumbs to ensure a golden-brown crisp finish to the food when it is cooked, not to create a soggy outer covering. When quantities of food are to be crumbed, it is best to use one person for each individual operation.

### Method

1. Season all the raw foods.

2. Dip them into sieved flour and shake or knock off any surplus.
3. Pass through beaten egg; wipe off all excess between the fingers.
4. Coat with fresh or dried breadcrumbs.
5. Pat gently with a palette knife and, where required (escalopes, cutlets, etc.), mark a trellis pattern with the edge of the knife.
6. Place on trays. Do not pile them up as this causes sticking.

*Note.* Excessive flour will accept too much egg, and this causes a type of batter to form around the food. The steam created during cooking will leave any uncooked flour separate from the food.

---

# COLD BUFFET

## 312 COLD BUFFET PREPARATIONS

To cover this subject thoroughly, one could easily write a separate volume.

The techniques used in preparing cold buffet foodstuffs call for a lot of experience and skill, so only the basic factors are mentioned, together with a few recipes. This should give a slight insight into this fascinating work.

---

## 313 White basic cold sauce    Chaud-froid blanc
(2 pints)                  (1 litre)

### Method (a)

1. Reduce $1\frac{1}{2}$ pints (750 ml) chicken velouté (368) with $\frac{3}{4}$ pint (375 ml) chicken stock (347) until it masks the back of a ladle.
2. Add $\frac{1}{4}$–$\frac{1}{2}$ pint (125–250 ml) of double cream to enrich and whiten the mixture. Reboil, then add 1 oz (25 g) leaf gelatine which has previously been soaked and well squeezed. Thoroughly dissolve the gelatine.
3. Pass the mixture through a clean tammy cloth (étamine).

### Method (b)

1. Reduce $1\frac{1}{2}$ pints (750 ml) chicken velouté (368) with 1 pint (500 ml) chicken jelly (315) until it masks the back of a ladle.
2. Finish as above with the same quantity of cream.

### For fish

Substitute fish velouté (624) and fish stock (356) using Method (a).

## 314 Brown basic cold sauce    Chaud-froid brun
(2 pints)                  (1 litre)

### Method

1. Reduce $1\frac{3}{4}$ pints (875 ml) demi-glace (369) with 1 pint (500 ml) aspic jelly (315) to $1\frac{3}{4}$ pints (875 ml). Remove any scum or fat and pass the mixture through a very fine strainer. Add 2 fl. oz (50 ml) madeira or port wine to finish.
2. Test for setting by placing a little on a plate in the refrigerator.
3. If a stronger set is required, add a little strained, soaked and dissolved gelatine.

### For duck

1. Refine the demi-glace with duck stock before starting to make the chaud-froid.
2. Finish with the strained juice of 2 oranges.

## For game

1. Prepare as for duck, using game stock, and omit the orange juice.

## For fish

1. The demi-glace is prepared from Lenten espagnole (367) and Fumet de poisson (357).
2. Reduce with Fish aspic jelly (316).

*Note.* In the preparation of all chaud-froid sauces, all fat and scum must be removed when reducing, or they will ruin the cold dish by remaining in the form of frozen granules of fat.

## 315 Aspic jelly

### Method

1. Prepare aspic jelly in the same manner as for Basic consommé (419), using a strong stock of the type of aspic required: beef, chicken, game, etc.
2. Soak 1½ oz per quart (40 g per litre) of leaf gelatine for 4–5 minutes then squeeze out all the water. Add to the clarified stock 15 minutes before ready.
3. Pass through a jelly bag, repassing the first ½ pint (300 ml).
4. Check for its setting quality by placing a small amount of the jelly in a saucer in the refrigerator.
5. Where a stronger setting aspic is required (for croûtons, lining of moulds, etc.), increase the amount of gelatine accordingly.

## 316 Fish aspic jelly

### Method

1. Take 2 pints or 1 litre of the court-bouillon (626) in which the fish has been cooked. If no wine has been used in cooking, add 2 fl. oz (50 ml for litre) of white or red wine, according to the colour of the jelly.
2. Soak 1½ oz per quart (40 g per litre) leaf gelatine for 4–5 minutes, then squeeze out all the water.
3. Place the cool liquid in a thick pan, add the gelatine and 2 loosened egg whites.
4. Place to boil and whisk occasionally until it is boiling. Then remove the whisk and do not stir again.
5. Allow to simmer for 15 minutes.
6. Pass and test, as for aspic jelly (315).

## 317 COMMODITIES USED FOR COLD BUFFET DECORATION

### Truffles

(a) Truffles are cut into very thin slices, then into fine strips for outline work, (b) cut into very thin slices, then into the exact shapes for a mosaic pattern or with a shaped cutter into crescents, etc. for bold relief decoration, or (c) whole prime truffles or slices are used for garnishing.

### Pimentoes

These are used for outline or 'filled in' decoration.

### Cucumber or leek

The peel from cucumbers or leeks is used after it has been removed with a peeler from the cucumber or the green part of washed leeks. It is then blanched for 10 seconds in boiling water and refreshed.

The peel is then cut into fine long strips for the stalks or stems used in floral decoration, and in strips of 3–5 mm, then cut well on the slant, to produce the leaves.

The thin end of the cucumber is scrolled with a scrolling knife, cut lengthwise, then into thin slices for border decoration.

### Radishes

Radishes are cut whole or in halves into thin slices; they may be scrolled if desired. They are used for flowers and border decoration.

They can be carved with the point of a knife, so that when they are opened, by leaving in cold water, they give the effect of a rose.

### White of hard-boiled egg

This is cut into very thin slices, then by cutter into various shapes (floral, mosaic, crescents) for edge decorations.

### Tongue or ham

Ham or tongue is cut into thin slices, then into shaped pieces, by knife or cutter, for mosaic and 'filled in' work.

### Carrot

The red part of cooked carrot, cut in very thin slices, is used for cut-out decoration.

**Yolk of egg**

The sieved yolk of hard-boiled egg, mixed to a paste with a little creamed butter or double-strength aspic jelly, is piped into small dots of various sizes to represent mimosa or for flower centres.

When mixed with double-strength aspic to a paste, spread on the back of a silver dish and set in the refrigerator, it may be cut out into shapes or designs. Yolk can also be coloured before setting.

## 318 TYPES OF DECORATION

(a) Decorative effect is achieved by neatness and colour contrast, i.e. by the use of well-turned cooked vegetable bundles or bouquets, with green vegetables, tomatoes, etc. as garnishes.

(b) A picture or outline creation is achieved to best effect by using fine truffle work on a white background. In some cases, one part may be filled in with other commodities.

(c) Designs are made by neat and precise cut-out decoration (into crescents, diamonds, dots, squares, mosaic) using ham, tongue, cucumber peel, white of egg, etc.

(d) Designs are also made with a filled-in picture of contrasting colours outlined in a fine truffle border, pimento, cucumber peel, yolk of egg mixture (natural and coloured), tomato, etc. being used for the filled-in part.

(e) Single flower or floral sprays are made with cucumber peel for the stems and leaves. Petals are cut out from white of egg (or coloured), pimento, tomato, etc. Yolk of egg mixture can be piped as mimosa, and ribbon bows at the bottom of sprays can be cut from pimento.

(f) Small, effective designs are achieved by using blanched tarragon leaves and chervil sprays in flower pots of pimento on small individual portions, as in Suprême de volaille.

For original decorative creations, lined decorated moulds and effects, great care should be exercised in the setting strengths of the jellies and chaud-froid used, to avoid disaster in the finished product.

## 319                                        Poularde Vendôme

**Method**

1. Insert the legs of a cleaned 5–6 lb (2–2·5 kg) boiling chicken, then place the chicken to boil; when cooked, allow it to go cold in the stock.

2. Drain the chicken and remove the breasts by cutting along the breast bone to a point 10 mm above the winglets. The breasts can then be cut into five thin slices on the slant, then trimmed to a pear shape; these suprêmes should then be placed on a wire grill.

3. Place the chicken carcass on an inverted silver dish and fill in the cavity on the breast with a mousse of foie gras or mock foie gras (325) and, with a warm wet palette knife, reform the foie gras into the perfect shape of the chicken. Place it in the refrigerator to set.

4. Sauce over (nappé) the poularde and the suprêmes with white chaud-froid sauce, at setting point (it is usually necessary to repeat this operation 2 or 3 times until a nice even surface has been obtained) then place to set in the refrigerator.

5. Trim the edges of the suprêmes evenly, then decorate the poularde and suprêmes according to choice, making sure that all the decoration is passed through double-strength aspic before placing it in position. Place in the refrigerator to set.

6. Nappé the poularde and suprêmes 3 or 4 times with aspic jelly at setting point until they are coated with 3 mm of jelly. Place in the refrigerator to set and, at the same time, line a large oval silver flat dish with aspic jelly 3 mm thick and place it to set.

7. Serve by placing the chicken to one end of the oval flat dish with the vent 10 mm clear of the collar of the dish, then place the suprêmes around in front of the chicken, fan-wise, leaving a gap of 10 mm between the suprêmes.

8. Finish by piping around the base of the chicken and around the suprêmes with finely-chopped aspic jelly, using a bag and a 5 mm plain tube.

**Poularde rose de mai**

Proceed as for Vendôme (319), substituting Mousse de jambon tomatée (325, footnote).

| 320  Chicken breasts in aspic with tarragon | Suprême de volaille à l'estragon |

**Method**

1. Take a cold boiled chicken, remove the breasts and the skin and remove the skin and bone from the legs.

2. In a silver entrée dish or plat-en-terre, place the cut-up leg portions of the chicken, then place the cut portions of breast neatly on top.

3. Decorate the chicken with blanched and refreshed tarragon leaves passed through jelly and place it in the refrigerator to set.

4. Nappé with tarragon-flavoured aspic jelly at setting point, then allow it to set.

5. Finish around the edge of the dish with a 10 mm cordon of chopped aspic jelly, and serve on an underflat with a doily.

**321**　　　　　　　　**Canard ou caneton Montmorency**

**Method**

1. Clean and truss the duck then plain roast and allow to go cold.
2. Remove the breasts and cut each breast into 4 or 5 thin suprêmes; place these on to a wire grill.
3. Replace the cavity on the breast with mousse of foie gras (325) and place to set in the refrigerator on an inverted silver flat dish.
4. Nappé the suprêmes and the duck with brown chaud-froid sauce at setting point, repeating 2 or 3 times to obtain an even surface. Place the duck to set in refrigerator.
5. Decorate the duck and the suprêmes with leaves, stalks and stoned halves of tinned cherries dipped in aspic, then set in the refrigerator.
6. Nappé 3 or 4 times with aspic jelly at setting point and reset.
7. Serve on a large oval silver flat dish lined with aspic jelly set 3 mm thick. Arrange the suprêmes around the duck, fan-wise, and finish around the base with chopped aspic jelly.

**322**　　　　　　　　**Côtelette d'agneau froide**

**Method**

1. Prepare and roast two eight-bone best ends of lamb and allow them to go cold.
2. Cut down between the bones, trim the cutlets and place them on a wire grid.
3. Nappé with brown chaud-froid at setting point. Repeat this operation until a coating of sauce 3 mm thick has been obtained then set the lamb in the refrigerator.
4. Decorate each cutlet according to choice, then set them in the refrigerator.
5. Nappé several times with aspic jelly at setting point until a glaze 3 mm thick is achieved, then place the cutlets to set in the refrigerator.
6. Line a round plain or fancy charlotte mould with double strength aspic to a depth of 10 mm in the bottom, then place to set in a deep tray of ice water.
7. When set, place a smaller mould inside to allow a gap of 10 mm all round between the moulds. Fill this gap with double aspic at setting point and allow it to set firm by placing ice water in the empty mould in the centre.
8. When set, remove the inner mould by filling it with hot water and emptying it immediately; this will release the mould. Decorate the jelly with suitable colourful decoration dipped in double aspic, then re-set in the refrigerator. Fill the centre with cooked peas bound with jelly, or cooked macédoine of vegetables bound with mayonnaise collée and place them to set in the refrigerator. Line a round flat silver dish with aspic jelly 3 mm deep and set in the refrigerator.
9. Serve with the vegetable mould turned out (dip in hot water for one second) and placed in centre of the flat dish with two rows of the jellied cutlets around it, and cutlet frills on the cutlets. Finish with chopped aspic jelly, using a 5 mm plain tube, around the edge.

**323**　　　　　　　　**Caneton à l'orange**

Proceed as for Canard ou caneton Montmorency (321) as far as 3 in the method. Without removing the skin, cut the breast to obtain 6–8 thin small slices from each breast.

4. Fill the cavity in the breast with Mousse of foie gras (325) just to the level of the breast bone and shape it with a warm wet palette knife.
5. Replace the thin slices of duck back to the position from which they were removed, over-lapping to allow 10 mm of the previous slice to show.
6. Decorate down the centre of the breast with segments of orange, free of skin and pith, dipped in double strength aspic jelly, then set in the refrigerator.
7. Glaze the duck several times with aspic jelly at setting point then place in the refrigerator. At the same time, line an oval dish 3 mm thick with port wine aspic jelly.
8. When set, serve the duck on the jellied dish with small bouquets of jellied orange segments or orange baskets around.
9. Finish around the base with finely chopped aspic jelly, using a 5 mm plain tube.

**324**　　　　　　　　**Caneton à l'orange et aux cerises**

Proceed as for Caneton à l'orange. When decorating, add halved cocktail cherries down the centre of the orange segments, and to the bouquets of orange or the orange baskets.

## 325 BASIC COLD MOUSSE PREPARATION

The main ingredient, the first on the list of ingredients, is that by which the mousse is named, e.g. foie gras, ham, salmon, pheasant, chicken, seafood. It is always cooked and, where applicable, free of skin, shell or bone.

| 8 portions | Ingredients | 10 couverts |
|---|---|---|
| 1 lb | main ingredient | 560 g |
| ¼ pint (5 fl. oz) | aspic jelly, i.e. chicken, fish | 170 ml |
| ¼ pint (5 fl. oz) | velouté (chicken, fish) | 170 ml |
| ¾ pint (15 fl. oz) | double cream | 525 ml |
| 2 level teaspoons | salt* | 8 g |
| ½ level teaspoon | ground white pepper | 2 g |

\* slightly less for ham. Béchamel may be substituted for velouté.

### Method

1. Cut the main ingredient into small dice or flakes and pound in a mortar to a paste. Alternatively, pass it through a very fine mincer blade and work to a paste in a basin with a spatule, then add the seasoning.
2. Gradually add the cold velouté or béchamel, mixing thoroughly, then rub the mixture through a very fine sieve. Replace it into a clean basin.
3. Half whip the cream, but not on ice.
4. Stir in the liquid aspic jelly and well mix. For mousse of a pink colour, i.e. ham, salmon, lobster, add a few drops of cochineal to give a good pink colour.
5. Fold in the half whipped cream immediately, mixing until it is thoroughly absorbed. Slowness in mixing or ice-cold cream will set the gelatine too quickly.
6. Pour into (a) a prepared mould lined (chemisée) with aspic jelly 5 mm thick and decorated (see method 6, 322) or into (b) a timbale or soufflé case with an oiled band of greaseproof paper 25 mm above the top edge of the dish.

Tap the mould or dish very gently on a cloth to remove any small pockets or pleats in the mixture.

7. Set it in the refrigerator for 2–3 hours.
8. Serve, if moulded in aspic, by dipping the mould for 1 second only in hot water and turning it out on to a round silver flat dish, previously lined and set with 3 mm of aspic jelly. When in a timbale or soufflé case, remove the paper band and decorate the top of the mousse with truffle, pimento, white of egg, etc., passed through double aspic. When set, lightly coat the surface of the mousse with aspic. Place the mousse on a round flat dish on a doily.

*Note.* Where the mousse is used in the preparation of other dishes, an additional ingredient is sometimes added, e.g. Mousse de jambon tomatée indicates the flavour, includes tomato (added in a small quantity in the form of a purée) as well as ham.

---

## 326 GENERAL RECEPTION BUFFET ITEMS – PRODUCTION

The amounts of the various types of food or articles of food produced will vary considerably since they depend on the kind of buffet required.

The governing factors are usually (a) the price to be charged, (b) the duration of the buffet and (c) the type of clientele attending the buffet.

---

### Sandwiches

The standard 3½ lb (1½ kg) sandwich loaf, when trimmed and cut lengthwise, will produce 12–14 slices, according to freshness, which, when buttered and filled, produces 6 or 7 tiers. Trim the edges of the bread with a sharp tranchelard, then cut into 10 finger-type sandwiches or cut into 4 sections and divide each section, corner to corner, to provide triangular pieces. Produces 60 or 70 finger pieces or 96–112 triangles. The average portion is 3 fingers or 4 triangles.

### Variety of fillings

Ham, ox-tongue, chicken, liver pâté, smoked salmon, creamed cheese, egg, egg and mayonnaise, cucumber, tomato, purée of sardine, etc.

### Bridge rolls        Petits pains

If these are not made, they are bought by the dozen.

They are produced in two ways: in open halves, or split, with filling between.

### Types of fillings

Sieved or chopped egg and mayonnaise, smoked salmon, crab and mayonnaise, piped purée of mousse of foie gras (325), mousse of terrine de foie (325), mouse of ham (325), purée of sardine. One whole bridge roll or two halves is normally served per portion.

### Assorted canapés        Canapés assortis

See notes on canapés (110).

Three pieces of canapé is the normal sized portion.

## Bouchées

Bouchées are prepared in sizes varying from 30–45 mm in diameter. They are baked, the centres are removed and the 'caps' retained.

## Fillings

Fillings are generally cut into 5 mm dice or served in a purée form; when bound with a sauce, the sauce is generally finished with cream.

Chicken: chicken and mushroom (with Sauce suprême, 400)
Chicken: chicken and mushroom (with Sauce kari, 413)
Veal and ham: veal, ham and mushroom (with Sauce suprême, 400)
Veal and ham: veal, ham and mushroom (with Sauce kari, 413)
Shrimps or prawns: shrimps, prawns and mushroom (with Sauce crevettes, 628)

Lobster: lobster and mushroom (with Coulis de homard, 629)
Chipolata or sausage rolls (1300), made small, 50–60 mm long.

**Hot hors d'oeuvre**          **Hors d'oeuvre chauds**
These are served only in certain types of reception buffets. See Hot hors d'oeuvre (111).

## 327 COCKTAIL RECEPTION BUFFET

Generally, the following are served in separate dishes on large, flat under-dishes on dish papers: potato crisps (Pommes chips), cocktail gherkins, cocktail onions, a variety of olives (Spanish queen, black, stuffed), fried salted nuts (almond, cashew, etc.), cheese straws, a variety of canapés (110), small 30 mm bouchées (326), hot grilled chipolata sausages.

---

## 328 LARDER GARNISHES AND PREPARATIONS

### KITCHEN

Brunoise: meat and poultry
Butters: savoury (112–118)
Capers
Chipolata and other sausages (264)
Giblets and bones of poultry and game; bones only of fish
Julienne: Ham, ox-tongue, truffle, white of egg, chicken, game, beetroot, gherkin
Lardons and diced pork
Olive stones
Oysters: opened, with or without shells
Quenelles: soup, fish, chicken, veal (150, 283)
Salpicon: cooked dice of ham, ox-tongue, poultry, beef, veal, pork, seafoods, truffle
Scallops (small pieces cut on the slant): cooked poultry, ham, ox-tongue, seafood, veal, game
Seafoods: picked shrimps, prawns, crayfish, halves and slices of lobster
Slices: ham, truffle, pickled walnut

Stuffings: see 291, 292, 293, 294, 295, 296, 297 and 298
Sieved egg: yolk and white, separated
Tinned fish: anchovy fillets, sardines

## 329 CONVENIENCE FOODS USED IN THE LARDER

1 Aspic jelly crystals
2 Bottled foods: olives, gherkins, pickled cabbage, rollmop herrings, meat and fish pastes, cocktail onions, cherries, etc.
3 Canned foods: fish, seafoods, vegetables, fruits, meat, ham, smoked ham, offals, Frankfurter sausages, oysters, foie gras, truffles
4 Frozen foods: meat, fish, shellfish, vegetables, cooked preparations, poultry, game
5 Herbs: loose dried and tins or packets
6 Meat preparations: sausages, brawn, cold meats
7 Sauces: tomato ketchup, chilli, horseradish, etc.

# Kitchen Section
(general information)

102

# Kitchen Section

## 330 Use of equipment

At first, it is difficult for the student of cookery to understand why so many varieties and sizes of equipment are necessary. But by general reasoning and with the knowledge given by skilled personnel, the need to use the correct equipment in the proper manner soon becomes apparent. It is essential, for the chef to work correctly and efficiently, that all equipment is at all times well maintained and kept clean.

Skilful cookery calls for the correct use of temperatures, whether they are freezing, chilled, warm or hot. To freeze or chill is reasonably easy, as the result can be seen or felt. Warm temperatures are used rather restrictedly and they are mainly applied to warm sauces. The most difficult to understand is the use of hot temperatures, as they can be applied in so many different ways, as in the following:

### (a) Open top stoves

Heated by gas or electricity, these are used mainly for individual items or for cooking in small quantities. Even with this limitation, provision is made for quicker cooking on certain of the rings or elements, and use should be made of this.

### (b) Solid top ranges

Designed for cooking in quantity, these require considerably more skill in use than open top stoves. The greatest heat lies in the centre of the cooking surface and the degree of heat is first determined by regulating the supply, i.e. by opening the tap to the maximum or only in part.

The area of the range used will give different temperatures, i.e. the centre, being hottest, will be used for fast boiling, frying or setting, and the outer parts of the surface will be used for simmering, sweating or poaching.

When really fierce direct heat is required, the centre rings can be removed and in some cases the cooking appliance can then be propped on part of one of the rings. This is done to spread the flame wider by allowing extra air to meet the gas supply. With electric solid top ranges, this is not possible.

### Ovens

The temperature of the oven is controlled by a regulator or thermostat control, the setting of which regulates the amount of fuel to give an approximate temperature. Generally, the difference tolerance is from 0–5°C (0–10°F).

This range of difference has little effect for general use. However, in pastry ovens, an oven thermometer is fitted to give the exact temperature within the oven.

Apart from the temperature selected, the position used in the oven is a separate factor affecting the degree of heat and this arises from the temperature being higher at the top than at the lower part of the oven. Furthermore, since the ceiling or roof of the oven acts as a deflector of heat, the top of the oven is used when the foodstuff requires colouring or setting.

Where a general even temperature is required, the centre position is used, and the lower part of the oven is generally used for braising, stewing, or where a slower heat is required to cook the bottom surface of foods.

Specialised ovens may have other features, according to type.

### Stewpans, sauteuse, plat à sauter, etc.

These vary in size and are made to specific shapes, like a sauteuse which is so designed with sloping sides for tossing foods easily, or for easy clearance of the bottom and side surfaces with a spatule or whisk.

The selection of the correct size is most important, as too large a size can result in excessive quantities of food being lost on the surface of the utensil.

### Frying, omelet and pancake pans

These utensils, particularly frying pans, are found in many sizes, with various built-in features, such as sloping and belly (rounded) sides.

Pancake pans have a very shallow side for ease in turning the pancake.

None of these pans should be washed. Cleaning is effected with sawdust, salt and clean cloths or paper; this means the surface is never moist and this is essential to prevent food sticking to the surface.

### Knives

To assist in the skilful cutting, shaping, filleting or channelling of foods, many sizes and types of knives are used.

The use of the wrong type of knife will have many effects, e.g. the point of a small knife is used for turning foods to various shapes; a larger or wider blade would leave undesirable wide ridges.

Certain operations, such as filleting, call for the use of a flexible blade, while cutting, for instance, needs a more rigid blade.

Generally a longer bladed knife with a degree of flexibility is required for carving to give a wide slice of meat.

Palette knives are designed with blunt edges for the turning, shaping etc. of foods without cutting into the surface.

Various other specially designed knives are used for the cutting of garnishes, the opening of oysters, and so on.

### Small equipment

Whisks, spoons, spatules, slices, etc., are made in a very wide range of sizes in different materials.

Using the wrong sizes can result in the equipment breaking, or the bending of the wires when a light whisk, designed for use in cream, whites of egg, etc. is used in a thick sauce. Using a heavy, rigid whisk results in waste of time and energy, together with a loss in volume of the finished foodstuff.

### Steaming ovens

Great care is required when opening steaming ovens. They should never be opened in one movement, but should be released gradually to allow excess steam pressure to escape; this reduces the risk of scalding the face, hands or arms.

The pressure and water level in the oven should be checked while the food is cooking.

### Machinery

The machinery used in the kitchen includes general purpose mixers, mincing machines, high speed chopping machines, automatic slicers, etc. They should never be used until adequate knowledge of the operation has been gained under supervision.

Always check that all safety devices are working and in the correct position and never feed foods into machines by hand while they are switched on.

The correct fitments for loading and feeding should always be used; the use of spoon handles, etc. will result in accidents and damage to the machines.

When not in use, the power supply should be disconnected or turned off.

Cleaning should be done immediately after use.

### Deep fryers

Great care needs to be exercised in the use of deep fryers, whether they are specially built fryers or movable fritures.

The heat required should only be maintained for the period the fryer is in use. At other times, it should be reduced or turned off.

A properly designed piece of equipment to fry in or on should always be used. Care is required, when draining, to avoid oil or fat falling on the floor.

Movable fritures should only be moved when the frying medium is cool. At other times, the temperature is adjusted by reducing the heat supply.

After use, the fryer is cooled, drained and cleaned and the strained oil or fat is replaced.

### Salamanders and grills

Great care is required when using these because of the very high temperatures produced.

With salamanders, often only part of the available heat is required, so use should be made of the movable bars.

After the foodstuff has been sealed or set, it is often necessary to move it to a cooler part of the grill.

---

## 331 HYGIENE IN THE KITCHEN

The main aim of kitchen hygiene is to prevent the contamination of foods. Those most likely to become contaminated are made-up dishes, such as meat pies, brawn and corned or pressed beef, and milk products such as custards, trifles and synthetic cream.

The conditions which encourage bacterial growth are warmth, moisture, time and those certain types of food as have been mentioned.

Cooked and prepared foods which will not be heated immediately before use are liable to become dangerously contaminated, as are foodstuffs that have to be handled in preparation after being cooked. If these foodstuffs are left about in a warm temperature, any bacteria introduced from the hands will multiply and the food so infected may cause food poisoning.

## Cold storage

Meats that are cooked on the day before use should first be cooled quickly in a well-ventilated cold or cool room and then kept in a refrigerator until required.

Stews, gravies and similar liquid foods should be placed in shallow containers to assist quick cooling.

All uncanned cooked meats should be stored in a refrigerator. Extreme cold will not kill bacteria, but it will prevent their multiplying, and this is why foods susceptible to spoilage should be stored at a low temperature. It cannot be over-emphasised, however, that this food should not be brought into a warm room earlier than is absolutely necessary or any bacteria present may start to multiply.

Refrigerators should be cleaned and defrosted regularly and should not be overcrowded.

Hot foods should never be placed in a refrigerator because they are liable to cause condensation on the cold foods and so assist in the growth of bacteria.

Milk should always be kept in a cold or cool room.

## Cooking

Adequate cooking will destroy most dangerous bacteria, but not the poisonous toxins which may have been formed if food has been left in a warm kitchen. Made-up dishes, such as pies, may not be sufficiently heated in the centre to destroy dangerous bacteria.

## 332 Hygiene as a preventative measure

It is obvious that the cleanliness of the skin, and particularly the hands, is of paramount importance, for the hands are the most usual means of transfer of dangerous bacteria to foods.

The hands must be kept clean by frequent and thorough washing with plenty of soap and hot water. The nails should be kept short, well scrubbed and scrupulously clean.

Washing of the hands after using the wc and before eating should be routine for everyone, but it is even more important for those who handle food.

Individual towels should always be used for drying the hands. These may be ordinary towels, provided they are changed frequently and kept separately, paper towels, which can be destroyed immediately after use, the continuous roller towel, which provides a portion of clean towel for each individual, or a hot air dryer.

All cuts, burns and abrasions should be covered immediately with clean waterproof dressing. A cotton bandage is too porous to give any protection against danger to food, or to the affected part for that matter.

Food should not be touched by hand more than is absolutely necessary, nor should the parts of crockery, cutlery and glasses which come into contact with food or the mouth.

Coughing and sneezing over food must be avoided as well as licking the fingers and touching the nose.

## Food preparation rooms

Food preparation rooms should be well ventilated and a high standard of cleanliness should be maintained. Floors should be kept free from cracks and easily washed down.

Table tops and similar working surfaces should be made of metal or glazed ware or plastic as they are much more hygienic than wood and easily kept clean.

---

### 333 'MISE EN PLACE'

Efficiency in the kitchen requires methodical working. An important part of this is to have the correct 'mise en place'; this is applied in many different ways, as follows:

(a) **Service:** To prepare in advance all equipment required for the keeping of food at the serving temperature, and this includes all the necessary dishes, plates, doilys, dish papers, etc., the small equipment required for actual serving, or finishing off dishes, and any small garnishes of food which may be used to complete dishes, such as chopped and picked parsley, lemon wedges, croutons, etc., and various sauces, toast, etc. that may be required.

(b) To prepare in advance all the ingredients and equipment used in the production of a dish, mixture, etc. before cooking.

(c) To prepare in advance at various stages in the preparation; this is particularly related to banquet production.

(d) To be more modern it includes the preparation in advance of blast frozen foods.

## 335 Cleaning and preparation of vegetables

### (a) Potatoes

Place the potatoes in a sink and cover them with cold water. For small quantities, remove the dirt with a scrubbing brush. For large quantities, tumble them about in the sink with a short bristle broom which is kept for this purpose.

Remove the peel with a vegetable peeler, or tumble them in a peeling machine; all the eyes are removed without digging deep holes in the potatoes. Rewash, place them in a container and cover them with cold water. If not required immediately, store the potatoes in refrigeration at 3–4°C (38–40°F).

### (b) Onions and shallots

With a small knife, remove the outer dry skin, cut the minimum off the root end and straighten the top end.

Shallots and button onions are easier to peel if they are first placed in a basin of luke-warm water.

### (c) Carrots, turnips and swedes

These are cleaned in the same way as potatoes, and carrots are peeled thinly with a vegetable peeler while turnips and swedes are peeled thickly with a knife. Rewash all these vegetables before using them.

### (d) Leeks

Cut off the minimum from the root end and remove the discoloured leaves from the top end. Remove one outer layer of skin. Trim the leeks to a point in the centre approximately 40 mm beyond the white part. The top green part is kept for general stocks if it is not too dark.

From a point 10 mm from the root end, split the leek through the centre towards the green end.

Soak them in cold salt water for a few minutes to loosen the dirt, then wash them under running water, loosening the leaves with the fingers, until they are thoroughly clear of all dirt. Resoak if necessary.

### (e) Celery

Pull away any discoloured parts from the celery and thoroughly wash to use for stocks or mirepoix.

With a knife, trim the root end clean to a point. If the outer stems are coarse or of a bad colour, remove, wash and use them for stocks, soups, etc.

Finish cleaning the outside of the stems with a peeler to leave a good white surface, then cut away and discard the green top of the celery (this is usually very bitter).

Soak the celery heads in cold water to loosen the inner dirt. If not required as whole heads, separate the stems and wash.

### (f) Peeling of tomatoes

With a knife point, cut away the 'eye' (the stalk base) from the tomato. Place them in a clean frying basket, immerse in boiling water for 5–10 seconds, until the skin will pull away; do not leave longer than necessary as the flesh quickly cooks and goes soft. Remove the skin.

### (g) Peeling and cooking of mushrooms

Wash the mushrooms well in cold water to remove any dirt or sand; drain thoroughly.

Remove the stalk, then, with the point of a knife, remove the skin.

For 'turning', do not remove the stalk. Hold the stalk in one hand, then, with the point of a small knife, just pass through the skin and turn the hand in a circular motion, at the same time moving the other hand in the opposite direction (outward turning). For inward turning, the hand holding the knife is turned to the left instead of the right.

Cut away the base and stalk of the mushroom.

**Mushrooms cooked white**                **Champignons à blanc**

**Method**

1. Add to a sauteuse that the mushrooms will half fill 10 mm of water, ½–1 oz (15–30 g) butter, a teaspoon of salt, and the juice of ½ lemon per pound of mushrooms.
2. Boil the liquid; add the sliced, whole, turned or scolloped (cut in sections on the slant) mushrooms.
3. Simmer for 6–7 minutes then use as required.

*Note.* This is generally used in dishes and sauces which are white or cream in colour.

**Sauté**

**Method**

1. After preparing the mushrooms, cut them in slices, scollops or, if small, leave them whole.
2. Melt 1½ oz (40 g) butter or bacon fat in a frying pan and add the prepared mushrooms.

3. Sauté gently for 5–6 minutes to a pale golden colour; do not dry out.

*Note.* Sauté mushrooms are generally used in dishes or sauces which are predominantly brown in colour, or they are served as a garnish with shallow-fried foods.

## Grilling

### Method

1. Use open mushrooms. After preparing, place them on a well-greased or oiled tray, the light side uppermost.
2. Season them with salt and pepper then brush over liberally with oil or clean fat.
3. Grill gently for 2–3 minutes on each side.

The preparation of other vegetables is dealt with under Vegetable dishes.

## 336 Other preparations

### 1. Picked parsley

Remove the small sprigs, approximately 25 mm in diameter, of parsley from the main stalk, leaving 10 mm of stem on each sprig.

### 2. Chopped parsley

Remove all the leaves from the stalks; wash well and dry in a cloth. Using a large knife, chop the parsley evenly into a concassé (roughly chopped) or until finely chopped.

### 3. Pluche of parsley

This consists of the very small individual tips of the leaves. Place them in a conical strainer then dip it in boiling water, then into cold water.

### 4. Lemons

These are prepared by: (a) Cutting in half; cut each end of the lemon straight, cut through in half then trim the edge, (b) Cutting in wedges or sections; trim off the ends straight, cut lengthways into 4, 6 or 8 equal pieces, and remove the piece of centre skin and the seeds, (c) Slicing; cut off the ends straight, stand on one end, then, with the top of a fillet knife, cut away the outer skin and pith, following the shape of the fruit, and then cut across the lemon into thin even slices, (d) Removing the zest, the yellow skin, which is removed with a peeler for flavouring, (e) Grating the yellow skin, which is removed on a grater for flavouring, (f) Extracting the juice by squeezing the lemon by hand or extractor, then straining.

### 5. Tomatoes

Tomatoes are prepared as follows: (a) In cases; cut out the eye, then, from the opposite end of the raw or peeled tomato, cut across one-quarter of the way down the tomato, remove the seeds with a teaspoon and retain the covers (caps). (b) By dicing; cut the peeled tomatoes in half. Squeeze out the seeds, press the halves flat and cut into 5 or 10 mm dice. (c) Concassé à cru (roughly chopped); prepare as for diced in (b), press and chop through into rough 10 mm squares. (d) Julienne, prepare as for diced (b) then, when pressed, cut across in very thin strips.

## 337 Cooked diced tomato                    Tomates concassées

### Method

1. Melt 1 oz (30 g) butter in a sauteuse and add 1 oz (30 g) finely chopped shallot or onion.
2. Sweat the shallot/onion slowly for 5–6 minutes, without colouring.
3. Prepare 1 lb (450 g) tomatoes into rough dice (336, 5) and add to the shallot/onion.
4. Add 1 level teaspoon (3 g) salt and $\frac{1}{4}$ teaspoon (1 g) ground white pepper. Cook slowly until most of the moisture has evaporated.

## 338 Basic mushroom farce                    Duxelle

| | Ingredients | |
|---|---|---|
| 1 lb | mushroom stalks and trimmings | 450 g |
| 4 oz | finely chopped onion | 110 g |
| 2 oz | butter | 55 g |
| 2 level teaspoons | salt | 6 g |
| $\frac{1}{2}$ level teaspoon | ground white pepper | 2 g |

### Method

1. Melt the butter in a shallow pan, add the onion and cook slowly (sweat) for 5–6 minutes, without colouring.
2. Wash, drain, then finely chop the mushroom stalks and trimmings.
3. Add to the onion, season then cook steadily for 10–15 minutes until the moisture has been evaporated.
4. Place in a basin, cover it with buttered paper and cool.
5. Store in refrigeration until required.

## 339 Croûtons

For use in the kitchen, these are prepared from bread in many ways. The most common are as follows:
(a) The crust is removed from the sandwich loaf which is then cut into 5 mm slices, then into 5 mm strips and finally into 5 mm dice. Well cover the bottom of a clean frying

pan with butter or white fat and heat it. Add the croûtons and toss them repeatedly until they are a light golden brown. Drain and sprinkle with a little salt. They can be used as a garnish for soups.

(b) The bread is cut in various-shaped larger dice or bâtons according to the recipe and cooked in the same manner as (a).

(c) The bread is cut round, oblong, oval or heart shaped then fried golden brown in butter or white fat.

Alternatively, they can be dipped in melted butter or margarine, then coloured a light golden brown under the salamander and drained.

Other kinds are shown under specific recipes.

## 340 Vegetable and herb flavourings

### (a) Bed of roots

This is comprised of slices of carrots and onions cut to varying thickness, according to the recipe, to cover the base of the pan used. Add bayleaves, peppercorns and other herbs, according to the recipe. The bed is used to protect the base of the foods being cooked and to give them flavour.

### (b) Mirepoix

Mirepoix is a rough 10–25 mm dice of carrots, onions, celery and, in some cases, bacon trimmings.

### (c) Bouquet garni

This is various size bundles or faggots of bayleaves, thyme and celery placed inside an outer layer of leek leaves, then tied with string. It is used to flavour.

## 341 Blanc or Court-bouillon for vegetables, calf's head, etc.

| | Ingredients | |
|---|---|---|
| 4 quarts | cold water | 4 litres |
| 3 | lemons (juice) | 3 |
| 2 oz | salt | 50 g |
| 2 oz | flour | 50 g |

### Method

Mix the flour to a smooth paste with cold water. Add the remainder of the water and bring to the boil, adding the salt and lemon juice, and boil for 5 minutes.

*Note.* The vegetables, i.e. salsify, parsnips, Jerusalem artichokes, artichoke bottoms, cardon, calves head, calves feet and sheeps trotters are added to the boiling blanc and gently simmered until tender.

## 342 CUTS OF PREPARED VEGETABLES

### (a) Julienne (very fine strips)

1. Cut the vegetables across in 40 mm lengths.
2. Cut lengthways into very thin slices (2 mm).
3. Cut the slices lengthways into 2 mm thin strips.

### (b) Brunoise (very small dice)

1. Cut the vegetables into convenient size lengths.
2. Cut lengthways into thin slices 3 mm thick.
3. Cut the slices lengthways into strips 3 mm thick.
4. Cut the strips across into small dice 3 mm.

### (c) Macédoine (5 mm dice)

1. Cut the vegetables into convenient size lengths.
2. Cut lengthways into 5 mm thick slices.
3. Cut the slices lengthways into strips 5 mm thick.
4. Cut the strips across into 5 mm dice.

### (d) Jardinière (bâtons)

1. Cut the vegetables across in 25 mm lengths.
2. Cut lengthways into slices 5 mm thick.
3. Cut the slices lengthways into strips 5 mm thick.

The English term bâton is used loosely; bâtons can be cut smaller or larger than above.

### (e) Paysanne

Due to the different shape of various vegetables, the finished cut of paysanne is achieved in the following manner:

#### Carrots, turnips, etc.

1. Cut lengthways into 10 mm thick slices.
2. Cut the slices lengthways into 10 mm thick strips.
3. Lightly trim off the pointed edges lengthways.
4. Slice across the strips thinly into 2 mm slices.

#### Cabbage, leeks, etc.

1. Cut the leaves into suitable lengths.
2. Cut lengthways into strips 10 mm wide.
3. Cut across the strips into 10 mm squares.

#### Celery

1. Separate the stems, cut into suitable lengths.
2. Cut lengthways into strips 10 mm wide.
3. Cut the strips across into 10 mm squares, or shred across the strips.

## (f) Tourné (turned):

### Potatoes

1. Select potatoes of an even size or of a size that can be divided into 2 pieces to avoid excess waste.
2. Cut a little off each end to give a square cut.
3. Using the point of a small knife, trim to the size and shape of a 2 oz egg (55 g), i.e. barrel shape.

### Carrots, turnips, etc.

1. Cut across the thicker end of the vegetable, then, working downwards, cut into 40 mm lengths for general garnish purposes. Sometimes the lengths may be shorter if they are to be used for specific garnishes.
2. Divide each length into sections lengthways. The number will vary according to the diameter of the vegetable.
3. Then turn to a barrel shape, as for potatoes, to give a finished size of 40 × 10 mm at the widest part of the turned vegetable, i.e. the centre.
4. For shorter lengths, the width will be in proportion.

## (g) Cutting with cutters

Ball and oval cutters are used for various small garnishes, particularly those made from potatoes and those to be used in soups.

When using cutters, the first edge entering the vegetable should do so at an angle to ensure that the complete depth of the cutter goes into the vegetable. Turn the cutter, then even pieces of vegetable will be obtained. A little practice in use is necessary to obtain a good result.

## 343 Choux paste                                Pâte à choux

| | Ingredients | |
|---|---|---|
| 1 pint | water | 1 litre |
| 10 oz | cake flour | 500 g |
| 8 oz | butter or margarine | 400 g |
| 2 level teaspoons | salt | 10 g |
| 1 level teaspoon | caster sugar | 5 g |
| 8–9 | eggs | 14–16 |

### Method

1. Place the water, butter, salt and sugar to boil in a saucepan.
2. Remove from the heat and add the sieved flour. Mix with a wooden spatula.
3. Replace over the heat and stir continuously until the mixture (panade) leaves the sides of the pan clean.
4. Remove from the heat and place on a triangle to cool slightly.
5. Add the eggs one at a time, thoroughly mixing evenly. For smaller quantities, beat the eggs and add a little at a time.
6. When the paste is ready, the mixture should just drop from the spatule.

*Note.* For some uses in the kitchen, the mixture may be adjusted to include more flour.

# Stocks - Essences - Glaze - Thickenings - Sauces

# Basic Stocks - Glaze - Essences

## 345 White beef stock — Fonds blanc de boeuf

| 1 gallon | Ingredients | 5 litres |
| --- | --- | --- |
| 4 lb | beef shin bones | 2 kg |
| 8 oz | carrots | 250 g |
| 8 oz | onions (stuck with two cloves) | 250 g |
| 4 oz | leek | 125 g |
| 4 oz | celery | 125 g |
| small sprig | thyme | small sprig |
| 1 oz | parsley stalks | 30 g |
| 12 | peppercorns (white) | 15 |
| 1 | bayleaf | 1 |
| 1¼ gallon | water | 6·25 litres |

### Method

1. Wash the bones and saw them into 100 mm lengths. Crack them open with a cleaver or chopper, remove the bone marrow and place it in cold water in the refrigerator.
2. Place the bones in a stock pot and cover with the cold water.
3. Bring to the boil then skim off all scum.
4. Add a further 2 pints (1 litre) of cold water and skim off all the fat. Wipe the inside of the stock pot with a clean wet cloth.
5. Add the remainder of the prepared ingredients (335).
6. Reboil, skim, then simmer gently for 6–8 hours; remove the vegetables when cooked.
7. During cooking, the stock should be skimmed frequently to remove all fat and scum.
8. Pass through a gauze strainer, reboil, skim and use as required.

## 346 White veal stock — Fonds blanc de veau

### Method

1. Prepare as for 'White beef stock' (345), replacing the beef shin bones with veal bones.

## 347 White poultry stock — Fonds blanc de volaille

### Method

1. Prepare as for White beef stock (346), replacing the beef shin bones with chicken or turkey bones, necks and giblets. For a strong stock, increase the bones by 50%.

2. Alternatively, use a 4–5 lb (2 kg) prepared boiling fowl, and remove it when cooked.

## 348 Rich white stock – unclarified consommé

### Method

1. Prepare as for White beef stock (345), adding 3 lb (1·5 kg) of shin of beef and 2 lb (1 kg) chicken bones.
2. Remove the shin of beef when cooked.

## 349 Brown beef stock — Fonds brun de boeuf

### Method

1. Use the same ingredients as for White beef stock (345), except that the bones should preferably be of a more meaty type, i.e. sirloin, rib, etc.
2. Chop the bones into 100 mm pieces. Place in a roasting tray and place in the centre of the oven at 230°C (450°F) to colour brown. Déglace (swill out) the tray.
3. Prepare the vegetables into a mirepoix (340b) and fry in a little fat which has been extracted from the bones.
4. Then proceed as for White beef stock (344).

## 350 Brown veal stock — Fonds brun de veau

### Method

Prepare as for Brown beef stock (349), replacing the beef bones with veal bones and trimmings.

## 351 Brown game stock — Fonds brun de gibier

### Method

1. Prepare as for Brown beef stock (349), replacing the beef bones with raw game bones or trimmings, including neck of venison. Add 4 oz (125 g) of mushroom trimmings.
2. Alternatively, quickly roast 2 lb (1 kg) of old pheasant and use this for the stock. Remove it when cooked.

## 352 Rich brown stock — Estouffade

### Method

1. Prepare as for Brown beef stock (349), adding 3 lb (1·5 kg) of shin beef and 2 lb (1 kg) veal bones. Roast and colour with the other bones.
2. Remove the shin of beef when cooked.

| 353 Meat glaze | Glace de viande |
| 354 Poultry glaze | Glace de volaille |
| 355 Game glaze | Glace de gibier |

**Method**

1. For Glace de viande, use beef stock; for the other glazes, use the appropriate stocks.

2. Reduce the strained stock in a wide pan over a fast heat.

3. When the stock is reduced to around 5 mm in depth, and is beginning to thicken, re-strain into a smaller shallow pan.

4. Continue to reduce until the liquid thickens like a syrup. Pass through a fine strainer into a china basin. Allow to cool, then store in the refrigerator.

5. The glaze is used to enrich sauces and for finishing or flavouring sauces and dishes.

### 356 White fish stock  Fonds de poisson blanc

| 1 gallon | Ingredients | 4 litres |
|---|---|---|
| 6 lb | suitable fish bones* | 2·4 kg |
| 6 oz | onions | 150 g |
| 1 oz | white mushroom trimmings | 25 g |
| ½ oz | parsley stalks | 15 g |
| 1 | lemon | 1 |
| 1 | bayleaf | 1 |
| small sprig | thyme | small sprig |
| 12 | white peppercorns | 15 |

\* i.e. Dover sole, turbot, whiting, brill, halibut.

**Method**

1. Wash and roughly chop the bones. Place them into a saucepan with the remainder of the ingredients, using only the juice of the lemon.

2. Bring to the boil, remove the scum and simmer gently for 20 minutes.

3. Pass through a gauze strainer, reboil and skim. Use as required.

### 357 Fish essence  Fumet de poisson

| 1 quart | Ingredients | 1 litre |
|---|---|---|
| 1½ lb | suitable fish bones | 600 g |
| 2 oz | butter | 50 g |
| 2 oz | shallots/onion | 50 g |
| ½ | lemon (in juice) | ½ |
| ¼ pint | dry white wine | 125 ml |
| 2 pints | fish stock (356) | 1 litre |

**Method**

1. Peel the shallots/onion and shred finely. Sweat in the butter in a suitable size saucepan for 2–3 minutes, without colouring.

2. Wash the fish bones, chop roughly then add them to the shallot and lemon juice. Cover with a lid and sweat on the side of the stove, or in an oven at 150°C (300°F) for 6–7 minutes.

3. Add the white wine and reduce by half, then add the fish stock.

4. Boil, skim and simmer for 20 minutes. Pass through a gauze strainer. Reboil, skim and use as required.

### 358 Fish glaze  Glace de poisson

**Method**

Reduce the fish stock in the same manner as other stocks to make glaze (353, 354, 355).

## 359 BASIC THICKENINGS

### 360 Roux

Roux is a combination of melted fat and flour, the flour being added to the melted fat and cooked with or without colouring. Mixing the flour into the fat allows the flour to cook evenly and, when stock is added, to make a smooth sauce. The roux is prepared in the following manner:

#### (a) White roux  Roux blanc

1. Heat 1 lb (450 g) margarine, stir in 1 lb (450 g) flour and thoroughly mix.

2. Cook slowly in the lower part of an oven at 150°C (300°F) or on the side of the stove (never over direct heat).

3. The roux is cooked when the mixture turns sandy in texture. Do not allow it to colour.

4. It is used for basic white sauce.

#### (b) Blond roux  Roux blond

1. Prepared and cooked in the same manner as for white roux, with the faintest tint of colouring.

2. It is used in the preparation of velouté and tomato sauce.

### (c) Brown roux                                    Roux brun

1. Prepared and cooked in the same manner as for white roux. The fat used should be good dripping from roast meat. Increase the flour by 25%.

2. Cook to a light brown colour.

3. It is used for basic brown sauce (Espagnole) and brown soups such as kidney, liver, etc.

### 361 Panada                                        Panade

Used as a binding or thickening agent in various preparations. The following are those mostly used:

#### (a) Bread panada                                 Panade au pain

| Ingredients | | |
|---|---|---|
| 8 oz | white breadcrumbs | 225 g |
| ½ pint | milk | 280 ml |
| ½ oz | butter | 15 g |
| 1 teaspoon | salt | 3 g |

**Method**

1. Boil the milk and butter then add the breadcrumbs and salt.

2. Mix with a wooden spatule. Cook on the side of the stove until the mixture leaves the side of the pan clean.

3. Place in a basin and cover the surface with melted butter to prevent skin forming.

4. Allow it to cool and use as required.

#### (b) Flour panada                                  Panade à la farine

| Ingredients | | |
|---|---|---|
| ½ pint | water | 280 ml |
| 2 oz | butter | 55 g |
| 5 oz | flour | 140 g |
| 1 teaspoon | salt | 3 g |

**Method**

1. Boil the butter, water and salt in a saucepan.

2. Add the sieved flour and mix thoroughly off the heat.

3. Replace over the heat and boil until the mixture leaves the sides of the pan clean.

4. Place in a shallow tray or pie dish and butter the surface to prevent skinning.

5. Allow it to cool and use as required.

#### (c) Frangipane panade                            Panade à la frangipane

| Ingredients | | |
|---|---|---|
| 4 oz | flour | 110 g |
| ½ pint | milk | 280 ml |
| 3 oz | butter | 85 g |
| 4 | egg yolks | 4 |

| 1 teaspoon | salt | 3 g |
|---|---|---|
| ¼ teaspoon | ground white pepper | 1 g |
| ¼ teaspoon | nutmeg | 1 g |

**Method**

1. Sieve the flour, salt, pepper and nutmeg together into a basin.

2. Gradually stir in the melted butter then the boiling milk.

3. Pass through a conical strainer into a clean saucepan.

4. Using a wooden spatule, stir in the egg yolks.

5. Stir continuously over the heat until the mixture thickens and reboils.

6. Place in a shallow tray or pie dish; butter the surface.

7. Use as required after the mixture has cooled.

#### (d) Rice panada                                   Panade au riz

| Ingredients | | |
|---|---|---|
| 8 oz | rice | 225 g |
| 1½ pints | consommé (unclarified) (348) | 840 ml |
| 1 oz | butter | 30 g |
| 2 teaspoons | salt | 6 g |

**Method**

1. Boil the stock, add the salt and the picked washed rice then reboil.

2. Add the butter, then cover with a buttered paper and lid and cook in the bottom of an oven at 160°C (325°F) or on the side of the stove for 45 minutes.

3. Rub through a sieve. Return to a clean pan and stir until it reaches boiling temperature.

4. Place on a shallow tray and butter the surface. Allow to cool.

### 362 Starch thickenings

(a) Arrowroot: produced from the ground pith of the roots of the maranta plant.

(b) Cornflour: produced from maize (Indian corn).

(c) Fécule: produced from potatoes and rice.

**Method**

1. Always dissolve the thickening in cold liquid until it becomes smooth.

2. Whisk the liquid when it is boiling, then pour in the dissolved thickening.

3. Continue to whisk or stir until it is reboiling, allow it to simmer on the side of the stove for a few minutes, then pass it through a conical strainer if it is required as a sauce.

### 363 Liaison thickenings

These types of thickenings are used to finish sauces and soups as follows, the quantities as per recipe:

### (a) Butter and cream

**Method**

1. Add the cream to the boiling liquid and reboil.
2. Remove from the heat then gradually stir or toss in the butter.
3. Do not allow to reboil.

### (b) Yolks of egg and cream

**Method**

1. Mix the yolks of egg and cream in a basin with a whisk.
2. Remove the pan containing the cooked food and sauce, sauce or soup from the heat.
3. Add a little of the sauce or liquid to the liaison, then pour or shake the liaison into the sauce or liquid to mix them together thoroughly.
4. Do not reboil, but keep it hot in a bain marie just below boiling point.

### (c) Blood

**Method**

1. Add 1 part of vinegar to 15 parts of blood, mix well to prevent coagulation, then pass the liquid through a fine strainer.
2. Then finish as for (b).

### 364 Butter and flour                           Beurre manié

| Ingredients | | |
|---|---|---|
| 4 oz | butter | 110 g |
| 3 oz | flour | 85 g |

**Method**

1. Cream the butter in a basin.
2. Add the sieved flour, absorb, then work it into a smooth paste.
3. Add to the boiling liquid in small pieces, the size of a hazel nut, shaking the liquid to dissolve the flour.
4. Return to boiling point. Do not continue to boil.

### 365 BASIC SAUCES

A variety of thickenings are used in producing sauces, many passing through various stages of refinement to produce other sauces. The following chart illustrates the stages used.

#### STRUCTURE OF SAUCES

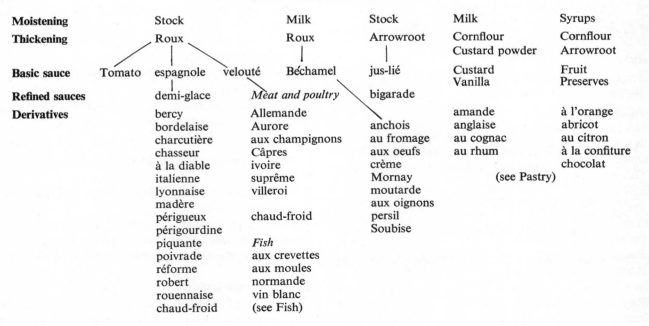

| | | | | | | |
|---|---|---|---|---|---|---|
| **Moistening** | | Stock | Milk | Stock | Milk | Syrups |
| **Thickening** | | Roux | Roux | Arrowroot | Cornflour Custard powder | Cornflour Arrowroot |
| **Basic sauce** | Tomato | espagnole    velouté | Béchamel | jus-lié | Custard Vanilla | Fruit Preserves |
| **Refined sauces** | | demi-glace | *Meat and poultry* | bigarade | | |
| **Derivatives** | | bercy | Allemande | | amande | à l'orange |
| | | bordelaise | Aurore | anchois | anglaise | abricot |
| | | charcutière | aux champignons | au fromage | au cognac | au citron |
| | | chasseur | Câpres | aux oeufs | au rhum | à la confiture |
| | | à la diable | ivoire | crème | | chocolat |
| | | italienne | suprême | Mornay | | |
| | | lyonnaise | villeroi | moutarde | (see Pastry) | |
| | | madère | | aux oignons | | |
| | | périgueux | chaud-froid | persil | | |
| | | périgourdine | | Soubise | | |
| | | piquante | *Fish* | | | |
| | | poivrade | aux crevettes | | | |
| | | réforme | aux moules | | | |
| | | robert | normande | | | |
| | | rouennaise | vin blanc | | | |
| | | chaud-froid | (see Fish) | | | |

## 366 White sauce — Béchamel

| 1 quart | Ingredients | 1 litre |
|---|---|---|
| 4 oz | margarine | 100 g |
| 4 oz | flour | 100 g |
| 1 | onion (studded with 1 clove) | 1 |
| 2 pints | milk | 1 litre |

### Method

1. Prepare a white roux (360a), with the margarine and flour.
2. Boil the milk.
3. Allow the cooked roux to cool slightly then add a quarter of the milk. Mix thoroughly with a wooden spatule over the heat until reboiling and very smooth.
4. Gradually add the remainder of the milk, mixing and reboiling each time before adding more milk.
5. Add the studded onion. Cover with a lid and cook gently in the bottom of an oven at 150°C (300°F) or on the side of the stove for 30 minutes.
6. Remove the onion. Pass the sauce through a conical strainer then cover the surface of the sauce with melted margarine. Use as required.

## 367 Brown sauce — Espagnole

| 1 quart | Ingredients | 1 litre |
|---|---|---|
| 4 oz | meat dripping | 100 g |
| 5 oz | flour | 125 g |
| 4 oz | carrots | 100 g |
| 4 oz | onions | 100 g |
| 1 oz | bacon trimmings | 25 g |
| 1 oz | tomato purée | 25 g |
| 3 pints | brown stock | 1·5 litres |

### Method

1. Prepare a brown roux (360c) with the dripping and flour.
2. Boil the stock.
3. Allow the cooked roux to cool slightly. Add the tomato purée, then add one-quarter of the stock. Mix thoroughly with a wood spatule over the heat, until reboiling and very smooth.
4. Gradually add the remainder of the stock, mixing and reboiling each time before adding more stock.
5. Prepare the carrots and onions into a mirepoix (340), fry with the bacon trimmings to a light golden brown, then add to the sauce.
6. Simmer gently for 4–5 hours, removing all scum and fat as it arises. The quantity should now be approximately 2 pints (1 litre). For Lenten espagnole, cook only for 1 hour.
7. Pass through a conical strainer and reboil. Use as required.

## 368 Velouté (Veal, chicken, mutton, fish)

| 1 quart | Ingredients | 1 litre |
|---|---|---|
| 4 oz | margarine | 100 g |
| 4 oz | flour | 100 g |
| 2 pints | stock (of the nature of the velouté, i.e. chicken) | 1 litre |

### Method

1. Prepare a blond roux (360b), with the margarine and flour.
2. Boil the stock. Allow the cooked roux to cool slightly.
3. Add one-quarter of the stock, mix thoroughly with a wooden spatule over the heat, until reboiling and very smooth.
4. Gradually add the remainder of the stock, mixing and reboiling each time before adding more stock.
5. Cover with a lid, cook gently in the bottom of an oven at 150°C (300°F) or on the side of the stove for 1 hour.
6. Pass through a conical strainer, cover the surface with melted margarine. Use as required.

## 369 Half glaze sauce — Sauce demi-glace

| 1 quart | Ingredients | 1 litre |
|---|---|---|
| 2 pints | espagnole (367) | 1 litre |
| 2 pints | estouffade (352) | 1 litre |
| 2¼ fl. oz | Madeira wine | 60 ml |

### Method

1. Boil the espagnole and estouffade together; remove all scum.
2. Gradually reduce to 2 pints (1 litre), removing all fat during the process.
3. Pass through a tammy cloth or fine strainer. Add the wine and mix the liquid. Butter the surface. Use as required.
4. When the sauce is used as a base for other sauces, the wine is omitted.

*Note.* When Sauce demi-glace tomatée is required, add 2 oz (50 g per litre) of tomato purée during the reduction process.

## 370 Tomato sauce — Sauce tomate

| 1 quart | Ingredients | 1 litre |
|---|---|---|
| 1 oz | fat bacon trimmings | 25 g |
| 2 oz | margarine | 50 g |
| 4 oz | onions | 100 g |
| 4 oz | carrots | 100 g |
| 4 oz | flour | 100 g |
| 6 oz | tomato purée | 150 g |
| ¼ oz (2 teaspoons) | salt | 5 g |
| 2 teaspoons | ground white pepper | 1 g |
| 1 small | bouquet garni (340) | 1 small |
| 2 pints | white beef stock (345) | 1 litre |

## Method

1. Cut the prepared vegetables and bacon trimmings into rough 10 mm dice.

2. Melt the margarine in a thick-bottomed saucepan, add the bacon and lightly fry to extract the fat.

3. Add the vegetables and fry them to a very light golden brown.

4. Stir in the flour to form a roux, cook in an oven at 150°C (300°F) or on the side of the stove, as for Blond roux (360b).

5. Allow to cool slightly then add the tomato purée and one quarter boiling stock. Mix thoroughly with a wooden spatule over the heat until smooth.

6. Gradually add the remainder of the stock, reboiling and mixing before adding more stock. Add the seasoning and bouquet garni then simmer gently for 1 hour.

7. Pass through a fine conical strainer with pressure.

8. Reboil, check the seasoning and consistency (the sauce should mask a ladle).

## DERIVATIVE SAUCES MADE FROM DEMI-GLACE

### 371 Bercy sauce — Sauce Bercy

| 1 quart | Ingredients | 1 litre |
| --- | --- | --- |
| 4 oz | finely chopped shallots | 100 g |
| 2 oz | butter | 50 g |
| ¼ oz | chopped parsley | 6 g |
| ½ pint | white wine | 250 ml |
| 1 teaspoon | glace de viande (353) | 3 g |
| 2 pints | demi-glace (369) | 1 litre |

## Method

1. Reduce the shallots and white wine together.

2. Add the demi-glace and the glace de viande, bring to the boil and simmer for 10 minutes.

3. Add the parsley and correct the seasoning.

4. Finish the sauce with the butter off the heat, shaking in a little at a time.

### 372 Bordelaise sauce — Sauce bordelaise

| 1 quart | Ingredients | 1 litre |
| --- | --- | --- |
| 4 oz | finely chopped shallots | 100 g |
| 3 oz | bone marrow | 75 g |
| ½ pint | red wine | 250 ml |
| 1 teaspoon | glace de viande (353) | 3 g |
| ¼ | lemon (in juice) | ¼ |
| 2 pints | demi-glace (369) | 1 litre |

## Method

1. Reduce the shallots and red wine together.

2. Add the demi-glace and simmer for 10 minutes.

3. Add the glace de viande and correct the seasoning.

4. Finish the sauce with half the marrow, chopped finely, and the lemon juice.

5. The poached slices of marrow are placed on the meat before saucing over.

### 373 Charcutière sauce — Sauce charcutière

## Method

1. Prepare as for Sauce Robert (384), adding 3 oz per 2 pints (75 g per litre) of gherkins cut in 25 mm julienne or thin slices (rondelles).

### 374 Chasseur sauce — Sauce chasseur

| 1 quart | Ingredients | 1 litre |
| --- | --- | --- |
| 1 oz | finely chopped shallots | 25 g |
| 6 oz | closed mushrooms | 150 g |
| 12 oz | tomatoes | 300 g |
| 1 oz | butter | 25 g |
| ¼ oz (2 teaspoons) | chopped parsley | 6 g |
| 1 teaspoon | chopped tarragon | 3 g |
| ½ pint | white wine | 250 ml |
| 2 pints | demi-glace (369) | 1 litre |

## Method

1. Sweat the shallots in the butter in a sauteuse for 2–3 minutes.

2. Add the cleaned sliced mushrooms and cook gently for 3–4 minutes.

3. Add the white wine and reduce by half.

4. Add the tomato concassé (336, 5c) and cook gently.

5. Add the parsley and tarragon.

6. Add the demi-glace, reboil and simmer for 10 minutes.

7. Correct the seasoning and consistency.

8. Finish with butter, if desired, tossed into the sauce in small pieces of 2 oz (50 g).

## 375 Devilled sauce — Sauce à la diable

| 1 quart | Ingredients | 1 litre |
|---|---|---|
| 2 oz | chopped shallots | 50 g |
| 2 oz | butter | 50 g |
| ⅛ oz (teaspoon) | crushed peppercorns | 3 g |
| ¼ pint | vinegar | 125 ml |
| ¼ pint | white wine | 125 ml |
| 2 pints | demi-glace (369) | 1 litre |

### Method

1. Place the shallots, crushed peppercorns, and vinegar in a sauteuse and reduce until nearly dry.
2. Add the white wine and reduce by a half.
3. Add the demi-glace, reboil and simmer for 10 minutes.
4. Correct the seasoning with a point of cayenne pepper.
5. Pass through a fine strainer and finish the sauce with the butter, in small pieces, off the heat.
6. Serve with a pinch of parsley on the top, to indicate that this is a hot flavoured sauce.

## 376 Italian sauce — Sauce italienne

| 1 quart | Ingredients | 1 litre |
|---|---|---|
| 2 oz | finely chopped shallots | 50 g |
| 8 oz | finely chopped mushroom trimmings | 200 g |
| 4 oz | finely chopped lean ham | 100 g |
| 2 oz | butter | 50 g |
| 1 lb | tomatoes | 400 g |
| ¼ oz (2 teaspoons) | chopped parsley | 6 g |
| teaspoon | chopped tarragon | 3 g |
| ¼ pint | white wine | 125 ml |
| 2 pints | demi-glace (369) | 1 litre |

### Method

1. Sweat the shallots in the butter in a sauteuse for 2–3 minutes. Add the mushroom and cook for 4–5 minutes.
2. Add the wine and reduce by a half.
3. Prepare the tomatoes into concassé (336, 5c).
4. Add the diced tomato and ham. Moisten with the demi-glace, and simmer for 8–10 minutes.
5. Correct the seasoning and add the chopped herbs.

*Note.* When used in fish dishes, omit the ham.

## 377 Brown onion sauce — Sauce lyonnaise

| 1 quart | Ingredients | 1 litre |
|---|---|---|
| 8 oz | finely shredded onions | 200 g |
| 2 oz | butter | 50 g |
| ⅛ pint (2½ fl. oz) | white wine | 60 ml |
| ⅛ pint (2½ fl. oz) | vinegar | 60 ml |
| 2 pints | demi-glace (369) | 1 litre |

### Method

1. Gently cook the onions in the butter in a sauteuse until tender, light brown but not crisp. Start quickly and then allow to cook gently for 6–7 minutes.
2. Moisten with the vinegar and reduce; add the white wine and reduce again.
3. Add the demi-glace, reboil and simmer for 10 minutes.
4. Correct the seasoning and serve.

## 378 Madeira sauce — Sauce madère

| 1 quart | Ingredients | 1 litre |
|---|---|---|
| 2 oz | butter | 50 g |
| ½ pint | estouffade (352) | 250 ml |
| ¼ pint | Madeira wine | 125 ml |
| 2 pints | demi-glace (369) | 1 litre |

### Method

1. Reduce the demi-glace and estouffade together to slightly below 2 pints (1 litre).
2. Add the madeira wine; this will correct the consistency.
3. Pass through a tammy cloth or fine strainer.
4. Reboil, finish the sauce, off the heat, with the butter in small pieces; mix well.

## 379 Truffle sauce — Sauce Périgueux

### Method

1. Prepare as for Sauce madère (378).
2. Finish with 2½ fl. oz (60 ml per litre) of truffle essence and 1½ oz (35 g per litre) of finely chopped truffles.

## 380 Truffle and foie gras sauce — Sauce périgourdine

### Method

1. Prepare as for Sauce madère (378).
2. Finish the sauce with 3 oz (75 g per litre) purée of foie gras and 1½ oz (35 g per litre) of finely chopped truffle.

## 381 Piquant sauce — Sauce piquante

| 1 quart | Ingredients | 1 litre |
|---|---|---|
| 2 oz | finely chopped shallots | 50 g |
| 4 oz | chopped gherkins | 100 g |
| 1 teaspoon | chopped parsley | 2 g |
| ½ teaspoon | chopped tarragon | 1 g |
| ¼ pint | white wine | 125 ml |
| ¼ pint | vinegar | 125 ml |
| 2 pints | demi-glace (369) | 1 litre |

### Method

1. Reduce the shallots and vinegar together, add the white wine and reduce again.
2. Add the demi-glace, reboil and simmer for 10 minutes.
3. Add the gherkins, parsley and tarragon.

## 382 Poivrade sauce      Sauce poivrade

| 1 quart | Ingredients | 1 litre |
|---|---|---|
| 4 oz | carrots | 100 g |
| 4 oz | shallot/onion | 100 g |
| 2 oz | celery | 50 g |
| 4 oz | butter | 100 g |
| 36 | crushed peppercorns | 30 |
| 1 | bayleaf | 1 |
| small sprig | thyme | small sprig |
| ½ oz | parsley stalks | 10 g |
| 3 fl. oz | vinegar | 75 ml |
| ¼ pint | marinade (303) | 125 ml |
| 2 pints | demi-glace (369) | 1 litre |

### Method

1. Cut the prepared vegetables into rough 5 mm dice.

2. Fry them in half the butter, colouring slightly.

3. Add thyme, bayleaf and parsley stalks.

4. Moisten with the vinegar and marinade.

5. Reduce, add the demi-glace then allow to simmer for 10 minutes.

6. Add the crushed peppercorns and simmer for 10 minutes more.

7. Pass with pressure through a fine conical strainer.

8. Finish with the other half of butter, off the heat, adding it in small pieces and mixing well.

*Note.* For game, add 8 oz (200 g) chopped game bones before moistening.

## 383 Reform sauce      Sauce Réforme

| 1 quart | Ingredients | 1 litre |
|---|---|---|
| 3 oz | julienne of ox-tongue | 75 g |
| 4 oz | julienne of gherkins | 100 g |
| 2 oz | julienne of white of egg | 50 g |
| 3 oz | julienne of mushroom | 75 g |
| 1 oz | julienne of truffle | 25 g |
| 1 oz | butter | 25 g |
| 1 pint | sauce poivrade (382) | ½ litre |
| 1 pint | demi-glace (369) | ½ litre |

### Method

1. Wash then peel the mushrooms. Slice them across thinly, then cut them into julienne. Cook slowly in the butter in a sauteuse for 5–6 minutes.

2. Add the remainder of the garnish.

3. Boil the sauces together, skim, then pass the liquid through a strainer over the garnish. Sometimes the garnish is bound with only a little of the sauce and the remainder is then used to surround the cooked cutlets.

## 384 Robert sauce      Sauce Robert

| 1 quart | Ingredients | 1 litre |
|---|---|---|
| 4 oz | finely chopped onion | 100 g |
| 2 oz | butter | 50 g |
| ½ teaspoon | sugar | 1 g |
| 1 teaspoon | glace de viande (353) | 3 g |
| 1 teaspoon | prepared English mustard | 3 g |
| 3 fl. oz | white wine | 75 ml |
| 2 pints | demi-glace (369) | 1 litre |

### Method

1. Sweat the onion in half of the butter, in a sauteuse, for 5–6 minutes. Do not colour.

2. Add the white wine and reduce.

3. Add the demi-glace and simmer for 10 minutes.

4. Skim, add the glace de viande, mustard and sugar.

5. Finish the sauce with 1 oz (25 g) butter, in small pieces, off the heat.

## 385 Rouennaise sauce      Sauce rouennaise

| 1 quart | Ingredients | 1 litre |
|---|---|---|
| 4 oz | finely chopped shallots | 100 g |
| 2 oz | butter | 50 g |
| 3 oz | sieved duck livers | 75 g |
| 1 teaspoon | glace de viande (353) | 3 g |
| ½ | lemon (in juice) | ½ |
| ¼ pint | red wine | 250 ml |
| 2 pints | demi-glace (369) | 1 litre |

### Method

1. Reduce the shallots and the red wine together until nearly dry.

2. Add the demi-glace and the glace de viande; simmer for 10 minutes.

3. Pass through a chinois and reheat with the ducks livers, taking care not to overheat. The sauce must not boil.

4. Add the lemon juice and correct the seasoning with a good turn of the peppermill.

5. Finish the sauce by adding the butter in small pieces. Mix thoroughly.

## DERIVATIVE SAUCES MADE FROM BÉCHAMEL

### 386 Anchovy sauce — Sauce anchois

| 1 quart | Ingredients | 1 litre |
|---|---|---|
| 1½ pints | béchamel (366) | 750 ml |
| ½ pint | fish stock (356) | 250 ml |
| 2½ fl. oz | anchovy essence or | 60 ml |
| 2 oz | purée of anchovy* | 50 g |

\* Three parts fillet of anchovy to one part butter passed through a very fine sieve.

#### Method

1. Boil the béchamel and fish stock in a saucepan.
2. Remove from the heat, add the anchovy essence or purée of anchovy and mix well. Correct the seasoning, adding a point of cayenne pepper.
3. Pass the sauce through a fine conical strainer, then coat the surface with butter.

Anchovy sauce is served with poached fish and fried fish preparations.

### 387 Cheese sauce — Sauce au fromage

| 1 quart | Ingredients | 1 litre |
|---|---|---|
| 1½ pints | béchamel (366) | 750 ml |
| ½ pint | milk | 250 ml |
| 12 oz | grated cheese (Gruyère, Cheddar) | 300 g |

#### Method

1. Boil the béchamel and milk together in a saucepan.
2. Remove from the heat. Add the grated cheese, whisking to dissolve. Correct the seasoning, adding a point of cayenne pepper. Pass through a fine conical strainer and coat the surface with butter.

Served mainly with vegetables, marrow, celery, cauliflower.

### 388 Egg sauce — Sauce aux oeufs

| 1 quart | Ingredients | 1 litre |
|---|---|---|
| 1½ pints | béchamel (366) | 750 ml |
| ½ pint | milk | 250 ml |
| 6 | hard-boiled eggs | 5 |
| 2 level teaspoons | salt | 5 g |
| ½ level teaspoon | ground white pepper | 1 g |

#### Method

1. Boil the béchamel and milk in a saucepan.
2. Whisk in the seasoning and correct.
3. Pass the liquid through a fine conical strainer. Add the hard-boiled eggs which have been cut into 5 mm dice. Butter the surface. Served with boiled or poached fish.

### 389 Cream sauce — Sauce crème

| 1 quart | Ingredients | 1 litre |
|---|---|---|
| 1½ pints | béchamel (366) | 750 ml |
| ½ pint | milk | 250 ml |
| ¼ pint | cream | 125 ml |
| 2 level teaspoons | salt | 5 g |
| ½ level teaspoon | ground white pepper | 1 g |

#### Method

1. Boil the béchamel and milk together in a thick saucepan, whisking to mix; reduce the liquid slightly.
2. Add the seasoning and cream and reboil. Pass the liquid through a fine conical strainer. Butter the surface. Cream sauce is used extensively as a sauce, or it can be mixed with prepared foods, particularly vegetables.

### 390 Mornay sauce — Sauce Mornay

| 1 quart | Ingredients | 1 litre |
|---|---|---|
| 1½ pints | béchamel (366) | 750 ml |
| ½ pint | milk, fish, stock, vegetable stock | 250 ml |
| 2 oz | Gruyère or Cheddar cheese | 50 g |
| 2 oz | Parmesan cheese | 50 g |
| 4 oz | butter | 100 g |
| 2 | yolks of egg | 2 |
| 1 level teaspoon | salt | 3 g |
| point | cayenne pepper | pointe |

#### Method

1. Boil the béchamel with the moistening agent (stock), according to the type required, e.g., for fish Mornay, use fish stock.
2. Whisk well, remove from the heat, add and thoroughly dissolve the grated cheese, then add the yolks and mix well together.
3. Add the butter in small pieces to absorb easily, stirring continuously, then add the seasoning. Correct the consistency and the seasoning.
4. Pass the liquid through a tammy cloth or very fine conical strainer. Butter the surface.

### 391 Mustard sauce — Sauce moutarde

| 1 quart | Ingredients | 1 litre |
|---|---|---|
| 1¾ pints | béchamel (366) | 875 ml |
| ¼ pint | milk | 125 ml |
| 1 oz | butter | 25 g |
| ½ oz | English mustard | 15 g |
| 2 level teaspoons | salt | 5 g |

#### Method

1. Boil the béchamel and milk together in a saucepan, whisking to mix, then add the salt.

2. Pass through a fine conical strainer and butter the surface.

3. Mix the mustard and butter to a paste. Add and, thoroughly mix to the sauce only when required for serving. Adding earlier may result in the sauce going a little thin in consistency.

The sauce is served with grilled herrings.

### 392 Onion sauce — Sauce aux oignons

| 1 quart | Ingredients | 1 litre |
|---|---|---|
| 1¾ pints | béchamel (366) | 875 ml |
| ¼ pint | milk | 125 ml |
| 2 lb | onions | 800 g |
| 3 oz | butter | 75 g |
| 2 level teaspoons | salt | 5 g |
| ½ level teaspoon | ground white pepper | 1 g |

**Method**

1. Cut the peeled onions into 5 mm dice. Melt the butter in a saucepan and add the onion.
2. Cover with a lid and sweat slowly for 8–10 minutes. Add a little water and simmer for 10 minutes. Reduce the moisture until almost dry.
3. Boil the béchamel and milk together in a separate saucepan, mixing well. Pass through a fine conical strainer on to the onions, add the seasoning and mix.
4. Butter the surface. Serve with roast mutton.

### 393 Parsley sauce — Sauce persil

| 1 quart | Ingredients | 1 litre |
|---|---|---|
| 1½ pints | béchamel (366) | 750 ml |
| ½ pint | milk | 250 ml |
| 2 oz | chopped parsley | 50 g |
| 2 level teaspoons | salt | 5 g |
| ½ teaspoon | ground white pepper | 1 g |

**Method**

1. Boil the béchamel and milk together, whisking to mix.
2. Add the seasoning, then pass through a fine conical strainer.
3. Place the chopped parsley in a conical strainer, dip in boiling water for 5–6 seconds, remove, drain the water, add to the sauce and mix in. Butter the surface. Served with boiled or poached fish and vegetables.

### 394 Soubise sauce — Sauce Soubise

**Method**

1. Prepare as for Onion sauce (392).
2. Rub through a very fine sieve. Reboil and adjust the consistency according to its use.

---

## DERIVATIVE SAUCES MADE FROM VELOUTÉ

### 395 Allemande sauce — Sauce allemande

| 1 quart | Ingredients | 1 litre |
|---|---|---|
| 2 pints | chicken or veal velouté (368) | 1 litre |
| 1 pint | chicken or veal stock (347 and 346) | ½ litre |
| ¼ pint | mushroom liquor | 125 ml |
| ½ | lemon (in juice) | ½ |
| 6 fl. oz | double cream | 150 ml |
| 5 | yolks of egg | 4 |
| 1 level teaspoon | salt | 3 g |
| ¼ level teaspoon | ground white pepper | 1 g |

**Method**

1. Pour the velouté, stock and mushroom liquor into a thick bottomed sauté pan.
2. Reduce over a good heat to 1½ pints (¾ litre), add half the cream, reboil then slightly reduce. During the reducing period, keep the sauce free from the bottom with an iron spatule or a stiff whisk. Remove from the heat.
3. Pour a little of the sauce on to a liaison of the yolks of egg and the remainder of the cream, mixing well. Whisk into the sauce then add the lemon juice.
4. Correct the seasoning of the sauce, adding a point of cayenne pepper.
5. Pass through a tammy cloth or fine conical strainer. Cover the surface with melted butter. Do not reboil. Allemande sauce is used for coating certain prepared foods and in other sauces.

### 396 Aurore sauce — Sauce aurore

| 1 quart | Ingredients | 1 litre |
|---|---|---|
| 1½ pints | chicken or veal velouté (368) | 750 ml |
| 1 pint | chicken or veal stock (347 and 346) | 500 ml |
| 4 oz | tomato purée | 100 g |
| 2 oz | butter | 50 g |
| 1 level teaspoon | salt | 3 g |
| ¼ teaspoon | ground white pepper | 1 g |

**Method**

1. Place all the ingredients, except the butter, in a thick bottomed sauté pan.

2. Reduce quickly over a fast heat, freeing the sauce from the pan with a metal spatula or a stiff whisk.

3. When reduced to 2 pints (1 litre), remove from the heat.

4. Pass through a tammy cloth or fine conical strainer.

5. Add the butter, off the heat, in small pieces, absorbing thoroughly. Butter the surface.

### 397 Mushroom sauce — Sauce aux champignons

| 1 quart | Ingredients | 1 litre |
|---|---|---|
| 1½ pints | chicken or veal velouté (368) | 750 ml |
| 1 pint | chicken or veal stock (347 and 346) | 500 ml |
| 8 oz | closed white mushrooms | 200 g |
| 2 oz | butter | 50 g |
| 2 fl. oz | cream | 50 ml |
| 2 | yolks of egg | 2 |
| 2 level teaspoons | salt | 5 g |
| ¼ level teaspoon | ground white pepper | 1 g |

#### Method

1. Reduce the velouté and stock in a thick bottomed sauté pan to 2 pints (1 litre). Keep the sauce free from the pan with a metal spatula or a stiff whisk.

2. Wash, peel and thinly slice the mushrooms. Add the peelings to the reduction in 1.

3. Melt the butter in a sauteuse, add the mushrooms, cover and sweat slowly for 6–7 minutes, without colouring.

4. Season the sauce and pass it through a tammy cloth or fine conical strainer. Add the mushrooms then butter the surface. Mushroom sauce is used with poultry or meat.

### 398 Caper sauce — Sauce aux câpres

| 1 quart | Ingredients | 1 litre |
|---|---|---|
| 1½ pints | mutton velouté (368) | 750 ml |
| 1 pint | mutton stock (from meat) | 500 ml |
| 3 oz | capers | 75 g |
| 1 level teaspoon | salt | 3 g |
| ¼ teaspoon | ground white pepper | 1 g |

#### Method

1. Reduce the velouté and stock to 2 pints (1 litre).

2. Add the seasoning and pass through a tammy cloth or fine conical strainer. Add the capers and butter the surface.
    Served with boiled leg of mutton.

### 399 Ivory sauce — Sauce ivoire

#### Method

1. Prepare as for Suprême sauce (400).

2. Finish with 2 teaspoons of meat glaze (353) to give a pale ivory tint. It is served generally with chicken.

### 400 Suprême sauce — Sauce suprême

| 1 quart | Ingredients | 1 litre |
|---|---|---|
| 1½ pints | chicken velouté (368) | 750 ml |
| 1 pint | chicken stock (347) | 500 ml |
| 2 oz | white mushroom trimmings | 50 g |
| ¼ pint | cream | 125 ml |
| 1 level teaspoon | salt | 3 g |
| ¼ level teaspoon | ground white pepper | 1 g |

#### Method

1. Reduce the velouté, stock and mushroom trimmings in a thick bottomed sauté pan to 2 pints (1 litre), using a metal spatula or a stiff whisk to prevent it sticking.

2. Whisk in the cream and seasoning. Pass through a tammy cloth or a fine conical strainer then butter the surface.

3. If desired, the sauce may be finished with 2 oz (50 g) of butter.

### 401 Villeroi sauce — Sauce Villeroi

#### Method

1. Prepared as for Allemande sauce (395). When reducing, add a little ham and truffle essence.

    It is used mainly for coating cooked foods, such as poached chicken, prior to finishing according to recipe.

---

## WARM SAUCES

### 402 Hollandaise sauce — Sauce hollandaise

| 1 quart | Ingredients | 1 litre |
|---|---|---|
| 2 lb | butter | 800 g |
| 8 | yolks of egg | 7 |
| 24 | white peppercorns | 20 |
| 2 fl. oz | vinegar | 50 ml |
| 1–2 level teaspoons | salt | 3–5 g |
| point | cayenne pepper | pointe |
| ¼ | lemon (in juice) | ¼ |

#### Method

1. Crush the peppercorns with the base of a sauteuse then place them in a sauteuse with the vinegar. Reduce until almost dry and then allow to cool completely.

2. Add the yolks of eggs and 2 tablespoons of cold water.

3. Stand in a bain-marie of hot water, whisking vigorously; do not allow to become too hot.

4. The sabayon (whipped yolks) is cooked when it has thickened and naps the back of a spoon.

5. Gradually whisk in the melted butter, avoiding the residue, then add the seasoning and lemon juice. The amount of salt will depend on the type of butter used.

6. Pass through muslin and keep at blood heat in a separate bain-marie.

7. If desired, the reduction may be omitted.
   Served with fish, eggs, vegetables.

### 403 Béarnaise sauce                    Sauce béarnaise

| 1 quart | Ingredients | 1 litre |
|---|---|---|
| 2 lb | butter | 800 g |
| 1 oz | finely chopped shallots | 25 g |
| ½ oz | tarragon stalks | 10 g |
| dessertspoon | chopped tarragon leaves | 5 g |
| dessertspoon | chopped parsley | 3 g |
| 24 | white peppercorns | 20 |
| 2 fl. oz | vinegar | 50 ml |
| 12 | yolks of egg | 10 |
| 1–2 level teaspoons | salt | 3–5 g |

**Method**

1. Place the crushed peppercorns, chopped tarragon stalks, chopped shallots and vinegar in a sauteuse and reduce slowly by three-quarters. Allow to cool completely.

2. Add the yolks of egg, stand in a bain-marie of water and whisk vigorously until the yolks are very thick. Do not allow to get too hot.

3. Gradually whisk in the melted butter, avoiding the residue. Correct the seasoning, which will depend on the type of butter used.

4. Pass through muslin, then add the chopped tarragon and parsley. Store at blood heat in a separate bain-marie. Overheating will cause the sauce to curdle. Served with fish or meat, particularly grills.

### 404 Choron sauce                       Sauce Choron

**Method**

1. Prepare as for Sauce béarnaise (403).

2. Add 2 oz (50 g per litre) of tomato purée to the reduction.
   Served mainly with grills.

### 405 Mousseline sauce                    Sauce mousseline

**Method**

1. Prepare as for Sauce hollandaise (402).

2. Add 25% of the volume of the sauce of soft whipped cream, at the moment of serving.

### 406 Paloise sauce                       Sauce paloise

**Method**

Prepare as for Sauce béarnaise (403), using mint stalks and chopped mint leaves in place of tarragon.

### 407 Foyot or Valois sauce              Sauce Foyot ou Valois

**Method**

Prepare as for Sauce béarnaise (403). When finished, add 2 teaspoons meat glaze (353).

### 408 Melted butter                       Beurre fondu

**Method**

1. Melt the required amount of butter in a bain-marie and allow it to stand for a few minutes.

2. Pass through muslin, leaving the residue.

### 409 THICKENED GRAVY                     JUS-LIÉ

**Method**

1. Prepare a brown veal stock (350).

2. Strengthen the flavour by adding 25–50% extra chicken bones, and necks that have been lightly roasted.

3. Add a little tomato debris. Thicken with 1 oz (30 g) of diluted arrowroot per qt/litre and allow to simmer for 15 minutes.

4. Pass through a gauze strainer, reboil, skim, season and adjust colour.

*Note.* The term Jus-lié tomaté is applied when tomato purée is added to give a tomato flavour.

## OTHER HOT SAUCES

### 410 Apple sauce                         Sauce aux pommes

| 1 quart | Ingredients | 1 litre |
|---|---|---|
| 4 lb | cooking apples | 1·6 kg |
| 4 oz | butter | 100 g |
| 4 oz | sugar | 100 g |

**Method 1**

1. Remove the skin from the apples, core and cut them into 8 sections.

2. Melt the butter in a sauteuse, add the apples and 2–3 tablespoons of water.

3. Cover, cook steadily until soft, then drain.

4. Pass through a sieve and add the sugar.

**Method 2**

1. Wash and quarter the apples and remove the core.

2. Place in a saucepan with 10 mm of water, bring to the boil and cook until soft. Drain well, pass through a sieve then add the sugar.

### 411  Bread sauce                     Sauce au pain

| 1 quart | Ingredients | 1 litre |
|---|---|---|
| 2 pints | milk | 1 litre |
| 6 oz | white breadcrumbs | 150 g |
| 2 oz | butter | 50 g |
| 2 oz | onion | 50 g |
| 2 level teaspoons | salt | 5 g |
| point | cayenne pepper | pointe |

### Method

1. Place the milk to boil in a saucepan with the onion studded with 2 cloves.

2. Whisk in the breadcrumbs then simmer on the side of the stove for 5–6 minutes and remove the onion.

3. Mix in the seasoning. Place the butter on top in small pieces to prevent skinning.

4. Mix well when serving, adjusting the consistency if necessary.

Served with roast chicken and roast game.

### 412  Cranberry sauce              Sauce aux airelles

| 1 quart | Ingredients | 1 litre |
|---|---|---|
| 2 lb | cranberries | 800 g |
| 8 oz | sugar | 200 g |
| ½ oz | arrowroot | 15 g |
| ½ pint | water | 250 ml |

### Method

1. Wash the cranberries and place them into a saucepan (not aluminium). Add the sugar and water.

2. Bring to the boil and simmer for 8–10 minutes until the fruit is soft.

3. Thicken with the diluted arrowroot and reboil for 1–2 minutes.

Serve the sauce with roast turkey.

### 413  Curry sauce                        Sauce kari

| 1 quart | Ingredients | 1 litre |
|---|---|---|
| 8 oz | finely chopped onions | 200 g |
| 2 oz | first-class dripping | 50 g |
| 2 oz | flour | 50 g |
| 1 oz | curry powder | 25 g |
| 4 oz | chopped apple | 100 g |
| 4 oz | chopped chutney | 100 g |
| 1 oz | desiccated coconut | 25 g |
| 2 oz | tomato purée | 50 g |
| 2 oz | sultanas | 50 g |
| 2 level teaspoons | salt | 5 g |
| 2½ pints | white beef stock (345) | 1·25 litres |
| ½ | lemon (in juice) | ½ |
| 1 clove | garlic | 1 clove |

### Method

1. Melt the dripping in a thick bottomed saucepan, add the onions, and cook gently for 7–8 minutes, without colouring. Add the peeled, chopped garlic.

2. Stir in the curry powder, then the flour. Cook in the bottom of the oven at 150°C (300°F) for 7–10 minutes, until it becomes sandy in texture.

3. Allow to cool slightly, add the tomato purée and one-quarter of the boiling stock. Reboil, mixing thoroughly.

4. Gradually add the remainder of the stock, reboiling each time before adding more stock.

5. Add the remainder of the ingredients; stir until reboiling. Simmer gently for 1 hour.

6. Skim well, correct seasoning and consistency to mask a ladle. Butter the surface.

Used with a large variety of dishes.

When used with poached eggs, the sauce is passed through a fine conical strainer, the garnish being likely to break the soft eggs.

---

## OTHER COLD SAUCES

**Served in small quantities**

### 414  Cumberland sauce

| 1 pint | Ingredients | ½ litre |
|---|---|---|
| 1 lb | red currant jelly | 400 g |
| 1 oz | finely chopped shallots | 25 g |
| ¼ pint | port wine | 125 ml |
| 2 small | oranges | 2 small |
| 1 | lemon (in juice) | 1 |
| ¼ teaspoon | dissolved English mustard | 1 g |

### Method

1. Cover the shallots with water in a small sauteuse, bring to the boil and simmer slowly for 2–3 minutes, then refresh and drain.

2. Remove the orange zest with a peeler. Cut into a fine short julienne, blanch, refresh and drain.

3. Heat the red currant jelly, to melt to a smooth consistency, in a saucepan. Stir in the port wine, mustard, orange and lemon juice.

4. Pass through a fine strainer then add the julienne of orange zest. It is served with venison and ham.

### 415 Horseradish sauce      Sauce raifort

| 1 pint | Ingredients | ½ litre |
|---|---|---|
| 8 oz | horseradish | 200 g |
| ¾ pint | cream | 375 ml |
| 1 fl. oz | vinegar | 25 ml |
| 1 level teaspoon | salt | 2 g |
| point | cayenne pepper | pointe |

**Method**

1. Wash the horseradish, trim the top and bottom, then peel.
2. Grate or scrape in long shreds and soak the shreds in the vinegar.

3. Softly whip the cream, add the horseradish and seasoning.

Served with roast beef.

### 416 Mint sauce      Sauce menthe

| 1 pint | Ingredients | ½ litre |
|---|---|---|
| 4 oz | fresh mint | 100 g |
| 2 oz | castor sugar | 50 g |
| 1 pint | vinegar | ½ litre |

**Method**

1. Wash the mint and shake off the water. Remove the leaves from the stalks.
2. Sprinkle the sugar on the mint and finely chop.
3. Mix with the vinegar in a basin.

# Soups

# Soups

# Les Potages

**417 Classification of soups**

The various soups fall into the following categories:

**(a) Clear soups**                                        **Consommé**

These are made from a very good basic stock (of the nature required) which is clarified, passed and then garnished with ingredients in keeping with the name and nature of the consommé.

**(b) Thickened passed soups**       **Purées, veloutés, crèmes**

**Purées**

These are made from a base of vegetables and a moistening of stock or water. Those of a farinaceous nature, i.e. with a base of pulses, or potatoes, require no other thickening agent, while those of an aqueous nature, i.e. with a base of carrots, turnips, celery, watercress, etc., require one.

The following are used with purées in the quantities given in the recipes: rice, cream of rice, potatoes, bread croûtons.

Finish the purées with butter, off the fire, at the moment of serving. If no other garnish is added to the finished purée, fried croûtons are served separately.

**Veloutés**

Veloutés are generally composed as follows:

25% purée of the ingredients of the nature of the soup,
25% velouté of the nature of the soup,
50% stock of the nature of the soup.

A liaison of yolks of egg and cream – 3 yolks and $\frac{1}{4}$ pint cream per quart (3 yolks and 125 ml per litre) – is added to the prepared soup just before serving, and various garnishes in keeping with the name and nature of the soup, are also added.

**Crèmes**

These soups differ from veloutés in that:

1. Milk replaces 50% of the moistening agent and in some cases is the sole moistening agent.
2. A clear béchamel is used in place of the basic velouté.
3. The soup is finished with cream only.

**Cullises**                                               **Coulis**

Cullises are made from a base of poultry, game or fish.

Rice is used as the thickening agent for poultry, and lentils for game or game espagnole.

For fish, a clear panada (comprising 5 oz bread per pint of milk per lb of fish, 250 g bread per litre per 400 g of fish) is used as the thickening agent.

The cullises are finished with butter, off the fire, at the moment of serving, and garnished with dice or julienne or quenelles of the ingredient used.

**Bisques**

These are made from a base of shell-fish which are sautéd with a mirepoix in butter, flambéed with brandy and white wine, moistened with half fish stock and half white stock, then tomatoes and/or tomato purée are added together with bouquet-garni, and then rice is used as the thickening agent. After 20 minutes of cooking, the shellfish are taken out and 3 oz (75 g) per quart (litre) of the flesh is placed aside for garnish. The remainder are crushed in a mortar and placed back to reboil with the liquid. The bisque is passed, finished with butter and cream then garnished with the flesh. Fish velouté may also be used as a thickening agent.

**(c) Thickened unpassed soups**        **Potages de légumes**

These are soups made from a mainly vegetable base, the garnishes of which are cut in a neat and uniform size. The soups are unpassed and obtain their thickening from the amount of garnish.

**Broths**

Broths are made from a good basic stock of beef, chicken or mutton which is garnished and thickened with a brunoise of vegetables, diced meat or chicken and also rice or pearl barley.

**(d) Foreign soups**                      **Potages étrangers**

These are soups of a foreign origin which do not fall into the previous categories. They are prepared in accordance with the recipe.

**418 Portions of soups**

The amount of soup normally served may vary from between 7 to 10 fl. oz (200 to 280 ml) per portion. The recipes given are based on the maximum quantities, i.e. 2 quarts for 8 portions and 3 litres for 10 portions.

## 419 Basic clear soup — Consommé clarifié

| 2 quarts (8) | Ingredients | 3 litres (10) |
|---|---|---|
| 1 lb | shin of beef | 600 g |
| 4 oz | carrots | 150 g |
| 4 oz | onions | 150 g |
| 4 oz | leeks | 150 g |
| 2 oz | celery | 75 g |
| 4 oz | tomato débris | 150 g |
| 2 | whites of egg | 3 |
| 24 | white peppercorns | 30 |
| small sprig | thyme | small sprig |
| 1 | bayleaf | 1 |
| 2 level teaspoons | salt | 8 g |
| 5 pints | white stock | 4 litres |

### Method

1. Mince or finely chop the shin of beef.
2. Mix the beef and the white of egg with a little cold water or stock in the bottom of a saucepan.
3. Add the cleaned and coarsely shredded vegetables, seasoning and the other ingredients, except the stock.
4. Mix well, then add the stock (cold), mixing thoroughly.
5. Place on a fire and bring slowly to the boil, stirring frequently until boiling.
6. When the consommé reaches the boil, reduce to a very gentle simmer for 3–4 hours. Do not stir after boiling.
7. Pass through a clean damp serviette or double muslin with care.
8. Reboil and correct the seasoning; remove all fat and use kitchen paper to finish.

If desired, half the quantity of onion may be left unpeeled (just topped and tailed) washed, cut in half across and then coloured brown on the top of a cleaned stove. These, added to the consommé, give it colour.

9. The flavour of the consommé will be improved by adding a small amount of lightly roasted chicken carcasses.

Before serving, a little sherry and a garnish, according to the type of soup, are added. Cheese straws are served separately.

## 420 Chicken consommé — Consommé de volaille

Prepare as for basic consommé, using chicken stock.

## 421 — Consommé Alexandra

This is chicken consommé which is thickened with seed tapioca (1 oz per quart, 25 g per litre), julienne of chicken (1 oz, 25 g), quenelles for soup (40–50) and julienne of cooked lettuce (1 oz, 25 g).

*Note.* The tapioca is whisked into the consommé and cooked for 10 minutes.

## 422 — Consommé alphabétique

Prepare as for basic consommé and garnish it with alphabet letters made from Italian paste. These are purchased, and cooked in boiling salt water for 5–6 minutes. Wash well, drain, add to consommé.

## 423 — Consommé aux diablotins

Prepare as for basic consommé and garnish it with 5–6 diablotins per portion. Cut them round, 10 mm in diameter, from thinly sliced bread then dip them in melted butter, then in Parmesan cheese and toast till they are golden brown. They are served separately in a sauceboat.

## 424 — Consommé aux profiteroles

This is basic consommé garnished with 10 profiteroles per portion. The profiteroles are made from choux paste (343). Pipe it out on trays, with a 3 mm plain tube the size of a pea, then bake at 200°C (400°F) for 5–6 minutes. Serve them separately, in a sauceboat.

## 425 — Consommé brunoise

Brunoise is a basic consommé which is garnished with a brunoise of mixed vegetables (4 oz per quart, 100 g per litre). Blanch the brunoise, refresh, drain, cover with a little of the consommé then simmer for 15 minutes.

## 426 — Consommé Carmen

For Carmen, prepare a basic consommé and garnish it with 1 oz of each per quart (25 g of each per litre) 5 mm-diced tomato, julienne of pimento and plain boiled rice.

*Note.* When preparing the basic consommé, add 2 oz per quart of tomato purée (50 g per litre) to the clarification.

## 427 — Consommé Caroline

Caroline is a chicken consommé which is garnished with lozenges of royale (445) and plain boiled rice (1 oz per quart, 25 g per litre) and finished with a pluche of chervil.

## 428 — Consommé Célestine

This is a basic consommé; garnish it with a julienne of pancakes containing chopped parsley, allowing one 150 mm pancake for 2–3 portions. Omit the sugar from the pancake mixture.

## 429 — Consommé aux cheveux d'ange

Prepare a chicken consommé and garnish it with cooked vermicelli. Crush the twirls of vermicelli lightly, cook in boiling salt water for 4–5 minutes and thoroughly wash and drain it.

**430** Consommé en gelée (cold)

For Consommé en gelée, add a little sherry to a basic consommé and $\frac{1}{2}$ oz per quart (12 g per litre) of soaked gelatine to set the consommé into a good jelly when cold.

**431** Consommé froid (cold)

Prepare a cold consommé as for 'en gelée', but omit the gelatine. A good consommé should just set into a natural light jelly form.

**432** Consommé Judic

Prepare as for chicken consommé and garnish it with cooked julienne of lettuce, julienne of mushroom cooked 'à blanc' (335 g) and 1 oz per quart (25 g per litre) quenelles for soups.

**433** Consommé julienne

Julienne is a basic consommé which is garnished with a julienne of cooked vegetables. See Consommé brunoise (425).

**434** Consommé à la madrilène

Hot Consommé à la madrilène is a basic consommé garnished with 1 oz each per quart (25 g per litre) of julienne of tomato (336, 5d), julienne of pimento and julienne of boiled celery. Cold Consommé madrilène is served with garnish and a little sherry in the consommé which is generally set in consommé cups to assure the equal division of the garnish.

An infusion of tomato purée is added to the basic consommé (see 426).

**435** Consommé aux pâtes d'Italie

Prepare as for basic consommé and garnish it with any various small shapes of Italian paste, cooked for 5–6 minutes in boiling salt water, washed well and drained. Use 1 oz of paste per quart of consommé (25 g per litre).

**436** Consommé paysanne

Prepare as for basic consommé and garnish it with a paysanne of cooked vegetables. See Consommé brunoise (425).

**437** Consommé printanière

Printanière is a basic consommé garnished with small pea-sized balls of carrot and turnip (2 oz per quart, 50 g per litre) which are blanched, refreshed and cooked in a little of the consommé, 1 oz per quart consommé (25 g per litre). Small diamonds of plain boiled French beans and peas are then added.

**438** Consommé printanière royale

This is made as for Consommé printanière (437) with the addition of diamonds or dice of royale (445).

**439** Consommé queue de boeuf

This is a basic consommé garnished with small pieces of ox-tail tips (2–3 pieces per portion) and pea-sized balls of carrot and turnip (2 oz per quart, 50 g per litre) which are all blanched, refreshed, then simmered in the consommé until they are cooked.

**440** Consommé royale

For Consommé royale, garnish a basic consommé with ordinary royale (445), cut into 5 mm dice, 5 mm diamonds, or 10 mm lozenges. Place the royale in a basin in cold water until required.

**441** Consommé au sagou

Garnish a basic consommé with 1 oz per quart (25 g per litre) of sago. Whisk the sago into boiling salt water, simmer for 10–15 minutes until cooked, i.e. transparent, then wash well in a conical strainer until free of the gum deposit.

**442** Consommé au tapioca

Prepare as for Consommé au sagou, substituting tapioca cooked for 10 minutes in place of sago.

**443** Consommé aux vermicelli

Garnish a basic consommé with 2 oz per quart (50 g per litre) of vermicelli, prepared as for Consommé aux cheveux d'ange (429).

**444** Consommé Xavier

Boil a basic consommé, pull it to the side of the stove and stir with a ladle while running through a coarse conical strainer 2 beaten eggs per quart/litre. Do not boil afterwards. This consommé is also known as Consommé aux oeufs filets.

**445 Royales for consommé, 8–10 portions**

**Ordinary royale**

| | Ingredients | |
|---|---|---|
| $\frac{1}{4}$ pint | cool consommé | 125 ml |
| 2 | whole eggs | 2 |
| 2 | yolks of egg | 2 |

**Method**

1. Mix the eggs and yolks, then add the cold consommé, mixing well.
2. Pass through a chinois and place in dariol moulds.

133

3. Place the moulds in a tray of water (bain-marie) and bake in a moderate oven at 150°C (300°F). Cover with greased paper or a loose lid.

4. Take care not to boil and, when set, allow them to cool in the moulds.

5. When cold, cut the royale into cubes, diamonds or lozenges and use them to garnish a prepared consommé.

## Cream royale

Proceed as for ordinary royale, substituting cream for the consommé.

## Chicken royale

| | Ingredients | |
|---|---|---|
| 2 oz | cooked white of chicken | 50 g |
| 1 oz | cold béchamel | 25 g |
| 2 fl. oz | double cream | 50 ml |
| 1 | whole egg | 1 |
| 1 | yolk of egg | 1 |
| ¼ teaspoon | salt | 1 g |
| few grains | ground white pepper | pointe |

### Method

1. Pound the chicken and béchamel and dilute them with the cream.

2. Pass them through a very fine sieve, then add the beaten egg and yolk.

3. Proceed as for ordinary royale.

## Fish royale

| | Ingredients | |
|---|---|---|
| 2 oz | cooked white or shell fish | 50 g |
| 1 oz | cold béchamel | 25 g |
| 2 oz | double cream | 50 g |
| 1 | whole egg | 1 |
| 2 | yolks of egg | 2 |
| ¼ teaspoon | salt | 1 g |
| point | cayenne pepper | pointe |

### Method

As for Chicken royale.

## Carrot royale (Crécy)

| | Ingredients | |
|---|---|---|
| 3 oz | plain boiled red of carrot | 75 g |
| 1 oz | cold béchamel | 25 g |
| 2 oz | double cream | 50 ml |
| 1 | whole egg | 1 |
| 2 | yolks of egg | 2 |
| few grains | sugar | few grains |
| ¼ teaspoon | salt | 1 g |
| few grains | ground white pepper | few grains |
| 2–3 drops | cochineal | 2–3 drops |

### Method

As for Chicken royale

## Other royales are game, spinach, foie gras, etc.

| | Ingredients | |
|---|---|---|
| 3 oz | purée of desired base | 75 g |
| 1 oz | cold béchamel | 25 g |
| 2 fl. oz | double cream | 50 ml |
| 1 | whole egg | 1 |
| 2 | yolks of egg | 2 |
| | seasoning according to base | |

### Method

As for Chicken royale.

---

## THICKENED PASSED SOUPS

### 446 Purées

### 447 Artichoke                        Purée d'artichaut

| 2 quarts (8) | Ingredients | 3 litres (10) |
|---|---|---|
| 1¾ lb | Jerusalem artichokes | 1 kg |
| 1¼ lb | peeled potatoes | 700 g |
| 2 oz | onion | 70 g |
| 2 oz | leek | 70 g |
| 1 + 2 oz | butter | 35 + 70 g |
| 5 pints | white beef stock (345) | 3·5 litres |
| ½ oz | salt | 15 g |
| ¼ level teaspoon | ground white pepper | 2 g |
| small | bouquet garni | small |
| | diced croûtons (339a) | |

### Method

1. Finely shred the cleaned onion and leek and sweat them in 1 oz (35 g) butter in a saucepan for 4–5 minutes without colouring.

2. Add the roughly diced peeled artichokes and potato.

3. Moisten with the boiling stock and the other ingredients, except the second amount of butter and croûtons.

4. Bring to the boil, then remove all the scum. Allow to boil steadily with a cover for 35–40 minutes, then remove the bouquet garni.

5. Rub through a sieve. Reboil, correct the seasoning and

consistency. If a little thin, thicken with a little diluted potato fecule.

6. Pass through a conical strainer with pressure.

7. Reboil, skim, then finish off the heat with the remainder of the butter, well mixed in.

8. Serve in a soup tureen on a round salver or plate and doily. Serve the croûtons in a sauceboat on an underdish with a doily.

## 448 Carrot — Purée de carottes

| 2 quarts (8) | Ingredients | 3 litres (10) |
|---|---|---|
| 1¾ lb | peeled carrots | 1 kg |
| 4 oz | rice (Carolina) | 140 g |
| 2 oz | onions | 70 g |
| 2 oz | leek | 70 g |
| 1 + 2 oz | butter | 35 + 70 g |
| 5 pints | white beef stock (345) | 3·5 litres |
| ½ oz | salt | 15 g |
| ½ level teaspoon | ground white pepper | 2 g |
| small | bouquet garni | small |
| | diced croûtons (339a) | |

### Method

1. Finely shred the cleaned onion and leek and sweat them in 1 oz (35 g) of the butter in a saucepan without colouring.

2. Add the roughly shredded carrots and rice.

3. Then proceed to finish and serve as for Purée d'artichaut (447, from 3).

## 449 Cauliflower — Purée Dubarry

The ingredients used are as for Purée d'artichaut (447), but the artichoke is replaced by the same quantity of trimmed cauliflower, including the stalk but not the leaf.

### Method

1. As for Purée d'artichaut (447), replacing artichoke in the method with roughly chopped cauliflower.

## 450 Mixed vegetable — Purée de légumes

| 2 quarts (8) | Ingredients | 3 litres (10) |
|---|---|---|
| 1 lb | peeled carrot | 560 g |
| 8 oz | peeled turnip | 280 g |
| 1¼ lb | peeled potato | 700 g |
| 2 oz | cleaned onion | 70 g |
| 2 oz | cleaned leek | 70 g |
| 2 oz | cleaned celery | 70 g |
| 1 + 2 oz | butter | 35 + 70 g |
| 5 pints | white beef stock (345) | 3·5 litres |
| ½ oz | salt | 15 g |
| ½ level teaspoon | ground white pepper | 2 g |
| small | bouquet garni | small |
| | diced croûtons (339a) | |

### Method

1. Finely shred the cleaned onion and leek and sweat them

in 1 oz (35 g) of the butter in a saucepan for 3–4 minutes without colouring.

2. Add the roughly shredded carrot, turnip and celery and sweat them with the other vegetables for a further 5 minutes, without colouring, then add the roughly cut pieces of potato.

3. Proceed to finish and serve as for Purée d'artichaut (447, from 3).

## 451 Potato — Purée Parmentier

| 2 quarts (8) | Ingredients | 3 litres (10) |
|---|---|---|
| 1½ lb | peeled potatoes | 840 g |
| 6 oz | leeks | 210 g |
| 1 + 2 oz | butter | 35 + 70 g |
| 1 oz | potato fécule | 35 g |
| ¼ pint | milk | 175 ml |
| ½ oz | salt | 15 g |
| ½ level teaspoon | ground white pepper | 2 g |
| 1 small | bouquet garni | 1 small |
| 5 pints | white beef stock (345) | 3·5 litres |
| | diced croûtons (339a) | |

### Method

1. Finely shred the cleaned leeks and sweat them in 1 oz (35 g) of the butter in a covered saucepan for 4–5 minutes without colouring.

2. Add the roughly diced potato, bouquet garni, seasoning and boiling stock. Bring to the boil, then remove the scum.

3. Boil fairly quickly, with a cover on, for 30 minutes.

4. Remove the bouquet garni. Rub through a sieve.

5. Reboil, thicken with the fecule diluted in the milk, correcting the seasoning.

6. Pass through a fine conical strainer; correct the seasoning.

7. Finish off the heat with the 2 oz (70 g) butter, blending thoroughly.

8. Serve in a soup tureen on a round salver with a doily. Serve the croûtons in a sauceboat on an underdish with a doily.

## 452 Watercress — Purée cressonnière

### Method

1. Prepare and serve as for Purée Parmentier (451), adding 8 oz (280 g) watercress to the ingredients.

2. Remove the best small leaves of the watercress for 1 oz (35 g) garnish. Place in a conical strainer, dip in boiling water for 5 seconds, then refresh and set aside.

3. Add the remainder of the watercress leaves and stalks to the soup with the stock.

4. When serving, garnish the soup with the blanched leaves. No croûtons are served.

## 453 Pulse

| Green pea soup | Purée St Germain |
|---|---|
| Yellow pea soup | Purée de pois jaune |
| White haricot bean soup | Purée soissonnaise |
| Red lentil soup | Purée de lentilles |

| 2 quarts (8) | Ingredients | 3 litres (10) |
|---|---|---|
| 12 oz | pulse, according to type | 420 g |
| 4 oz | onion (studded with one clove) | 140 g |
| 3 oz | carrot | 100 g |
| 4 oz | bacon or ham bone | 140 g |
| 2 oz | butter | 70 g |
| small | bouquet garni | small |
| 3 level teaspons | salt | 12 g |
| ½ level teaspoon | ground white pepper | 2 g |
| 5 pints | water | 3·5 litres |
| | diced croûtons (339a) | |

### Method

1. Pick, wash and soak the pulse for 12 hours.

2. Rewash and place to cook in clean cold water.

3. Bring to the boil and remove the scum which rises to the surface.

4. Add the vegetables, bouquet garni and ham bone.

5. Allow to simmer for 1 hour, then add the seasoning.

6. Allow to cook until tender (approximately 1½–2 hours).

7. Remove the garnish and pass through a sieve with pressure.

8. Reboil, skim, correct the seasoning and consistency, and finish, off the heat, with butter.

9. Pass through a chinois and serve in a soup tureen on a salver with a doily.

Serve the croûtons in a sauceboat on an underflat with a doily.

*Note.* For lentil soup, increase the amount of lentils by 25%.

## 454 Turnip

| | | Purée freneuse |
|---|---|---|
| 2 quarts (8) | Ingredients | 3 litres (10) |
| 1¼ lb | peeled turnips | 700 g |
| 1¼ lb | peeled potatoes | 700 g |
| 4 oz | leeks | 140 g |
| 1 + 2 oz | butter | 35 + 70 g |
| ½ oz | salt | 15 g |
| ¼ level teaspoon | ground white pepper | 2 g |
| 5 pints | white beef stock (345) | 3·5 litres |
| small | bouquet garni | small |
| | diced croûtons (339a) | |

### Method

1. Shred the cleaned leeks and roughly dice the turnips.

2. Melt the butter in a saucepan, add the leeks, sweat a little, then add the turnips.

3. Allow to sweat gently with the lid on, without colouring, for 6–7 minutes. Add the roughly cut potato.

4. Moisten with the boiling stock, reboil, add the bouquet garni, season and simmer for 30–40 minutes.

5. Pass through a sieve with pressure, reboil, then correct the seasoning and consistency.

6. Pass through a fine conical strainer, reboil and skim.

7. Serve in a soup tureen on a salver with a doily. Serve the croûtons in a sauceboat on an underflat and a doily.

---

## VELOUTÉS – CRÈMES

### 455 Cream of asparagus · Crème d'asperges

| 2 quarts (8) | Ingredients | 3 litres (10) |
|---|---|---|
| 6 oz | white of leek | 210 g |
| 2 oz | onion | 70 g |
| 2 oz | butter | 70 g |
| 14 oz | tinned asparagus tips | 500 g |
| small | bouquet garni | small |
| 3 pints | chicken or veal stock (347/6) | 2 litres |
| 1½ pints | béchamel (366) | 1 litre |
| ¼ pint | cream | 175 ml |
| ½ oz | salt | 15 g |
| ½ level teaspoon | ground white pepper | 2 g |

### Method

1. Finely shred the cleaned onion and leek and sweat them in the butter in a covered saucepan for 5–6 minutes without colouring.

2. Moisten with the boiling stock, then add the seasoning and bouquet garni.

3. Cut the asparagus into 5 mm dice from the heads downwards to half the length of the tips. Place aside for garnish. Add the remainder to the soup.

4. Simmer for 30 minutes, then remove the bouquet garni.

5. Pass through a sieve. Reboil with the béchamel.

6. Pass through a fine conical strainer. Reboil, skim, correct the seasoning and consistency to the thickness of single cream.

7. Stir in the cream, add the garnish of diced asparagus. Serve in a soup tureen on a salver with a doily.

### Note

1. When fresh asparagus is used, take a 1 lb bundle for 8 portions ($\frac{1}{2}$ kg for 10 portions).

2. Remove the side offshoots to a depth of 50–75 mm from the head of the asparagus, then scrape the stalks at the points from which the shoots were removed.

3. Wash, then tie the asparagus into a bundle, and cut the bundle 75–85 mm from the head.

4. Cook the asparagus tips in boiling salt water for 10–18 minutes; refresh, drain and cut into 5 mm dice for garnish.

5. The white part of the stalks is roughly cut into 25 mm lengths and added to the stock at (2) in previous recipe and simmered for 1 hour. The soup is then finished in the same manner.

**Crème Gosford**

### Method

For each 1 quart of Crème d'asperges, add this garnish.

Boil $\frac{1}{4}$ pint milk, 'rain' in 1 oz seed tapioca, whisk and allow to simmer for 10 minutes, stirring occasionally. Add to the soup when finishing. (Use 25 g tapioca in 125 ml milk per litre of crème d'asperges.)

### 456                       Velouté Agnès Sorel

| 2 quarts (8) | Ingredients | 3 litres (10) |
| --- | --- | --- |
| 2 pints | chicken velouté (368) | 1·4 litres |
| 2½ pints | chicken stock (347) | 1·75 litres |
| 4 oz | closed mushrooms | 140 g |
| 2 oz | cooked ox-tongue | 70 g |
| ½ oz | salt | 15 g |
| ½ level teaspoon | ground white pepper | 2 g |
| 4 | yolks of egg | 5 |
| ¼ pint | cream | 175 ml |

### Method

1. Wash and peel the mushrooms, and cut them into julienne and cook 'à blanc' (335 g).

2. Place the trimmings into a saucepan with the velouté and stock. Boil, remove the scum and reduce the liquid to just below 4 pints (3 litres), then add and correct the seasoning.

3. Mix the yolks of eggs and cream together. Pour a little of the soup on to the liaison, mixing well, then whisk the liaison into the soup off the heat.

4. Pass through a very fine conical strainer, add the julienne of mushroom and the ox-tongue, which has also been cut into julienne.

5. Serve in a soup tureen on a salver with a doily.

### 457                       Velouté Bagration

| 2 quarts (8) | Ingredients | 3 litres (10) |
| --- | --- | --- |
| 2 pints | veal velouté (368) | 1·4 litres |
| 2½ pints | white veal stock (346) | 1·75 litres |
| 2 oz | macaroni | 70 g |
| ½ oz | salt | 15 g |
| ½ level teaspoon | ground white pepper | 2 g |
| 4 | yolks of egg | 5 |
| ¼ pint | cream | 175 ml |

### Method

1. Boil the velouté and stock in a saucepan. Remove the scum and reduce to just below 4 pints (3 litres), then add the seasoning and correct.

2. Pour a little of the soup on to the liaison of yolks of egg, and cream them together. Mix the liaison well into the soup with a whisk, off the heat.

3. Pass through a very fine conical strainer.

4. Garnish with the macaroni, which has been cooked in boiling salt water for 20 minutes, refreshed, then cut into 10 mm lengths.

5. Serve in a soup tureen on a salver with a doily.

### 458  Cream of carrot               Crème de carotte

| 2 quarts (8) | Ingredients | 3 litres (10) |
| --- | --- | --- |
| 1¼ lb | peeled carrots | 700 g |
| 4 oz | leeks | 140 g |
| 1 oz | butter | 35 g |
| ½ oz | salt | 15 g |
| ½ level teaspoon | ground white pepper | 2 g |
| 3 pints | white beef stock (345) | 2 litres |
| 1½ pints | béchamel (366) | 1 litre |
| small | bouquet garni | small |
| ¼ pint | cream | 175 ml |

### Method

1. Cut 2 oz (70 g) of the carrots for garnish with a pea-sized scoop cutter, or into 5 mm dice. Plain boil and refresh, then set aside for the garnish.

2. Finely shred the cleaned leek and sweat in the butter in a covered saucepan for 3–4 minutes. Add the remainder of the roughly shredded carrot and sweat for 4–5 minutes, without colouring.

3. Moisten with the boiling stock, reboil, remove any scum, then add the seasoning and bouquet garni.

4. Simmer for 35–40 minutes, until the carrot is soft.

5. Pass through a sieve with pressure. Reboil, and add the béchamel, mixing thoroughly.

6. Pass through a fine conical strainer. Reboil, skim, then correct the seasoning and consistency. Garnish with the cooked dice or balls of carrot and finish with the cream.

7. Serve in a soup tureen on a salver with a doily.

## Cream of carrot and rice      Crème Crécy

**Method**

1. Prepare Crème Crécy in the same manner as Cream of carrot (458), omitting the béchamel, and thicken it with 2 oz cream of rice and 1¼ pints milk (70 g rice to 1 litre milk). Dilute then boil the rice in the soup for 7–8 minutes before passing.

2. Add the additional garnish of 2 oz (70 g) of plain boiled patna rice.

## 459 Cream of cauliflower      Crème Dubarry

| 2 quarts (8) | Ingredients | 3 litres (10) |
|---|---|---|
| 1½ lb | cauliflower | 700 g |
| 4 oz | leek | 140 g |
| 1 oz | butter | 35 g |
| ½ oz | salt | 15 g |
| ¼ level teaspoon | ground white pepper | 2 g |
| 3 pints | white beef stock (345) | 2 litres |
| 1¼ pints | béchamel (366) | 1 litre |
| small | bouquet garni | small |
| ¼ pint | cream | 175 ml |

**Method**

1. Wash and prepare the cauliflower, removing most of the green part of the leaves (the leaf stalks may be used).

2. Select some of the buds to use as a garnish (2 oz for 8 portions, 70 g for 10 portions).

3. Chop the remainder of the cauliflower coarsely.

4. Shred the onions and leeks finely and sweat them in butter. Add the chopped cauliflower and sweat it for five minutes without colouring.

5. Add the stock, bouquet garni and seasoning, then simmer for 20–30 minutes.

6. Pass through a fine sieve.

7. Reboil the purée and mix in the béchamel sauce.

8. Reboil, and correct the seasoning and consistency. Pass through a chinois.

9. Reboil. Draw to the side of the stove, stir in the cream and add the garnish of plain boiled small buds of cauliflower (5 mm in size).

10. Serve in a soup tureen on a salver with a doily.

## 460 Cream of celery      Crème de céleri

**Method**

1. Prepare and serve as for Cream of cauliflower (459), replacing the cauliflower with the same quantity of celery.

2. After cleaning the celery, take the centre stems and cut 2 oz (70 g) into 25 mm coarse julienne, then plain boil and use as garnish for the finished soup.

## 461 Cream of chicken      Crème reine
##      Crème de volaille
## Velouté of chicken      Velouté de volaille

| 2 quarts (8) | Ingredients | 3 litres (10) |
|---|---|---|
| 2 pints | chicken velouté (368) | 1·4 litres |
| 2½ pints | chicken stock (347) | 1·75 litres |
| ½ oz | salt | 15 g |
| ¼ level teaspoon | ground white pepper | 2 g |
| 2 oz | white mushroom trimmings | 70 g |
| 2 oz | cooked white of chicken | 70 g |
| ¼ pint | cream | 175 ml |
| 4 | yolks of egg | 5 |

**Method**

1. Place the washed mushroom trimmings in a saucepan with the velouté and stock, bring to the boil, remove any scum and reduce to just below 4 pints (3 litres).

2. For Velouté de volaille, pour this mixture on to the liaison of yolks and cream. For Crème de volaille, finish with the cream only.

3. Pass the liquid through a very fine conical strainer.

4. Add the garnish of the cooked chicken, cut in 25 mm julienne or 5 mm dice, and correct the seasoning and consistency.

5. Serve in a soup tureen on a salver with a doily.

## 462      Velouté de concombre

**Method**

1. Prepare as for Velouté de volaille.

2. Peel 1 lb (560 g) cucumber and cut out with a pea-sized ball scoop 2 oz (70 g). Plain boil the cucumber for 5 minutes, refresh, and keep for the garnish.

3. Cook the remainder of the roughly chopped cucumber in the stock for 15 minutes, before adding the velouté to reduce the liquid. Pass the mixture through a sieve, then finish as for Velouté de volaille, using the cucumber garnish in place of chicken.

# 463 Cream of cucumber — Crème Doria

## Method

1. Prepare as for Velouté de concombre, finishing with cream only, and the garnish.

# 464 — Crème Germiny

| 2 quarts (8) | Ingredients | 3 litres (10) |
|---|---|---|
| 4 pints | chicken consommé or chicken stock | 3 litres |
| 12 | yolks of egg | 15 |
| ¼ pint | cream | 175 ml |
| 1–2 level teaspoons | salt | 4–8 g |
| ⅛ level teaspoon | ground white pepper | ½ g |
| 8 oz | sorrel | 280 g |
| 2 oz | butter | 70 g |

## Method

1. Thoroughly wash the sorrel after picking to remove any weeds. Roll the leaves and shred them finely across.

2. Sweat the sorrel gently in half the butter, with a cover, for 4–5 minutes, then cover with a little of the consommé and simmer for a further 4–5 minutes. Set aside for the garnish.

3. Boil the remainder of the consommé, add the seasoning, then pour it on to the liaison of yolks of egg and cream. Pass the mixture through a very fine conical strainer. Do not reboil; correct the seasoning.

4. Add the garnish of the cooked sorrel.

5. Serve in a soup tureen on a salver with a doily.

# 465 Cream of leek — Crème de poireaux

## Method

1. Prepare as for Cream of cauliflower, substituting 1½ lb (840 g) leek for the cauliflower.

2. Before coarsely shredding the cleaned leeks, select 2 oz (70 g) of white of leek for the garnish, cut it into 25 mm julienne, plain boil, refresh, then drain.

3. Add the white of leek to the finished cream soup when serving.

# 466 Cream of mixed vegetables — Crème de légumes

| 2 quarts (8) | Ingredients | 3 litres (10) |
|---|---|---|
| 8 oz | carrots | 280 g |
| 8 oz | turnips | 280 g |
| 4 oz | leek | 140 g |
| 4 oz | onion | 140 g |
| 4 oz | celery | 140 g |
| 1 oz | butter | 35 g |
| ½ oz | salt | 15 g |
| ½ level teaspoon | ground white pepper | 2 g |
| 3½ pints | white beef stock (345) | 2·25 litres |
| 1¼ pints | béchamel (366) | 1 litre |
| ¼ pint | cream | 175 ml |
| small | bouquet garni | small |
| | diced croûtons (339a) | |

## Method

1. Clean the vegetables and cut them into small pieces.

2. Melt the butter in a saucepan, add the shredded leeks and chopped onions and sweat them a little, with a cover on.

3. Add the remainder of the cut vegetables and allow them to sweat gently with the lid on for 4–5 minutes. Do not allow them to colour.

4. Moisten with the boiling stock, reboil, season, add the bouquet garni and allow them to simmer for 35–40 minutes.

5. Pass through a sieve, reboil and add the béchamel.

6. Correct the seasoning and consistency.

7. Pass through a chinois, reheat, add the cream and serve in a soup tureen on a salver with a doily.

Diced fried croûtons of bread are served in a sauceboat on an underdish with a doily.

# 467 Cream of mushroom — Crème de champignons

| 2 quarts | Ingredients | 3 litres |
|---|---|---|
| 2 oz | butter | 70 g |
| 6 oz | white of leek | 210 g |
| 2 oz | onion | 70 g |
| 3 oz | closed mushrooms | 100 g |
| 8 oz | mushroom stalks | 280 g |
| 3 pints | chicken or veal stock (347/6) | 2 litres |
| 1½ pints | béchamel | 1 litre |
| ¼ pint | cream | 175 ml |
| ½ oz | salt | 15 g |
| ½ level teaspoon | ground white pepper | 2 g |
| small | bouquet garni | small |

## Method

1. Finely shred the washed and prepared leeks and onions.

2. Sweat them slowly in the butter, covered with a lid, without colouring. Add the bouquet garni and stock.

3. Add the washed mushroom stalks and peelings, bring to the boil, season with salt and pepper, and boil gently for 35–40 minutes.

4. After peeling and washing the whole mushrooms, cut into 5 mm dice and cook 'à blanc'.

5. Add the prepared béchamel to the soup, reboil, pass the mixture through a machine or a fine sieve with pressure, then through a fine conical strainer.

6. Adjust the seasoning and consistency if required.

7. Reboil, add the garnish of cooked mushrooms, then finish the soup at the last moment with the cream.

8. Serve in a soup tureen on a salver with a doily.

*Note.* Cream soups should barely mask the back of spoon

### 468  Cream of green peas (fresh)  Crème St Germain

| 2 quarts | Ingredients | 3 litres |
|---|---|---|
| 1¼ lb | shelled peas | 700 g |
| 2 oz | onion | 70 g |
| small | bouquet garni | small |
| 1¼ pints | béchamel | 875 ml |
| 1½ pints | white stock | 1 litre |
| ¼ pint | cream | 175 ml |
| ½ oz | salt | 15 g |
| ½ level teaspoon | ground white pepper | 2 g |
| | diced croûtons (339a) | |

#### Method

1. Blanch the shelled peas in boiling salt water for 2 minutes, then refresh and drain.
2. Place in a saucepan with the boiling stock, onion, seasoning and bouquet garni.
3. Simmer until the peas are quite soft (approximately 20 minutes) then remove the bouquet garni.
4. Pass through a sieve with pressure.
5. Reboil with the béchamel then correct the seasoning and consistency.
6. Pass through a fine conical strainer, reboil, and finish with the cream.
7. Serve the soup in a soup tureen on a salver with a doily, with the croûtons in a sauceboat on an underdish with a doily.

### 469  Cream of green peas  Crème St Germain

#### Method

1. Prepare a Purée St Germain (453).
2. Finish with ¼ pint (175 ml) of cream.

### 470  Crème Balvet  Crème jubilée

#### Method

1. Mix together 3 parts Crème St Germain (469) with 1 part basic consommé (419).
2. Add a garnish of vegetables as served in Croûte-au-pot (507).

### 471  Crème camélia

#### Method

1. Prepare a Purée St Germain (453).
2. Boil ¼ pint (175 ml) of milk, rain in 2 oz (70 g) of seed tapioca, stir, simmer for 10 minutes then add to the soup.
3. Plain boil 2 oz (70 g) of julienne of leek, drain and add to the soup with 2 oz (70 g) of julienne of cooked chicken.
4. Finish with ¼ pint (175 ml) of cream.
5. Serve in a soup tureen on a salver with a doily.

### 472  Crème Lamballe

#### Method

1. Prepare a Purée St Germain (453).
2. Boil ¼ pint (175 ml) of milk, rain in 2 oz (70 g) of seed tapioca, stir, simmer for 10 minutes then add to the soup.
3. Finish the soup with 2 oz (70 g) of butter, off the heat, and ¼ pint (175 ml) of cream.
4. Serve in a soup tureen on a salver with a doily.

### 473  Crème Longchamps

#### Method

1. Prepare a Crème St Germain (469)
2. Lightly crush 2oz (70 g) vermicelli, drop it into boiling salt water and simmer for 5 minutes. Refresh, drain and add to the soup.
3. Serve in a soup tureen on a salver with a doily.

### 474  Cream of potato  Crème Parmentier

| 2 quarts (8) | Ingredients | 3 litres (10) |
|---|---|---|
| 2 lb | peeled potatoes | 1·12 kg |
| 6 oz | leeks | 210 g |
| 3 oz | butter | 100 g |
| 1 oz | potato fécule | 35 g |
| ½ oz | salt | 15 g |
| ½ level teaspoon | ground white pepper | 2 g |
| small | bouquet garni | small |
| 3½ pints | white stock | 2·4 litres |
| ½ pint | milk | 350 ml |
| ¼ pint | cream | 175 ml |
| | diced croûtons (339a) | |

#### Method

1. Clean and coarsely shred the leeks.
2. Melt half the butter in a saucepan, add the leeks, cover and sweat for 4–5 minutes without colouring.
3. Moisten with the stock and add the roughly cut pieces of potato.
4. Bring to the boil, season, add the bouquet garni and allow to boil for 30 minutes.
5. Pass through a sieve, reboil then add three-quarters of the previously boiled milk.
6. Thicken the mixture with the fécule diluted in the remainder of the cold milk.
7. Reboil, correct the seasoning and pass through a chinois.
8. Finish with the remainder of the butter stirred in off the heat, and add the cream.
9. Serve in a soup tureen on a salver with a doily and serve the croûtons in a sauceboat on an underdish with a doily.

## 475 Cream of sweetcorn — Crème Washington / Crème de maïs

| 2 quarts (8) | Ingredients | 3 litres (10) |
|---|---|---|
| 6 oz | white of leek | 210 g |
| 2 oz | onion | 70 g |
| 2 oz | butter | 70 g |
| ½ oz | salt | 15 g |
| ½ level teaspoon | ground white pepper | 2 g |
| 14 oz | tinned creamed sweetcorn | 500 g |
| 3 pints | chicken or veal stock | 2 litres |
| 1½ pints | béchamel | 1 litre |
| ¼ pint | cream | 175 ml |
| small | bouquet garni | small |

### Method

1. Shred the prepared leeks and onions and sweat them in a covered pan in the butter.
2. Moisten with the boiling stock, then add the bouquet garni and the salt and pepper.
3. When boiling, add a half of the creamed corn and simmer for 15–20 minutes.
4. Add the béchamel, reboil, then pass through a sieve or soup machine.
5. Pass through a fine conical strainer, reboil, correct the seasoning and consistency (thickness of single cream).
6. Add the garnish of the remaining creamed corn, then finish with the cream.
7. Serve in a soup tureen on a salver with a doily.

## 476 Tomato soup

| 2 quarts (8) | Ingredients | 3 litres (10) |
|---|---|---|
| 2 oz | fat bacon trimmings | 70 g |
| 3 oz | butter | 100 g |
| 8 oz | onions | 280 g |
| 8 oz | carrots | 280 g |
| 4 oz | flour | 140 g |
| 12 oz | tomato purée or | 420 g |
| 1¾ lb | fresh tomatoes | 1 kg |
| ½ oz | salt | 15 g |
| ½ level teaspoon | ground white pepper | 2 g |
| 5 pints | white stock | 3·5 litres |
| ¼ pod | garlic | pointe |
| small | bouquet garni | small |
| | diced croûtons (339a) | |

### Method

1. Clean and prepare the vegetables and cut them into 10 mm mirepoix.
2. Heat the butter and fry the bacon bits; add the mirepoix and fry them gently.
3. Add the flour and mix well to make a roux.
4. Allow the roux to cook gently in the oven at 150°C (300°F) until blond.
5. After the roux has cooled a little, gradually work in the tomato purée and the boiling stock.
6. Reboil, skim, add the bouquet garni and garlic and seasoning.
7. Allow to simmer for 1 hour.
8. Pass through a sieve, reboil, skim, correct the seasoning and consistency.
9. Pass through a fine conical strainer and reboil.
10. Serve in a soup tureen on a salver with a doily. Serve the croûtons in a sauceboat on an underdish and a doily.

## 477 Cream of tomato — Crème de tomate

### Method

1. Prepared and served as for Tomato soup (476).
2. Finish with ¼ pint (175 ml) of cream.

*Note.* The soup can be finished with ½ pint (350 ml) of boiling milk, provided that the amount of stock used has been reduced by the same quantity.

## 478 — Crème andalouse

### Method

1. Prepare as for Crème de tomate (477).
2. Garnish with 2 oz (70 g) each of plain boiled patna rice and julienne of red pimento. Crème andalouse is not served with croûtons.

## 479 — Crème bretonne

### Method

Mix together 3 parts Purée soissonnaise (453) with 1 part Crème de tomate (477); serve the soup with croûtons.

## 480 — Crème Carmen

### Method

1. Prepare as for Crème de tomate (477).
2. Garnish with 4 oz (140 g) tomatoes prepared into 5 mm dice, and 2 oz (70 g) julienne of red pimento; do not serve with croûtons.

## 481 — Crème portugaise

### Method

Prepare as for Crème de tomate (477) and garnish with 2 oz (70 g) of plain boiled patna rice.

## 482 Crème Solférino

**Method**

1. Mix together equal quantities of Crème Parmentier (474) and Crème de tomate (477).
2. Garnish with 2 oz (70 g) pea-size balls of plain boiled carrot and 2 oz (70 g) 5 mm dice of fried potatoes.

## 483 Creme Waldèze

**Method**

1. Prepare as for Crème de tomate (477).
2. Garnish with 2 oz (70 g) seed tapioca cooked for 10 minutes in ¼ pint (175 ml) milk.

## 484 Cream of turnip — Crème freneuse

| 2 quarts (8) | Ingredients | 3 litres (10) |
| --- | --- | --- |
| 1½ lb | peeled turnips | 700 g |
| 4 oz | leek | 140 g |
| 1 oz | butter | 35 g |
| ½ oz | salt | 15 g |
| ½ level teaspoon | ground white pepper | 2 g |
| 3 pints | white stock | 2 litres |
| 1½ pints | béchamel | 1 litre |
| small | bouquet garni | small |
| ¼ pint | cream | 175 ml |

**Method**

1. Cut 2 oz (70 g) of the peeled turnip into pea-sized balls or 5 mm dice for the garnish. Plain boil for 12 minutes, refresh and drain.
2. Shred the cleaned leeks and sweat them in the butter in a covered pan for 4–5 minutes, without colouring.
3. Add the roughly chopped turnip, bouquet garni, seasoning and stock. Bring to the boil, remove the scum and simmer for 35–40 minutes. Remove the bouquet garni.
4. Pass through a sieve with pressure, reboil, then add the béchamel and stir until boiling. Pass through a fine conical strainer.
5. Check the seasoning and consistency. Finish with the cream and garnish.
6. Serve in a soup tureen on a salver with a doily.

## 485 Cream of watercress — Crème cressonnière

**Method**

1. Prepare a Purée cressonnière (452).
2. Finish with ¼ pint (175 ml) of cream.
3. Serve in a soup tureen on a salver with a doily.

---

## 486 THICKENED UNPASSED SOUPS — POTAGE DE LÉGUMES

### 487 Potage à l'aurore

| 2 quarts (8) | Ingredients | 3 litres (10) |
| --- | --- | --- |
| 4 oz | pearl barley | 140 g |
| 1 oz | butter | 35 g |
| 3 oz | celery | 100 g |
| 2 oz | tomato purée | 70 g |
| ½ oz | salt | 15 g |
| ½ level teaspoon | ground white pepper | 2 g |
| 5 pints | white stock | 3·5 litres |
| small | bouquet garni | small |

**Method**

1. Pick, wash and soak the barley for 2 hours.
2. Boil the stock and add the barley, bouquet garni and seasoning.
3. Reboil, cover and allow to simmer very gently for 3 hours, skimming frequently.
4. Clean and prepare the celery and cut it into paysanne.
5. Sweat the celery in the butter and moisten with a little stock; allow it to cook for 20 minutes.
6. Add the tomato purée and the celery to the soup, after removing the bouquet garni.
7. Reboil the soup and correct the seasoning and consistency.
8. Serve in a soup tureen on a salver with a doily.

### 488 Potage bonne femme

| 2 quarts (8) | Ingredients | 3 litres (10) |
| --- | --- | --- |
| 1 lb | peeled potatoes | 560 g |
| 6 oz | leeks | 210 g |
| 3 oz | butter | 100 g |
| ½ oz | salt | 15 g |
| ½ level teaspoon | ground white pepper | 2 g |
| 2 dessertspoons | chopped parsley | 10 g |
| ½ teaspoon | chervil pluche | 1 g |
| 1 | bayleaf | 1 |
| 1 oz | potato fécule and | 35 g |
| ½ pint | milk or | 350 ml |
| ¼ pint | cream | 175 ml |

**Method**

1. Thoroughly clean the leeks and cut them paysanne-style.

2. Melt one-third of the butter and add the leeks. Allow them to sweat, with the lid on, without colouring.

3. Moisten with the boiling stock, add the bayleaf and seasoning.

4. Add the potatoes, cut paysanne-style, and the chervil and parsley.

5. Reboil, and allow to simmer for 20 minutes; remove the bayleaf.

6. Add the cream, correct the seasoning and consistency, or, in place of the cream, add two-thirds of the milk, boiled and then thickened with the fecule and diluted with the remaining one-third of cold milk.

7. Finish with the remaining two-thirds of the butter off the heat.

8. Serve in a soup tureen on a salver with a doily. Serve with separate dry, toasted flute bread slices.

### 489 Potage cultivateur

| 2 quarts (8) | Ingredients | 3 litres (10) |
|---|---|---|
| 8 oz | carrot | 280 g |
| 4 oz | turnip | 140 g |
| 4 oz | leek | 140 g |
| 2 oz | onions | 70 g |
| 8 oz | peeled potatoes | 280 g |
| 1½ oz | butter | 50 g |
| 2 oz | streaky bacon | 70 g |
| ½ oz | salt | 15 g |
| ½ level teaspoon | ground white pepper | 2 g |
| 4 pints | white stock | 3 litres |
| small | bouquet garni | small |

#### Method

1. Peel and chop the onion. Clean and wash the other vegetables and cut them into paysanne, keeping each one separate.

2. Thinly slice the bacon, then shred finely across.

3. Gently fry the bacon in the butter; add the chopped onions and leeks.

4. Fry gently, then add the carrots and turnips and allow them to sweat with the lid on until tender (12–15 minutes).

5. Moisten with the boiling stock and add the potatoes and bouquet garni.

6. Reboil, season and allow to simmer for 30 minutes; remove the bouquet garni.

7. Correct the seasoning and consistency and serve in a soup tureen on a salver with a doily.

### 490 Potage paysanne

| 2 quarts (8) | Ingredients | 3 litres (10) |
|---|---|---|
| 6 oz | carrot | 210 g |
| 4 oz | turnip | 140 g |
| 4 oz | leek | 140 g |
| 4 oz | onion | 140 g |
| 4 oz | celery | 140 g |
| 3 oz | cabbage | 100 g |
| 12 oz | peeled potatoes | 400 g |
| 2 oz | peas | 70 g |
| 2 oz | haricots verts | 70 g |
| 2 oz | butter | 70 g |
| ½ oz | salt | 15 g |
| ½ level teaspoon | ground white pepper | 2 g |
| 4 pints | white stock | 3 litres |
| small | bouquet garni | small |

#### Method

1. Clean and wash all the vegetables. Chop the onion and cut the remainder of the vegetables into paysanne, keeping them separate. Cut the beans into small diamonds.

2. Melt the butter in a saucepan, add the leek and onion and sweat them for 2–3 minutes, then add the carrot, turnip and celery. Sweat these with a cover on for 12–15 minutes without colouring.

3. Add the stock, seasoning and bouquet garni, bring to the boil, remove any scum, and simmer for 10 minutes.

4. Add the paysanne of potato, cut slightly thicker.

5. After 5 minutes, add the cabbage, beans and peas and allow it to simmer for a further 20 minutes. Remove the bouquet garni.

6. Correct the seasoning and consistency and remove all the fat.

7. Serve in a soup tureen on a salver with a doily.

### 491 Potage thourins

| 2 quarts (8) | Ingredients | 3 litres (10) |
|---|---|---|
| 1¼ lb | onions | 700 g |
| 2 oz | butter | 70 g |
| ½ oz | salt | 15 g |
| ½ level teaspoon | ground white pepper | 2 g |
| 2½ pints | white stock | 1·75 litres |
| 1½ pints | béchamel | 1 litre |
| 3 | yolks of egg | 4 |
| ¼ pint | cream | 175 ml |

#### Method

1. Peel then finely shred the onions.

2. Melt the butter in a saucepan, add the onions, cover and sweat them gently for 6–7 minutes.

3. Moisten with the stock, add the seasoning and simmer for 15–20 minutes.

4. Mix in the passed béchamel and simmer for a further 10 minutes. Correct the seasoning.

5. Pour on to a liaison of the yolks of egg and cream. Do not boil.

6. Serve the soup in a soup tureen on a salver with a doily, and serve toasted sliced bread flutes in a sauceboat, on an underdish, with a doily.

## 493 Scotch broth

| 2 quarts (8) | Ingredients | 3 litres (10) |
|---|---|---|
| 2 oz | carrot | 70 g |
| 2 oz | turnip | 70 g |
| 2 oz | onion | 70 g |
| 2 oz | leek | 70 g |
| 2 oz | cabbage | 70 g |
| 2 oz | celery | 70 g |
| ½ oz | salt | 15 g |
| ¼ level teaspoon | ground white pepper | 2 g |
| 2 oz | pearl barley | 70 g |
| dessertspoon | chopped parsley | 5 g |
| 4 pints | mutton broth | 3 litres |

## Method

1. Bring the stock to the boil and skim off any scum.

2. Add the picked, washed and soaked barley and allow it to simmer for one hour.

3. Clean and prepare the vegetables and cut them into brunoise (342b).

4. After the barley has had one hour's cooking, add the vegetables.

5. Add the seasoning and allow to simmer for 30 minutes, then skim, and add the parsley.

6. Correct the seasoning and consistency.

   If desired, ¼ pint boiled milk or cream per gallon (30 ml per litre) may be added to the finished soup.

7. Serve in a soup tureen on a salver with a doily.

## 494 Mutton broth

### Method

1. Prepare and serve as for Scotch broth (493).

2. Blanch and refresh 1 lb (560 g) scrag of mutton and add it to the stock with the barley. When the broth is ready, remove the scrag and cut 4 oz (140 g) of the meat into 5 mm dice and add it to the broth.

## 495 Barley broth

### Method

Prepare and serve as for Scotch broth (493), using white beef stock in place of mutton stock.

## 496 Chicken broth

### Method

1. Prepare the ingredients as for Scotch broth (493).

2. Replace the barley with patna rice and the mutton stock with chicken stock.

3. Boil the stock, add the brunoise of vegetables, simmer for 10 minutes, then add the picked and washed rice. Reboil and simmer for a further 20 minutes.

4. Finish as from 6 in method of Scotch broth (493), adding 4 oz (140 g) of 5 mm dice of boiled chicken.

## 497 Rabbit broth

### Method

Prepare and serve as for Chicken broth (496), replacing the chicken stock with rabbit stock and the garnish of chicken with rabbit.

---

## 498 FOREIGN SOUPS — POTAGES ÉTRANGERS

### 499                              Bortsch polonaise

| 2 quarts (8) | Ingredients | 3 litres (10) |
|---|---|---|
| 5 oz | raw beetroot | 175 g |
| 4 oz | white cabbage | 140 g |
| 4 oz | onion | 140 g |
| 4 oz | carrot | 140 g |
| 4 oz | leek | 140 g |
| 2 oz | celery | 70 g |
| 1 oz | fennel | 35 g |
| 2 oz | streaky bacon | 70 g |
| 1½ lb | flat ribs of beef | 840 g |
| 1 lb | duck | 560 g |
| 2 oz | pork chipolata sausages | 70 g |
| 4 pints | basic consommé (419) | 3 litres |
| small | bouquet garni | small |

## Method

1. Clean and prepare the vegetables and duck.

2. Cut all the vegetables into julienne.

3. Sweat the julienne in butter in a saucepan, moistening with the consommé.

4. Add the duck (which has been coloured in a fast oven), beef, herbs, seasoning and bouquet garni.

5. Skim well and allow to simmer until the duck and meat are cooked. Remove the bouquet garni.

6. Remove the duck and meat. Poach the chipolatas for 10 minutes and drain.

7. Finely shred the streaky bacon and add it to the consommé.

8. Cut the duck and meat into small 10 mm scallops and the sausages into thin slices.

9. Add the garnish, then correct the seasoning and consistency.

10. Serve in a soup tureen on a salver with a doily.

The following is served separately: 1 jug of sour cream or ½ pint (350 ml) whipped cream to which lemon juice is added, 1 jug of beetroot juice, made by grating raw beetroots, adding a little water and squeezing through a cloth, and 1 dish of small forcemeat patties (Pâté à bortsch).

## 500 Cocky-leeky

| 2 quarts (8) | Ingredients | 3 litres (10) |
|---|---|---|
| 4 pints | chicken consommé | 3 litres |
| 8 oz | white of leek | 280 g |
| 4 oz | cooked white of poached chicken | 140 g |
| 1 oz | butter | 35 g |
| 4 oz | prunes | 140 g |

### Method

1. Cook the soaked prunes as for compote.

2. Cut the prepared leeks into julienne.

3. Sweat the leeks in butter in a saucepan until tender, without colouring, for 10–12 minutes.

4. Moisten with the boiling consommé.

5. Reboil and simmer for 20 minutes.

6. Cut the chicken garnish into 100 mm scallops and add to the soup.

7. Add the prunes, cut in 5 mm dice. If desired, the prunes may be served separately in a dish.

8. Serve the soup in a tureen on a salver with a doily.

## 501         Potage minestrone

| 2 quarts (8) | Ingredients | 3 litres (10) |
|---|---|---|
| 2 oz | fat bacon | 70 g |
| 2 oz | onion | 70 g |
| 3 oz | leek | 100 g |
| 2 oz | celery | 70 g |
| 4 oz | carrot | 140 g |
| 4 oz | turnip | 140 g |
| 2 oz | cabbage | 70 g |
| 4 oz | peeled potatoes | 140 g |
| 2 oz | haricot beans | 70 g |
| 1 oz | butter | 35 g |
| 1 oz | tomato purée or | 35 g |
| 4 oz | tomatoes in concassé | 140 g |
| 1½ oz | spaghetti | 50 g |
| 1½ oz | patna rice | 50 g |
| ½ oz | salt | 15 g |
| ¼ level teaspoon | ground white pepper | 2 g |
| 3 oz | Parmesan cheese | 100 g |
| 2 dessertspoons | chopped parsley | 8 g |
| ¼ pod | garlic | ¼ pod |
| 4 pints | white stock | 3 litres |

### Method

1. Soak the haricot beans for 8 hours. Cover with fresh water and cook separately for approximately 1½ hours, until tender, and add them to the finished soup.

2. Clean and wash the vegetables and cut them into paysanne, keeping them separate. Chop the onion.

3. Melt the butter in a saucepan, add half the shredded fat bacon, then gently fry to extract the fat.

4. Add the onion and leek and sweat them gently for 2–3 minutes.

5. Add the carrot, turnip and celery and sweat these with a cover for 4–5 minutes, without colouring.

6. Add the tomate concassée or purée, moisten with the boiling stock, reboil and simmer for 15 minutes.

7. Add the seasoning, the picked and washed rice, the spaghetti broken into 25 mm lengths, the potato and cabbage and simmer for 10 minutes.

8. Add the peas and simmer for a further 15 minutes. Add the remainder of the fat bacon, finely chopped with the garlic and parsley, and the cooked haricot beans.

9. Correct the seasoning and consistency.

10. Serve in a soup tureen on a salver with a doily and the grated Parmesan cheese in a sauce boat, on an underdish, with a doily.

## 502 Mock turtle soup (thick)     Potage fausse tortue

| 2 quarts (8) | Ingredients | 3 litres (10) |
|---|---|---|
| 4 oz | calf's head or | 140 g |
| 1 | calf's foot | 1 |
| 2 oz | lean ham | 70 g |
| 3 oz | butter | 100 g |
| 3 oz | flour | 100 g |
| 1 oz | tomato purée | 35 g |
| 2 oz | mushrooms | 70 g |
| ½ oz | salt | 15 g |
| ½ level teaspoon | ground white pepper | 2 g |
| 1 fl. oz | Madeira wine | 35 ml |
| 5 pints | rich brown stock (352) | 3·5 litres |
| ½ pkt | turtle herbs | ½ pkt |
| | **Garnish** | |
| 1½ oz | chicken quenelles (283) | 50 g |
| 2 | hard boiled yolks of egg | 3 |
| 6 | rognons de coq | 8 |
| 3 | crêtes de coq | 4 |
| 1½ oz | small button onions | 50 g |

### Method

1. Soak the calf's head or foot for 3–4 hours, then rewash, blanch and refresh.

2. Place to boil in a saucepan, with the stock, and simmer until the head/foot is cooked (approximately 1½ hours), adding the turtle herbs during the last 15 minutes of cook-

ing. Remove the flesh, cut it into 10 mm dice for the garnish, and strain the stock.

3. Wash and peel the mushrooms and cut them into 5 mm dice. Cut the ham into 5 mm dice.

4. Melt the butter in a saucepan, add the mushrooms and ham, and cook them slowly for 5–6 minutes; drain them and set aside for the garnish.

5. Return the fat to the saucepan, add the flour and cook to a blond roux. Allow to cool.

6. Add the tomato purée. Gradually add the boiling stock, then season and simmer for 2 hours, removing all the fat and scum.

7. Pass through a very fine conical strainer, reboil and skim.

8. Add the garnish of 10 mm diced calf's head or foot, the diced ham, mushrooms, 5 mm diced hard-boiled yolk of egg, poached quenelles, cooked rognons and crêtes de coq, and the small button onions, glazed golden brown.

9. Serve in a soup tureen on a salver with a doily; add the wine at the last moment.

*Note.* The button onions, crêtes and rognons de coq are often omitted in modern trade practice.

### 503 Mulligatawny

| 2 quarts (8) | Ingredients | 3 litres (10) |
|---|---|---|
| 8 oz | onions | 280 g |
| 2 oz | butter | 70 g |
| 1 oz | curry powder | 35 g |
| 2½ oz | flour | 85 g |
| 1 oz | desiccated coconut | 35 g |
| 5 oz | apple | 175 g |
| 2 oz | tomato purée | 70 g |
| 2 oz | patna rice | 70 g |
| ½ oz | salt | 15 g |
| 2 oz | chopped chutney | 70 g |
| 1 | bayleaf | 1 |
| 4½ pints | brown stock | 3·15 litres |
| ½ pod | garlic | ½ pod |

**Method**

1. Peel and finely chop the onions and gently sweat them in the butter in a saucepan, colouring slightly.

2. Mix in the curry powder, then the flour, and cook in the oven at 150°C (300°F) for 7–8 minutes. Cool slightly.

3. Add the tomato purée and gradually work in the boiling stock. Add the salt, chopped garlic, soaked coconut, chopped chutney and the peeled and finely chopped apple and bayleaf.

4. Reboil and simmer for 40–45 minutes. During this time,

plain boil the rice in salted water for 15–16 minutes, until just cooked. Thoroughly wash out the starch, drain and place it aside for garnish.

5. Pass the soup through a sieve or a soup machine, then, with pressure, through a conical strainer.

6. Reboil, check the seasoning and consistency, skim, then add the garnish of rice.

   If desired, the soup may be finished with ¼ pint (175 ml) of cream.

7. Serve in a soup tureen on a salver with a doily.

### 504 Thick ox-tail     Potage queue de boeuf lié

| 2 quarts (8) | Ingredients | 3 litres (10) |
|---|---|---|
| 12 oz | ox-tail tips | 420 g |
| 8 oz | carrot | 280 g |
| 8 oz | onion | 280 g |
| 3 oz | meat dripping | 100 g |
| 3 oz | flour | 100 g |
| 2 oz | tomato purée | 70 g |
| ½ oz | salt | 15 g |
| ½ level teaspoon | ground white pepper | 2 g |
| small | bouquet garni | small |
| 5 pints | brown stock | 3·5 litres |
| | **Garnish** | |
| 2 oz | carrot balls | 70 g |
| 2 oz | turnip balls | 70 g |

**Method**

1. Cut the ox-tail tips into 10 mm pieces long then fry them quickly in a little of the dripping and drain. Cook for 2–2½ hours in a little of the stock.

2. Add this dripping to the remainder in a saucepan. Peel the carrot and onion, cut into 10 mm rough dice and dry them until golden brown.

3. Add the flour and cook in the oven until light brown and sandy in texture. Cool slightly.

4. Add the tomato purée, gradually stir in the boiling stock, then add the seasoning and bouquet garni.

5. When boiling, simmer for 3–3½ hours, removing any scum and fat.

6. Cook the garnish of pea-sized carrots and turnips separately in boiling salt water for 20 and 15 minutes respectively, then drain them.

7. Pass the soup through a sieve, then through a fine conical strainer.

8. Reboil, skim and correct the seasoning and consistency. Garnish with the ox-tail tips (the liquor strained into the soup) and the balls of cooked carrot and turnip.

9. Serve in a soup tureen on a salver with a doily.

## 505 Clear turtle soup

Tortue claire

| 2 quarts | Ingredients | 3 litres |
|---|---|---|
| 2 oz | turtle meat | 70 g |
| 4 pints | basic consommé (419) | 3 litres |
| ½ pkt | turtle herbs | ½ pkt |
| 2 oz | carrot balls | 70 g |
| 2 oz | turnip balls | 70 g |
| 1 oz | arrowroot | 35 g |
| 3 fl. oz | sherry | 100 ml |

### Method

1. Boil the prepared consommé, infuse with the ½ bag of turtle herbs and let it stand for 15 minutes. Repass the consommé.

2. Reboil, thicken with the arrowroot diluted in water to the consistency of thin oil, simmer for 2 minutes and check the seasoning.

3. Plain boil the pea-sized balls of carrot and turnip for 20 and 15 minutes respectively, drain, then add them to the soup.

4. Add the sherry and the cooked turtle meat, cut in 10 mm dice at the moment of service.

5. Serve in a soup tureen on a salver with a doily. Serve lemon wedges and cheese straws separately.

### Cooking of turtle meat

1. Soak the dried turtle meat in cold water for 36–48 hours, changing the water.

2. Thoroughly clean the turtle meat and well cover with water. Boil and skim. Add a little carrot, onion and celery and simmer for approximately 4 hours until the point of a knife will easily penetrate the meat.

3. Cut the meat into 10 mm dice and strain the liquor over it.

---

## 506 UNCLASSIFIED SOUPS

### 507

Croûtes-au-pot

### Method

1. Prepare as for Petite marmite (508).

2. Cut the root vegetables into 5 mm dice, then cut the cabbage, celery and leeks, into a paysanne.

3. For the croûtons, cut off the corners from a sandwich loaf, lengthways, to form a triangular shape with a 25 mm base. Then cut these lengths into 5 mm slices, nipping out the soft centre of bread. Colour these in the oven on a baking sheet until crisp and light golden brown.

### 508

Petite marmite

| 2 quarts (8) | Ingredients | 3 litres (10) |
|---|---|---|
| 4 pints | basic consommé (419) | 3 litres |
| 1 lb | lean beef | 560 g |
| 8 oz | flat ribs of beef | 280 g |
| 8 oz | marrow bones | 280 g |
| 3 oz | leeks | 100 g |
| 4 oz | carrots | 140 g |
| 4 oz | turnips | 140 g |
| 4 oz | heart of cabbage | 140 g |
| 4 oz | very small button onions | 140 g |
| 2 oz | heart of celery | 70 g |
| 4 | chicken necks | 5 |
| 4 | chicken gizzards | 5 |
| 8 | chicken winglets | 10 |

### Method

1. Trim the chicken winglets at each end and cut them into halves.

2. Cut away the flesh of the gizzards from the side skin.

3. Blanch the two lots of beef, chicken necks, winglets and gizzard flesh. Thoroughly wash and drain them.

4. Clean and wash the vegetables. Turn the carrots and turnips 25 mm long, or cut out with an olive cutter. Cut the leek and celery into paysanne.

5. Place the consommé to boil in an earthenware marmite, add the chicken necks, beef, gizzard flesh and bones tied in muslin. Simmer for 45 minutes.

6. Add the chicken winglets, carrots, turnips, leeks, onions and celery and simmer for a further 1¼ hours.

7. Blanch the cabbage, refresh, squeeze into 10 mm small balls. Place in a sauteuse. Moisten with the fat skimmings from the consommé, cover and braise for 20 minutes.

8. Remove the muslin of bones, the chicken necks and beef. Cut the beef into 10 mm dice, remove any marrow from the bones, and slice; add both to the soup.

9. Prepare the bread flutes as in 3 in method of Croûtes-au-pot (507). Dip the flutes in 'dégraissage', the fat skimmed from the soup, and lightly grill till golden brown.

10. Serve the soup in the earthenware marmite on a salver, wrapped around with a serviette. Serve the croûtons in a sauceboat on an underdish with a doily.

## 509        Pot-au-feu

| 2 quarts (8) | Ingredients | 3 litres (10) |
|---|---|---|
| 4 pints | basic consommé | 3 litres |
| 1½ lb | flat ribs of beef | 840 g |
| 4 oz | carrots | 140 g |
| 4 oz | turnips | 140 g |
| 3 oz | leeks | 100 g |
| 4 oz | celery | 140 g |
| 4 oz | cabbage | 140 g |
| 4 oz | very small button onions | 140 g |

### Method

1. Blanch the flat ribs, wash well and drain.

2. Boil the consommé in an earthenware marmite, add the beef and simmer gently for 2½ hours, skimming occasionally.

3. Turn the cleaned carrots and turnips 25 mm long. Cut the cleaned cabbage, celery and leeks into 10 mm squares and add them to the consommé. Half braise the button onions 'à blanc' and add to the consommé and simmer for one more hour.

4. Cut the beef into 10 mm dice for the garnish. Skim off all the fat, correct the seasoning and quantity. .

5. Serve in the earthenware marmite, with a serviette wrapped around, on a salver.

6. Serve the following garnish separately in small dishes on an underflat with dish paper:

| | Garnish | |
|---|---|---|
| 2 oz | gherkins | 70 g |
| 2 oz | coarse salt | 70 g |
| 15 | small forcemeat patties | 20 |

## 510        Poule-au-pot

### Method

1. Use and prepare the ingredients as for Petite marmite (508), omitting the beef, marrow bones and basic consommé and replacing them with a cleaned 3 lb (1·5 kg) boiling fowl and chicken consommé.

2. Blanch the chicken, necks, prepared gizzards and winglets, wash well and drain.

3. Boil the chicken consommé in an earthenware marmite, add the chicken, necks and gizzards and simmer for 30 minutes.

4. Add the chicken winglets, carrots, turnips, leeks, celery and button onions and simmer for a further 1–1¼ hours. Remove all the fat from the soup.

5. Prepare the cabbage as for Petite marmite.

6. Remove the chicken when cooked. Cut 4 oz (140 g) of the skinned white of chicken into 10 mm scallops and return to the soup as garnish.

7. Complete and serve as from 8 in method of Petite marmite.

## 511   Brown onion soup      Soup à l'oignon

| 2 quarts (8) | Ingredients | 3 litres (10) |
|---|---|---|
| 4 pints | rich brown stock or basic consommé | 3 litres |
| 1 lb | onions | 560 g |
| 1½ oz | butter | 50 g |
| 2 oz | arrowroot | 70 g |
| 3 oz | grated cheese | 100 g |
| ½ oz | salt | 15 g |
| ½ level teaspoon | ground white pepper | 2 g |
| 3 oz | bread flutes | 100 g |

### Method

1. Peel, wash and finely shred the onions.

2. Gently cook the onions in the butter in a saucepan until tender (10–12 minutes). Colour them to a light golden brown, but do not allow them to go crisp.

3. Add the onions to the boiling stock or consommé, reboil and season (if using consommé, check whether it is already seasoned). Skim and simmer for 15 minutes.

4. Dilute the arrowroot with water, stir into the boiling soup and simmer for a further 5 minutes.

5. Pour the soup into individual-portion marmites. Cover the surface with neatly arranged toasted bread flutes. These are thin slices cut from 25 mm-diameter French bread, or from the corners of sandwich loaves, and toasted until light golden brown.

6. Liberally sprinkle the surface of the soup with grated cheese.

7. Place in a tray of hot water in a hot oven to colour the cheese, or finish under the salamander.

8. To serve, wipe the marmites and place them on a flat dish with dish paper.

## 512   Liver soup      Soupe aux foies

| 2 quarts (8) | Ingredients | 3 litres (10) |
|---|---|---|
| 8 oz | carrot | 280 g |
| 8 oz | onion | 280 g |
| 3 oz | meat dripping | 100 g |
| 3 oz | flour | 100 g |
| 2 oz | tomato purée | 70 g |
| 12 oz | liver | 420 g |
| ½ oz | salt | 15 g |
| ½ level teaspoon | ground white pepper | 2 g |
| small | bouquet garni | small |
| 5 pints | brown stock | 3.5 litres |

### Method

1. Fry the liver quickly in a little of the fat, then drain.

2. Place the drained fat with the remainder to melt in a saucepan.

3. Peel, wash and cut the carrot and onion into rough 10 mm dice. Fry in the fat to a light golden brown.

4. Add the flour, mix, then cook in the oven to a light brown colour. Allow to cool.

5. Add the tomato purée, then gradually add the boiling stock. Reboil, add the seasoning, bouquet garni and the fried piece of liver.

6. Simmer for $2\frac{1}{2}$–3 hours. Remove the liver, cut half the amount into 5 mm dice and set aside for garnish, and finely chop the remainder and return it to the soup.

7. Pass the soup through a sieve, then through a fine conical strainer.

8. Reboil, skim and correct the seasoning and consistency.

9. Serve in a soup tureen on a salver with a doily.

## 513 Kidney soup      Soupe aux rognons

**Method**

1. Prepare and serve as for Liver soup (512).
2. Replace the liver with ox-kidney.

## 514 THE USE OF CONVENIENCE SOUPS

Convenience soups are being more widely used today in different levels of catering. One distinct advantage of their use is that the various packets of soup base give the exact quantities required, when they are mixed with water. The finished soup can be improved considerably by the following methods:

(a) For types other than cream soups:

Use a good basic stock, i.e. white or brown, according to the nature and colour of the soup.

(b) For cream soups:

1. Sweat a little shredded leek in butter, add a white stock, simmer for 20 minutes, then strain.

2. Reboil, thicken with the soup-base diluted with fresh milk.

3. Finish the soup with a little cream.

# Egg dishes

152

153

# Egg dishes

## 515 EGG DISHES

With this group of dishes, it is essential that all the garnishes, preparations and sauces, where appropriate, are ready in advance.

Well-prepared and presented egg dishes require last minute cooking and finishing, or drying out, shrivelling and other forms of deterioration take place.

## 516 POACHED EGGS      OEUFS POCHÉS
## FIRM BOILED EGGS      OEUFS MOLLETS
## MOULDED EGGS      OEUFS MOULÉS

The following recipes given for poached eggs may be applied to the other two methods of cooking eggs using the same ingredients and methods.

## 517 Basic preparation of poached eggs      Oeufs pochés
**Method**

1. Fill a pan with water to a depth of 50–75 mm and add $\frac{1}{20}$ part of vinegar. Place to boil.
2. When boiling, break the eggs on the flat part of the handle, and open the shells to release the eggs just above the surface of the water.
3. Reboil, remove from the heat and allow to poach on the side of the stove for 3 minutes. Lift from the liquid with a perforated spoon into a basin of cold water.
4. Using a knife, lightly trim off any loose edges to give a uniform round shape.
5. Before use, carefully place the eggs into boiling salted water for 45–60 seconds to reheat, then drain and use as required.

## 518 Basic preparation of boiled eggs      Oeufs mollets
**Method**

1. Select eggs without cracks in the shell and plunge them into enough boiling water to cover the eggs. When cooking a quantity, the eggs are placed in a frying basket for easy removal.
2. Boil gently to the following degree:
(a) Very soft-boiled (Oeuf à la coque) 2 minutes.
(b) Soft-boiled (Oeuf à la coque) 3–4 minutes.
(c) Firm-boiled (Oeuf mollet) 5½–6 minutes.
(d) Hard-boiled (Oeuf dur) 9–10 minutes.

## 519 Basic preparation of moulded eggs (hot)    Oeufs moulés
**Method**

1. Using a brush, grease the dariol or fluted moulds with butter to give a good coating then season the moulds with mixed salt and ground white pepper.
2. Break the eggs into the moulds and place them into a shallow pan with hot water half-way up the moulds. Bring the water to boiling point, cover the pan and cook in an oven at 150°C (300°F), or on the side of the stove, until set (5–6 minutes).
3. Release the top edge of the egg with the point of a knife; the egg should then unmould easily.

## 520      Oeufs pochés à la reine

| 8 portions | Ingredients | 10 couverts |
|---|---|---|
| 8 | poached eggs (517) | 10 |
| 6 oz | cooked boiled chicken | 210 g |
| 1 pint | sauce suprême (400) | 700 ml |
| 2 fl. oz | cream | 70 ml |
| 8 | short paste tartlets | 10 |

**Method**

1. Cut the cooked chicken into 5 mm dice and place in a saucepan. Add sufficient of the sauce to bind then heat it to boiling point and season.
2. Add the cream to the remainder of the sauce and heat it to boiling point.
3. Warm the tartlets in an oval earthenware dish. Divide the diced chicken equally into the tartlets.
4. Place the hot drained eggs on the chicken and mask over with the sauce suprême.
5. Serve on an underflat with dish paper.

## 521      Oeufs pochés Argenteuil
**Method**

1. Use the same ingredients as for Oeufs pochés à la reine (520), omitting the cooked chicken and adding a 14 oz (500 g)

tin of asparagus tips or the equivalent of cooked fresh asparagus tips.

2. Cut the asparagus tips 40 mm from the head and place them in a buttered dish to heat. Cut the remainder of the stems into 5 mm dice, bind them with a little sauce suprême, and heat.

3. Fill the stems into the warm tartlet cases in an earthenware dish.

4. Place the hot drained eggs on top and mask over with the sauce, with cream added. Garnish on top of the eggs with the hot asparagus tips.

5. Serve on an underflat and dish paper.

## 522       Oeufs pochés à l'aurore

| 8 portions | Ingredients | 10 couverts |
|---|---|---|
| 8 | poached eggs (517) | 10 |
| 8 | short paste tartlets | 10 |
| 1 pint | sauce aurore (396) | 700 ml |

**Method**

1. Warm the tartlets in an earthenware dish.

2. Place a dessertspoon of sauce in each tartlet.

3. Dress the hot drained eggs in the tartlets.

4. Mask over with the sauce, enough to cover the base of the dish also.

5. Serve on an underflat with dish paper.

## 523       Oeufs pochés bénédictine

| 8 portions | Ingredients | 10 couverts |
|---|---|---|
| 8 | poached eggs (517) | 10 |
| 8 | small brioche or tartlet | 10 |
| 4 oz | lean cooked ham | 140 g |
| 1 pint | sauce hollandaise (402) | 700 ml |

**Method**

1. Cut 1 or 2 slices of ham, then cut 8 or 10 diamonds 25 × 10 mm. Cut the remainder into small dice.

2. Remove the soft centre from the brioche and warm the case. Warm the tartlets, if used. Place in an earthenware dish.

3. Mix a little of the sauce with the diced ham to bind, then fill into the brioche or tartlets.

4. Place the hot drained egg on top. Mask over with the sauce, covering the base of the dish, then place a diamond of ham on top of each egg.

5. Serve on an underflat with dish paper.

## 524       Oeufs pochés bergère

| 8 portions | Ingredients | 10 couverts |
|---|---|---|
| 8 | poached eggs (517) | 10 |
| 6 oz | cooked lamb | 210 g |
| 4 oz | duxelle (338) | 140 g |
| 1 pint | Mornay sauce (390) | 700 ml |
| 2 oz | Parmesan cheese | 70 ml |

**Method**

1. Cut the lamb into 5 mm dice; mix it with the duxelle and heat.

2. Place in small mounds as a base for each of the eggs in an earthenware dish. Place the hot drained eggs on top.

3. Mask over with the sauce so that it covers the base of the dish. Sprinkle evenly with the Parmesan cheese and colour golden brown under the salamander, or in the top of an oven at 230°C (450°F).

4. Serve on an underflat with dish paper.

## 525       Oeufs pochés à l'indienne
##       Oeufs pochés Bombay
##       Oeufs pochés Madras

| 8 portions | Ingredients | 10 couverts |
|---|---|---|
| 8 | poached eggs (517) | 10 |
| 8 oz | patna rice | 280 g |
| 1 pint | curry sauce (413) | 700 ml |
| 2 teaspoons | chopped parsley | 5 g |

**Method**

1. Pick and wash the rice. Cook in plenty of boiling salted water for 16–18 minutes until just cooked. Place a colander over the saucepan and thoroughly wash away all starch from the rice under running water.

2. Well drain the rice. Place in a shallow buttered tray, cover with a buttered paper and heat through in the oven at 150°C (300°F).

3. Dress the rice loosely in an earthenware dish and place the hot drained eggs on top. Mask over with the strained sauce then sprinkle a little parsley on the centre of each egg.

4. Serve on an underflat with dish paper.

## 526       Oeufs pochés chasseur

| 8 portions | Ingredients | 10 couverts |
|---|---|---|
| 8 | poached eggs (517) | 10 |
| 8 | short paste tartlets | 10 |
| 4 oz | closed mushrooms | 140 g |
| 4 oz | chicken livers | 140 g |
| 1 pint | sauce chasseur (374) | 700 ml |
| 2 teaspoons | chopped parsley | 5 g |
| 2 oz | butter | 70 g |

## Method

1. Wash the mushrooms, peeling them if necessary, and cut them into small scallops. Sauté slowly in half the butter for 5–6 minutes, then season.

2. Cut the cleaned chicken livers into 10 mm scallops. Season and sauté rapidly in the remainder of the butter over a fierce heat for 2–3 minutes.

3. Mix the mushrooms and chicken livers with a little of the sauce to bind, then fill into the warmed tartlets.

4. Place into a hot earthenware dish then place the hot drained eggs in the tartlets. Mask over with the boiling sauce and sprinkle with chopped parsley.

5. Serve on an underflat with dish paper.

### 527          Oeufs pochés Mornay

| 8 portions | Ingredients | 10 couverts |
|---|---|---|
| 8 | poached eggs (517) | 10 |
| 1 pint | Mornay sauce (390) | 700 ml |
| 2 oz | parmesan cheese | 70 g |

### Method

1. Place a little of the sauce on an earthenware dish and place the hot, well-drained eggs on top.

2. Mask the sauce over the eggs, covering the base of the dish, and sprinkle evenly with the cheese.

3. Colour a light golden brown under the salamander.

4. Serve on an underflat with dish paper.

### 528          Oeufs pochés florentine

### Method

1. Prepare 2 lb (1 kg) spinach as for Épinards en branche (1017).

2. Place the buttered spinach in an earthenware dish and place the well drained eggs on top, then finish as for Oeufs pochés Mornay (527).

### 529          Oeufs pochés Otéro

| 8 portions | Ingredients | 10 couverts |
|---|---|---|
| 8 | poached eggs (517) | 10 |
| 1 pint | Mornay sauce (390) | 700 ml |
| 8 × 6–7 oz | large potatoes | 10 × 170–200 g |
| 2 oz | Parmesan cheese | 70 g |
| 1½ oz | butter | 50 g |
| 1 | yolk of egg | 1 |

### Method

1. Scrub the large even-shaped potatoes and place them in a tray on a shallow bed of coarse salt.

2. Bake them in the centre to lower part of the oven at 180–190°C (350–375°F) for approximately 1–1¼ hours, turning them over after 35 minutes. Test with the point of a knife, which should penetrate to the centre of the potato without undue pressure, then remove them from the oven.

3. Cut across one-third of the way down the length of the potato, the base being the flatter, deep part.

4. Remove the cooked potato with a dessertspoon, retaining the larger piece, i.e. the base.

5. Pass the potato through a sieve with pressure, mix with the butter, add 3 level teaspoons (10 g) salt, ½ level teaspoon (2 g) white pepper and the yolk of an egg. Mix well.

6. Using a piping bag and a 10 mm star tube, pipe a scroll of the potato around the top edge of the baked potato base casing. Dry slightly in the hot oven and egg wash.

7. Put a tablespoon of the sauce in the casing and place the hot, well-drained eggs on top.

8. Mask over the eggs with the sauce to the level of the potato, then sprinkle evenly with the cheese.

9. Colour them golden brown under the salamander, or in the top of a hot oven.

10. Serve on a hot, flat dish with dish paper and garnish between the potatoes with washed sprigs of parsley.

### 530          Oeufs pochés portugaise

| 8 portions | Ingredients | 10 couverts |
|---|---|---|
| 8 | poached eggs (517) | 10 |
| 8 × 2½ oz | large tomatoes (M) | 10 × 70 g |
| 1 pint | tomato sauce (370) | 700 ml |
| 1 oz | finely chopped onion | 35 g |
| 1 oz | butter | 35 g |
| 2 teaspoons | chopped parsley | 5 g |
| ½ pod | garlic | ½ pod |

### Method

1. Remove the stalk base (eye) of the tomato then blanch in boiling water for 6–10 seconds, refresh and peel them.

2. From the opposite end to the stalk base, cut across the tomato approximately three-eighths of the way down. Remove the seeds from all pieces with a teaspoon.

3. Place the larger base cases in a buttered shallow tray or sauteuse, season lightly and brush with melted butter.

4. Cut the smaller pieces of tomato into 10 mm dice.

5. Sweat the onion in the butter in a small covered saucepan for 4–5 minutes, without colouring.

6. Add the finely chopped garlic and tomato sauce, boil, add the diced tomato and simmer for 5 minutes.

7. Heat the tomato cases in a cool oven at 120°C (250°F)

for 2–3 minutes; do not overcook as this causes the cases to collapse.

8. Place the tomato cases into a hot earthenware dish and place one hot well-drained egg in each. Mask over with the sauce, so that it covers the base of the dish, and sprinkle a little chopped parsley in the centre of each egg.

9. Serve on an underflat with dish paper.

## 531 Oeufs pochés princesse

**Method**

1. Place the hot drained eggs into warm short-paste tartlets in a hot earthenware dish.

2. Mask over with Sauce suprême (400), covering the base of the dish.

3. Garnish the top of each egg with 2 or 3 short asparagus tips, heated in butter.

4. Serve on an underflat on a dish paper.

## 532 Oeufs pochés Washington

| 8 portions | Ingredients | 10 couverts |
|---|---|---|
| 8 | poached eggs (517) | 10 |
| 8 | short paste tartlets | 10 |
| 1 × 14 oz | tin creamed corn | 500 g |
| 1 pint | sauce suprême (400) | 700 ml |
| 2 fl. oz | cream | 70 ml |
| 2 teaspoons | chopped parsley | 5 g |

**Method**

1. Drain the creamed corn and place it into a saucepan, with just enough sauce to bind the corn. Bring to the boil.

2. Warm the tartlet cases in an earthenware dish and three-quarters fill with the corn.

3. Add the remainder of the corn and cream to the boiling sauce, mask the sauce over the eggs and cover the base of the dish.

4. Place a sprinkling of parsley on the centre of each egg.

5. Serve on an underflat with dish paper.

## 533 BASIC PREPARATION OF OEUFS EN COCOTTE

**Method**

1. Using a clean brush, well grease the egg cocottes with butter. Lightly season with mixed salt and white pepper (4 to 1). For recipes requiring a preparation in the base of the cocotte, take a slightly larger size.

2. Break the eggs into the prepared cocottes and place them into a shallow pan with hot water half-way up the side of the cocottes.

3. Bring to the boil, cover and allow to cook on the side of the stove or in the oven at 150°C (300°F) for 3–4 minutes, until lightly set. Finish as per recipe.

## 534 Oeufs en cocotte à la crème

**Method**

1. Prepare as for Oeufs en cocotte (533).

2. When cooked, mask over the egg surface with a dessert-spoon of hot cream.

3. Wipe around the cocottes. Serve on an underflat on a dish paper.

## 535 Oeufs en cocotte au jus

**Method**

1. Prepare as for Oeufs en cocotte à la crème (534).

2. Replace the cream with boiling jus-lié (409).

## 536 Oeufs en cocotte à la reine

| 8 portions | Ingredients | 10 couverts |
|---|---|---|
| 8 | eggs | 10 |
| 1 oz | butter | 35 g |
| 4 oz | cooked poached chicken | 140 g |
| ¼ pint | sauce suprême | 175 ml |
| 3 fl. oz | cream | 100 ml |

**Method**

1. Cut the chicken into 5 mm dice and place it in a small saucepan. Add sufficient sauce to bind the chicken, heat it to boiling point and season.

2. Butter and season the cocottes and divide the prepared chicken into them to a depth of approximately 5 mm.

3. Break in the eggs and cook them as in basic preparation (533).

4. Mask the eggs with the hot cream.

5. Serve on an underflat with dish paper.

## 537 Oeufs en cocotte bergère

| 8 portions | Ingredients | 10 couverts |
|---|---|---|
| 8 | eggs | 10 |
| 1 oz | butter | 35 g |
| 4 oz | cooked lamb | 140 g |
| ¼ pint | jus-lié (409) | 175 m |
| 2 fl. oz | meat glaze (353) | 70 ml |

**Method**

1. Prepare as for Oeufs en cocotte à la reine (536), replacing the chicken and sauce with 5 mm of diced lamb and jus-lié.

2. When cooked, run a thread (cordon) of hot meat glaze around the white of each egg.

### 538 Oeufs en cocotte petit duc

| 8 portions | Ingredients | 10 couverts |
|---|---|---|
| 8 | eggs | 10 |
| 2 oz | butter | 70 g |
| 8 oz | asparagus tips | 280 g |
| ¼ pint | sauce périgueux (379) | 175 ml |

**Method**

1. Cut the cooked or tinned asparagus tips 40 mm long from the head and the remainder into 5 mm dice. Heat both lots in a little butter.

2. Grease and season the cocottes. Divide the diced asparagus into the bottom of each cocotte.

3. Break in the eggs and cook them as in basic preparation (533).

4. Mask the eggs with the boiling sauce and place 2–3 hot asparagus tips across the yolk.

5. Serve on an underflat with dish paper.

### 539 Oeufs en cocotte portugaise

| 8 portions | Ingredients | 10 couverts |
|---|---|---|
| 8 | eggs | 10 |
| 2 oz | butter | 70 g |
| 1 lb | tomatoes | 560 g |
| 1 oz | finely chopped onion | 35 g |
| ½ pod | garlic | ½ pod |
| ¼ pint | tomato sauce (370) | 175 ml |

**Method**

1. Prepare the onion, tomatoes and half the butter into cooked Tomate concassée (337), adding the finely chopped garlic.

2. Place this mixture into the bottoms of the prepared greased and seasoned cocottes.

3. Cook as in basic preparation (533).

4. Run a thread of the sauce around the white of the eggs when cooked. Wipe the cocottes.

5. Serve on an underflat with dish paper.

## 540 BASIC PREPARATION OF SCRAMBLED EGGS — OEUFS BROUILLÉS

It is normal trade practice to serve this type of egg dish individually so that only the garnishes are given in the recipes, and these should be used with the basic preparation.

| 8 portions | Ingredients | 10 couverts |
|---|---|---|
| 16 | eggs | 20 |
| 4 oz | butter | 140 g |
| 4 level teaspoons | salt | 15 g |
| ½ level teaspoon | ground white pepper | 2 g |
| 2 fl. oz | cream (if desired) | 70 ml |

**Method**

1. Break the eggs into a basin, whisk lightly until all the whites are thoroughly broken down and mixed in, then add the seasoning.

2. Melt half the butter in a sauteuse, pour in the eggs and stir with a wooden spatule over a medium heat. Continue stirring, clearing the sides and bottom edges of the sauteuse until the eggs are a light creamy consistency, then remove them from the heat.

3. Thoroughly mix in the remainder of the butter until it is all absorbed. Stir in the cream, if used.

4. Serve in a loose dome shape in individual hot egg dishes placed on an underflat with dish paper.

### 541 Scrambled eggs with mushrooms — Oeufs brouillés aux champignons

| 8 portions | Additional ingredients | 10 couverts |
|---|---|---|
| 12 oz | closed mushrooms | 280 g |
| 1½ oz | butter | 50 g |
| 2 teaspoons | chopped parsley | 5 g |

**Method**

1. Wash, peel, then thinly slice the mushrooms.

2. Melt the butter in a sauteuse then add the mushrooms and a little salt and white ground pepper. Cover and cook gently for 5–6 minutes, until tender. Keep hot.

3. Prepare the basic scrambled eggs (540).

4. Serve the egg in a loose dome shape in individual hot egg dishes, and place the divided mushrooms in the centre on top. Sprinkle the mushroom with a little chopped parsley.

5. Place the dishes on an underflat with dish papers.

### 542 Scrambled eggs with croûtons — Oeufs brouillés aux croûtons

**Method**

1. Prepare 1 dessertspoon of 5 mm diced fried, bread croûtons, and four 25 mm triangular croûtons per portion (dip the triangular croûtons in melted butter and lightly grill or fry on each side).

2. Prepare the basic scrambled eggs (540).

3. Serve in a loose dome shape in individual hot egg dishes, with the diced croûtons in the centre on top of the eggs and the triangular ones spaced evenly around the edges.
4. Place on an underflat with dish paper.

### 543 Scrambled eggs with fresh herbs — Oeufs brouillés aux fines herbes

**Method**

1. Wash, drain and finely chop enough fresh parsley, chives, tarragon and chervil to allow ½ a teaspoon per portion.
2. Prepare the basic scrambled eggs (540).
3. Stir in the chopped herbs, when the eggs are cooked, with the butter.
4. Serve in a loose dome shape in individual hot egg dishes on an underflat with dish paper.

### 544 Scrambled eggs with chicken livers — Oeufs brouillés aux foies de volaille

**Method**

1. Clean, then cut into 10 mm scallops, 1 oz (30 g) of chicken livers per portion.
2. Barely cover the bottom of a frying pan with oil, heat until smoking, add the livers and lightly season with salt and milled pepper. Toss them over a fierce heat for 2–3 minutes then place them into a saucepan and add enough demi-glace (369) to bind.
3. Serve the eggs in a loose dome shape in hot egg dishes, with the chicken livers on top in the centre. Sprinkle the liver with chopped parsley.
4. Place on an underflat with dish paper.

### 545 Scrambled eggs with ham — Oeufs brouillés au jambon

**Method**

1. Cut one 25 × 10 mm wide diamond of sliced ham, and ½ oz (15 g) of lean 5 mm diced ham per portion.
2. Prepare the basic scrambled eggs (540), and add the diced ham, when the eggs are cooked, with the butter.
3. Serve the eggs in a loose dome shape in hot individual egg dishes and place a diamond of ham in the centre.
4. Place on an underflat with dish paper.

### 546 Scrambled egg with asparagus — Oeufs brouillés aux pointes d'asperges

**Method**

1. Heat in butter 3–4 asparagus tips per portion.
2. Prepare the basic scrambled eggs (540).
3. Serve the eggs in a loose dome shape in hot individual egg dishes, and arrange asparagus tips on top in the centre.
4. Place on an underflat with dish paper.

### 547 — Oeufs brouillés chasseur

**Method**

1. Prepare a garnish of chicken livers as for Oeufs brouillés aux foies de volaille (544) and add half this quantity of mushrooms, as prepared in Oeufs brouillés aux champignons (541).
2. Serve as for Oeufs brouillés aux foies de volaille (544).

*Note.* May be bound with Sauce chasseur (374).

### 548 — Oeufs brouillés à la forestière

**Method**

1. Prepare half the quantity of mushrooms as for Oeufs brouillés aux champignons (541).
2. Cut ½ oz (15 g) streaky bacon into very small lardons 10 × 3 × 3 mm. Blanch, drain, lightly fry, then mix it with the cooked mushrooms.
3. Prepare the basic scrambled eggs (540).
4. Serve the eggs in a loose dome shape in hot individual egg dishes and place the garnish on top, in the centre. Sprinkle the garnish with a little chopped parsley.
5. Place on an underflat with dish paper.

### 549 Scrambled egg with tomato — Oeufs brouillés aux tomates

**Method**

1. Using 2 lb (1 kg) tomatoes, 2 oz (70 g) finely chopped onion and 2 oz (70 g) butter, prepare a cooked Tomate concassée (337).
2. Prepare and serve the basic scrambled eggs (540). Place the garnish of cooked tomato on top in the centre and sprinkle the garnish with chopped parsley.

**550**                              Oeufs brouillés portugaise

**Method**

1. Prepare as for scrambled egg with tomato (549).

2. When cooking the tomato, add 1 pod of peeled and finely chopped garlic to the onion.

## 551 BASIC PREPARATION OF      OMELETTES OMELETS

The cooking of omelets calls for some degree of skill and quick movement, and practice is the only method whereby a satisfactory standard can be attained. It is vital that everything is prepared and available before cooking.

Omelets are classified as follows:

(a) rolled omelets, where the garnish is cooked with the eggs.

(b) rolled omelets, where the garnish is placed inside and/ or on top; when the garnish is inside, the omelets are known as stuffed (fourrées) omelets.

(c) flat omelets, mainly cooked thus because the extensive garnish, or its shape, prevents rolling.

(d) sweet omelets, which vary in preparation according to the recipe.

**Method**

1. Clean the omelet pan thoroughly with a cloth. If necessary, first place a little oil in the pan with coarse salt. Heat until smoking, knock out the salt, wipe with paper then a cloth.

2. Use 2–3 eggs per portion. Break the eggs into a wooden or china basin and add a few grains of salt and ground white pepper.

3. Beat the eggs vigorously with a fork until the whites are thoroughly broken down with the yolks. Failure to mix well results in white streaks in the cooked omelet.

4. Heat the cleaned omelet pan, add ½ oz (15 g) of butter per portion and move the butter around to prevent the butter colouring in any part of the pan.

5. When the butter is foaming, but not coloured, pour in the eggs quickly then, using a fork in the right hand, move the mixture in a circular motion until it becomes a light creamy texture.

6. Stop stirring, set over the gas for 5 seconds only, remove from the heat and tap the pan on the edge of the stove.

7. Holding the omelet pan in the left hand, slightly raise the handle, then, with the inside of the fork, begin to roll the edge nearest the handle towards the opposite side, until just over halfway across. Where a garnish is placed inside an omelet, it is added into the cavity at this stage.

8. Knock the base of the handle with the clenched right hand; this will make the far side of the omelet come up and roll inwards.

9. Still keeping the handle upwards, press the two rolled edges together in a straight line with the back of the fork. Return the pan over the gas, holding the handle upwards in the right hand, and set the omelet into shape for 5 seconds.

10. Hold a warm oval dish in the left hand at an angle of 45° then roll the omelet on to the centre of the dish and serve immediately.

11. Should the omelet be slightly mis-shapen, place a clean cloth over its surface and correct the shape.

**552 Plain omelet**                **Omelette nature**

**Method**

Prepare and serve as for basic omelet (551).

**553 Mushroom omelet**      **Omelette aux champignons**

**Method**

1. Prepare the same quantity of mushroms as in Scrambled eggs with mushrooms (541, 1 and 2 in method).

2. Prepare and serve as for basic omelet (551), adding the cooked mushrooms to the butter when it is melted.

**554 Shrimp omelet**          **Omelette aux crevettes**

**Method**

1. Allow 1 oz (30 g) peeled pink shrimps per portion and add sufficient shrimp sauce (628), or cream sauce (389), to bind them. Heat together until boiling point.

2. When rolling the omelet, add a dessertspoon of the shrimps and complete the omelet.

3. Make a 25 mm incision in the centre of the omelet.

4. Place another dessertspoon of shrimps on top, sprinkle them with chopped parsley and serve.

*Note.* The incision allows the sauce to drain into the omelet.

**555 Omelet with chicken**      **Omelette aux foies de**
     **livers**                                    **volaille**

**Method**

1. Prepare the same quantity of chicken livers as in Scrambled eggs with chicken livers (544).

2. Prepare as for basic omelet (551).

3. Make a 25 mm incision in the centre of the omelet, place a tablespoon of the chicken liver in the centre of the omelet and sprinkle it with chopped parsley.

### 556 Cheese omelet        Omelette au fromage

**Method**

1. Allow 1 oz (30 g) of grated Parmesan cheese per portion.
2. Prepare as for basic omelet (551), and, when the mixture is creamy, sprinkle the eggs with half the cheese.
3. Complete the omelet and, when finished, sprinkle the surface evenly with the remainder of the cheese.

### 557 Omelet with fresh herbs     Omelette aux fines herbes

**Method**

1. When mixing the eggs, add 1 teaspoon of finely chopped fresh herbs (parsley, chives, tarragon, chervil) for each portion.
2. Prepare as for basic omelet (551).

### 558 Ham omelet         Omelette au jambon

**Method**

1. Cut one 25 × 10 mm wide diamond of sliced ham, and ½ oz (15 g) of lean 5 mm diced-ham per portion.
2. Prepare as for basic omelet, adding the diced ham to the butter when it is melted. Complete the omelet and, when finished, decorate in the centre with a diamond of ham.

### 559 Bacon omelet         Omelette au lard

**Method**

1. Allow 1 oz (30 g) of sliced and skinned streaky bacon per portion and cut it into 5 mm strips.
2. Prepare the mixture as for basic omelet (551) and add the bacon to the melted butter. Fry gently for 1 minute, turn up the gas and complete making the omelet.

### 560 Tomato omelet       Omelette aux tomates

**Method**

1. Take 2 lb (1 kg) tomatoes, 2 oz (70 g) finely chopped onions and 2 oz (70 g) butter, and prepare them into a cooked Tomates concassées (337).
2. Prepare as for basic omelet (551). When half rolled, add a dessertspoon of the cooked tomato then complete the omelet.

3. Make a 25 mm incision in the centre of the omelet and place a dessertspoon of the tomato on top. Sprinkle the tomato with chopped parsley.

### 561 Kidney omelet       Omelette aux rognons

**Method**

1. Allow 1 oz (30 g) lambs kidneys per portion.
2. Cut the kidneys in half, lengthways, remove the skin, cut out the core, then cut them into 10 mm scallops.
3. Just cover the base of a frying pan with oil, heat until smoking, add the kidney and season with salt and milled pepper. Fry over a fierce heat for 2–3 minutes then place it in a saucepan and add sufficient demi-glace (369) to bind.
4. Prepare as for basic omelet (551).
5. Make a 25 mm incision in the centre of the omelet, place a tablespoon of the kidney in the centre and sprinkle it with chopped parsley.

### 562            Omelette bonne femme

**Method**

1. Allow ½ oz (15 g) closed mushrooms per portion and prepare and cook them as in Scrambled egg with mushrooms (541, 1 and 2 in method).
2. Allow ½ oz (15 g) cooked shredded onion per portion (565).
3. Allow ½ oz (15 g) skinned and sliced streaky bacon per portion and cut it into 5 mm strips.
4. Prepare as for basic omelet (551). Add the bacon to the melted butter and cook it gently for 1 minute; turn up the heat, add the onion and mushroom and complete the omelet.

### 563            Omelette chasseur

**Method**

1. Allow 1 oz (30 g) of chicken livers per portion and prepare them as in Scrambled egg with chicken livers (544).
2. Allow ½ oz (15 g) of closed mushrooms per portion and prepare and cook them as in 541, then add them to the livers.
3. Prepare as for basic omelet (551). Make a 25 mm incision in the centre of the omelet, place a tablespoon of the garnish in the centre of the omelet and sprinkle it with chopped parsley. Cover the base of the dish with a thin sauce demi-glace (369).

**564 Spinach omelet**     **Omelette à la florentine**

**Method**

1. Allow 2 lb (1 kg) fresh spinach, prepared as for Épinards en branche (1017).
2. Prepare as for basic omelet (551); when half rolled, place a tablespoon of the hot leaf spinach inside the cavity then complete the omelet.

**565 Onion omelette**     **Omelette lyonnaise**

**Method**

1. Peel and finely shred 1 lb (560 g) of onions.
2. Melt 2 oz (70 g) of butter in a frying pan, add the onions and cook them gently for 7–8 minutes to a light golden-brown colour, tossing frequently.
3. Prepare as for basic omelet (551), adding a dessertspoon of the cooked onion to the butter when it is melted.

**566 Potato omelet**     **Omelette Parmentier**

**Method**

1. Allow 2 oz (55 g) per portion of peeled potato cut into 5 mm dice and thoroughly dried on a cloth.
2. Heat 3 mm of oil in a frying pan. When smoking, add the potato and fry it rapidly until a light golden-brown colour then drain in a colander.
3. Prepare as for basic omelet (551), adding a tablespoon of the cooked potato to the butter when it is melted.

**567 FLAT OMELETS**

Few omelets fall into this category and the best known are given in the following recipes.

**Method of preparation**

1. The garnish is usually added to the butter when it is melted.
2. Prepare as for basic omelet (551) to the end of 6 in the method.
3. After tapping the pan to free the bottom of the omelet, lightly push the loose edges inwards with the back of the fork, then toss the omelet over on to the other side.
4. Replace over the gas for 10 seconds to set.
5. Slide the omelet out on to a service plate, cover and serve immediately. Flat omelets are not generally served on silver.

**568 Spanish omelet**     **Omelette à l'espagnole**

**Method**

1. Prepare 1 lb (560 g) tomatoes into 5 mm raw dice (336, 5b). Prepare and cook 8 oz (280 g) onions as for Omelette lyonnaise (565). Cut 4 oz (140 g) of tinned red pimento into 25 mm julienne.
2. Prepare as for flat omelet (567), adding the garnish to the butter when it is melted.

**569**     **Omelette à la fermière**

**Method**

1. For each portion, cut ½ oz (15 g) of lean ham into 5 mm dice and add it to the butter when melted.
2. Add ½ teaspoon (1 g) of chopped parsley to each portion of eggs.
3. Prepare as for flat omelet (567).

**570**     **Omelette à la paysanne**

**Method**

1. For each portion, prepare 2 oz (55 g) peeled potatoes as for Omelette Parmentier (566) and 2 oz (55 g) of onion as for Omelette lyonnaise (565).
2. Cut ½ oz (15 g) of skinned and sliced streaky bacon into 5 mm strips across the width.
3. Add the strips of bacon to the melted butter in the omelet, fry gently for 1 minute then add the potato and onion. Turn up the gas and finish as for flat omelet (567).

**571 SWEET OMELETS**

There are very few of this type of omelet. Those which are not true omelets, but which bear the name, are dealt with in the Pastry section.

**572 Jam omelet**     **Omelette à la confiture**

**Method**

1. Select a jam that is well jellied, i.e. apricot, red currant jelly, gooseberry, blackcurrant.
2. Prepare as for basic omelet (551), then, when half rolled, place a dessertspoon of the jam in the cavity, and complete the omelet.
3. Sprinkle the omelet surface with castor sugar, using a dredger. With a previously heated red-hot poker, mark a trellis pattern, with 25 mm divisions, across the omelet and serve.

**573 Rum omelet**              **Omelette au rhum**

**Method**

1. Prepare as for Jam omelet (572), using apricot jam.
2. The omelet is finished in the restaurant by pouring 1 fl. oz (30 ml) of rum over the omelet and flaming (flambé).

**574 BASIC PREPARATION OF OEUFS SUR LE PLAT**

**Method**

1. Thickly butter the special fireproof egg dishes and sprinkle lightly with mixed salt and pepper (4 to 1).
2. Heat on the side of the stove then break in 1 or 2 eggs, according to portion. Set the yolks in the centre of the dish by holding in position, if necessary.
3. Place on a baking sheet and cook in the oven at 150°C (300°F), or under a cool salamander, until the white is just set.
4. Serve immediately on an underflat with a doily.

**575**          **Oeufs sur le plat à la crème**

**Method**

Prepare as for basic preparation (574). When nearly cooked, mask over with a tablespoon of cream.

**576**          **Oeufs sur le plat au beurre noir**

**Method**

1. Prepare as for basic preparation (574).
2. Melt 1 oz (30 g) per portion of butter in a frying pan, heat it until the butter turns dark brown, then add 1 teaspoon of vinegar. Pour the mixture over the egg.

**577**          **Oeufs sur le plat aux crevettes**

**Method**

1. Allow 1 oz (30 g) of peeled pink shrimps per portion, add sufficient shrimp sauce (628), or cream sauce (389) to bind them, then heat to boiling point.
2. Prepare as for basic preparation (574); when cooked, place a tablespoon of the garnish on the side of the yolk and sprinkle the garnish with chopped parsley.

**578**          **Oeufs sur le plat aux foies de volaille**

**Method**

1. Allow 1 oz (30 g) of chicken livers per portion and prepare them as in recipe 544, 1 and 2 in method.

2. Prepare as for basic preparation (574); when cooked, place a tablespoon of the garnish on the side of the yolk and sprinkle the garnish with chopped parsley.

**579**          **Oeufs sur le plat au lard**

**Method**

1. Allow two small slices of skinned streaky bacon per portion and grill them very lightly on both sides.
2. Prepare as for basic preparation (574). When heating the egg dishes, lay in the 2 slices of bacon, break the egg or eggs on top and complete cooking.

**580**          **Oeufs sur le plat Bercy**

**Method**

1. Allow 2 chipolata sausages per portion.
2. Grill them till golden-brown, allowing 3 minutes on each side under a moderate salamander.
3. Prepare as for basic preparation (574). When cooked, place a grilled sausage on each side of the yolk and cover the white with boiling tomato sauce (370).

**581**          **Oeufs sur le plat chasseur**

**Method**

1. Allow 1 oz (30 g) of chicken livers per portion and prepare them as in recipe 544.
2. Allow ½ oz (15 g) closed mushrooms per portion. Prepare and cook them as in recipe 541, add them to the livers and bind with Sauce madère (378).
3. Prepare as for basic preparation (574). When cooked, place a tablespoon of the garnish alongside the yolk and sprinkle it with chopped parsley.

**582**          **Oeufs sur le plat Meyerbeer**

**Method**

1. Allow one small lambs kidney per portion. Cut through the kidney three-quarters of the way towards the core, remove the skin then cut out the core. Place a skewer through the kidney to keep it open. Season with salt and pepper and brush it with oil. Place the cut side down on a tray, then grill for 3–4 minutes and turn over and grill the other side for 3–4 minutes.
2. Prepare as for basic preparation (541).
3. Serve half a grilled kidney on each side of the yolk. Cover the white with Sauce Périgueux (379).

## 583                  Oeufs sur le plat Opéra

**Method**

1. Allow 1 oz (30 g) of chicken livers per portion. Prepare and cook them as in recipe 544, binding with Sauce madère (378).
2. Heat 2–3 asparagus tips per portion in butter.
3. Prepare as for basic preparation (541).
4. Serve the chicken livers on one side of the yolk, the asparagus tips on the opposite side.

## 584               Oeufs sur le plat portugaise

**Method**

1. Take 2 lb (1 kg) tomatoes, 2 oz (70 g) finely chopped onion and 2 oz (70 g) butter.
2. Prepare into a cooked Tomates concassées (337), adding ½ a pod of peeled, very finely chopped garlic.
3. Prepare as for basic preparation (541).
4. Serve a dessertspoon of the garnish on each side of the yolk and sprinkle it with chopped parsley.

## 585 FRIED EGGS             OEUFS FRITS

**Method**

1. Allow 1 or 2 eggs per portion.
2. Melt ½ oz (15 g) butter or clarified bacon fat in an omelet pan, break in the eggs and season them lightly with a little mixed salt and ground white pepper.
3. Cook over moderate heat until the white is just set, then lift them with a slice or palette knife on to a hot service plate and serve immediately.

## 586 Fried eggs with bacon       Oeufs frits au lard

**Method**

1. Prepare the eggs as in recipe 585.
2. Garnish with 2–3 grilled slices of bacon. (Generally, back and streaky bacon are both served.) Place the skinned and sliced bacon on trays and grill on each side for 1–2 minutes under a moderate salamander.

## 587 Fried eggs, French style      Oeufs frits à la française

**Method**

1. Heat enough oil in a frying pan to give a depth of 25 mm. During heating, insert a wooden spatula in the oil to remove any moisture.
2. Break each egg separately into a saucer and season with mixed salt and ground white pepper.

3. When the oil shows a light blue vapour, add the egg. Quickly envelop the yolk by shaping the white around it with the spatula. Fry until golden brown for 2–3 minutes.
4. Remove with a slice and drain on a cloth.
5. Used generally for garnish.
6. When served as an egg dish, place 2 eggs on a hot silver flat dish on a doily and serve hot Tomato sauce (370) in a sauceboat on an underdish with a doily.

## UNCLASSIFIED EGG DISHES

## 588                        Oeufs à l'aurore

**Method**

1. Prepare as for Oeufs Chimay (589), replacing the Sauce Mornay with Sauce aurore (396). When preparing the Sauce aurore, whisk in two yolks of eggs before passing the sauce.

## 589                          Oeufs Chimay

| 8 portions | Ingredients | 10 couverts |
|---|---|---|
| 8 | hard boiled eggs | 10 |
| 8 oz | mushrooms or trimmings | 280 g |
| 2 oz | finely chopped onion | 70 g |
| 1 oz | butter | 35 g |
| 2 oz | Parmesan cheese | 70 g |
| 1 pint | sauce mornay (390) | 700 ml |

**Method**

1. Make a duxelle (338) from the butter, onion and mushrooms.
2. Cut the shelled eggs in halves, lengthways, remove the yolk, cut it into rough 5 mm dice and mix it with the duxelle. Check the seasoning.
3. Using a dessertspoon, fill the egg whites, in a dome shape, with the mixture.
4. Place the halves of egg into a buttered oval earthenware dish. Mask the eggs with the sauce and cover the base of the dish. Sprinkle evenly with the cheese.
5. Colour golden brown under a moderate salamander, finish in a moderate oven for 1–2 minutes to heat through.
6. Serve on an underflat with dish paper.

## 590 Egg croquettes            Croquettes d'oeufs

| 8 portions | Ingredients | 10 couverts |
|---|---|---|
| 12 | hard boiled eggs | 15 |
| 1¼ pints | sauce béchamel (366) | 875 ml |
| 8 oz | white breadcrumbs | 280 g |
| 2 | eggs | 3 |
| 2 | yolks of egg | 3 |
| ½ oz | salt | 20 g |
| ½ level teaspoon | ground white pepper | 2 g |
| 3 oz | flour | 100 g |

## Method

1. Reduce the béchamel by just over one-third in a thick-bottomed shallow pan.

2. Add the shelled eggs cut into a rough 5 mm dice with the seasoning. Reboil, add the yolks of egg, mix thoroughly and remove from the heat.

3. Pour on to a greased tray and cover with a greased paper. Allow to go cold.

4. Divide into 16 or 20 pieces. Using the flour mould, egg and crumb into croquettes 50 × 25 mm in diameter. (See 310.)

5. Deep fry, at 180°C (360°F), 8–10 pieces at a time then drain.

6. Serve on a hot flat dish on dish paper and garnish with sprigs of fried parsley. Serve ½ pint (350 ml) of Tomato sauce (370) or Piquant sauce (381) in a sauceboat on an underdish with a doily.

## 591 Curried eggs — Oeufs à l'indienne

| 8 portions | Ingredients | 10 couverts |
| --- | --- | --- |
| 8 | hard boiled eggs | 10 |
| 8 oz | patna rice | 280 g |
| 1 pint | curry sauce (413) | 700 ml |
| 2 teaspoons | chopped parsley | 5 g |

## Method

1. Rain the picked and washed rice into plenty of salted water. Stir until reboiling, then boil gently for 16–18 minutes until just cooked. Thoroughly wash off the starch under cold water and drain well.

2. Place the rice in a shallow buttered tray and cover it with a buttered paper. Heat it in the bottom of an oven at 120–150°C (250–300°F).

3. Place the shelled hard-boiled eggs into boiling salted water for 1 minute to reheat.

4. Dress the rice loosely in an earthenware or silver dish. Cut the eggs in halves lengthways and dress, flat side down, on the rice.

5. Mask over with the boiling curry sauce. Sprinkle the chopped parsley on the centre of each half egg.

## 592 Scotch eggs

| 8 portions | Ingredients | 10 couverts |
| --- | --- | --- |
| 8 | hard boiled eggs | 10 |
| 1½ lb | pork sausage meat (263) | 840 g |
| 3 oz | flour | 100 g |
| 8 oz | white breadcrumbs | 280 g |
| 2 | eggs | 3 |

## Method

1. Divide the sausage meat into 3 oz (85 g) pieces, flatten to 10 mm in thickness and wrap around the shelled hard-boiled egg.

2. Using a little flour, mould between the hands to eliminate all cracks in the sausage meat.

3. Pass through the beaten eggs and breadcrumbs then lightly roll between the hands to firm the crumbs.

4. Deep fry at 140°C (280°F) for 10 minutes, to a golden brown colour. Do not use a higher temperature.

5. Drain then serve on a hot flat dish on a dish paper garnished with sprigs of fried parsley. Serve separately, in a sauceboat on an underdish with a doily, ½ pint (350 ml) of Tomato (370) or Piquant sauce (381).

6. When served cold, garnish with a salad and serve Sauce vinaigrette (7).

## 593 Egg mayonnaise — Mayonnaise d'oeuf
## Method

1. When served as an egg dish, allow 1–2 eggs per portion. Prepare as for Hors d'oeuvre (71).

# Farinaceous dishes

# Farinaceous dishes

## 594 FARINACEOUS DISHES

This group of dishes contains a considerable amount of starch foods which possess little individual flavour. For this reason it is essential that the following points are observed.
(a) The finished dish must be very hot.
(b) The amount of seasoning should be adequate.
(c) Sauces and fillings should be highly flavoured and seasoned. Although normally only found on luncheon menus, these dishes, particularly spaghetti, are also used considerably as garnishes.

The quantities given in the recipes are those required for serving the dish as a main course; when used as a garnish, two-thirds of the amount is sufficient.

---

## SPAGHETTI

### 595 Spaghetti au gratin

| 8 portions | Ingredients | 10 couverts |
|---|---|---|
| 10 oz | spaghetti | 350 g |
| 2 oz | butter | 70 g |
| 4 oz | grated Parmesan cheese | 140 g |
| ½ oz | salt | 20 g |
| ½ level teaspoon | milled pepper | 2 g |
| ¼ level teaspoon | grated nutmeg | 1 g |
| 1½ pints | cream sauce (389) | 1 litre |

### Method

1. Drop the spaghetti into plenty of boiling salted water, reboil and allow to cook gently, stirring occasionally to separate the strands.
2. After 16–18 minutes, test it by biting a piece of the spaghetti. If it is cooked, a suspicion of firmness should remain. Drain in a colander.
3. If it is not needed immediately, place under running cold water to clear the starch then drain thoroughly in a colander. Reheat in boiling salted water for 1 minute when required, then drain.
4. Melt the butter in a clean shallow pan, add the sphaghetti and season it with salt and milled pepper. Lightly fork it over until it becomes very hot. Add half the cheese and the boiling sauce and combine them thoroughly. Correct the seasoning.
5. Place the spaghetti into a buttered earthenware dish and sprinkle the surface evenly with the remaining cheese.
6. Colour golden brown under the salamander or at the top of an oven at 200°C (400°F).
7. Serve on an underdish with dish paper.

### 596 Spaghetti bolonaise

| 8 portions | Ingredients | 10 couverts |
|---|---|---|
| 10 oz | spaghetti | 350 g |
| 3 oz | butter | 100 g |
| 3 oz | grated Parmesan cheese | 100 g |
| 8 oz | lean beef (good quality) | 280 g |
| 2 oz | finely chopped onion | 70 g |
| ½ pod | garlic | ½ pod |
| 1 oz | fat bacon | 35 g |
| ¾ oz | salt | 25 g |
| 1 level teaspoon | milled pepper | 3 g |
| 1 pint | demi-glace (369) | 700 ml |

### Method

1. Place 1 oz (35 g) of the butter in a saucepan, add the finely chopped fat bacon and cook it gently for 2 minutes. Add the finely chopped onion, cover the pan and sweat the onion for 4–5 minutes, then add the peeled finely chopped garlic.
2. Mince the beef on a 3 mm cutter, or chop finely, add it to the onion and stir over a fierce heat until the meat separates
3. Add the demi-glace and half the salt and pepper, boil then simmer gently for 1½ hours, stirring occasionally. Correct the sauce with a little stock if it is too thick.
4. Cook the spaghetti as for Spaghetti au gratin (595) to include 3 in method.

### 5. Service method A

Melt the remainder of the butter in a shallow pan, add the spaghetti and the remainder of salt and pepper and lightly fork the spaghetti over. Add the sauce and combine. Serve the spaghetti in a hot earthenware of silver entree dish, on an underflat with dish paper, with the cheese in a sauceboat on an underdish with a doily.

169

## 6. Service method B

As for A, with both the sauce and cheese served in sauceboats.

### 597                             Spaghetti génoise

#### Method

1. Prepare and serve as for Spaghetti au gratin (595).
2. When combining with the sauce, add 4 oz (140 g) of 5 mm diced mushrooms, cooked 'à blanc' (335g).

### 598                             Spaghetti italienne

| 8 portions | Ingredients | 10 couverts |
|---|---|---|
| 10 oz | spaghetti | 350 g |
| 2 oz | butter | 70 g |
| 4 oz | grated Parmesan cheese | 140 g |
| ½ oz | salt | 15 g |
| ½ level teaspoon | milled pepper | 2 g |
| 3 fl. oz | cream | 110 ml |

#### Method

1. Cook the spaghetti as for Spaghetti au gratin (595) to include 3 in method.
2. Melt the butter in a shallow pan, add the spaghetti and seasoning with half of the cheese, then add the cream and fork the spaghetti over until very hot.
3. Serve it in a loose dome shape in a hot earthenware or silver entrée dish on an underflat with dish paper and serve the remainder of the cheese in a sauceboat on an underdish with a doily.

### 599                             Spaghetti milanaise

#### Method

1. Prepare and serve as for Spaghetti napolitaine (600). When the spaghetti is mixed with the sauce, add the following additional garnish: 2 oz (70 g) each of julienne of ox-tongue, cooked ham and cooked mushroom. The mushroom is cooked 'à blanc' (335g).

### 600                             Spaghetti napolitaine

| 8 portions | Ingredients | 10 couverts |
|---|---|---|
| 10 oz | spaghetti | 350 g |
| 3 oz | butter | 100 g |
| 3 oz | grated Parmesan cheese | 100 g |
| 2 oz | finely chopped onion | 70 g |
| 1 lb | tomatoes | 560 g |
| ½ oz | salt | 15 g |
| ½ level teaspoon | milled pepper | 2 g |
| 1½ pints | tomato sauce (370) | 1 litre |

#### Method

1. Using 1 oz (35 g) of the butter, the tomatoes and onion, prepare a cooked Tomates concassées (337).
2. Cook the spaghetti as for Spaghetti au gratin (595) to include 3 in the method.
3. Melt the remainder of the butter in a shallow pan, add the spaghetti, season, then add the sauce and the cooked tomato. Heat them together until very hot.
4. Serve in a loose dome shape in a hot earthenware or entrée dish on an underflat with dish paper with the cheese in a sauceboat on an underdish with a doily.

### 601                             Spaghetti sicilienne

#### Method

1. Prepare and serve as for Spaghetti italienne (598).
2. Before serving, lightly fork in the following garnish: 2 oz (70 g) finely chopped onion, sweated in 1 oz (35 g) of butter, and 4 oz (140 g) of chicken livers, cut into 5 mm dice and fried rapidly in ½ oz (20 g) butter for 2–3 minutes.

## MACARONI

### 602 Macaroni cheese               Macaroni au gratin

#### Method

1. Prepare and serve as for Spaghetti au gratin (595), replacing the spaghetti with macaroni. When the macaroni is cooked, cut it into approximate 50 mm lengths. Add a level teaspoon of mixed English mustard to the sauce when combining.

### 603 Other macaroni dishes

#### Method

Prepare and serve the macaroni in the same manner as any spaghetti recipes given.

## NOODLES

### 604 Noodles                             Nouilles

| 8 portions | Ingredients | 10 couverts |
|---|---|---|
| 8 oz | strong flour | 280 g |
| 3 level teaspoons | salt | 10 g |
| 2 | eggs | 3 |
| 2 | yolks of egg | 2 |
| 2 tablespoons | olive oil | 50 ml |

## Method

1. Sieve the flour and salt on to the table and make a bay in the centre.

2. Beat the eggs, yolks and oil together and pour the mixture into the bay.

3. Absorb the flour and work into a firm smooth dough. Should the flour be very dry, add 1 tablespoon of milk or water. Divide the mixture into two pieces.

4. Cover completely with a cloth to prevent crusting and let it stand for 15–20 minutes.

5. Using strong flour, dust the board or table, roll each piece into a long thin roll and flatten the roll with the palm of the hand. With a rolling pin, roll out into a rectangle 450 × 200 mm.

6. Hang over a pole to dry, or suspend over the edge of the table with the rolling pin over one end.

7. After 8–10 minutes, dust with flour on both sides then fold the 200 mm width over twice, to reduce to 50 mm. Cut this into 5 mm strips and shake them loosely on to a tray.

8. Place a suitable size pan to boil with 125–150 mm of water with a little salt added. When the water is boiling, drop in the noodles. Reboil, lightly stir, then boil gently for 7 minutes, stirring occasionally.

9. Drain in a colander, or refresh and drain if not required immediately.

## 605 Buttered noodles    Nouilles au beurre

| 8 portions | Ingredients | 10 couverts |
|---|---|---|
| 8 oz flour mix | basic noodles (604) | 280 g flour mix |
| 3 oz | butter | 100 g |
| 3 oz | grated Parmesan cheese | 100 g |
| ½ oz | salt | 20 g |
| ½ level teaspoon | milled pepper | 2 g |
| ¼ level teaspoon | grated nutmeg | 1 g |

## Method

1. Prepare and cook the noodles as in recipe 604.

2. Melt the butter in a shallow pan, add the drained noodles and sprinkle them with the salt, pepper and nutmeg. Fork over gently until thoroughly hot.

3. Serve the noodles in a loose dome shape in a hot earthenware or entrée dish on an underflat with dish paper with the cheese in a sauceboat on an underdish with a doily.

## 606 Buttered green noodles    Nouilles vertes au beurre

### Method

1. When preparing the noodles, add 2 oz (70 g) of very dry spinach purée to the eggs and oil and mix them thoroughly.

2. Then proceed as for Nouilles au beurre (605).

## RAVIOLI

## 607 Ravioli paste    Pâte à ravioli

| 8 portions | Ingredients | 10 couverts |
|---|---|---|
| 8 oz | strong flour | 280 g |
| 3 level teaspoons | salt | 10 g |
| 1¼ fl. oz | olive oil | 50 ml |
| 3¾ fl. oz | cold water | 130 ml |

### Method

1. Sieve the flour and salt on to a table and make a bay. Mix the oil and water together and pour it all into the bay

2. Absorb the flour and knead it to a very smooth dough. Cover completely with a cloth and let it stand for 30 minutes.

## 608 Preparation of ravioli

### Method

1. Divide the rested dough into 2 pieces and cover one.

2. Dust one piece with flour and roll it very thin into a rectangle. Roll this on to the rolling pin, then unroll it on to an oiled piece of greaseproof paper.

3. Brush off any surplus flour and brush the surface with beaten egg.

4. Place the ravioli filling (609) in a piping bag with a 10 mm plain tube.

5. Pipe the filling in small pieces, the size of a hazel nut, 30 mm apart in straight lines down and across the paste.

6. Roll out the other half of the paste to the same size. Roll it on to the rolling pin, then gradually unroll it so that it covers the other piece of paste; allow it to drop between the small mounds of filling. Do not stretch the paste.

7. Using the blunt wide end of a piping tube, press gently between the mounds of filling to seal the two layers of paste.

8. Using a serrated pastry wheel, run along all the edges to trim off all excess paste, which can then be discarded.

9. Run the wheel across between the mounds, then up in the opposite direction to divide the rectangle into 30 mm squares.

10. Pull the paper on to a tray.

11. Place 100–125 mm of water to boil in a suitable pan, adding a little salt. When the water is boiling, pick up the paper at each end, drop one end into the water, then just move the paper in the water to release the ravioli. This eliminates having to pick up each ravioli.

12. Reboil, then simmer for 7 minutes. Lift the ravioli out of the water with a spider and drain it well. Place into a buttered earthenware dish or dishes.

13. Mask over with ½ pint (350 ml) of jus-lié (409) and sprinkle the surface evenly with 2 oz (70 g) grated Parmesan cheese. Colour golden brown under the salamander, then heat in a moderate oven for 2 minutes.

14. Serve on an underflat with dish paper.

### 609  Ravioli filling

**Farce à ravioli**

| 8 portions | Ingredients | 10 couverts |
|---|---|---|
| 8 oz | braised beef or veal | 280 g |
| 2 oz | calves brain (cooked) | 70 g |
| 1 lb | spinach | 560 g |
| 2 oz | finely chopped onion | 70 g |
| 1 oz | butter | 35 g |
| 3 level teaspoons | salt | 10 g |
| ½ level teaspoon | milled pepper | 2 g |
| 2 tablespoons | demi-glace (369) | 50 ml |
| 1 pod | garlic | 1 pod |

### Method

1. Sweat the onion in the butter in a covered pan for 5–6 minutes, then add the peeled, finely chopped garlic and cook them for 2 minutes.

2. Thoroughly wash the spinach and cook it in a little salted boiling water for 10 minutes. Refresh drain and thoroughly squeeze out the water.

3. Roughly dice the meat and add the onion with the spinach, seasoning, brain and sauce. Raise to boiling point.

4. Pass through a 3 mm mincer blade and place the mixture into a basin.

*Note.* Other types of fillings are made by replacing the beef or veal with chicken, cheese or foie gras.

## CANNELONI

### 610

**Canneloni**

| 8 portions | Ingredients | 10 couverts |
|---|---|---|
| 8 oz flour mix | ravioli paste (607) | 280 g flour mix |
| 8 portion mix | ravioli filling (609) | 10 portion mix |
| 2 oz | grated Parmesan cheese | 70 g |
| ½ pint | jus-lié (409) | 350 ml |

### Method

1. Roll out the paste into a very thin rectangle. Dust liberally with strong flour for easy rolling.

2. Roll the paste on to the rolling pin and unroll it on to an oiled sheet of greaseproof paper. Brush off excess flour.

3. Trim the edges with a serrated pastry wheel, then cut it into 60 × 60 mm squares with the wheel. Cut through the incisions in the paste with a pair of scissors to divide the paper into 4 pieces for easy moving.

4. Hold the paper and release the paste into 100–125 mm of boiling salted water and simmer for 7 minutes. With a spider, lift out into a bowl of cold water.

5. Drain the paste on a cloth, spread over or pipe the filling along the edge of the paste, then roll it up.

6. Place the canneloni into a buttered earthenware dish, the seams underneath. Mask over with the jus-lié and sprinkle evenly with the cheese.

7. Colour golden brown in the top of the oven at 200°C (400°F); finish under the salamander if necessary.

8. Serve on an underflat with dish paper.

### 611

**Capelletti al sugo**

| 8 portions | Ingredients | 10 couverts |
|---|---|---|
| 8 oz flour mix | noodle paste (604) | 280 g flour mix |
| 8 portion mix | ravioli filling (609) | 10 couvert mix |
| 1 lb | tomatoes | 560 g |
| ½ pint | jus-lié (409) | 350 ml |
| 2 oz | grated Parmesan cheese | 70 g |

### Method

1. Dust the noodle paste with strong flour and roll it out as thin as possible.

2. Cut out circles of the paste with a 50 mm fluted cutter, then egg-wash the paste.

3. Place the filling in a piping bag with 10 mm plain tube and pipe a mound 25 mm in diameter × 10 mm high in the centre of each circle of paste.

4. Fold one edge of the paste over to meet the other edge and press the edges firmly all round to seal them together.

5. Drop into 100–125 mm of boiling salted water, reboil and simmer for 7 minutes.

6. Lift from the water with a spider, drain well and arrange them half overlapping in a buttered earthenware dish.

7. Prepare the tomatoes into a raw 10 mm dice (336, 5b).

8. Sprinkle the diced tomato over the capelletti, mask over with the jus-lié and sprinkle evenly with the cheese. Brown in the top of the oven at 200°C (400°F).

9. Serve on an underflat with a dish paper.

# GNOCCHI

## 612     Gnocchi parisienne

| 8 portions | Ingredients | 10 couverts |
|---|---|---|
| ½ pint | milk | 350 ml |
| 4 oz | margarine | 140 g |
| 5 oz | flour | 175 g |
| 3 level teaspoons | salt | 10 g |
| 4 | eggs | 5 |
| 1 pint | cream sauce (389) | 700 ml |
| 4 oz | grated Parmesan cheese | 140 g |

### Method

1. Using the milk, margarine, flour, salt and eggs, prepare a choux paste (343). Note that milk is used in place of water.

2. Add half the cheese to the mixture and place it into a piping bag with a 10 mm plain tube.

3. Boil 50–75 mm of water in a shallow pan then remove from the heat. Dip a small knife point in the water. Rest the piping bag on the edge of the pan. Press the piping bag gently and cut the mixture off at 10 mm intervals with the wet knife point.

4. Replace the pan over the heat until nearly boiling, then reduce the heat and poach the gnocchi for 3–4 minutes. Do not boil.

5. Drain the gnocchi carefully in a colander. Return to the pan, add the cream sauce and mix them lightly by moving the pan.

6. Carefully spoon the gnocchi and sauce into a buttered earthenware dish and sprinkle the surface evenly with the remainder of the cheese.

7. Colour golden brown in the top of an oven at 200°C (400°F) and finish, if necessary, under the salamander.

8. Serve on an underflat with dish paper.

## 613     Gnocchi piedmontaise

| 8 portions | Ingredients | 10 couverts |
|---|---|---|
| 2 lb | potatoes (large) | 1 kg |
| 8 oz | flour | 280 g |
| 2 oz | butter | 70 g |
| 3 level teaspoons | salt | 10 g |
| ½ level teaspoon | ground white pepper | 2 g |
| few grains | grated nutmeg | pointe |
| 2 | eggs | 3 |
| 2 | yolks of egg | 2 |
| 2 oz | grated Parmesan cheese | 70 g |
| 1 pint | tomato sauce (370) | 700 ml |

### Method

1. Scrub the potatoes and place them in a shallow tray on a bed of coarse salt. Bake in the centre of an oven at 200°C (400°F) for 1¼–1½ hours; turn them over during cooking.

2. Cut the potatoes in halves, remove the potato from the casings with a spoon and pass this through a sieve with pressure.

3. Place in a basin and add the seasoning and butter. Mix in the sieved flour and beaten egg to bind.

4. Mould the mixture in small quantities, keeping the remainder warm. Dust a board with a little flour, roll the mixture into a round strip 25 mm in diameter then divide it at 10 mm intervals.

5. Using a little flour, mould these pieces into small round balls. Press on one side with the thumb, then mark the thinner side with the back of a fork to form a shell.

6. Place 50–75 mm of water to boil in a shallow pan, adding a little salt. When the water boils, add the gnocchi, bring back to boiling point, reduce the heat and poach gently for 5–6 minutes.

7. Carefully lift out with a perforated spoon, then drain and place into a buttered earthenware dish.

8. Thin the sauce slightly with a little stock, then mask over the gnocchi. Sprinkle the surface with the cheese.

9. Colour golden brown in the top of an oven at 200°C (400°F) or under a moderate salamander.

10. Serve on an underdish with dish paper.

## 614     Gnocchi à la romaine

| 8 portions | Ingredients | 10 couverts |
|---|---|---|
| 8 oz | semolina | 280 g |
| 2 oz | butter | 70 g |
| 6 oz | grated Parmesan cheese | 210 g |
| Few grains | grated nutmeg | few grains |
| 2 | yolks of egg | 3 |
| 2 pints | milk | 1·4 litres |

### Method

1. Boil the milk in a thick bottomed saucepan.

2. Rain in the semolina, stir with a wooden spatule until boiling and add the seasoning. Simmer for 10 minutes.

3. Remove from the heat, add 4 oz (140 g) of cheese, the butter and egg yolks and mix thoroughly.

4. Place into a buttered shallow tray, spreading evenly to a depth of 10 mm and cover with a greased paper.

5. When cold, heat the base of the tray for 2–3 seconds to release. Remove the paper and turn out the contents on to a board.

6. Using a 50 mm round fluted cutter dipped in hot water, cut out crescents 25 mm wide in the centre. Remould the trimmings and use these for more crescents. It may also be cut in 40 mm circles instead of crescents.

7. Neatly arrange the gnocchi in a buttered earthenware dish, slightly overlapping.

8. Brush over with melted butter, sprinkle evenly with the remainder of the cheese.

9. Colour light golden brown in the top of an oven at 200°C (400°F) Finish, if necessary, under a moderate salamander.

10. Serve on an underflat with dish paper.

*Note.* Sauce tomate (370) may be served separately if desired.

## RICE

### 615 Braised rice           Riz pilaff

| 8 portions | Ingredients | 10 couverts |
|---|---|---|
| 8 oz | patna-type rice | 280 g |
| 2 oz | finely chopped onion | 70 g |
| 4 oz | butter | 140 g |
| 3 level teaspoons | salt | 10 g |
| ½ level teaspoon | milled pepper | 2 g |
| 16 fl. oz | chicken or white veal stock | 560 ml |
| ½ | bayleaf | ½ |

**Method**

1. Melt half the butter in a sauteuse, add the onion, cover and sweat gently for 4–5 minutes, without colouring.

2. Add the picked and washed rice and stir with a wooden spatule over a low heat until all the grains are coated with butter.

3. Add the boiling stock and bayleaf and stir until boiling. Cover with a buttered paper and lid.

4. Place in the bottom of an oven at 180°C (350°F) for approximately 15 minutes. Test a few grains between the teeth. A slight firmness of the rice should remain when cooked.

5. Remove the paper and bayleaf. Turn out immediately into another sauteuse to prevent overcooking.

6. Add the remainder of the butter and fork the rice over lightly to separate the grains. Correct the seasoning.

7. Serve in a loose dome shape in a hot earthenware or entrée dish on an underflat with dish paper.

8. Riz pilaff can be flavoured with saffron, which is then infused in the stock.

### 616           Riz pilaff au fromage

**Method**

1. Prepare and serve as for Riz pilaff (615).

2. When the rice is cooked and the butter is being added, mix in 3 oz (110 g) of grated Parmesan cheese.

### 617           Riz pilaff aux champignons

**Method**

1. Prepare and serve as for Riz pilaff (615).

2. When the rice is half cooked, add 6 oz (210 g) of prepared white closed mushrooms cut into 5 mm dice and cooked 'à blanc' (335 g).

### 618           Riz à l'orientale

**Method**

1. Prepare and serve as for Riz pilaff (615).

2. When cooked, mix in with the butter 2 oz (70 g) of plain boiled peas, 2 oz (70 g) of 5 mm diced red pimento and 8 oz (280 g) of tomatoes prepared in 5 mm raw dice (336, 5b).

### 619           Risotto

| 8 portions | Ingredients | 10 couverts |
|---|---|---|
| 8 oz | Italian or Carolina rice | 280 g |
| 2 oz | finely chopped onion | 70 g |
| 4 oz | butter | 140 g |
| 2 oz | grated Parmesan cheese | 70 g |
| 3 level teaspoons | salt | 10 g |
| ½ level teaspoon | milled pepper | 2 g |
| 24 fl. oz | chicken or white veal stock | 840 ml |
| ½ | bayleaf | ½ |

**Method**

1. Melt half the butter in a sauteuse, add the onion, cover and sweat for 4–5 minutes, without colouring.

2. Add the picked and washed rice and stir over a gentle heat until the grains are coated with butter.

3. Add two thirds of the boiling stock, the seasoning and bayleaf, stir until boiling, then cover with a buttered paper and lid.

4. Simmer very gently on a low heat or on the side of the stove, gradually adding more of the stock after 10 minutes, to keep the rice very moist.

5. Test after 14–15 minutes. When cooked, add the remainder of the butter and cheese and fork them lightly together to mix.

6. Serve in a hot earthenware dish on an underdish with paper.

*Note.* Both Riz pilaff and Risotto may have various other foods added as a garnish to the rice, e.g. mushrooms, chicken livers, etc.

# Fish dishes

# Fish dishes

## 620 FISH DAYS

The fish dishes in this section allow a very wide variety of methods of use, preparation and cooking of fish.

The different cuts and preparations used in the recipes have generally been dealt with in the Larder Section (148), while any individual preparation is included in the recipes.

## 621 Portions of fish, guidance weights

Darne: 5–6 oz (140–170 g). For these slices, allow 12 oz (340 g) of uncleaned fish, i.e., 12 portions from an 8 lb (4 kg) fish.

Fillets: 2 per portion taken from a 1¼–1½ lb (560–575 g) fish.

Herring and mackerel: as for whiting.

Smelts: 6–7 small or 4–5 large per portion.

Soles, whole: 10–12 oz (280–340 g) uncleaned weight.

Suprêmes: 4–5 oz (115–140 g) from fillets. For this size fillet for turbot, halibut, brill, etc. allow 12 oz (340 g) of uncleaned fish, i.e. 12 portions from an 8 lb (4 kg) fish.

Trout, individual portion: 5–7 oz (140–200 g).

Whitebait: 4–5 portions per pound (i.e. 90–110 g per portion).

Whiting,: for 2 fillets per portion, allow 8–10 oz (225–280 g).

Whiting, served whole: 6–8 oz (170–225 g).

## 622 METHODS OF COOKERY APPLIED TO FISH

### (a) Boiling

Whole fish, such as salmon, salmon trout, turbot and trout, and slices of salmon, cod, turbot, halibut and brill are all normally boiled.

Various cooking liquids are used, in the process and the most popular are found in these notes.

Whole fish are placed in a cold cooking liquid which is then gently raised to boiling temperature.

Cuts of fish are placed into a liquid. which is already boiling. This helps to set the natural albumen, thus preventing it from gradually emerging from the cut of fish and spoiling the finished appearance.

### (b) Poaching

When large whole fish are poached, a bed of roots is placed under the fish to prevent burning, while fillets or cuts are placed in a buttered shallow pan or tray, with or without a garnish. Fish stock and often wine are then added to come about three-quarters of the way up the depth of the fish. The pan is covered with a buttered paper and gradually brought to boiling point, then cooked in the lower part of an oven at 160–180°C (325–350°F), timed as per recipe. When cooked, the natural flakes of the fish should just begin to separate when pressed with the finger.

The cooking liquid and garnish, where used, are then reduced in quantity and added to the sauce to be served with the dish.

This method of cooking fish lends itself particularly well to assist in retaining the shape of the fish or fish preparation.

### (c) Braising

Slices or whole fish are sometimes braised, and for the latter a bed of roots is placed beneath the fish. A buttered shallow-type pan is used, the size and depth depending on the type of fish to be cooked. Fish stock and wine is then added to a depth of approximately 25 mm, and the pan is covered with a thickly buttered paper. The fish is then brought to boiling point, then braised in the lower part of the oven at 160°C (325°F). During cooking, it should be basted with the liquor frequently, and, when cooked, the liquor is reduced and added to the sauce to be served.

### (d) Grilling

Very little true grilling of fish is practised today. When the method is used, the prepared fish is thoroughly dried on a cloth, seasoned, then passed through flour, the excess flour being knocked off. It is then brushed liberally with oil and placed between the pre-heated special type double-hinged fish grills for ease in turning. This grill is placed across the main grill bars and turned over half-way through the cooking period.

The most widely used method of grilling fish is to dry and season the prepared fish then pass it through flour, removing the excess. A trellis pattern 25 mm apart is marked with a pre-heated poker on both sides of the fish. The fish is liberally brushed with oil, placed on oiled shallow trays and cooked under a salamander, being turned over half way through the cooking period.

### (e) Shallow frying

Small, whole fish, cuts and fillets are cooked by this method, and the finished dish is then termed 'à la meunière'. When salmon trout are cooked thus, they are split open from the back and cooked flat.

The fish is dried, seasoned and passed through flour, the excess flour being removed. It is then shallow fried in oil, or oil and butter, on both sides, the presentation side cooked first. In suprêmes or fillets of fish, this is the side that was removed from next to the bone.

The cooked fish is then placed on a dish, garnished according to name, sprinkled with chopped parsley and lemon juice, then masked over with nut butter (beurre noisette).

### (d) Deep frying

Fillets, small whole fish, cuts and various cooked fish preparations are used in this method. After preparation, and before cooking, fish is coated with one of the following.
  (i) Flour, milk, then flour ('à la française').
 (ii) Flour, egg and breadcrumbs ('panée à l'anglaise').
(iii) With a frying batter.

The coating used, when deep fat at the correct temperature is used, will set quickly, thus preventing the natural moisture of the fish from entering the frying medium, and vice-versa.

When cooked, the fish is drained, served on a hot flat dish on a dish paper and garnished with fried sprigs of parsley and sometimes wedges of lemon. An appropriate sauce is usually served separately.

### 623 BASIC PREPARATIONS RELATED TO FISH DISHES

Fish stock (Fonds de poisson) (356)
Fish essence (Fumet de poisson) (357)
Fish glaze (Glace de poisson) (358)

### 624 Fish velouté           Velouté de poisson

| 1 quart | Ingredients | 1 litre |
| --- | --- | --- |
| 4 oz | margarine | 100 g |
| 4 oz | flour | 100 g |
| 2 pints | fish stock | 1 litre |

**Method**

1. Melt the margarine in a saucepan, add the flour and mix them thoroughly.

2. Cover and cook in the lower part of the oven at 160–180°C (325–350°F) until sandy in texture and very lightly coloured, i.e. a blond roux. Allow to cool.

3. Add one-third of the boiling stock, place to boil and stir well with a wooden spatule until it is boiling and completely smooth. Gradually add the remainder of the stock, boiling each time before adding more.

4. Cover and simmer in the lower part of the oven at 160°C (325°F), or on the side of the stove, for 30 minutes.

5. Pass through a fine conical strainer into a clean container and butter the surface.

### 625 Court-bouillon for white fish

| 1 quart | Ingredients | 1 litre |
| --- | --- | --- |
| 2 pints | water | 1 litre |
| ½ pint | milk | 250 ml |
| 1 oz | salt | 25 g |
| ½ | lemon (in juice) | ½ |
| ½ | bayleaf | ½ |

**Method**

1. Place all the ingredients in a shallow pan, bring to boiling point, then use as required.

*Note.* The liquid should be deep enough to cover the fish to be cooked.

### 626 Court-bouillon for salmon, salmon trout and shellfish

| 1 quart | Ingredients | 1 litre |
| --- | --- | --- |
| 2 pints | water | 1 litre |
| 2½ fl. oz | vinegar | 60 ml |
| 2 oz | carrot | 50 g |
| 2 oz | onion | 50 g |
| ¼ oz | parsley stalks | 5 g |
| ½ oz | salt | 10 g |
| ½ | bayleaf | ½ |
| small | sprig thyme | small |
| 10 | white peppercorns | 10 |

**Method**

1. Shred the peeled carrot and onion. Place all the ingredients in a saucepan.

2. Bring to the boil, skim, then simmer for 30 minutes.

3. Pass through a fine strainer, reboil and use.

### SAUCES FOR FISH

### 627 Mushroom sauce (for fish)     Sauce aux champignons

**Method**

1. Prepare as for Sauce aux champignons (397), replacing the chicken velouté with fish velouté (624).

## 628 Shrimp sauce — Sauce aux crevettes

| 1 quart | Ingredients | 1 litre |
|---|---|---|
| 1½ pints | fish velouté (624) | 750 ml |
| ½ pint | fish stock (356) | 250 ml |
| ¼ pint | cream | 125 ml |
| 1 oz | butter | 25 g |
| 4 oz | peeled pink shrimps | 100 g |
| 3 level teaspoons | salt | 7 g |
| few grains | cayenne pepper | pointe |

### Method

1. Boil the velouté and stock together and reduce by one-quarter.

2. Pass through a fine conical strainer or tammy cloth into a clean sauteuse, add the cream and reboil.

3. Pass a quarter of the shrimps and the butter through a very fine sieve. Gradually toss into the sauce off the heat. Add the seasoning and correct.

4. Stir in the remainder of the shrimps.

## 629 Basic lobster sauce — Coulis de homard

| 1 quart | Ingredients | 1 litre |
|---|---|---|
| 1 × 1½ lb | live lobster | 1 × 600 g |
| 6 oz | carrot | 150 g |
| 4 oz | onion | 100 g |
| 2 oz | celery | 50 g |
| 4 oz | tomato purée | 100 g |
| 1 small | bouquet garni | 1 small |
| 1½ pints | fish velouté (624) | 750 ml |
| 1½ pints | fish stock (356) | 750 ml |
| 2 fl. oz | brandy | 50 ml |
| 4 fl. oz | white wine | 100 ml |
| 2 fl. oz | olive oil | 50 ml |
| 3 level teaspoons | salt | 7 g |
| few grains | cayenne pepper | pointe |

### Method

1. Spike the live lobster by passing the point of a large knife through the shell between the eyes.

2. Chop away the claws and legs with the end of the blade.

3. Cut through the shell at the beginning of the tail, leaving the tail whole. Divide the upper part of the shell in two pieces, lengthways.

4. Remove the sac, the small bag containing gravel, from behind each of the eyes and discard.

5. From these upper pieces of the shell (carapace), remove the coral and stomach and pass them through a fine sieve with 2 oz (50 g) of butter. Refrigerate for use in finishing the sauce.

6. Heat the oil in a saucepan until a light blue vapour appears, then add the pieces of lobster and fry them quickly for 1–2 minutes. Add the cleaned vegetables, cut in rough

10 mm dice, cover with a lid and sweat on a reduced heat for 4–5 minutes.

7. Add the brandy and flame it, then add the white wine, tomato purée, fish stock and bouquet garni. Boil, cover, then simmer for 25–30 minutes.

8. Remove the tail and claws of the lobster from the liquid, crack the shells and remove the flesh (also removing the flesh from the claw joints) and place it aside for other uses. Return the crushed shell to the cooking liquid and simmer for a further 15 minutes.

9. Pass the liquid and vegetables through a sieve.

10. Pour the passed liquid into a thick bottomed shallow pan, add the velouté and reduce to 2 pints (1 litre), stirring often to prevent burning.

11. Add the salt and cayenne to season then pass through a tammy cloth or very fine conical strainer. Reboil then butter the surface.

12. To finish, a little cream usually is added, according to use, then the sauce is finished with the butter off the heat.

## 630 White wine sauce — Sauce vin blanc

| 1 quart | Ingredients | 1 litre |
|---|---|---|
| 1½ pints | fish velouté (624) | 750 ml |
| 1 pint | fish stock (356) | 500 ml |
| ¼ pint | dry white wine | 125 ml |
| ¼ pint | cream | 125 ml |
| 8 oz | butter | 200 g |
| 2 oz | mushroom trimmings | 50 g |
| 3 level teaspoons | salt | 7 g |
| few grains | cayenne pepper | pointe |
| ½ | lemon (in juice) | ½ |

### Method

1. Place the velouté, stock, wine and the washed mushroom trimmings in a thick bottomed shallow pan. Boil, then reduce by one-quarter.

2. Remove from the heat and gradually toss in the butter in small pieces, absorbing each piece before adding more.

3. Whisk in the cream, season, then add the lemon juice. Correct the seasoning and the consistency, which should be that of single cream. The sauce should barely mask the back of a ladle.

4. Pass through a tammy cloth or very fine strainer. Butter the surface.

## 631 White wine sauce (for glazing) — Sauce vin blanc à glacer

### Method

1. Prepare as for White wine sauce (630), but whisk in a prepared 2 egg yolk sabayon (632) before passing the sauce.

2. When prepared in quantity, the butter and sabayon may be replaced with an equal quantity of Sauce hollandaise (402).

### 632 Preparation of sabayon for fish sauces

**Method**

1. Place the yolks of eggs in a sauteuse, add half the quantity of cold water, and whisk them together.

2. Place the sauteuse in a bain-marie over a gentle heat. Whisk the yolks continuously until they thicken, but are quite smooth.

3. The sabayon is used in the sauce to quicken the glazing process in order to prevent the sauce boiling, which would separate the butter.

---

## 633 BOILED FISH DISHES

### 634 Preparation of baby or chicken turbot

| | |
|---|---|
| | Turbotin |
| Turbot | Turbot |
| Brill | Barbue |
| Halibut | Flétan |

These are all prepared, cooked and served in the same manner.

**Method**

1. Wash the fish and place it on a board. Using a large knife, cut through the skin of the white side straight down the centre of the fish, then through the tail.

2. Using the wide end of the blade, gradually chop along the centre line, through the bone, towards the head.

3. Cut behind the head, across to the centre bone, to remove the larger half of the fish. Cut across the smaller half at the top of the flesh, where it meets the stomach cavity.

4. Chop away the side fin bones.

5. Mark, then cut the fish through into portions on the bone (tronçons).

6. Wash well in cold water to remove any clotted blood and soak the fish in cold salted water if it needs to be whitened.

### 635 Boiled Turbot (slices)     Tronçon de turbot poché

**Method**

1. Prepare a court-bouillon (625) in a shallow pan.

2. When boiling, add the slices of turbot, reboil, then allow to poach gently on a reduced heat for 8–12 minutes, according to thickness. The flesh will just ease from the bone when cooked.

3. Remove with a fish slice and drain.

4. Serve on a serviette or directly on a hot flat oval dish. Remove the dark skin.

5. Garnish along the side of the fish with 2 small plain boiled turned potatoes per portion and place a spring of parsley on either side.

6. Serve with an appropriate sauce in a sauceboat on an underdish with a doily, e.g. Sauce hollandaise (402) or mousseline (405).

### 636 Boiled cod slices     Darne de cabillaud pochée

**Method**

1. Wash the cod and place it on a board. Cut off the head then remove the fins with a knife or scissors and lightly trim along the edges of the belly.

2. With a sharp large knife, cut the fish through into slices 20–25 mm in thickness, according to size.

3. Roll the belly flaps inwards, tie the slices with string and rewash them in cold water.

4. Prepare a court-bouillon (625) in a shallow pan.

5. When it is boiling, carefully add the slices of cod then reboil and poach gently on a reduced heat until cooked (8–10 minutes). The centre bone will ease clear when the fish is cooked; remove this bone when serving.

6. Serve as for boiled turbot (635), as from 4 in method.

7. Any of these sauces may be served separately: egg (388), parsley (393), shrimp (628), mushroom (627).

### 637 Boiled salmon slices     Darne de saumon pochée

**Method**

1. Use a salmon of between 8–12 lb (4–5·5 kg) for this method to obtain suitably-sized slices.

2. Clean as described in cleaning of fish (148).

3. With a large knife, cut the salmon into slices from just

over 10 mm to up to 25 mm thick, according to the size of the fish.

4. Prepare a court-bouillon (626) in a shallow pan.

5. When boiling, carefully add the slices of salmon, reboil, then poach gently on a reduced heat for 5–7 minutes, according to thickness. The centre bone will ease clear when cooked.

6. Serve as for boiled turbot (635), as from 4 in method. Remove the centre bone and place parsley in this cavity.

7. On the underflat, with the sauce, serve a shallow dish of sliced peeled cucumber sprinkled with chopped parsley.

Sauce hollandaise (402), or Sauce mousseline (405) are usually served separately.

## 638 Cooking of whole salmon

### Method

1. Prepare a court-bouillon (626) and strain it into a salmon fish kettle with the drainer inserted.

2. Clean the salmon as described in cleaning of fish (148)

3. Place into the fish kettle, checking that the liquid covers the fish.

4. Raise the liquid gently to boiling point, remove the scum, then gently simmer on a reduced heat for the following approximate times, according to the weight of the fish:

7–9 lb (3–4 kg) 15 minutes

10–14 lb (4·5–6 kg) 18–20 minutes

15–20 lb (6·5–9 kg) 22–25 minutes

Allow the salmon to go cold in the court-bouillon.

## 639 Cold salmon — Saumon froid

| 8 portions | Ingredients | 10 couverts |
|---|---|---|
| 2½–3 lb | prepared salmon | 1·4–1·7 kg |
| 4 × 2 oz | tomatoes | 5 × 55 g |
| 1 | lettuce | 1 large |
| ½ | cucumber | ¾ |
| 4 | hard boiled eggs | 5 |
| 3 pints | court-bouillon (626) | 1·5 litres |
| ½ pint | sauce mayonnaise (1) or verte (3) | 350 ml |

### Method

1. If the salmon is to be cooked in one piece, cut the piece from the tail end or the centre. If for slices (darne), preference should be for the centre of the fish. The slices may be cut for 1 or 2 portions each.

2. Cook the salmon in the court-bouillon as in 637 for slices or 638 for whole or pieces, then allow it to go cold.

3. Remove the skin, then scrape away the brown part which covers the flesh. Remove the centre bone from the slices.

4. Dress the salmon on an oval silver flat dish.

5. Peel the cucumber, slice it thinly and arrange the slices half overlapping each other along the slices, or down the centre if the fish is left in one piece.

6. Garnish around the sides of the salmon with sections of the prepared lettuce, quarters of peeled tomatoes and quarters of shelled hard-boiled eggs. Serve the sauce in a sauceboat on an underdish with a doily.

## POACHED FISH DISHES

While the recipes for poached fish given here are given only for fillets of sole, they may be used for other cuts of white fish such as suprême de turbot, flétan, barbue, cabillaud and aigrefin; quenelles may also be prepared by these methods.

When soles are served, they are prepared thus: skin both sides and remove the side fins with a pair of scissors. Cut off the head, clean the stomach cavity, then wash the fish well to remove any blood. Cook as per recipe. When cooked, place each sole on an upturned oval silver flat dish. With the edge of a palette knife, pull out the fin bones from each side of the fish, then break off the piece of backbone that protrudes from the wider end. Proceed to finish as per recipe.

## 640 Fillets of sole, white wine sauce — Filets de sole au vin blanc

| 8 portions | Ingredients | 10 couverts |
|---|---|---|
| 4 × 1¼–1½ lb | soles | 5 × 550–650 g |
| 1 oz | butter | 35 g |
| 1 oz | finely-chopped shallot | 35 g |
| ½ pint | fish stock | 350 ml |
| ¼ | lemon (in juice) | ⅓ |
| 2 fl. oz | white wine | 70 ml |
| 8 | fleurons (puff paste crescents) | 10 |
| 1 pint | white wine sauce (630) | 700 ml |

### Method

1. Grease a shallow pan or tray with the butter and sprinkle in the finely-chopped shallot.

2. Skin both sides of the soles then fillet, trim and wash them.

3. Arrange them in the tray, cut side uppermost, and season them very lightly with salt.

4. Sprinkle with the wine then add the fish stock and lemon juice. Cover with a buttered paper.

5. Gently raise to boiling point, cook in the lower part of the oven at 160–180°C (325–350°F) for 5–7 minutes. When cooked, the fish should just begin to flake when it is pressed.

6. Strain off the stock and reduce it to an essence then add it to the white wine sauce.

7. Place a little sauce on a hot oval silver flat dish and arrange the fillets side by side down the dish.

8. Mask the fillets with the remainder of the sauce. Place the fleurons around the edges of the fillets, inside the collar of the dish.

### 641 Filets de sole Véronique

| 8 portions | Ingredients | 10 couverts |
|---|---|---|
| 4 × 1¼–1½ lb | soles | 5 × 550–650g |
| 1 oz | butter | 35 g |
| 8 oz | white grapes | 280 g |
| ½ | lemon (in juice) | ½ |
| ½ pint | fish stock | 350 ml |
| 2 fl. oz | white wine | 70 ml |
| 1 pint | sauce vin blanc à glacer (631) | 700 ml |

#### Method

1. Prepare as for Filets de sole vin blanc up to and including 6 in method. The fillets of sole may be folded, if desired, for better presentation.

2. To fold the fillets, make a 3 mm-deep incision across the fillets on the side from which the skin was removed. To ensure uniformity in size, only fold under part of the smaller fillets.

3. Blanch the grapes in boiling water for 6–10 seconds, then refresh them and remove the skin and seeds.

4. To serve, place a little of the sauce on an oval flat dish and dress the drained fillets on it in an oval shape, slightly overlapping the ends. Mask the fillets with the sauce and glaze to a light golden brown under a very fast salamander.

5. Arrange the grapes in a dome shape in the centre of the fillets. If desired, the grapes may be placed on the fillets before glazing, but the finished dish is not so effective.

### 642 Filets de sole Suchet

#### Method

1. Prepare as for Filets de sole vin blanc (640).

2. Cut 2 oz (70 g) each of prepared carrot, leek, celery and turnip into a very fine julienne. Blanch them for 5 minutes then refresh and drain them and sprinkle over the fish before poaching.

3. Reduce the garnish and cooking liquor; do not strain. When it is nearly dry, add it to the white wine sauce. Finish as per recipe, omitting the fleurons.

### 643 Filets de sole fermière

#### Method

1. Prepare as for Filets de sole Suchet (642).

2. Cut the vegetables into a paysanne instead of julienne.

3. When serving, fleurons are placed around the outer edge of the fish, after masking it with the sauce.

### 644 Filets de sole Lydia

| 8 portions | Ingredients | 10 couverts |
|---|---|---|
| 4 × 1¼–1½ lb | sole | 5 × 550–650 g |
| 1 oz | butter | 35 g |
| 1 oz | finely chopped shallots | 35 g |
| 4 oz | peeled pink shrimps | 140 g |
| 1 × 14 oz tin | asparagus tips | 1 × 500 g |
| ½ | lemon (in juice) | ½ |
| 2 fl. oz | white wine | 70 ml |
| ½ pint | fish stock | 350 ml |
| 1 pint | sauce vin blanc à glacer (631) | 700 ml |

#### Method

1. Prepare as for Filets de sole vin blanc (640) up to and including 6 in method.

2. Place a little of the sauce on an oval silver flat dish and arrange the fillets down the dish. Place 2–3 hot buttered asparagus tips (fresh, if available) on each portion, with a bouquet of shrimps.

3. Mask over with the sauce and glaze under a very hot salamander.

### 645 Filets de sole Bercy

| 8 portions | Ingredients | 10 couverts |
|---|---|---|
| 4 × 1¼–1½ lb | sole | 5 × 550–650 g |
| 1 oz | butter | 35 g |
| 2 oz | finely chopped shallot | 70 g |
| 3 tablespoons | finely chopped parsley | 20 g |
| ½ | lemon (in juice) | ½ |
| 2 fl. oz | white wine | 70 ml |
| ½ pint | fish stock | 350 ml |
| 1 pint | sauce vin blanc à glacer (631) | 700 ml |

## Method

1. Grease a shallow pan or tray with the butter.
2. Skin both sides of the soles then, fillet, trim and wash them.
3. Sprinkle the shallot into the tray, lay the fillets on top, sprinkle them with the parsley and season lightly.
4. Add the wine, lemon juice and fish stock. Cover with a buttered paper and gently raise to boiling point.
5. Place in the lower part of an oven at 160–180°C (325–350°F) to poach for 5–7 minutes.
6. Run off the cooking liquor into a sauteuse and reduce it to an essence. Add it to the sauce and correct the seasoning.
7. Place a little of the sauce on an oval silver flat dish. Arrange the fillets down the dish, mask them with the remainder of the sauce and glaze under a very hot salamander.

### 646        Filets de sole à la bonne femme

## Method

1. Prepare and serve as for Filets de sole Bercy (645).
2. Wash, peel and thinly slice 8 oz (280 g) of white closed mushrooms and sprinkle them over the fillets before cooking.

### 647        Filets de sole d'Antin
###        Filets de sole Bréval

## Method

1. Prepare and serve as for Filets de sole à la bonne femme (646).
2. Blanch and skin 8 oz (280 g) of tomatoes then remove the seeds and cut them into 10 mm dice. Sprinkle the dice over the fillets before cooking.

### 648        Filets de sole Mornay

| 8 portions | Ingredients | 10 couverts |
|---|---|---|
| 4 × 1¼–1½ lb | soles | 5 × 550–650 g |
| 1 oz | butter | 35 g |
| 2 oz | grated Parmesan cheese | 70 g |
| ¼ | lemon (in juice) | ¼ |
| ½ pint | fish stock | 350 ml |
| 1 pint | Mornay sauce (390) | 700 ml |

## Method

1. Skin both sides of the soles, then fillet, trim and wash them.
2. Prepare the Mornay sauce for fish (390).
3. Place the fillets in a greased shallow pan or tray and very lightly season them with salt.
4. Add the lemon juice and fish stock, cover with a but-

tered paper, and gently raise to boiling point. Then place the fish in the lower part of an oven at 160–180°C (325–350°F) to cook for 5–7 minutes.
5. Strain the cooking liquor into a sauteuse, reduce it to an essence then add it to the sauce.
6. Place a little of the sauce on an oval flat dish and arrange the fillets down the dish. Mask the remainder of the sauce over the fillets and evenly sprinkle the surface with the cheese.
7. Colour (gratinate) till golden brown under a moderate salamander.

### 649        Filets de sole à la florentine

## Method

1. Prepare and serve as for Filets de sole Mornay (648).
2. Prepare 2 lb (1 kg) spinach into buttered leaf spinach (1017).
3. Dress the spinach down the centre of the dish, place the fillets on top and finish with the sauce and cheese. Gratinate under the salamander.

### 650        Filets de sole Cubat

## Method

1. Prepare 8 oz (280 g) of mushroom trimmings or stalks into a duxelle (338).
2. Prepare the fish as for Filets de sole Mornay (648).
3. When serving, either (a) place the duxelle flat on the dish or (b) bind with a spoonful of the sauce and, with a piping bag and a 10 mm star tube, pipe a scroll of duxelle on top of each fillet, then in both cases finish as for Mornay.

### 651        Filets de sole Otéro

### 652        Paupiettes de sole Otéro

## Method

1. Prepare all the ingredients as for Filets de sole Mornay (648).
2. Scrub 1 large potato per portion, and place it on a tray on coarse salt. Bake it in the oven at 200°C (400°F) for 1–1¼ hours. Cut off one-third of the potato across. With a spoon, scoop out the centre of the potato and pass it through a sieve. Add 1½ oz (50 g) of butter, salt and pepper to season, then mix in 1 yolk of egg.
3. With a piping bag and a 10 mm star tube, pipe a border around the edge of the potato cases (the deeper part) and

185

finish with a small rosette at each end. Partially dry the potato under the salamander, then egg-wash.

4. Skin the soles on both sides then fillet, trim and wash them.

5. For fillets, make a small incision and fold the fillets in halves. For paupiettes, flatten the fillets slightly, then spread ½ oz (15 g) fish farce (149) on the side from which the skin was removed. Then, starting at the wider end of the fillet, roll the fillet up to form the paupiette.

6. Place the fish into a shallow pan or tray, season lightly and add the lemon juice and fish stock. Poach for 5–7 minutes in the oven at 160–180°C (325–350°F).

7. Reduce the cooking liquor to an essence and add it to the mornay sauce.

8. Place a spoonful of sauce in the bottom of each potato case then insert the fish. Mask over with the sauce to the level of the bottom edge of the potato.

9. Sprinkle evenly with the cheese, then gratinate under a moderate salamander.

10. Serve on a hot oval silver flat dish on a dish paper and garnish in between the potatoes with sprigs of picked parsley.

## 653 Filets de sole Dugléré

| 8 portions | Ingredients | 10 couverts |
|---|---|---|
| 4 × 1¼–1½ lb | soles | 5 × 550–650 g |
| 2 oz | finely chopped shallots | 70 g |
| 2 oz | butter | 70 g |
| 1 lb | tomatoes | 560 g |
| 3 level teaspoons | salt | 10 g |
| 2 tablespoons | chopped parsley | 20 g |
| ½ | lemon (in juice) | ½ |
| 2½ fl. oz | dry white wine | 85 ml |
| ¼ pint | cream | 175 ml |
| ½ pint | fish stock | 350 ml |
| ¾ pint | fish velouté (624) | 525 ml |
| few grains | cayenne pepper | pointe |

### Method

1. Skin the soles on both sides then fillet, trim and wash them.

2. Butter a shallow pan or tray and sprinkle in the shallot. Place the fillets in top of the shallot and season. Sprinkle with the chopped parsley and the tomato, which should be prepared into raw 10 mm dice after skinning and removing the seeds.

3. Add the lemon juice, wine and fish stock. Cover with a buttered paper.

4. Raise gently to boiling point then cook in the lower part of an oven at 160–180°C (325–350°F) for 5–7 minutes.

5. Run off the cooking liquor and garnish into a sauteuse, reduce by a half, add the strained velouté, reboil and reduce it, if necessary, to masking consistency.

6. Remove from the heat, toss in the butter in small pieces and absorb it into the sauce. Add the cream and correct the seasoning.

7. Place a little of the sauce on a hot oval silver dish, arrange the fillets down the dish and mask them over with remainder of the sauce. Sprinkle the surface with chopped parsley.

## 654 Filets de sole à l'indienne

## 655 Paupiettes de sole à l'indienne

| 8 portions | Ingredients | 10 couverts |
|---|---|---|
| 4 × 1¼–1½ lb | soles | 5 × 550–650 g |
| 8 portions | riz pilaff (615) | 10 couverts |
| 1 pint | curry sauce (413) | 700 ml |
| ½ pint | fish stock | 350 ml |
| 2 teaspoons | chopped parsley | 5 g |

### Method

1. Prepare the sauce.

2. Skin the soles on both sides and fillet, trim and wash them.

3. Prepare the fillets, either (a) folded or (b) in paupiettes (see 5 in method of 651 and 652).

4. Place the fish in a buttered shallow pan or tray and season it lightly.

5. Prepare the Riz pilaff (615).

6. Add the fish stock to the fish then cover it with a buttered paper. Gently raise to boiling point and cook in the lower part of the oven at 160–180°C (325–350°F) for 5–7 minutes.

7. Run off the cooking liquor into a sauteuse, reduce to an essence, then add it to the curry sauce.

8. To serve, lightly press the cooked Riz pilaff into a border mould and turn it out on to a hot oval or round silver flat dish.

9. Dress the folded fillets or paupiettes inside the rice border, mask over with the sauce, and also run sauce around the outside of the rice. Sprinkle the fish with chopped parsley.

## 657        Poisson grillé St Germain

Generally, fillets or suprêmes of any white fish may be prepared in this manner.

### Method

1. Clean and prepare the fish into fillets or suprêmes.
2. Dry it on a cloth and season with a little salt and white pepper. Pass it through flour, removing any excess, then through melted butter or margarine and finally white breadcrumbs.
3. Lightly pat with a palette knife.
4. Lightly mark a 25 mm spaced trellis pattern on the fish with a hot poker. Place the fish on to a well-greased tray and brush it over with melted butter.
5. Grill on both sides under a moderate salamander for a total time of approximately 5–6 minutes for fillets and, 6–8 minutes for suprêmes. Brush them over with melted butter when cooked.
6. Serve on a hot oval flat dish and garnish each side with sprigs of parsley. Serve a sauceboat of Sauce béarnaise (403) on an underdish with a doily.

## 658        Poisson caprice

### Method

1. Prepare and cook the fish as for Poisson grillé St Germain (657).
2. With each portion, serve a half of a peeled banana, cut on the slant. Pass the banana through flour, place it on an oiled tray, brush it over with oil then lightly dredge with caster sugar. Grill to a light golden brown under a hot salamander.
3. Dress the fish on a hot oval silver dish, with the banana on top. Serve a sauceboat of Sauce Robert (384) on an underdish with a doily.

## 659        Filets de sole grillés

## 660        Filets de plie grillés

### Method

1. Skin the soles on both sides and fillet, trim, wash and drain them. Fillet the place, remove the dark skin, then wash and drain.
2. Dry the fish on a cloth, season with a little salt and white pepper and pass through flour, removing any excess.

3. If not being true grilled, mark a trellis pattern across the fish with a hot poker.
4. Brush the fish with oil and place it on a greased tray.
5. Grill for 2½–3 minutes on each side under a hot salamander then brush over with melted butter.
6. Serve the fish on a hot oval silver flat dish and garnish it with sprigs of picked parsley and lemon wedges along the sides. Serve any of the savoury butters (112–118) or a suitable sauce, e.g. Sauce diable (375), separately.

## 661        Tronçon de turbot grillé

### Method

1. Prepare the turbot into slices (634).
2. Prepare and serve as for Filets de sole grillés (659).
3. When grilling, allow 4–5 minutes each side, according to the thickness.

## 662 Grilled sole        Sole grillée

## 663 Grilled small plaice        Petite plie grillée

### Method

1. Trim the tail and fins of the fish, cut off the head and clean the stomach cavity of congealed blood. In the case of sole, remove the dark skin.
2. Then prepare and serve as for Filets de sole grillés (659). When grilling, allow 3½–4 minutes on each side.

## 664 Grilled cod steak        Darne de cabillaud grillée

### Method

1. Prepare the cod as in recipe 636 up to and including 3 in the method.
2. Dry the fish on a cloth then season and flour it. Mark a trellis pattern across the fish with a hot poker.
3. Brush over with oil and place it on a greased tray. Grill for 4–5 minutes on each side under a moderate salamander brush the cod with oil while cooking.
4. Serve on a hot flat oval dish. Remove the string and centre bone and place a sprig of parsley in the centre cavity and wedges of lemon along the side. Serve any of the savoury butters (112–118) or an appropriate sauce, such as Sauce diable (375), separately.

## 665 Grilled salmon steak — Darne de saumon grillée

**Method**

1. Clean the salmon as described in 148.
2. Cut it into slices for 1 or 2 portions.
3. Then proceed to prepare and cook as for grilled cod steak (664), allowing approximately 5 minutes on each side; brush liberally with oil while grilling.
4. Serve on a hot oval flat dish, remove the centre bone, garnish with sprigs of parsley and wedges of lemon. Serve a dish of sliced cucumber on an underflat with a doily, together with an appropriate sauce, e.g. Sauce verte (3) or a savoury butter (112–118).

## 666 Grilled herring — Hareng grillé

**Method**

1. Remove the scales by scraping along the skin with a knife, held at an angle to the fish, from the tail to the head.
2. Trim the tail and fins with scissors and cut off the head. Remove the stomach and congealed blood; be careful not to remove the roe. Wash the fish well and drain.
3. Make 3–4 incisions approximately 25 mm long and to a depth of 3 mm in the thicker part of the flesh.
4. Dry on a cloth then season with salt and white pepper. Flour and brush over with oil and place the fish on a greased tray. Cover the tail with a slice of potato while grilling, to prevent burning. Grill on each side for approximately 4 minutes then brush over with butter.

5. Arrange the fish in line on a hot oval flat silver dish and garnish it with sprigs of parsley and lemon wedges. Serve Sauce moutarde (391) in a sauceboat on an underflat with a doily.

## 667 Grilled mackerel — Maquereau grillé

**Method**

1. Cut off the head, remove the stomach and scrape away the dark skin of the stomach lining.
2. Pass the knife point along each side of the back bone, clip free close to the tail. Trim the tail across, wash well and drain.
3. Dry on a cloth, season with salt and white pepper and pass through flour, removing any excess.
4. Brush well with oil, place the cut side down on a greased tray.
5. Grill under a moderate salamander till a light golden brown, (2½–3 minutes) on each side.
6. Dress with the cut side showing on a hot oval silver flat dish and brush the fish with butter. Garnish with sprigs of parsley and wedges of lemon.

## 668 — Maquereau grillé Mirabeau

**Method**

1. Prepare and grill as for grilled mackerel (667).
2. Serve the fish on a hot oval silver flat dish. Place two anchovy knots, a slice of Beurre maître d'hôtel (116), and 2 stoned olives on each mackerel, omitting the lemon.

## 669 SHALLOW FRIED FISH

Fillets and suprêmes of any white fish, and suprêmes of salmon, can be shallow fried. Individual trout are cooked whole, and larger trout and salmon trout are split down the back and opened flat.

## 670 — Poisson meunière

**Method**

1. Prepare the fish according to the type used and wash and drain it.
2. Dry it on a cloth, season with salt and white pepper and pass through flour at the moment of cooking, removing all surplus flour.
3. Previously heat sufficient oil in a frying pan. When a blue vapour appears, lay the fish in the oil, presentation side first. In the case of fillets and suprêmes, this is the surface removed from the bone.

4. Fry quickly over a fast heat to a golden brown on each side (generally 2–3 minutes each side). For trout, reduce the heat when it is coloured and allow 3–4 minutes on each side.
5. Cut away the skin and pith from some lemons and cut them into slices, allowing 2 slices per portion.
6. Serve the fish neatly arranged across a hot oval silver flat dish with the sliced lemon on the fish.
7. Sprinkle all over liberally with chopped parsley, then with a squeeze of lemon juice.
8. Melt ¾–1 oz (20–30 g) of butter per portion, allow to

foam, then, when just beginning to turn nut brown (beurre noisette), mask completely over the fish.

*Note.* If desired, a thread (cordon) of jus-lié may be run around the dish before masking with the butter.

## 671          Poisson belle meunière

**Method**

1. Peel some tomatoes and cut them into 5 mm slices (serve 2 slices per portion) and arrange them overlapping on a greased tray. Season them with salt and pepper, sprinkle them with melted butter and heat them for 1–2 minutes in a cool oven, while the fish is cooking.
2. Prepare and grill in advance one medium mushroom per portion (977).
3. Wash 1–2 soft roes per portion; drain and dry them on a cloth. Season then pass them through flour. Place them on a greased tray, brush them well with oil and grill till they are golden brown (2–3 minutes). Prepare and cook in advance.
4. Serve the fish as for Poisson meunière (670), replacing the lemon slices with the sliced tomato in the centre of the fish, and the mushroom and roes on each side.

## 672          Poisson bretonne

**Method**

1. Prepare and serve as for Poisson meunière (670), omitting the lemon slices.
2. For 8 (10) portions, allow 3 oz (100 g) of picked pink shrimps and 8 oz (280 g) of closed white mushrooms.
3. Wash and slice the mushrooms and place them in a sauteuse with 1 oz (35 g) butter and some seasoning. Cover and cook slowly for 8–10 minutes.
4. When serving, sprinkle the shrimps and mushrooms over the fish then complete the dish as for Poisson meunière.

## 673          Poisson Doria

**Method**

1. Prepare and serve as for Poisson meunière (670), omitting the lemon slices.
2. For 8 (10) portions, peel one medium to large cucumber, cut it across into 25 mm lengths, then cut across into 6 sections 25 mm long; turn these to a small barrel shape. Melt 1½ oz (50 g) of butter in a sauteuse, add the cucumber,

season it with salt and pepper and cover with a lid. Cook gently for 6–7 minutes to finish with a glaze.
3. When serving, sprinkle the fish with the cucumber before the parsley.

## 674          Poisson grenobloise

**Method**

1. Prepare and serve as for Poisson meunière (670). After cutting away the rind and pith of the lemon, cut between the skin divisions to produce segments and allow 3–4 segments per portion.
2. Prepare and fry some croûtons, cut 25 × 5 × 5 mm, allowing 7–8 per portion.
3. When serving, sprinkle the fish with the lemon segments, croûtons and a teaspoon of capers per portion, before sprinkling with the parsley.

## 675          Filets de sole Murat

| 8 portions | Ingredients | 10 couverts |
|---|---|---|
| 4 × 1¼ lb | soles | 5 × 560 g |
| 6 | cooked artichoke bottoms | 8 |
| 1¼ lb | peeled potatoes | 1 kg |
| 3 oz | butter | 100 g |
| 3 fl. oz | oil | 100 ml |
| 1 | lemon (in juice) | 1½ |
| ½ oz | chopped parsley | 20 g |

**Method**

1. Skin the soles on both sides then fillet, trim, wash and drain them.
2. Cut into 50 × 5 × 5 mm goujonnettes and dry them on a cloth.
3. Cut out the potatoes with an olive-shaped scoop cutter. Place these into a shallow pan and, barely cover with water. Bring to the boil rapidly and drain.
4. Heat a little of the oil in a frying pan until it smokes, then add the potatoes and fry them rapidly until light golden brown. Drain, replace in the pan, season, add a ½ oz (20 g) of butter, finish to cook in an oven at 150°C (300°F) for 6–7 minutes.
5. Cut the artichoke bottoms into 8 sections across on the slant. Lightly season them then sauté in a little butter.
6. Heat sufficient oil to cover the bottom of a frying pan and when smoking, add one layer only of the fish, which should be previously passed through seasoned flour. Fry the fish over a fierce heat until golden brown then remove with a slice direct to a hot shallow earthenware dish; keep the fish hot. Cook the remainder of the fish and add it to the rest in the dish.

7. Sprinkle the potatoes and artichokes over the fish, then sprinkle with the chopped parsley, then the lemon juice; finish by masking over with the nut butter (beurre noisette).

8. Place the dish on an underflat with dish paper.

**676**  Filets de sole Cécilia

**Method**

1. Prepare and shallow fry the fish as for Poisson meunière (670).

2. Dress in a buttered earthenware oval dish, place 2–3 buttered asparagus tips on each portion then sprinkle with Parmesan cheese and melted butter.

3. Gratinate under a moderate salamander.

4. Serve on an underflat with dish paper.

---

## DEEP FRIED FISH

### 677 Frying batters
Pâtes à frire

| (A)  8 portions | Ingredients | 10 couverts |
|---|---|---|
| 8 oz | strong flour | 280 g |
| ½ oz | yeast | 20 g |
| 2 level teaspoons | salt | 8 g |
| ½ level teaspoon | sugar | 2 g |
| 2 level desertspoons | olive oil | 20 ml |
| ½ pint | water | 350 ml |

**Method**

1. Sieve the flour and salt into a basin and make a bay.

2. Dissolve the yeast and sugar in a quarter of the water, raised to blood heat, and pour it into the bay.

3. Add the remainder of the water and oil, gradually absorb the flour into it to mix it into a smooth batter, beating well.

4. Cover the basin with a cloth and put it in a warm temperature, but never near a direct heat, to prove.

5. Before using, knock back the batter and check the consistency: it should just coat the article to be fried. Flour varies and will sometimes require a little extra water.

| (B)  8 portions | Ingredients | 10 couverts |
|---|---|---|
| 8 oz | strong flour | 280 g |
| 2 level teaspoons | salt | 8 g |
| 2 dessertspoons | olive oil | 20 ml |
| 1 | egg yolk | 1 |
| 1 | egg white | 2 |
| ½ pint | water | 350 ml |

**Method**

1. Sieve the flour and salt into a basin and make a bay.

2. Add the egg yolk, oil and water; mix them together, then gradually absorb the flour into a smooth batter, beating well. Cover the basin with a cloth.

3. Allow to rest for 1 hour. Just before using, add the stiffly-whipped white of egg, folding in with a wooden spoon

### (C)  with baking powder

| 8 portions | Ingredients | 10 couverts |
|---|---|---|
| 8 oz | strong flour | 280 g |
| ¾ oz | baking powder | 30 g |
| 2 level teaspoons | salt | 8 g |
| ½ level teaspoon | sugar | 2 g |
| ½ pint | water | 350 ml |

**Method**

1. Sieve the flour and salt into a basin and make a bay.

2. Add three-quarters of the water and sugar and gradually absorb the flour into a smooth batter, beating thoroughly. Cover and allow to rest for 1½–2 hours.

3. 10–15 minutes before using, dissolve the baking powder in the remainder of the water and thoroughly mix into the batter.

4. If required in a hurry, dissolve the powder in all of the water and mix sufficiently to blend all the ingredients, but do not overbeat.

**678 Fried fillets of sole**  Filets de sole frits

**679 Fried fillets of plaice**  Filets de plie frits

**Method**

1. Skin the soles on both sides then fillet, trim, wash and drain them. Fillet the plaice and remove the dark skin then trim, wash and drain it.

2. Dry the fish on a cloth and season it with salt and white pepper. Pass through flour, removing the excess, then through beaten egg and white breadcrumbs (panée à l'anglaise).

3. Gently pat the fillets with a palette knife to prevent loose crumbs.

4. Deep fry at 180°C (360°F) for 3–4 minutes until golden brown then drain.

5. Serve on a hot oval silver flat dish with dish paper. Arrange the fillets, crossing each other in pairs, down the dish. Garnish with sprigs of picked parsley and lemon wedges. Serve a sauceboat, on an underdish with a doily, of an appropriate sauce, e.g. Tartare (4) Rémoulade (5).

## 680 Fried sole — Sole frite

## 681 Fried small plaice — Petite plie frite

**Method**

1. Skin the soles on both sides and trim off the fins of the sole and plaice with scissors and square off the tails. Cut off the heads, clean out the stomach cavity then thoroughly wash and drain the fish.

2. Then proceed as for fried fillets of sole (678). Allow 5–7 minutes frying time, according to thickness; for large soles (2 portions) allow 8–10 minutes at 170°C (340°F).

## 682 Fried plaited fillet of sole — Filets de sole frits en tresse

**Method**

1. Skin the soles on both sides then fillet, trim, wash and drain them.

2. Cut twice through the fillets lengthways to within 10 mm of one end to make three long pieces; plait these pieces neatly.

3. Then finish as from 4 in method of fried fillet of sole (678).

## 683 — Goujons de sole frits

**Method**

1. Skin the soles on both sides, then fillet, trim, wash and drain them.

2. Cut the fillets across, on the slant, into lengths 75 × 10 mm wide.

3. Dry these pieces on a cloth then season, flour, egg and crumb, then roll them lightly.

4. Cook and serve as from 4 in method of fried fillet of sole (678).

## 684 — Goujonnettes de sole frites

**Method**

Prepare, cook and serve as for Goujons de sole frits (683), but cut the fillets smaller (50 × 5 × 5 mm).

## 685 — Sole Colbert

**Method**

1. Skin the soles on both sides, cut off the fins with scissors and trim the tail. Cut off the head, clean out the stomach cavity, then wash and drain the fish.

2. Cut down the centre of the sole, as if to fillet, from a point 25 mm from the top to within 10 mm of the tail. Ease the flesh as for filleting to half way to the outer edge. Cut through the backbone at each end and the centre.

3. Dry on a cloth, open the flesh to the sides to reveal the bone. Season, flour, egg and crumb. Deep fry at 180°C (360°F) for 5–7 minutes, according to size, and drain.

5. With a small knife, ease out the bone, cut off the fried pané and replace over the cavity.

6. Serve on a hot flat oval dish with dish paper. Place 2 slices of parsley butter (116), in the centre opening and garnish with fried sprigs of parsley and lemon wedges.

## 686 — Goujons de turbot frits

**Method**

1. Cut the skinned fillet of turbot into 75 × 10 × 10 mm strips. Start at the thinner end of the fillet and, when approaching the thicker part, divide each strip into two pieces, thus reducing the thickness of the fillet to 10 mm.

2. Finish and serve as from 3 in method of Goujons de sole frits (683).

## 687 — Poisson frit à la française

**Method**

1. May be applied to fillets, cuts and small whole fish.

2. Clean and prepare the fish then wash and drain it.

3. Dry the fish on a cloth, season, pass through flour, milk, then flour for a second time.

4. Deep fry fillets at 180°C (360°F) for 3–5 minutes and cuts at 170–175°C (340–350°F) for 6–9 minutes, according to thickness.

5. Drain, serve on a hot oval silver flat dish on dish paper and garnish the fish with fried sprigs of parsley and lemon wedges. An appropriate sauce may be served separately.

## 688 Fried whitebait — Blanchaille frite

**Method**

1. Pick out any weed, etc. from the fish then thoroughly wash, drain and dry it in a cloth.

2. Prepare and fry 'à la française' at 180°C (360°F) for about

1 minute, until golden brown. Then drain and lightly sprinkle with a mixture of salt and cayenne pepper (ratio of 10 to 1).

3. Serve on a hot oval flat dish on a dish paper in a loose dome-shaped mound garnished with sprigs of fried parsley and lemon wedges. Brown bread and butter is served on a dish with a doily.

## 689            Poisson frit à l'Orly

**Method**

1. Generally applied to fillets and suprêmes of various white fish.

2. Place the cleaned and prepared fish on a shallow tray, season it with salt and white pepper and sprinkle a little lemon juice, coarsely chopped parsley and a little oil over it. Marinade for 15 minutes.

3. Dip the fish into frying batter to coat then drop it into the frying fat or oil at 180°C (360°F) turning it with a spider during frying. Fry fillets for 3–5 minutes and suprêmes for 5–7 minutes. Drain well.

4. Serve the fish on a hot oval flat dish with dish paper and garnish on the side with sprigs of fried parsley and lemon wedges. Serve hot tomato sauce (370) in a sauceboat on an underdish with a doily.

## 690 Fried smelts          Éperlans frits

**Method**

1. Square the tails and cut off all fins with scissors. With the fingers, carefully pull away the gills. Make a small 25 mm incision in the belly and remove the intestines. Then thoroughly wash and drain the fish.

2. Dry on a cloth then season, flour, egg and crumb and roll the fish.

3. With a cloth, wipe the heads and tails clean of crumbs.

4. Fry and serve as for fried fillets of sole (678), from 4 in method.

## 691 Fried fillets of whiting      Filets de merlan frits

**Method**

1. Prepare the fillets of whiting as in Larder section (148).

2. Finish and serve as for fried fillets of sole (678) from 2 in method.

## 692 Fried curled whiting        Merlan en colère

**Method**

1. Prepare the whiting as in Larder section (148).

2. Dry on a cloth then season, flour, egg and crumb it.

3. Check that the tail still passes through the eye socket.

4. Place the curled whiting, backs down, into a frying basket and deep fry at 170°C (340°F) for 7–8 minutes. Drain well.

5. Serve the whiting on a hot oval flat dish on dish paper and arrange them on the dish with their backs uppermost. Garnish with sprigs of fried parsley and wedges of lemon along the side. Serve an appropriate sauce, e.g. Tartare (4) or Rémoulade (5) in a sauceboat on an underdish with a doily.

## 693            Merlan en lorgnette

**Method**

1. Square off the tails and cut off all fins with scissors. Remove the eyes with a small knife.

2. Pass a filleting knife along each side of the backbone as for filleting, but do not remove the head. With the scissors, clip the backbone free close to the head.

3. Dry on a cloth then season, flour, egg and crumb. Roll the fillets from the tail towards the head and secure each fillet with a cocktail stick, to represent a pair of spectacle frames.

4. Proceed to fry and serve as for Merlan en colère (692) from 4 in method. Remove the cocktail sticks when drained.

## 694            Merlan en buisson

**Method**

1. Prepare the whiting as for Merlan en lorgnette (693), 1 and 2 of method.

2. Cut the fillets, from the attached head, into 3 or 4 strips.

3. Dry the fish on a cloth, season, carefully flour, egg and crumb, rolling each strip of fish with the hand.

4. Lay in a frying basket to represent an octopus.

5. Fry and serve as for Merlan en colère (692)

## 696 Cooking of lobsters (boiling)

**Method**

1. Prepare a court-bouillon (626), or alternatively, prepare an acidulated liquor of 2 fl. oz (50 ml) to 2 pints (1 litre) of water, adding $\frac{1}{2}$ oz (10 g) of salt.
2. Wash the live lobsters, holding them by the back. Spike them by passing the point of a large knife through the shell between the eyes.
3. Plunge them into the boiling liquid, cover and allow to boil steadily for 15–25 minutes for $\frac{3}{4}$ lb (340 g) to $1\frac{1}{2}$ lb (680 g) sizes. When possible, allow lobsters to cool in the liquid.

## 697 Cleaning preparation of cooked lobster (halves)

**Method**

1. With the end of the blade of a large knife, chop away the claws and legs, close to the body.
2. Pull away the small lower pincer claws. Crack the claws and joints at the widest part and carefully remove the flesh, in one piece if possible.
3. Insert the point of the knife in the natural small recess halfway between the point of the head and commencement of tail. Cut through the centre of the shell towards the tip of the head, then down the centre in the opposite direction through the tail.
4. Remove the two halves of the sac (the small bag containing gravel) located behind the eyes and discard it.
5. With a knife point, remove the dark excreta line (trail) from the tail; wash the lobster if necessary.

## 698     Homard Mornay

| 8 portions | Ingredients | 10 couverts |
|---|---|---|
| 4 × $\frac{3}{4}$–1 lb | cooked lobsters | 5 × 350–450 g |
| 2 oz | grated Parmesan cheese | 70 g |
| 2 oz | butter | 70 g |
| 1 pint | Mornay sauce (390) | 700 ml |

**Method**

1. Prepare the lobster into cleaned halves (697). Remove the tail from the shell and cut it into 5–6 pieces on the slant.
2. Wash the shells then invert them and dry them on a tray.
3. Thickly grease a sauteuse with the butter, add all the lobster flesh, cover with a lid and heat through for 5–7 minutes in an oven at 160–175°C (325–350°F).

4. Turn the shells when dry and place a little sauce at the bottom. Replace the tail pieces in the correct position, as before cutting. Place the claw and joint flesh in the top part of the shell.
5. Mask over with the remainder of the sauce, to fill the shells, and sprinkle the surface evenly with the cheese.
6. Gratinate golden brown under a moderate salamander.
7. Serve on a hot oval silver flat dish with dish paper and garnish around the sides with sprigs of picked parsley.

## 699     Homard cardinal

**Method**

Prepare and serve as for Homard Mornay (698). Use a sauce made of 1 part Sauce Mornay (390) and 3 parts Coulis de homard (629); finish the sauce with a little butter.

## 700     Bouchée de homard

| 8 portions | Ingredients | 10 couverts |
|---|---|---|
| 8 oz flour mix | puff paste | 280 g flour mix |
| 3 × 1 lb | cooked lobster | 4 × 420 g |
| $\frac{3}{4}$ pint | coulis de homard (629) | 525 ml |
| $\frac{1}{4}$ pint | cream | 175 ml |
| 2 oz | butter | 70 g |

**Method**

1. Prepare the puff paste into 8 (or 10) bouchées (1282) 70 mm in diameter. Bake them at 190°C (375°F) for 25–30 minutes, until golden brown and crisp. Remove the centres, retaining the 'caps'.
2. Remove the flesh from the cooked lobsters, cut the tail in half lengthways and remove the trail. Wash, drain and cut all the flesh into 10 mm scallops.
3. Boil the sauce with the cream, reduce slightly then remove it from the heat. Add the butter a little at a time, until absorbed.
4. Add the lobster and heat it until it is nearly boiling. Fill it into the bouchées then place the 'caps' on at an angle.
5. Serve them on a hot oval silver flat dish on dish paper and garnish between them with sprigs of parsley.

## 701 Lobster patties

| 8 portions | Ingredients | 10 couverts |
|---|---|---|
| 8 oz flour mix | puff paste | 280 g flour mix |
| 2 × 1 lb | cooked lobster | 2 × 560 g |
| $\frac{1}{2}$ pint | coulis de homard (629) or béchamel (366) | 350 ml |

## Method

1. Boil the sauce, add the lobster flesh (prepared as in 700, 2 in method), and raise to boiling point. Place to cool, covered with a greased paper, in a shallow tray.

2. Prepare 8 (or 10) patties 60 mm in diameter (1283), using the lobster filling.

3. When rested, egg-wash the surface. Bake at 190°C (375°F), first at the top of the oven to set and lightly colour, then in the lower part of the oven for 20–25 minutes.

4. Serve the patties on a hot flat dish on a doily and garnish between them with sprigs of parsley.

## 702 Mussels                                                          Moules

### Method

1. Scrape the shells of the mussels with a small knife to remove all barnacles and weed. Discard any mussels with an open or damaged shell. Soak them in cold water, then drain.

2. Place 1 oz (25 g) of finely chopped shallot or onion in a saucepan for each 1 quart (litre) of mussels.

3. Cover with a well-fitting lid, place over a fierce heat to cook, until all the shells open (approximately 5–6 minutes) then remove.

4. Remove the mussels from the shells, pull away the beard and tongue.

## 703                                               Moules à la marinière

| 8 portions | Ingredients | 10 couverts |
|---|---|---|
| 4 pints | mussels | 3 litres |
| 2 oz | finely chopped shallots | 70 g |
| 2 oz | butter | 70 g |
| 1½ oz | flour | 55 g |
| 3 level teaspoons | salt | 10 g |
| ½ level teaspoon | ground white pepper | 2 g |
| 2 dessertspoons | chopped parsley | 10 g |
| ½ | lemon (in juice) | ½ |
| ¼ pint | dry white wine | 175 ml |
| 2 fl. oz | cream | 70 ml |

### Method

1. Place the shallots, wine, lemon juice and three-quarters of the parsley in a saucepan. Add the cleaned mussels (702, 1 in method).

2. Cover with a lid, place over a fierce heat and cook until all shells have opened (5–6 minutes) then remove them from the fire.

3. Remove the mussels from the saucepan and place them in a basin. Tilt the saucepan and allow it to stand, while preparing the mussels, so that any grit will fall to the bottom of the liquid.

4. Remove the mussels from the shells, pull away the tongue and beard. Replace each mussel into a half shell, place them into a deep dish, preferably a timbale or entrée dish, and cover and keep warm.

5. Carefully run off the liquor into a sauteuse, leaving any grit behind.

6. Adjust the quantity to 1 pint (700 ml) by adding a little fish stock if necessary, then bring to the boil, mix the butter and sieved flour to a smooth paste (Beurre manié) and add it to the liquor in small quantities. Whisk until boiling.

7. And sufficient of the seasoning to taste and finish with the cream.

8. Reboil the sauce, pour it over the mussels and sprinkle the surface with the remainder of the parsley. Place on an underdish with a doily and serve.

## 704 Fried mussels                                          Moules frites

### Method

1. Clean and cook the mussels (702).

2. Lightly flour, egg and crumb.

3. Deep fry at 180°C (360°F) for 2–3 minutes, until golden brown, then drain.

4. Serve in a loose dome shape on a hot flat dish on dish paper; garnish with fried sprigs of parsley and lemon wedges. Serve Sauce tartare (4) in a sauceboat on an underdish with a doily.

## 705 Cooked fish croquettes                    Croquettes de poisson

## Cooked fish cutlets                             Côtelettes de poisson

## Cooked fish médaillon                          Médaillons de poisson

Any poached or boiled white fish or salmon may be used, the fish used always being included in the name of the dish, e.g. Côtelettes de saumon, sauce piquante (381).

### Method 1

| 8 portions | Ingredients | 10 couverts |
|---|---|---|
| 1 lb | cooked fish (free of skin and bone) | 560 g |
| 1 lb | peeled potatoes | 560 g |
| 4 level teaspoons | salt | 15 g |
| ½ level teaspoon | ground white pepper | 2 g |
| 2 dessertspoons | chopped parsley | 8 g |
| 2 | eggs | 3 |

### Basic mixture

1. Cut the potatoes into evenly sized pieces, place them in a saucepan and cover with cold water. Boil, skim, cover with a lid and cook for 18–20 minutes.

2. Drain and dry off on a slow heat. Pass through a sieve with pressure and return to the cleaned pan.

3. Add the seasoning, chopped parsley and the fish; combine lightly with a spatule over the heat and add the beaten egg.

4. Place into a shallow tray to cool, covered with a greased paper.

## Method 2

| 8 portions | Ingredients | 10 couverts |
|---|---|---|
| 1 pint | béchamel (366) | 700 ml |
| 1½ lb | cooked fish (free of skin and bone | 840 g |
| 4 level teaspoons | salt | 15 g |
| ½ level teaspoon | ground white pepper | 2 g |
| 2 dessertspoons | chopped parsley | 8 g |
| 3 | yolks of egg | 4 |

### Basic mixture

1. Pour the béchamel into a thick bottom plat à sauter, reduce by a half, keeping freely moving with a spatule to prevent burning. Alternatively, prepare the béchamel double-thick to the required quantity.

2. Add the flaked fish, seasoning and parsley. Carefully combine with a spatule and heat to boiling point. Remove from the heat and stir in the yolks.

3. Turn out on to a buttered shallow tray and cover with a buttered paper, to cool.

### Method

1. Divide either mixture into 2 oz (55 g) pieces (allow 2 pieces per portion).

2. Mould into the desired shape (see 310, Moulding of cooked food preparations).

3. Deep fry at 180°C (360°F), until golden brown, for 2–3 minutes.

4. Serve on a hot flat oval dish on paper; garnish with sprigs of fried parsley. For cutlets, place frills on the pieces of macaroni. Serve an appropriate sauce e.g. Piquante, (381), Tomate (370), etc. in a sauceboat on an underdish with a doily.

## 706        Coquilles de poisson Mornay

Any poached or boiled white fish or salmon may be used for this recipe, and the type of fish should always be indicated in the name of the dish, e.g. Coquilles de turbot Mornay.

| 8 portions | Ingredients | 10 couverts |
|---|---|---|
| 1½ lb | cooked fish (free of skin and bone) | 840 g |
| 2 lb | peeled potatoes | 1 kg |
| 2 oz | grated Parmesan cheese | 70 g |
| 1 pint | Mornay sauce (390) | 700 ml |

### Method

1. Prepare the potatoes into basic duchesse mixture (1089).

2. Using a piping bag and a 10 mm star tube, pipe a scrolled border around 8 or 10 scallop shells, finishing with a rosette at the point.

3. Place on a baking sheet and dry under a moderate salamander until just beginning to colour.

4. Carefully break the fish into large flakes, add a little of the sauce and gently heat the mixture almost to boiling point.

5. Divide the fish equally into the shells and mask the remainder of the sauce over it. Sprinkle the surface evenly with the cheese.

6. Gratinate under a moderate salamander until golden brown then place in a moderate oven for 1–2 minutes.

7. Serve the shells on a hot flat dish with a doily and garnish between them with sprigs of parsley.

## 707    Preparation of scallops

### Method

1. Check the scallops for freshness: the shell should be firmly closed.

2. Place the shells on a closed top stove or in a moderate oven for a few seconds to start opening.

3. Open the shell, free the scallop with a small knife and put it into a basin of salted cold water.

4. Remove the trail and rinse the scallop; retain the white body and orange coloured roe.

5. Place these into a sauteuse with sufficient water to cover, a squeeze of lemon juice and a little salt.

6. Bring to the boil, skim them, simmer for 6–8 minutes. Then refresh and trim away any grisle.

## 708        Coquilles St Jacques Mornay

### Method

1. Prepare the scallops (1 per portion) as in 707.

2. Cut the body and the roe, on the slant into 4 pieces each. Heat them in a little butter in a sauteuse.

3. Then prepare and serve as for Coquilles de poisson Mornay (706).

*Note.* Other variations of this dish can be made by changing the sauce used, e.g. Coquilles St Jacques Bercy, Bonne femme, etc.

## 709                                               Brochette de fruits de mer

| 8 portions | Ingredients | 10 couverts |
|---|---|---|
| 8 oz | small closed mushrooms | 280 g |
| 1½ oz | butter | 55 g |
| 8 oz | scallops | 280 g |
| 1 quart | mussels | 1·5 litre |
| 8 oz | scampi | 280 g |
| 8 portions | riz pilaff (615) | 10 couverts |
| 1 pint | white wine sauce (630) | 700 ml |

### Method

1. Prepare the scallops (707) and cut them into 5 mm thick slices on the slant.

2. Prepare the mussels (702)

3. Place the scampi in a sauteuse, cover with water, boil and refresh.

4. Wash, peel and slowly cook the mushrooms in the butter in a covered sauteuse for 5–6 minutes.

5. Prepare the sauce and braised rice.

6. Place the mushrooms, mussels, scampi and pieces of scallops alternately on to 8 (or 10) serving skewers. Place these on a buttered tray and sprinkle them liberally with melted butter.

7. Lightly grill them on all sides under a very moderate salamander for 5–6 minutes then brush them with butter.

8. Serve the braised rice levelled on a hot oval silver flat dish and place the skewers on top. Serve the sauce in a sauce-boat on an underdish with a doily.

## 710  Smoked poached haddock

### Method

1. Allow 6–8 oz (170–225 g) of haddock per portion.

2. Cut off all fins from the fish and trim off the thin part near the end from which the head was removed. Divide into portions according to its size.

3. Cover the fish with ½ milk and ½ water in a shallow pan. Boil, skim then simmer the fish until cooked (5–7 minutes). The bone should pull clear when it is cooked.

4. Serve in a hot earthenware dish, placed on an underdish with dish paper, with a little of the cooking liquor, brush with melted butter and garnish with a sprig of parsley.

## 711  Fish kedgeree                Cadgerée de poisson

Although any poached or boiled white fish can be used in kedgeree, the dish is normally associated with salmon or poached smoked haddock; the name of the dish should state the fish used in the recipe, e.g. Cadgerée de saumon.

| 8 portions | Ingredients | 10 couverts |
|---|---|---|
| 2 lb | fish | 1 kg |
| 3 oz | butter | 100 g |
| 4 | hard boiled eggs | 5 |
| 12 oz of rice | riz pilaff (615) | 420 g of rice |
| 1 pint | curry sauce (413) | 700 ml |
| 1 dessertspoon | chopped parsley | 5 g |

### Method

1. Poach, then drain the fish, remove all bone and skin and flake it lightly.

2. Prepare the rice into Riz pilaff.

3. Cut the eggs into 10 mm rough dice.

4. Heat the butter in a shallow pan, add the rice, fish and eggs and combine them carefully to avoid breaking the fish into too small pieces. Correct the seasoning,

5. Serve in a loose dome shape, in a hot earthenware dish, sprinkled with chopped parsley. Place the dish on an underflat with dish paper. Serve the boiling sauce in a sauce-boat on an underflat and doily.

## 712  Fish pie

Any poached or boiled white fish or salmon may be used.

| 8 portions | Ingredients | 10 couverts |
|---|---|---|
| 1¼ lb | cooked fish (free of skin and bone) | 700 g |
| 4 oz | mushrooms | 140 g |
| 1¼ lb | peeled potato | 840 g |
| 2 | yolks of egg | 3 |
| 2 oz | butter | 70 g |
| 3 level teaspoons | salt | 10 g |
| ½ level teaspoon | ground white pepper | 2 g |
| 2 dessertspoons | chopped parsley | 10 g |
| 1 pint | cream sauce (389) | 700 ml |
| 2 | hard boiled eggs | 3 |

### Method

1. Cut the potatoes in pieces of an even size, then plain boil, drain, dry off and pass them through a sieve with pressure.

2. Add the butter and yolks of egg and mix well.

3. Prepare the mushrooms into 5 mm dice and cook 'à blanc' (335 g).

4. Bring the sauce to the boil, add the lightly flaked fish, mushrooms, parsley, seasoning and the eggs, cut into 5 mm dice, and reboil. Place the mixture in a buttered pie dish so that it half fills the dish.

5. Using a piping bag and a 10 mm star tube, pipe the potato across the surface of the mixture, finishing with rosettes around the edge. Brush the potato with egg wash.

6. Place in a shallow tray with water, and colour golden

brown at the top of an oven at 220–230°C (425–450°F).
7. Place a pie collar around the pie dish and serve it on an underflat with dish paper. Brush the potato surface with melted butter.

## 713 Raie au beurre noir

| 8 portions | Ingredients | 10 couverts |
|---|---|---|
| 2 × 1½ lb | wings of skate | 2 × 840 g |
| 4 oz | butter | 140 g |
| 1 oz | capers | 35 g |
| 2 dessertspoons | chopped parsley | 10 g |
| 2 tablespoons | vinegar | 40 ml |

### Method

1. If the dark skin is not already removed from the skate, pass the point of a knife under the first 10 mm of the thick side. Hold the skin with a cloth and pull it off towards the outer thin part of the wings. Wash the fish.
2. Cut the wings into 4–5 portions of equal weight.
3. Place in a shallow pan and cover with a court-bouillon (626). Bring to the boil, skim, then simmer for 8 to 10 minutes. The fish should just begin to come clear of the bone.
4. Remove with a slice, drain well, place on to a hot oval flat silver dish and sprinkle the fish with the capers and parsley.
5. Heat the butter until a dark brown, add the vinegar, then mask the liquid over the fish.

## 714 Merlan à l'anglaise

## 715 Éperlans à l'anglaise

### Method

1. Allow one 7–8 oz (200–225 g) whiting per portion or 4–5 smelts per portion, according to size.
2. Split the fish down the back by passing the knife point along each side of the backbone. Cut the bone, close to the head and tail and remove it; also remove the eyes. Ungutted fish should be used.
3. Remove the gut, and any small bone along the outer edge of the fish not previously removed then wash, drain and dry the fish on a cloth.
4. Season the fish then pass it through flour, egg and fresh white breadcrumbs.
5. Pat with a palette knife to flatten the crumbs then mark a 10 mm trellis pattern across the cut side of the fish.
6. Place enough of a mixture of half oil and half butter in a frying pan to cover the base. Heat, then add the fish,

cut side down first, and shallow fry golden brown on each side.
7. Serve on a hot oval flat dish, the cut side uppermost. Place 2 slices of parsley butter (116) on each of the whiting and a half slice on each smelt; garnish with sprigs of parsley.

## 716 Merlan à l'italienne

### Method

1. Prepare the whiting as for recipe 714, up to and including 3 in the method.
2. Butter an oval earthenware dish or dishes, place a little Sauce italienne (376) on the dish, place the fish on top and pour the sauce over it so that it is covered.
3. Sprinkle the surface lightly with white breadcrumbs and Parmesan cheese then melted butter.
4. Cook at the top of an over at 180–190°C (350–375°F) for 8–10 minutes. Clean around the edge of the dish with a wet cloth then place it on an underdish with dish paper and serve.

## 717 Merlan au gratin

| 8 portions | Ingredients | 10 couverts |
|---|---|---|
| 8 × 7–8 oz | whiting | 10 × 200–225 g |
| 16 | medium closed mushrooms | 20 |
| 1 oz | finely chopped shallots | 35 g |
| 3 oz | butter | 100 g |
| 2 oz | white breadcrumbs | 70 g |
| 2 fl. oz | dry white wine | 70 ml |
| 1 | lemon (in juice) | 1 |

### Method

1. Prepare the whiting as for recipe 714, up to and including 3 in the method.
2. Well grease a number of earthenware dishes (the whiting is usually cooked in 1 or 2 portion dishes).
3. Turn the mushrooms and half cook them 'à blanc' (335 g).
4. Wash the trimmings and stalks then finely chop them.
5. Sprinkle the bottom of the dish or dishes with the shallot and chopped mushroom. Place the whiting on top, cut side showing, and season it with a little salt and white pepper.
6. Sprinkle with the lemon juice and wine. Place two turned mushrooms on each fish.
7. Sprinkle the surface evenly with breadcrumbs to give it a thin coat, then sprinkle with the melted butter.
8. Cook in the top of an oven at 180–190°C (350–375°F) for 8–10 minutes. Clean around the edge of the dishes. Sprinkle the surface with melted butter.
9. Serve on an underflat with dish paper.

**718 Cold half lobster**             **Demi-homard froid**

**Method**

1. Allow a half of a 12 oz–1 lb (350–450 g) lobster per portion, preparing the halves as in 697.

2. Fill the cavity of the shell with a few capers and place the claw on top.

4. Dress the shells on a cold oval silver flat dish and garnish each one with a quarter of prepared lettuce, ½ hard-boiled egg and sections of peeled tomato. Serve Mayonnaise sauce (1) in a sauceboat on an underdish with a doily.

**719 Cold fish and shellfish salads**
    **Cold fish and shellfish mayonnaise**

When preparing the following as a main fish course, double the ingredients quoted in the hors d'oeuvre recipes.

**Fish salad (79)**              **Salade de poisson**

**Fish mayonnaise (80)**         **Mayonnaise de poisson**

**Lobster salad (81)**           **Salade de homard**

**Lobster mayonnaise (82)**      **Mayonnaise de homard**

**Crab salad (81)**              **Salade de crabe**

**Crab mayonnaise (82)**         **Mayonnaise de crabe**

**Prawn salad (81)**             **Salade de crevettes roses**

**Prawn mayonnaise (82)**        **Mayonnaise de crevettes roses**

**720**                          **Filets de sole Dugléré froids**

**Method**

1. Prepare and cook the fillets of sole as for Filets de soles duglère (653), up to and including 4 in method. Allow the fillets to go cold.

2. Reduce the cooking liquor and garnish until almost dry then allow it to go cold.

3. Replace the fish velouté with the same quantity of Mayonnaise sauce (1).

4. Add the mayonnaise, then the cream, to the reduction and, correct the seasoning.

5. Dress the fillets of sole in an earthenware dish, mask over with the sauce and sprinkle the surface with chopped parsley. Place the dish on an underflat with dish paper.

# Entrées - Relevés - Roasts

202

# Entrées, Relevés and Roasts

Certain points about these categories of dishes need to be explained and clarified before the individual recipes are started, so that the dishes are made, used and served correctly.

It is accepted that an entrée is the first course following the fish, although more than one entrée can be included in the same menu. Entrées are normally cut portions or preparations of meat, poultry and game, while uncut portions (i.e. either whole or large joints of meat, poultry and game) are regarded as relevés, or 'relieving', dishes.

The garnishes used in entrées, relevés and roasts contribute enormously to the effect of their final presentation, and the following factors should help the student of cookery achieve the best effects:

(a) the quantity of garnish should be adequate for the number of portions to be served;

(b) where gravies or sauces are served with the course, it is usual for additional quantities to be served separately in sauceboats;

(c) garnishes should be positioned with the food so that the effect is not lost after the first portions of the food have been served. When garnishes are prepared separate from the main ingredient, they are usually arranged in rows along each side of the dish, in bouquets around the dish or, in a few cases, sprinkled over the top of the food;

(d) for eye-appeal, artistic use should be made of the available colours in a garnish;

(e) chopped parsley should be used for contrast and should not be used indiscriminately.

The number of garnishes is legion, so that only a certain number is given here, consideration having been made for popularity and variety.

## 722 GARNISHES FOR SMALL ENTRÉES

The recipe preparation numbers and quantities (for garnish per one portion) are given with the following garnishes, which are related to various groups of dishes, indicated as follows:

N, Noisette; T, Tournedos; E, Escalope de veau; G, Grenadin de veau; M, Médaillon de ris de veau.

*Note.* A demi-glace base sauce is generally served with tournedos and jus-lié with noisettes and veal.

**Arlésienne** (N and T) 3 slices of fried egg plant (967), 5–6 rings of French fried onions (1049) and 1 dessertspoon of cooked tomate concassée (337), the tomato served on top.

**Beauharnais** (N and T) 2 stuffed mushrooms (978) and buttered quarters of 1 artichoke (961).

**Bohémienne** (N) $\frac{1}{2}$ oz (15 g) riz pilaff (615), 5–6 rings of French fried onions (1049) and 1 dessertspoon of cooked tomate concassée (337), the tomato served on top.

**Bolonaise** (E, G and M) 1 oz (30 g) spaghetti bolonaise (596).

**Castillane** (T and N) 2 half-size pommes croquettes (1092), 5–6 rings of French fried onions (1049) and 1 dessertspoon of cooked tomate concassée, the tomato served on top.

**Chartres** (T and N) 2 half-size pommes fondantes (1114), 2 stuffed mushrooms (978) and a quarter of braised lettuce (1039); place blanched tarragon leaves across the entrée.

**Catalane** (T and N) 1 small grilled tomato (1072) inside a buttered artichoke bottom (961).

**Choisy** (T and N) 1 quarter of braised lettuce (1039) and 2 half-size pommes château (1111).

**Choron** (T and N) 1 buttered artichoke bottom (961) filled with buttered peas (1053) and 7–8 pieces pommes noisettes (1122).

**Fleuriste** (T and N) 1 poached tomato, filled with jardinière of vegetables (1035), and 2 half-size pommes château (1111).

**Fontainebleau** (T and N) 2 small bouchées of duchesse potatoes (40 mm in diameter) filled with jardinière of vegetables (1035).

**Judic** (T and N) 1 stuffed tomato (duxelle) (1074), one-quarter of braised lettuce (1039) and 2 half-size pommes château (1111).

**Médicis** (T and N) 1 buttered artichoke bottom (961) filled with small balls of glazed carrots, turnips (1043) and peas, 7 to 8 pieces of pommes noisettes (1122) and 1 dessertspoon of sauce Choron (404) on the entrée.

**Milanaise** (E, G and M) 1 oz (30 g) spaghetti milanaise (599).

**Montpensier** (N and T) 1 buttered artichoke bottom (961), filled with 2–3 buttered asparagus tips (965), and 7–8 pieces pommes noisette (1122), with julienne of truffle placed on the entrée after it has been masked with sauce.

**Napolitaine** (E, G and M) 1 oz (30 g) spaghetti napolitaine (600).

**Niçoise** (T and N) 1 small poached tomato (1073), 1 oz (30 g) buttered French beans (1031) and 2 half-size pommes château (1111).

**Opéra** (N and T) 1 small short paste tartlet filled with 1 oz (30 g) of scalloped fried chicken livers bound with sauce madère (378) and 1 bouchée of pommes duchesse (40 mm in diameter) filled with 3–4 buttered asparagus tips (965).

**Princesse** (E, G and M) 1 buttered artichoke bottom (961), filled with 3–4 buttered asparatus tips (965), and 7–8 pieces of pommes noisette (1122).

**Rachel** (N and T) 1 buttered artichoke bottom (961) filled with 3–4 slices of poached bone marrow.

**Rossini** (N and T) 1 slice of foie gras, tossed in butter on top, slices of truffle, cordon of meat glaze around.

**St Germain** (N and T) 1 buttered artichoke bottom (961) containing purée of 2 oz (55 g) fresh peas piped to a dome shape.

**Sicilienne** (E, G and M) 1 oz (30 g) spaghetti sicilienne (601).

**Sévigné** (N and T) 1 quarter of braised lettuce (1039), 3–4 grilled mushrooms (977) and 2 half-size pommes château (1111).

**Tyrolienne** (N and T) 6–8 rings of French fried onions (1049) and 1 dessertspoon of cooked tomate concassée (337) served on top of the entrée.

**Viennoise** (E) (à la carte) Sieved yolk, white of egg and chopped parsley in rows at the ends of the dish, a slice of peeled lemon on the escalope, with paupiette of anchovy and stoned olive, jus-lié and beurre noisette over it. (Table d'hôte) Yolk, white and chopped parsley may be placed on the lemon with the anchovy and olive.

---

## 723 GARNISHES FOR JOINTS OF MEAT AND POULTRY

Most of these garnishes are suitable for serving with various joints of lamb, beef and veal and, in some cases, with chicken when it is roasted, braised or poêlé.

**Allemande** 1 oz (30 g) nouilles au beurre (605), one rosette of mashed potato (1079) and jus-lié.

**Ancienne** (for chicken or veal) 4–5 white glazed button onions (724a) and 3–4 small white button mushrooms cooked à blanc (335 g).

**Arlésienne** As for small entrée with jus-lié.

**Boulangère** 1 portion pommes boulangère (1135), the meat to be finished cooking on top of the potatoes, and jus-lié.

**Bruxelloise** 1 small or half endive braisée (1013) 5–6 small choux de Bruxelles au beurre (991), 2 half-size pommes château (1111), and jus-lié.

**Bourguignonne** 4–5 button onions glazed brown (724b), 1 oz (30 g) scallops of closed mushrooms (sauté) (335g), 1 oz (30 g) lardons of bacon (sauté) (724d) and jus-lié.

**Bourgeoise** 4–5 turned carottes glacées (969), 4–5 turned navets glacés (1043), 1 oz (30 g) buttered peas (1053) and jus-lié.

**Bouquetière** 4–5 turned carottes glacées (969), 4–5 turned navets glacés (1043), 1 oz (30 g) buttered peas (1053), 1 oz (30 g) buttered haricots verts (1031), buds of cauliflower Mornay (995) or cauliflower or masked with Hollandaise sauce (402), 1 small tomate pochée (1073), 2 half-size pommes château (1111), 4–5 button onions glazed brown (724b) and jus-lié.

**Clamart** 1 small short paste tartlet or 1 buttered artichoke bottom (961) filled with 1 oz (30 g) petits pois à la française

(1056) or purée of buttered peas (1055) with 2 half size pommes château (1111) and jus-lié.

**Concorde** 4–5 turned carottes glacées (969), 1 oz (30 g) buttered peas (1053), 1 rosette of mashed potato (1079) and jus-lié.

**Dubarry** 1 small ball of chou-fleur Mornay (995), 2–3 half-size pommes château (1111) and jus-lié.

**Favorite** 1 buttered artichoke bottom (961) cut into quarters, 1 small portion braised celery (974), 2 half-size pommes château (1111) and jus-lié.

**Flamande** 1 half-size petits choux braisés (986), 4–5 turned carottes glacées (969), 4–5 turned navets glacés, 1 slice of sausage (cooked and served with cabbage) and 2 half size pommes persillées (1078).

**Fleuriste** As for small entrée with jus-lié.

**Freneuse** 6–7 turned navets glacés (1043), 2 half-size Pommes château (1111) and jus-lié.

**Judic** As for small entrée, with jus-lié.

**Jardinière** 2 oz (55 g) jardinière de légumes (1035) with jus-lié.

**Macédoine** 2 oz (55 g) macédoine de légumes (1036) with jus-lié.

**Maryland** (chicken) 1 grilled slice of bacon, 2 small corn croquettes (1042), ½ banana, fried or grilled in butter, and sherry and cream sabayon.

**Nivernaise** same as Bourgeoise, with the addition of 3–4 button onions glazed brown (724b) and jus-lié.

**Nouilles (aux)** 1 oz (30 g) nouilles au beurre (605) with jus-lié.

**Primeurs (aux)** 4–5 turned Carottes glacées (969), 4–5 turned navets glacés (1043), 1 oz (30 g) buttered peas (1053) and 1 oz (30 g) haricots verts au beurre (1031) cut in 10 mm diamonds.

**Soissonnaise** 1 oz (30 g) haricots blancs au beurre (1026) and jus-lié.

**Vichy** 2 oz (55 g) carottes Vichy (970), and jus-lié.

---

## 724 PREPARATION OF GARNISHES

The methods described cover various items of garnish not covered in the other recipes given.

(a) **White glazed**      **Petits oignons glacés**
    **button onions**                **à blanc**

**Method**

1. Place the peeled button onions in a suitable plat à sauter, just cover with water and add a little butter, salt and pepper. Boil then cook for 15–16 minutes until tender; during the last few minutes rapidly reduce all the liquid to form a glaze, without colouring.

(b) **Brown glazed button**      **Petits oignons glacés**
    **onions**                       **à brun**

**Method**

1. Prepare and cook as for 'à blanc' (a), adding a little sugar.

2. When the cooking liquor has formed a glaze, allow the onions to colour golden brown. Move the handle of the pan in a circular movement to roll the onions in the glaze to obtain an even colour.

(c) **Poached bone marrow**

**Method**

1. Cut the bone marrow in 10 mm slices.

2. Drop into a shallow pan of boiling salted water.

3. Remove from the heat then allow to poach for 1–2 minutes.

4. Only place to cook when required.

(d) **Lardons of bacon (sauté)**

**Method**

1. Remove the rind and smoked surface from streaky bacon and cut it into 5 mm thick slices then into 5 mm strips, for general use. Other sizes are also used.

2. Place it in a shallow pan, cover with water and boil, refresh then drain.

3. Add a little clean bacon fat or butter.

4. Toss over the heat, until a very light golden brown, without crisping or drying out.

**(e) Duchesse potato bouchées (Mixture 1089)**

**Method**

1. Grease a baking sheet.
2 With a piping bag and a 10 mm star tube, pipe a 40 mm circle or oval, then pipe over this to raise an outer wall 40 mm high, leaving a space in the centre for garnish.
3. Dry in a moderate oven at 175°C (347°F), egg-wash, then colour a light golden brown.

---

## 725 THE APPLICATION OF ROASTING

The types of meat, poultry and game used for roasting, together with the various methods of preparation, are dealt with under individual headings, e.g. beef, veal, in the Larder Section.

The under surface of joints of meat needs some sort of protection during roasting to prevent frying. This can be achieved, according to the size of the joint, by:

(a) placing small joints on wire trivets,
(b) placing larger joints on chopped bones of the meat, after the joint has been boned:
(c) laying the joint on a bed of thickly-cut slices of carrots and onions; this is particularly used for many kinds of relevés;
(d) laying the joint on thick slices of potato; this is usually used for large plain roasts, such as ribs of beef.

**Method**

1. Evenly sprinkle the article to be roasted with salt all over.
2. Place it in a suitable size roasting tray. Smear the top surface all over with clean dripping or fat. Use method (a) (b) (c) or (d) as above, to protect the joint. Poultry and game are turned on their side.
3. Place in a hot oven at 230–260°C (450–500°F) for 10–15 minutes to seal the pores of the meat (this retains the natural juices). In the case of very small birds, such as poussin or quail, the sealing process is effected on top of the stove.
4. Reduce the heat. The temperature used will vary considerably from 150–200°C (300–400°F), according to the size and thickness. In a few cases of very large items, i.e. large turkeys, the temperature may even be lower.
5. During cooking, baste the meat frequently, depending on the size. Poultry and game are turned from one leg over to the other leg, then finally on to the back to colour the breast. Where a 'bard' of fat bacon is used on certain game, it is removed just before cooking is finished to colour the breast.
6. The following methods are used to test when the meat is cooked.
(i) Press red meats, such as beef, with the finger or the edge of a roasting fork. The pressure should produce a pink blood, which denotes the meat is ready (underdone).
(ii) Pierce white meats, such as veal, lamb and pork, with a roasting fork or trussing needle. The liquid or juice which is released should be quite clear; if any pink is present, further cooking is necessary.
(iii) In the case of chicken and other poultry pass a fork through the back of the carcass above the leg and hold the vent over a plate: the natural juices should be clear. Alternatively pierce the drumstick close to the thigh; the juice should be clear if the meat is cooked. The latter method is used for turkey.
7. Remove the meat, poultry or game. Remove the trivet or potato if used.
8. Set the tray on the stove until the juices form a caramelised sediment, i.e. when the fat clears and just begins to show a light blue vapour.
9. Run off the fat and retain the sediment. Moisten the tray with brown stock; if for roast gravy (jus de rôti) allow ¾ pint (530 ml) for each 8–10 covers. If used for jus-lié, add a little stock first, then the required quantity of jus-lié. Allow to simmer gently for 4–5 minutes to dissolve the sediment. Fast boiling will emulsify any fat.
10. Pass through a gauze strainer into a bain-marie container. Reboil, skim off all fat. Correct the seasoning with salt if necessary. Add a little gravy browning in a ladle if necessary.

# GUIDANCE CHART FOR ROASTING TIMES

**Beef**  15–20 minutes setting time,
plus 15 minutes per lb weight (33 min/kg).

**Lamb**  15–20 minutes setting time,
plus 20 minutes per lb weight (44 min/kg).

**Mutton**  20 minutes setting time,
plus 20–25 minutes per lb weight (44–55 min/kg).

**Veal**  20 minutes setting time,
plus 25 minutes per lb weight (55 min/kg).

**Pork**  25 minutes setting time,
plus 30 minutes per lb weight (66 min/kg).

*Note.* Exceptions to these times are the roasting of contre-filet and faux filet which are thin in comparison to their weight, and therefore need only to be roasted for just over half the normal roasting time.

Where certain joints have a stuffing placed inside, the cooking time requires to be increased by 5 minutes per lb weight (11 min/kg).

## Poultry

All poultry, irrespective of size, is roasted for approximately one-third of the total cooking time on each leg and one-third on the back to finish and colour the breast.

Chicken  20 minutes per lb weight (44 min/kg) when drawn.

Duck  25 minutes per lb weight (55 m n/kg) when drawn.

Turkey  15–16 minutes per lb weight (33–35 min/kg) when drawn.

When very small chicken, i.e. poussin, are roasted, the tray is set on top of the stove first until the poussin begin to fry, then placed in the oven.

## 726 Carving of roast meats poultry and game

### Method

1. Irrespective of the shape or type, except in short-cut saddles, meat is always carved against the grain.
2. For pork, remove the crackling before carving and cut it into thin pieces. Loin of pork should be cut across, slightly on the slant to give a wider slice. Legs of pork are carved by starting at the knuckle end and cutting in thin slices with the knife at an angle of 45°. When the slices begin to widen, start slicing to the bone from each side in turn, for uniformity of size.
3. Legs of lamb and mutton are carved as for pork. To carve best ends, cut through between the rib bones where they are closer together. Remove a bone, if necessary, to cut evenly sized portions.

Saddles are carved (a) English style, by removing the meat from the saddle, then slicing across, slightly on the slant (this is usually applied to long cut saddles), and (b) French style, used for carving short-cut saddles, by passing the knife along the length of the saddle close to the back-bone, then down and underneath to where the side fat commences, the slices being cut 4–6 mm thick along the whole length of the saddle ('en aiguillette').

Unboned shoulders of lamb and mutton require considerable skill in carving. First start slicing at the knuckle end, on the slant, then, when the bone is met, cut at a greater angle from both sides of the shoulder.

4. Beef, whether on the bone, or boned, is cut very thin against the grain. In the case of ribs, remove each rib bone as each becomes clear of meat, to facilitate carving the next slice.
5. Turn chicken, duck and pheasant on the side when carving. Pass the knife through the skin at the top of the leg, where it joins the body, then turn it around to ease the leg clear of the body. When the leg is served (which is unusual in the case of pheasant) make a 20 mm incision through the natural joint where the drumstick bone joins the thigh.

Cut off the wing in a straight line parallel to the breast bone to allow the knife to come down through the natural ball and socket joint between the wing and the breast. Turn the carcass on end and chop off the back part of the carcass. Cut the breast lengthways, through the bone, into 2, 3 or 4 pieces, according to size.

6. Legs of turkey are removed in the same manner as chicken. The bone is then removed and the flesh cut on the slant in thin slices.

The breast is carved in thin slices, the slices kept a regular size during carving.

## 727 Serving of roast meats, poultry and game

1. The roasted item may be served whole, carved or portioned.
2. Portions should be arranged neatly on a hot oval dish and masked over with a little roast gravy.
3. All roast meats should be garnished with washed, picked watercress and additional gravy should be served in a sauceboat on an underdish with a doily.
4. Place the appropriate garnish on the dish being served. In some cases, other garnishes are served in extra sauceboats.

**728 Adjuncts for roast meat, game and poultry**

Beef: Yorkshire pudding, horseradish sauce or scraped horseradish, jus rôti.

Mutton, leg: red currant jelly, jus rôti.

Mutton, shoulder: onion sauce, jus rôti.

Lamb: mint sauce, jus rôti.

Veal: boiled bacon, jus rôti. (This joint is usually stuffed.)

Venison: red currant jelly, sour cream sauce, jus rôti.

Pork: sage and onion stuffing, apple sauce, jus rôti.

Chicken: pommes chips, grilled bacon, bread sauce, watercress, jus rôti.

Duck: apple sauce, sage and onion stuffing, jus rôti, watercress.

Turkey: grilled sausages, cranberry sauce, bread sauce, pommes chips, jus rôti, watercress, braised chestnuts.

Pigeon: croûton, watercress, pommes paille, jus rôti.

Goose: apple sauce, sage and onion stuffing, chestnut purée, jus rôti, watercress.

Poussin: as for chicken.

Guinea fowl: bread sauce, pommes chips, watercress, jus rôti.

Pheasant, grouse, partridge, quail: bread sauce, fried breadcrumbs, watercress, bird dressed 'en croûte' with farce au gratin, pommes chips or gaufrette, jus rôti.

Wild duck: orange sauce, watercress, orange salad, jus rôti.

---

## 729 THE APPLICATION OF BOILING

Care should be taken with the way in which boiling is carried out, since meat and poultry can become tough and hard, or tender, and may lose or retain their flavour and nutriment during the boiling process. One of the distinct advantages of boiling is that meat loses less weight during this cooking process than during any other, and, also, the water in which the meat is cooked can be turned to a useful purpose, i.e. for stock.

A number of basic points should be observed when boiling meat, and these are indicated here:

1. The water should always cover the article being cooked; hot water should be used to keep the level constant, as cold will lower the temperature.

2. It is advisable to add a flavouring, such as bouquet garni, onion, carrot, leek, celery, etc., which will flavour the meat and the stock.

3. After being brought to boiling point, the liquid should not boil briskly but should bubble very slowly on the side of the stove. In other words, the liquid should gently simmer.

4. Boiling is used to achieve one of two distinct results: to retain as much of the natural juices in the meat by placing the meat in boiling water (the boiling water will seal the pores and cut ends and coagulate the albumen), or to extract the juices and to mix them with the liquid by placing the meat in cold water which is then brought slowly to the boil. Salt meats, such as pickled silverside, salt pork, ham, tongue and smoked meats, should be put into cold water and brought slowly to the boil.

5. The time for boiling meats should be approximately 20–25 minutes per lb (45–55 min/kg) plus 15–20 minutes longer. Fowls take from 1½ hours, according to size and age. All salt and smoked meats should be soaked overnight in cold running water to extract excess salt and to help soften the meat.

The types of meat and poultry which can be boiled, together with the various methods of preparation, are dealt with under individual headings, e.g. beef, lamb, in the Larder Section.

---

**730 Adjuncts for boiled meats**

Beef (fresh): cabbage, carrots, turnip, leeks, celery, onions and liquor;

(salted): dumplings, carrots.

Mutton: caper sauce and vegetable garnish, turnips, button onions, celery.

Veal (breast): parsley sauce, boiled bacon.

Pork (pickled): pease pudding, carrots, liquor.

Rabbit: pickled pork and onion sauce

Chicken and fowl: sauce suprême and rice, or pickled pork and parsley sauce and rice.

Turkey: celery sauce or sauce suprême.

See under the individual headings in the Larder Section for the types of meat that can be poêlé, and for the various methods of preparing them.

**Method**

1. Carefully select a suitable pan with a tight fitting lid and of a size to just hold the joint or article of poultry.

2. Prepare a bed of roots (340) which will just cover the bottom of the pan.

3. Season the meat or poultry all over. Place it on the bed of roots (place poultry on the leg side).

4. Smear it all over with butter then cover tightly with the lid.

5. Commence cooking in the centre of the lower part of the oven at 220°C (425°F). After 15 minutes, reduce the heat to 160–175°C (325–350°F), according to the size of the meat. Use the lower heat for larger articles.

6. During cooking, baste frequently, turning the mea-over. For poultry, turn over on to the other leg after onet third of the cooking time, then on to the back after two-thirds of the cooking time. Cooking times are approximately the same as these for roasting and the meat is tested in the same manner.

7. 10–15 minutes before it has finished cooking, remove the cover, baste frequently to colour very lightly and glaze the meat.

8. Remove the meat and poultry when cooked. Set the pan on the stove until the fat becomes clear, then run off.

9. Add wine or stock to 'déglacer' the pan, reduce, then add ¾ pint (525 ml) of jus-lié, reboil and pass through a gauze strainer.

10. Reboil, skim to remove all fat and correct the season-ing.

---

## 732 BEEF—ROASTS, RELEVÉS, ENTRÉES

**733 Roast ribs of beef**      Côtes de boeuf rôties

**734 Roast sirloin of beef (on the bone)**      Aloyau de boeuf rôti

**Method**

1. Prepare the ribs of beef as in 165 and 179; or

2. Prepare the sirloin of beef as in 164.

3. Prepare and roast as described in 725.

4. Carve and serve as described in 726, method 4.

5. Garnish on the side with Yorkshire pudding and sprigs of watercress. Serve, on an underdish with a doily, sauce-boats of roast gravy and horseradish sauce (415).

**735 Roast boned sirloin of beef**      **Contrefilet de boeuf rôti**
                                       **Faux-filet de boeuf rôti**

**Method**

1. Prepare the sirloin of beef (164) for contrefilet or faux filet.

2. Prepare and roast as in 725c.

3. When cooked, remove the meat, then proceed as from 8 in method of 725 to produce jus de rôti or jus-lié as required.

**736 Yorkshire pudding 8–10 portions**

| | Ingredients | |
|---|---|---|
| 6 oz | flour | 170 g |
| 2 oz | first-class dripping | 55 g |
| 3 level teaspoons | salt | 10 g |
| 2 | eggs | 2 |
| ½ pint | milk | 280 ml |

**Method**

1. Sieve the flour and salt into a basin and make a well.

2. Beat the eggs then add half the milk to them. Pour this mixture into the well, absorb the flour with a whisk and beat it until smooth. Gradually add the remainder of the milk.

3. Pass through a fine conical strainer into a clean basin then allow it to rest for 1 hour.

4. For individual puddings, use bun frame trays, placed on a baking sheet. Alternatively, use an omelette or a similar-sized frying pan.

5. Melt the dripping and pour it into the moulds or pans to give a 3 mm depth.

6. Using a ladle, pour the mixture into the moulds or pans to a depth of 10 mm.

7. Place in the centre to top of the oven at 200°C (400°F).

8. Cook for 15–17 minutes for individual portions and 20–25 minutes for larger ones, until golden brown and crisp.

## 737  Roast fillet of beef      Filet de boeuf rôti

### Method

1. Prepare the fillet of beef (163). Usually the fillet is finished piqué.

2. Prepare and roast as in 725c. Start the roasting tray on top of the stove and set the fillet, then roast.

3. When cooked, remove the fillet then proceed as from 8 in method of 725 to produce jus de rôti or jus-lié as required.

## 738      Filet de boeuf portugaise

### Method

1. Prepare, cook and finish with jus-lié as in 737.

2. Cut across the fillet to produce 5 mm thick slices.

3. Dress the slices half overlapping down the centre of a hot oval silver flat dish.

4. Garnish along one side with 1 each Tomate farcie (duxelle) (1074) and 2–3 half-size Pommes château (1111) per portion and along the opposite side in a mound.

5. Mask over the fillet with jus-lié and sprinkle the potatoes with chopped parsley. Serve a sauceboat of jus-lié on an underdish with a doily.

*Note.* For various other garnishes for filet, contrefilet and faux filet, see garnishes (723).

## 739  Boiled beef (French style)      Boeuf bouilli à la française

| 8 portions | Ingredients | 10 couverts |
|---|---|---|
| 2½ lb | flat ribs or thin flank | 1·4 kg |
| 3 oz | carrot | 100 g |
| 3 oz | onion stuck with clove | 100 g |
| small | bouquet garni | small |
| 1 oz | salt | 35 g |
| 8 | white pepper corns | 10 |
| | garnish | |
| 6 oz | turned carrots | 210 g |
| 6 oz | turned turnips | 210 g |
| 6 oz | button onions | 210 g |

### Method

1. Place a pan of white stock or water to boil.

2. Add the whole carrots and onions (stuck with the cloves).

3. Add the salt, peppercorns and the bouquet garni.

4. Place the joint (tied and rolled if necessary) in the boiling liquor and allow it to cook for about 3 hours.

5. Place the turned vegetables and the peeled button onions in muslin bags to cook with the beef after 2 hours.

6. Carve the meat in medium to thick slices across the grain and mask it with a little liquor. Serve garnished with the vegetables

7. Freezing salt, gherkins and pickled red cabbage should be available at table.

## 740  Boiled salt beef and dumplings

| 8 portions | Ingredients | 10 couverts |
|---|---|---|
| 2½ lb | pickled silverside or brisket | 1·4 kg |
| 6 oz | turned or young carrots | 210 g |
| 6 oz | button onions | 210 g |
| 8 oz (flour mix) | suet paste (1143) | 280 g (flour mix) |
| 2 teaspoons | chopped parsley | 5 g |

### Method

1. Beef should be left in brine from 7–10 days, according to size, for a good flavour and colour.

2. Soak the beef in cold water for 1–2 hours to remove any excess salt from the brine.

3. Place the meat in a saucepan and cover it with cold water. Bring to the boil, skim then simmer for 1 hour.

4. Add the prepared carrots and onions and simmer for a further 45 minutes.

5. Divide the suet paste into 16 or 20 pieces and, using a little flour, roll the pieces between the palms of the hands into small dumplings. Drop into the boiling liquor and simmer for 20–25 minutes.

6. Test the meat with a trussing needle, which should penetrate to the centre of the joint without pressure.

7. Carve the beef in thin slices against the grain. Dress the slices, slightly overlapping, on a hot oval flat silver dish.

8. Place the dumplings along each side of the meat and arrange the carrots and onions at opposite ends of the dumplings. Sprinkle chopped parsley on the carrots and onions. Mask over with a little of the strained liquor. Serve a sauceboat of the liquor separately on an underdish with a doily.

## 741  Braised beef      Boeuf braisé

The types of beef used for braising are dealt with under Preparation of beef joints in the Larder section.

| 8 portions | Ingredients | 10 couverts |
|---|---|---|
| 2½ lb | prepared beef | 1·4 kg |
| 4 oz | carrot* | 140 g |
| 4 oz | onion* | 140 g |
| 1 oz | celery* | 35 g |
| ½ pod | garlic | ½ pod |

| | | | | | |
|---|---|---|---|---|---|
| 4 teaspoons | salt* | 15 g | 2 oz | dripping | 70 g |
| ½ level teaspoon | milled pepper* | 2 g | 1 lb | cabbage | 560 g |
| 2 oz | dripping | 70 g | 4 level teaspoons | salt | 15 g |
| 2 oz | tomato purée | 70 g | ½ level teaspoon | milled pepper | 2 g |
| 1 oz | arrowroot | 35 g | 6 fl. oz | beer | 210 ml |
| 2½ pints | brown stock | 1·75 litres | 1½ pints | demi-glace | 1 litre |
| small | bouquet garni | small | ½ pint | brown stock | 350 ml |
| ¼ pint | red or white wine* | 175 ml | 2 teaspoons | chopped parsley | 5 g |
| | (* used in marinade) | | | | |

## Method 1

1. Prepare the joints (preferably 5–7 lb, 2–3 kg) and bone and tie them. If of a lean nature, the joints are piquéed with strips of larding bacon which have been soaked in brandy and seasoned with pepper, nutmeg and spice.

2. Marinade the joints with the thick sliced carrots, onions, etc. for 6 hours.

3. Line the bottom of a greased braising pan (just sufficiently large enough to contain the joints) with the vegetables of the marinade.

4. Allow to fry gently on the side of the stove.

5. Quickly fry off the drained and seasoned joints until they are coloured and sealed on all sides.

6. Place them on the bed of vegetables, add the wine and reduce quickly.

7. Add the stock, tomato purée and crushed garlic.

8. Reboil, skim and add the seasoning; cover the pan.

9. Place in a slow oven (covered) to cook for approximately 3 hours at 150°C (300°F).

10. Remove the joints, reboil the sauce, skim and reduce it to two-thirds of the amount. Correct the seasoning and thicken with the diluted arrowroot.

11. If the joints are to be served whole, they should be placed back in the oven for 20 minutes with a basting of a little of the sauce to give them a good glaze.

12. To serve, cut the meat in medium-thick slices and arrange them slightly overlapping on a hot oval silver flat dish, mask them with the strained jus-lié.

13. An appropriate garnish is served with the beef, such as aux nouilles, Bourgeoise or Bourguignonne (723).

## Method 2 (quicker)

The meat is not marinaded and the vegetables are cut into mirepoix. These are fried off and added to the fried-off joints in the braising pan. The remainder of the method is as before. This method is quicker but lacks the same finish.

## 742          Carbonnade de boeuf à la flamande

| 8 portions | Ingredients | 10 couverts |
|---|---|---|
| 2 lb | prepared beef | 1·125 kg |
| 12 oz | onions | 420 g |

## Method

1. Prepare the beef (topside, silverside or chuck steak) by cutting it into small steaks; flatten them slightly with a cutlet bat.

2. Peel and finely shred the onions.

3. Sauté the onions until light brown but not crisp then place them in the braising pan.

4. Sauté the seasoned steaks quickly to colour on each side and add them to the onions.

5. Pour off the fat and déglacé the pan with the beer; add the déglaçage to the onions.

6. Reduce the onions, steaks and beer together, then add the prepared demi-glace, thinned with the stock.

7. Bring to the boil, cover with a greased paper and lid. Then place in a slow oven to cook for approximately 2–2½ hours at 150–160°C (300–325°F).

8. Prepare the cabbage into small braised cabbage balls (987) or trim, shred into strips 5 mm wide, blanch for 2–3 minutes, refresh; add the cabbage to the steaks 15–20 minutes before the steaks are cooked.

9. Remove all fat from the sauce then correct the consistency so that it will just mask the steaks. Correct the seasoning.

10. Serve the steaks in a hot earthenware or silver entrée dish, mask them with the sauce and shredded cabbage or place the small cabbages along the side. Place on an underdish with dish paper. Sprinkle the steaks with chopped parsley.

## 743 Braised steaks          Steak braisé

### Method 1

| 8 portions | Ingredients | 10 couverts |
|---|---|---|
| 2 lb | prepared topside or thick flank | 1·125 kg |
| 4 oz | carrot | 140 g |
| 4 oz | onion | 140 g |
| 1 oz | celery | 35 g |
| 2 oz | dripping | 70 g |
| 2 oz | flour | 70 g |
| 2 oz | tomato purée | 70 g |
| 4 level teaspoons | salt | 15 g |
| ½ level teaspoon | milled pepper | 2 g |
| ¼ pod | garlic | ¼ pod |
| small | bouquet garni | small |
| 2½ pints | brown stock | 1·75 litres |

211

## Method

1. Cut the beef into 8 or 10 evenly sized steaks and flatten them slightly with a wet cutlet bat.

2. Heat the dripping in a plat-à-sauter; when it is smoking, add the seasoned steaks, fry them golden brown and remove them.

3. Add the carrot, onion and celery cut into rough 10 mm dice and fry till golden brown. Stir in the flour and cook the roux in the oven at 150°C (300°F).

4. Allow the roux to cool and add the tomato purée. Gradually add the boiling stock, then the bouquet garni and fried steaks.

5. Boil, then cover with a greased paper and lid. Braise in the lower part of the oven at 150–160°C (300–325°F) for 2–2½ hours, until tender.

6. When cooked, remove the steaks to a clean pan. Boil the sauce, remove all the fat and correct the consistency and seasoning. Pass through a fine conical strainer over the steaks and reboil.

7. Serve in a hot entrée or earthenware dish and sprinkle the surface with chopped parsley.

*Note.* The steaks are generally served with a suitable vegetable garnish, e.g. Jardinière.

### Method 2

| 8 portions | Ingredients | 10 couverts |
|---|---|---|
| 2 lb | prepared topside or thick flank | 1·125 kg |
| 2 oz | dripping | 70 g |
| 2 oz | tomato purée | 70 g |
| small | bouquet garni | small |
| 1½ pints | espagnole | 1 litre |
| 1 pint | brown stock | 700 ml |
| 4 level teaspoons | salt | 15 g |
| ½ level teaspoon | milled pepper | 2 g |

### Method

1. Prepare the steaks as for Method 1.

2. Heat the dripping in a plat-à-sauter; when it is smoking, add the seasoned steaks. Fry both sides golden brown.

3. Run off the fat. Add the espagnole, thinned with the stock, and the tomato purée and bouquet garni.

4. Boil, then cover with a greased paper and lid. Braise in the lower part of the oven at 150–160°C (300–325°F) for 2–2½ hours, until tender. Finish and serve as from 6 in Method 1.

## 744 Beef olives    Paupiettes de boeuf

| 8 portions | Ingredients | 10 couverts |
|---|---|---|
| 2 lb | prepared topside made into beef paupiettes (159 and 160) | 1·125 kg |
| 4 oz | carrots | 140 g |
| 2 oz | tomato purée | 70 g |
| 4 oz | onions | 140 g |
| small | bouquet garni | small |
| ½ pod | garlic | ½ pod |
| 4 level teaspoons | salt | 15 g |
| ½ level teaspoon | milled pepper | 2 g |
| 1¼ pints | demi-glace | 1 litre |
| ½ pint | brown stock | 350 ml |
| **garnish** | | |
| 4 oz | turned carrots | 140 g |
| 4 oz | turned turnips | 140 g |
| 2 oz | shelled or frozen peas | 70 g |
| 2 teaspoons | chopped parsley | 10 g |

## Method

1. When preparing the paupiettes (159) a quarter of the meat, in the form of trimmings, is used in the stuffing (160).

2. Line a braising pan with the thick slices of carrot and onion.

3. Fry off the beef olives quickly and place them on the bed of vegetables.

5. Moisten with the stock and sauce, reboil then add the seasoning, bouquet garni, tomato purée and, crushed garlic.

6. Cover with a greaseproof paper and lid and place in the lower part of the oven to cook for 1½–2 hours at 150–160°C (300–325°F).

7. Remove the beef olives, take off the string and place them in a clean pan.

8. Skim off all fat from the sauce, correct the consistency so that it will mask a ladle and correct the seasoning. Pass the sauce through a fine conical strainer over the paupiettes.

9. Add the carrots cooked glacé (969), turnips cooked glacé (1043) and the peas boiled in salted water for 7–8 minutes and then drained.

10. Serve the paupiettes in a line in a hot entrée or earthenware dish, masked over with the sauce and garnish and sprinkled with chopped parsley. Place the dish on an under-flat with dish paper.

## 745 Braised ox-tails    Queue de boeuf braisée

| 8 portions | Ingredients | 10 couverts |
|---|---|---|
| 4 lb | ox-tails | 2·25 kg |
| 5 oz | carrots | 175 g |
| 5 oz | onions | 175 g |
| 2 oz | dripping | 70 g |
| 2 oz | tomato purée | 70 g |
| 1 oz | arrowroot | 35 g |
| 4 level teaspoons | salt | 15 g |
| ½ level teaspoon | milled pepper | 2 g |
| small | bouquet garni | small |
| ½ pod | garlic | ½ pod |
| 3 pints | brown stock | 2 litres |

| | Garnish | |
|---|---|---|
| 4 oz | turned carrots | 140 g |
| 4 oz | turned turnips | 140 g |
| 4 oz | button onions | 140 g |
| 2 oz | shelled or frozen peas | 70 g |
| 2 teaspoons | chopped parsley | 10 g |

## Method

1. Cut the ox-tails into segments, dividing them at the joints; the larger pieces should be cut in half. Trim off any excess fat.

2. Clean and prepare the vegetables and cut them into mirepoix.

3. Heat the fat until a blue haze appears, then quickly fry off the seasoned ox-tail and place it in a braising pan.

4. Fry off the mirepoix and add to the ox-tail.

5. Add the tomato purée, bouquet garni, crushed garlic and moisten with the boiling stock.

6. Reboil, skim and season.

7. Cover and place in a slow oven at 150°C (300°F) for approximately 3 hours, to braise the meat until tender.

8. Remove the meat and place it in a clean pan.

9. Skim the liquid, reduce it by one-third and correct the seasoning.

10 Thicken with the arrowroot diluted in cold water.

11. Pass the liquid through a fine chinois on to the meat.

12. Reboil, add the garnish of glazed carrots (969), glazed turnips (1043), brown glazed button onions (724b), and the peas, plain boiled for 7–8 minutes and drained.

13. Serve in a hot earthenware casserole or dish and sprinkle the surface with chopped parsley. Place on an underflat with a doily.

## 746 Stewed ox-tail     Ragoût de queue de boeuf

### Method

1. Use the same ingredients as for braised ox-tail (745), omitting the arrowroot and replace it with 2 oz (70 g) of flour.

2. Prepare as for braised ox-tail, adding the flour when the ox-tail has been fried; singe (i.e. cook and colour the flour) through the oven for 8–10 minutes at 160°C (325°F).

3. Finish and serve in the same manner. When the ox-tail is cooked and removed to a clean pan, reduce the sauce to just mask a ladle.

## 747 Brown beef stew     Ragoût de boeuf

| 8 portions | Ingredients | 10 couverts |
|---|---|---|
| 2½ lb | stewing beef | 1·4 kg |
| 4 oz | carrot | 140 g |
| 4 oz | onion | 140 g |
| 2 oz | dripping | 70 g |
| 2 oz | flour | 70 g |
| 2 oz | tomato purée | 70 g |
| 4 level teaspoons | salt | 15 g |
| ½ level teaspoon | pepper | 2 g |
| ½ pod | garlic | ½ pod |
| small | bouquet garni | small |
| 2½ pints | brown stock | 1·75 litres |
| 2 teaspoons | chopped parsley | 10 g |

### Method

1. Remove any gristle and surplus fat from the meat and cut it into 25 mm cubes. If prepared meat is used, reduce the quantity by 20 per cent.

2. Clean and prepare the vegetables and cut them into 10 mm mirepoix.

3. Heat the dripping in a shallow pan and quickly fry off the seasoned meat to colour and seal it.

4. Sprinkle the meat with flour, mixing well, and place it in the oven to singe at 200°C (400°F). Add the fried off mirepoix.

5. Work in the tomato purée and the boiling brown stock.

6. Reboil, add the crushed garlic, seasoning and bouquet garni.

7. Cover with a greased paper and a lid and place it in a slow to moderate oven, i.e. at about 150°C (300°F), to cook for approximately 2 hours; stir occasionally.

8. Remove the meat and place it in a clean pan.

9. Pass the sauce, then reboil and skim; correct the seasoning and consistency.

10. Pour the sauce over the meat.

11. Serve in a hot entrée or earthenware dish and sprinkle the surface with chopped parsley. Place on an underdish with paper.

## 748     Ragoût de boeuf au vin rouge

### Method

1. Prepare and serve as for Ragoût de boeuf (747).

2. When moistening, reduce the stock by ½ pint (350 ml) and replace it with red wine.

## 749     Ragoût de boeuf aux légumes

### Method

1. Prepare and serve as for Ragoût de boeuf (747).

2. When placing the meat into a clean pan, add the following garnish and combine.

| | | |
|---|---|---|
| 4 oz | turned glazed carrots (969) | 140 g |
| 4 oz | turned glazed turnips (1043) | 140 g |
| 4 oz | button onions glazed brown (724b) | 140 g |
| 3 oz | plain boiled peas | 100 g |

**750**             **Ragoût de boeuf aux champignons**

## Method

1. Prepare and serve as for Ragoût de boeuf (747).

2. When placing the meat into a clean pan, add 8 oz (280 g) of button or scalloped cleaned mushrooms which have been slowly fried in 1 oz (35 g) of butter.

**751**             **Sauté de boeuf**

| 8 portions | Ingredients | 10 couverts |
|---|---|---|
| 1¾ lb | tail of beef fillet (trimmed) | 1 kg |
| 2 fl. oz | olive oil | 70 ml |
| 2 oz | butter | 70 g |
| 4 level teaspoons | salt | 15 g |
| ½ level teaspoon | milled pepper | 2 g |
| 2 level teaspoons | chopped parsley | 10 g |
| ½ pint | red or white wine | 350 ml |
| 1 pint | demi-glace | 700 ml |

## Method

1. Cut the fillet into bâtons 50 × 10 × 10 mm or cubes (163) and season.

2. Heat the oil in a plat-à-sauter over a very fierce heat until smoking. Add the meat and sauté rapidly, keeping slightly underdone.

3. Remove the meat and keep it warm.

4. Run off any oil from the pan, add the wine and reduce it until it is almost dry.

5. Add the demi-glace, reboil and pass through a fine conical strainer into a clean pan.

6. Toss in the butter in small pieces, off the heat, then add the meat; do not reboil.

7. Serve in a hot entrée dish, sprinkled with chopped parsley. Place on an underdish with dish paper.

*Note.* Usually a prepared garnish of mushrooms, vegetables, etc. is added.

**752**             **Sauté de boeuf à la Strogonoff**

| 8 portions | Ingredients | 10 couverts |
|---|---|---|
| 1¾ lb | tail or fillet of beef (trimmed) | 1 kg |
| 2 oz | finely chopped onions | 70 g |
| 1½ fl. oz | olive oil | 50 ml |
| 1½ oz | butter | 50 g |
| 4 level teaspoons | salt | 15 g |
| ½ level teaspoon | milled pepper | 2 g |
| 2 teaspoons | chopped parsley | 10 g |
| 4 tablespoons | vinegar | 80 ml |
| 1 pint | double cream | 700 ml |

## Method

1. Cut the fillet into batons 40 × 5 × 5 mm and season.

2. Heat the oil and butter in a plat-à-sauter over a fierce heat. Add the meat and sauté rapidly, keeping the meat slightly underdone. Remove the meat and keep it warm.

3. Add the onion to the pan and cook it gently for 5–6 minutes without allowing it to crisp. Add the vinegar and reduce until almost dry.

4. Add the cream and boil for 3–4 minutes, to reduce slightly. Remove from the heat, add the meat and toss over to combine.

5. Serve in a hot entrée dish and sprinkle with chopped parsley. Place on an underdish with dish paper.

**753**             **Tournedos sauté**

| 8 portions | Ingredients | 10 couverts |
|---|---|---|
| 8 | tournedos (163) | 10 |
| 2 oz | first class dripping (or oil) | 70 g |
| 2 fl. oz | white wine | 70 ml |
| 1 pint | demi-glace | 700 ml |
| 2 teaspoons | chopped parsley | 10 g |
| 4 level teaspoons | salt | 15 g |
| ½ level teaspoon | milled pepper | 2 g |

## Method

1. Season the prepared tournedos.

2. Heat the dripping in a plat-à-sauter; when it is smoking, add the tournedos and set them on both sides quickly over a fierce heat.

3. Then sauté steadily for a further 3–4 minutes on each side for medium done.

4. Remove the tournedos and run off the fat from the pan.

5. Add the wine, déglacé the pan then add the demi-glace.

6. Reboil, skim and pass through a fine conical strainer.

7. Dress the tournedos on a hot flat dish and mask them over with the sauce. Sprinkle a little parsley on the centre of each.

*Note.* A lightly fried, or butter-dipped and grilled croûton the size of the tournedos may be placed under each, when serving. For various garnishes, see 722.

**754**             **Entrecôte sauté**

## Method

1. Proceed to cook and serve as for Tournedos sauté (753). Croûtons are not served.

2. After sealing the meat on both sides, the cooking time depends on the thickness of the entrecôte.

## 755           Entrecôte sauté bordelaise

**Method**

1. Cook the entrecôtes as in 754, replacing the demi-glace with Sauce bordelaise (372).

2. For serving, place the entrecôtes on a hot flat oval silver dish in a fan shape. Place on top 2–3 10 mm-thick slices of bone marrow poached in salted water for 2 minutes. Then mask over the meat with the sauce and sprinkle the marrow with chopped parsley.

## 756           Tournedos sauté chasseur

## 757           Entrecôte sauté chasseur

| 8 portions | Ingredients | 10 couverts |
|---|---|---|
| 8 | tournedos (163) or entrecôte (164) | 10 |
| 2 oz | first class dripping (or oil) | 70 g |
| 6 oz | closed mushrooms | 210 g |
| 2 oz | finely chopped shallots | 70 g |
| 1 lb | tomatoes | 560 g |
| 1 oz | butter | 35 g |
| 4 level teaspoons | salt | 15 g |
| ½ level teaspoon | milled pepper | 2 g |
| 1 level teaspoon | chopped tarragon | 3 g |
| 2 level teaspoons | chopped parsley | 5 g |
| 2 fl. oz | white wine | 70 ml |
| 1 pint | demi-glace or jus-lié | 700 ml |

**Method**

1. Prepare the shallots by peeling and chopping them finely.

2. Peel wash and slice the mushrooms.

3. Blanch, refresh and peel the tomatoes. Cut them in half across, remove the pips and core, and cut the flesh into 10 mm dice (concassé).

4. Heat the fat in a sauté pan and quickly sauté the steaks.

5. When cooked, remove to the serving dish and place it in a warm place.

6. Pour off the fat, add the butter and shallots and gently sauté. When it is just colouring, add the mushrooms.

7. Sauté the mushrooms for 3–4 minutes, add the white wine to déglacé, reduce then add the tomatoes.

8. Cook together gently, shaking the sauté pan.

9. Add the prepared sauce, reboil, add the tarragon and half of the parsley.

10. Correct the seasoning and the consistency.

11. Pour the sauce over the steaks and serve sprinkled with the chopped parsley.

## 758 Hamburg or Vienna steak (194)     Bitok de boeuf

## 759 Russian minced steak (193)     Bitok à la russe

**Method**

1. Melt sufficient first class dripping in a sauté pan to give a depth of 3 mm.

2. Add the steaks when it is smoking. Cook them steadily for 4–5 minutes till they are a very light golden brown on each side.

3. Dress them slightly overlapping on a hot flat dish and mask them with 1 pint (700 ml) of an appropriate sauce, e.g. Sauce smitaine (760).

## 760           Sauce smitaine

| 1 quart | Ingredients | 1 litre |
|---|---|---|
| 4 oz | finely chopped onions | 100 g |
| 2 oz | butter | 50 g |
| 1 level teaspoon | paprika pepper | 2 g |
| 2½ fl. oz | vinegar | 60 ml |
| 2½ fl. oz | white wine | 60 ml |
| 2 pints | cream or cream sauce (389) | 1 litre |

**Method**

1. Melt the butter in a saucepan, add the onions, cover the pan and gently sweat them for 7–8 minutes without colouring.

2. Add the paprika and cook it slowly for 1 minute. Add the vinegar and reduce it until nearly dry. Add the wine and reduce it by a half.

3. Add the cream or cream sauce, boil, then simmer for 10 minutes. Correct the seasoning, especially if cream is used.

## 761 Goulash of beef           Goulash de boeuf

| 8 portions | Ingredients | 10 couverts |
|---|---|---|
| 2½ lb | stewing beef | 1·4 kg |
| 8 oz | finely chopped onion | 280 g |
| 3 oz | lard | 100 g |
| 2 oz | flour | 70 g |
| 4 oz | tomato purée | 140 g |
| 3 level teaspoons | salt | 15 g |
| 1 oz | paprika pepper | 35 g |
| 2½ pints | white stock | 1·75 litres |
| 16 | turned potatoes (half size) | 20 |
| 2 teaspoons | chopped parsley | 10 g |
| ½ pod | garlic | ½ pod |
| ¼ pint mix | choux paste (343) | 175 ml |

**Method**

1. Cut away any sinew or excess fat from the meat then cut it into 25 mm cubes. If prepared meat is used, reduce the quantity by 20 per cent.

2. Heat the fat in a shallow pan, add the seasoned meat, fry it quickly to set it, then colour it a light golden brown.

3. Add the onion, cover with a lid and sweat for 7–8 minutes, stirring occasionally.

4. Add the paprika and sweat for 1 minute. Add the flour then cover and cook in an oven at 150°C (300°F) for 10 minutes.

5. Add the tomato purée then gradually add the boiling stock.

6. Boil. Add the crushed chopped garlic. Cover the pan with a lid and place it in the bottom of an oven at 150°C (300°F) to cook for 2 hours until the meat is tender.

7. Blanch the potatoes for 4–5 minutes, drain and add them to the goulash 30 minutes before the meat is expected to be cooked.

8. Remove from the oven and skim off any fat. Correct the consistency of the sauce: if it is too thick, add a little stock; if it is too thin, pour off some sauce and reduce. (Never reduce the sauce with the meat or the meat will shred and burn.)

9. Fifteen minutes before the meat is ready, place a shallow pan of water to heat, then, before it has boiled, remove it to the side of the stove.

10. Place the choux paste into a piping bag with a 10 mm plain tube. Rest the bag on the side of the pan. Gently press, then, with a small knife occasionally dipped in the water, cut off the paste at 10 mm intervals to form small gnocchi. Replace the pan over a gentle heat to poach for 4–5 minutes. Do not allow the water to boil, or the gnocchi will 'blow'.

11. Serve the goulash in a hot entrée or earthenware dish. Place the well drained gnocchi along each side and sprinkle chopped parsley along the centre. Place the dish on an underflat with dish paper.

## 762 Curried beef                                Kari de boeuf

| 8 portions | Ingredients | 10 couverts |
|---|---|---|
| 2½ lb | stewing beef | 1·4 kg |
| 2 oz | dripping | 70 g |
| 2 oz | flour | 70 g |
| 1½ oz | curry powder | 50 g |
| 1 lb | finely chopped onion | 560 g |
| 4 oz | finely chopped apple | 140 g |
| 2 oz | finely chopped chutney | 70 g |
| 1 oz | tomato purée | 35 g |
| 1½ oz | desiccated coconut | 50 g |
| 4 level teaspoons | salt | 15 g |
| ½ level teaspoon | ground white pepper | 2 g |
| 2 level teaspoons | chopped parsley | 10 g |
| 1 pod | garlic | 1 pod |
| 1 | bayleaf | 1 |
| ½ | lemon (in juice) | ½ |
| 2 pints | brown stock | 1·4 litres |

## Method

1. Cut away any sinew or excess fat from the meat and cut it into 25 mm cubes. If prepared meat is used, reduce the quantity by 20 per cent.

2. Heat the dripping in a pan and fry the seasoned meat till lightly coloured. Add the onions and cook them with the meat for 5–6 minutes, colouring lightly.

3. Add the curry powder and bayleaf and cook for a further 1–2 minutes. Sprinkle in the flour and mix well. Cook in the bottom of an oven at 150°C (300°F) for 6–7 minutes.

4. Add the tomato purée, chopped chutney, apple and the previously soaked coconut. Gradually add the boiling stock, boiling between each addition.

5. When boiling, add the finely chopped garlic and lemon juice. Cover with a greased paper and lid and place the pan in the bottom of an oven at 150°C (300°F) to cook for 2–2¼ hours, stirring occasionally. The meat should be easily penetrated with a fork when cooked. Correct the seasoning and consistency and remove all the fat. If the sauce is too thick, add a little stock.

6. Serve in a hot entrée or earthenware dish and sprinkle the surface with chopped parsley. Place the dish on an underflat with dish paper. Serve loosely, in a similar dish or dishes, plain boiled rice (763), and, if desired, saffron braised rice (615) garnished with blanched sultanas. Toasted Bombay duck and golden brown papadums, fried at 180°C (350°F) and well drained, are served separately, placed on a flat dish with a doily.

## 763 Plain boiled rice

| 8 portions | Ingredients | 10 couverts |
|---|---|---|
| 12 oz | patna rice | 420 g |
| 1 oz | salt | 35 g |
| ½ | lemon (in juice) | ½ |

## Method

1. Place 1 gallon (5 litres) of water to boil and add the salt and lemon juice.

2. Wash the rice and rain it into the boiling water. Stir until reboiling.

3. Simmer for 16–17 minutes then test a few grains between the teeth: a little firmness should remain in the centre of the grain when it is cooked.

4. Place a colander over the pan and run cold water over it until all the starch has been washed clear.

5. Drain the rice thoroughly for a few minutes then place it in a shallow tray on a damp cloth. Heat this in an oven at

90°C (200°F), or in a hot plate, then loosely separate the grains with a fork.

## 764 Minced beef · Hachis de boeuf

### Method 1, using raw beef

| 8 portions | Ingredients | 10 couverts |
|---|---|---|
| 2 lb | lean minced beef | 1·125 kg |
| 8 oz | finely chopped onion | 280 g |
| 2 oz | dripping | 70 g |
| 1 oz | tomato purée | 35 g |
| 4 level teaspoons | salt | 15 g |
| ½ level teaspoon | ground white pepper | 2 g |
| 1 pint | demi-glace | 700 ml |
| 1¾ lb | peeled potatoes (duchesse, 1089) | 1 kg |
| 1 teaspoon | chopped parsley | 5 g |

### Method

1. Melt the fat in a saucepan, add the onion and cook it gently for 7–8 minutes, colouring slightly.
2. Add the minced beef and continue to stir over a fast heat until the meat stiffens and separates.
3. Add the seasoning, tomato purée, then the boiling demi-glace.
4. Reboil, cover, place in the bottom of an oven at 150° (300°F) and cook for 1–1¼ hours, stirring occasionally.
5. Skim off all the fat then correct the seasoning and consistency.
6. Pipe a scrolled border of potato round an entrée or earthenware dish; dry it slightly in the oven, eggwash then colour it golden brown under a salamander.
7. Place the cooked beef inside the border. Sprinkle the parsley in a line down the centre of the meat. Place the dish on an underflat with dish paper.

### Method 2, using cooked beef

1. Replace the minced raw beef with 1½ lb (850 g) of cooked beef cut into 5 mm dice.
2. Prepare and serve as for Method 1; allow only 15 minutes for cooking in the oven.

## 765 Minced beef with dumplings

### Method

1. Use the same ingredients as for minced beef (764, method 1), omitting the duchesse potato.
2. Prepare as for minced beef (764, method 1).
3. Thirty minutes before the meat is cooked, place it into an earthenware casserole.
4. Prepare an 8 oz (280 g) flour mix of suet paste (1143).

5. Divide this into 16 or 20 pieces and mould them into small round dumplings. Place the dumplings on the minced beef and cover it with a thickly greased paper and lid.
6. Continue to cook in the oven, removing the lid and paper 10 minutes before the meat is cooked to lightly colour the dumplings.
7. To serve, remove any fat, sprinkle the surface with chopped parsley then replace the cover. Place the casserole on an underflat with dish paper.

## 766 Braised ox-tongue · Langue de boeuf braisée au madère

| 8 portions | Ingredients | 10 couverts |
|---|---|---|
| 1 × 2½ lb | ox-tongue | 1 × 1·4 kg |
| 2 oz | carrot | 70 g |
| 2 oz | onion | 70 g |
| 1 | bayleaf | 1 |
| 8 | white peppercorns | 10 |
| 1¼ pints | sauce madère (378) | 840 ml |
| ¼ pint | brown stock | 175 ml |

### Method

1. To obtain the correct flavour and a good red colour, the ox-tongue requires 10–12 days in brine. (See brine for red meats, 195.)
2. Wash the ox-tongue and place it to boil with cold water. Skim the surface then add the carrot, onion, bayleaf and peppercorns, cover the pan with a lid.
3. Cook slowly for 2–2½ hours then test the meat with a needle: it should penetrate through the thickest part of the tongue without pressure.
4. Plunge the ox-tongue into cold water, remove the skin, and trim away any gristle and windpipe from the back of tongue.
5. Place it in a shallow braising pan, mask it over with the Sauce madère, slightly thinned out with brown stock, and braise it gently for 20–30 minutes, glazing from time to time with the sauce.
6. Cut the tongue in thin slices and serve each slice overlapping the meat on a hot oval dish. Mask it over with the strained sauce and place garnish alongside.

### Garnishes

**aux nouilles**: 1 oz (30 g) of Nouilles au beurre (605) per portion.

**aux ravioli**: 3–4 pieces of ravioli (608) per portion.

**aux épinards**: a small portion Épinards à la crème (1019) in a scrolled dome shape, with a 25 mm triangular butter-fried croûton on top, per portion.

## 767 Fried ox-liver — Foie de boeuf sauté

| 8 portions | Ingredients | 10 couverts |
|---|---|---|
| 1½ lb | ox liver | 840 g |
| 4 oz | dripping | 140 g |
| 4 oz | flour | 140 g |
| 4 level teaspoons | salt | 15 g |
| ½ level teaspoon | milled ground pepper | 2 g |

### Method

1. Trim the liver of as much vein and gristle as possible, then pull the skin off. (See 184.)

2. Cut the liver on the slant in 5 mm thick slices.

3. Heat enough fat to just cover the bottom of a pan, and lay the slices of seasoned and floured liver in it. The liver must only be seasoned and floured immediately before cooking, for the seasoning and flour will cause the liver to bleed if left for any time.

4. Fry the liver quickly to colour light brown on both sides; do not overcook.

5. To serve, arrange the slices, slightly overlapping, on a hot oval flat dish and surround them with demi-glace sauce (369).

Ox-liver is usually served with Sauce lyonnaise.

## 768 — Foie de boeuf lyonnaise

### Method

1. Prepare and serve as for Foie de boeuf sauté (767), masking over with a pint (700 ml) of Sauce lyonnaise (377) and sprinkling the surface with chopped parsley.

## 769 Savoury meat roll

| 8 portions | Ingredients | 10 couverts |
|---|---|---|
| 1¼ lb | lean minced beef | 700 g |
| 4 oz | onion | 140 g |
| 1½ oz | dripping | 50 g |
| 5 oz | bread | 175 g |
| 8 oz | cooked boiled carrot | 280 g |
| 5 oz | cooked boiled turnip | 175 g |
| 4 level teaspoons | salt | 15 g |
| ½ level teaspoon | ground white pepper | 2 g |
| ½ level teaspoon | powdered sage | 2 g |
| 2 level teaspoons | chopped parsley | 15 g |
| 1 pint | demi-glace | 700 ml |

### Method

1. Finely chop the onions and sweat them gently, without colouring, until tender.

2. Soak the bread and squeeze out the moisture.

3. Pass the meat through the fine plate of the mincer.

4. Press the surplus moisture from the carrots and turnips, then mix them with the meat, bread, onions, seasoning and the sage (all cold).

5. Pass again through the mincer.

6. Mould the mixture into a roll 60 mm in diameter, making sure there are no cracks.

7. Place the roll on a greased baking dish and baste it with a little fat.

8. Cook in a moderate oven for 1¼–1½ hours.

9. Roll it in breadcrumbs and brown off in the oven.

10. Allow to set for 20 minutes and carve in 10 mm thick slices.

11. Serve the slices, slightly overlapping, on a hot oval flat dish, mask over with the boiling sauce and sprinkle the parsley in a line down the centre.

## 770 Cottage pie

There is a slight controversy among some chefs regarding the basic ingredient of this dish, but it is generally recognized that Cottage pie is made from beef, while Shepherd's pie is made from lamb or mutton.

### Method 1, using raw beef

| 8 portions | Ingredients | 10 couverts |
|---|---|---|
| 2 lb | lean stewing beef | 1·125 kg |
| 4 oz | finely chopped onion | 140 g |
| 1 oz | dripping | 35 g |
| 2 lb | peeled potatoes | 1·125 kg |
| 4 level teaspoons | salt | 15 g |
| ½ level teaspoon | ground white pepper | 2 g |
| 2 level teaspoons | chopped parsley | 10 g |
| ½ pint | demi-glace | 350 ml |

### Method

1. Either cut the meat into very small dice, or finely mince it.

2. Heat the dripping in a saucepan, add the onion and fry it gently for 5–6 minutes. Add the meat and seasoning and fry them together until the meat separates.

3. Add the sauce, bring to the boil, cover and cook in the bottom of an oven at 150°C (300°F) for 1¼ hours.

4. Remove any fat, correct seasoning and add the parsley. Place into one or more greased pie dishes.

5. While the meat is cooking, cut the potatoes into evenly sized pieces. Place these in a saucepan, cover with water, add a little salt, boil, then simmer for 18–20 minutes. Drain, dry off on the stove, pass through a sieve and mix; if a little dry, add a little butter to bind.

6. Using a piping bag and 10 mm star tube, pipe the potato over the meat so that the meat is neatly covered.

7. Place the pie dishes in a shallow tray with water (bain-marie) and put the tray in the top of an oven at 200–220°C (400–425°F) to colour pies golden brown.

8. Brush the surface with melted butter.

9. To serve, place the pie dishes on an underflat with dish paper with a pie frill around each dish.

## Method 2, using cooked meat

1. Prepare and serve as for Method 1, replacing the raw beef with 1½ lb (840 g) of cooked beef.
2. After adding the sauce, cook for only 15–20 minutes in the oven.

## 771 Beef croquettes — Croquettes de boeuf

## 772 Beef médaillons — Médaillons de boeuf

| 8 portions | Ingredients | 10 couverts |
|---|---|---|
| 1¼ lb | lean cooked meat | 700 g |
| 4 oz | finely chopped onion | 140 g |
| 1 oz | dripping | 35 g |
| 2 teaspoons | chopped parsley | 5 g |
| 4 level teaspoons | salt | 15 g |
| ½ level teaspoon | ground white pepper | 2 g |
| ½ pint | espagnole | 350 ml |
|  | **Panée** |  |
| 8 oz | white breadcrumbs | 280 g |
| 2 oz | flour | 70 g |
| 2 | eggs | 3 |

## Method

1. Either mince the meat or cut it into 3 mm dice.
2. Heat the dripping in a thick shallow pan, add the onions and fry them gently for 5–6 minutes, colouring lightly.
3. Add the meat and seasoning and fry them with the onions for 2 minutes. Add the sauce, boil and reduce the sauce by a half. Use an iron spatula to prevent burning.
4. Place the mixture in a shallow tray, cover with a greased paper and allow it to go cold.
5. Divide into 16 or 20 equal pieces, moulding them to the desired shape. (310).
6. Pass each piece through the flour, beaten egg and crumbs, then reshape them.
7. Deep fry at 180°C (360°F), and drain.
8. Serve on a hot flat dish with dishpaper and garnish them with sprigs of fried parsley. Serve an appropriate sauce, such as piquante (381), separately, in a sauceboat on an underdish with a doily.

## 773 Durham cutlets

| 8 portions | Ingredients | 10 couverts |
|---|---|---|
| 1 lb | lean cooked beef | 560 g |
| 2 oz | finely chopped onion | 70 g |
| 1 oz | dripping | 35 g |
| 1 lb | peeled potatoes | 560 g |
| 2 teaspoons | chopped parsley | 5 g |
| 4 level teaspoons | salt | 15 g |
| ½ level teaspoon | ground white pepper | 2 g |

| 8 oz | **Panée** white breadcrumbs | 280 g |
|---|---|---|
| 2 oz | flour | 70 g |
| 2 | eggs | 2 |

## Method

1. Cut the potatoes in evenly sized pieces then plain boil, drain, dry off on the stove, and pass them through a sieve.
2. Cut the beef into 3 mm dice or mince.
3. Heat the dripping in a pan, add the onions and cook them for 5–6 minutes, colouring lightly.
4. Add the meat, potato, seasoning and parsley and mix them thoroughly together.
5. Divide the mixture into 16 or 20 equal pieces of 2 oz (55 g) and mould them into cutlets (see 310).
6. Pass the cutlets through flour, beaten egg and crumbs. Reshape them and place a small piece of macaroni in the end of each cutlet.
7. Finish and serve as for beef croquettes (771) from 7 in method. Place a cutlet frill on each.

## 774 Cornish pasties

### Method 1, using raw meat

| 8 portions | Ingredients | 10 couverts |
|---|---|---|
| 1 lb | lean beef | 560 g |
| 10 oz | peeled potato | 350 g |
| 2 oz | finely chopped onion | 70 g |
| 1 oz | dripping | 35 g |
| 2 teaspoons | chopped parsley | 5 g |
| 4 level teaspoons | salt | 15 g |
| ½ level teaspoon | ground white pepper | 2 g |
| 8 oz (flour mix) | Puff or rough puff paste (1141/2) | 350 g (flour mix) |
| 2½ fl. oz | brown stock | 85 ml |

## Method

1. Sweat the onion in the dripping for 6–7 minutes without colouring. Allow it to go cold.
2. Cut the beef and potato into 5 mm dice, add the onion, parsley and seasoning, then moisten with the stock.
3. Dust the pastry with flour and roll it out 3 mm thick. Cut eight or ten 150 mm-diameter circles and eggwash the edges.
4. Divide the filling equally and place each portion on one-half of the circle of pastry. Fold the pastry over to meet the other edge.
5. Place the pasties on to a greased baking sheet, sprinkled with water, with the sealed edge uppermost. Crinkle the edge with the fingers. Brush with eggwash and prick each side with a fork.
6. Allow to rest for 30–60 minutes. Start to cook at the top

of an oven at 190°C (375°F). When the pastry just shows signs of colouring, move the pasties to a lower position and reduce the temperature to 130°C (275°F) to cook for approximately 1¼ hours

7. Serve them on a hot flat dish on a dish paper and garnish them with picked parsley. Serve a separate sauceboat of demi-glace or jus-lié.

### Method 2, using cooked meat

1. Prepare and serve as for Method 1.

2. Use cooked beef, reducing the quantity by 20 per cent, replace the brown stock with espagnole, and use cooked boiled potatoes.

3. When baking the pasties, use the same oven positions, retain a temperature of 190°C (375°F) and cook for 25–30 minutes.

### 775 Tripe and onions

| 8 portions | Ingredients | 10 couverts |
| --- | --- | --- |
| 2 lb | tripe | 1·125 kg |
| 1 lb | onions | 560 g |
| 2 oz | cornflour | 70 g |
| 2 teaspoons | chopped parsley | 5 g |
| 4 level teaspoons | salt | 15 g |
| ½ level teaspoon | ground white pepper | 2 g |
| 1 pint | milk | 2 g |
| 1 pint | water | 700 ml |

### Method

1. Wash the tripe well then blanch and refresh it.

2. Place it in a clean shallow pan and cover with the milk and water. Bring to the boil, skim the surface, then add the seasoning and the peeled shredded onions.

3. Simmer for 1½–2 hours until the tripe is soft then correct the seasoning.

4. Dilute the cornflour in a little water and run it into the cooking liquor, shaking the pan to keep the sauce smooth.

5. Reboil and simmer for 5–10 minutes; correct the consistency.

6. Serve the tripe and onions in a hot earthenware casserole, sprinkle with chopped parsley and cover the dish. Place the dish on an underdish with a doily.

### 776 Beef hot pot

| 8 portions | Ingredients | 10 couverts |
| --- | --- | --- |
| 2½ lb | stewing beef | 1·4 kg |
| 8 oz | onions | 280 g |
| 1 oz | dripping | 35 g |
| 2 teaspoons | chopped parsley | 5 g |
| 4 level teaspoons | salt | 15 g |
| ½ level teaspoon | ground white pepper | 2 g |
| 2½ lb | potatoes (medium) | 1·4 kg |
| 1 pint | brown stock | 700 ml |

### Method

1. Trim away any bone, sinew or surplus fat from the beef and cut it into 25 mm cubes. If prepared meat is used, reduce the quantity by 20 per cent.

2. Peel and finely shred the onions.

3. Wash, peel and rewash the potatoes, then cut them into 3 mm-thick slices.

4. Grease an earthenware casserole.

5. Place a layer of sliced potatoes and onions in the casserole.

6. Add a layer of seasoned meat, then add a layer of onions and parsley.

7. Add a layer of potatoes and finish on the top with the slices neatly arranged, each overlapping like slates on a roof. Brush the surface with melted dripping.

8. Three-quarters fill the casserole with the boiling stock and reboil.

9. Press the tops down gently with a slice, place the hot pot in an oven at 150°C (300°F) and cook it for 2–2½ hours.

10. From time to time during cooking, the tops must be pressed down gently to prevent them becoming dry and crisp.

11. When cooked, i.e. with the top golden brown and the meat cooked and just moist, carefully clean the dish and serve after sprinkling the surface with chopped parsley. Place on an underdish with a doily.

### 777 Steak pie

| 8 portions | Ingredients | 10 couverts |
| --- | --- | --- |
| 8 oz flour mix | puff pastry (1141) or short paste (1138) | 280 g flour mix |
| 8 portions | pie filling (307) | 10 couverts |
| 1 | egg | 1 |

### Method

1. Prepare the meat and other ingredients as for Steak and kidney pie filling (307), replacing the quantity of kidney with the same amount of beef.

2. If desired, the finished pie can be cooked from raw meat. Preferably the steak should be cooked separately for 1 hour, as described in 307, as this does not dry the paste so easily during baking.

3. Place the prepared meat in a pie dish with enough of the cooking liquor to come three-quarters of the way up the meat.

4. Dust the table with flour and roll the paste outwards from the centre in both directions till it is 5 mm thick. Place an inverted pie dish, of the size being used, on the paste and cut the paste 25 mm larger all round.

5. Cut enough paste from the remainder for a 20 mm-wide band for the pie edging. Moisten the edge of the pie dish with water and press the band edging firmly into position all round the edge, sealing the two ends together with water.

6. Egg-wash the band of paste, place the paste which has been cut out for a cover carefully into position, on the reverse side to the side on which it was rolled. Using the hands, press lightly towards the centre of the pie, then press the edges firmly on to the egg-washed band. With the point of a knife angled outwards at 45°, cut away any excess paste from the pie dish.

7. From the remaining paste, cut strips 25 mm wide of similar thickness, then cut eight or ten leaves on the slant, approximately 55 mm long from point to point. Mark the leaf veins on the paste with the back of a knife.

8. Seal around the edge of the paste on the pie dish with the thumb and finger and crinkle or mark the edge with the back of a knife. Brush the surface with eggwash, then place the leaves, equally spaced, into position in the centre of the paste; egg-wash the leaves.

9. Roll the paste trimmings to 1·5 mm thick and cut out three plain circles of paste 35, 50 and 60 mm in diameter. Place these on top of each other with the smallest circle on top. Bring the edges of the bottom circle together and press them firmly together at the centre. Make two incisions crossways along the paste opposite to the joined edges. Fold back two layers of the paste to form a rose and trim away any excess paste from the bottom.

10. Egg-wash the rose, then make a small hole in the centre of the leaves by pressing with the finger; place the rose in this position.

11. Allow to rest for at least 1 hour; longer if possible.

12. Place the pie dish on a baking sheet and put it towards the top of an oven at 200°C (400°F) for approximately 10–15 minutes until the paste has begun to rise and set in position. Reduce the temperature to 160°C (325°F) if partly cooked meat is used. When raw meat is used, move to the lower part of the oven and reduce to 140°C (280°F).

13. Bake partly cooked meat for 1¼ hours and raw meat for 2 hours. To check when the meat is cooked, run the point of a knife around under the edge of the paste and lift one end with a palette knife; the meat should begin to shred when pressed between the fingers. Check the level of the cooking liquor.

14. Serve the pie on an underflat, on a dish paper, and place a pie collar around the pie dish.

## 778 Steak and kidney pie

### Method

Prepare, cook and serve as for Steak pie (777), using the filling for Steak and kidney pie (307).

## 779 Steak, kidney and mushroom pie

### Method

1. Prepare and serve as for Steak and kidney pie (778).

2. Before covering, add 4 oz (140 g) of washed and sliced closed mushrooms lightly cooked in 1 oz (35 g) of butter.

## 780 Steak and kidney pudding

| 8 portions | Ingredients | 10 couverts |
|---|---|---|
| 12 oz flour mix | suet paste (1143) | 420 g flour mix |
| 8 portions | pudding filling (308) | 10 couverts |

### Method

1. Cut one-quarter of the paste and place it aside for covering the pudding.

2. Mould the remainder in a ball, well dust it with flour and press the clenched fist in the centre to press the paste in the shape of a pocket.

3. Dust the inside of the pocket with flour and roll it until it is large enough to line the basin being used.

4. Thickly grease a 2 pint pudding basin for 8 portions or a 2½ pint (1·5 litre) basin for 10.

5. Place the pocket of paste in the basin and press it to the sides of the basin and to the top edge.

6. Fill with the steak and kidney. Moisten the top edge of the paste with water.

7. Roll the other piece of paste into a ball, then roll in both directions from the centre to a size 10 mm larger than the top of the basin.

8. Place the suet paste cover on top and firmly press the two edges together to seal them. Cover with a double thickness of heavily-greased greaseproof paper and twist the edges to seal.

9. Steam for 4 hours. To serve, wipe the basin clean and place it on an underflat with a doily. Wrap a clean serviette around the dish and pin it to fasten it in position.

*Note.* For variations, see notes at end of filling 308.

| 782 Roast leg of lamb | Gigot d'agneau rôti |
|---|---|
| 783 Roast shoulder of lamb | Épaule d'agneau rôtie |
| 784 Roast saddle of lamb | Selle d'agneau rôtie |
| 785 Roast loin of lamb | Longe d'agneau rôtie |

**Method**

1. Prepare leg of lamb as in 203, shoulder as in 202b, saddle as in 204a and b, and loin as in 205.
2. Prepare and roast them as described in 725a, b and c.
3. Carve and serve as described in 726, 3.
4. Garnish the joints with sprigs of picked watercress and, on an underdish with a doily, serve a sauceboat of mint sauce (416). When roast leg of mutton is served, the mint sauce is replaced by onion sauce (392).

*Note.* When the lamb is stuffed, the name of the dish indicates as much, e.g. Longe d'agneau farcie rôtie.

When roasting lamb, a little rosemary sprinkled on the joints imparts a very fine flavour. Small incisions are sometimes cut in the skin of the joint and small pieces of garlic inserted.

**786 Roast best end of lamb**      **Carré d'agneau rôti**

**Method**

1. Prepare the best end (209).
2. Season the joint, place it in a roasting tray, fat side down, then roast it as described in 725 for approximately 45–55 minutes. Turn over during roasting.
3. Carve and serve as described in 726, 3. Place cutlet frills on the bones.
4. Garnish with sprigs of watercress and serve a sauceboat of mint sauce (416) on an underflat with a doily.

**787**      **Carré d'agneau à la boulangère**

**Method**

1. Prepare a dish of Pommes boulangère (1135), allowing half the quantity as a garnish.
2. Finish cooking the lamb on the potatoes for the last 15–20 minutes.
3. Carve the joint as described in 726, 3. Place the pieces of lamb, slightly overlapping, on a hot oval silver flat dish and put a cutlet frill on each bone. Serve the garnish along the side.

*Note.* For other garnishes, see 723.

**788**      **Carré d'agneau persillé**

**Method**

1. Prepare the best end (209).
2. Roast as for Carré d'agneau rôti (786).
3. Ten minutes before the meat is cooked, press a 5 mm covering of parsley crumbs over the complete surface of the fat side of the best end. Return it to the oven to finish cooking and colour the crumbs a light golden brown.
4. Carve as described in 726, 3, and serve on a hot oval silver dish with roast gravy.

**Parsley crumbs** for 1 best end

Mix 3 oz (85 g) of fresh white breadcrumbs with 3 tablespoons (15 g) of chopped parsley, ¼ pod of finely chopped garlic, a little salt and pepper, then bind this mixture with 3 oz (85 g) of melted butter.

| 789 Leg, loin, saddle, best end of lamb poêlé | Gigot, longe, selle, carré d'agneau poêlé |
|---|---|

**Method**

1. Select a suitable pan, slightly larger than the joint, with a tight-fitting lid.
2. Prepare the joint as follows: leg as in 203, loin as in 205, saddle as in 204a and b, and best end as in 209.
3. Cut a 5 mm-thick bed of roots (340) for lining the bottom of the pan. Place the seasoned joint on top and smear it all over with butter.
4. Heat the pan for 1 minute on top of the stove then place it in the lower part of an oven at 200–220°C (400–425°F) for 15–20 minutes. Lower the temperature, according to size of joint, to 175–190°C (350–375°F). Cook for the same length of time as for roasting. (See guidance times, 725.)
5. Turn the joint during cooking and baste it every 12–15 minutes. Ten to fifteen minutes before it is cooked, remove the cover and lightly colour the presentation side of the joint.
6. Remove the joint and keep it warm. Set the pan on the stove until the fat clears, run off the fat and moisten it with 1 pint (700 ml) of jus-lié for each 8 (or 10) portions to be served. Reboil, simmer, then strain.
7. Serve the joint whole or in slices; see 726 for the method of carving.
8. Garnish the meat according to the name of dish (see garnishes 723). Mask the meat with jus-lié if it is sliced, or

surround the base of the dish with it. Serve additional jus-lié in a sauceboat on an underflat with a doily.

## 790  Boiled leg of mutton, caper sauce  Gigot de mouton bouilli (lamb may also be used), sauce câpre

| 8 portions | Ingredients | 10 couverts |
|---|---|---|
| 2½ lb | leg of mutton or lamb | 1·4 kg |
| 6 oz | turned turnips | 210 g |
| 6 oz | button onions | 210 g |
| 1 head | celery | 1 large head |
| 4 level teaspoons | salt | 15 g |
| 8 | white peppercorns | 10 |
| 1 | bayleaf | 1 |
| 1 pint | caper sauce (791) | 700 ml |
| 2 teaspoons | chopped parsley | 5 g |

### Method

1. Place a pan of water to boil and add the salt, bayleaf and peppercorns.

2. When boiling, add the prepared leg of mutton or lamb (203) then reboil, skim, cover the pan and simmer for 30 minutes.

3. Add the cleaned, trimmed and peeled celery and simmer for a further 30 minutes. Add the turned turnips and peeled button onions tied in a muslin.

4. Simmer for a further 30 minutes, test the joint by passing a trussing needle through the thickest part of the leg. The needle should penetrate without undue pressure, and no sign of blood should appear. Cook the meat until tender, allowing 20 min per lb (45 min per kg), plus 20 minutes.

5. Serve by carving the leg as described in 726, 3; arrange the slices, slightly overlapping, on a hot flat silver dish. Arrange the celery, cut into 50 mm-long sections, along each side of the meat, with the turnips and button onions on each side of the celery. Mask over with a little of the boiling strained liquor and sprinkle chopped parsley on the onions and turnips. Serve the sauce in a sauceboat on an underflat with a doily.

## 791  Caper sauce  Sauce câpre

| 1 quart | Ingredients | 1 litre |
|---|---|---|
| 4 oz | margarine | 100 g |
| 4 oz | flour | 100 g |
| 2 oz | capers | 50 g |
| 2 pints | mutton stock | 1 litre |

### Method

1. Make a velouté (368) with the stock obtained from the meat after one hour's cooking and the fat and flour. Cook the velouté, and correct the seasoning and consistency.

2. Pass it through a fine conical strainer then add the capers.

## 792  Fried lamb cutlet  Côtelette d'agneau sautée

## 793  Noisette d'agneau sautée

## 794  Filet mignon sauté

### Method

1. Prepare the best end into cutlets (209), noisette or filet mignon (205).

2. Heat enough first class dripping in a sauté pan to give a depth of 3 mm. When the fat is smoking, add the meat, seasoned with salt and milled pepper.

3. Sauté quickly on each side to seal the meat, then reduce the heat to cook it steadily for 2–4 minutes on each side until it is golden brown (approximately 9–10 minutes in all).

4. Arrange the cutlets neatly on a hot oval silver flat with an appropriate garnish (722). Mask the meat and the base of the dish with jus-lié.

## 795  Fried breadcrumbed cutlet  Côtelette d'agneau panée

### Method

1. Prepare the best end into cutlets (209) and season them with salt and milled pepper.

2. Pass them through flour, beaten egg and white breadcrumbs. Tidy the shape with a palette knife and mark a 10 mm trellis pattern.

3. Shallow fry the cutlets in first class dripping or oil in a sauté pan over a moderate heat to prevent the crumbs over-colouring. Cook for approximately 5 minutes on each side; when pressed, the cutlets should be firm with no pink blood apparent.

4. Dress them slightly overlapping each other on a hot oval silver dish with an appropriate garnish, i.e. any of the spaghetti garnishes or Princesse (722).

5. Surround the base of the dish with jus-lié and mask the cutlets with a little Beurre noisette. Serve a sauceboat of jus-lié.

## 796  Côtelette d'agneau Réforme

### Method

1. Prepare and cook as for Côtelette d'agneau panée (795).

2. Serve the cutlets slightly overlapping each other on a hot oval dish. Place the Reform garnish, bound with a little of the Reform sauce (383), along the side and surround with the sauce. Finish with a little Beurre noisette.

## 797       Kebab d'agneau à l'orientale

| 8 portions | Ingredients | 10 couverts |
|---|---|---|
| 8 portions | kebab d'agneau (217) | 10 couverts |
| 8 portions | riz à l'orientale (618) | 10 couverts |
| ¾ pint | jus-lié | 525 ml |
| 2 oz | dripping | 70 g |

### Method

1. Heat the dripping in a sauté pan, add the kebab and gently sauté it for approximately 10 minutes, turning it on to all sides with a palette knife.

2. To serve, place the rice in a hot oval flat dish or an earthenware dish so that it forms a bed the width of the skewers. Place the kebab on top of the rice and surround the base of the dish with jus-lié. Serve the remainder of the jus-lié in a sauceboat on an underflat with a doily.

### 798 Fried lambs liver       Foie d'agneau sauté

### 799 Fried lambs liver and bacon       Foie d'agneau au lard

These are prepared and cooked as for Foie de veau au lard (852).

### 800 Braised loin or chump chop       Chop d'agneau braisée

| 8 portions | Ingredients | 10 couverts |
|---|---|---|
| 8 | loin or chump chops (205 and 204) | 10 |
| 6 oz | carrot | 210 g |
| 6 oz | onion | 210 g |
| 2 oz | dripping | 70 g |
| 2 oz | flour | 70 g |
| 1½ oz | tomato purée | 50 g |
| 2 teaspoons | chopped parsley | 5 g |
| 4 level teaspoons | salt | 15 g |
| ½ level teaspoon | pepper | 2 g |
| 2 pints | brown stock | 1·4 litres |
| small | bouquet garni | small |

### Method

1. Heat the dripping in a sauté pan and, when it is smoking, add the seasoned chops. Fry quickly to a light colour and seal them on both sides; remove them from the pan.

2. Add the peeled carrot and onion, cut in rough 10 mm dice, and fry them until they are a light golden brown. Replace the chops in the pan.

3. Sprinkle with the flour, shaking the pan, then pass through an oven at 150°C (300°F) for 6–7 minutes to singe the flour.

4. Add the tomato purée, bouquet garni and gradually add the boiling stock. Stir until boiling then skim away any scum and fat.

5. Cover with a greased paper and lid. Braise in the lower part of an oven at 150°C (300°F) for 1¼ hours until tender.

6. Remove the chops to a clean pan, skim off all fat from the sauce, then correct the seasoning and consistency. Pass the liquid through a fine conical strainer over the chops and reboil.

7. Serve the meat in a hot entrée or earthenware dish, mask over with the sauce and sprinkle the surface with chopped parsley. Place the dish on an underflat with dish paper.

*Note.* This dish is generally served with a vegetable garnish such as jardinière or buttered peas.

### 801       Chop d'agneau Champvallon

| 8 portions | Ingredients | 10 couverts |
|---|---|---|
| 8 × 4–5 oz | chops (usually chump, 204) | 10 × 110–140 g |
| 8 oz | onions | 280 g |
| 2 lb | peeled potatoes (large) | 1·125 kg |
| 2 lb | tomatoes | 1·125 kg |
| 3 oz | dripping | 100 g |
| 2 teaspoons | chopped parsley | 5 g |
| 4 level teaspoons | salt | 15 g |
| ½ level teaspoon | milled pepper | 2 g |
| 1½ pints | jus-lié | 875 ml |

### Method

1. Finely shred the peeled onions, lightly sauté them in half the dripping, then drain.

2. Prepare the tomatoes into 10 mm raw concassé.

3. Season the chops and sauté them quickly in the remainder of the dripping, on both sides, to a light golden brown.

4. Place a little of the onion in the bottom of a greased oval earthenware casserole. Place the chops on top, slightly overlapping each other.

5. Sprinkle the chops with the remainder of the onion, then the tomato.

6. Mask over with the jus-lié. Cut the potatoes in 5 mm thick slices and arrange them, half overlapping, on top of the other ingredients.

7. Bring to the boil and cover the casserole with the lid. Braise in the centre of the oven at 150°C (300°F) for 1¼–1½ hours. Fifteen minutes before cooked, remove the cover, brush the potato with melted butter and colour golden brown.

8. To serve, sprinkle the surface with chopped parsley, replace the cleaned lid and place the casserole on an underflat with dish paper.

### 802 Loin chop toad-in-the-hole

| 8 portions | Ingredients | 10 couverts |
|---|---|---|
| 8 portions | Yorkshire pudding mix (736) | 10 couverts |

| 8 | loin chops (205) | 10 |
| 4 oz | dripping | 140 g |
| 4 level teaspoons | salt | 15 g |
| ½ level teaspoon | milled pepper | 2 g |
| ¾ pint | jus-lié | 525 kg |

## Method

1. Season the chops. Heat a quarter of the fat in a sauté or frying pan and, when it is smoking, quickly fry the chops for 1 minute on each side to seal the meat.

2. Place the chops in a suitably sized roasting tray which allows a space of 20 mm all around between the chops.

3. Pour the remainder of the melted warm fat over the chops, then run the Yorkshire pudding mix between them.

4. Place in the centre of an oven at 190–200°C (375–400°F) and cook for 25–30 minutes until the batter is crisp. During cooking, brush the chops with a little melted butter or fat.

5. To serve, cut through the batter to form equal squares; arrange these neatly on a hot oval flat dish. Serve the jus-lié in a sauce boat on an underflat with a doily.

## 803             Côtelette d'agneau Soubise

| 8 portions | Ingredients | 10 couverts |
| --- | --- | --- |
| 8 × 3½ oz | lamb cutlets (209) | 10 × 100 g |
| 8 oz | finely chopped onion | 280 g |
| 1 oz | butter | 35 g |
| 1½ oz | grated Parmesan cheese | 50 g |
| 2 oz | dripping | 70 g |
| 6 level teaspoons | salt | 20 g |
| 1 level teaspoon | milled pepper | 3 g |
| 1 | yolk of egg | 1 |
| ½ pint | Mornay sauce (390) | 350 ml |
| ¾ pint | jus-lié | 525 ml |
| ¼ pint | béchamel (366) or | 175 ml |
| 2 oz | (cream of rice) | 70 g |
| ¼ pint | (white stock ) | 175 ml |

## Method

1. Melt the butter in a saucepan, add the onion, then cover and sweat gently for 10–12 minutes without colouring.

2. Add the béchamel seasoned with one-third of the salt and pepper. If using stock, add the stock, reboil, stir in the rice and cook it gently for 6–7 minutes.

3. Add the yolk of egg. Pass the mixture through a fine sieve and place it to one side, covered with a greased paper.

4. Heat the dripping in a sauté pan; when it is smoking, add the seasoned cutlets and sauté them gently for 2–3 minutes on each side, keeping them underdone.

5. Place the cutlets on a shallow tray. With a piping bag and a 10-mm star tube, pipe a scroll of the Soubise mixture on each of them.

6. Mask the cutlets with the Mornay sauce and sprinkle the surface evenly with the cheese.

7. Place in the top of an oven at 230°C (450°F) for 4 minutes to colour golden brown and finish cooking the cutlets. If necessary, finish to colour under a salamander.

8. Serve the cutlets in rows on a hot oval silver flat dish; surround the base with jus-lié. Serve the remainder of the jus-lié in a sauceboat on an underflat with a doily.

## 804 Brown lamb stew          Navarin d'agneau

| 8 portions | Ingredients | 10 couverts |
| --- | --- | --- |
| 2½ lb | middle neck (208) and breast of lamb (206) | 1·4 kg |
| 4 oz | carrot | 140 g |
| 4 oz | onion | 140 g |
| 2 oz | dripping | 70 g |
| 3 oz | flour | 100 g |
| 1 oz | tomato purée | 35 g |
| 2 teaspoons | chopped parsley | 5 g |
| 4 level teaspoons | salt | 15 g |
| ½ level teaspoon | ground white pepper | 2 g |
| ½ pod | garlic | ½ pod |
| small | bouquet garni | small |
| 2½ pints | brown stock | 1·75 litres |
| | **Garnish** | |
| 4 oz | turned carrots | 140 g |
| 4 oz | turned turnips | 140 g |
| 8 oz | ½ size turned potatoes | 280 g |
| 4 oz | button onions | 140 g |
| 3 oz | shelled or frozen peas | 100 g |

## Method

1. The proportion of breast of lamb should not exceed one-third of the total weight of meat used. Preparation numbers are given in ingredients.

2. Clean and prepare the carrot and onion into rough 10 mm dice.

3. Heat the dripping in a shallow pan and, when it is smoking, add the seasoned meat. Quickly sauté to seal and colour golden brown then remove it and place aside.

4. Add the mirepoix, fry it golden brown then replace the meat.

5. Sprinkle with the flour, shaking the pan to combine. Place in an oven at 200°C (400°F) for 6–7 minutes to singe the flour.

6. Add the tomato purée and gradually add the stock, stirring the mixture till it is reboiling. Add the crushed garlic and bouquet garni.

7. Cover the pan with a greased paper and lid and place it in the bottom of an oven at 150°C (300°F) for 1¼ hours.

8. Cook the carrots glacés (969), the turnips glacés (1043), the button onions glacés à brun (724b); plain boil the peas for 7–8 minutes and refresh; part boil the potatoes for 8–10 minutes and drain.

225

9. Remove the meat to a clean shallow pan, removing any breast bones, and add all the garnish except the peas.

10. Reboil the sauce, removing all fat with a ladle; adjust the consistency by reducing it, if necessary, so that it will mask the back of the ladle. If it is too thick, add a little stock. Correct the seasoning.

11. Pass the liquid through a fine conical strainer over the meat and garnish. Reboil, cover and cook for a further 20–25 minutes in the oven.

12. Remove any fat and serve in an earthenware casserole or dish. Sprinkle the surface with the peas, heated in a little butter, and the chopped parsley. Place the dish on an underflat with dish paper.

*Note.* When the garnish is added, the dish is usually named Navarin d'agneau printanière or aux légumes.

## 805 Curried lamb        Kari d'agneau

### Method

1. Prepare and serve as for Kari de boeuf (762), replacing the beef with the same quantity of lamb. Boned shoulder (202) cut in 25 mm cubes is usually used. If the meat has been prepared, reduce the quantity by 20 per cent.

2. The cooking time is reduced to $1\frac{1}{2}$–$1\frac{3}{4}$ hours.

## 806 White lamb stew        Blanquette d'agneau

| 8 portions | Ingredients | 10 couverts |
|---|---|---|
| 2½ lb | stewing lamb | 1·4 kg |
| 4 oz | onion (stuck with clove) | 140 g |
| 4 oz | carrot | 140 g |
| 4 oz | butter | 70 g |
| 2 oz | flour | 70 g |
| 2 teaspoons | chopped parsley | 5 g |
| 4 level teaspoons | salt | 15 g |
| ½ level teaspoon | ground white pepper | 2 g |
| small | bouquet garni | small |
| 2 pints | water | 1·4 litres |
| ¼ pint | cream | 175 ml |
| | **Garnish** | |
| 4 oz | bread | 140 g |
| 2 oz | butter | 70 g |

### Method

1. Boned shoulder of lamb is normally used for this recipe. Prepare the meat (202) and cut it into 40 mm cubes. If the meat has already been prepared, reduce the quantity by 20 per cent.

2. Place the lamb in a pan, cover it with water then blanch, refresh and drain.

3. Place back in the cleaned pan and add the measured water. Reboil, then wipe the sides of the pan clean with a damp cloth.

4. Add the carrot, onion, bouquet garni and seasoning. Cover the pan and allow it to simmer for 1 hour.

5. Melt the butter, add the flour and cook it as for blond roux (360b).

6. Gradually add all the stock from the lamb to the roux, then boil and simmer for a few minutes.

7. Place the lamb into a clean pan. Pass the sauce through a fine conical strainer directly onto the meat.

8. Reboil, cover with a greased paper and lid and simmer for a further 30 minutes or until it is cooked.

9. Skim off any fat and correct the consistency of the sauce to mask the back of a ladle; if it is too thin, run some off and reduce. Add the cream and reboil.

10. Cut the bread into 5 mm slices then into heart-shaped croûtons approximately 50 mm long × 30 mm at the wide end. Dip them in the melted butter and grill till they are a light golden brown on each side.

11. Serve the meat and sauce in a hot entrée or earthenware dish on an underflat with dish paper. Dip the points of the croûtons in the sauce, then in chopped parsley. Arrange them evenly spaced around the edge of the blanquette with the pointed ends facing the centre.

## 807        Blanquette d'agneau à l'ancienne

### Method

1. Prepare and serve as for Blanquette d'agneau (806).

2. When placing the lamb in a clean pan at 7 in method, add the following garnish for 8 or 10 portions: 6 oz (210 g) of peeled button onions boiled for 7–8 minutes then drained; 4 oz (140 g) of button white mushrooms, peeled or turned and half-cooked 'à blanc' (335g).

## 808 Lancashire hot pot

### Method

1. Prepare and serve as for Beef hot pot (776).

2. Replace the beef with mutton or lamb, using 2 parts middle neck and 1 part breast. For preparation, see 208 and 206.

3. The cooking time is reduced to $1\frac{1}{2}$–$1\frac{3}{4}$ hours.

4. Add a teaspoon (4 ml) of Worcester sauce to the stock before adding it to the meat.

## 809 Shepherds pie

**Method**

1. Prepare and serve as for Cottage pie (770), replacing the beef with lamb.

2. Use jus-lié or demi-glace.

## 810 Minced lamb        Hachis d'agneau

**Method**

Prepare and serve as for Hachis de boeuf (764), replacing the beef with lamb.

## 811 Braised lambs tongues     Langue d'agneau braisée

| 8 portions | Ingredients | 10 couverts |
|---|---|---|
| 2 lb | lambs tongues | 1·125 kg |
| 4 oz | carrot | 140 g |
| 4 oz | onion | 140 g |
| 1½ oz | tomato purée | 50 g |
| 1 oz | dripping | 35 g |
| 2 teaspoons | chopped parsley | 5 g |
| 4 level teaspoons | salt | 15 g |
| ½ level teaspoon | ground white pepper | 2 g |
| 1½ pints | jus-lié | 1 litre |
| small | bouquet garni | small |

**Method**

1. Wash the tongues, then blanch and refresh, and trim away any attached wind pipe and gristle.

2. Peel the carrots and onions and cut them into 10 mm mirepoix.

3. Melt the dripping in a shallow pan, add the mirepoix, fry till golden brown and run off any excess fat.

4. Add the tongues, tomato purée, jus-lié and bouquet garni. Add the seasoning if the jus-lié is not seasoned.

5. Bring to the boil and cover with greased paper and a lid. Braise in the bottom of an oven at 150°C (300°F) for 1½ hours. Test the meat by prodding the thickest part with a trussing needle; it should pass through the meat without pressure.

6. Take out the tongues, remove the skin and cut them in halves lengthways. Arrange them neatly in a hot entrée dish.

7. Pass the sauce, then skim it, correct the seasoning and consistency, and mask it over the tongues and sprinkle the surface with chopped parsley. A garnish is usually served alongside, e.g. jardinière, or paysanne of vegetables cooked glacé, or a purée of green peas (St Germain) (1055).

*Note.* If desired, brown stock thickened with diluted arrow-root (¾ oz per pint, 40 g per litre) may be used in place of jus-lié.

## 812 Braised lambs hearts     Coeur d'agneau braisé

**Method**

1. Prepare the ingredients as for Braised lambs tongues (811), omitting the tongues.

2. Allow 1 × 4 – 4½ oz (110 – 125 g) lambs hearts per portion.

3. Cut a conical-shaped piece out of the top of the heart to remove the tubes. Tie across the heart with string.

4. Cook and serve as for Braised lambs tongues (811).

## 813 Braised stuffed lambs hearts     Coeur d'agneau farci braisé

**Method**

1. Prepare and serve as for Braised lambs hearts (812).

2. Before tying, place a little stuffing (216) in the cavity from which the tubes were removed.

## 814        Rognons sautés

| 8 portions | Ingredients | 10 couverts |
|---|---|---|
| 16 × 2 oz | lambs kidneys | 20 × 55 g |
| 2 fl. oz | oil | 70 ml |
| 1 pint | demi-glace | 700 ml |
| 2 fl. oz | Madeira wine | 70 ml |
| 2 teaspoons | chopped parsley | 5 g |
| 4 level teaspoons | salt | 15 g |
| ½ level teaspoon | milled pepper | 2 g |
|  | **Garnish** |  |
| 4 oz | bread | 140 g |
| 2 oz | butter | 70 g |

**Method**

1. Prepare the lambs kidneys for sauté (212).

2. Heat the oil in a large sauté pan; when it is smoking, add the cut kidneys and sauté them very rapidly over a fierce heat. If necessary, cook a half at a time. Sauté for 4–5 minutes then place them aside to keep warm in a clean pan.

3. Déglacé the pan with the wine, add the demi-glace and reboil. Pass through a fine conical strainer over the kidneys. Do not reboil.

4. Prepare the heart-shaped croûtons (806, 10 in method).

5. Serve the kidneys and sauce in a hot entrée dish on an underflat with dish paper. Dip the points of the croûtons in the sauce, then in the chopped parsley. Arrange the croûtons around the kidneys with the points to the centre.

## 815 Rognons sautés turbigo

**Method**

1. Prepare and serve as for Rognons sautés (814).
2. Add the following garnish, previously prepared and cooked, to the kidneys before adding the sauce:
8 oz (280 g) small whole, or scallops of mushrooms sauté (335g). 8 oz (280 g) pork chipolata sausages, each twisted in 3 pieces and grilled for 5–6 minutes on all sides, then divided.

## 816 Bordure de rognons

**Method**

1. Prepare the kidneys as for Rognons sautés (814), adding only half the sauce.
2. Prepare 8 or 10 portions of Riz pilaff (615).
3. To serve, lightly press the rice into a greased savarin or border moulds and turn on to a hot flat dish. Place the kidneys in the centre and sprinkle them with chopped parsley. Surround the rice with the remainder of the sauce, slightly thinned with stock. No croûtons are used.

## 817 Braised lambs sweetbreads     Ris d'agneau braisé

**Method**

1. Clean and prepare the sweetbreads (214).
2. Cook as for ris de veau braisé (847), using lambs sweetbreads.

## 818 Bouchées de ris d'agneau

**Method**

1. Prepare and cook the sweetbreads as for Ris d'agneau braisé (817).
2. Finish as for Bouchées de ris de veau (851).

## 819 Irish stew

| 8 portions | Ingredients | 10 couverts |
|---|---|---|
| 2½ lb | stewing lamb | 1·4 kg |
| 8 oz | onions | 280 g |
| 8 oz | leeks | 280 g |
| 8 oz | white cabbage | 280 g |
| 6 oz | celery | 210 g |
| 2 lb | peeled potatoes | 1·125 kg |
| 8 oz | button onions | 280 g |
| 4 teaspoons | chopped parsley | 10 g |
| 4 level teaspoons | salt | 15 g |
| ½ level teaspoon | ground white pepper | 2 g |
| small | bouquet garni | small |
| 2 pints | water | 1·4 litres |

**Method**

1. Prepare the lamb: middle neck as in 208 and breast as in 206, the proportion of breast, if used, not exceeding one-third of the total weight of meat. Blanch, refresh, wash thoroughly and drain.
2. Place the lamb in a shallow pan, cover with water, bring to the boil and skim the surface. Add the seasoning and bouquet garni then cover and allow to simmer for 20 minutes.
3. Turn 16 or 20 three-quarter size turned potatoes from the peeled potatoes.
4. Clean and finely shred the onion, leek, celery and cabbage; add these to the meat with the potato trimmings.
5. Reboil, cover and cook steadily for 40 minutes.
6. Remove the meat to a clean pan. Rub the cooked vegetables and liquor through a sieve, then pass the liquid over the meat through a coarse conical strainer. If desired, do not pass the vegetables and liquor.
7. Reboil, then add the button onions and turned potatoes, both having been previously blanched and drained.
8. Cover with a paper and lid, then simmer for a further 30–35 minutes, until the meat, onions and potatoes are cooked.
9. Correct the seasoning and consistency of the liquor, which should be like a sauce.
10. Serve in a hot entrée dish and sprinkle the surface liberally with the parsley. Place the dish on an underflat with dish paper.

| | | | |
|---|---|---|---|
| **821 Roast leg of veal** | Cuissot de veau rôti | **829 Fried veal cutlet** | Côte de veau sautée |

**822 Roast loin of veal**       Longe de veau rôtie

**Method**

1. Prepare the leg of veal (222).
2. Prepare the loin of veal (225).
3. Prepare and roast them as described in 725c.
4. Carve as for leg of pork in 726, 2.
5. Serve the meat with slices of boiled bacon and veal stuffing (241) and garnish with picked watercress.
6. Place the stuffing to cook 30–35 minutes before the meat is ready. Melt a little fat in a frying pan and press the stuffing into the pan to a depth of 20 mm. Moisten the surface with fat from the meat and cook the stuffing to a light golden brown colour in the oven at 180°C (350°F). Then cut it into wedge-shaped pieces.
7. Arrange the slices of veal and bacon alternately on a hot dish and place the stuffing alongside them. Mask the meat with broken roast gravy, i.e. jus de rôti, with a little demi-glace added.

**823 Roast stuffed loin of veal**       Longe de veau farcie rôtie

**824 Roast stuffed breast**       Poitrine de veau farcie rôtie
     **of veal**

**Method**

1. Prepare the loin (225) or breast (224), placing a 25 mm diameter roll of veal stuffing (241) down the centre of the meat before rolling and tying it.

**825**       Cuissot de veau poêlé

**826**       Longe de veau poêlée

**827**       Carré de veau poêlé

**828**       Épaule de veau poêlée

**Method**

1. Prepare the veal; leg as in 222, loin as in 225, carré as in 226, and shoulder as in 223.
2. Cook and serve in the same manner as Lamb poêlé (789).

**830**       Grenadin de veau sauté

**Method**

1. Prepare the veal: cutlets as in 226 and grenadin as in 222.
2. Season with salt and milled pepper on both sides.
3. Heat sufficient oil and butter in a sauté pan and add the cuts of veal. Sauté them steadily for 5–6 minutes on each side. To test when the meat is ready, press the veal with the finger; it should be firm to the touch with no trace of blood.
4. Serve the cutlets neatly arranged on a hot oval flat dish surrounded with jus-lié. Mask the veal with ½ oz (15 g) per portion of Beurre noisette.

Veal cutlets are usually served garnished (722).

**831**       Côte ou grenadin de veau Zingara

**Method**

1. Prepare and cook the veal as for Sauté (829 and 830) and serve it on a hot oval flat dish.
2. Prepare a garnish of 2 oz (55 g) each of julienne of cooked ham, cooked ox-tongue, mushroom cooked 'à blanc' (335g) and ½ oz (15 g) of julienne of truffle for each 8 or 10 portions.
3. Prepare 1 pint (700 ml) of Sauce madère (378).
4. Add enough of the sauce to the garnish to loosen it, then heat it and mask it over the veal. Surround the veal with the remainder of the sauce.

**832**       Côte ou grenadin de veau en papillote

**Method**

1. Prepare the veal: for cutlets, as in 226, for grenadin as in 222, then as for en papillote as in 227.
2. Place the paper casings containing the veal on suitably sized flat dishes lightly brushed with oil.
3. Cook them in the centre of an oven at 175–190° (350–375°F) for approximately 15 minutes. By this time, the paper should have risen and just begun to colour. If not, increase the heat for 2–3 minutes.
4. Serve immediately on the same dish, placing a cold dish underneath. Serve a sauceboat of jus-lié on an underflat with a doily.

## 833 Fried crumbed veal cutlet     Côte de veau panée

**Method**

1. Prepare the veal cutlets (226) and season them with salt and milled pepper.
2. Panée à l'anglaise (311).
3. Cook and serve them as for Côte de veau sautée (829). Care is necessary, when cooking not to use too much heat as this can cause overcolouring of the crumbs. The cutlets are usually served garnished (722).

## 834 Fried veal escalope     Escalope de veau sautée

**Method**

1. Prepare the veal escalopes (222) and season them with salt and milled pepper.
2. Heat sufficient oil and butter to cover the base of a sauté pan. Lightly flour the veal and place it in the butter.
3. Cook gently for 3–4 minutes on each side to colour a light golden brown. Too much heat will cause excessive shrinkage of the veal.
4. Serve the escalopes on a hot oval flat dish, slightly overlapping; surround them with jus-lié and mask over with Beurre noisette. They are usually garnished (722).

## 835 Fried crumbed veal escalope     Escalope de veau panée

**Method**

1. Prepare the escalopes (222) and season them with salt and milled pepper.
2. Panée à l'anglaise (311).
3. Then cook and serve as for Escalope de veau sautée (834). They are usually garnished (722).

## 836 Escalope of veal, Viennese style     Escalope de veau viennoise

**Method**

1. Prepare and serve as for Escalope de veau panée (835).
2. For both 8 and 10 portions, prepare the following garnish: 3–4 hard boiled eggs, the yolk and white passed separately through a coarse sieve; 8–10 slices of lemon, free of skin and pith; 8–10 paupiettes of anchovy; 8–10 stoned olives; chopped parsley.
3. For 'à la carte' service, arrange rows of the white of egg, chopped parsley and yolk of egg at each end of the dish. Place the cooked escalopes slightly overlapping down the centre and put a slice of lemon on each of them, with the anchovy wrapped around the olive on top.

4. Before masking with the Beurre noisette, squeeze a little lemon juice over the escalopes. Surround the base with jus-lié.
5. For 'table d'hôte' service, the egg and parsley may be mixed together and placed on the lemon before the anchovy and olive.

## 837     Médaillon de ris de veau pané

**Method**

1. Prepare the sweetbreads in slices (236).
2. Panée à l'anglaise (311).
3. Cook and serve as for Escalope de veau sautée (834) from 2 in method).
   The dish is usually garnished (702), i.e. Médaillon de ris de veau princesse.

## 838 White veal stew     Blanquette de veau

**Method**

1. Prepare and serve as for Blanquette d'agneau (806). The cooking time is reduced to approximately 1–1¼ hours.
2. Boned shoulder (223), or quasi (222) is normally used for stewing.

## 839     Blanquette de veau à l'ancienne

**Method**

Prepare and serve as for Blanquette d'agneau à l'ancienne (807). The veal used is the same as in the previous recipe.

## 840     Blanquette de veau valencienne

**Method**

1. Prepare and serve as for Blanquette de veau à l'ancienne (839).
2. Serve 8 or 10 portions of Riz pilaff (615) separately in a timbale or an entrée dish on an underflat with dish paper. Sprinkle the top of the rice with 2 oz (55 g) of julienne of smoked or cooked ox-tongue.

## 841 Fricassée of veal     Fricassée de veau

| 8 portions | Ingredients | 10 couverts |
| --- | --- | --- |
| 2½ lb | stewing veal | 1·4 kg |
| 3 oz | butter | 100 g |
| 3 oz | flour | 100 g |
| 2 teaspoons | chopped parsley | 5 g |
| 4 level teaspoons | salt | 15 g |
| ¼ level teaspoon | ground white pepper | 2 g |
| 2 pints | white veal stock | 1·4 litres |
| ¼ pint | cream | 175 ml |
| 2 | yolks of egg | 3 |
| small | bouquet garni | small |

| | Garnish | |
|---|---|---|
| 4 oz | bread | 140 g |
| 2 oz | butter | 70 g |

## Method

1. Usually quasi (222) or boned shoulder of veal (223) is used. Prepare and cut the meat into 40 mm cubes. Where prepared veal is used, reduce the quantity by 20 per cent.

2. Heat the butter in a shallow pan, add the seasoned veal and cook it, without colouring, over the heat until the veal stiffens.

2. Sprinkle with the flour and lightly singe it for 5–6 minutes in an oven at 150°C (300°F).

4. Gradually stir in the boiling stock so that it forms a smooth sauce. If desired, omit the flour and stock and substitute an equal quantity of thin veal velouté.

5. Add the bouquet garni, cover with a greased paper and lid and cook in an oven for 50–60 minutes.

6. Put the meat in a clean pan then remove any fat from the sauce and correct its seasoning and consistency. The sauce should be thin.

7. Reboil, skim and remove from the heat. Mix the yolks of egg and cream together.

8. Remove the pan from the stove, move the pan in a circular movement while adding the liaison of cream and yolks. Do not reboil, or the sauce will curdle.

9. Cut the bread into 5 mm slices, then into 50 mm-long heart-shaped croûtons; dip them in melted butter and grill them till they are a light golden brown on both sides.

10. Serve the fricassée in an entrée or earthenware dish. Dip the points of the croûtons in the sauce, then into the parsley, and space evenly around the edge of the fricassée with the points to the centre. Place the dish on an underflat with dish paper.

## 842　　　　Fricassée de veau à l'ancienne

## Method

1. Prepare and serve as for Fricassée de veau (841).

2. After 30 minutes cooking time, move the meat into a clean pan and add, for 8 or 10 portions, 6 oz (210 g) of peeled button onions, boiled for 7–8 minutes and drained; 4 oz (140 g) of button white mushrooms, peeled or turned and half cooked 'à blanc' (335g). Cook the fricassée for a further 20–25 minutes, and finish as from 8 in 841.

## 843　Brown veal stew　　　　Ragoût de veau

## Method

1. Prepare and serve as for Ragoût de boeuf (747), replacing the beef with stewing veal.

2. Reduce the cooking time to approximately 1 hour. Other variations, given in 748, 749 and 750, may be applied to veal.

## 844　　　　Paupiette de veau

## Method

1. Prepare and serve as for Paupiette de boeuf (744), replacing the beef with veal when making the paupiettes (159).

2. Reduce the cooking time to 1–1¼ hours.

## 845　　　　Osso bucco

| 8 portions | Ingredients | 10 couverts |
|---|---|---|
| 8 × 6 oz | pieces of veal knuckle | 10 × 170 g |
| 8 oz | finely chopped onions | 280 g |
| 2 oz | butter | 70 g |
| 1¾ lb | tomatoes | 1 kg |
| 1 oz | tomato purée | 35 g |
| 2 teaspoons | chopped parsley | 5 g |
| 4 level teaspoons | salt | 15 g |
| ½ level teaspoon | milled pepper | 2 g |
| 1 pod | garlic | 1 pod |
| 1½ pints | white veal stock (346) | 1 litre |

## Method

1. Prepare the knuckle of veal (221).

2. Melt the butter in a shallow pan, then add the seasoned pieces of knuckle of veal, and cover the pan and allow them to sweat on both sides until lightly coloured.

3. Add the onion; continue to sweat with the veal until very lightly coloured.

4. Add the finely chopped garlic, tomato purée, wine and stock. Bring to the boil and skim.

5. Prepare the tomatoes into 10 mm concassé (336, 5b) and add them to the veal. Cover and braise in the lower part of the oven for 1¼ hours. The meat should then begin easily to move away from the bone.

6. Remove the veal to a hot entrée dish, cover and keep warm.

7. Slightly reduce the cooking liquor, which should have thickened slightly with the tomato and natural gelatine from the veal. Correct the seasoning.

8. Mask the liquor over the veal and sprinkle the surface with the chopped parsley. Place the dish on an underflat with paper.

## 846 Calf's brains in black butter — Cervelle au beurre noir

**Method**

1. Prepare and clean the brains (230), allowing one set of brains per portion.

2. Place the brains in a sauteuse and cover them with a court-bouillon (626).

3. Bring to the boil, skim then poach gently for 10–12 minutes.

4. Drain and cut the brains into 10 mm-thick slices on the slant. Fry these slices quickly in butter in a sauté pan.

5. Arrange the slices neatly, half overlapping, in an entrée dish; sprinkle them liberally with coarsely chopped parsley.

6. Heat 1½ oz (45 g) of butter per portion in a frying pan until nearly black; add a teaspoon of vinegar, then mask the mixture over the brains. Place the dish on an underflat with paper.

## 847 Braised veal sweetbreads — Ris de veau braisé

**Method**

1. Prepare the sweetbreads (236) and place them on a bed of roots (340a) in a shallow pan.

2. Cover with white veal stock (346) then add a little salt and ground white pepper.

3. Boil and skim. Add a bouquet garni and cover the pan with a greased paper and lid. Braise in the lower part of the oven at 150°C (300°F) for approximately 1 hour.

4. Allow to cool in the liquor. Sweetbreads are not usually served plain braised.

5. When served plain, remove the sweetbreads to an entrée dish and keep them hot.

6. Reduce the cooking liquor by one-third, thicken it slightly with diluted arrowroot, pass it through a fine strainer and mask it over the sweetbreads. Sprinkle the surface with chopped parsley.

## 848 — Ris de veau braisé poulette

| 8 portions | Ingredients | 10 couverts |
|---|---|---|
| 2 lb | veal sweetbreads | 1·125 kg |
| 8 oz | closed white mushrooms | 280 g |
| 2 teaspoons | chopped parsley | 5 g |
| 4 level teaspoons | salt | 15 g |
| ½ level teaspoon | ground white pepper | 2 g |
| 2 | yolks of egg | 3 |
| 1½ pints | veal or chicken velouté (368) | 1 litre |
| ¼ pint | cream | 175 ml |
| | **Garnish** | |
| 4 oz | bread | 140 g |
| 2 oz | butter | 70 g |

**Method**

1. Prepare the sweetbreads (236) and place them into a shallow braising pan.

2. Peel or turn the mushrooms (if large, cut them in scallops), half-cook them 'à blanc' (335 g) and sprinkle them over the sweetbreads.

3. Mask over with the boiling strained velouté, boil and cover with a greased paper and lid.

4. Braise in the lower part of an oven at 150°C (300°F) for approximately one hour. Remove any fat from the sauce.

5. Add a little of the sauce to the liaison of yolks and cream and run this mixture into the sauce, shaking the pan to mix them together. Do not reboil.

6. Serve in a hot entrée dish and garnish with heart-shaped croûtons grilled in butter, the ends dipped in the sauce and chopped parsley. Place the croûtons around the sides with the points to the centre. Place the entrée dish on an underflat with dish paper.

## 849 — Ris de veau braisé princesse

**Method**

1. Prepare and serve as for Ris de veau braisé poulette (848).

2. Garnish between the croûtons with 3–4 hot buttered aparagus tips (965) per portion.

## 850 — Ris de veau braisé au madère

| 8 portions | Ingredients | 10 couverts |
|---|---|---|
| 2 lb | veal sweetbreads | 1·125 kg |
| 8 oz | closed mushrooms | 280 g |
| 1 oz | butter | 35 g |
| 2 teaspoons | chopped parsley | 5 g |
| 1½ pints | sauce madère (378) | 1 litre |
| | **Garnish** | |
| 4 oz | bread | 140 g |
| 2 oz | butter | 70 g |

**Method**

1. Prepare the sweetbreads (236) and place them into a shallow braising pan.

2. Peel or turn the mushrooms (if they are large, cut them into scallops), lightly sauté them in the butter and add them to the sweetbreads.

3. Mask over with the boiling strained sauce and boil.

4. Cover with a greased paper and lid and braise in the lower part of an oven at 150°C (300°F) for 1 hour. Remove any fat from the sauce.

5. Serve in a hot entrée dish and garnish with heart-shaped

croûtons grilled in butter, the points dipped in the sauce and parsley. Place the entrée dish on an underflat with dish paper.

## 851 Bouchée de ris de veau

| 8 portions | Ingredients | 10 couverts |
|---|---|---|
| 8 | puff paste bouchées (1282) | 10 |
| 2 lb | veal sweetbreads | 1·125 kg |
| 1¼ pints | sauce suprême (400) | 875 ml |
| 8 oz | closed white mushrooms | 280 g |

### Method

1. Prepare and braise the sweetbreads (847) then drain them and cut them into 10 mm scallops.

2. Peel or turn the mushrooms (cut them into scallops if they are large) and cook 'à blanc' (335g). Drain then add them to the sweetbreads in a sauteuse.

3. Bind with the boiling sauce suprême and correct the seasoning.

4. Fill the hot pastry cases with the mixture and place the pastry cover on top, at an angle.

5. Serve the bouchées on a hot round or oval flat dish with a doily. Garnish between them with sprigs of fresh parsley.

## 852 Calf's liver and bacon    Foie de veau au lard

| 8 portions | Ingredients | 10 couverts |
|---|---|---|
| 1½ lb | calf's liver | 850 g |
| 16 | slices of streaky bacon | 20 |
| 3 oz | dripping | 100 g |
| 3 oz | flour | 100 g |
| 4 level teaspoons | salt | 15 g |
| ½ level teaspoons | milled pepper | 2 g |
| 1 pint | jus-lié | 700 ml |

### Method

1. Prepare and cut the liver as in 235 and sprinkle with the seasoning.

2. Heat enough of the dripping to just cover the base of a frying pan and add the lightly floured liver. Flour the liver just before cooking it.

3. Fry it quickly for 2 minutes on each side.

4. Lightly grill the bacon on a tray for 1 minute on each side.

5. Serve the slices of liver, slightly overlapping, on a hot flat oval dish and place 2 slices of bacon crosswise on each portion. Surround the liver with jus-lié and serve the remainder in a sauceboat on an underflat with a doily.

## 853 Pojarski de veau, sauce smitaine

| 8 portions | Ingredients | 10 couverts |
|---|---|---|
| 8 | pojarski de veau (240) | 10 |
| 1 fl. oz | oil | 35 ml |
| 1 oz | butter | 35 g |
| 2 teaspoons | chopped parsley | 5 g |
| 1 pint | sauce smitaine (760) | 700 ml |

### Method

1. Prepare the veal pojarski as in 240.

2. Heat the oil and butter in a sauté pan, add the pojarski and cook very gently for 4–5 minutes on each side till very lightly coloured. Excess heat will cause excessive shrinkage and crusting.

3. Arrange the veal neatly on a hot oval flat dish and mask over with the boiling sauce. Place a pinch of chopped parsley in the centre of each pojarski.

## 854 Calf's head, vinaigrette sauce    Tête de veau vinaigrette

| 8 portions | Ingredients | 10 couverts |
|---|---|---|
| 1 medium | calf's head | 1 large |
| 4 oz | tomatoes | 140 g |
| 1 oz | finely chopped onion | 35 g |
| 2 teaspoons | chopped parsley | 5 g |
| 1 oz | salt | 35 g |
| 1 | hard boiled egg | 1 |
| ¼ pod | garlic | ¼ pod |
| ½ pint | vinaigrette sauce (7) | 350 ml |
| small | bouquet garni | small |

### Method

1. Prepare the calf's head (232). When cutting it into portions, remove the ears.

2. Prepare 4 quarts (5 litres) of blanc (341). Add the calf's head, salt and bouquet garni to it when it boils.

3. Reboil, cover and simmer for approximately 1½ hours. A needle should easily penetrate the flesh when it is cooked.

4. Clean and cook the brain (230).

5. Remove the tongue and place it in cold water; remove the skin and trim the shape. Replace in the blanc to reheat.

6. Cut the tomatoes into a 5 mm raw concassé (336, 5c); place this in a basin and add the coarsely sieved hard-boiled egg, onion, parsley, finely chopped garlic and the vinaigrette. Mix well and place it in a sauceboat on an underflat with a doily.

7. Place the portions of calf's head into a hot entrée or earthenware dish. Cut the tongue and brain in slices and arrange them on each side. Place the dish on an underflat with dish paper; serve the sauce separately.

**855  Veal and ham pie (with gammon)**
  **Veal and bacon pie (with bacon)**

**Method**

1. Prepare the 8 or 10 portions of pie (309).
2. Cover with puff pastry, cook and serve as for Steak pie (777), from 4 in the method. Allow approximately 1¾ hours cooking time.

*Note.* When required for serving cold, place 3 soaked sheets of gelatine on top of the filling before covering. Alternatively, add aspic jelly to the pie when it is cooked and allow it to set.

For Raised veal and ham pie, see the Pastry section.

---

## 856  PORK, HAM—ROASTS, RELEVÉS, ENTRÉES

| | |
|---|---|
| **857  Roast leg of pork** | **Cuissot de porc rôti** |
| **858  Roast loin of pork** | **Longe de porc rôtie** |
| **859  Roast spare ribs** | **Basse-côte de porc rôtie** |

**Method**

1. Prepare the leg as in 246, the loin as in 251 and the spare ribs as in 249.
2. Prepare and roast the joint as described in 725b.
4. Prepare, cook and finish the garnish of sage and onion stuffing (294), placing it in a greased tray to a depth of 10 mm. Moisten the surface with fat from the pork and start to cook it 25–30 minutes before the meat is ready. Cook it in the centre of an oven at 180°C (350°F) until it is a light golden brown.
4. Prepare the apple sauce (410).
5. Carve the pork as described in 726, 2.
6. To serve, arrange the slices of pork, slightly overlapping, on a hot flat oval dish, placing the pieces of crackling along the side and the squares of stuffing opposite. Mask the meat with boiling roast gravy and garnish with sprigs of watercrews. Serve the apple sauce and extra gravy in a sauceboat on an underflat with a doily.

**860  Boiled leg of pork**　　　**Cuissot de porc bouilli**

**Method**

1. Place a suitable size pan of water to boil and add 1½ oz of salt per gallon (10 g per litre), together with 4 oz (110 g) each of peeled carrots and onions, stuck with cloves, 1 bayleaf and 8–10 white peppercorns.
2. When boiling, add the prepared leg of pork (246). Reboil, skim, cover and simmer gently until cooked. Allow 25 min per lb (44 min per kg), plus 25 minutes. Test the meat with a trussing needle by prodding the thickest part of the leg: the juice that emerges should be colourless when the meat is cooked; if it is pink, continue simmering.

3. One hour before the meat finishes cooking, add the following garnish, tied in a muslin for easy removal, for both 8 and 10 portions: 6 oz (200 g) each of turned carrots, peeled button onions, 2 leeks and 2 small hearts of celery (the latter two having been previously trimmed and cleaned).
4. To serve, carve the pork as described in 726, 2 and arrange the slices neatly overlapping each other on a hot oval silver dish. Mask over with a little of the strained cooking liquor and garnish along the sides with bouquets of the turned carrots and button onions, with the leeks and celery cut into sections and folded. Sprinkle the carrots with chopped parsley. Serve separately, on an underdish and a doily, a dish of pease pudding (purée of yellow peas) (1063) and a sauceboat of the strained liquor.

**861  Boiled ham, parsley**　　　**Jambon bouilli, sauce**
  **sauce**　　　　　　　　　　　　　　　　　　**persil**

**Method**

1. Prepare the ham for cooking according to the cut used (267–270). Soak the joints to extract any excess salt, then wash them.
2. Place the ham into cold water, bring to the boil and skim the surface. Proceed to cook, carve and serve as for boiled pork (860), removing the skin before carving.
3. With the ham, serve, in addition, parsley sauce (393).
*Note.* The ham may also be garnished with broad beans (1021).

**862  Braised ham**　　　　　　　　　　**Jambon braisé**

**Method**

1. Prepare and cook the ham as in 861, omitting the vegetables for garnish.
2. Remove the ham from the liquor when it is barely cooked. Then remove the skin and place the ham into a shallow braising pan, the fat side uppermost, and add approximately 10 mm of the liquor.

3. Press cloves into the fat in rows 25 mm apart and at intervals of 25 mm. Sprinkle the ham with brown sugar.

4. Place it in the centre of an oven at 200°C (400°F) to colour it a golden brown. Baste it frequently with the liquor.

5. Cut the ham into thin slices and arrange each slice neatly overlapping the next on a hot oval silver dish. Mask over with boiling Sauce madère (378). Serve on the side of the ham an appropriate garnish, as following:

Jambon braisé aux nouilles: 1 oz (30 g) Nouilles aux beurre (605) per portion;

Jambon braisé aux ravioli: 3–4 pieces of ravioli (608) per portion;

Jambon braisé aux épinards: small portion of Épinards à la crème (1019), scrolled in a dome shape with a 25 mm triangle of butter-fried croûton on top, per portion.

## 863                       Jambon sous la cendre

**Method**

1. Prepare the ham or gammon by either open-boning or tunnel-boning.

2. Trim away any rough edges to form an even shape and remove any skin from the trimmings. Use the trimmings with an equal quantity of lean veal to make a farce as for Beef paupiettes (160), omitting the beef.

3. Place the farce in the centre of the ham in the place from which the bone has been removed. Roll the ham to form an even shape then tie it tightly and place it in a muslin, tying the ends.

4. Cook as for boiled ham (861), without the garnish. Remove when barely cooked and allow to go cold.

5. Remove the muslin and skin from the ham.

6. Roll out a piece of puff paste 5 mm thick. Place the ham on the paste and completely envelop the ham with it. Finish with the seam of the paste where it is joined underneath. Lightly squeeze the ends of the paste to seal them together, tucking the ends underneath in the process.

7. Place on a greased tray. Egg-wash the paste all over, decorate with pastry leaves and brush it with egg-wash. Let it stand for 1–2 hours.

8. Bake in the centre of an oven at 200°C (400°F) for approximately 15 minutes, until the paste is set, then reduce to 160°C (325°F) and cook for a further 45 minutes.

9. Serve on a hot flat dish on a dish paper and garnish the ham with sprigs of parsley. Serve Sauce madère (378) in a sauceboat on an underflat with a doily.

## 864            Paupiettes de jambon sous la cendre

| 8 portions | Ingredients | 10 couverts |
|---|---|---|
| 1½ lb | gammon | 840 g |
| 4 oz | lean veal | 140 g |
| | beef paupiette farce (minus the beef) (160) | |
| 8 oz flour mix | puff paste | 280 flour mix |
| 2 oz | butter | 70 g |
| 2 oz | carrot | 70 g |
| 2 oz | onion | 70 g |
| 2 oz | leek | 70 g |
| 2 oz | celery | 70 g |
| ¼ pint | white wine | 175 ml |
| ¾ pint | sauce madère (378) | 525 ml |

**Method**

1. Cut the gammon in thin slices, trim the slices and use the trimmings with the veal and other ingredients of the paupiette farce to prepare the stuffing.

2. Make into paupiettes as for beef (159).

3. Melt half the butter in a sauteuse, add the paupiettes, cover the sauteuse then sweat them slowly for 12 to 15 minutes to shrink slightly. Allow to cool, then remove the string.

4. Clean the vegetables, cut them into brunoise and sweat them in a sauteuse in the remainder of the butter for 6–7 minutes, without colouring. Add the wine, reduce the liquid until dry then allow to go cold.

5. Dust the paste with flour, roll out till 3 mm thick then cut it into 110–125 mm squares and egg-wash the edges.

6. Sprinkle the centre of the paste with the brunoise and place a paupiette on top. Envelope the paupiette with the paste, sealing the ends and turning them into the join.

7. Place them on a greased baking sheet with the sealed edge underneath. Egg-wash, decorate with two small pastry leaves, then egg-wash the leaves. Let them stand for 1 hour.

8. Bake them in the centre to top of an oven at 200°C (400°F) for 10–15 minutes to set and lightly colour. Then move them to a lower position in the oven, reduce the temperature to 140°C (280°F) and cook for a further 1 hour. Test when they are cooked with a needle: it should penetrate without undue pressure.

9. Serve them on a hot flat dish on a dish paper and garnish between them with sprigs of parsley. Serve the sauce in a sauceboat on an underflat with a doily.

## 865 Côte de porc flamande

| 8 portions | Ingredients | 10 couverts |
|---|---|---|
| 8 × 4–4½ oz | pork chops | 10 × 110–125 g |
| 1½ lb | apples (russet type) | 850 g |
| 2 oz | butter | 70 g |
| 2 oz | dripping | 70 g |
| 4 level teaspoons | salt | 15 g |
| ½ level teaspoon | milled pepper | 2 g |
| 1 level teaspoon | caster sugar | 4 g |
| ¼ level teaspoon | ground cinnamon | 1 g |

### Method

1. Prepare the pork (250) and season it with the salt and milled pepper.
2. Peel and core the apples then cut them into 6 or 8 sections. Melt the butter in an earthenware casserole, add the apples, sugar and cinnamon; lightly toss over.
3. Heat the dripping in a sauté pan, add the meat and sauté it quickly on each side for 2–3 minutes till a light golden brown. Arrange the meat neatly on the apples, the slices slightly overlapping.
4. Cover, place in the lower part of an oven at 180–190°C (350–375°F) and cook for 10–12 minutes until the apples are just soft and the meat cooked.
5. Clean the casserole and place it on an underflat with dish paper.

## 866 Raised pork pies

See Pastry section.

## 867 Sausage toad-in-the-hole

| 8 portions | Ingredients | 10 couverts |
|---|---|---|
| 16 × 2 oz | pork sausages | 20 × 55 g |
| 8 portions | Yorkshire pudding mix (736) | 10 couverts |
| 3 oz | dripping | 100 g |
| ¾ pint | jus-lié | 525 ml |

### Method

1. Add the dripping to a suitably sized roasting tray. When it is melted, add the sausages and cook them gently, till they are very lightly coloured and set, for 2–3 minutes.
2. Allow them to cool slightly and arrange them in pairs, with a space of 25 mm between them all round. Run the Yorkshire pudding mixture in between the sausages.
3. Place in the centre of an oven at 190–200°C (375–400°F) and cook for 20–25 minutes until the batter is crisp.
4. To serve, cut through the batter to form squares of the same size. Arrange these neatly on a hot oval flat dish. Serve the jus-lié in a sauceboat on an underflat with a doily.

## 868 POULTRY AND GAME—ROASTS, RELEVÉS, ENTRÉES

### 869 Roast chicken — Poulet rôti

### 870 Roast baby chicken — Poussin rôti

### Method

1. Prepare the chicken or poussin for roasting (273).
2. Season inside and all over with a little salt. If desired, a little rosemary may be placed inside the carcass for flavour.
3. Place the chicken in a roasting tray on the leg side and smear it all over with first class dripping or white fat.
4. Small chickens, i.e. poussin, are heated in the tray on top of the stove until they start to fry.
5. Place the tray in the centre to top of the oven at 230°C (450°F), to set the chicken, for approximately 10 minutes, then reduce the heat to about 200°C (400°F) according to size. Allow approximately 20 minutes cooking time per lb (44 minutes per kg) drawn weight. Do not reduce the heat when cooking poussin.
6. During roasting, the chicken or poussin should have one-third of the cooking time on each leg and the rest of time on the back to colour the breast. Baste it frequently during cooking.
7. To test the chicken see 725, 6iii. Remove the chicken from the tray and keep it warm. Set the sediment in the tray until the fat clears then run off the fat and add ¾ pint (525 ml) of good brown stock strengthened with the lightly roasted neck and giblets.
8. Simmer this for 5–6 minutes then pass it through a gauze strainer and reboil. Remove all the fat, correct the seasoning and colour by adding a few drops of gravy browning if necessary.
9. Remove the string from the chicken. Serve it whole or cut (726, 5) on a hot oval flat dish garnished with pommes chips on each side and sprigs of watercress in front. Serve the roast gravy and bread sauce (411) in sauceboats on an underflat with a doily.

### 871 Roast chicken with bacon — Poulet rôti au lard

### Method

Prepare, cook and serve the chicken as for Poulet rôti (869). Garnish it with 1 slice of grilled streaky bacon per portion placed across the breast of the chicken.

## 872 Roast stuffed chicken, English style     Poulet rôti à l'anglaise

### Method

1. When preparing the chicken, fill it with Farce à l'anglaise (291), leaving a gap between the stuffing and the breast bone to allow the heat to penetrate.

2. Allow 5 minutes per lb (11 minutes per kg) extra cooking time during roasting. Cook and serve the chicken as for Poulet rôti (869).

## 873 Roast stuffed chicken, American style     Poulet rôti à l'américaine

### Method

Prepare, cook and serve the chicken as for Poulet rôti à l'anglaise (872), using Farce à l'américaine (292) for the stuffing.

## 874 Roast stuffed chicken, Californian style     Poulet rôti californienne

### Method

Prepare, cook and serve the chicken as for Poulet rôti à l'anglaise (872), using Farce à la californienne (293) for the stuffing.

## 875 Roast stuffed poussin, Polish style     Poussin rôti polonaise

### Method

1. Place one portion for each cover of Farce au gratin (296) inside each poussin.

2. Prepare, cook and serve the poussin as for Poussin rôti (870).

3. Before serving, mask over with Polonaise: melt 1 oz (30 g) of butter per portion, add ½ oz (15 g) of white breadcrumbs, fry them till light golden brown then add one-quarter of a coarsely sieved hard-boiled egg and a teaspoon (2 g) of chopped parsley. Serve only roast gravy, separately.

## 876     Poulet poêlé

### Method

1. Prepare the chicken with the legs entered (273).

2. Select a pan with a tightly fitting lid, slightly larger than the chicken, and place a bed of roots (340a) in the base. Lay the seasoned chicken on one leg on the bed and smear it all over with butter.

3. Then cook as for Lamb poêlé (789). Turn over on to the other leg, then on to the back during cooking. Allow 25 minutes cooking time per lb of prepared weight (55 minutes per kg).

4. If stuffed with braised rice, etc., allow an extra 5 minutes cooking per lb weight (11 minutes per kg).

The chicken is usually served garnished (723).

## 877 Boiled chicken with rice     Poulet poché au riz, sauce suprême

| 8 portions | Ingredients | 10 couverts |
|---|---|---|
| 2 × 3 lb | boiling chicken | 2 × 1·7 kg |
| 4 oz | carrot | 140 g |
| 4 oz | onion | 140 g |
| 4 oz | celery | 140 g |
| 2 oz | leek | 70 g |
| 1 oz | salt | 35 g |
| 8 | white peppercorns | 10 g |
| 1 | bayleaf | 1 |
| 8 portions | riz pilaff (615) | 10 couverts |
| 1¼ pints | sauce suprême (400) | 875 ml |

### Method

1. Prepare the chicken with the legs entered (273).

2. Cover the chicken, in a pan of a suitable size, with approximately 6 pints (4 litres) of water.

3. Bring to the boil, skim the surface, then, wipe the edges of the pot with a damp cloth. Add the cleaned vegetables, salt, peppercorns and bayleaf.

3. Reboil, cover, then simmer gently for approximately 1½ hours. Larger or older fowl will take longer. Test the meat with a trussing needle: the needle should penetrate the thickest part of the leg without pressure, and the juice released should have no colour; if it is pink, continue cooking.

5. Prepare the sauce and rice so that they are ready when the chicken is cooked. Use stock from the chicken after it has been cooking 45 minutes. Replace the stock taken from the chicken with enough water to re-cover it.

6. Remove the skin from the chicken if it is served whole. To cut it in portions, cut the skin where the leg joins the breast, then carefully ease the legs away. Chop off the bone at the end of the drumsticks and make a 10 mm incision through the joint of the drumstick and thigh then remove the skin.

7. Remove the skin from the wing and breast. For smaller chicken, pass the knife along the breast bone, then down through the natural joint between the wing and breast. For larger chicken, cut the wings off by passing the knife in line with the breast bone, at a point halfway between the wing and breast bone. Turn the carcass on its end, chop away the back part and serve the breast in one piece or cut it lengthways into two pieces.

8. Place the braised rice in a hot entrée or earthenware dish and arrange the chicken on top; if cut, place with the legs in the centre, the breast on top and the wings on each side. Mask over with the sauce and place the dish on an underflat with dish paper.

*Note.* Sauce ivoire (399) may be used instead of suprême for variation.

### 878           Poulet poché princesse

#### Method

1. Prepare, cook and serve as for Poulet poché au riz, sauce suprême (877).
2. Place 3–4 hot buttered asparagus tips per portion around the edge of the dish after masking the chicken with the sauce.

### 879 Chicken in casserole or cocotte     Poulet en casserole ou en cocotte

| 8 portions | Ingredients | 10 couverts |
| --- | --- | --- |
| 2 × 2½–3 lb | roasting chicken | 2 × 1·4–1·7 kg |
| 4 oz | carrot | 140 g |
| 4 oz | onion | 140 g |
| 2 oz | celery | 70 g |
| 4 oz | butter | 140 g |
| 2 teaspoons | salt | 15 g |
| ½ level teaspoon | milled pepper | 2 g |
| 2 teaspoons | chopped parsley | 5 g |
| 1 pint | jus-lié | 700 ml |
| small | bouquet garni | small |

#### Method

1. Prepare the chicken with the legs entered (273).
2. Clean and cut the vegetables into 5 mm slices and place them in the base of a greased casserole or cocotte with the bouquet garni. Add the seasoned chickens, turned on to the leg, and smear them all over with the butter.
3. Set lightly on top of the stove to heat the receptacle. Cover with the lid and place in the centre of an oven at 230°C (450°F) for the first 15 minutes. Reduce the temperature to 200°C (400°F) and cook for 25 minutes per lb prepared weight (55 min per kg). Turn the chickens over on to the other leg, then the back, basting frequently. Just before cooked, remove the cover and baste and glaze the chicken till lightly coloured. Test as for roasting (725, 6 iii).
4. Remove the chicken and keep it hot. Set the receptacle on the stove until the fat clears, then run it off.
5. Add the jus-lié, reboil, simmer for 5 minutes then pass it through a gauze strainer. Reboil and remove any fat.

6. Clean the receptacle and replace the chicken with the string removed. Mask it over with the jus-lié, sprinkle with chopped parsley and cover. Place on an underflat with dish paper. The dish is usually served with one of the garnishes listed below.

*Note.* When cooked in quantity, a braising pan is used for cooking and the chicken is then served in a casserole or cocotte. Pigeon and pheasant may be served in the same manner.

#### Garnishes

**aux chipolatas**: 3–4 half-sized pieces of grilled pork chipolata sausages per portion.

**bonne femme**: 1 oz (30 g) button onions glazed brown (724b), 1 oz (30 g) lardons sautés (724d) and 1 oz (30 g) pommes cocotte (quarter size pommes château, 1125) per portion.

**Champeaux**: as for Bonne femme; déglacé the cocotte with 1 fl. oz (30 ml) of white wine per portion.

**grand-mère**: 1½ oz (45 g) 10 mm diced or scalloped mushrooms sauté (335g) and 1 oz (30 g) buttered fried croûtons (339), cut 25 × 5 × 5 mm per portion.

**mascotte**: half an artichoke bottom per portion, cut in sections and lightly fried in butter with 1 oz (30 g) cocotte potatoes (1125) and 1 slice of truffle.

**Parmentier**: 2 oz (55 g) Pommes Parmentier (1119) sprinkled with chopped parsley per portion.

**paysanne**: 2 oz (55 g) per portion of glazed mixed paysanne of carrot, turnip, onion, leek and celery.

### 880 Sauté of chicken         Poulet sauté

| 8 portions | Ingredients | 20 couverts* |
| --- | --- | --- |
| 2 × 2½–3 lb | roasting chicken | 5 × 1·125–1·350 kg |
| 3 oz | butter | 210 g |
| 2 teaspoons | chopped parsley | 10 g |
| 4 level teaspoons | salt | 30 g |
| ½ level teaspoon | milled white pepper | 4 g |
| 1¼ pints | jus-lié or demi-glace | 2 litres |

\* The size of chicken used produces 4 portions, so to provide true metric quantities, the unit of 20 couverts is used in all recipes for Poulet sauté.

#### Method

1. Cut the prepared and cleaned chickens for sauté (275).
2. Lightly fry off the chopped pieces of carcass, neck and giblet in a little fat and mirepoix of carrot, onion and

238

celery. Drain off any fat and moisten with the jus-lié or demi-glace. Boil, then simmer for 45 minutes and strain.

3. Heat the butter in a suitably sized sauté pan over a fast heat. Add the seasoned cut pieces of chicken and colour them till light golden brown.

4. Cover with a lid and cook in an oven at 200°C (400°F) for 25–30 minutes, removing the wing and breast pieces after 20 minutes.

5. Remove the chicken to an entrée dish; cover and keep it warm.

6. Drain off the fat from the sauté pan, add the jus-lié or demi-glace. Boil, simmer for 5 minutes then pass through a fine conical strainer. Reboil, correct the seasoning and consistency and then skim off any fat.

7. Mask this over the chicken and sprinkle the surface with chopped parsley. Serve on an underflat with dish paper.

## 881        Poulet sauté au vin

**Method**

1. Prepare and serve as for Poulet sauté (880).

2. After draining off the fat at 6 in method, deglacé the pan with ¼ pint (8) or 350 ml (20) of white wine before adding the jus-lié or demi-glace.

## 882        Poulet sauté aux champignons

**Method**

1. Prepare and serve as for Poulet sauté (880)

2. Wash and peel 8 oz (8) or 560 g (20) of small closed mushrooms – if large, cut them in scallops – and lightly sauté them for 5–7 minutes in the fat drained from the chicken at 6 in method.

3. Sprinkle the mushrooms over the chicken before masking it with the jus-lié or demi-glace.

## 883        Poulet sauté bonne femme

**Method**

1. Prepare and serve as for Poulet sauté (880).

2. Before masking the chicken with the sauce, sprinkle bonne femme garnish over the chicken. (See garnishes at foot of 879.)

## 884        Poulet sauté chasseur

| 8 portions | Ingredients | 20 couverts |
|---|---|---|
| 8 portions | as for poulet sauté (880) | 20 couverts |
| 8 oz | button mushrooms | 560 g |
| 1 lb | tomatoes | 1·125 kg |

| 1 oz | finely chopped shallots | 70 ml |
| 1 teaspoon | finely chopped tarragon | 8 g |
| ¼ pint | white wine | 350 ml |

**Method**

1. Prepare as for Poulet sauté (880) to 5 (inclusive) in method.

2. After removing the chicken, add the shallots to the fat in the sauté pan and cook gently for 3–4 minutes. Add the washed and sliced mushrooms, cover with a lid, cook slowly for 5–6 minutes, then run off any excess fat.

3. Add the wine then reduce the liquid by two-thirds. Add the jus-lié or demi-glace, reboil and correct the seasoning.

4. Skim, add the tomatoes, prepared in 10 mm concassé, reboil and add the chopped tarragon.

5. Mask this over the chicken, sprinkle with the chopped parsley. Serve on an underflat with dish paper.

## 885        Poulet sauté Doria

**Method**

1. Prepare and serve as for Poulet sauté (880).

2. After masking with the sauce, sprinkle with small turned pieces of glazed cucumber. For quantity and method of preparation see Poisson Doria (673). Double the quantity in the metric to give 20 portions.

## 886        Poulet sauté mascotte

**Method**

1. Prepare and serve as for Poulet sauté (880).

2. After masking with the sauce, sprinkle with mascotte garnish. (See garnishes at foot of 879.)

## 887        Poulet sauté Parmentier

**Method**

1. Prepare and serve as for Poulet sauté (880).

2. After masking with the sauce, place on each side of the chicken 2 oz (55 g) per portion of Pommes Parmentier (1119) and sprinkle them with the chopped parsley.

## 888        Poulet sauté portugaise

| 8 portions | Ingredients | 20 couverts |
|---|---|---|
| | As for poulet sauté (880) | |
| 2 oz | finely chopped onion | 140 g |
| 1½ lb | tomatoes | 1·7 kg |
| 8 oz | small closed mushrooms | 560 g |
| 1 pod | garlic | 2 large pods |
| ¼ pint | white wine | 375 ml |
| ¾ pint | tomato sauce (to replace ½ the jus-lié) | 1 litre |

## Method

1. Prepare as for Poulet sauté (880) to 5 (inclusive) in method.
2. After removing the chicken, add the onion to the fat in the sauté pan and cook gently for 3–4 minutes. Add the washed and sliced mushrooms, cover with a lid and cook slowly for 5–6 minutes, then run off the fat.
3. Add the wine and finely chopped garlic; then reduce the liquid by two-thirds. Moisten with the tomato sauce and half the quantity of jus-lié. Do not use demi-glace.
4. Reboil, correct the seasoning, then skim. Add the tomatoes which have been prepared into 10 mm concassé. Reboil.
5. Mask over the chicken and sprinkle the surface with the chopped parsley. Serve on an underflat with dish paper.

## 889        Suprême de volaille sauté au beurre

### Method

1. Prepare the Suprême de volaille (276).
2. Heat sufficient butter to cover the base of a sauté pan to a depth of 3 mm.
3. Season the chicken with salt and milled pepper. Pass through flour, knocking off all excess.
4. Place the chicken into the hot butter and sauté over a closed fire for 4–5 minutes on each side till a very light golden brown.
5. Dress fanwise on a hot oval dish, or on a round flat dish in a circle, each suprême slightly overlapping the next.
6. Surround the base of the dish with jus-lié. Heat ½ oz (15 g) of butter per portion in a frying pan; when a nut colour (noisette), mask it over the suprêmes. Serve additional jus-lié in a sauceboat on an underflat with a doily.

## 890        Suprême de volaille pané

### Method

1. Prepare and serve as for Suprême de volaille sauté au beurre (889).
2. Before cooking, season the chicken with salt and milled pepper and panée à l'anglaise (311).
3. This dish is always served with a garnish (722).

## 891        Suprême de volaille viennoise

### Method

1. Prepare the suprêmes (276). Carefully flatten them out with a wet cutlet bat until they are very thin.

2. Then prepare and serve as for Escalope de veau viennoise (836).

## 892        Suprême de volaille Maryland

### Method

1. Prepare and cook the suprêmes as for Suprême de volaille pané (890).
2. Place on each suprême a half of grilled banana, with one slice of grilled streaky bacon across the banana.
3. Place two half size corn croquettes (1042) per portion along the sides, with Pommes paille (1101) at each end.
4. Mask over with ½ oz (15 g) Beurre noisette per portion.
5. In a sauceboat, on an underflat with a doily, serve a sherry and cream sabayon, or jus-lié.
6. To prepare the sabayon, place 3 yolks of egg (4 for 10 portions), ¼ pint (175 ml) of cream and 2 fl. oz (70 ml) of sherry in a sauteuse and prepare as for sabayon (632).

## 893 Chicken cutlets      Côtelette de volaille

### Chicken croquettes      Croquette de volaille

### Chicken médaillon      Médaillons de volaille

### Method

1. Prepare the basic mixture (284).
2. Panée à l'anglaise (311) to the desired shape (310).
3. Cutlets or médaillons may be deep or shallow fried. Croquettes are always deep fried.
4. Deep fry 8–10 pieces at a time at 180°C (360°F) for 2–3 minutes, until golden brown, then drain. Serve on a hot oval flat dish on a dish paper and garnish with sprigs of fried parsley. Cutlets have cutlet frills placed on the mock bone. Serve an appropriate sauce e.g. piquante, madère.
5. To shallow fry, heat sufficient clean dripping or oil in a sauté pan to cover the base to a depth of 3 mm.
6. Add the cutlets or médaillon and cook them quickly on a closed fire on both sides till a light golden brown.
7. Serve them on a hot oval or round flat dish, slightly overlapping. Place cutlet frills on the mock bone. Surround the base of the dish with jus-lié and serve additional jus-lié in a sauceboat on an underflat with a doily.
8. When shallow fried, a garnish is generally placed alongside (e.g. Côtelette de volaille princesse). For garnishes, see 722.

*Note.* Chicken and ham cutlets and croquettes are prepared and served in the same manner. For basic mixture, see 285.

## 894 Cromesquis de volaille

**Method**

1. For 8 to 10 portions, prepare the following: basic chicken cutlet mixture (284); basic pancakes (1394), omitting the sugar; basic frying batter (677).

2. Lay the pancakes on the table and place a 20 mm-thick roll of the cutlet mixture on the pancakes. Roll the pancake and trim the ends across with a knife. If desired, the rolls of the mixture may be wrapped in pig's caul (the membrane lining of the stomach, cleaned and prepared).

3. Pass these cromesquis through the frying batter and deep fry them at 180°C (360°F) until golden brown. It is necessary during frying to move the cromesquis around to obtain an even colouring.

4. Drain and serve on a hot flat dish on a dish paper. Garnish with sprigs of fried parsley and serve an appropriate sauce, e.g. tomate, piquante separately.

*Note.* Cromesquis may be made from various types of meat: this is prepared as for the basic croquette mixture of the type of meat used.

## 895 Fricassée of chicken — Fricassée de volaille

| 8 portions | Ingredients | 20 couverts* |
|---|---|---|
| 2 × 2½–3 lb | roasting chicken | 5 × 1·125–1·350 kg |
| 3 oz | butter | 210 g |
| 3 oz | flour | 210 g |
| 2 teaspoons | chopped parsley | 10 g |
| 4 level teaspoons | salt | 30 g |
| ½ level teaspoon | ground white pepper | 4 g |
| 2 pints | chicken stock (347) | 2·8 litres |
| ¼ pint | cream | 350 ml |
| 2 | yolks of egg | 5 |
| small | bouquet garni | large |
| | **Garnish** | |
| 2 oz | butter | 140 g |
| 4 oz | bread | 280 g |

\* The size of chicken used produces 4 portions, so to provide true metric quantities, the unit of 20 couverts is used.

**Method**

1. Cut the prepared chicken as for sauté (275).

2. Prepare the chicken stock from the carcass and giblets.

3. Prepare and serve as for Fricassée de veau (841), using the chicken and chicken stock in place of veal and veal stock.

4. Reduce the cooking time to 45–50 minutes.

## 896 Fricassée de volaille à l'ancienne

**Method**

1. Prepare and serve as for Fricassée de volaille (895).

2. After 25 minutes cooking time, move the pieces of chicken into a clean pan. Add, for 8 or 20 portions, 6 oz (420 g) of peeled button onions, boiled for 7–8 minutes, then drained and 4 oz (280 g) of whole button mushrooms, peeled or turned and half cooked à blanc (335g).

3. Cook for a further 20–25 minutes, then finish as in 895.

## 897 Curried chicken — Kari de volaille

| 8 portions | Ingredients | 20 couverts* |
|---|---|---|
| 2 × 2½–3 lb | roasting chicken | 5 × 1·125–1·350 kg |
| 2 oz | first class dripping | 140 g |
| 2 oz | flour | 140 g |
| 1½ oz | curry powder | 100 g |
| 4 oz | chopped apple | 280 g |
| 2 oz | chopped chutney | 140 g |
| 1 lb | finely chopped onions | 1 kg |
| 1½ oz | desiccated coconut | 100 g |
| 1 oz | tomato purée | 70 g |
| 2 teaspoons | chopped parsley | 10 g |
| 4 level teaspoons | salt | 30 g |
| small | bouquet garni | 30 g |
| 2 pints | chicken or white stock | 2·8 litres |
| ½ | lemon (in juice) | 1 |
| 1 pod | garlic | 2 pods |
| 12 oz | patna rice | 840 g |

\* The size of chicken used produces 4 portions, so to provide true metric quantities, the unit of 20 couverts is used

**Method**

1. Cut the prepared chicken as for sauté (275).

2. Heat the dripping in a shallow pan, add the seasoned pieces of chicken, fry them quickly to a light golden brown and remove them to a pie dish or tray.

3. Add the onions to the fat and cook them steadily for 7–8 minutes, colouring them slightly, then add the chicken.

4. Sprinkle with the curry powder, then the flour, and singe in an oven at 150°C (300°F) for 7–8 minutes.

5. Add the tomato purée and gradually stir in the boiling stock. Mix in the chopped apple, chopped chutney, garlic, bouquet garni, lemon juice and the coconut (previously soaked in water for a few minutes and drained).

6. When boiling, cover with a greased paper and lid. Cook in the lower part of an oven at 150°C (300°F) for 45–50 minutes. Test the chicken by piercing the drumstick with a fork; it should penetrate without pressure.

7. Remove the bouquet garni and correct the seasoning and consistency. If the sauce is a little thin, run it off into a separate pan and reduce till it masks the back of a spoon; if too thick, add a little stock.

241

8. Serve in a hot entrée dish and sprinkle the surface with chopped parsley. Place on an underflat with dish paper.

9. Garnish with hot plain boiled rice (763) in an entrée dish on an underflat with dish paper and/or saffron braised rice. Serve Bombay duck and pappadums separately. (For preparation, see Curried beef, 762.)

## 898                Pojarski de volaille, sauce smitaine

**Method**

1. Prepare the required number of chicken pojarski (282).

2. Cook and serve as for Pojarski de veau (853).

## 899                Brochette de foies de volaille

| 8 portions | Ingredients | 10 couverts |
|---|---|---|
| 8 | brochette de foies de volaille (280) | 10 |
| 8 portions | riz pilaff (615) | 10 couverts |
| 1 pint | sauce madère (378) | 700 ml |
| 2 oz | first class dripping or oil | 70 g |

**Method**

1. Prepare the brochette, the sauce and the braised rice.

2. Heat the dripping or oil in a plat sauté until lightly smoking. Add the brochettes and sauté them quickly for 5–6 minutes, turning them on all sides.

3. Dress the braised rice 20–25 mm in depth in a hot entrée dish to form a bed on which to place the brochettes. Pour a little of the sauce around the base of the rice. Serve the entrée dish on an underflat with dishpaper, and serve the remainder of the sauce in a sauceboat.

## 900                Pilaff de foies de volaille

| 8 portions | Ingredients | 10 couverts |
|---|---|---|
| 1½ lb | chicken livers | 840 g |
| 2 fl. oz | oil | 70 g |
| 2 teaspoons | chopped parsley | 5 g |
| 4 level teaspoons | salt | 15 g |
| ½ level teaspoons | milled pepper | 2 g |
| 1 pint | demi-glace | 700 ml |
| 2 fl. oz | Madeira wine | 70 ml |
| 8 portions | riz pilaff (615) | 10 couverts |

**Method**

1. Carefully cut away the gall bladder and any stained parts from the liver.

2. Prepare the sauce and the braised rice.

3. Heat half the oil in a sauté pan; when it is smoking, add half the livers and fry them over a very fierce heat for 3–4 minutes, tossing them over during cooking. Place aside and cook the remainder.

4. Déglacé the pan with the wine, add the demi-glace, then boil and strain and add half the sauce to the liver. Do not reboil, or the blood will coagulate.

5. Lightly press the braised rice into a greased border mould. Turn it out on to a hot oval or round flat dish. Carefully dress the livers inside the rice and sprinkle them with chopped parsley. Surround the base of the rice with the remainder of the sauce.

## 901                Hachis de volaille duchesse

| 8 portions | Ingredients | 10 couverts |
|---|---|---|
| 1½ lb | boiled chicken (free of skin and bone) | 840 g |
| 1¼ pints | sauce suprême (400) | 875 ml |
| 2 lb | peeled potatoes (prepared into duchesse mixture, 1089) | 1·125 kg |
| 1 oz | butter | 35 g |
| 4 level teaspoons | salt | 15 g |
| ½ level teaspoon | ground white pepper | 2 g |
| 1 | egg | 1 |

**Method**

1. Prepare the sauce and duchesse potato mixture.

2. Cut the skinned and boned chicken into 5 mm dice.

3. Using a piping bag with a 10 mm-star tube, pipe a scrolled border of the potato around the edge of an entrée or earthenware dish. If desired, it may be prepared in small dishes for 1 or 2 portions. Dry the potato in an oven at 150°C (300°F) – then egg-wash the surface.

4. Butter a shallow pan, add the chicken and seasoning. Cover with a buttered paper and lid. Heat in an oven at 150°C (300°F) for 4–7 minutes. Add the sauce to bind to a medium-loose texture.

5. Colour the potato border golden brown under a moderate salamander. Fill inside the border with the chicken mixture. Serve on an underflat with dish paper.

*Note.* Turkey may be used instead of chicken.

## 902                Hachis de volaille Colbert

**Method**

1. Prepare and serve as for Hachis de volaille (901). Place a hot drained poached egg on top of each portion.

## 903                Hachis de volaille princesse

**Method**

Prepare and serve as for Hachis de volaille (901). Place 3–4 hot buttered asparagus tips (965) on top of each portion.

## 904          Émincé de volaille duchesse

**Method**

1. Prepare and serve as for Hachis de volaille (901). Cut the chicken into 10 mm scallops.
2. May also be served Colbert (902) or Princesse (903).

## 905          Émincé de volaille gratiné

**Method**

1. Prepare as for Émincé de volaille duchesse (904).
2. Mask the finished chicken with a thin coating of sabayon or Mornay sauce and sprinkle it with Parmesan cheese. Colour golden brown under a moderate salamander.

## 906          Poulet à la king

**Method**

1. Prepare and serve as for Émincé de volaille duchesse (904).
2. When reducing the velouté for the sauce suprême, add 2 fl. oz (70 ml) of whisky or brandy.
3. To finish, place 3 mm-thick strips of pimento in a trellis pattern across the chicken.

*Note.* Alternatively, the finish may include a thin coating of sabayon over the chicken, glazed under the salamander, then finished with the pimento.

## 907          Crêpe de volaille

| 8 portions | Ingredients | 10 couverts |
|---|---|---|
| 1¼ lb | boiled chicken (free of skin and bone) | 700 g |
| ¾ pint | sauce suprême (400) | 525 ml |
| ¾ pint | pancake batter (1394) | 525 ml |
| ¾ pint | sauce Mornay (390) | 525 ml |
| ¼ pint | milk | 175 ml |
| 1 oz | butter | 35 g |
| 4 level teaspoons | salt | 15 g |
| ½ level teaspoons | ground white pepper | 2 g |
| 2 oz | Parmesan cheese | 70 g |

**Method**

1. Prepare the pancake batter, omitting the sugar. Cook 16 or 20 pieces (1394).
2. Cut the chicken into 5 mm dice and place into a sauteuse greased with the butter. Season, then cover with a buttered paper and lid. Heat in the oven at 150°C (300°F) for 6–7 minutes. Add the sauce suprême to bind to a medium-loose texture.
3. Lay the pancakes flat on the table and equally divide the chicken mixture on to one half of the pancakes. Fold the pancake over and place them overlapping in a buttered oval earthenware dish or number of dishes.

4. Boil the milk and add it to the sauce Mornay to thin it. Mask the mixture over the pancakes and cover the base of the dish or dishes.
5. Sprinkle evenly with the cheese and colour the surface a light golden brown under a moderate salamander. Pass through an oven at 150°C (300°F) for 2 minutes to thoroughly heat through. Serve on an underflat with dish paper.

## 908          Crêpe de volaille princesse

**Method**

1. Prepare and serve as for Crêpe de volaille (907).
2. Before coating with the sauce Mornay, place 3–4 asparagus tips on each portion of pancakes.

## 909   Chicken vol-au-vent      Vol-au-vent de volaille

| 8 portions | Ingredients | 10 couverts |
|---|---|---|
| 8 oz (flour mix) | puff paste (1141) | 280 g (flour mix) |
| 1½ lb | boiled chicken (free of skin and bone) | 840 g |
| 1¼ pints | sauce suprême (400) | 875 ml |
| 4 level teaspoons | salt | 15 g |
| ½ level teaspoon | ground white pepper | 2 g |
| 1 | egg | 1 |
| 1 fl. oz | oil | 35 ml |
| few | sprigs of parsley | few |

**Method**

1. Prepare the puff paste (1141). Dust it with flour and roll it evenly in all directions until 5 mm thick.
2. For individual vol-au-vent, cut out with a 95 mm fluted cutter. Larger cases may be cut for 2–4 portion vol-au-vent.
3. Turn the circles of paste over and place on a clean baking sheet. Sprinkle them with water and allow them to rest for at least 1 hour in a cool place.
4. When ready to bake, brush over with the beaten egg. Dip a 75 mm plain cutter in oil, then press two-thirds through the paste, leaving an equal border all round.
5. Bake at the top of an oven at 190–200°C (380–400°F) for 15–20 minutes, until the paste has risen and set into shape. Then move to a lower part of the oven and cook for a further 15 minutes, until the paste is quite crisp.
6. Remove the centre cap and discard the inner uncooked part of the case.
7. Cut the chicken into 10 mm scallops, place it into a buttered saucepan, season, cover and heat in a bain-marie tray. When hot, add the sauce and keep it boiling in the bain-marie.
8. To serve, fill the warm pastry cases with the mixture to a slight dome shape. Place the pastry 'cap' on at an angle.

9. Place on a hot flat dish with dish paper and garnish between with sprigs of parsley.

## 910 Chicken and mushroom vol-au-vent      Vol-au-vent de volaille aux champignons

### Methods

Prepare and serve as for Vol-au-vent de volaille (909). Add 4 oz (140 g) of prepared button mushrooms cooked 'à blanc' (335 g).

## 911      Vol-au-vent de volaille régence

### Method

1. Prepare and serve as for Vol-au-vent de volaille aux champignons (910). Add to the chicken and mushroom 3 teaspoon-size poached chicken quenelles (283) per portion and place a slice of truffle dipped in butter on top of each portion of chicken before adding the 'cap'.

*Note.* In these dishes, the weight of cooked chicken, free of skin and bone, represents approximately one-third of the undrawn weight, i.e. a 4½ lb or (2 kg) boiling fowl will produce 1½ lb (670 g) of cooked flesh.

## 912      Ballotine de volaille

| 8 portions | Ingredients | 10 couverts |
|---|---|---|
| 8 | ballotine of chicken (279) | 10 |
| 4 oz | carrot | 140 g |
| 4 oz | onion | 140 g |
| 2 oz | first class dripping | 70 g |
| 4 level teaspoons | salt | 15 g |
| ½ level teaspoon | ground white pepper | 2 g |
| small | bouquet garni | small |
| 1½ pints | jus-lié | 1 litre |
| | **Garnish** | |
| 4 oz | turned carrots | 140 g |
| 4 oz | turned turnips | 140 g |
| 3 oz | shelled or frozen peas | 100 g |
| 4 oz | button onions | 140 g |

### Method

1. Peel and wash the carrot and onion and cut it into 5 mm-thick slices. Place into a suitable size sauté pan with the bouquet garni.

2. Heat the dripping in a frying pan, add the seasoned ballotine and colour to a light golden brown on all sides. Place the ballotine on top of the bed of roots.

3. Add the boiling jus-lié, then reboil, skim and cover with a greased paper and lid.

4. Place in the lower part of an oven at 150°C (300°F) and braise for 35–45 minutes, basting with the liquor a few times during cooking. Test the meat with a trussing needle, which should easily penetrate.

5. Remove the ballotine from the sauce and, after taking off the string, place it into a clean pan.

6. Add the glazed carrots (969), glazed turnips (1043) and button onions cooked 'glacés à brun' (724b).

7. Reboil the sauce, remove all fat and check the seasoning and consistency. Pass it through a gauze strainer over the ballotine, garnish then reboil.

8. Serve in a hot entrée dish and sprinkle with the peas (plain boiled for 7–12 minutes in salt water and drained). Place on an underflat with dish paper.

## 913 Chicken pie

## 914 Chicken and mushroom pie

### Method

1. Prepare the chicken pie filling (305).

2. Using the same amount of puff paste, cover as for Steak pie (777). Let the paste stand in a cool place for at least 1 hour; then egg-wash the surface.

3. Place on a baking tray, commence cooking in the top of an oven at 190–200°C (380–400°F) for 15–20 minutes, until the paste rises and sets in shape.

4. Move to a lower part of the oven, reduce the temperature to 140°C (280°F) and continue cooking for a further 1¼ hours. If necessary, cover the paste with greaseproof paper when it is coloured golden brown.

5. To test, cut under the paste at one end of the pie and pass a small knife into a leg piece of chicken: the knife should easily penetrate the meat. Check the level of stock, which should two-thirds fill the pie dish.

6. Serve on a flat oval dish on dish paper. Place a pie frill around the pie dish.

## 915 Roast duck or duckling      Canard ou caneton rôti

| 8 portions | Ingredients | 10 couverts |
|---|---|---|
| 2 × 3 lb | duckling | 2 × 1·7 kg |
| 2 oz | first class dripping | 70 g |
| 8 level teaspoons | salt | 30 g |
| 1 level teaspoon | milled pepper | 4 g |
| ¾ pint | brown stock | 525 ml |
| 8 portions | sage and onion stuffing (294) | 10 portions |
| ½ pint | apple sauce (410) | 350 ml |
| ½ bunch | watercress | ½ bunch |

### Method

1. Clean and prepare the ducks for roasting (288).

2. Prepare and cook the duck and make the gravy as for Poulet rôti (869), allowing 25 minutes, per lb of drawn

weight (55 minutes per kg). If desired, the stuffing may be placed inside the duck. When it is stuffed, allow an additional 5 minutes per lb (11 minutes per kg).

3. If the stuffing is cooked separately, place it into a greased shallow tray or frying pan 10 mm in depth, mask over with fat from the roast duck and place the pan to cook at the top of the same oven for 30 minutes before the duck is ready.

4. To serve, remove the string from the duck, place on a hot oval flat dish, with a little of the gravy. Place the pieces of stuffing along each side, the watercress sprigs in front. Serve roast gravy and apple sauce in sauceboats on an underflat with dish paper.

5. To cut a duck in portions, allow the duck to rest and set for 10 minutes after cooking. Turn it on to one leg, run a knife along the skin at the top of the leg, where it meets the breast, so that it cuts through the skin, then lift away the leg. Repeat the process on the other leg. Turn the carcass on to the back, then cut off the wings on a straight line half-way between the winglet bone and the breast bone. Chop away the back part of the carcass and divide the breast in two pieces lengthways.

## 916        Caneton bigarade

| 8 portions | Ingredients | 10 couverts |
|---|---|---|
| 2 × 3 lb | duckling | 2 × 1·7 kg |
| 4 oz | carrot | 140 g |
| 4 oz | onion | 140 g |
| 2 oz | butter | 70 g |
| 8 level teaspoons | salt | 30 g |
| 1 level teaspoon | milled pepper | 4 g |
| 1 | bayleaf | 1 |
| small sprig | thyme | small sprig |
| 3 medium | oranges | 4 |
| 1 | lemon | 1 |
| 2 fl. oz | port wine | 70 ml |
| ¾ pint | jus-lié | 525 ml |
| 1 oz | sugar | 35 g |

### Method

1. Clean, singe and truss the ducklings (288).

2. Grease a braising pan and line it with the thick slices of peeled carrot, onion, thyme and bayleaf.

3. Add the seasoned ducklings and lay them on their legs.

4. Smear them with butter, cover with greaseproof paper and a lid.

5. Set to cook on the stove then place in a moderate oven at 180°C (350°F).

6. Allow 10 minutes on each leg and finish on their backs, giving 35–40 minutes cooking time in all, according to the size. The ducklings must be underdone.

7. Finely peel the oranges and lemons of their zest and cut it into very fine julienne. Blanch for 3 minutes and refresh.

8. Carefully cut the pith from the oranges and cut out the segments as for orange salad; squeeze out the juice.

9. When the ducklings are ready, remove and pour off the fat from the braisière.

10. Add the jus-lié, simmer for 5 minutes, strain and carefully skim.

11. Caramelise the sugar, then add the wine, lemon and orange juice.

12. Reduce the liquid, add the jus-lié, reboil, correct the seasoning and consistency.

13. Serve the duckling on a dish garnished with the segments of orange and pour the sauce over them. Sprinkle the reheated zest on the duckling.

14. The duckling is served carved very thin; the legs are not served but are used for other dishes.

## 917        Caneton aux petits pois

### Method

1. Prepare and cook the ducks 'poêlé', as in Caneton bigarade, up to and including 5 in method. Allow 25 minutes per lb of drawn weight (55 min per kg). Test the meat by inserting a needle in the leg: no blood should appear. Turn the ducks, during cooking, on to the legs and back.

2. When cooked, remove the ducks and pour off the fat.

3. Moisten the braising pan with ¾ pint (525 ml) of jus-lié, reboil, simmer for 5 minutes then pass through a gauze strainer.

4. Remove the string from the ducks. Serve in a cocotte, mask with jus-lié, garnish alongside with 10 oz (350 g) of shelled or frozen peas prepared à la française (1056).

## 918 Roast turkey        Dindonneau rôti

### Method

1. Clean and prepare the turkey (289).

2. Stuff it with chestnut stuffing (298) and Farce à l'anglaise (291). (For the method of stuffing, see 299.)

3. Roast as for chicken. Commence cooking at 220°C (425°F) to seal and set, then reduce the temperature to 160–180°C (325–350°F), according to the size. Allow 14–15 minutes per lb of stuffed prepared weight (30–33 min per kg). Baste and turn frequently during cooking. Test the meat with a trussing needle through the thickest part of the thigh: the juice emerging should be colourless when the turkey is cooked.

4. Allow the turkey to rest and set for 30 minutes before carving.

5. Set the roasting tray on the stove, until the fat clears. Run off the fat and add $\frac{3}{4}$ pint (525 ml) of brown stock. Boil, simmer for 5 minutes then pass it through a gauze strainer. Reboil, skim off all fat and season.

6. Carve the turkey by removing the legs; bone out the thighs with a small knife. Cut the thigh and breast flesh in evenly sized thin slices.

7. Dress some of each stuffing on a hot oval flat dish; place the dark flesh on top, then the white flesh. Mask with boiling gravy.

8. Garnish along each side with braised chestnuts (2 per portion) (298, 1–3 in method) and 2 pieces of grilled pork chipolata sausage per portion. Garnish with sprigs of watercress. Serve, in sauceboats on an underflat with a doily, additional roast gravy and $\frac{1}{2}$ pint (350 ml) of cranberry sauce (412).

---

## 919 ROASTING OF GAME (FEATHERED VARIETIES)                GIBIER A PLUME

**Method**

1. Prepare, clean and truss the bird, placing a thin slice of fat bacon (bard de lard) across the breast, to cover, as a protection during roasting.

2. Season with salt and milled pepper, inside and out. Place the bird on one leg in a roasting tray and smear it all over with butter or first class dripping.

3. Set the tray on top of a stove until it starts frying.

4. Then place it at the centre to top of the oven at 230°C (450°F) to set. Small game birds are roasted at this temperature throughout. For larger varieties, e.g. pheasant, the heat is reduced after 10–15 minutes to 200°C (400°F).

5. During roasting, the bird is turned on to the other leg, then on to the back. 5–10 minutes before roasting is complete the bacon is removed to allow the breast to colour. The bird should be basted frequently to prevent the flesh becoming dry. Approximate times, with the degree of cooking necessary, are given at the end of method.

6. Remove the bird from the tray. Set the tray on the stove until the fat clears, then run it off.

7. Moisten the sediment with $\frac{3}{4}$ pint (525 ml), per 8 (10) portions, of good brown stock or game stock. Boil, then simmer this for 5 minutes, then pass it through a gauze strainer; reboil, remove all the fat, season and colour golden brown.

8. For each portion, cut a bread croûton 50 × 30 mm wide and 5 mm thick, trim the corners and cut out a small 5mm wedge at the centre of the sides. Lightly fry in butter, then spread, with Farce de gibier (297) in a slight dome shape,

9. To serve, remove the string and place the bird on a hot oval flat dish. Put the croûtons in front of the bird, game chips to the rear and sprigs of watercress in between them. Mask the bird with $\frac{1}{2}$ oz (15 g) of Beurre noisette per portion. On an underflat with dish paper, place sauceboats of

roast gravy, bread sauce (411), and golden brown butter-fried breadcrumbs.

**Approximate roasting times**

**Grouse**: underdone; 15–20 minutes according to size.

**Guinea fowl**: as for chicken, by weight.

**Hazel hen**: very slightly underdone; 25–35 minutes, according to size.

**Partridge**: not underdone; 15–25 minutes, according to size.

**Pheasant**: not underdone; as for chicken, by weight.

**Plover**: not underdone; 14–16 minutes.

**Quail**: not underdone; 8–10 minutes.

**Snipe**: slightly underdone; 7–8 minutes.

**Wild duck and teal**: underdone; 16–20 minutes, according to size.

**Woodcock**: slightly underdone; 6–7 minutes.

## 920                                    Faisan en cocotte

**Method**

Prepared, cooked and garnished as for Poulet en cocotte (879).

## 921                                    Cailles aux raisins

**Method**

1. Clean and prepare the quails with the legs entered.

2. Butter-roast the quails in a cocotte for 8–10 minutes at 220°C (425°F).

3. Run off the fat, add $\frac{1}{2}$ fl. oz (15 ml) of brandy for each

quail and a little roast gravy. Add a garnish of 2 oz (55 g) of peeled and stoned grapes per portion.

4. Cover the cocotte, and serve it on an underflat with dish paper.

## 922 Salmis of game — Salmis de gibier

| 8 portions | Ingredients | 10 couverts |
|---|---|---|
| 2 × 2½ lb | pheasant or | 2 × 1·4 kg |
| 4 × 12–14 oz | partridge | 5 × 340–390 g |
| 4 oz | onion | 140 g |
| 4 oz | carrot | 140 g |
| 2 oz | celery | 70 g |
| 2 oz | butter | 70 g |
| 8 oz | button mushrooms | 280 g |
| 8 oz | button onions | 280 g |
| 2 teaspoons | chopped parsley | 5 g |
| ¼ pint | red wine | 175 ml |
| 1½ pints | demi-glace | 1 litre |
| ½ pint | game or brown stock | 350 ml |
| small | bouquet garni | small |
| | **Garnish** | |
| 4 oz | bread | 140 g |
| 2 oz | butter | 70 g |
| 8 portions | Farce au gratin (296) | 10 couverts |

### Method

1. Cooked game is usually used: if not, prepare the game as for roast, and cook.

2. Cut the birds into portions as for chicken (726, 5).

3. Chop the carcass, neck etc. into pieces.

4. Melt the butter in a sauteuse or a thick-bottomed pan and add the chopped carcass and the cleaned carrot, onion and celery cut in rough 10 mm dice. Colour to a light golden brown.

5. Drain off any surplus fat, add the wine and reduce the liquid by a half. Add the demi-glace and stock.

6. Wash and peel the mushrooms. Add the trimmings and bouquet garni to the sauce and simmer for 1 hour.

7. Sauté the mushrooms (335g) and peel and cook the button onions 'glacés à brun' (724b). Add both to the cut game in a clean shallow pan.

8. Pass the sauce through a very fine strainer or tammy cloth over the game.

9. Heat to boiling point then correct the seasoning and consistency. Cover with a greased paper and lid and cook in an oven at 150°C (300°F) for 20 minutes.

10. Prepare 8–10 heart-shaped croûtons and lightly fry or grill them in the butter to a golden brown. Spread them with the warm Farce au gratin in a slight dome shape.

11. Serve the salmis in an entrée dish and sprinkle with chopped parsley. Place the croûtons equally spaced around, with the points to the centre. Place the dish on an underflat with dish paper.

## 923 GROUND-GAME (FURRED) — GIBIER À POIL

### Jugged hare — Civet de lièvre

| 8 portions | Ingredients | 10 couverts |
|---|---|---|
| 5 lb | young hare | 2·8 kg |
| 8 portions | ingredients of marinade (303) | 10 couverts |
| 2 oz | first class dripping | 70 g |
| 1½ oz | flour | 50 g |
| 2 oz | tomato purée | 70 g |
| 1¼ pints | brown stock | 875 ml |
| | **Garnish** | |
| 8 oz | button onions | 280 g |
| 8 oz | button mushrooms | 280 g |
| 8 oz | streaky bacon | 280 g |
| 4 oz | bread | 140 g |
| 2 oz | butter | 70 g |
| 2 teaspoons | chopped parsley | 5 g |

### Method

1. Skin the hare and collect the blood in a basin (301). Cut it into pieces (302).

2. Place in a basin and cover with the marinade. Place in refrigeration to marinade for 5–12 hours.

3. Drain in a colander, retaining the liquid.

4. Heat the dripping in a shallow pan; when it is smoking, add the hare and fry it quickly to colour on all sides.

5. Sprinkle with the flour, shaking to mix. Place in an oven to singe for 8–10 minutes at 150°C (300°F).

6. Add the tomato purée and gradually stir in the boiling stock. Add the vegetables and liquor of the marinade.

7. Boil and skim, then cover with a greased paper and lid. Place in the bottom of an oven at 150°C (300°F) to simmer for 35–45 minutes. Test the meat by prodding the leg with a fork; it should penetrate without undue pressure.

8. Remove the hare to a clean shallow pan. Add the bacon, cut in lardons 25 × 5 × 5 mm and blanched and lightly fried, the washed and peeled or turned mushrooms lightly fried in the bacon fat, and the peeled button onions cooked 'glacés à brun' (724b).

9. Cut the bread into heart-shaped croûtons, dip them in melted butter and grill both sides till golden brown.

10. Reboil the sauce, correct the seasoning, remove to the side of the stove and pour in the blood, shaking the pan to mix. Pass the sauce through a fine conical strainer over the hare, and garnish it.

11. Serve in a hot entrée dish. Dip the points of the croûtons in the sauce, then in the parsley, and space them evenly around the dish with the points to the centre. Place on an underflat with dish paper. Serve a sauceboat of red currant jelly on a flat dish with a doily.

## 924 RABBIT ENTRÉES

For this group of dishes, the rabbit is prepared as described in 301; for cutting into portions, see 302.

## 925 White rabbit stew — Blanquette de lapin

**Method**

Cook and serve as for Blanquette d'agneau (806), using rabbit in place of lamb. Adjust the cooking time to approximately 1¼ hours.

## 926 — Fricassée de lapin

**Method**

Cook and serve as for Fricassée de volaille (895). Adjust the cooking time to approximately 1¼ hours.

## 927 Brown rabbit stew — Ragoût de lapin

**Method**

Cook and serve as for Ragoût de boeuf (747). Adjust the cooking time to approximately 1¼ hours.

## 928 Curried rabbit — Kari de lapin

**Method**

1. Cook and serve as for Kari de volaille (897). Adjust the cooking time to approximately 1¼ hours.

## 929 Rabbit and bacon pie

**Method**

Prepare, cook and serve as for Chicken pie (913), replacing the chicken with rabbit.

# Grills

# Grills

## 930 GENERAL NOTES

The methods of producing the various dishes in this section will vary according to the type of equipment used, as is fully explained in the section on grilling in Methods of Cookery.

Apart from the garnishes given in the recipes, the practice of the trade, particularly in those restaurants whose grills are their speciality, is to add a garnish of grilled tomatoes, mushrooms and various fried potatoes to the main dish.

## LAMB

**931 Grilled lamb cutlets** — Côtelettes d'agneau grillées

**932 Grilled lamb chop** — Chop d'agneau grillée

**933 Grilled lamb crown chop**

**934 Grilled chump chop**

**935 Grilled noisette of lamb** — Noisette d'agneau grillée

**936 Grilled fillet of lamb** — Filet mignon grillé

### Method

1. Prepare the cutlets as in 209, the other various cuts as in 205, and the chump chop as in 204.
2. Season with salt and milled pepper on both sides and brush with oil.
3. Place on the grill bars or under a salamander and grill quickly on both sides for the first 2–3 minutes to seal the meat. Continue grilling over or under a more moderate heat until the meat is firm to the touch and no blood emerges when pressure is applied. Total approximate grilling times are as follows:

Cutlets: 7–8 minutes

Double cutlets: 10–12 minutes

Lamb chop: 12–14 minutes

Crown chop: 14–16 minutes

Chump chop: 11–12 minutes

Noisette of lamb: 8–10 minutes

Filet mignon: 7–8 minutes

4. Serve on a hot oval silver flat dish and garnish with sprigs of picked watercress, or the garnish according to the name of the recipe.

### Garnishes: per portion

**Vert-pré:** 2 oz (55 g) Pommes paille (1101); watercress; parsley butter (116).

**aux champignons:** 2 oz (55 g) Champignons grillés (977); 2 oz (55 g) Pommes paille (1101); watercress.

**Paloise:** (filet mignon and noisette): 2 oz (55 g) Pommes noisette (1122); Sauce paloise (406).

**Henry IV** (filet mignon and noisette): 3 oz (85 g) Pommes Pont Neuf (1105); watercress.

## 937 Mixed grill

| 8 portions | Ingredients | 10 couverts |
|---|---|---|
| 8 | lamb cutlet | 10 |
| 8 × 2 oz | pork sausage or | 10 × 55 g |
| 16 × 1 oz | pork chipolatas | 20 × 30 g |
| 8 | lambs kidney | 8 |
| 1 lb | open mushrooms | 560 g |
| 2 fl. oz | oil | 70 ml |
| 8 × 2 oz | tomatoes | 10 × 55 g |
| 8 | slices streaky bacon | 10 |
| 1 lb | peeled potatoes, Pommes paille (1101) | 560 g |
| 1 bunch | watercress | 1 bunch |
| 6 oz | parsley butter (116) | 210 g |

### Method

1. Prepare the lamb cutlets (209) and season them with salt and milled pepper.
2. Wash and peel the mushrooms and season them with salt and milled pepper. Place them on an oiled tray, dark side down, then liberally brush them with oil.
3. Cut out the stalk base (eye) from the tomatoes, then turn over and make two incisions crossways on the top. Season, place on an oiled tray and brush them with oil.
4. Prepare the kidneys for grilling (212) then season and brush with oil.
5. Place the sausages on an oiled tray and brush them with oil. Place the slices of bacon on a tray.
6. Prepare and fry the straw potatoes (1101).
7. Grill the sausages on all sides for 10 minutes (chipolatas for 6–7 minutes), cutlets for 7–8 minutes, kidneys 7–8

minutes, tomatoes and mushrooms 6–7 minutes, bacon 1–1½ minutes each side.

7. Serve the cutlets in pairs running down the centre of a hot oval flat dish, with the bones crossing and cutlet frills on the bones. Put the sausages and kidneys on opposite sides of the cutlets, with the bacon crossed in the centre on each side. Place the tomatoes on each side of the bacon, with the mushrooms on top, and place the straw potatoes at each end of the dish with watercress on each side of them. Cut the parsley butter in 5 mm slices and place in the grilled kidneys.

## 938 Grilled kidneys        Rognons grillés

**Method**

1. Prepare for grilling (212) two lambs kidneys per portion.
2. Season them with salt and milled pepper and brush them with oil. Place the cut side down on a grill or grilling tray.
3. Grill quickly, allowing 3½–4 minutes on each side.
4. Remove the kidneys from the skewer and place them on to a hot flat oval dish, cut side showing. Place straw potatoes (1101), at each end, watercress on each side, and place a 5 mm slice of parsley butter (116) in each kidney.

## 939 Grilled calf's liver and bacon      Foie de veau grillé au lard

**Method**

1. Prepare the calf's liver (235), cut to allow 2 slices per portion of 3 oz (85 g).
2. Season with salt and milled pepper and brush with oil. Place on very hot grill bars and cook quickly for 2–2½ minutes on each side.
3. Serve on a hot oval flat dish with 2 slices of grilled streaky or back bacon placed on top. Garnish with picked watercress.

## BEEF

| | |
|---|---|
| **940 Grilled minute steak (164)** | **Entrecôte minute grillé** |
| **941 Grilled sirloin steak (164)** | **Entrecôte grillé** |
| **942 Grilled double sirloin steak (164)** | **Entrecôte double grillé** |
| **943 Grilled tournedos (163)** | **Tournedos grillé** |
| **944 Grilled chateaubriand (163)** | **Chateaubriand grillé** |
| **945 Grilled T-bone steak (164)** | |

## 946 Grilled porterhouse steak (164)

## 947 Grilled fillet steak (163)

## 948 Grilled rump steak (162)

**Method**

1. Prepare the various steaks (see the reference number at the end of English title).
2. Season with salt and milled pepper on both sides and brush over with oil.
3. Place on the hot grill bars; turn, after a quarter of the grilling time, so that the grill marks form a trellis pattern. When half the grilling time has elapsed, turn over and cook the other side in the same manner. The degree to which the steaks are cooked depends on customers' instructions.
4. While grilling calls for a lot of experience, the following points should give some assistance.

(a) **Rare (au bleu)**: very underdone; the meat is very soft to the touch, very red blood coming from the meat.

(b) **Underdone (saignant)**: the meat should be slightly resilient to finger pressure, with red blood coming from the meat.

(c) **Medium or just done (à point)**: the meat should be fairly firm to finger pressure, with a slight springiness; a little pink to red blood should emerge.

(d) **Well done or well cooked (bien cuit)**: the meat should be firm to finger pressure; no blood should emerge.

The part of the grill used will vary according to thickness of the steak and the degree to which it needs to be cooked.

5. Serve the steak on a hot oval flat dish and garnish it with watercress, Pommes pailles (1101) or Pommes allumettes (1102) and a suitable savoury butter, e.g. parsley, or a warm butter sauce, e.g. Béarnaise (403) Choron (404) or Valois (407).

When designated Henry IV, garnish the steak with watercress and Pommes Pont Neuf (1105).

## PORK

## 949        Crépinette de porc grillée

**Method**

1. Prepare the Crépinette (261).
2. Brush it with oil, grill over a moderate heat, moving to mark a trellis pattern on each side. It should be grilled for approximately 10–12 minutes and the meat, when pressed should be firm to the touch.

3. Serve on a hot flat oval dish and garnish with watercress. Serve an appropriate sauce, e.g. Charcutière (373), or Robert (384) in a sauceboat on an underflat with a doily.

## 950 Grilled pork chop  Côte de porc grillée
**Method**

1. Prepare the pork chops (250).
2. Grill and serve as for Côte de veau grillée (953) from 2 in method. The chops are grilled until well done (13–15 minutes). Serve an appropriate sauce separately, e.g. Apple (410), Charcutière (373), Robert (384).

## 951  Côte de porc normande
**Method**

1. Prepare and grill as for Côte de porc grillée (950).
2. For each portion of pork, peel and core a 4 oz (110 g) apple and cut it through into 6 sections.
3. Place on a buttered tray, lightly sprinkle with a little caster sugar and cinnamon mixed together. Sprinkle with melted butter and white bread crumbs.
4. Cook under a moderate salamander for 4–5 minutes, to a light golden brown.
5. Serve the grilled chops on a hot oval flat dish and garnish on the side with the apple sections and picked watercress.

## 952 Grilled pork sausages  Saucissons de porc grillés
**Method**

1. To prevent the skins bursting, the sausages may be placed in a shallow pan, covered with cold water, blanched rapidly, refresh and drained. Allow 4 oz (110 g) sausages per portion.
2. Prepare, cook and serve as for Crépinette de porc (949). May also be served with two slices per portion of grilled bacon.

## VEAL

## 953 Grilled veal cutlet  Côte de veau grillée
**Method**

1. Prepare the veal cutlets (226) and season them with salt and milled pepper on both sides.
2. Brush with oil, place on the hot grill bars, set on each side to seal for 2–3 minutes, then move to a more moderate part of the grill to cook for 11–13 minutes in all. Should be firm to finger pressure, with no trace of blood, when cooked.

3. Serve on a hot oval flat dish; garnish with straw potatoes (1101) and watercress. In a sauceboat on an underflat with a doily serve an appropriate sauce, e.g. Bercy (371), Italienne (376), Périgueux (379).

## HAM

## 954 Grilled ham  Jambon grillé
**Method**

1. Prepare the slices of ham or gammon for grilling (267) and season them with milled pepper.
2. Brush with oil, place on the grill bars and then move so that a trellis marking is formed. Turn over and repeat the process on other side. Grilling time is approximately 5–6 minutes.
3. Serve on a hot flat oval dish; garnish with straw potatoes (1101) and picked watercress. In a sauceboat on an underflat with a doily, serve an appropriate sauce, e.g. Madère (378) Charcutière (373).

## 955 Grilled ham and pineapple  Jambon grillé aux ananas
**Method**

1. Prepare and grill the ham as for Jambon grillé (954).
2. For each portion, allow one 10 mm slice of prepared pineapple, fresh or canned. Cut the slices in halves and place them on a shallow tray. If fresh, dust heavily with icing sugar; if canned, add a little sugar to the syrup, reduce it until it becomes thick and mask it over the pineapple. Cook and colour golden brown under a hot salamander for 2–3 minutes.
3. Serve the grilled ham on a hot oval flat dish. Place the pineapple overlapping on top, and garnish on the side with picked watercress. In a sauceboat on an underflat with a doily, serve Sauce Madère (378).

## CHICKEN

## 956 Grilled chicken  Poulet grillé
**Method**

1. For each four portions, use a 2½ lb (1·125 kg) roasting chicken, prepared for grilling (274).
2. Season with salt and milled pepper and brush with oil.
3. Place on the hot grill bars, skin side first, or mark a trellis pattern on the skin side with a hot poker.
4. Melt enough first class dripping in a roasting tray to

cover the surface and place the chicken in it, skin side down.

5. Cook in the centre to top of the oven at 220–230°C (425–450°F) for approximately 30 minutes, turning and basting with the fat. Test through the thigh with a cook's fork: the juice emerging should be colourless. Colour golden brown.

6. Serve on a hot oval flat dish; garnish on each side with straw potatoes and with watercress at each end. Serve a sauceboat of Sauce diable (375), on an underflat with a doily.

*Note.* When designated 'au lard', add 1 grilled slice of streaky bacon per portion and lay it across the chicken.

Leg (cuisse) or wing (aile) of chicken may be prepared and served in the same manner.

**957** Poulet grillé Robinson

**Method**

1. Prepare, cook and serve, as for Poulet grillé (956). Add, alongside the additional garnish, 1 grilled tomato, 1 slice of grilled bacon and 2 grilled mushrooms, placed on the tomato, per portion.

**958 Grilled devilled chicken** Poulet grillé diable

**Method**

1. Prepare, cook and serve as for Poulet grillé (956).

2. When cooked, brush the chicken with thin English mustard and dip it in white breadcrumbs. Sprinkle with melted butter or chicken fat and colour golden brown on both sides under a moderate salamander.

# Vegetables

256

# Vegetables

# Légumes

## 959 GENERAL NOTES

All vegetables should be fresh when they are cooked, and green vegetables in particular should be used before they have deteriorated in quality and become dry, decayed or discoloured.

Plenty of boiling water, in about the ratio of 6–10 parts water to vegetable, should be used (except in the case of spinach) for boiling and blanching. The use of such a large amount of water may be questioned by some on the basis that the vegetables may lose some of their nutritional value, but it does produce a well-presented vegetable.

All scum must be removed during cooking to prevent discolouration, and the vegetables must be well drained before serving.

Root vegetables (with the exceptions of new potatoes, leeks and celery) are generally placed to boil in cold water, and those grown above the ground are placed in boiling water.

Vegetables which are cooked before they are required for service should be refreshed, drained and refrigerated, then reheated as required, according to recipe.

---

## PREPARATION AND COOKING OF INDIVIDUAL VEGETABLES

### 960 Globe artichokes                    Artichauts en branche

**Method**

1. For a satisfactory result, it is essential that the globe artichokes are very fresh and not discoloured. Allow 1 per portion.
2. Cut off approximately 20 mm from the top of the artichoke and trim the edges of the leaves with a pair of scissors.
3. Cut away the stalk, where it joins the base, and place a slice of lemon under the base and secure it by tying with string in opposite directions across the artichoke.
4. Plunge into boiling salted water, reboil, skim, then cook gently, turning occasionally for 20–30 minutes. Test when they are ready with the point of a small knife: it should penetrate the base without undue pressure.
5. Remove the artichokes from the water with a slice then drain them. Remove the string and lemon. Lift out the centre with a fork. Scrape away the fur from the base, leaving clean.
6. Replace the centre in an inverted position, with a small sprig of parsley on top.
7. Serve on a hot dish, on a serviette. In a sauceboat on an underflat with a doily serve an appropriate sauce, e.g. Hollandaise (402), Mousseline (405), Beurre fondu (408).

*Note.* May also be served cold, in which case they are refreshed before finishing. Serve Vinaigrette (7) separately.

### 961 Artichoke bottoms                    Fonds d'artichauts

**Method**

1. Cut away the stalk from the base and trim away at least one layer of the base leaves.
2. Cut across the artichoke 20 mm from the base. With a small sharp knife, trim around the edge of the artichoke, then around the top edge and across the bottom to leave a good round smooth shape. If necessary, the base surface may be finished with a vegetable peeler.
3. Immediately rub the base surface with lemon to prevent discolouration
4. Place the artichokes into sufficient boiling blanc (341) to cover them. Reboil, skim, and simmer for 20–30 minutes until tender (test with the point of a knife).
5. Refresh, then, with the thumb, push out the fur centre to leave a clean surface.
6. When used whole, as part of a garnish, place them on a buttered tray, season with salt and pepper and sprinkle with melted butter. Cover with a buttered paper and heat through for 3–4 minutes in an oven at 150°C (300°F).

When served as a vegetable and for certain garnishes, the bottoms are cut into quarters, or sections, on the slant, then seasoned and lightly sautéd in butter.

## 962 Jesuralem artichokes in cream sauce — Topinambours à la crème

| 8 portions | Ingredients | 10 couverts |
|---|---|---|
| 2½ lb | Jerusalem artichokes | 1·4 kg |
| 2 oz | butter | 70 g |
| 4 level teaspoons | salt | 15 g |
| ½ level teaspoon | ground white pepper | 2 g |
| ½ pint | cream sauce (389) | 350 ml |
| ¼ pint | cream | 175 ml |

### Method

1. Wash the artichokes, remove the skin with a peeler and rewash. If necessary, cut and trim the edges to an even size.
2. Place into a boiling blanc (341), reboil and simmer until cooked (approximately 30 minutes). Test when they are ready with a knife point, which should penetrate easily.
3. Thoroughly drain, add to the butter in a shallow pan, season, heat, add the cream and sufficient thin cream sauce to bind loosely.
4. Serve in a hot vegetable dish and sprinkle with chopped parsley.

## 963 — Topinambours au gratin

1. Prepare and cook, as for Topinambours à la crème (962), replacing the cream sauce with thin Sauce Mornay (390).
2. Place in a vegetable dish, sprinkle evenly with about 1 oz (35 g) Parmesan cheese and colour golden brown under a moderate salamander.

## 964 Asparagus — Asperges

### Method

1. The thickness of the stalks varies. Allow 6–8 stalks of 10 mm in diameter, or the equivalent of smaller stalks.
2. Using a blunt knife, or the back of a knife, carefully remove the leaf shoots, commencing 25 mm from the top of the head. The stems are rather brittle, so the stalk should only be raised slightly from the board, and little pressure applied.
3. Scrape the white part of the stems with the knife blade or with a peeler.
4. Wash in cold water and place the sticks together in 2–4 portion bundles. Tie with string 40 mm from the head and approximately 125 mm down. Cut through the white part of the stalks 175 mm from the head to trim to an even length.
5. Place in a shallow pan of boiling salted water, reboil, skim and simmer gently for approximately 15 minutes, turning while cooking. Test when they are ready by piercing the green part with a knife point: it should penetrate without pressure.
6. Lift the asparagus carefully from the water with a slice and drain it on a cloth. Serve on an asparagus stand or serviette on a hot oval flat dish Remove the string. Serve a suitable sauce, such as Hollandaise (402), Mousseline (405) or Beurre fondu (408) in a sauceboat on an underflat with a doily.

*Note.* May be refreshed, drained, then served cold in the same manner, with Sauce vinaigrette (7).

## 965 Buttered asparagus tips — Pointes d'asperges au beurre

### Method

1. Young thin stemmed asparagus, called sprew (sprue) is used. Cut them in the bundles to a length 60 mm from the head, then plain boil them for 6–8 minutes, and refresh and drain.
2. Reheat in butter in a shallow pan covered with a buttered paper.
3. The tips are generally used as a garnish, although they are sometimes served as a vegetable.

## 966 Stuffed egg plant — Aubergine farcie

| 8 portions | Ingredients | 10 couverts |
|---|---|---|
| 4 | aubergines | 5 |
| 3 oz | butter | 100 g |
| 8 oz | mushrooms/stalks | 280 g |
| 2 oz | finely chopped shallot/onion | 70 g |
| 1 lb | tomatoes | 560 g |
| 3 oz | breadcrumbs | 100 g |
| 2 dessertspoons | chopped parsley | 10 g |
| 4–5 level teaspoons | salt | 15–20 g |
| ½ level teaspoon | white pepper | 4 g |
| ¼ pint | demi-glace (thin) | 175 ml |

### Method

1. Remove the stalk and cut the aubergine in two lengthways. Insert the point of a knife 5 mm from the edge and run it around the vegetable, then insert it at intervals of 10 mm, in both directions, to a depth of 5 mm.
2. Deep fry at 175°C (350°F) for 2–3 minutes, until the centre of the aubergine is fairly soft. Drain.
3. With a spoon, scoop out the centre of the aubergine and finely chop.
4. Sweat the shallot/onion in half the butter for 4–5 minutes, without colouring. Add the washed and finely chopped mushrooms and cook for a further 5–6 minutes.
5. Prepare the tomatoes into 10 mm concassé, add to the mushrooms with the seasoning, parsley and half the crumbs, mixing thoroughly.

6. Place the filling into the aubergine cases, on a greased tray, and smooth it to a slight dome shape with a palette knife.

7. Sprinkle with the remainder of the crumbs and melted butter. Colour golden brown under a salamander.

8. Serve in a row in a hot vegetable dish and surround them with the boiling thin demi-glace.

### 967 Fried egg plant — Aubergine frite
**Method**

1. Remove the peel with a vegetable peeler.

2. Cut into 5 mm thick slices. If small, cut on the slant, to increase the size of slice.

3. Dip in milk, drain, then pass through flour. Shake off any surplus flour by placing them on a sieve.

4. Deep fry at 180°C (360°F), moving while frying for 2–3 minutes, until golden brown. Drain and lightly season with salt.

5. Generally used as a garnish. When served as a vegetable, allow half an aubergine per portion and serve them on a hot flat or vegetable dish on a doily.

### 968 Broccoli — Brocoli
**Method**

1. Prepare the broccoli spears by trimming the stem to 50 mm beneath the leaf. Trim away any discoloured parts. Thoroughly wash in cold salted water.

2. Cook, finish and serve as for various methods of cauliflower (994–1000). Cook in shallow trays or pans for 15–18 minutes.

*Note.* When frozen spears are used, the cooking time may be reduced by 3–4 minutes.

### 969 Buttered carrots — Carottes au beurre / Carottes glacées

| 8 portions | Ingredients | 10 couverts |
|---|---|---|
| 2 lb | carrots | 1·125 kg |
| 2 oz | butter | 70 g |
| 2 teaspoons | chopped parsley | 5 g |
| 4 level teaspoons | salt | 15 g |
| 1 level teaspoon | sugar | 4 g |
| ½ level teaspoon | ground white pepper | 2 g |

**Method**

1. Wash, peel and rewash the carrots. Starting at the thicker end, cut them into 40 mm lengths, then divide these lengthways into 4–6 sections. Allow 7–8 pieces per portion.

2. Turn to a barrel shape. The carrots may also be cut into 5 mm dice or 25 × 5 × 5 mm batons.

3. Place in a shallow pan, just cover with water, add salt, pepper, sugar and butter.

3. Boil, skim, cover and allow to cook steadily for 25–30 minutes. Remove the cover and test them with a knife point; it should penetrate without undue pressure.

4. Increase the heat to rapidly evaporate the liquor until only a coating glaze remains.

5. Serve in a loose dome shape in a hot vegetable dish, sprinkled with chopped parsley. Place on an underflat with dish paper.

### 970 Vichy carrots — Carottes Vichy
**Method**

1. Use the same ingredients as for Carottes glacées (969). Select carrots approximately 25 mm in diameter.

2. Wash, peel and rewash the carrots then cut them into 3 mm-thick slices across the carrots.

3. Cook and serve as for Carottes glacées (969). If available, use Vichy water in place of ordinary water.

### 971 — Carottes royale
**Method**

Prepare and serve as for Carottes Vichy. Finish, off the heat, with a liaison of 2 yolks (3 for 10 portions) and ½ pint (350 ml) of cream.

### 972 Creamed carrots — Carottes à la crème
**Method**

1. Prepare and cook as for Carottes glacées (969).

2. When glazed, add ¾ pint (525 ml) of thin Cream sauce (389).

*Note.* The sauce should only be added at the point of service, or it will tend to become coloured by the juice of the carrots.

### 973 Purée of carrots — Purée de carottes

| 8 portions | Ingredients | 10 couverts |
|---|---|---|
| 2½ lb | carrots | 1·4 kg |
| ½ oz | salt | 20 g |
| ½ level teaspoon | ground white pepper | 2 g |
| 2 oz | butter | 70 g |

**Method**

1. Wash, peel and rewash the carrots, then cut them into evenly size pieces.

2. Place them in a saucepan and barely cover with cold water. Bring to the boil, skim, add the seasoning, then boil gently for 25–30 minutes, until tender.

3. Thoroughly drain, pass through a coarse sieve or fine mincer blade.

4. Melt the butter in a saucepan, add the purée, stir over the heat to evaporate any excess moisture and correct the seasoning.

5. Serve in a scrolled dome shape in a hot vegetable dish with a pinch of chopped parsley in the centre.

## 974 Braised celery — Céleri braisé au jus

| 8 portions | Ingredients | 10 couverts |
|---|---|---|
| 2 large or 4 small | celery heads | 3 large or 5 small |
| 4 oz | carrot | 140 g |
| 4 oz | onion | 140 g |
| 8 oz | beef suet trimmings | 280 g |
| 2 teaspoons | chopped parsley | 5 g |
| ½ oz | salt | 20 g |
| ¼ level teaspoon | white pepper | 2 g |
| ½ | bayleaf | 1 |
| small sprig | thyme | small sprig |
| ½ | lemon (in juice) | 1 |
| 1 pint | white stock | 700 ml |
| ½ pint | demi-glace or jus-lié | 350 ml |

**Method**

1. Trim off the celery, where the green commences and pull off any withered stems. Trim the root to a point.

2. Wash thoroughly and trim a little with a vegetable peeler.

3. Blanch for 5 minutes in boiling salted water to which the lemon juice has been added.

4. Refresh and wash thoroughly under running water to remove any dirt.

5. Line a braising pan with slices of beef suet trimmings and with the 5 mm-thick slices of peeled carrots, onions, thyme and bayleaf.

6. Pack in the celery, half cover with the seasoned stock and cover with more slices of suet.

7. Bring to the boil, cover with greaseproof paper and a lid.

8. Place in a moderate oven at 150°C (300°F) to cook for 1–1¼ hours.

9. Drain. If small, cut the celery in halves lengthways and, if large, in quarters lengthways. In both cases turn the ends under to give a length of 60–75 mm pieces.

10. Strain the cooking liquor, reduce to an essence, add to the demi-glace or jus-lié.

11. Serve the celery in a hot vegetable dish, mask over with the sauce, place a pinch of chopped parsley in the centre of each piece. Place on an underflat with dish paper.

## 975 — Céleri braisé à la moelle

**Method**

1. Prepare, cook and serve as for 974.

2. Before masking with the sauce, place 1–2 slices of poached bone marrow (724c) on each piece of celery. Use demi-glace.

## 976 — Céleri braisé, Sauce crème

**Method**

Prepare, cook and serve as for Céleri braisé au jus (974). Substitute Sauce crème (389) for demi-glace or jus-lié.

## 977 Grilled mushrooms — Champignons grillés

**Method**

1. Use 3 oz (85 g) open grilling mushrooms per portion.

2. Wash and peel the mushrooms and cut off the stalks level with the mushroom head.

3. Place the heads on an oiled tray, dark side down. Liberally brush with oil or fat and season with salt and milled pepper.

4. Grill under a moderate salamander for 2–2½ minutes, turn over, season and grill the other side for the same time.

5. Serve with the dark side showing in a hot vegetable dish. Brush over with melted butter and garnish with sprigs of parsley. Place the dish on an underflat with dish paper.

## 978 Stuffed mushrooms — Champignons farcis

| 8 portions | Ingredients | 10 couverts |
|---|---|---|
| 1½ lb | large mushrooms | 840 g |
| 3 oz | butter | 100 g |
| 2 oz | finely chopped onion/shallot | 70 g |
| 4 level teaspoons | salt | 15 g |
| ½ level teaspoon | ground white pepper | 2 g |
| 2 oz | breadcrumbs | 70 g |

**Method**

1. Select 3–4 regular shaped mushrooms per portion.

2. Wash and peel the mushrooms and cut away the stalk. Grill (977) or sauté in a little dripping.

3. Wash the remainder and finely chop them with the peelings and stalks.

4. Use half the butter, onion and chopped mushroom to prepare a duxelle (338).

5. With a spoon, place the duxelle on the dark side of the mushrooms in a dome shape.

6. Sprinkle with the crumbs and the remainder of the melted butter.

7. Colour slightly under a moderate salamander.

8. Serve in a hot vegetable dish, garnished with sprigs of parsley. Place on an underflat with dish paper.

## 979 Cabbage — Chou vert, nature, à la presse

**Method**

1. The amount required per portion will vary according to the quality. Good cabbage will yield approximatey 3 portions per pound (6–7 portions per kg).

2. Cut away the base stalk and remove any discoloured parts of the leaves.

3. Cut into quarters and cut away the centre stalk and any heavy thick leaf stalk. Wash thoroughly in salted cold water.

4. Plunge into plenty of boiling salted water (2 oz salt per gallon, 15 g per litre). Reboil and remove any scum; turn the cabbage over with a spider during cooking. Allow to boil steadily for 15–20 minutes. Test by pressing the thickest stalk between the finger and thumb: it should be soft.

5. Drain in a colander and press out all water. Place on a plate, the larger leaves underneath, and cover with another plate and press.

6. Turn the plates upside down, remove the top plate, and cut the cabbage into neat size wedges.

7. Serve on a hot vegetable dish, on an underflat with dish paper.

*Note.* If prepared in advance, refresh and drain and reheat in a steamer for 10 minutes.

## 980 Buttered cabbage — Choux au beurre

**Method**

1. Prepare and cook as for Chou vert (979), then refresh and press to drain.

2. Lightly chop into rough 25 mm squares. Toss the cabbage in melted butter in a plat sauté or poêlé and season with salt and milled pepper. Do not colour.

4. Serve loosely in a hot vegetable dish and brush with melted butter. Place on an underflat with dish paper.

## 981 Creamed cabbage — Choux à la crème

**Method**

1. Prepare and cook as for Chou vert (979) then refresh and press to drain.

2. Very finely chop the cabbage or pass through a 5 mm mincer blade.

3. Heat a little butter in a saucepan, add the cabbage, dry off any moisture and season with salt and milled pepper.

4. Add sufficient Sauce crème (389) to just bind together.

5. Serve in a hot vegetable dish, scrolled in a dome shape, with one 25 mm triangular butter-fried croûton per portion placed along the centre. Place on an underflat with dish paper.

## 982 — Choux à l'étuvée

**Method**

1. Prepare the cabbage as for Chou vert (979) Shred into 10 mm-wide strips across the cabbage.

2. Melt 1 oz (30 g) of butter per 1 lb (450 g) of prepared cabbage in a shallow braising pan. Add the cabbage and season it with salt and milled pepper.

3. Add 2½ fl.oz (70 ml) of white stock per lb (450 g) of cabbage. Cover with a buttered paper and lid and boil. Cook in the bottom of an oven at 150°C (300°F) for 30–40 minutes, stirring during cooking.

4. Serve in loose dome shape in a hot vegetable dish on an underflat with dish paper.

## 983 Spring greens — Choux de printemps

**Method**

1. Prepare, cook and serve as for Chou vert (979), or Choux au beurre (980).

2. Allow only 10–12 minutes cooking time.

## 984 — Choux à la flamande

| 8 portions | Ingredients | 10 couverts |
|---|---|---|
| 2½ lb | red cabbage | 1·4 kg |
| 3 oz | butter | 100 g |
| 4 oz | onion (stuck with cloves) | 140 g |
| 8 oz | cooking apples | 280 g |
| 1 oz | sugar | 35 g |
| ½ oz | salt | 20 g |
| ½ teaspoon | ground white pepper | 2 g |
| ½ pint | vinegar | 350 ml |

**Method**

1. Cut away the base stalk and remove any discoloured part of the leaves. Cut in quarters and remove the centre and the thick parts of the stem. Wash well.

2. Finely shred the cabbage across.

3. Grease an earthenware casserole or tin-lined braising pan (aluminium will cause discolouration) with the butter.

4. Add the onion, sugar, salt, pepper and vinegar.

5. Cover with a greased paper and lid. Place to cook in the

bottom of an oven at 150°C (300°F) for approximately 1¼ hours. Fork over 2–3 times during cooking and add a little stock if necessary.

6. Peel and core the apples then cut them into 5 mm dice. Mix this into the cabbage and cook for a further 30 minutes, until soft.

7. Serve in a loose dome shape in a hot vegetable dish on an underflat with dish paper.

### 985 Braised sauerkraut — Choucroute braisée

| 8 portions | Ingredients | 10 couverts |
| --- | --- | --- |
| 2 lb | prepared sauerkraut | 1·125 kg |
| 4 oz | carrot | 140 g |
| 4 oz | onion (stuck with clove) | 140 g |
| 2 oz | butter | 70 g |
| 8 oz | streaky bacon | 280 g |
| 12 | white peppercorns | 15 |
| small | bouquet garni | small |
| 12 | juniper berries | 15 |
| ½ pint | white stock | 350 ml |

#### Method

1. Grease a casserole or braising pan with the butter and add the sauerkraut (prepared pickled white cabbage).

2. Add the stock, boil, then add the peeled carrot, onion stuck with clove, bouquet garni, the bacon with rind removed, the peppercorns and juniper berries tied in muslin for easy removal.

3. Boil and cover with a greased paper and lid. Braise in the bottom of an oven at 150°C (300°F) for 2½–3 hours, turning during cooking; add a little stock if necessary. Remove the bacon when cooked.

4. Serve in a loose dome shape, garnished with rings of carrot and thin 50 mm-long slices of bacon, in a hot vegetable dish.

*Note.* When served as an entrée, double the quantity of bacon, add 2 frankfurter sausages per portion 30 minutes before the cabbage is cooked and serve the sausages on top of the cabbage.

### 986 Braised cabbage — Choux braisés

| 8 portions | Ingredients | 10 couverts |
| --- | --- | --- |
| 3½ lb | cabbage | 2 kg |
| 4 oz | carrot | 140 g |
| 4 oz | onion | 140 g |
| 4 oz | streaky bacon | 140 g |
| ½ oz | salt | 20 g |
| ½ teaspoon | ground white pepper | 2 g |
| small | bouquet garni | small |
| ¾ pint | white stock | 525 ml |
| ½ pint | demi-glace | 350 ml |

#### Method

1. Trim away any discoloured parts of the leaves and cut off the base stem.

2. Cut the centre stem away by cutting a conical piece 50–75 mm deep out of the base.

3. Separate the leaves and wash the cabbage well. Blanch in boiling salted water for 5 minutes, refresh and drain.

4. Lay 8 or 10 of the largest leaves on the table and place another smaller leaf on top. Divide the remainder of the cabbage equally and place it in the centre of each leaf. Season with salt and pepper.

5. Envelope the centre with the leaves and mould into a ball. Place in a cloth and squeeze out the excess water.

6. Peel the carrot and onion, cut them into slices and place them in the bottom of a shallow braising pan.

7. Place the cabbage on top, with the bacon and bouquet garni, and moisten with the stock (preferably slightly fatty).

8. Boil, then cover with a buttered paper and lid and braise in the bottom of an oven at 150°C (300°F) for 1–1¼ hours.

9. Remove the cabbage to a hot vegetable dish. Reduce the cooking liquor rapidly to an essence then add it to the boiling demi-glace.

10. Place a small 25 mm-square thin slice of the bacon, with a slice of the carrot cut with a small fluted cutter, on each portion of cabbage and surround them with the sauce. Place on an underflat with dish paper.

### 987 Stuffed cabbage (small) — Petits choux farcis

#### Method

1. Prepare, cook and serve as for Choux braisés (986).

2. Before enveloping at 5 in method, place a small ball (1 oz (30 g)) of pork sausage meat (263) in the centre.

*Note.* May be prepared in larger sizes if required, and the stuffing may be varied, e.g. Riz pilaff (615).

### 988 Brussels sprouts — Choux de Bruxelles

| 8 portions | Ingredients | 10 couverts |
| --- | --- | --- |
| 2½ lb | Brussels sprouts salt | 1·4 kg |

#### Method

1. Remove any discoloured leaves with a small knife.

2. Carefully trim the base stalk and make crossed incisions in the base with the point of the knife. Do not cut down into the sprouts, as this will cause them to break apart during cooking.

3. Thoroughly wash in cold salted water.

4. Plunge into 8–10 times their own volume of boiling salted water. (2 oz salt per gallon, 15 g per litre).

5. Reboil rapidly, adjust the heat to boil gently for 12–16 minutes, according to size. Remove all scum during cooking. Test when they are ready with the point of a knife; it should penetrate without undue pressure.

6. Finish as required by recipe. If not required immediately, refresh, drain and refrigerate.

## 989        Choux de Bruxelles nature

**Method**

Prepare and cook the sprouts (988) and drain them thoroughly in a colander. Serve in a loose dome shape in a hot vegetable dish. Place on an underflat with dish paper.

## 990        Choux de Bruxelles au gratin

**Method**

1. Prepare and cook the sprouts (988) and drain them thoroughly in a colander.

2. Place them in a buttered earthenware dish and brush them with melted butter. Sprinkle evenly with grated cheese.

3. Colour a light golden brown under a moderate salamander, place the dish on an underflat with dish paper.

## 991        Choux de Bruxelles au beurre

**Method**

1. Prepare and cook the sprouts (988) and drain them thoroughly in a colander.

2. Serve them in a hot vegetable dish and brush them liberally with melted butter. Place the dish on an underflat with dish paper.

## 992        Choux de Bruxelles sautés au beurre

**Method**

1. Prepare and cook the sprouts (988) and drain them thoroughly in a colander.

2. Melt 2 oz (70 g) of butter in a plat sauté or poêlé and add the sprouts. Season with a little milled pepper.

3. Toss over and sauté until just beginning to lightly colour.

4. Serve in a loose dome shape in a hot vegetable dish on an underflat with dish paper.

## 993        Choux de Bruxelles Mornay

**Method**

1. Prepare and cook the sprouts (988) and drain them thoroughly in a colander.

2. Place them in a shallow pan, add ¾ pint (525 ml) of thin (i.e. half the normal thickness) Sauce Mornay (390).

3. Carefully mix by lightly moving around. Place in a buttered earthenware dish.

4. Sprinkle evenly with grated cheese and colour to a light golden brown under a moderate salamander. Serve on an underflat with dish paper.

## 994 Cauliflower        Chou-fleur nature

| 8 portions | Ingredients | 10 couverts |
|---|---|---|
| 2 × 1¾ lb | cauliflower | 2 × 1 kg |
|  | salt |  |

**Method**

1. Cut away the base of the stem, just below where the inside young green leaves join the stem.

2. With a small knife, cut out a small conical-shaped piece of the base stem and pierce up the centre with the knife point. This allows the water to penetrate during cooking.

3. With the point of a knife, shave off any dark spots on the white surface (flower). Soak in cold salt water for 10–15 minutes to drive out any caterpillars.

4. Cook in plenty of boiling salted water and remove all scum. Cover with a cloth or wet paper, with the flower side uppermost, for 16–20 minutes, according to size. Test with a knife point through the base of the stem: it should penetrate without undue pressure.

5. Remove from the water carefully with a small spider or slice and drain on a cloth.

6. Serve either whole on a serviette on a hot round flat dish or portioned in a hot vegetable dish on an underflat with dish paper.

*Note.* Cauliflower is generally served with a sauce, in which case the term 'nature' is dropped and the sauce named, i.e. Sauce hollandaise (402), Mousseline (405) Beurre fondu (408), Sauce crème (389), Sauce au fromage (387).

## 995        Chou-fleur Mornay     Chou-fleur au gratin

**Method**

1. Prepare and cook the cauliflower (994) then drain and place it in a buttered vegetable or earthenware dish. It can be served either whole or portioned.

2. Mask the cauliflower and cover the base of the dish with Sauce Mornay (390) and sprinkle the surface evenly with grated cheese. Colour golden brown under a very moderate salamander or at the top of an oven at 200°C (400°F). Place the dish on an underflat with dish paper.

## 996            Chou-fleur milanaise

### Method

1. Prepare and cook the cauliflower (994) then drain and place it (either whole or portioned) in a buttered vegetable or earthenware dish.

2. Brush liberally with melted butter and sprinkle evenly and liberally with grated cheese.

3. Colour light golden brown under a moderate salamander. Place the dish on an underflat with dish paper.

## 997 Buttered cauliflower      Chou-fleur au beurre

### Method

Prepare and cook the cauliflower (994) then drain and place it in a hot vegetable dish, whole or portioned, and brush with melted butter. Place on an underflat with dish paper.

## 998            Chou-fleur persillé

### Method

Prepare as for Chou-fleur au beurre (997), sprinkle with chopped parsley.

## 999            Chou-fleur sauté au beurre

### Method

1. Prepare and cook the cauliflower (994) then drain and cut it into portions.

2. Carefully sauté in butter in a frying pan to lightly colour on all sides.

3. Serve on a hot vegetable dish on an underflat with dish paper. Brush the cauliflower with melted butter.

## 1000            Chou-fleur à la polonaise

### Method

1. Prepare and cook the cauliflower (994) then drain and, if desired, lightly sauté it in butter.

2. Place in a hot vegetable dish, whole or portioned, and mask it over with the polonaise (1001). Place on an underflat with dish paper.

## 1001            Polonaise

| 8 portions | Ingredients | 10 couverts |
|---|---|---|
| 3 oz | butter | 100 g |
| 1 oz | fresh white breadcrumbs | 35 g |
| 2 | hard-boiled eggs | 3 |
| 3 dessertspoons | chopped parsley | 10 g |

### Method

1. Pass the egg through a coarse sieve.

2. Heat the butter in a frying pan, add the crumbs, fry them until a light golden brown, then add the sieved egg and parsley and mask it over the prepared foodstuff.

## 1002 Sea kale            Choux de mer

| 8 portions | Ingredients | 10 couverts |
|---|---|---|
| 2½ lb | sea kale | 1·4 kg |
| 1 | lemon (in juice) | 1 |
|  | salt |  |

### Method

1. Clean the root with a small knife, removing the least amount possible. Trim off any discoloured leaves.

2. Wash carefully in salted cold water and tie in bundles.

3. Place into boiling salted water containing the lemon juice. Boil, skim and cook gently until tender (approximately 15–18 minutes).

4. Remove with a slice and drain on a cloth.

5. Serve on a serviette on a hot oval flat dish. Serve an appropriate sauce, such as Hollandaise (402), Mousseline (405), Beurre fondu (408), in a sauceboat on an underflat with a doily.

## 1003            Choux de mer au gratin
##                     Choux de mer Mornay

### Method

1. Prepare and cook the sea kale (1002) then drain it thoroughly and arrange it neatly in a buttered vegetable or earthenware dish.

2. Mask over with a thin Mornay sauce (390) and sprinkle the surface evenly with grated cheese. Colour golden brown under a moderate salamander. Place on an underflat with dish paper.

## 1004 Marrow            Courge
## Baby marrow            Courgette

| 8 portions | Ingredients | 10 couverts |
|---|---|---|
| 2½ lb | marrow | 1·4 kg |
|  | salt |  |

## Method

1. If courgettes are used, reduce the quantity by 20 per cent.

2. Trim the ends with a knife and remove the skin with a vegetable peeler.

3. Cut in halves lengthways and remove the seeds with a spoon.

4. If necessary, cut larger marrows again down the length. Cut them into even 50 mm squares and lightly trim the corners round.

5. Plunge into plenty of boiling salted water, reboil, skim and boil them gently for 10–12 minutes (slightly less for baby marrow). Test with the point of a knife: a slight firmness should remain in the marrow.

6. Remove with a spider, drain on a cloth and serve in a hot vegetable dish. Place on an underflat with dish paper.

May be served with Sauce crème (389) or Sauce au fromage (387).

## 1005        Courge au beurre

### Method

Prepare, cook and serve as for 1004. Dress slightly overlapping and brush over with melted butter.

## 1006        Courge milanaise

### Method

Finish as for Courge au beurre (1005). Sprinkle evenly with grated Parmesan cheese and colour golden brown under a moderate salamander. Place on an underflat with dish paper.

## 1007        Courge Mornay

### Method

1. Prepare and cook (1004) and place it in a buttered vegetable or earthenware dish. Mask with Sauce Mornay (390) and sprinkle evenly with cheese.

2. Colour golden brown under a moderate salamander. Place on an underflat with dish paper.

## 1008 Stuffed marrow        Courge farcie

| 8 portions | Ingredients | 10 couverts |
|---|---|---|
| 2 lb | marrow | 1·125 kg |
| 2 oz | finely chopped onion | 70 g |
| 1 oz | butter or dripping | 35 g |
| 8 oz | pork sausage meat (263) | 280 g |
| 6 oz | white breadcrumbs | 210 g |
| 3 dessertspoons | chopped parsley | 10 g |
| ½ oz | salt | 20 g |
| ¼ teaspoon | ground white pepper | 2 g |
| ½ pod | garlic | ½ pod |
| ½ pint | demi-glace | 350 ml |
| 4 oz | carrot | 140 g |
| 4 oz | onion | 140 g |

### Method

1. Wash, peel and rewash the marrow.

2. Split in halves lengthways.

3. Remove the seeds by scooping out with a spoon, blanch in boiling water for 4 minutes, refresh, then place the halves in a shallow braising pan/tray on a thin bed of roots.

4. Fry the chopped onion in a little fat till a pale golden brown, add the sausage meat and stir over the fire with a spatule to separate the meat. Add the finely chopped garlic and cook for a further 5 minutes.

5. Add the salt, pepper and chopped parsley and three-quarters of the breadcrumbs. Mix them well together and, if necessary, add a little demi-glace to bind the stuffing.

6. Place the stuffing into the cavity of the marrow and smooth it to a dome shape with a palette knife. Sprinkle with the remaining crumbs and a little melted butter.

7. Moisten the bottom of the pan with 5 mm of white stock. Cook in the oven at 200–220°C (400–425°F) for 35–40 minutes, then test through the marrow with the point of a knife.

8. Serve on hot vegetable dish in halves, or each half cut into portions. Brush over with melted butter, sprinkle with chopped parsley and run a little thin demi-glace around the base. Place on an underflat with dish paper.

## 1009 Fried baby marrow        Courgette frite

| 8 portions | Ingredients | 10 couverts |
|---|---|---|
| 2 lb | baby marrow | 1·125 kg |
| 6 oz | flour | 210 g |
| ½ pint | milk | 350 ml |

### Method

1. Cut off the ends of the baby marrow and remove the skin with a peeler.

2. Cut across into 5 mm thick slices; if very small, cut them on the slant to enlarge the slices.

3. Dip in the milk, then in the flour, shaking off the excess flour on a sieve.

4. Fry in small batches in deep fat at 180°C (360°F); move around to colour them a golden brown.

5. Drain and season them with salt. Serve in a hot vegetable or flat dish on a dish paper.

## 1010        Courge à la provençale

| 8 portions | Ingredients | 10 couverts |
|---|---|---|
| 2 lb | marrow | 1·125 kg |
| 2 lb | tomatoes | 1·125 kg |
| 4 oz | finely chopped onion | 140 g |
| 4 fl. oz | oil | 140 ml |
| 2 pods | garlic | 2 pods |
| 4 teaspoons | chopped parsley | 10 g |
| ½ oz | salt | 20 g |
| ½ teaspoon | milled pepper | 2 g |

**Method**

1. Trim away the ends of the marrow and remove the skin with a peeler.

2. Cut in quarters lengthways and scrape away all the seeds. Cut across in 5 mm-thick slices.

3. Prepare the tomatoes into 10 mm raw concassé (336,5c).

4. Cook the onion in the oil in a sauteuse for 6–7 minutes, without colouring.

5. Add the peeled, finely chopped garlic and the marrow. Toss over the heat for 1–2 minutes then season with salt and pepper.

6. Sprinkle in the tomato, cover, cook in the oven at 160°C (325°F) or on the side of the stove for approximately 30 minutes, until the marrow is soft.

7. Serve in a loose dome shape in a hot vegetable dish; sprinkle the surface with chopped parsley. Place on an underflat with dish paper.

## 1011        Ratatouille

| 8 portions | Ingredients | 10 couverts |
|---|---|---|
| 1 lb | baby marrow | 560 g |
| 1 lb | aubergine | 560 g |
| 4 oz | finely shredded onion | 140 g |
| 1 lb | tomatoes | 560 g |
| 2 teaspoons | chopped parsley | 5 g |
| ½ oz | salt | 20 g |
| ½ level teaspoon | milled pepper | 2 g |
| 1 pod | garlic | 1 large pod |
| 4 fl. oz | oil | 140 ml |

**Method**

1. Trim away the ends of the baby marrow and aubergine. Remove the skin with a peeler. Cut both into 5 mm-thick slices; if not very small, cut them in halves lengthways, then cut across in 5 mm slices.

2. Prepare the tomatoes into 10 mm raw concassé (336,5c).

3. Cook the shredded onion in the oil in a sauteuse for 6–7 minutes, without colouring.

4. Add the peeled, finely-chopped garlic, marrow and aubergine. Toss over the heat for 1–2 minutes then season with salt and pepper.

5. Finish and serve as from 6 in method of Courge provençale (1010).

## 1012   Stuffed cucumber      Concombre farci

**Method**

1. Trim the ends of 3 medium cucumbers for 8, or 4 cucumbers for 10 portions. Remove the skin with a peeler.

2. Cut across the cucumber into 30 mm lengths. Scoop out the centre with a ball scoop to a depth of two-thirds the thickness.

3. Blanch in boiling water for 5 minutes, then refresh and drain well.

4. Place in a buttered shallow pan or tray and season with salt and pepper.

5. Prepare a farce as for stuffed marrow (1008), adding 4 oz (140 g) of washed chopped mushroom to the onion at 4 in method. Replace the sausage meat with finely minced or chopped cooked meat.

6. With a bag and a 20 mm plain tube, fill the cucumber cases to a dome shape. Sprinkle with breadcrumbs and melted butter.

7. Cook and colour slightly in the top of an oven at 200°C (400°F) for 5 minutes.

8. Serve in a hot vegetable dish and surround them with thin demi-glace.

## 1013        Endive belge à l'étuvée

| 8 portions | Ingredients | 10 couverts |
|---|---|---|
| 2½ lb | Belgian endive (chicory) | 1·4 kg |
| 1 | lemon (in juice) | 1 |
| ½ oz | salt | 20 g |
| ½ teaspoon | ground white pepper | 2 g |
| 2 teaspoons | chopped parsley | 5 g |
| 3 oz | butter | 100 g |

**Method**

1. Remove any discoloured leaves and very lightly trim the base clean.

2. Blanch for 2–3 minutes in boiling water containing half the lemon juice. Refresh and drain.

3. Grease a shallow pan or tray (not aluminium) with half the butter. Lay in the endive, season, add the remainder of the lemon juice and about 5 mm of white stock.

4. Cover with a greased paper and lid. Boil, place in the bottom of an oven at 150°C (300°F) to cook (approximately 50–60 minutes).

5. Serve in a hot vegetable dish. Brush with the remainder of the butter and sprinkle with the chopped parsley. Place the dish on an underflat with dish paper.

## 1014 Endive belge au jus

**Method**

1. Prepare and cook the endives (1013) and place them in a hot vegetable dish. Reduce the cooking liquor to an essence and add it to ¼ pint (175 ml) of jus-lié.
2. Mask the endive with the liquid and sprinkle it with chopped parsley.

## 1015 Endive belge Mornay

**Method**

1. Prepare and cook the endives (1013), then drain and place them in a buttered vegetable or earthenware dish.
2. Mask with Sauce Mornay (390) and sprinkle the surface evenly with grated cheese. Colour golden brown under a moderate salamander. Place the dish on an underflat with dish paper for serving.

## 1016 Endive meunière

**Method**

1. Prepare and cook the endives (1013) and drain them thoroughly.
2. Shallow fry in butter to a light golden brown then place them into a hot vegetable dish.
3. Sprinkle with chopped parsley and a little lemon juice. Mask over with Beurre noisette, allowing ½ oz (15 g) per portion.

## 1017 Buttered leaf spinach Épinards en branche

**Method**

1. Allow 8 oz (225 g) of spinach per portion; if the quality is below par, the quantity needs to be increased.
2. Remove any discoloured parts of the leaves, and the stems to within 10 mm of the leaf.
3. Wash several times in cold water until all grit and sand is removed, then drain.
4. Place into approximately 100 mm of boiling water in a wide pan, pressing the spinach well down.
5. Reboil rapidly and cook for 4–8 minutes (the latter time is for older winter spinach).
6. Refresh under running cold water, then drain and squeeze into balls to remove excess water.
7. Heat 2 oz (70 g) of butter for each 8–10 portions in a frying pan or plat sauté, then add the loosened spinach. Season with salt, milled pepper and a little grated nutmeg.
8. Toss or fork over until hot; do not colour.
9. Serve loosely in a hot vegetable dish on an underflat with dish paper.

## 1018 Spinach purée Épinards en purée

**Method**

1. Prepare, cook and drain the spinach (1017), then rub it through a sieve or pass it through a fine mincer blade.
2. Heat 1½ oz (50 g) of butter per 8–10 portions in a sauteuse and add the purée. Season with salt, milled pepper and a little grated nutmeg.
3. Stir over the heat with a spatule until it is thoroughly hot.
4. Serve in a scrolled dome shape in a hot vegetable dish on an underflat with dish paper.

## 1019 Creamed spinach purée Épinards en purée à la crème

**Method**

1. Prepare as for spinach purée (1018); when reheated, add approximately ½ pint (350 ml) of béchamel or half the quantity of cream.
2. Serve as for spinach purée, with a little hot cream around the base. Place two 5 mm thick 25 mm triangular butter-fried bread croûtons per portion on top and around the edge.

## 1020 Épinards aux fleurons

**Method**

Prepare, cook and serve as for 1019, replacing the croûtons with fleurons (small puff paste crescents or flowers, etc., 1511).

## 1021 Broad beans Fèves

**Method**

1. Allow 10 oz (280 g) of broad beans per portion.
2. Remove the beans from the casings and wash them.
3. Plunge them into plenty of boiling salted water, reboil, skim and boil steadily for approximately 18–20 minutes.
4. Unless very young, refresh, remove the skin, reheat in boiling salted water and drain.
5. Serve in a loose dome shape in a vegetable dish, on an underflat with dish paper.

*Note.* When frozen beans are used, blanch for 5–6 minutes, refresh, skin and cook them in boiling salted water for 6–7 minutes.

## 1022 Buttered broad beans — Fèves au beurre

**Method**

1. Prepare and cook the beans (1021) and drain them.
2. Melt 2 oz (70 g) of butter per 8–10 portions in a sauteuse. Add the beans and toss them very lightly to coat with butter.
3. Serve in a loose dome shape in a hot vegetable dish on an underflat with dish paper.

## 1023 — Fèves persillées

**Method**

Prepare as for Fèves au beurre (1022); sprinkle the beans liberally with chopped parsley when serving.

## 1024 — Fèves à la crème

**Method**

Prepare and serve as for Fèves au beurre (1022), adding ¾ pint (525 ml) of Sauce crème (389), or cream, for each 8–10 portions. Sprinkle with chopped parsley when served.

## 1025 White haricot beans — Haricots blancs

| 8 portions | Ingredients | 10 couverts |
|---|---|---|
| 12 oz | white haricot beans | 420 g |
| 2 oz | carrot | 70 g |
| 2 oz | onion (stuck with clove) | 70 g |
| 2 oz | bacon bone or trimmings | 70 g |
| ½ oz | salt | 20 g |

**Method**

1. Pick over and wash the beans. Soak in four times the volume of cold water for 8–12 hours.
2. Rewash, place them in a saucepan and well cover with cold water. Boil, remove all scum, add the peeled carrot, onion and bacon bone, then cover the pan.
3. Allow to simmer for approximately 2 hours, until the beans are soft. Add the salt approximately half an hour before the beans are cooked. (Added at an earlier stage, the salt tends to harden the beans.)
5. Drain and use.

## 1026 — Haricots blancs au beurre

**Method**

1. Prepare and cook the beans (1025) then drain them and toss in 3 oz (85 g) of butter.
2. Serve in a hot vegetable dish and sprinkle them with chopped parsley. Place the dish on an underflat with dish paper.

## 1027 — Haricots bretonne

**Method**

1. Prepare and cook the beans (1025) and drain them. Prepare 1 lb (560 g) of tomatoes in 10 mm raw concassé for each 8–10 portions.
2. Add to the beans ¾ pint (525 ml) of Tomato sauce (370) and the diced tomato; reboil.
3. Serve in a loose dome shape in a hot vegetable dish; sprinkle with chopped parsley. Place the dish on an underflat with dish paper.

## 1028 — Haricots lyonnaise

**Method**

1. Prepare and cook the beans (1025) and drain them. Add ¾ pint (525 ml) of Sauce lyonnaise (377) and mix thoroughly together.
2. Serve in a loose dome shape in a hot vegetable dish on an underflat with dish paper. Sprinkle the beans with chopped parsley.

## 1029 — Flageolets à la crème

**Method**

1. Soak and cook the same quantity of flageolet beans as for Haricots blancs (1025).
2. Drain, then add ¾ pint (525 ml) of Sauce crème (389) for each 8–10 portions.
3. Serve in a loose dome shape in a hot vegetable dish on an underflat with dish paper. Sprinkle the beans with chopped parsley.

## 1030 French beans — Haricots verts

| 8 portions | Ingredients | 10 couverts |
|---|---|---|
| 2½ lb | French beans | 1·4 kg |
| | salt | |

**Method**

1. Remove the top and tail of the beans, breaking them off with the fingers; avoid waste. Wash and drain.
2. If very young small beans, leave them whole. Those of a medium size are cut down the centre, lengthways. Larger beans are cut down the centre lengthways, then across in the centre.
3. Plunge into plenty of boiling salted water, reboil rapidly, remove all scum during cooking.
4. Boil steadily for approximately 15 minutes, drain in a colander. Finish as per recipe.

## 1031 Haricots verts au beurre

**Method**

1. Prepare and cook the beans (1030) and drain them thoroughly.

2. Serve them in a dome shape in a hot vegetable dish on an underflat with dish paper. Brush them liberally with melted butter.

## 1032 Haricots verts sautés au beurre

**Method**

1. Prepare and cook the beans (1030) and drain them thoroughly.

2. Heat 2 oz (70 g) butter for each 8–10 portions in a frying pan or plat sauté, then add the beans and season them with milled pepper. Toss over, do not colour.

3. Serve in a loose dome shape in a hot vegetable dish on an underflat with dish paper.

## 1033 Haricots verts au gratin

**Method**

1. Prepare, and finish in the sauté pan, as for 1032, adding ½ pint (350 ml) of Sauce crème (389) and ¼ pint (175 ml) of cream. Thoroughly combine.

2. Place the beans in a buttered vegetable or earthenware dish and sprinkle them evenly with Parmesan cheese Colour light golden brown under a moderate salamander. Serve the dish on an underflat with dish paper.

## 1034 Runner beans

**Method**

1. Use the same quantities as for Haricots verts (1030).

2. Thoroughly wash the beans. If they are young, pull off the ends and side string; otherwise remove the side string with a peeler.

3. Cut at an angle to give thin slices approximately 50–75 mm long.

4. Cook as for Haricots verts then drain and serve them in a hot vegetable dish on an underflat with dish paper.

## 1035 Mixed vegetables — Jardinière de légumes

## 1036 — Macédoine de légumes

| 8 portions | Ingredients | 10 couverts |
|---|---|---|
| 12 oz | carrot | 420 g |
| 8 oz | turnip | 280 g |
| 4 oz | French beans | 140 g |
| 4 oz | shelled or frozen peas | 140 g |
| 2 oz | butter | 70 g |
| ½ oz | salt | 20 g |
| ½ teaspoon | ground white pepper | 2 g |
| 1 teaspoon | sugar | 5 g |

**Method**

1. Wash and peel the carrots and turnips; rewash them. Cut them into batons 25 × 5 × 5 mm for Jardinière or into 5 mm dice for Macédoine.

2. Cook them separately, glazed. (For carrot see 969, for turnip, 1043.)

3. Prepare the French beans and cut them into 10 mm-long diamonds; cook them as in 1030 and drain.

4. Cook the peas in boiling salted water for 7–10 minutes, then drain.

5. Combine the vegetables and add the remainder of the butter.

6. Serve in a loose dome shape in a hot vegetable dish on an underflat with dish paper.

## 1037 Jardinière de légumes à la crème

## 1038 Macédoine de légumes à la crème

**Method**

1. Prepare and cook as in 1035 and 1036.

2. Add ¾ pint (525 ml) of Sauce crème (389) and mix thoroughly.

3. Serve as for 1035 and 1036 and sprinkle with chopped parsley.

## 1039 Braised lettuce — Laitue braisée

| 8 portions | Ingredients | 10 couverts |
|---|---|---|
| 4 | 'hearty' lettuce | 5 |
| 3 oz | onion | 100 g |
| 3 oz | carrot | 100 g |
| ½ oz | salt | 20 g |
| ½ teaspoon | ground white pepper | 2 g |
| ½ pint | fatty white stock | 350 ml |
| ¼ pint | demi-glace or jus-lié | 175 ml |

**Method**

1. Remove the withered and discoloured leaves and carefully trim the base of the lettuce.

2. Place the lettuce in a bowl of cold salted water to stand for 10 minutes.

3. Wash thoroughly by holding the base of the lettuce and plunging up and down in the water.

4. Drain well and place in boiling salted water for 3 minutes to blanch.

5. Refresh and wash again.

6. Press the lettuce gently to expel the water.

7. Line the bottom of a greased braising pan with the thick slices of carrot and onion, then add the bouquet garni.

8. Pack in the lettuce and half cover it with the seasoned stock to moisten. Cover the pan with greased paper and a lid.

9. Bring to the boil and place in a moderate oven for 45 minutes to braise.

10. When cooked, remove the lettuce, cut each in two, folding each piece neatly in half.

11. Place the portions in a hot vegetable dish.

12. Strain the stock, skim off all grease, reduce and add to the sauce to be used, i.e. jus-lié, demi-glace. Serve the lettuce masked with the sauce. Place on an underflat with dish paper.

## 1040 Corn on the cob                                   Maïs

**Method**

1. Remove the coarser leaves, cut the top from the head, then trim the stump. Allow 1 head per portion.

2. Cook in boiling salted water, to which a small amount of lemon juice has been added, for approximately 20 minutes

3. Drain well, then pull back some of the leaves to reveal the maize.

4. Serve, on a serviette, on a hot flat oval dish. Serve melted butter (408), in a sauceboat on an underflat with a doily.

## 1041                                        Maïs à la crème

**Method**

1. Prepare and cook the corn (1040). Remove the corn kernels (maize) with a fork.

2. Place in a sauteuse, add enough cream to come half way up the corn, then bring to the boil and simmer for 5 minutes.

3. Serve in a hot vegetable dish on an underflat with dish paper.

*Note.* Tinned corn kernels are normally used.

## 1042 Corn croquettes                       Croquettes de maïs

| 8 portions | Ingredients | 10 couverts |
| --- | --- | --- |
| ¾ pint | béchamel | 525 ml |
| 12 oz (drained) | corn kernels (maize) | 420 g |
| 2 | yolks of egg | 3 |
| 4 level teaspoons | salt | 15 g |
| ½ level teaspoon | ground white pepper | 2 g |
| 6 oz | white breadcrumbs | 210 g |
| 2 | eggs | 3 |

**Method**

1. Boil the béchamel in a thick sauteuse and reduce the quantity by one-third.

2. Add the drained corn, salt and pepper and stir the mixture with a wooden spatule until reboiling. Then stir in the yolks of egg and move the sauteuse from the stove.

3. Place the corn in a shallow buttered tray, cover with a buttered paper and allow to cool.

4. Divide into 24–30 pieces and mould them into croquettes (310).

5. Panée with the egg and crumbs (311).

6. Deep fry 8 or 10 pieces at a time at 180°C (360°F) then drain. Serve on a hot vegetable flat dish or with dish paper. Garnish with sprigs of fried parsley.

## 1043 Buttered turnips                    Navets au beurre (glacés)

## 1044 Buttered swedes                    Rutabagas au beurre (glacés)

| 8 portions | Ingredients | 10 couverts |
| --- | --- | --- |
| 2½ lb | turnips or swedes | 1·4 kg |
| 2 oz | butter | 70 g |
| 2 teaspoons | chopped parsley | 5 g |
| 4 teaspoons level | salt | 15 g |
| ½ level teaspoon | sugar | 2 g |
| ½ level teaspoon | ground white pepper | 2 g |

**Method**

1. Wash the turnips or swedes, thickly peel them with a knife and rewash.

2. Cut them into 40 mm lengths, then across into 10 mm-thick slices, then into 10 mm-wide pieces. Turn to a barrel shape with the point of a small knife.

3. Place into a shallow pan, barely cover with water, then add the salt, sugar, pepper and butter.

4. Boil, skim and cover and cook turnips steadily for 15 minutes, swedes for 20 minutes. Test when they are ready with a knife point.

5. Remove the cover and increase the heat to rapidly evaporate the liquor to form a glaze.

6. Serve in a loose dome shape, sprinkled with chopped parsley in a hot vegetable dish, placed on an underflat with dish paper.

## 1045 Purée of turnips                          Purée de navet

## 1046 Purée of swedes — Purée de rutabaga

| 8 portions | Ingredients | 10 couverts |
| --- | --- | --- |
| 2½ lb | turnips or swedes | 1·4 kg |
| 1 lb | peeled potatoes | 560 g |
| 2 oz | butter | 70 g |
| 2 teaspoons | chopped parsley | 5 g |
| 4 level teaspoons | salt | 15 g |
| ½ level teaspoon | ground white pepper | 2 g |

### Method

1. Wash the turnips or swedes, thickly peel them with a knife, rewash and cut them into rough 25 mm cubes.

2. Place into a saucepan and cover with cold water. Cut the potatoes into evenly sized pieces, place them in a pan and cover with cold water.

3. Place both to boil, skim then add the salt. Cover the pans and simmer for 20 minutes. Test when they are cooked with the point of a knife: it should penetrate the vegetable.

4. Drain off the water, using the cover. Dry off on the side of the stove.

5. Pass both vegetables through a sieve with pressure.

6. Place both in a clean saucepan and add the butter and pepper. Stir over the heat until thoroughly hot.

7. Serve scrolled to a dome shape in a hot vegetable dish, with a pinch of parsley in the centre. Place the dish on an underflat with dish paper.

## 1047 — Navets à la crème

### Method

Prepare, cook and serve as for Navets glacés (1043). When glazed, add ¾ pint (525 ml) of thin Sauce crème (389).

## 1048 Shallow fried onions — Oignons sautés / Oignons lyonnaise

| 8 portions | Ingredients | 10 couverts |
| --- | --- | --- |
| 4 lb | onions | 2·25 kg |
| 4 oz | first class dripping | 140 g |
| ⅓ oz | salt | 20 g |
| ½ teaspoon | ground white pepper | 2 g |
| 2 teaspoons | chopped parsley | 5 g |

### Method

1. Peel and wash the onions, cut them in halves from the top down, then cut away the root and finely shred.

2. Melt the dripping in a frying pan, add the onions and season. Fry gently, tossing over frequently, and allow them to cook for approximately 12–15 minutes, until tender and golden brown. Drain off any excess fat.

3. Serve in a vegetable dish and sprinkle them with chopped parsley. They are generally used as a garnish.

## 1049 French fried onions — Oignons frits à la française

| 8 portions | Ingredients | 10 couverts |
| --- | --- | --- |
| 2½ lb | medium to large onions | 1·4 kg |
| ⅝ pint | milk | 350 ml |
| 6 oz | flour | 210 g |
| ½ oz | salt | 20 g |

### Method

1. Peel and wash the onions and cut them across in slices 3 mm thick.

2. Remove the small centre rings (use these for other purposes). Separate the onion rings.

3. Dip in the milk, drain, then in the flour, shaking off any excess on a sieve.

4. Deep fry in 3–4 lots at 180°C (360°F) until crisp and golden brown. Drain, then season with the salt.

5. Serve in a loose dome shape in a vegetable or flat dish on dish paper.

## 1050 Braised onions — Oignons braisés

| 8 portions | Ingredients | 10 couverts |
| --- | --- | --- |
| 16 × 2 oz | onions | 20 × 55 g |
| 2 oz | dripping | 70 g |
| 2 teaspoons | chopped parsley | 5 g |
| 4 level teaspoons | salt | 15 g |
| 1 level teaspoon | sugar | 4 g |
| ½ level teaspoon | ground white pepper | 2 g |
| 1½ pints | white stock | 1 litre |
| ⅝ pint | demi-glace | 350 ml |

### Method

1. Peel the onions, removing only a little of the root, and wash.

2. Blanch in boiling salt water for 10 minutes and drain.

3. Heat the fat in a shallow pan or tray, then add the onions, seasoning and sugar. Lightly fry, turning them till coloured a light golden brown.

4. Add enough stock to come half way up the onions, and boil. Cover the pan with a greased paper and lid.

5. Braise in the bottom of an oven at 150°C (300°F) for approximately 1¼ hours, until tender. Test when they are cooked with knife point; it should penetrate the onions without undue pressure.

6. Remove the onions to a vegetable dish and keep them warm. Reduce the cooking liquor rapidly to an essence and add it to the demi-glace.

7. Mask this over the onions and place a pinch of chopped parsley on each onion. Place on an underflat with dish paper.

### 1051 Stuffed onions                                    Oignons farcis
**Method**

1. Prepare, cook and serve as for Oignons braisés (1050).
2. Prepare a half quantity of stuffing as for Courge farcie (1008).
3. After blanching the onions for 15 minutes (instead of 10 minutes), remove the centre. With a piping bag and a 20 mm plain tube, fill with the stuffing. Do not fry off.

### 1052 Peas                                              Petits pois

| 8 portions | Ingredients | 10 couverts |
|---|---|---|
| 4 lb | peas (in pod) or | 2·25 kg |
| 1¼ lb | peas (frozen) | 700 g |
| 2 sprigs | mint | 3 sprigs |

**Method**

1. Remove the fresh peas from the pods, discarding any bad ones, and wash them.
2. For both fresh and frozen peas, place them into boiling salted water with the mint. Reboil and skim, then cook them gently for 7–8 minutes (frozen), 15–16 minutes (fresh) and drain them in a colander. If required cold, refresh and drain. Finish as per recipe.

### 1053 Buttered peas                          Petits pois au beurre
**Method**

1. Prepare and cook the peas (1052) and drain them. Replace in the saucepan and add 2 oz (70 g) of butter, 1 teaspoon (5 g) each of salt and caster sugar, per 8 or 10 portions.
2. Toss over lightly to mix, until very hot. Serve in a loose dome shape in a hot vegetable dish on an underflat with dish paper.

### 1054                                     Petits pois à la menthe
**Method**

Prepare, cook and serve as for Petits pois au beurre (1053). Place 2 blanched and refreshed mint leaves per portion on top of the peas.

### 1055 Purée of fresh peas               Purée de pois frais
**Method**

1. Prepare and cook the peas (1052). If they are to be served as a vegetable for a main dish, increase the quantity by 25 per cent.
2. Refresh and drain, then rub them through a sieve. Heat 2 oz (70 g) of butter in a pan, add the purée and 1 teaspoon (5 g) each of salt and caster sugar per 8 or 10 portions.
3. Thoroughly mix with a spatule over the heat until hot.
4. Serve scrolled to a dome shape in a hot vegetable dish on an underflat with dish paper.

### 1056 Peas, French style               Petits pois à la française

| 8 portions | Ingredients | 10 couverts |
|---|---|---|
| 4 lb | peas (in pod) or | 2·25 kg |
| 1¼ lb | frozen peas | 700 g |
| 4 oz | small button or silver onions | 140 g |
| 2½ oz | butter | 85 g |
| ¾ oz | flour | 25 g |
| 4 level teaspoons | salt | 15 g |
| ½ level teaspoon | ground white pepper | 2 g |
| ½ level teaspoon | caster sugar | 2 g |
| 1 small | lettuce | 1 |

**Method**

1. Remove the fresh peas from the pod, discarding any bad ones, and wash them.
2. Remove any discoloured leaves from the lettuce, cut it in quarters, then wash and drain. Shred the lettuce finely across into a julienne. Peel and wash the button onions.
3. Place the peas, button onions, lettuce, salt, pepper, sugar and half the butter in a shallow pan or casserole. (If frozen peas are used, boil the onions for 10 minutes.)
4. Add sufficient white stock or water to come half way up the peas. Boil and cover, then place in the bottom of an oven at 150°C (300°F) to braise for 25–30 minutes, until tender. Test when the onions are cooked with the point of a knife.
5. Mix the remainder of the butter with the flour to a paste (Beurre manié). Shake into the peas in very small pieces, reboil, but do not allow to continue boiling.
6. Serve in the casserole on a hot vegetable dish on an underflat with dish paper.

### 1057                          Petits pois à la flamande
Petits pois et carottes panachées
**Method**

1. Prepare and cook the peas as for Petits pois au beurre (1053). Reduce the quantity by 40 per cent.
2. Peel and wash 1 lb (560 g) of carrots for 8 or 10 portions. Cut them in 25 mm lengths, then into sections, and turn them to a small barrel shape.

3. Cook as for Carottes glacées (969) then combine them with the peas.

4. Serve in a loose dome shape on a hot vegetable dish on an underflat with dish paper.

## 1058 Petits pois bonne femme

**Method**

1. Prepare, cook and serve as for Petits pois à la française (1056).

2. Add, when boiling, 3 oz (100 g), for 8 or 10 portions, of blanched and very lightly fried lardons of bacon, to flavour the peas.

## 1059 Stuffed pimentos Piments farcis

| 8 portions | Ingredients | 10 couverts |
|---|---|---|
| 8 × 3½ oz | red or green pimentos | 10 × 100 g |
| 3 oz | carrot | 100 g |
| 3 oz | onion | 100 g |
| ½ oz | salt | 20 g |
| ½ teaspoon | ground white pepper | 2 g |
| ¼ pint | white stock | 525 ml |
| small | bouquet garni | small |
| 8 portions | riz pilaff (615) | 10 couverts |

**Method**

1. Dip the pimentos in deep fat at 180°C (350°F) for 1 minute, or brush with oil and lightly grill under the salamander, in order to remove the skin.

2. Peel, cut out the stalk and remove all the seeds with a teaspoon.

3. Peel and wash the carrot and onion, cut them in thin slices, place them in a 150 mm deep pan and add the bouquet garni.

4. With a dessertspoon, fill the pimentos with the braised rice, which should be approximately three-quarters cooked. If desired, 2–4 oz (70–140 g) of chopped cooked ham or meat, diced cooked mushrooms, or 10 mm raw diced tomato may be added to the rice.

5. Place on the bed of roots in the pan and add the stock. Boil, season, then cover with a buttered paper and lid.

6. Braise in the bottom of an oven at 150°C (300°F) for approximately 45–50 minutes.

7. Serve neatly arranged in a hot vegetable dish on an underflat with dish paper.

## 1060 Buttered parsnips Panais au beurre

| 8 portions | Ingredients | 10 couverts |
|---|---|---|
| 2½ lb | parsnips | 1·4 kg |
| 2 oz | butter | 70 g |
| ½ oz | salt | 20 g |
| ½ teaspoon | ground white pepper | 2 g |

**Method**

1. Wash the parsnips, trim each end with a knife, peel, then rewash.

2. Starting at the thick end, cut them across into 40 mm lengths.

3. Cut these into 4, 6 or 8 sections down the length into evenly sized pieces. With a small knife, cut out the hard centre pieces.

4. Place in a shallow pan and add enough water to come three-quarters of the way up the parsnips.

5. Add the remainder of the ingredients, then boil, skim and cover. Cook steadily for 15 minutes, remove the cover and rapidly reduce the cooking liquor until it has evaporated. Test the vegetables with the knife point.

6. Serve in a loose dome shape in a hot vegetable dish on an underflat.

## 1061 Panais persillés

**Method**

Prepare, cook and serve as for Panais au beurre (1060) and sprinkle them with chopped parsley.

## 1062 Panais rissolés

**Method**

1. Prepare the parsnips as for Panais au beurre (1060), to include 3 in method.

2. Blanch for 2–3 minutes in boiling salted water then drain in a colander.

3. Toss over in 3 oz (100 g) of butter or first class dripping in a sauté pan or tray, until lightly coloured.

4. Season with the salt and pepper and finish to cook for 15–20 minutes in the centre of an oven at 190–200°C (375–400°F) until tender.

5. Serve, sprinkled with chopped parsley, in a hot vegetable dish on an underflat with dish paper.

## 1063 Pease pudding Purée de pois jaunes

## 1064 Purée of green peas Purée St Germain

| 8 portions | Ingredients | 10 couverts |
|---|---|---|
| 1 lb | yellow split peas (1063) | 560 g |
| 1 lb | green split peas (1064) | 560 g |
| 2 oz | carrot | 70 g |
| 2 oz | onion (stuck with clove) | 70 g |
| 2 oz | bacon bone or trimmings | 70 g |
| 2 oz | butter | 70 g |
| ½ oz | salt | 20 g |
| ½ teaspoon | ground white pepper | 2 g |

## Method

1. Prepare and cook the peas as for Haricots blancs (1025), keeping the amount of water low.
2. When cooked, thoroughly drain in a colander.
3. Rub through a sieve, place into a clean pan, add the butter and pepper.
4. Stir with a spatule over the heat until hot.
5. Usually used as a garnish, piped in scrolls with a 10 mm star tube, or served in a vegetable dish, scrolled to a dome shape.

## 1065 Leeks        Poireaux

| 8 portions | Ingredients | 10 couverts |
|---|---|---|
| 3 lb (8 × 6 oz) | leeks | 1·7 kg (10 × 170 g) |
| | salt | |

## Method

1. Remove one layer of the skin from the leeks and very lightly trim across the root. Cut off the green leaves 25 mm above where the white part finishes, cutting to a point.
2. Cut down the centre of the leek, commencing 10 mm from the root. Thoroughly wash and soak if necessary to remove all dirt or mud.
4. Tie in bundles of 3–4 with a string 10 mm from each end.
5. Plunge into plenty of boiling salted water. Reboil rapidly, then skim and boil gently for 20–25 minutes until tender. Test with knife point; it should penetrate the leek without pressure.
6. Drain, cut through the remaining uncut 10 mm to divide the leeks in halves. Fold the green part underneath. Dress in a vegetable dish and finish as per recipe.

## 1066 Leeks, Cream sauce        Poireaux, sauce crème

### Method

Prepare and cook the leeks (1065). Serve in a hot vegetable dish. Mask over with ½ pint (350 ml) of sauce crème (389). Place a pinch of chopped parsley on the centre of each piece.

## 1067        Poireaux milanaise

### Method

1. Prepare and cook the leeks (1065). Dress them neatly in rows in a vegetable dish, brush them with melted butter and sprinkle evenly with grated cheese.
2. Colour lightly under a moderate salamander. Place the dish on an underflat with dish paper.

## 1068 Braised leeks        Poireaux braisés

### Method

1. Prepare the leeks as for 1065. Blanch for 2–3 minutes in salted water and refresh, then drain.
2. Place in a shallow pan and add three-quarters of their depth of greasy white stock. Add salt and pepper to season and bring to the boil.
3. Cover with a buttered paper and lid. Braise in the bottom of an oven at 150°C (300°F) for 50–60 minutes. Finish as per recipe.

## 1069        Poireaux au jus

### Method

1. Prepare and braise the leeks (1068).
2. When cooked, remove from the pan, divide them in halves, fold the green underneath the white part and place them in a hot vegetable dish.
3. Remove the fat from the stock and reduce it to an essence. Add this to ½ pint (350 ml) of jus-lié and mask it over the leeks. Place a pinch of chopped parsley on each leek. Serve the dish on an underflat with dish paper.

## 1070 Salsify        Salsifis

### Method

1. Allow 4 oz (110 g) per portion. Wash the salsify, scrape or peel to remove the skin, rewash and cut them in 50–60 mm lengths.
2. Plunge them immediately into enough blanc (341) to cover them, reboil, then simmer for 40–45 minutes, until cooked. Test with knife point, which should penetrate without undue pressure.
3. Thoroughly drain in a colander. Finish as per recipe. Salsify may be finished as for any of the cauliflower recipes (994 to 1000 inclusive).

## 1071        Salsifis frits

### Method

1. Prepare and cook the salsify (1070), thoroughly drain and wipe it with a cloth.
2. Pass through frying batter (677), deep fry at 180°C (360°F) until golden brown, then drain and lightly season with salt.
3. Serve on a hot flat dish on dish paper. Garnish with sprigs of fried parsley.

276

## 1072 Grilled tomatoes        Tomates grillées

**Method**

1. Select medium-sized tomatoes. With the point of a knife, remove the stalk base (eye).
2. Invert, then make two 10 mm incisions, crosswise, to just penetrate through the skin.
3. Place on an oiled tray, brush over with oil, season with salt and pepper.
4. Grill under a moderate salamander for 4–6 minutes, according to firmness.
5. Generally used as a garnish.

## 1073 Poached tomatoes        Tomates pochées

**Method**

1. Select small tomatoes. Remove the stalk base (eye) with the point of a knife.
2. Blanch them in boiling water for 6–10 seconds, then refresh and remove the skins.
3. Placing them on the base side, pack closely in a buttered sauteuse or tray and season with salt and pepper.
4. Place a small knob of butter on each tomato and cover them with a buttered paper.
5. Cook in an oven at 150–160°C (300–325°F) for 4–6 minutes until just soft but not collapsed.
6. Generally used as a garnish.

## 1074 Stuffed tomatoes (duxelle)    Tomates farcies (duxelle)

| 8 portions | Ingredients | 10 couverts |
|---|---|---|
| 2 lb (16 × 2 oz) | tomatoes (MM) | 1·1 kg (20 × 55 g) |
| 1 oz | finely chopped onion | 35 g |
| 6 oz | mushroom stalks or trimmings | 210 g |
| 1 oz | butter | 35 g |
| 2 oz | chopped ham | 70 g |
| 2 oz | white breadcrumbs | 70 g |
| 2 teaspoons | chopped parsley | 5 g |
| 4 level teaspoons | salt | 15 g |
| ½ level teaspoon | ground white pepper | 2 g |
| ¼ pint | jus-lié | 175 ml |

**Method**

1. Wash the tomatoes and remove the stalk base (eye).
2. Cut across to remove one-quarter of the tomato and retain it for the caps. Remove the centre pulp and seeds, pass it through a conical strainer and retain the juice.
3. Place the tomato cases in a greased tray and season them lightly with a little salt and pepper.
4. Sweat the onion in the butter in a sauteuse for 4–5

minutes, without colouring. Add the washed and finely chopped mushrooms and cook it for a further 5–6 minutes

5. Add the seasoning, crumbs, ham, chopped parsley and the strained juice and thoroughly mix them together. If the mixture is a little tight, add a spoonful of the jus-lié.
6. Pass the tomato cases through an oven at 150°C (300°F) for 2 minutes only.
7. With a piping bag and a 10 mm star tube, pipe the mixture into the cases to just above the top edge.
8. Place the 'caps' on at a slight angle and brush them with melted butter. Cook in the oven at 150°C (300°F) for 3–4 minutes until only just soft.
9. Serve in a hot vegetable dish on an underflat with dish paper. Surround the base of the tomatoes with the jus-lié.

*Note.* Stuffed tomatoes are used extensively for garnish.

## 1075        Tomates farcies à la provençale

| 8 portions | Ingredients | 10 couverts |
|---|---|---|
| 1½ lb (8 × 3 oz) | tomatoes (M) | 850 g (10 × 85 g) |
| 2 oz | finely chopped onion | 70 g |
| 3 oz | butter | 100 g |
| 8 oz | white breadcrumbs | 280 g |
| 4 teaspoons | chopped parsley | 10 g |
| 4 level teaspoons | salt | 15 g |
| ½ level teaspoon | ground white pepper | 2 g |
| 1 pod | garlic | 1 pod |

**Method**

1. Wash the tomatoes and remove the stalk base (eye).
2. Cut them across in halves and remove the seeds and centre core with a spoon.
3. Place the halves on a greased tray and place it in an oven at 150°C (300°F) for 2 minutes to slightly soften the tomatoes.
4. Melt the butter in a sauteuse, add the onion, cover, then sweat them for 5–6 minutes, colouring very lightly.
5. Add the peeled and finely chopped garlic, then sweat for a further 3–4 minutes.
6. Add the remainder of the ingredients and mix them thoroughly.
7. Fill the tomato cases, using a dessert spoon, with the prepared crumbs in a dome shape.
8. Sprinkle with a little melted butter, return to the oven for 4–5 minutes to complete cooking and lightly colour the crumbs.
9. Serve in a hot vegetable dish on an underflat with dish paper.

# Potatoes

# Potatoes

# Pommes de terre

## 1076  Plain boiled potatoes — Pommes nature

| 8 portions | Ingredients | 10 couverts |
|---|---|---|
| 4 lb | potatoes | 2·25 kg |
| ½ oz | salt | 20 g |

**Method**

1. Wash, peel and rewash small evenly sized potatoes.
2. If necessary, trim them to an even shape and size; do not turn.
3. Place them in a saucepan, cover with cold water and add the salt. Boil, remove all scum, cover and simmer for approximately 20 minutes. Test with the point of a knife: it should penetrate without undue pressure.
4. Using the cover, drain off all water and replace the pan on the stove to dry off any excess moisture.
5. Serve in a hot vegetable dish, with an underflat, on a dish paper.

## 1077 — Pommes au beurre

**Method**

Prepare, cook and serve as for Pommes nature (1076). Brush liberally with melted butter.

## 1078 — Pommes persillées

**Method**

1. Prepare the potatoes, turning three pieces per portion the size of a 2 oz (55 g) egg; cook and serve as for Pommes nature (1076).
2. Brush liberally with melted butter and sprinkle with chopped parsley.

## 1079  Mashed potatoes — Pommes purée

**Method**

1. Prepare and cook as for Pommes nature (1076). If larger potatoes are used, cut them into evenly sized pieces. For the best results in all mashed potatoes, a floury type should be used, e.g. King Edward.
2. When dried off, pass small quantities at a time through a sieve with pressure. Do not rub the potatoes through the sieve, as this will cause a rubbery mixture.
3. Replace in a clean saucepan, add 2 oz (70 g) of butter, ½ level teaspoon (2 g) of ground white pepper and a pinch of grated nutmeg for each 8 or 10 portions.
4. Thoroughly mix with a wooden spatule over the heat, then gradually add approximately ¼ pint (175 ml) of boiling milk.
5. Serve in a scrolled dome shape in a hot vegetable dish, on an underflat with dish paper.

## 1080 — Pommes purée à la crème

**Method**

Prepare, cook, serve as for Pommes purée (1079); surround the base with a little hot cream.

## 1081 — Pommes mousseline

**Method**

1. Prepare, cook and serve as for Pommes purée (1079).
2. At the moment of serving, fold in ¼ pint (175 ml) of soft whipped cream.

## 1082 — Pommes purée au gratin

**Method**

1. Prepare, cook and serve as for Pommes purée (1079).
2. When scrolled, sprinkle evenly with grated cheese and melted butter and gratiné under a moderate salamander.

## 1083  Snow potatoes — Pommes à la neige

**Method**

1. Prepare and cook as for Pommes nature (1076).
2. When dried off, pass the potatoes through a coarse wire sieve, or potato ricer, direct into a hot vegetable dish, in a mound like snow. Do not shape.

## 1084  New potatoes — Pommes nouvelles

The sources of supply of new potatoes vary considerably today, and this has caused some rethinking about the usual methods of preparation. For a good presentation, many types of new potatoes need peeling before use; those with a very fine soft skin may be cooked and peeled after cooking, but they are few in number.

| 8 portions | Ingredients | 10 couverts |
|---|---|---|
| 2½ lb | new potatoes | 1·4 kg |
| ½ oz | salt | 20 g |
| 2–3 | sprigs of mint | 3–4 |

## Method

1. Scrub the potatoes clean (peel if necessary) and rewash.

2. Place in a saucepan, cover with boiling water and add the salt. Boil, skim, add the mint and simmer for approximately 20 minutes. Test with the point of a knife: it should easily penetrate the potato.

3. If not previously peeled, drain the potatoes, cool them slightly, then peel and place them in a pan of cold water. Bring to the boil, skim off any scum and add a little salt.

4. In both cases, drain with the lid of the pan. Serve in a hot vegetable dish, finishing the potatoes according to the name of the recipe, on an underflat with dish paper.

### 1085      Pommes nouvelles au beurre

## Method

Prepare, cook and serve as for Pommes nouvelles (1084). Brush the potatoes liberally with melted butter.

### 1086      Pommes nouvelles à la menthe

## Method

Prepare, cook and serve (1084). Brush the potatoes liberally with melted butter and decorate on top with two blanched and refreshed mint leaves per portion.

### 1087      Pommes nouvelles persillées

## Method

Prepare, cook and serve the potatoes (1084). When drained, place them in a sauteuse with 2 oz (70 g) of butter per 8 or 10 portions and season with a little ground white pepper. Sprinkle with 3 dessertspoons (10 g) of chopped parsley and roll the potatoes gently around to coat them with the butter and parsley.

### 1088      Pommes nouvelles rissolées

## Method

1. Prepare and cook the potatoes (1084) and drain them.

2. Melt 2 oz (70 g) of first class dripping in a frying pan and add the potatoes to it.

3. Roll the potatoes in the fat over a fairly fast heat to colour them a light golden brown. Drain, add 1 oz (35 g) of butter for 8 or 10 portions and roll the potatoes in it to coat them.

4. Serve in a loose dome shape in a hot vegetable dish; sprinkle with chopped parsley. Place the dish on an underflat with dish paper.

### 1089    Duchess potatoes, basic mixture    Pommes duchesse

| 8 portions | Ingredients | 10 couverts |
|---|---|---|
| 4 lb | potatoes | 2·25 kg |
| 2 oz | butter | 70 g |
| ½ oz | salt | 20 g |
| ¼ level teaspoon | ground white pepper | 2 g |
| few grains | grated nutmeg | few grains |
| 2 | yolks of egg | 3 |

## Method

1. Wash, peel and rewash the potatoes and cut them into evenly sized pieces.

2. Place in a saucepan, cover with cold water and add the salt.

3. Bring to the boil and skim, then cover the pan and allow them to simmer for approximately 20 minutes, until cooked.

4. Using the cover, drain off all the water. Return the pan to the stove to thoroughly dry off any moisture.

5. Pass through a sieve with pressure; do not rub through.

6. Return to a clean pan, add the butter, pepper and nutmeg. Thoroughly mix with a wooden spatula over the heat, until hot. Add the yolks of egg and mix well. This is the prepared basic mixture.

7. Half fill a piping bag with a 10 mm star tube, with the basic mixture, and pipe the potato in slightly spiralled mounds 40 mm in diameter, 50 mm high, on to lightly greased baking sheets. Allow two pieces per portion.

8. Place in the centre of an oven at 190–200°C (375–400°F), to dry the outer surface, for 2–3 minutes.

9. Brush all over with egg wash then return to the oven for 3–4 minutes to colour the potatoes a golden brown.

10. Serve in a hot vegetable or flat dish on a dish paper. Garnish in between with sprigs of parsley.

### 1090      Pommes marquise

## Method

1. Prepare, cook and serve as for Pommes duchesse (1089).

2. When piping the potato, keep the sides straight, instead of in a spiral, and leave a small hole in the centre, so that the shape resembles a nest.

3. After egg-washing at 9 in method, fill the centre with cooked Tomato concassé (337). Allow 8 oz (280 g) of tomato per 8 or 10 portions.

## 1091          Pommes Berny

**Method**

1. Prepare a basic duchess mixture (1089), adding $\frac{1}{2}$ oz (20 g) of finely chopped truffle to the mixture.

2. With a little flour, roll the potato into a cylindrical shape and divide it into 24 or 30 pieces. Roll these into small balls (serve 3 per portion).

3. Pass through beaten egg and 6 oz (210 g) chopped almonds.

4. Deep fry 8–10 pieces at a time at 180°C (360°F) until golden brown, then drain. Serve in a hot vegetable or flat dish on a dish paper. Garnish with sprigs of fried parsley.

## 1092 Croquette potatoes     Pommes croquettes

**Method**

1. Prepare a basic duchess mixture (1089).

2. With a little flour, roll out and divide into 24–30 pieces. Roll these into balls, eliminating all cracks, then into a cylinder shape 50 mm long × 25 mm in diameter.

3. Pass through beaten egg and 6 oz (200 g) for 8–10 portions, of white breadcrumbs.

4. Finish and serve as for Pommes Berny (1091) from 4 in method.

## 1093          Pommes brioche

**Method**

1. Prepare a basic duchess mixture (1089).

2. Roll out three-quarters of the mixture and divide it into 16–20 pieces (serve 2 per portion). Roll these pieces into 50 mm balls, place them on a greased baking sheet and press the top with the thumb to indent slightly.

3. Roll out the remainder of mixture and divide it into 16–20 pieces. Roll these into small 20 mm balls and place one on top of each base to form a small brioche.

4. Finish and serve as for Pommes duchesse (1089) from 8 in method.

## 1094          Pommes galette

**Method**

1. Prepare a basic duchess mixture (1089).

2. With a little flour, form it into a roll and divide it into 16 or 20 pieces (serve 2 per portion).

3. Mould these into balls 50 mm in diameter, then lightly flatten them with a palette knife until they are 20 mm thick. Mark across with a 10 mm trellis pattern.

4. Place on a greased and lightly floured baking sheet.

5. Finish and serve as for Pommes duchesse (1089) from 8 in method. When served, brush over with melted butter.

## 1095          Pommes St Florentin

**Method**

1. Prepare a basic duchess mixture (1089), adding 3 oz (100 g) of chopped ham per 8 or 10 portions.

2. Finish as for Pommes Berny (1091) from 2 in method. Replace the chopped almonds with crushed vermicelli.

## 1096          Pommes Lorette

| 8 portions | Ingredients | | 10 couverts |
|---|---|---|---|
| 3 lb | potatoes into duchess mix | | 1·7 kg |
| 3 oz | butter ⎤ | | 100 g |
| 7½ oz | flour ⎟ for | | 250 g |
| 4 level teaspoons | salt ⎬ choux | | 15 g |
| 6 | eggs ⎟ paste | | 7 |
| ¾ pint | water ⎦ | | 525 ml |

**Method**

1. Prepare a basic duchess mixture (1089).

2. From the other ingredients, prepare a stiff choux paste (343).

3. Gradually mix the paste into the potato until they are thoroughly combined.

4. With a little flour, roll lengthwise until 25 mm in diameter and divide this into 24–30 pieces, cutting well on the slant. Then roll to a cigar shape approximately 60 mm long. Fry 8–10 pieces at a time at 160°C (320°F) for approximately 5–6 minutes. Turn, during frying, until golden brown on all sides.

5. Drain, then arrange them in a hot vegetable or flat dish on a dish paper. Garnish with sprigs of fried parsley.

## 1097          Pommes dauphine

**Method**

1. Prepare a basic duchess and choux paste mixture as for Pommes lorette (1096).

2. Prepare greased pieces of paper on a tray.

3. Mould the mixture into a dessertspoon, using the side of the pan, to form a rounded surface. With another spoon dipped in water, cut the mixture out of the dessert-spoon and place it on the paper (8–10 pieces per piece of paper). Allow 3 pieces per portion.

4. Remove the paper carefully, releasing one end into the fat. Deep fry and serve as for Pommes Lorette (1096).

## 1098 Pommes chips

**Method**

1. Wash, peel and rewash selected medium-size potatoes.
2. Cut them in thin slices (1 mm thick) with a mandolin. Wash thoroughly, drain and dry in a cloth.
3. Deep fry at 180°C (360°F), moving the potatoes around until a light golden brown. Drain thoroughly and sprinkle lightly with salt.

Pommes chips are used mainly for garnish purposes and cocktail side dishes.

## 1099 Pommes gaufrettes

**Method**

1. Prepare and cook as for Pommes chips (1098).
2. Use the corrugated blade on the mandolin, and turn each slice of the potato at right angles after each cut to produce corrugations in the form of a trellis pattern on each slice.

## 1100 Pommes cheveux

**Method**

1. Cut the peeled potatoes in very thin slices on a mandolin, then cut the slices across into a very fine julienne.
2. Wash thoroughly, drain and dry in a cloth. Deep fry at 180°C (360°F) until light golden brown. Drain well, lightly sprinkle with salt. Pommes cheveux are used as a garnish.

## 1101 Straw potatoes Pommes paille

**Method**

1. Cut the peeled potatoes in 1·5 mm slices on a mandolin, then cut along the slices into 1·5 mm julienne. Finish as for Pommes cheveux (1100) from 2 in method.

## 1102 Matchstick potatoes Pommes allumettes

**Method**

1. Allow 8 oz (225 g) of potatoes per portion. Wash, peel, and rewash the potatoes.
2. Trim on all sides to give straight edges. Cut into slices 50 mm long × 3 mm thick, then cut lengthways into 3 mm-thick pieces, to give a finished size of 50 × 3 × 3 mm.
3. Wash well, drain and dry in a cloth. Deep fry at 180°C (360°F) until golden brown.
4. Drain well and sprinkle lightly with salt. Serve in a hot vegetable or flat dish on a dish paper.

## 1103 Pommes mignonnettes

**Method**

1. Allow 8 oz (225 g) of potatoes per portion. Wash, peel and rewash them.
2. Trim on all sides to give straight edges. Cut in slices 50 mm long × 5 mm thick. Then cut lengthways 5 mm thick, to give a finished size 50 × 5 × 5 mm.
3. Wash and well drain. Deep fry to blanch at 140°C (280°F) until just cooked (test by pressing between the fingers) then remove them from the frying medium.
4. To finish, re-fry the potatoes at 180°C (360°F) until golden brown, then drain and sprinkle lightly with salt.
5. Serve in a hot vegetable or flat dish on a dish paper.

## 1104 Fried potatoes Pommes frites

**Method**

Prepare, blanch and re-fry to finish as for Pommes mignonnettes (1103). Cut the potatoes into pieces 50 × 10 × 10 mm.

## 1105 Pommes Pont Neuf

**Method**

1. Wash, peel and rewash fairly large potatoes.
2. Cut them 60 × 20 × 20 mm. Blanch at 140°C (280°F) for 6–7 minutes.
3. Finish and serve as for Pommes mignonnettes (1103) from 4 in method.

## 1106 Pommes bataille

**Method**

1. Use fairly large potatoes. Serve 8 oz (225 g) per portion.
2. Trim the potatoes on all sides, then cut them into 20 mm dice; wash and drain.
3. Deep fry to blanch at 140°C (280°F) until cooked (approximately 6–7 minutes).
4. Finish and serve as for Pommes mignonnettes (1103) from 4 in method.

## 1107 Pommes copeaux

**Method**

1. Wash, peel and rewash selected large potatoes.
2. Cut them in 20 mm-thick slices and trim the edges straight with a knife. Using a peeler, make 150–175 mm lengths to represent shavings; wash and drain.

3. Deep fry at 180°C (360°F) until golden brown, then drain and season lightly with salt.

4. Serve in a hot vegetable or flat dish on a dish paper.

## 1108 Steamed potatoes — Pommes vapeur

**Method**

1. Allow 8 oz (225 g) of potatoes per portion. Wash, peel and rewash.

2. Turn them to a barrel shape the size of a 2 oz (55 g) egg.

3. Place in a steamer tray, on a cloth, and season them lightly with salt. Cover with a clean cloth.

4. Steam for approximately 20 minutes, then test with a knife point; it should easily penetrate the potato.

5. Serve in a hot vegetable dish and garnish with sprigs of picked parsley. Place the dish on an underflat with dish paper.

## 1109 Sauté potatoes — Pommes sautées

| 8 portions | Ingredients | 10 couverts |
| --- | --- | --- |
| 4 lb | potatoes | 2·25 kg |
| 4 oz | first class dripping | 140 g |
| 2 oz | butter | 70 g |
| 2 teaspoons | chopped parsley | 5 g |
| ½ oz | salt | 20 g |
| ½ level teaspoon | ground white pepper | 2 g |

**Method**

1. Select medium-size potatoes, approximately 45 mm in diameter. Scrub the potatoes.

2. Place in a steamer tray and steam them for approximately 20 minutes. Do not overcook. The potatoes may be boiled in the skins if desired.

3. Allow to cool then peel them cleanly with a small knife. Cut into 5 mm slices on to plates.

4. Melt the dripping in a clean frying pan. When lightly smoking, add the sliced potatoes until they half fill the pan. Season with salt and pepper.

5. Fry the potatoes quickly, turning the potatoes 4 or 5 times, with a toss of the pan, during cooking.

6. When the potatoes are golden brown, drain them in a colander, with a pie dish beneath.

7. Re-toss in the frying pan with the butter.

8. Serve in a loose dome shape in a hot vegetable dish and sprinkle with the chopped parsley. Place the dish on an underflat with dish paper.

## 1110 — Pommes lyonnaise

**Method**

1. Prepare and cook 4 oz (140 g) of onions for 8 or 10 portions as for Oignons lyonnaise (1048).

2. Sprinkle the onions into the Pommes sautées (1109) at 7 in method and serve.

## 1111 — Pommes château

| 8 portions | Ingredients | 10 couverts |
| --- | --- | --- |
| 4 lb | potatoes | 2·25 kg |
| 3 oz | first class dripping | 100 g |
| 1 oz | butter | 35 g |
| ½ oz | salt | 20 g |
| ½ level teaspoon | ground white pepper | 2 g |
| 2 teaspoons | chopped parsley | 5 g |

**Method**

1. Select suitably sized potatoes and wash, peel and rewash them. Turn them to a barrel shape the size of a 2 oz (55 g) egg; allow 3 pieces per portion.

2. Place them in a wide shallow pan and barely cover them with cold water. Boil rapidly over a very fast heat then drain in a colander.

3. Heat the dripping in a roasting tray until a blue haze appears. Add the blanched potatoes and fry them quickly, turning with a slice until a light golden brown.

4. Drain off any excess fat then season them. Place in the centre to top of an oven at 200°C (400°F) to finish cooking (approximately 20 minutes). Shake the potatoes over during cooking. Colour them a light golden brown.

5. Serve in a loose dome shape in a hot vegetable dish. Brush over with the melted butter and sprinkle with chopped parsley. Place the dish on an underflat with dish paper.

*Note.* The potatoes are prepared half the normal size for garnishes.

## 1112 — Pommes flamande

**Method**

1. Prepare, cook and serve as for Pommes berrichonne (1117), omitting the lardons.

2. When cooked, add 4 oz (140 g) of 25 mm-long turned glazed carrots (969).

## 1113 — Pommes rissolées

**Method**

1. Prepare, cook and serve the potatoes as for Pommes

château (1111). The potatoes should be of a 2 oz (55 g) even round shape, or they can be turned. Colour them to a golden brown.

## 1114 Fondant potatoes　　　　Pommes fondantes

**Method**

1. Prepare the potatoes as for Pommes château (1111) up to and including 3 in method, only slightly colouring them.
2. Drain off any excess fat then moisten the tray with a good white stock which comes half way up the potatoes.
3. Brush the potatoes with melted butter and cover them with a buttered paper. Place in the centre of an oven at 200°C (400°F) and cook for approximately 20 minutes until soft. Brush with melted butter during cooking. Remove the paper 5 minutes before cooked to colour them a light golden brown.
4. Serve in a hot vegetable dish. Brush them with melted butter and sprinkle with chopped parsley. Place the dish on an underflat with dish paper.

## 1115　　　　Pommes crétan

**Method**

Prepare, cook and serve the potatoes as for Pommes fondantes (1114). Before placing them in the oven, sprinkle the potatoes with a little finely chopped and sieved fresh thyme.

## 1116　　　　Pommes Champignol

**Method**

1. Prepare, cook and serve the potatoes as for Pommes fondantes (1114). Before placing them in the oven, sprinkle the potatoes with 3 oz (100 g) of grated cheese for 8 or 10 portions; do not cover but allow the cheese to glaze light golden brown during cooking.
2. When serving, omit the chopped parsley.

## 1117　　　　Pommes berrichonne

**Method**

1. Prepare, cook and serve the potatoes as for Pommes fondantes (1114).
2. Prepare and blanch 2 oz (70 g) of small lardons of bacon, and peel 4 oz (140 g) of very small button onions per 8 or 10 portions.
3. Add these to the potatoes when lightly colouring the potatoes in the fat.

## 1118　　　　Pommes au lard

**Method**

Prepare, cook and serve as for Pommes berrichonne (1117). Cut the potatoes into 20 mm dice instead of turning them, and double the quantity of lardons.

## 1119　　　　Pommes Parmentier

| 8 portions | Ingredients | 10 couverts |
| --- | --- | --- |
| 4 lb | potatoes | 2·25 kg |
| 4 oz | first class dripping | 140 g |
| 1 oz | butter | 35 g |
| ½ oz | salt | 20 g |
| ½ level teaspoon | ground white pepper | 2 g |
| 2 teaspoons | chopped parsley | 5 g |

**Method**

1. Select large potatoes and wash, peel and rewash them.
2. Trim them on all sides to give straight edges then cut them into 20 mm dice.
3. Place in a wide shallow pan and barely cover with cold water. Boil rapidly over a very fast heat then drain in a colander.
4. Heat the dripping in a clean frying pan until a blue haze appears, then add the diced potato. Fry rapidly and toss over to colour a light golden brown; drain off any excess fat.
5. Season them with the salt and pepper and place in the centre of an oven at 180–200°C (365–400°F) to finish cooking, for approximately 12–15 minutes.
6. Serve in a loose dome shape in a hot vegetable dish. Brush the potatoes with melted butter and sprinkle them with chopped parsley. Place the dish on an underflat with dish paper.

## 1120　　　　Pommes bordelaise

**Method**

Prepare, cook and serve as for Pommes Parmentier (1119). Sprinkle 1 pod of peeled and finely chopped garlic on the potatoes before placing them in the oven.

## 1121　　　　Pommes bretonne

| 8 portions | Ingredients | 10 couverts |
| --- | --- | --- |
| 4 lb | potatoes | 2·25 kg |
| 1 lb | tomatoes | 560 g |
| 4 oz | onions | 140 g |
| 3 oz | first class dripping | 100 g |
| 1 oz | butter | 35 g |
| ½ oz | salt | 20 g |
| 2 teaspoons | ground white pepper | 5 g |
| ½ level teaspoon | chopped parsley | 2 g |
| ½ pod | garlic | ¼ pod |
| 1 pint | white stock | 700 ml |

## Method

1. Prepare as for Pommes Parmentier (1119) up to and including 4 in method. Colour the potatoes very lightly.

2. Place them in a shallow tray and season with salt and pepper.

3. Meanwhile, peel the onions, cut them into 3 mm dice and cook them in the butter. Prepare the tomatoes into 10 mm raw dice.

4. Sprinkle the onion and tomato over the potato and add the peeled and finely chopped garlic.

5. Moisten with the boiling stock to come approximately one-third up the potatoes.

6. Cook in the centre of an oven at 190–200°C (375–400°F) until cooked (approximately 15–20 minutes).

7. Serve in a loose dome shape in a hot vegetable dish. Brush the surface with melted butter and sprinkle with chopped parsley.

## 1122 Pommes noisette

| 8 portions | Ingredients | 10 couverts |
|---|---|---|
| 4 lb | potatoes | 2·25 kg |
| 4 oz | first class dripping | 140 g |
| 1 oz | butter | 35 g |
| ½ oz | salt | 20 g |
| ½ level teaspoon | ground white pepper | 2 g |
| 2 teaspoons | chopped parsley | 5 g |

## Method

1. Use large potatoes and wash, peel and rewash them.

2. With a 15 mm ball cutter, cut the potatoes into balls. When using the scoop, the first edge should enter the potato at an angle of 45°; press inwards, until the opposite edge is level with the edge of the outside of the potato, then turn and twist the scoop to produce a ball of potato.

3. Place the potato balls in a wide shallow pan and barely cover them with cold water. Boil on a very fast heat and drain them immediately in a colander.

4. Heat the dripping in a frying pan; when it starts to smoke, add the potato balls, fry them rapidly until a light golden brown then drain off the surplus fat.

5. Season the potatoes, add the butter and cook them in the centre of an oven at 190–200°C (375–400°F) for 10–12 minutes until soft.

6. Sprinkle with the chopped parsley and serve in a loose dome shape in a hot vegetable dish on an underflat with dish paper.

## 1123 Pommes parisienne

## Method

1. Prepare, cook and serve the potatoes as for Pommes noisettes (1122).

2. When cutting, use a 20 mm ball scoop.

3. When coloured at 4 in method, transfer the potato balls to a shallow tray. When cooked, add 2 fl. oz (70 ml) of slightly thinned meat glaze. Roll the potatoes to coat with the glaze.

## 1124 Pommes olivette

## Method

Prepare, cook and serve the potatoes as for Pommes noisettes (1122). When cutting the potatoes, use a 30 mm long oval scoop.

## 1125 Pommes cocotte

## Method

Prepare and cook as for Pommes château (1111), turning the potatoes to approximately one-quarter of the size. Pommes cocotte are used for garnishing purposes.

## 1126 Pommes en robe de chambre

## Method

1. Select one large 7–8 oz (200–225 g) potato per portion.

2. Scrub well to clean. Steam for 25 minutes, or until cooked.

3. With a knife point, cleanly remove a 10 mm band of the skin from around the circumference.

4. Serve on a serviette on a hot vegetable or flat dish. Garnish between the potatoes with sprigs of parsley.

## 1127 Pommes à la crème

| 8 portions | Ingredients | 10 couverts |
|---|---|---|
| 4 lb | potatoes | 2·25 kg |
| 1 oz | butter | 35 g |
| ½ oz | salt | 20 g |
| ½ level teaspoon | ground white pepper | 2 g |
| ¾ pint | milk | 525 ml |

## Method

1. Select then wash medium size potatoes. Steam them for approximately 20 minutes, until only just cooked.

2. Peel the potatoes and cut them into 5 mm-thick slices. Place these in a buttered shallow pan (plat sauté).

3. Season, add the milk and bring gently to the boil. Cover and place on the side of the stove for 15 minutes to

allow the starch from the potatoes to thicken the milk. If desired, a part of the milk can be replaced with cream.

4. Serve in a loose dome shape in a hot vegetable dish on an underflat with dish paper.

## 1128          Pommes maître d'hôtel

### Method

Prepare, cook and serve as for Pommes à la crème (1127). Sprinkle the finished potatoes with chopped parsley.

## 1129          Pommes Delmonico

| 8 portions | Ingredients | 10 couverts |
|---|---|---|
| 4 lb | potatoes | 2·25 kg |
| 2 oz | butter | 70 g |
| 1 oz | grated cheese | 35 g |
| 1 oz | white breadcrumbs | 35 g |
| ½ oz | salt | 20 g |
| ½ level teaspoon | ground white pepper | 2 g |
| 1 pint | milk | 700 ml |

### Method

1. Select large potatoes, then wash, peel and rewash them. Trim the edges and cut them into 10 mm dice.

2. Place them in a wide shallow pan and barely cover with cold water. Boil rapidly on a very fast heat, drain in a colander then replace in the pan.

3. Add the milk and seasoning, bring to the boil, cover and simmer gently for approximately 30 minutes.

4. Carefully transfer the potatoes to a buttered earthenware dish and sprinkle them with the grated cheese and breadcrumbs, then with the melted butter.

5. Colour light golden brown under a moderate salamander or in the top of a hot oven.

6. Serve on an underflat with dish paper.

## 1130          Pommes dauphinoise

### Method

1. Use the same ingredients as for Pommes Delmonico (1129). Omit the breadcrumbs and treble the quantity of cheese, using gruyère.

2. Wash, peel and rewash small to medium potatoes. Cut across the width into 5 mm-thick slices.

3. Place the slices in a buttered shallow pan, then add the milk, salt, pepper and half the grated cheese.

5. Boil, cover and cook on the bottom of an oven at 150°C (300°F) for 30 minutes, until soft.

5. Finish and serve as for Pommes Delmonico (1129) from 4 in method, omitting the breadcrumbs.

## 1131   Baked jacket potatoes       Pommes au four

### Method

1. Select one large 7–8 oz (200–225 g) potato per portion and scrub it thoroughly to clean.

2. Place it in a tray on a shallow bed of coarse salt, or, alternatively, wrap in paper.

3. Bake in the centre to bottom of an oven at 190°C (375°F) for approximately 1 hour, turning after 30 minutes. Test when it is ready with the point of a knife: it should easily penetrate the potato.

4. Serve on a serviette on a hot flat dish and garnish with sprigs of parsley.

## 1132          Pommes en surprise

### Method

1. Prepare and cook as for Pommes au four (1131).

2. Cut off approximately one-quarter of each potato. With a dessertspoon, remove the potato from the casing and 'cap'.

3. Pass the potato through a sieve with pressure and place it in a saucepan with 2 oz (70 g) of butter per 8 or 10 portions; add a little salt, pepper and a few grains of nutmeg. Gradually add 3 fl. oz (100 ml) of cream. A little chopped ham and chopped chives or parsley may be added if desired.

4. With a piping bag and a 10 mm star tube, fill the casing, finishing with a raised scrolled edge on one side. Replace the cap at an angle.

5. Pass through an oven at 180°C (350°F) for 5–6 minutes to reheat.

6. Serve on a serviette on a hot flat dish and garnish with sprigs of parsley between the potatoes.

## 1133          Pommes Macaire

### Method

1. Prepare and cook as for Pommes au four (1131).

2. When cooked, cut the potatoes cross-ways in halves and remove the potato with a spoon. Pass through a coarse sieve with pressure and place into a basin.

3. For each 8 or 10 portions, add 2 oz (70 g) of butter, ½ oz (20 g) salt, ½ level teaspoon (2 g) of ground white pepper and 4 teaspoons (10 g) of chopped parsley; thoroughly mix them together with a spatule.

4. Melt 2 oz (70 g) of butter or first class dripping in a suitable size frying pan and press in the potato mixture to a thickness of 25 mm. Place in the centre to top of an oven at 200°C (400°F) to colour golden brown.

5. To serve, reverse on to a hot round flat dish and brush over the surface with melted butter.

6. Alternatively, at 4 in method, use a little flour, roll out the mixture and divide it into 16 or 20 pieces. Roll these into balls and gently flatten them with a palette knife till 20 mm thick. Mark a 10 mm trellis pattern across the surfaces.

7. Heat enough dripping to cover the bottom of a frying pan. Place the potatoes in, marked side down, and fry them on both sides to a light golden brown.

8. Serve in a hot vegetable dish on an underflat with dish paper.

## 1134 Pommes Byron

### Method

1. Prepare and cook as for Pommes Macaire (1133).

2. Mask over with cream to cover the potato and the base of the dish and sprinkle the surface evenly with grated cheese. Colour golden brown under a moderate salamander.

## 1135 Pommes boulangère

| 8 portions | Ingredients | 10 couverts |
|---|---|---|
| 4 lb | potatoes | 2·25 kg |
| 8 oz | onions | 280 g |
| 2 oz | first class dripping | 70 g |
| 1 oz | butter | 35 g |
| ½ oz | salt | 20 g |
| ½ level teaspoon | ground white pepper | 2 g |
| 2 teaspoons | chopped parsley | 5 g |
| ¾ pint | white stock | 525 ml |

### Method

1. Wash, peel and rewash medium-size potatoes.

2. Cut the potatoes into 3 mm-thick slices, with a mandolin. Retain 20 per cent of the best slices for covering purposes.

3. Peel the onions, cut them downwards in halves, cut away the root and shred them finely. Gently fry the onions in the dripping for 6–7 minutes without colouring.

4. Mix the onions with the 80 per cent of the potatoes and season with the salt and pepper.

5. Place into a buttered earthenware dish and press flat with a slice. Cover the complete surface with the 20 per cent more evenly shaped slices, the slices to overlap each other by three-quarters. Brush with melted butter.

6. Add the boiling stock to come half way up the potatoes. Place on a baking sheet, in the centre of an oven at 190–200°C (375–400°F).

7. Cook for 30–40 minutes; press the surface flat with the back of a slice every 10 minutes during cooking to prevent the potato curling up and burning.

8. Serve brushed over with melted butter and sprinkled with chopped parsley. Place the dish on an underflat with dish paper.

# Pastry Section

# Pastry Section

## 1136 GENERAL INFORMATION

In pastry work, it is necessary to understand certain basic factors in order to use effectively the recipes and the methods of cooking. The following information is offered for guidance.

### (a) The use of ingredients

Unlike other areas of cookery, correction cannot be easily made in pastry recipes. Many recipes are so finely balanced that even a small difference of ingredients – of weight or kind – may have disastrous results. All the ingredients, therefore, should be of the correct type, and carefully weighed or measured as specified in the recipes.

A comparison between two kinds of flour will well illustrate this difference between two similar ingredients. Strong flour (also referred to as hard flour because of the greater proportion of hard wheat used in the milling process) produces a much stronger gluten factor than other flours, and it is used, for this reason, when an aereated dough or paste is required, i.e. for yeast goods, puff paste and batters. Cake flour (sometimes referred to as soft flour), on the other hand, is milled with a greater proportion of soft wheat, and it will accept a greater amount of shortening, i.e. fat content, as is required in various recipes; it is, however, quite unsuitable for yeast goods, etc. because of its low gluten content. As a result of this variation in types of flour, and the quantities of different wheats used in milling blended flours, the quantities of liquids given in the recipes will always be approximate.

Sugar, too, is processed into various types. It is essential that caster sugar is used in certain recipes, because it dissolves easily into the other ingredients to form a very smooth texture. In liquids, especially sauces and milk puddings, granulated sugar may be used satisfactorily; this is generally more economical in price. Cube sugar should always be used for boiling, since it is generally accepted that it is refined to a greater degree and will therefore produce less impurities: the major factor causing boiled sugar to granulate (turn).

Eggs are assumed in the recipes to be of 2 oz (55 g) in weight each. In those recipes where the balance is very fine, a liquid weight or measure is given.

### (b) The use of oven temperatures

It is necessary to use the correct temperatures, together with the correct oven position during cooking, to achieve the desired results from the recipes.

Pastry ovens are fitted with oven thermometers which should always be read. Thermostat temperatures are only regarded as accurate to within 5°C (10°F). In certain instances, it is necessary to use 'top' heat, i.e. the baking tray or sheet is placed near the top of the oven, to make the mixture or paste rise or to colour an article. In other cases, 'bottom' heat is required to cook the underside of a paste or mixture or the contents between layers of paste. Sometimes both top and bottom heat are used at different stages in the baking process, and this will be indicated in the recipes.

---

## 1137 PASTES

**(Metric quantities are in an easily identified unit unless given to produce a specific amount of portions)**

### 1138 Short paste          Pâte à brisée

| | Ingredients | |
|---|---|---|
| 1 lb | cake flour | 500 g |
| 8 oz | margarine | 250 g |
| 1 level teaspoon | salt | 5 g |
| 5 fl. oz (approx) | water | 150 ml (approx) |

**Method**

1. Sieve the flour and salt together on to a slab or table.

2. Rub in the fat between the opened fingers until the flour becomes a fine sandy texture.

3. Make a bay in the centre, add three-quarters of the water and lightly absorb the flour from the centre. Add the remainder of the water as required to form into a medium stiff paste. Avoid over-mixing, as this causes toughness in the paste.

4. Cover and keep in a cool place or refrigerate until

needed for use. Short paste is used generally for pies (other than fruit), tartlets, pasties, etc. and for kitchen use.

## 1139 Sweet short paste (for covering fruit pies)

### Method

1. Prepare as for Pâte à brisée. Sprinkle 2 oz (60 g) caster sugar on the sieved flour and mix it in.

## 1140 Sugar paste (flans, tartlets)

Pâte sucrée
Pâte à foncer

| | Ingredients | |
|---|---|---|
| 1 lb | cake flour | 500 g |
| 8 oz | margarine | 250 g |
| 4 oz | caster sugar | 125 g |
| ½ level teaspoon | salt | 2 g |
| 2 | eggs | 2 large |

### Method

1. Sieve the flour and salt together on to a slab or table and make a bay in the centre.

2. Place the fat and sugar in the bay and cream them together until soft.

3. Add the eggs and mix them into the fat and sugar.

4. Lightly mix in the flour from the centre, to a smooth paste. Do not over-mix, or the paste may become greasy from the temperature of the hand.

5. Finish mixing the paste by 'scraping down' with a palette knife until it is smooth. Cover with a cloth and place it into refrigeration until firm enough to roll.

*Note.* For using the paste for lining tartlets, barquettes, etc. for pastries, increase the fat content by 25 per cent to give a shorter paste.

## 1141 Puff paste

Pâte feuilletée
Le feuilletage

| | Ingredients | |
|---|---|---|
| 1 lb | strong flour | 500 g |
| 1 lb | special pastry margarine* or butter | 500 g |
| 1 level teaspoon | salt | 5 g |
| 9½ fl. oz (approx.) | water (ice cold) | 300 ml (approx.) |
| ½ | lemon (in juice) | ½ |

### Method

1. Special pastry margarine,* being waxy in texture, is purchased for this purpose. When butter and the pastry margarine are used together, they must be thoroughly mixed and set in a refrigerator.

2. Sieve the flour and salt on to a slab or table and make a bay in the centre.

3. Add the cold water and lemon juice, absorb the flour from the centre and work it into a smooth medium dough. Cover with a cloth to prevent a skin forming and let it stand for 20 minutes.

4. After letting it rest, cut a cross three-quarters of the way through the dough, then, with a little flour, roll out the four prongs of paste in the form of a Maltese cross. The edges of the prongs should be thinner than the centre of the dough.

5. If the fat is very firm or hard, knead it to the same texture. as the dough.

6. Place the fat in the centre of the dough and fold in the four prongs of dough so that they completely envelope the fat.

7. Knock the paste gently with a rolling pin to flatten, then, using the minimum of flour for dusting, roll out in both directions to approximately 500 × 175 mm.

8. Brush off any surplus flour and fold the paste in three (1 turn). Turn the paste at right angles and roll out as before and complete the second turn. Cover with a cloth and refrigerate for 20 minutes to let it rest.

9. Give the paste two more turns and rest it for 20 minutes; then give the last two turns, making six in all. If being prepared some time in advance, give five turns and complete the last turn before using; this will make the paste more pliable.

*Note.* There are many ways of preparing puff paste, most of which require more skill than this method.

## 1142 Rough puff paste

| | Ingredients | |
|---|---|---|
| 1 lb | strong flour | 500 g |
| 12 oz | special pastry margarine or butter | 375 g |
| 1 level teaspoon | salt | 5 g |
| 9½ fl. oz (approx) | water (ice cold) | 300 ml (approx) |
| ½ | lemon (in juice) | ½ |

### Method

1. Sieve the flour and salt together. Break the firm fat into small pieces the size of a hazel nut. Do not rub in.

2. Make a bay in the centre and add the water and lemon juice.

3. Mix to a medium dough, then turn and rest the paste as for Puff paste (1141).

## 1143 Suet paste

| | Ingredients | |
|---|---|---|
| 1 lb | cake flour | 500 g |
| 8 oz | first class suet | 250 g |
| ¾ oz | baking powder | 25 g |
| 1 level teaspoon | salt | 5 g |
| 9 fl. oz (approx) | water | 280 ml (approx) |

### Method

1. Pick the suet free of all skin, add 25 per cent of the flour and chop it very fine.

2. Mix into the remainder of the flour, salt and baking powder sieved together.

3. Thoroughly combine and make a bay in the centre.

4. Add the water, absorb the flour from the centre and work the paste into a smooth medium dough. Cover with a cloth and use as required.

*Note.* Due to the presence of the baking powder, the paste should be mixed only when it is required for use.

## 1144 Hot water paste (for raised pies)

| | Ingredients | |
|---|---|---|
| 1 lb | cake flour | 500 g |
| 4 oz | lard | 125 g |
| 2 level teaspoons | salt | 10 g |
| 10 fl. oz | water | 315 ml |

### Method

1. Sieve the flour and salt together into a warm basin and make a bay in the centre.

2. Place the water and lard to boil, then pour into the bay.

3. Mix from the centre quickly with a wooden spatula.

4. Turn out on to the table and knead the paste until it is smooth in texture.

5. Use and mould while hot.

## 1145 Patty paste                                Pâte à pâté

| | Ingredients | |
|---|---|---|
| 1 lb | cake flour | 500 g |
| 3 oz | butter or margarine | 100 g |
| 3 oz | lard or chicken fat | 100 g |
| 1 level teaspoon | salt | 5 g |
| 1 | egg | 1 |
| 5 fl. oz (approx) | water | 150 ml (approx) |

### Method

1. Sieve the flour and salt together. Rub in the fat until the mixture becomes very fine, then make a bay in the centre.

2. Add the beaten egg and water. Absorb the flour from the centre and work it to a smooth medium dough.

3. Cover with a cloth and let it rest for 15–20 minutes before using.

## 1146 Choux paste (see 1368)                     Pâte à choux

## 1147 Ravioli paste                              Pâte à ravioli

See 607 for paste and 608 for making.

## 1148 Noodle paste                               Pâte à nouilles

See 604 for paste and making.

# 1149 CREAMS AND FILLINGS

## 1150 Pastry cream                               Crème pâtissière

| | Ingredients | |
|---|---|---|
| 1 pint | milk | 1 litre |
| 2½ oz | flour | 125 g |
| 4 oz | caster sugar | 200 g |
| 2 | eggs | 3 |
| 2 | yolks of egg | 4 |
| | vanilla pod or essence | |

### Method

1. Mix the eggs, yolks and sugar in a china basin with a whisk. Add the flour, absorb it and whisk it until smooth.

2. Place the milk to boil with the vanilla (1 pod or a few drops). Remove the pod when the milk is boiling.

3. Whisk the milk on to the mixture, return it to the pan and whisk continuously until it thickens and boils. Cover with a buttered paper.

*Note.* If prepared for later use, place the mixture in a china basin and cover it with a buttered paper.

## 1151 Whipped cream (sweetened)               Crème Chantilly

### Method

1. Place the cream in a china or stainless steel basin on crushed ice. If the cream has been previously well chilled, no ice is required.

2. Whisk until the cream begins to thicken, then add 2 oz of sieved icing sugar per pint (100 g per litre) and a few drops of vanilla essence.

3. Carefully continue whipping until the whisk just begins to leave a mark (this is piping consistency).

4. Store in refrigeration.

## 1152 Whipped synthetic cream (sweetened)

### Method

1. Place the synthetic cream in a basin and whisk quickly until it begins to thicken (soft-whipped), then add the sieved icing sugar as for fresh cream.

2. Continue whisking quickly until it is of piping consistency.

### 1153 Combination whipped cream

**Method**

1. To use fresh and synthetic cream together, whip each separately to the soft-whipped stage.

2. Add the sieved icing sugar and vanilla, mix them together and give only a few turns to the whisk to bring the cream to piping consistency.

### 1154 Butter cream        Crème au beurre

**Method 1**

| | Ingredients | |
|---|---|---|
| 1 lb | butter | 500 g |
| 8 oz | caster sugar | 250 g |
| 4 | yolks of egg | 5 |
| ½ pint | milk | 300 ml |
| 3–4 drops | vanilla essence | 4–5 drops |

**Method**

1. Place the yolks in a china basin and whisk in the caster sugar until light and creamy.

2. Boil the milk and vanilla and pour it on to the yolks and sugar.

3. Return to the pan and stir until slight thickening occurs; do not boil. Allow to go cold, then strain.

4. Cream the butter well, then gradually whisk in the custard base.

**Method 2, suitable for hot weather**

1. Place equal quantities of butter and sieved icing sugar in a basin.

2. Cream them well together until very light, then add a few drops of vanilla essence.

### 1155        Frangipane

| | Ingredients | |
|---|---|---|
| 1 lb | butter or margarine | 500 g |
| 1 lb | caster sugar | 500 g |
| 1 lb | ground almonds | 500 g |
| 4 oz | flour | 125 g |
| 8 | eggs | 9–10 |

**Method**

1. Cream the fat and sugar in a basin until very light and smooth.

2. Add the eggs, one at a time, and cream the mixture well before adding more. For small quantities, beat all the eggs together and add a little at a time.

3. Add the sieved flour and ground almonds mixed together. Mix until all the ingredients are thoroughly absorbed.

*Note.* Frangipane may be prepared well in advance and stored in refrigeration for subsequent use, at which time it should be returned to room temperature.

### 1156        Crème St Honoré

| | Ingredients | |
|---|---|---|
| 1 pint | milk | 1 litre |
| 4 oz | caster sugar | 200 g |
| 2½ oz | flour | 125 g |
| ½ oz | leaf gelatine | 25 g |
| 5 | yolks of egg | 9 |
| 10 | whites of egg | 18 |
| 3–4 drops | vanilla essence | 5–6 drops |

**Method**

1. Soak the gelatine in cold water for 5 minutes, then drain it and squeeze out all water.

2. Prepare a pastry cream from the milk, sugar, flour, yolks and vanilla (1150).

3. When reboiled, add and thoroughly dissolve the soaked gelatine.

4. Stiffly whip the whites of eggs and fold them into the mixture while it is still hot.

### 1157 Lemon curd (for tartlets)

| | Ingredients | |
|---|---|---|
| 1 lb | butter | 500 g |
| 1 lb | caster sugar | 500 g |
| 4 | lemons | 5 |
| 4 | eggs | 5 |

**Method**

1. Mix the eggs and sugar in a clean saucepan (not aluminium) or bowl. Whisk together, then add the butter, grated lemon rind and strained juice.

2. Place in a bain-marie and allow the water to gently boil. Stir the mixture frequently until it thickens.

3. Strain and use as required.

### 1158 Lemon curd (for flans)

| 8 portions | Ingredients | 10 couverts |
|---|---|---|
| ½ pint | water | 350 ml |
| 2 oz | butter or margarine | 70 g |
| 3 oz | caster sugar | 100 g |
| 1¼ oz | cornflour | 45 g |
| 2 | lemons | 3 |
| 2 | yolks of egg | 3 |

The quantities given will fill a 200 or 225 mm flan for 8 or 10 portions respectively.

## Method

1. Dilute the cornflour with a little of the measured water.
2. Place the remainder of the water, butter, sugar, finely grated lemon rind and strained juice in a saucepan to boil.

3. Whisk this on to the diluted cornflour and return the mixture to the pan. Whisk continuously until the mixture reboils, then remove it from the stove.
5. Allow to cool slightly and whisk in the yolks quickly until thoroughly mixed. Add a few drops of yellow colouring if necessary to give a lemon colour. Use as required.

# 1159 OTHER PASTRY PREPARATIONS

## 1160 Almonds                                    Amandes

### Method

1. If the almonds are required blanched, dip them whole in boiling water for 2–3 minutes until the skins loosen, then refresh and remove skin.
2. Filleted almonds are first blanched, then cut in thin slices the length of the almonds.
3. Roasted almonds are flaked, chopped or filleted almonds placed on a clean baking sheet and carefully roasted to a very light brown in the oven at approximately 150°C (300°F). Desiccated or shredded coconut may be roasted in the same manner.

### Roasted salted almonds                    Amandes salées

### Method

1. Blanch 1 lb (450 g) of whole almonds in boiling water for 2–3 minutes until the skins loosen, then strain them and remove the skins.
2. Lightly whip 1 egg white in a basin and add the almonds. Sprinkle in 2 oz (55 g) of table salt, mix thoroughly, then lay on a clean baking sheet.
3. Roast in the centre of an oven at 160°C (325°F); shake the baking sheet to turn the almonds and colour them a light golden brown.
4. Serve in small dishes for cocktail receptions and on bars.

## 1161 Brandy butter

### Method

Cream together equal quantities of unsalted butter and sieved icing sugar until very light in texture. Add 4 fl. oz of brandy per pound of butter (140 ml per 500 g of butter). Serve piped, scrolled in a sauceboat, or use as required.

## 1162 Fondant

### Method

1. Place 7 lb (3 kg) of lump sugar in a clean copper basin or sugar boiler. Add 8 oz (225 g) of glucose and 2 pints (1·125 litres) of water.
2. Boil quickly to 120°C (240°F) (soft ball), removing any scum as it rises.
3. Allow to cool, then pour the mixture on to a marble slab and work with a fondant spatule until it turns white and solid. This operation may be carried out in a general purpose mixer basin with the spatule on a low speed.
4. Store in a clean container covered with a wet cloth.

## 1163 Marzipan (cooked)                        Massepain
### Method

1. Boil together 1 lb (450 g) of cube sugar and ¼ pint (140 ml) of water as for Fondant (1162), to 120°C (240°F) (soft ball).
2. Remove from the fire. With a wooden spatule, stir in 8 oz (225 g) of ground almonds and 3–4 drops of vanilla essence.
3. Add 2 yolks of egg and mix them in quickly. When cool enough, turn the mixture on to the table and work it smooth by hand.
4. Store in a damp cloth to prevent crusting.

## 1164 Marzipan (raw)

### Method

1. Pass through a fine sieve 1 lb (450 g) of icing sugar and 8 oz (225 g) of ground almonds.
2. Make a bay and add approximately 2 whites of egg and 3–4 drops of vanilla essence.
3. Mix together and work smooth by hand. This is suitable

for the making of marzipan fruits and flowers for petits fours and pastries.

4. Store in a damp cloth.

### 1165 Ordinary meringue

**Method**

1. Place 5 clean whites of egg in a bowl and quickly whip them until stiff, i.e. until they stand on the whisk.

2. Fold in 8 oz (225 g) of sieved caster sugar; avoid over-mixing.

3. For meringue shells, pipe out the mixture with a 15 mm plain tube, round or oval, on greaseproof paper lined on a baking sheet.

4. Cook and dry out slowly for 1½–2 hours in an oven or hot plate at 80°C (175°F).

5. Release the shells from the paper by running a little water on the hot baking sheet, underneath the paper.

*Note.* This type of meringue is used for flans and certain pastries.

### 1166 Swiss meringue

**Method**

1. Place 4 whites of egg and 8 oz (225 g) of sieved icing sugar in a clean basin with a few drops of acetic acid or lemon juice.

2. Whisk vigorously over a pan of hot water until the meringue will form a ribbon or bear its own weight.

3. Remove from the heat and continue to whisk until cold.

4. Pipe out with a star tube into fancy shapes on a lightly greased and floured baking sheet.

5. Cook in a very cool oven 80–90°C (175–200°F) for 20–30 minutes until dry.

### 1167 Praline

**Method**

1. Place in a clean copper bowl 8 oz (225 g) each of whole almonds and hazel nuts and add 1 lb (450 g) of caster sugar.

2. Place over a moderate heat and stir continuously with a wooden spatula until the sugar completely melts and turns to a nice brown colour.

3. Carefully turn out on to a lightly oiled baking sheet. Allow to go completely cold and set.

4. Crush finely with a rolling pin and pass through a coarse sieve. Store in a covered airtight tin.

Praline is a very fine flavouring used in buttercream, ice and pudding mixtures.

### 1168 White praline        Praline blanche

**Method**

1. Place 8 oz (225 g) of lump sugar and 5 fl. oz (140 ml) of water to boil in a clean sugar boiler.

2. Remove any scum, cook to 130°C (260°F) (hard ball), remove from the heat and stir in 4 oz (110 g) of ground almonds.

3. Mix well until the mixture turns sandy in texture then pass it immediately through a very coarse sieve.

4. When cold, store in an airtight tin. White praline is used where a light coloured praline is desired.

### 1169 Royal icing        Glace royale

**Method**

1. Place 3 whites of egg in a clean basin, add 1 lb (450 g) of sieved icing sugar and 3–4 drops of acetic acid or lemon juice.

2. With a wooden spatula, beat smooth until the icing will stand to a point on the spatula. Larger quantities are beaten by machine.

3. Always keep the bowl covered with a damp cloth after making the icing, as crusting quickly occurs.

*Note.* For a brilliant white, 1 or 2 grains of washing blue may be added.

### 1170 Stock syrup

**Method**

1. Boil together 16 oz (450 g) of granulated sugar with 1 pint (560 ml) of water.

2. The density of the syrup may be corrected by adding more sugar if it is required thicker, or more water if it is required thinner.

3. For the poaching of fruits and for soaking purposes, the syrup is flavoured with a little lemon zest, bayleaf and cinnamon stick, according to the flavour required.

*Note.* Stock syrup is used for many purposes in pastry work.

### 1171 Water icing

**Method**

1. Sieve the required amount of icing sugar into a china

basin and very carefully add a little hot water at a time to mix to the consistency of fondant, i.e. to coat the back of a spoon.

*Note.* The liquid used may be strained lemon or orange juice to give the required flavour. When these are used, correct the colour to lemon with 1 or 2 drops of yellow colour; for orange use yellow and cochineal.

## 1172 SWEET SAUCES

### 1173 Egg custard sauce

Sauce à l'anglaise

| 1 quart | Ingredients | 1 litre |
|---|---|---|
| 2 pints | milk | 1 litre |
| 4 oz | sugar | 100 g |
| ½ oz | cornflour | 15 g |
| 6 | yolks of egg | 5 |
| 6 drops | vanilla essence | 5 drops |

**Method**

1. Dilute the cornflour with a quarter of the milk and boil the remainder. Whisk the diluted cornflour into the boiling milk and stir until reboiling.
2. Mix the yolks of egg, sugar and vanilla essence in a basin.
3. Pour the thickened milk on to the egg yolks, whisking quickly.
4. Pour back into the saucepan and reheat near to boiling point to complete the thickening. Do not boil or the mixture will curdle.
5. Pass through a fine conical strainer; keep hot in a bain-marie below boiling point.

### 1174 Custard sauce

| 1 quart | Ingredients | 1 litre |
|---|---|---|
| 2 pints | milk | 1 litre |
| 2 oz | custard powder | 50 g |
| 4 oz | sugar | 100 g |
| 6 drops | vanilla essence | 5 drops |

**Method**

1. Dilute the custard powder in a basin with a quarter of the milk.
2. Boil the remainder of the milk and whisk in the diluted custard powder; whisk until reboiling.
3. Remove from the heat, add the sugar and vanilla essence and stir to dissolve.
4. Strain into a storage container, sprinkle the surface with milk or water to prevent a skin forming and cover with a lid. Keep hot in a bain-marie.

### 1175 Vanilla sauce

Sauce vanille

| 1 quart | Ingredients | 1 litre |
|---|---|---|
| 2 pints | milk | 1 litre |
| 2 oz | cornflour | 50 g |
| 4 oz | sugar | 100 g |
| 1 | lemon | 1 |
| 6 drops | vanilla essence | 5 drops |

**Method**

1. Remove the zest (outer skin) of the lemon with a peeler, put it in a saucepan with three-quarters of the milk and place it to boil.
2. Dilute the cornflour with the remainder of the milk, whisk it into the boiling milk and stir until reboiling.
3. Add the sugar and vanilla essence, cover and allow the lemon to infuse.
4. Pass through a fine conical strainer into a storage container. Sprinkle the surface with milk or water and cover the container. Keep hot in a bain-marie.

### 1176 Almond sauce

Sauce amande

**Method**

Prepare and finish as for Sauce vanille (1175). Replace the vanilla essence with sufficient almond essence to flavour.

### 1177 Brandy sauce

Sauce cognac

### 1178 Rum sauce

Sauce au rhum

### 1179 Sherry sauce

**Method**

1. Prepare and finish as for Sauce vanille (1175).
2. At the moment of service, add 4 fl. oz (100 ml) of the spirit or wine per quart (litre).

### 1180 Apricot glaze

**Method 1**

Warm pure apricot jam to boiling point, add 1 or 2 drops

of yellow colour if necessary, strain and use at boiling temperature. The glaze is suitable for flans, tartlets and bands.

## Method 2

1. Place 1 lb (450 g) of apricot jam in a saucepan, add ¼ pint (280 ml) fruit syrup of a suitable colour, or stock syrup and 4 oz (110 g) of sugar.
2. Boil, add a few drops of yellow colour and thicken with approximately 1 oz (30 g) of arrowroot diluted in a little water. The glaze should well coat the back of a spoon.
3. Pass through a fine conical strainer. Use at boiling temperature.

*Note.* The glaze will spread or coat easier and more evenly when used at boiling temperature.

### 1181 Apricot sauce        Sauce à l'abricot

#### Method

Prepare as for Apricot glaze, method 2; use 1 pint (560 ml) of syrup. The sauce should be of the consistency of oil.

### 1182 Jam sauce        Sauce à la confiture

| 1 quart | Ingredients | 1 litre |
|---------|-------------|---------|
| 1 lb | granulated sugar | 400 g |
| 1½ lb | jam (of desired flavour) | 600 g |
| 1½ oz | arrowroot | 40 g |
| 1 pint | water | 500 ml |

#### Method

1. Boil the water, jam and sugar and thoroughly dissolve.
2. Dilute the arrowroot in a little water, whisk it into the boiling liquid and stir until reboiling.
3. Simmer gently for a few minutes to clear.
4. Remove any scum and add a few drops of suitable colouring, e.g. cochineal with a red jam, to give a clear colour. Pass through a fine conical strainer into a storage container. Cover and keep hot in a bain-marie.

### 1183 Lemon sauce        Sauce citron

| 1 quart | Ingredients | 1 litre |
|---------|-------------|---------|
| 1 lb | granulated sugar | 400 g |
| 2 oz | arrowroot | 50 g |
| 4 | lemons | 4 |
| 1½ pints | water | 750 ml |

#### Method

1. Remove the zest of the lemons with a peeler, cut it into

a fine julienne, blanch in boiling water for 4–5 minutes, then refresh and drain.
2. Squeeze the juice of the lemons into a saucepan, add the sugar and water and boil it.
3. Whisk in the arrowroot diluted in a little water and stir until reboiling.
4. Add a few drops of yellow colour to give a lemon tint to the sauce.
5. Pass through a fine conical strainer into a storage container, then add the julienne of zest. Cover and keep hot in a bain-marie.

### 1184 Orange sauce        Sauce orange

#### Method

1. Prepare in the same way as for Lemon sauce (1183), replacing the lemons with oranges.
2. When adding the colouring also add a few drops of cochineal to give an orange tint.

### Marmalade sauce

#### Method

Prepare as for Jam sauce (1182), replacing the jam with marmalade. Care must be taken, when adding the diluted arrowroot, to stir quickly to prevent any lumps forming, as the sauce is not strained.

### 1185 Syrup sauce

| 1 quart | Ingredients | 1 litre |
|---------|-------------|---------|
| 2 lb | golden syrup | 800 g |
| 1½ oz | arrowroot | 40 g |
| 2 | lemons (in juice) | 2 |
| 1 pint | water | 500 ml |

#### Method

1. Boil the water, syrup and lemon juice in a saucepan.
2. Dilute the arrowroot in a little water, whisk into the boiling syrup and stir until reboiling.
3. Pass through a fine conical strainer into a storage container, adding a few drops of yellow colour if necessary. Cover the container and keep it hot in a bain-marie.

### 1186 Cold cream sauce        Sauce Chantilly
###      (for masking fruits)

#### Method

1. Prepare a 1 pint (½ litre) mix of Sauce vanille (1175). Allow it to go cold then pass it into a clean basin.

2. Add ½ pint (250 ml) of soft whipped cream or synthetic cream. Mix it in lightly and adjust the consistency so that it well masks the back of a ladle.

### 1187 Chocolate sauce — Sauce chocolat

| 1 quart | Ingredients | 1 litre |
|---|---|---|
| 2 pints | milk | 1 litre |
| 6 oz | granulated sugar | 150 g |
| 3 oz | block chocolate or | 75 g |
| 1½ oz | cocoa powder | 40 g |
| 1½ oz | cornflour | 40 g |
| 1 oz | butter | 25 g |

#### Method

1. Roughly slice the block chocolate and place it, or the cocoa powder, if used, in a saucepan. Add a quarter of the milk and bring to the boil, whisking to dissolve the chocolate.

3. Add the remainder of the milk and sugar, bring to the boil and whisk in the cornflour diluted with a little water.

4. Whisk until reboiling, then remove from the heat and add the butter. If necessary, adjust the colour with 1 or 2 drops of cochineal and gravy browning.

5. Pass through a fine conical strainer into a storage container. Sprinkle the surface with milk or water, then cover the container and keep hot in a bain-marie.

### 1188 Suchard sauce — Sauce Suchard

| 1 quart | Ingredients | 1 litre |
|---|---|---|
| 2¼ lb | granulated sugar | 900 g |
| 6 oz | cocoa powder | 150 g |
| 1½ pints | water | 750 ml |

#### Method

1. Half fill a saucepan with all the ingredients.

2. Bring to the boil, stirring occasionally. Allow to simmer gently for 40–50 minutes until the sauce thickens enough to just mask a ladle.

3. Pass through a fine conical strainer into a storage container, cover it and keep hot in a bain-marie.

The sauce is used for various ice dishes, beignets soufflés, etc.

### 1189 Melba sauce — Sauce Melba

#### Method 1

1. Pass 1 lb (450 g) of fresh raspberries through a hair sieve and stir in approximately 1¼ lb (550 g) of sieved icing sugar to bring them to a thick consistency.

2. Colour to a brilliant red with cochineal. Place in a stone jar or china basin, cover and keep in refrigeration. (Do not store in metal containers in case the sauce becomes discoloured.)

#### Method 2

| 1 quart | Ingredients | 1 litre |
|---|---|---|
| 1 lb | red currant jelly | 400 g |
| 1 lb | strawberry jam | 400 g |
| 1 lb | raspberry jam | 400 g |
| 1 oz (approx) | arrowroot | 25 g |
| 1 pint | water | 500 ml |

#### Method

1. Place all the ingredients except the arrowroot in a clean saucepan.

2. Stir occasionally until boiling, thicken with the diluted arrowroot, reboil, then check the consistency. (The sauce should mask the back of a spoon.)

3. Correct the colour to a brilliant red, if necessary, with a few drops of cochineal.

4. Allow to go cold, then pass through a very fine strainer to remove all the seeds and store in refrigeration.

### 1190 — Sauce sabayon

| 1 quart | Ingredients | 1 litre |
|---|---|---|
| 8 oz | caster sugar | 200 g |
| 8 | yolks of egg | 7 |
| 12 fl. oz | marsala | 300 ml |

#### Method

1. Place the yolks of egg in a well-tinned sauteuse or china basin, whisk in the sugar and two-thirds of the wine.

2. Whisk continuously over a pot of hot water or in a medium hot bain-marie until the mixture doubles in volume and thickens to well mask a spoon, i.e. to form a ribbon as the whisk is removed.

3. Remove from the heat, gradually whisk in the remainder of the marsala to adjust to a sauce consistency.

4. The sauce should only be prepared a minute or two before required. It is served with various hot sweet dishes, e.g. Pouding soufflé, Sauce sabayon.

The basic ingredients used in the making of yeast goods are flour, salt, yeast, water or milk, sugar and fat.

## Flour

Flour is milled from the endosperm of the wheat berry. It consists of starch, moisture, natural sugar, mineral salts, soluble and insoluble protein and a trace of natural oil. The insoluble protein forms gluten when moistened and this rubbery substance holds the gas produced in fermentation.

When flour is old and has been in store for a long time it becomes infested with weevils. They are not harmful but they live on the starch and protein of the flour. Flour so infested can be finely sieved and used, but is useless for making bread. Flour mite is another pest and it can only be removed by heat-treating the flour.

## Salt

Salt or sodium chloride is a mineral salt used in making bread. It strengthens the gluten, gives a whiter loaf, keeps the bread moist (because of its hygroscopic properties) and enhances the quality of the bread.

Salt has the beneficial effect of steadying the action of the yeast during fermentation, but it is a yeast poison. It should never be brought into direct contact with the yeast and should never be used in excessive quantities.

## Yeast

Yeast is a uni-cellar plant. In a suitable sugary medium, it reproduces by budding. During fermentation, the yeast cells feed on the natural sugar in the flour, and any added sugars, and split into carbon dioxide and alcohol.

Fermentation flavours are due to the presence of the alcohol. Yeast works best at a temperature of 25°C (80°F), at temperatures of 30°C (90°F) and above, yeast works very rapidly and soon becomes exhausted. Generally speaking, yeast is killed if exposed to a temperature of 50°C (120°F).

## Water

The temperature of the water used in making bread is assessed as follows: double the required dough temperature and subtract the temperature of the flour. For instance, if the dough temperature is to be 28°C (82°F) and flour temperature is 16°C (60°F), the water temperature will be 2 × 28°C (or 2 × 82°F) less 16°C (60°F) = 40°C (104°F).

## Sugar

Any form of sugar may be used in yeast goods. The concentration should not be too great or the activity of the yeast will be impaired. (Concentrated solutions inhibit any mould or bacterial activity.) Note that only milk sugar or lactose is not fermented by yeast.

## Fat

The fat used in bread-making is a great improver of the quality of the bread: the crumb is more silky, the crust short, it delays the bread becoming stale and increases the food value.

## Judging bread

Points to consider are:
1. Good shape and volume,
2. The colour and bloom on the crust,
3. The colour and silkiness of the crumb,
4. The texture of the crumb and the bread's slicing and buttering properties,
5. Flavour and moistures.

## Temperature and times of baking

| Rolls | 1½–2 oz | 230°C (450°F) for 10 minutes. |
|---|---|---|
| Bread | 1¾ lb | 230°C (450°F) for 45 minutes. |
| Buns | | 230°C (450°F) for 12–15 minutes. |
| Bread | 14 oz | 230°C (450°F) for 30 minutes. |

## 1192 Bread rolls

| | Ingredients | |
|---|---|---|
| 1 lb | strong flour | 500 g |
| ½ oz | yeast | 15 g |
| 1 oz | butter | 30 g |
| ¼ oz (1 level teaspoon) | salt | 4 g |
| ⅛ oz (1 level teaspoon) | sugar | 4 g |
| 8 fl. oz | warm water (37°C, 98°F) | 250 ml |

## Method

1. Mix the yeast and sugar with the tepid water and add sufficient flour to make a light batter. Place it to one side to allow it to ferment.

2. Sieve the flour and salt and rub in the butter. Make a bay in the centre.

PASTRY SECTION

3. Add the ferment and mix it to a medium dough, kneading thoroughly until the dough leaves the hands and table cleanly.

4. Cover it with a cloth and place it aside to prove, i.e. double its size.

5. 'Knock back' the dough again and then allow it to prove again.

6. Then 'knock it back' again and divide the dough into 8 or 10 pieces.

7. Mould the rolls into the shapes as required and then place them on a greased and floured baking sheet.

8. Cover with a cloth and put in a warm place to prove.

9. Egg-wash, place in a hot oven at 230°C (450°F) to bake and, if possible, have a dish of boiling water in the bottom of the oven.

10. After ten minutes, allow to dry out in a cooler part of the oven for approximately 3 minutes.

## 1193 Bridge rolls                                     Petits pains

| | Ingredients | |
|---|---|---|
| 1 lb | strong flour | 500 g |
| ¾ oz | yeast | 25 g |
| 2 oz | butter | 60 g |
| 1 | egg | 1 |
| 7½ fl. oz | milk | 230 ml |
| ¼ level teaspoon | salt | 2 g |
| ¼ level teaspoon | sugar | 2 g |

### Method

1. Prepare and make the dough as for Bread rolls (1192); add the egg to the flour and ferment at 3 in method.

2. When moulding at 7 in method, divide the dough into 16 or 20 pieces and mould them into finger shapes 75 mm long.

3. Place them on a lightly greased baking sheet and allow them to prove in a warm place, covered with a cloth.

4. When doubled in size, egg-wash and bake at the top of an oven at 260°C (500°F) for 10 minutes.

## 1194 Basic bun dough

| | Ingredients | |
|---|---|---|
| 1 lb | strong flour | 500 g |
| ½ oz | yeast | 15 g |
| 4 oz | butter or margarine | 125 g |
| 3 oz | caster sugar | 95 g |
| ¼ level teaspoon | salt | 2 g |
| 2 | eggs | 2 large |
| 5 fl. oz | water or milk | 155 ml |

### Method

1. Sieve the flour and salt into a basin and make a bay in the centre.

2. Dissolve the yeast in the tepid (blood heat) milk or water, pour it into the bay and work in a little of the flour to make a slack batter. Sprinkle on top with a little of the dry flour, cover the basin with a clean cloth and place it to prove in a warm place for 10–15 minutes.

3. When the proving has doubled the volume of the batter, add all the eggs at one time, absorb the flour and work very energetically until the paste is very elastic in texture.

4. Add the sugar and work the mixture again for a few minutes.

5. Cover the dough with the butter broken in small pieces, cover the basin with cloth and prove it in a warm place for 15–20 minutes.

6. When the dough has doubled in volume, work well together until all the liquid butter is completely absorbed, then use the dough as required.

## 1195 Currant buns (1 lb or 500 g basic mixture (1194))
### Method

1. Well mix 4 oz (125 g) of cleaned currants into the prepared basic bun dough (1194).

2. Divide the dough into 16 or 20 pieces.

3. Using the minimum of flour, mould the pieces into perfect balls by rolling them on the wooden board or table with the palm of the hand, then decreasing the pressure to form a smooth surface.

4. Place them on a greased baking sheet 60 mm apart, cover with a cloth and prove in a warm place for 10–15 minutes.

5. When the buns are doubled in size, bake them in a hot oven at 220–230°C (425–450°F) for 12–15 minutes. When cooked, brush over immediately with bun-wash. Allow them to cool on a wire grid.

## 1196 Bun-wash
### Method

Boil together 12 oz (360 g) of granulated sugar with ½ pint (300 ml) of water; use the wash while warm.

## 1197 Chelsea buns (1 lb or 500 g basic mixture (1194))
### Method

1. Using the minimum of flour, roll out the dough into a 5 mm-thick oblong shape 225–250 mm wide × 400 mm long.

2. Brush the dough with melted butter, sprinkle it with brown sugar, then with 4 oz (125 g) of mixed clean fruit

307

(currants, sultanas, mixed chopped peel) and the grated rind of 1 lemon.

3. Roll up the dough firmly and cut it into 16 or 20 equal pieces. Place these 25 mm apart in a well-greased deep baking tin.

4. Prove in a warm place for 15 minutes, covered with a cloth. When doubled in size, bake in a hot oven at 200–220°C (400–425°F) for 15–17 minutes.

5. When cooked, brush with bun-wash, allow to cool for 1 minute then dredge with caster sugar.

**1198 Doughnuts** (1 lb or 500 g basic mixture, (1194))

1. Using the minimum of flour, roll out the dough to 5 mm thick and cut out the doughnuts with a plain 50 mm cutter until all the dough is used.

2. Egg-wash all round the edges of half the pieces of dough, then place a little jam in the centre. Place the other half of the rings of bun dough on top and well press down the edges.

3. Place the doughnuts on a well-floured board, cover with a cloth and set to prove in a warm place until doubled in size (approximately 15 minutes).

4. Fry in hot 140°C (280°F) clean deep fat for 3–4 minutes on each side till golden brown.

5. Drain well, then roll them in granulated sugar with a little ground cinnamon mixed in ($\frac{1}{2}$ oz cinnamon per lb of sugar, 15 g per 500 g).

**1199 Swiss buns** (1 lb or 500 g basic mixture, (1194))

**Method**

1. Using the minimum of flour, roll the dough into a long roll and divide it into 16 or 20 pieces. Mould these to finger shapes 60 mm long.

2. Place them on a greased baking sheet 30 mm apart, cover with a cloth and prove in a warm place.

3. When doubled in size, bake at the top of an oven at 200–220°C (400–425°F) for 10–15 minutes.

4. Allow to cool, then glaze the surface of the buns with white fondant or water icing.

**1200 Bath buns** (1 lb or 500 g basic mixture, (1194))

**Method**

1. Add 4 oz (125 g) of cleaned mixed fruit (sultanas, currants, mixed peel) to the basic dough and mix thoroughly.

2. Break into 16 or 20 shaped pieces and put them on a greased baking sheet. Place to prove in a warm temperature.

3. When doubled in size, bake at the top of an oven at 200°C (400°F) for 12–15 minutes.

4. When cooked, brush over with bun-wash and sprinkle with pieces of broken sugar.

**1201 Hot cross buns** (1 lb or 500 g basic mixture, (1194))

**Method**

1. Add 1½ level teaspoons (5 g) mixed spice to 4 oz (125 g) of cleaned mixed fruit (sultanas, currants, mixed peel). Mix thoroughly to distribute the spice, which should be sprinkled in.

2. Finish as for Currant buns (1195) from 2 in method.

3. After proving at 4 in method, make deep impressions in the buns with the back of a knife in the shape of a cross.

**1202 Savarin paste**          **Pâte à savarin**

| | Ingredients | |
|---|---|---|
| 1 lb | strong flour | 500 g |
| ¾ oz | yeast | 25 g |
| 8 oz | butter or margarine | 250 g |
| 1 oz | sugar | 30 g |
| ½ level teaspoon | salt | 2 g |
| 6 large or 7 medium (12 fl. oz) | eggs | 7 large or 8 medium (375 ml) |
| 4 fl. oz | milk | 125 ml |

**Method**

1. Sieve the flour and salt together into a basin and make a bay in the centre.

2. Dissolve the yeast and sugar in the tepid milk and pour it into the bay. Work in a little of the flour to form a loose batter. Cover the bowl with a cloth and place it to prove in a warm temperature.

3. When the ferment has doubled its size, add the eggs to the paste all at once and work it vigorously until very elastic in texture and the paste leaves the hand clean.

4. Break the butter into pieces, place them on top of the dough, cover with a cloth and set to prove in a warm place.

5. When the paste has proven (doubled in size) 'knock back' thoroughly, absorbing all the butter. One-third fill four greased and floured 200 mm (225 mm for the metric quantity) savarin moulds with it.

6. Place the moulds on a baking sheet and prove in a warm place until the paste reaches the top of the mould.

7. Bake in the centre to top of an oven at 190–200°C (375–400°F) for 30–35 minutes. The savarin, if cooked, should lift from the mould and be coloured golden brown all around. Tip out on a wire cooling grid to cool.

**Finish of savarins**

**Method**

1. Place the cooked savarins on a pastry grid with a shallow tray beneath.
2. Using a ladle, soak them with boiling stock syrup (1170) until they become quite soft and spongy.
3. Brush the savarins with boiling apricot glaze (1180) all over until they are well covered.
4. Serve them on a round flat dish, surrounded with a sauce of the fruit being used as the filling.
5. When a cream filling, as in Chibouste, is used, no sauce is served.
6. When the savarin is designated Chantilly, it is also finished with rosettes of whipped cream on top of the paste (1 rosette per portion).

**1203 Fruit savarin**                       **Savarin aux fruits**

**Method**

Fill the centre of the prepared savarins with fruit salad with a little liqueur added and surround them with apricot sauce.

**1204 Apple savarin**                       **Savarin normande**

Fill the centre with sections of poached apples bound with apricot sauce and place the same sauce around the base.

**1205 Peach or apricot savarin**       **Savarin aux pêches ou aux abricots**

**Method**

Fill the centre with slices of peaches or apricots bound with apricot sauce with the same sauce around the base.

**1206 Cherry savarin**                   **Savarin Montmorency**

**Method**

Fill the centre with stoned and poached cherries bound with Melba sauce (1189), with a little kirsch added, and place sauce Melba around the base.

**1207**                                    **Savarin chibouste**

**Method**

Fill the centre with moulded tablespoons of Crème St Honoré (1156).

**1208**                                     **Babas (pâte à)**

**Method**

1. Prepare the paste as for Pâte à savarin (1202), add 4 oz (125 g) of cleaned currants to the paste and thoroughly combine them.
2. Grease and flour 18 to 20 dariole moulds and one-third fill them with the paste. Knock the moulds on the base to level the paste. Place them on a baking sheet.
3. Place to prove in a warm temperature until the paste reaches the top of the mould.
4. Bake at the centre to top of an oven at 200°C (400°F) for 20 minutes, then turn out on to a wire grill to cool. When cold, trim the wide end level.

**1209 Rum babas**                          **Babas au rhum**

**Method for finishing**

1. Boil the stock syrup (1170) and flavour it slightly with rum.
2. Place the prongs of a large fork in the widest end of the baba and completely immerse it into the syrup until it stops bubbling.
3. Remove from the syrup and stand on the base, slipping away the fork.
4. Sprinkle on top with neat rum then glaze with boiling apricot glaze (1180).
5. Decorate on top with a rosette of whipped cream with a half glacé cherry in the centre.
6. Serve on a round flat dish with a light rum-flavoured apricot sauce around.

**1210 Babas with fruit**                   **Babas aux fruits**

**Method**

1. Soak and glaze the babas as for Babas au rhum, omitting the rum.
2. Finish with a rosette of whipped cream with a half glacé cherry on top.
3. Serve the babas on a round flat in a circle, touching each other, with a dome-shaped mound of liqueur-flavoured fruit salad in the centre and a thin apricot sauce around.

**1211**                                    **Marignans à la crème**

**Method**

1. Prepare a basic Pâte à savarin (1202).
2. Grease and flour 18–20 large barquette moulds, half fill them with the paste and place them on a baking sheet. Place to prove in a warm temperature.
3. When the paste reaches the top edge of the moulds,

cook at the top of an oven at 200°C (400°F) for 18–20 minutes, until golden brown. Place on a wire grill to cool.

4. Soak with rum-flavoured stock syrup until spongy. Sprinkle the surface with neat rum and mask or brush over with boiling apricot glaze (1180).

5. With a sharp knife, make an incision across the marignan on the slant from the top outer edge to the opposite base edge; do not cut right through.

6. Slightly raise the top and, using a bag and a 10 mm star tube, fill inside with scrolled Crème Chantilly (1151). Decorate the top surface of each with a quarter of glacé cherry and 2 diamonds of angelica, one on each side.

7. Serve the marignans on a flat round salver with one end towards the centre. Cover the base of the dish with thin apricot sauce.

---

## BAKING POWDER GOODS

A good brand of baking powder should always be used for these products as many cheaper brands are adulterated. The best baking powder is that made by sieving many times together one part bicarbonate of soda with two parts cream of tartar.

---

### 1212 Basic mixture

| | Ingredients | |
|---|---|---|
| 1 lb | cake flour | 500 g |
| 1 oz | baking powder | 30 g |
| 3 oz | caster sugar | 95 g |
| 4 oz | butter or margarine | 125 g |
| 1 level teaspoon | salt | 4 g |
| 2 | eggs | 2 large |
| 5 fl. oz (approx) | milk | 150 ml (approx) |
| 3–4 drops | vanilla essence | 5 drops |

#### Method

1. Sieve the flour, salt and baking powder together three times to ensure even distribution.

2. Sprinkle the sugar in it, add the butter or margarine and rub it in between the opened fingers to a sandy texture, then make a bay.

3. Add the beaten eggs mixed with the milk and vanilla essence.

4. Absorb the flour from the centre, mixing very lightly to a soft smooth dough. Avoid over-mixing.

### 1213 Plain scone rounds

#### Method

1. Divide the basic mix (1212) into 4 pieces of even size and weight.

2. Using a little flour, mould round with the hand, then roll out in a circle, keeping the dough 20 mm thick.

3. Place the circles on a greased baking sheet and mark them across with the back of a knife. The impression of the knife should go half way through the dough.

4. Brush over with milk or milk and egg-wash. Bake at the top to centre of an oven at 190°C (375°F) for approximately 15–18 minutes, until light golden brown on the top and underneath surfaces. Cool on a wire grill.

*Note.* For sultana scone rounds, incorporate 4 oz (125 g) of cleaned sultanas at 3 in method of basic mixture, after rubbing in the fat.

### 1214 Plain scones

#### Method

1. Prepare the basic mixture (1212). Using a little flour, roll out until 20 mm thick.

2. With a plain cutter 50–55 mm in diameter dipped in flour, cut out 16 or 20 pieces. Lightly re-mix the trimmings and recut for use.

3. Place the scones on a greased baking sheet and brush them with milk or milk and egg-wash.

4. Bake at top to centre of an oven at 190°C (375°F) for 12–14 minutes, until light golden brown on the top and under surfaces. Cool on a wire grill.

*Note.* For sultana scones, incorporate 4 oz (125 g) of cleaned sultanas at 3 in method of basic mixture, after rubbing in the fat.

### 1215 Rock cakes

1. Prepare a basic mixture (1212), incorporating 4 oz (125 g) of cleaned sultanas and currants at 4 in method, after rubbing in the fat.

2. Divide the mixture into 16 or 20 equal sized rough pieces by squeezing the mixture through the thumb and finger of the closed hand. Place direct on to a greased baking sheet.

3. Sprinkle with caster sugar, using a dredger. Bake at the top to centre of oven at 190°C (375°F) for 12–14 minutes, until light golden brown on the top and under surfaces.

## 1216 Rice buns

### Method

1. Prepare a basic mixture (1212), substituting 2 oz (60 g) of ground rice for the same amount of the flour.

2. Divide the mixture into 16 or 20 equal pieces. Roll into balls, milk, or milk and egg-wash the top half and dip it in granulated sugar.

3. Place on a greased baking sheet, sugar surface upwards. Bake as for Plain scones (1214) at 4 in method.

## 1217 Raspberry buns

### Method

1. Prepare a basic mixture (1212) and divide it into 16 or 20 equal size pieces.

2. Using a little flour, roll them into balls. Milk, or milk and egg-wash the top half and dip it in granulated sugar.

3. Place on a greased baking sheet, sugar surface upwards. Make an indentation in the centre of each with the finger tip and pipe a little raspberry jam in the centre of each.

4. Bake as for Plain scones (1214) at 4 in method.

## 1218 Fairy cakes (basic mixture)

| | Ingredients | |
|---|---|---|
| 1 lb | butter or high quality margarine | 500 g |
| 1 lb | caster sugar | 500 g |
| 1½ lb | cake flour | 750 g |
| ¼ oz (2 level teaspoons) | baking powder | 7 g (1 level dessertspoon) |
| 8 | eggs | 9 |
| 5 fl. oz | milk | 155 ml |
| 4 drops | vanilla essence | 5 drops |

### Method

1. Sieve the flour and baking powder together 2 or 3 times on to a piece of paper.

2. In a mixing bowl, cream the butter and sugar to a very light texture. Add the eggs one at a time, creaming well between adding each egg. Add the essence.

3. Mix in one-quarter of the flour and powder, then gradually absorb the milk. Finish by folding in the remainder of the flour. Mix until the batter is clear of flour grains.

4. Place the mixture in a piping bag with a 10 mm plain tube and half fill 48 or 55 paper pastry cases 50 mm in diameter. Place them on a baking sheet 20 mm apart.

5. Bake at top to centre in an oven at 190°C (375°F) for 15–18 minutes until light golden brown and the centre of the top surface is just firm to the touch. Cool on wire grill.

## 1219 Cherry cakes

### Method

1. Prepare a basic mixture (1218). After clearing the mixture at 3 in method, add 4 oz (125 g) of washed, dried and finely chopped glacé cherries.

2. Before baking, place one-quarter of a glacé cherry on the centre of each cake.

## 1220 Citron cakes

### Method

1. Prepare a basic mixture (1218). After clearing the mixture at 3 in method, add 4 oz (125 g) of finely chopped citron peel.

2. Before baking, place a small thin slice of citron peel on the centre of each cake and dredge the surface with caster sugar.

## 1221 Sultana cakes

### Method

1. Prepare and finish as for Fairy cakes (1218). After clearing the mixture at 3 in method, add 4 oz (125 g) of cleaned sultanas.

## 1222 Caraway seed cakes

### Method

1. Prepare and finish as for Fairy cakes (1218). After clearing the mixture at 3 in method, sprinkle into the mixture ¼ oz (8 g) of caraway seeds.

2. After piping, dredge the top surface with caster sugar before baking.

## 1223 Queen cakes

| | Ingredients | |
|---|---|---|
| 1 lb | butter or high quality margarine | 500 g |
| 1 lb | caster sugar | 500 g |
| 1½ lb | cake flour | 750 g |
| ⅛ oz (1 level teaspoon) | baking powder | 3 g |
| 8 oz | sultanas | 250 g |
| 8 oz | currants | 250 g |
| 4 oz | chopped mixed peel | 125 g |
| 1 | grated rind of lemon | 1 |
| 8 | eggs | 10 |
| 5 fl. oz | milk | 155 ml |
| 4 drops | vanilla essence | 5 drops |

### Method

1. Prepare the ingredients and mix it as for fairy cakes (1218) to include 3 in method.

2. After clearing the mixture, add the cleaned mixed dried fruit and grated lemon rind.

3. With a piping bag and a 20 mm plain tube, half fill 50–55 greased and floured queen cake moulds (these are a tapered fluted mould).

4. Bake them at the centre to top of an oven at 190°C (375°F) for 20 minutes. Turn out of moulds on to a wire grill to cool.

## 1224 Victoria sandwich

| | Ingredients per sandwich | |
|---|---|---|
| 4 oz | butter or high quality margarine | 110 g |
| 4 oz | caster sugar | 110 g |
| 5 oz | flour | 140 g |
| ½ level treaspoon | baking powder | 2 g |
| 2 | eggs | 2 |
| 2 drops | vanilla essence | 2 drops |

### Method

1. Sieve the flour and baking powder together 2 or 3 times to mix thoroughly.

2. Cream the butter and sugar in a basin until very light in texture.

3. Gradually add the beaten eggs. Add the essence.

4. Lightly fold in the flour and baking powder and mix only until the mixture is clear of flour grains.

5. Equally divide into two 175 mm well greased and floured sponge tins. Tap on a cloth on the table to level the mixture. Place on a baking sheet.

6. Bake in the top of an oven at 180°C (350°F) for 12–15 minutes until the centre is springy to the touch.

7. Turn out on to a wire grill to cool.

8. Spread one half evenly with a smooth jam and place the other half on top. Lightly dredge the surface with icing sugar.

9. Serve on a flat round salver with a doily.

---

## 1225 MILK PUDDINGS

### 1226 Baked rice pudding     Pouding au riz à l'anglaise

| 8 portions | Ingredients | 10 couverts |
|---|---|---|
| 2 pints | milk | 1·4 litres |
| 4 oz | sugar | 140 g |
| 4 oz | Carolina rice | 140 g |
| 1 oz | butter or margarine | 35 g |
| few grains | salt | few grains |
| few grains | nutmeg | few grains |

### Method

1. Place the milk to boil in a thick-bottomed pan and add the few grains of salt.

2. When boiling, add the washed rice and stir until re-boiling. Cover and place in the bottom of an oven at 150°C (300°F) to cook for 30 minutes, stirring occasionally.

3. Add the sugar and stir to dissolve it, then pour the mixture into a buttered 2¾ pint (2 litre) pie dish. (It may be divided into a number of smaller pie dishes if required.)

4. Place a few small pieces of butter on the milk surface and lightly sprinkle with a few grains of nutmeg.

5. Place on a baking sheet, place in the centre to top of an oven at 150°C (300°F) for approximately 30–40 minutes, to colour the skin light golden brown. Keep in a warm place for 15 minutes before serving for the rice to finish absorbing the milk. Clean the rim of the pie dish.

6. Serve on an oval flat dish on a dish paper with a pie collar around the clean pie dish.

### 1227 Boiled rice pudding

### Method

Prepare as for Baked rice pudding (1226, 1 and 2 in method). Allow to cook in the oven or on the side of the stove for 45 minutes, then add the sugar.

## 1228 Rice for Condé, créole, moulds, etc.

| 8 portions | Ingredients | 10 couverts |
|---|---|---|
| 2 pints | milk | 1·4 litres |
| 4 oz | sugar | 140 g |
| 6 oz | Carolina rice | 210 g |
| few grains | salt | few grains |
| ½ | zest of lemon | ½ |

### Method

1. Remove the zest from the lemon with a peeler and tie it with string. Attach one end of the string to the handle of the saucepan for easy removal.

2. Add the milk and boil. Add the picked and washed rice and a few grains of salt.

3. Stir until reboiling then cover the pan with a buttered paper and lid. Place in the bottom of an oven at 150°C (300°F) to cook for 40 minutes. Stir occasionally.

4. Remove the cover and paper, add the sugar and stir to dissolve it.

5. Turn out into a basin and cover with a well buttered paper. Allow to cool and thicken.

*Note.* For sweets where whipped cream is to be added in considerable quantity, reduce the milk by 20 per cent.

## 1229          Pouding au riz à la française

| 8 portions | Ingredients | 10 couverts |
|---|---|---|
| 2 pints | milk | 1·4 litres |
| 4 oz | sugar | 140 g |
| 4 oz | Carolina rice | 140 g |
| 2 oz | butter | 70 g |
| 4 | yolks of egg | 5 |
| 4 | whites of egg | 5 |
| 4 drops | vanilla essence | 5 drops |
| few grains | grated nutmeg | few grains |

### Method

1. Boil the milk in a thick-bottomed pan, add the picked, washed rice and stir until reboiling.

2. Cover with a lid and gently simmer on the side of the stove, stirring occasionally for 35–40 minutes until the rice is soft.

3. Mix the yolks, sugar, vanilla and half the butter in a basin, then stir in half the rice. Return all to the saucepan containing the rest of the rice and stir it over the fire, without boiling to thicken. Remove from the stove.

4. Stiffly whip the whites of egg, then, with a wooden spoon, fold into the rice mixture.

5. Place into buttered pie dishes and put a few small knobs of the remaining butter on top. Evenly sprinkle the surface with a few grains of nutmeg.

6. Place the pie dishes in a tray of water to come half way up the dishes.

7. Place in the top of an oven at 220°C (425°F) to colour quickly. Clean the edge of the pie dishes.

8. Serve on an underflat with dish paper and pie frills around the dish.

*Note.* Sago, semolina and tapioca can all be prepared in the same manner, substituting the particular cereal for rice. The milk is boiled for 15 minutes less than in this recipe.

## 1230 Boiled or baked milk puddings

Sago, tapioca, semolina, ground rice.

| 8 portions | Ingredients | 10 couverts |
|---|---|---|
| 2 pints | milk | 1·4 litres |
| 4 oz | named cereal | 140 g |
| 4 oz | sugar | 140 g |
| 1 oz | butter | 35 g |
| few grains | salt | few grains |
| few grains | nutmeg | few grains |

### Method for boiled pudding

1. Place the milk and salt in a thick-bottomed pan, bring it to the boil, then rain in the cereal. Whisk continuously until reboiling.

2. Cover, simmer gently to cook for 10–15 minutes, then add the sugar.

### Method for baked pudding

1. Prepare as above. After adding the sugar, pour the mixture into suitably sized buttered pie dishes, and three-quarters fill them.

2. Place small pieces of the butter on top and lightly sprinkle the surface with nutmeg.

3. Place the pie dishes in a tray of water and colour them quickly in the top of an oven at 200°C (400°F) for 15–20 minutes.

4. Serve on an underflat with dish paper with pie collars around the cleaned pie dishes.

*Note.* When flavoured with lemon or orange, the grated zest of 1 fruit per 8–10 portions is added to the milk when it is placed to boil, e.g. Pouding de semoule à l'orange.

## 231 Macaroni pudding       Pouding au macaroni

| 8 portions | Ingredients | 10 couverts |
|---|---|---|
| 2 pints | milk | 1·4 kg |
| 4 oz | macaroni | 140 g |
| 4 oz | sugar | 140 g |

| 2 oz | butter | 70 g |
| few grains | nutmeg | few grains |
| 2 | eggs | 2 large |
| 4 drops | vanilla essence | 5 drops |

## Method

1. Place the macaroni in boiling water, reboil, cook for 10 minutes, refresh and cut into 25 mm lengths; drain.

2. Boil the milk, add the drained macaroni and stir it until reboiling. Cover and simmer for 30 minutes until soft.

3. Beat the eggs in a basin, add the sugar and vanilla and pour on the macaroni.

4. Three-quarters fill suitably sized greased pie dishes with the macaroni.

5. Place small pieces of butter on top and sprinkle lightly with the nutmeg.

6. Place in a tray of water and cook in the centre to top of an oven at 160°C (325°F) to set and colour golden brown, for approximately 20–25 minutes.

7. Serve the cleaned pie dishes on an underflat with dish paper and put pie frills around the dishes.

## 1232 Vermicelli pudding — Pouding aux vermicelli (aux vermicelles)

### Method

1. Prepare, cook and serve as for Macaroni pudding (1231), using vermicelli in place of macaroni.

2. Lightly crush the twists of vermicelli and blanch for only 4 minutes before refreshing.

## 1233 Cornflour mould, jam sauce

| 8 portions | Ingredients | 10 couverts |
| --- | --- | --- |
| 2 pints | milk | 1·4 litres |
| 3 oz | cornflour | 100 g |
| 4 oz | sugar | 140 g |
| 1 oz | butter | 35 g |
| 4 drops | vanilla essence | 5 drops |
| ¾ pint | jam sauce (1182) | 525 ml |

### Method

1. Dilute the cornflour with a quarter of the milk.

2. Place the remainder of the milk to boil, with the essence, in a thick-bottomed pan.

3. When boiling, whisk in the well-mixed diluted cornflour and whisk continuously until reboiling. Cook for 3–4 minutes.

4. Add the sugar and butter and whisk to dissolve them.

5. Pour into 8 or 10 individual 5 fl. oz (140 ml) wet moulds, or use larger moulds. Allow to go cold and refrigerate for 1 hour to chill.

6. Unmould by easing the mixture around the complete edge with the finger.

7. Serve turned out on to a round flat dish. Surround the base of the dish with the cold strained sauce.

*Note.* It may be prepared in various flavours.

## 1234 Rice mould — Pouding au riz moulé

| 8 portions | Ingredients | 10 couverts |
| --- | --- | --- |
| 2 pints | milk | 1·4 litres |
| 6 oz | Carolina rice | 210 g |
| 4 oz | sugar | 140 g |
| 4 drops | vanilla essence | 5 drops |
| 3 | yolks of egg | 4 |

### Method

1. Boil the milk in a thick-bottomed pan and add the picked and washed rice. Stir until reboiling, then cover and simmer for 40 minutes until soft, stirring occasionally.

2. Mix the yolks of egg, sugar and vanilla in a basin.

3. Pour on the rice, mixing during the process, then return to the stove and stir until the yolks thicken. Do not reboil.

4. Pour the rice into 8 or 10 individual 5 fl. oz (140 ml) wet moulds, or border moulds if they are to be served with poached fruits.

5. To serve, ease the edges, invert the moulds on to a flat round salver and surround with a thin strained jam sauce.

*Note.* When moulded in border moulds, turn out and place the stewed fruit in the centre.

## 1235 Semolina mould — Pouding semoule moulé

### Method

Prepare, cook and serve as for Rice mould (1234), replacing the rice with semolina. Cook for only 12–15 minutes after reboiling. Add the tied zest of 1 lemon to the milk and remove it before adding the milk to the yolks, sugar, etc.

## 1236 — Pouding brésilien

| 8 portions | Ingredients | 10 couverts |
| --- | --- | --- |
| 2 pints | milk | 1·4 litres |
| 6 oz | tapioca | 210 g |
| 4 oz | sugar | 140 g |
| 2 oz | butter | 70 g |
| 4 | yolks of egg | 5 |
| 4 drops | vanilla essence | 5 drops |
| 8 oz | sugar for caramel | 280 g |

### Method

1. Prepare the caramel as for Crème caramel (1239). Pour

into 8 or 10 individual 5 fl. oz (140 ml) moulds to cover the base to a depth of 5 mm.

2. Boil the milk, rain in the tapioca and whisk it until reboiling. Simmer for 10–12 minutes, stirring occasionally.

3. Mix the yolks of eggs, sugar, butter and vanilla in a basin and whisk on the cooked tapioca, mixing quickly.

4. Fill the moulds, place in a deep tray and add hot water to come half way up the moulds.

5. Cook in the centre to top of an oven at 190°C (375°F) for 20–25 minutes, until set firm in the centre.

6. To serve, ease from the edge of the mould and invert it on to a hot flat dish. In a sauceboat, on an underflat with a doily, serve custard (1174), or Sauce anglaise (1173).

## BAKED CUSTARD BASED SWEETS

### 1237 Baked egg custard        Crème renversée

| 8 portions | Ingredients | 10 couverts |
|---|---|---|
| 2 pints | milk | 1·4 litres |
| 4 oz | sugar | 140 g |
| 4 | eggs | 5 |
| 4 drops | vanilla essence | 5 drops |
| few grains | grated nutmeg | few grains |

### Method

1. Place the milk in a pan and warm it to blood heat.

2. Mix the eggs, sugar and vanilla in a basin until the whites are completely absorbed then pour on the warm milk, mixing during the process.

3. Strain into suitably sized buttered pie dishes and three-quarters fill; wipe the edges.

4. Place in a tray of water (bain-marie) and bake in the centre of an oven at 160°C (325°F) for 45–60 minutes until the custard is set firm in the centre. If the oven used is too hot, curdling will occur.

5. Clean the pie dishes and place them on an underflat with dish paper and pie frills around the pie dishes.

*Note.* When prepared for invalid diets, the egg content of this dish is reduced by 50 per cent.

### 1238 Bread and butter pudding

| 8 portions | Ingredients | 10 couverts |
|---|---|---|
| 2 pints | milk | 1·4 litres |
| 6 oz | bread (free of crust) | 210 g |
| 2 oz | butter | 70 g |
| 3 oz | sugar | 100 g |
| 2 oz | currants | 70 g |
| 2 oz | sultanas | 70 g |
| ½ oz | mixed peel (cut) | 20 g |
| 4 | eggs | 5 |
| 4 drops | vanilla essence | 5 drops |

### Method

1. Grease the pie dishes with a little butter and sprinkle the base with the washed, drained mixed fruit.

2. Cut the bread into 5 mm-thick slices and spread them thinly with butter. Cut them into 4 pieces, corner to corner, in triangles. Arrange these neatly in the pie dish, half overlapping each other.

3. Place the milk in a pan to heat to blood temperature.

4. Mix the eggs, sugar and vanilla in a basin and pour on the warm milk, mixing during the process, then strain.

5. Gradually pour the strained custard base over the bread and sprinkle or dredge a little caster sugar on the surface.

6. Place the pie dish in a tray of water (bain-marie) and place in the centre of an oven at 160°C (325°F) for cooking gently for approximately 1 hour until just set in the centre and coloured golden brown.

7. Clean the pie dish and serve it on an underflat with dish paper and a pie frill around the dish.

### 1239 Caramel cream        Crème caramel

| 8 portions | Ingredients | 10 couverts |
|---|---|---|
| 1½ pints | milk | 1·05 litres |
| 3 oz | sugar | 100 g |
| 6 | eggs | 8 |
| 3–4 drops | vanilla essence | 5 drops |
| 8 oz | sugar (for caramel) | 280 g |

### Method

1. To make the caramel, place the sugar in a clean sugar boiler or pan and add one-quarter of the amount of water. Boil, remove any scum and boil rapidly until the syrup just begins to colour. Carefully move the pan over the heat to evenly colour the sugar to a mid-brown caramel colour. Carefully add 1 or 2 dessertspoons of water, reboil and run the caramel into the base of 8 or 10 individual 5 fl. oz (140 ml) moulds to give a depth of 5 mm of caramel. Allow to set firm.

2. Heat the milk in a pan to blood temperature and pour it on to the beaten eggs, sugar and vanilla, mixing during the process; strain the liquid.

3. Place the moulds in a deep tray, fill them with the Crème renversée, then add enough hot water to the tray for the moulds to be half immersed in it.

4. Cook in the centre of an oven at 150°C (300°F) for 35–45 minutes, until set firm in the centre.

5. Remove from tray and allow to go cold.

6. To serve, loosen the edge of the custard with the finger. Invert on to a round flat salver, draining any caramel around the base of the dish to cover.

## 1240 Coffee caramel cream      Crème caramel moka
**Method**

Prepare, cook and serve as for Crème caramel (1239), adding sufficient coffee extract or essence to the prepared Crème renversée, at 2 in method, to flavour and give a coffee-coloured tint.

## 1241 Cabinet pudding      Pouding de cabinet

| 8 portions | Ingredients | 10 couverts |
|---|---|---|
| 1½ pints | milk | 1·05 litres |
| 4 (8 fl. oz) | eggs | 5 |
| 3 oz | sugar | 100 g |
| 5 oz | sponge cake (stale) | 175 g |
| 2 oz | currants | 70 g |
| 2 oz | sultanas | 70 g |
| ½ oz | mixed peel | 20 g |
| 4 drops | vanilla essence | 5 drops |

**Method**

1. Well grease 16 or 20 small dariole moulds (3 fl. oz or 85 ml size) with a brush and place them in a deep tray.

2. Cut the sponge cake into 5 mm dice. Wash and drain the fruit.

3. Equally divide the sponge and fruit into the moulds.

4. Heat the milk to blood temperature, pour it on to the beaten eggs, sugar and vanilla, mix well and strain.

5. Fill the moulds with the prepared Crème renversée. Add enough hot water to the tray to half immerse the moulds.

6. Cook in the centre of an oven at 160°C (325°F) for approximately 40 minutes, until set firm.

7. To serve, loosen the edge with the finger, invert, shake and place on a hot flat dish, In a sauceboat on an underflat with a doily serve any of the following sauces: Anglaise (1173), Apricot (1181), Custard (1174), Jam (1182).

## 1242 Diplomat pudding      Pouding diplomate
**Method**

1. Prepare and cook as for Cabinet pudding (1241), replacing the mixed dried fruit with 5 mm diced glacé or crystallised fruits.

2. Serve cold on a flat salver and surround the base with a thin cold red jam sauce.

## 1243      Crème au chocolat

| 8 portions | Ingredients | 10 couverts |
|---|---|---|
| 1½ pints | milk | 1·05 litres |
| 4 oz | sugar | 140 g |
| 1 oz | chocolate or cocoa powder | 35 g |
| 6 | eggs | 8 |
| ½ pint | chocolate sauce (1187) | 350 ml |
| ¼ pint | stock syrup (1170) | 175 ml |

**Method**

1. Take 8 or 10 individual 5 fl. oz (140 ml) moulds, brush them with plastic fat and then coat with caster sugar.

2. Place the chocolate/cocoa powder in a saucepan with the sugar and half the milk and whisk until boiling.

3. Beat the eggs in a basin, add the other half of the cold milk and whisk in the hot milk and chocolate, mixing well. Add 1–2 spots of cochineal and gravy browning if necessary to give a good chocolate colour. Strain the liquid.

4. Place the moulds in a deep tray. Fill the moulds. Cook as for Crème caramel (1239) then allow them to go cold.

5. Serve them cold on a round flat dish surrounded with strained chocolate sauce thinned with the stock syrup.

## 1244      Crème Ste. Claire
**Method**

1. Prepare and cook as for Crème caramel (1239), omitting the caramel. Grease and sugar the moulds.

2. When cold, serve on a cold round salver and mask over with Sauce Melba (1189) thinned with a little stock syrup (1170) to just mask. Decorate with a rosette of Crème Chantilly (1151).

## 1245      Petits pots à la crème

| 8 portions | Ingredients | 10 couverts |
|---|---|---|
| 1½ pints | milk | 1·05 litres |
| 6 oz | sugar | 210 g |
| 4 drops | vanilla essence | 5 drops |
| 3 | eggs | 4 |
| 4 | yolks of egg | 5 |

**Method**

1. Boil a quarter of the milk with the sugar and vanilla. Remove it from the stove and add the remainder of the milk to cool.

2. Mix the eggs and yolks in a basin until the whites are completely absorbed, pour on the milk, mix, then strain.

3. Place 8 or 10 of the larger size egg cocottes in a tray and fill them to the edge with the mixture. Half immerse the cocottes in water in the tray.

4. Cook in the centre of an oven at 150°C (300°F) for 30–35 minutes until set firm in the centre. The surface should not be coloured, but should shine because of the high sugar and yolk content.

5. Allow to go cold. To serve, clean the cocottes and place them on a flat dish with dish paper.

*Note.* For a richer mixture, part of the milk may be replaced with fresh cream. When prepared in larger quantities, variety may be given by serving three different flavours, i.e. Petits pots vanille, as given in recipe; Moka, by adding coffee extract to the custard before cooking; Chocolat, by adding 1 oz (35 g) of cocoa/chocolate powder to the milk and sugar when boiling.

### 1246  Queen of puddings     Pouding à la reine

| 8 portions | Ingredients | 10 couverts |
|---|---|---|
| 1 pint | milk | 700 ml |
| 8 oz | cake crumbs | 280 g |
| 4 + 6 oz (meringue) | caster sugar | 140 + 210 g (meringue) |
| 4 oz | butter | 140 g |
| 4 oz | red jam | 140 g |
| ½ oz | angelica | 20 g |
| ½ oz | glacé cherries | 20 g |
| 4 | eggs | 5 |
| 4 drops | vanilla essence | 5 drops |

**Method**

1. Boil the milk and remove it from the stove. Stir in the cake crumbs, vanilla, 4 oz (140 g) of the sugar, butter, then the egg yolks and mix them well.

2. Pour into a 2¾ pint (2 litre) buttered pie dish and half immerse this in a tray of warm water.

3. Cook in the centre to lower part of an oven at 160°C (325°F) for approximately 18–20 minutes until set firm in the centre.

4. Remove from the oven, cover the surface with the warmed, strained jam and allow to cool slightly.

5. Using the whites of egg and the 6 oz (210 g) of sugar, prepare an ordinary meringue (1165).

6. With a piping bag and 10 mm star tube, pipe a trellis pattern, with the lines 25 mm apart, across the jam surface. Then finish round with a scrolled edge and small rosettes of meringue.

7. Decorate the meringue edge with quarters of glacé cherries and small diamonds of angelica.

8. Colour the meringue light golden brown in the top of an oven at 190°C (375°F). Clean the pie dish.

9. Serve on an underflat on a dish paper with a pie frill around the dish.

---

## STEAMED PUDDINGS, ROLLS AND SPONGES

### 1247  General notes

The suet used in these dishes should be best kidney suet picked clear of all skin, tissue and red parts. The amount specified is weighed, then broken into small pieces for chopping, and part of the flour is used while chopping the suet so that it separates easily.

All the powders (baking powders, spices, salt, cocoa, etc.) used in the recipes should be sieved with the flour to mix them thoroughly. All dried fruit should be well washed and drained; if desired, it may be soaked overnight to swell the fruit. The pudding mixtures should be mixed just enough to combine the ingredients, but should never be overmixed; the consistency should be moist but not wet.

The moulds used should be well greased with clarified fat or butter, and, if desired, sprinkled with breadcrumbs. Greaseproof paper for the covering is treated similarly.

Cooking time depends on the size of the mould but should be approximately 2–2½ hours. A mixture made from 1 lb of base (i.e. flour or flour and breadcrumbs) will half-fill a standard sleeve mould and, with 2½ hours steaming, will swell and fill the mould, giving 12–16 portions according to the required size.

Fresh white breadcrumbs may be used in steamed puddings: 1 oz being approximately equivalent to 1 oz of flour.

### 1248  Basic steamed suet pudding

**Recipe A**

| 8 portions | Ingredients | 10 couverts |
|---|---|---|
| 8 oz | cake flour | 280 g |
| 8 oz | white breadcrumbs | 280 g |
| 8 oz | finely chopped suet | 280 g |
| 4 oz | caster sugar | 140 g |
| ⅛ oz (1 level teaspoon) | baking powder | 5 g |
| ½ level teaspoon | salt | 2 g |
| ⅛ oz (1 level teaspoon) | spice (to recipe) | 5 g |
| 1 | egg | 2 small |
| ½ pint | milk | 350 ml |

317

## Recipe B

| 8 portions | Ingredients | 10 couverts |
|---|---|---|
| 4 oz | cake flour | 140 g |
| 12 oz | white breadcrumbs | 420 g |
| 8 oz | finely chopped suet | 280 g |
| 4 oz | caster sugar | 140 g |
| ⅛ oz (1 level teaspoon) | baking powder | 5 g |
| ½ level teaspoon | salt | 2 g |
| ⅛ oz (1 level teaspoon) | spice (to recipe) | 5 g |
| 2 | eggs | 3 |
| ½ pint | milk | 350 ml |

### Method

1. Light the steamer to heat it ready for cooking.
2. Sieve the flour, salt, baking powder and spices, where used.
3. Mix in the suet, breadcrumbs and any fruit being used.
4. Make a bay in the centre, place the sugar in it. For treacle or syrup pudding, also add the ginger at this stage.
5. Add the beaten eggs and milk. Mix lightly to combine all the ingredients.
6. Three-quarter fill the prepared greased moulds or basins with the mixture.
7. Cover with a greased greaseproof paper and steam a 4½–5 oz (125 g) mould for 1 hour, a 1 lb (or 500 g) mould for 1¼ hours and a 2 lb (or 1 kg) mould for 2 hours.
8. To serve, invert the mould on to a hot flat dish and serve an appropriate sauce separately in a sauceboat on an underflat with a doily.

### 1249 Currant pudding

#### Method

Add to the basic recipe (1248) 8 oz (280 g) of cleaned currants and ⅛ oz – a level teaspoon (5 g) – of mixed spice. Sauces served are Custard (1174), Vanilla (1175) or Almond (1176).

### 1250 Sultana pudding

#### Method

Add to the basic recipe (1248) 8 oz (280 g) of cleaned sultanas and ⅛ oz (5 g) of cinnamon. Sauces served are Custard (1174), Vanilla (1175) or Almond (1176)

### 1251 College pudding

#### Method

Add to the basic recipe (1248) 6 oz (210 g) of cleaned currants, 2 oz (70 g) cut mixed peel, the grated rind of 1 lemon and ⅛ oz (5 g) of grated nutmeg. Sauces served are Custard (1174), Vanilla (1175) or Almond (1176).

### 1252 Mixed fruit pudding

#### Method

Add to the basic recipe (1248) 2 oz (70 g) each of cleaned currants, sultanas, raisins and mixed peel, the grated rind of 1 lemon and ⅛ oz (5 g) of mixed spice. Sauces served are Custard (1174), Vanilla (1175), Almond (1176) or Apricot (1181).

### 1253 Jam or marmalade pudding

#### Method

Use basic recipe (1248) Place 1 oz (30 g) of jam or marmalade per portion in the base of the greased mould or basin. Sauces served are Custard (1174), Jam (1182) or Marmalade (1184).

### 1254 Baroness pudding

#### Method

Add to the basic recipe (1248) 8 oz (280 g) of cleaned stoneless raisins and ⅛ oz (5 g) of mixed spice. Sauces served are Custard (1174) or Vanilla (1175).

### 1255 Fig or date pudding

#### Method

Add to the basic recipe (1248) 8 oz (280 g) of 5 mm diced washed figs or dates and ⅛ oz (5 g) of mixed spice. Serve Custard (1174) or Vanilla (1175) sauces.

### 1256 Ginger pudding

#### Method

Add to the basic recipe (1248) 4 oz (140 g) of golden syrup, 2 oz (70 g) of finely diced stem ginger and ⅛ oz (5 g) of ground ginger. Use the sauces as for fig pudding.

### 1257 Treacle pudding

#### Method

Add to the basic recipe (1248) 8 oz (280 g) of treacle and 1 oz (35 g) of finely diced candied lemon peel. Serve Custard (1174) Vanilla (1175) or Syrup (1185) sauces.

### 1258 Steamed apple pudding

| 8 portions | Ingredients | 10 couverts |
|---|---|---|
| 12 oz flour mix | suet paste (1143) | 420 g flour mix |
| 2 lb | cooking apples | 1·1 kg |
| 1½ + 4 oz | sugar | 50 + 140 g |
| 3 | cloves | 4 |

## Method

1. Prepare the suet paste (1143), adding the 1½ oz (50 g) of sugar to the flour to sweeten the paste. If small size puddings are to be made, increase the amount of suet paste by one-third.

2. Retain a quarter of the paste for the cover.

3. Using a little flour, roll the remainder into a ball. Form this into a pocket shape with hand, dust it with flour and roll it to the size of the basin. Making the lining in the form of a pocket prevents the paste from pleating.

4. Well grease a 2 pint (1½ litre) basin and add the paste. Press it evenly to the same thickness at the bottom and sides of the basin.

5. Peel, quarter and core the apples, and cut them into sections approximately 5 mm thick on the outer edge. Place them in the lined basin, sprinkle with the 4 oz (140 g) of sugar, then add the cloves, evenly placed to diffuse the flavour. Add ⅛ pint of water (85 ml for 10) and wet the edges of the top of the paste with water.

6. Roll the remaining paste in a ball and, with a little flour, roll it to the size required to cover the basin.

7. Place it over the apples, pressing firmly around the edges to seal them, then trim off any excess paste with a knife.

8. Cover with a thickly greased double greaseproof paper. Steam for 2 hours. Allow to stand for 1–2 minutes before serving.

9. If large, place the basin on a round salver with a doily and a serviette wrapped around the basin. If in individual puddings, turn out of the moulds on to a hot round salver. In a sauceboat on an underflat with a doily, serve Custard sauce (1174) or Sauce anglaise (1173).

*Note.* Variations can be made by using 25 per cent of cranberries, blackberries or rhubarb, reducing the apple by the same amount.

## 1259 Steamed jam roll

| 8 portions | Ingredients | 10 couverts |
|---|---|---|
| 12 oz flour mix | suet paste (1143) | 420 g flour mix |
| 8 oz | jam | 280 g |

### Method

1. Using a little flour, roll the paste into an oblong 300 × 250 mm wide (slightly larger for 10).

2. Wet the paste with water on the two sides and top edge. Spread the jam evenly with a palette knife to within 25 mm of the edges.

3. Roll from the bottom edge along the 250 mm width and squeeze the ends of the roll to seal the paste.

4. Wrap in a thickly greased double greaseproof paper and steam for 1½–2 hours.

5. To serve, unwrap the roll, rolling off the paper on a hot flat oval dish. With the seam underneath, cut the roll in slices on the slant and trim away the end edges. In a sauceboat on an underflat with a doily, serve Custard sauce (1174) or Sauce anglaise (1173).

## 1260 Steamed apple roll

### Method

Prepare, cook and serve as for Steamed jam roll (1259). In place of the jam, spread the following mixture: 2 lb (1·1 kg) of apples prepared as for pudding (1258), 4 oz (140 g) of brown sugar and ⅛ oz (5 g) of cinnamon.

*Note.* Variations can be made by using 25 per cent of cranberries, blackberries, sultanas, currants or raisins, reducing the apple by the same amount.

## 1261 Steamed syrup roll

### Method

Prepare, cook and serve the roll as for Steamed jam roll (1259). In place of jam, spread with the same quantity of warmed golden syrup and sprinkle it with 2 oz (70 g) of white breadcrumbs.

## 1262 Steamed mincemeat roll

### Method

Prepare, cook and serve the roll as for Steamed jam roll (1259). In place of jam, spread evenly with 1 lb (560 g) of mincemeat (1294).

## 1263 Steamed vanilla sponge (basic mixture)

### Recipe A

| 8 portions | Ingredients | 10 couverts |
|---|---|---|
| 7 oz | cake flour | 245 g |
| 6 oz | butter or margarine | 210 g |
| 6 oz | caster sugar | 210 g |
| ⅛ oz (1 level teaspoon) | baking powder | 5 g |
| 3 | eggs | 4 medium |
| 4 drops | vanilla essence | 5 drops |

319

**Recipe B**

| | | |
|---|---|---|
| 7 oz | cake flour | 245 g |
| 6 oz | butter or margarine | 210 g |
| 6 oz | caster sugar | 210 g |
| $\frac{1}{4}$ oz (2 level teaspoons) | baking powder | 10 g |
| 2 | eggs | 3 medium |
| 2 fl. oz | milk | 70 ml |
| 4 drops | vanilla essence | 5 drops |

**Method**

1. Light the steamer. With a brush and plastic fat, thickly grease 8 or 10 individual 5 fl. oz (140 ml) moulds.
2. Sieve the flour and baking powder two or three times to mix them evenly.
3. Cream the sugar and butter in a suitably sized basin (not aluminium) to a very light creamy texture. Add the beaten eggs a little at a time to avoid curdling. Mix in the essence.
4. For recipe A, mix in the flour until it is all absorbed and the mixture is clear of flour grains.
5. For recipe B, mix in half the flour, gradually absorb the milk, then the remainder of the flour, and mix until clear.
6. With a piping bag and large plain tube, pipe the mixture equally in the moulds until just over half full.
7. Cover the moulds with a greased greaseproof paper. Steam A for 40 minutes, B for 1 hour.
8. Turn out the sponges on to a hot flat dish by tapping the edge of the moulds. In a sauceboat on an underflat with dish paper, serve Custard sauce (1174) or Sauce anglaise (1173).

*Note.* If sleeve moulds are used, well grease the moulds, fill one half, fasten and steam for $1\frac{3}{4}$ hours.

### Steamed lemon sponge

**Method**

Add to the basic mix (1263) the grated rind of one lemon. The same sauces are served.

### 1264 Steamed golden sponge

**Method**

Prepare, cook and serve as for Vanilla sponge (1263). When the moulds are greased, pour in golden syrup to cover the base to a depth of 5 mm.

### 1265 Steamed red cap sponge – jam sponge

**Method**

Prepare as for Golden sponge (1264), replacing the syrup with strained or sieved raspberry jam.

### 1266 Steamed black cap sponge

Prepare, cook and serve as for Vanilla sponge (1263). Line the bottom of the greased moulds 5 mm deep with washed currants, loosely bound with blackberry or blackcurrant jelly.

### 1267 Steamed fruit sponges (various)

**Method**

Prepare, cook and serve as for Vanilla sponge (1263). Add the various additional ingredients as for steamed suet puddings of the corresponding fruits. Fruit sauces are also served.

### 1268 Steamed chocolate sponge

**Method**

Prepare, cook and serve as for Vanilla sponge (1263). Substitute 1 oz (35 g) of chocolate or cocoa powder for each 8 or 10 portions in place of the same quantity of flour. Chocolate sauce (1187) is served with the sponge.

### 1269 Steamed cherry sponge

**Method**

Prepare, cook and serve as for Vanilla sponge (1263), adding 4 oz (140 g) per 8 or 10 portions of washed and drained chopped glacé cherries to the mix. Serve Almond sauce (1176) with the sponge.

### 1270 Christmas pudding — Pouding de Noël

| 8 portions | Ingredients | 10 couverts |
|---|---|---|
| 3 oz | cake flour | 100 g |
| 3 oz | white breadcrumbs | 100 g |
| $3\frac{1}{2}$ oz | finely chopped suet | 120 g |
| 3 oz | sultanas | 100 g |
| $3\frac{1}{2}$ oz | currants | 120 g |
| 5 oz | stoneless raisins | 175 g |
| $1\frac{1}{2}$ oz | cut mixed peel | 50 g |
| $\frac{1}{4}$ oz | stoned prunes | 10 g |
| 1 oz | peeled apple | 35 g |
| $\frac{1}{4}$ oz | stem ginger | 10 g |
| $2\frac{1}{2}$ oz | Barbados sugar | 85 g |
| $\frac{1}{4}$ oz | ground almonds | 10 g |
| $\frac{1}{8}$ | grated zest of lemon | $\frac{1}{6}$ |
| $\frac{1}{8}$ | grated zest of orange | $\frac{1}{6}$ |
| few grains | salt | few grains |
| $\frac{1}{2}$ level teaspoon | mixed spice | 2 g |
| 1 | egg | 1 large or 2 small |
| 2 fl. oz | old ale | 70 ml |
| 1 level teaspoon | rum | 5 ml |
| 1 level teaspoon | brandy | 5 ml |
| 1 level dessertspoon | Madeira wine | 15 ml |
| 1 level dessertspoon | sherry | 15 ml |

## Method

1. Wash all the fruit, except the peel, ginger and apple. Thoroughly drain then dry in a cloth.

2. Finely chop the apple, prunes and ginger.

3. Thoroughly mix all the ingredients together, except the egg, beer, spirits and wine, in a basin.

4. When mixed, add the beaten egg, beer, etc., and continue to remix thoroughly.

5. Cover with a cloth and refrigerate for 8–12 hours to allow the fruit to swell and absorb the flavours.

6. Place the mixtures into a greased 2 pint or 1½ litre basin. Cover with greased double greaseproof paper and a cloth and tie it around with string.

7. Steam for 4–5 hours initially, then cool and store.

8. Steam for a further 2½–3 hours when required.

9. To serve, remove the cloth and paper, invert the pudding on to a hot flat dish, allow to stand for 2–3 minutes, then remove the basin. Sprinkle the top surface with caster sugar, place a sprig of holly in the centre. Serve in sauceboats, on an underflat with dish paper, rum sauce (1178) and brandy butter (1161).

---

## SOUFFLÉ PUDDINGS—POUDING SOUFFLÉ

### 1271 Vanilla soufflé pudding     Pouding soufflé vanille
The basic mixture will produce 8–10 portions.

| | Ingredients | |
|---|---|---|
| ¾ pint | milk | 420 ml |
| 4 oz | butter | 110 g |
| 4 oz | cake flour | 110 g |
| 4 oz | caster sugar | 110 g |
| 5 (10 oz) | eggs | 5 (280 g) |
| 4 drops | vanilla essence | 4 drops |

## Method

1. Place the milk and essence to boil in a saucepan or sauteuse.

2. In a basin, mix the butter, sugar and flour to a smooth paste.

3. Remove the milk from the heat, add the paste, break down and stir with a whisk. Replace over the heat and whisk continuously until reboiling; remove from the stove.

4. Cool slightly, add the separated yolks of egg one at a time, whisking well to mix them in.

5. Stiffly whip the whites of egg. Carefully fold them into the mixture with a wooden spoon until they are completely absorbed.

6. Using a small ladle or piping bag and a large plain tube, fill 8–10 greased and sugared 5 fl. oz (140 ml) individual or dariole moulds with the mixture. Tap the moulds on the table lightly to remove any pleats in the mixture.

7. Place the moulds in a deep tray, add enough hot water to come half way up the moulds and boil gently on the top of the stove until the mixture rises level with the top of the mould.

8. Cook in the centre of an oven at 200°C (400°F) for 20–22 minutes.

9. Serve only when required by inverting on to a hot flat dish. On an underflat with a doily serve a sauceboat of a suitable sauce, i.e. Sauce anglaise (1173), Chocolate (1187), Suchard (1188) or Sabayon (1190).

### 1272 Lemon soufflé pudding     Pouding soufflé au citron
## Method
Prepare, cook and serve as for Pouding soufflé vanille (1271), adding to the milk the grated rind of 1 lemon. This soufflé may also be served with lemon sauce (1183).

### 1273 Orange soufflé pudding     Pouding soufflé à l'orange
## Method
Prepare, cook and serve as for Pouding soufflé vanille (1271), adding to the milk the grated rind of 1 orange and 1–2 drops of cochineal and yellow colour to give an orange tint. It may be served with Orange sauce (1184) as well as those listed in 1271.

### 1274 Chocolate soufflé pudding     Pouding soufflé au chocolat
## Method
Prepare, cook and serve as for Pouding soufflé vanille (1271). Replace one-eighth of the flour with cocoa powder. Serve with Chocolate sauce (1187).

### 1275 Harlequin soufflé pudding     Pouding soufflé arlequin
## Method
1. Prepare equal half quantities of vanilla (1271) and chocolate soufflé pudding (1274).

2. One half fill the prepared moulds with vanilla base and one half with chocolate base.

3. Cook and serve as for Vanilla soufflé pudding (1271).

## 1276 Praline soufflé pudding
Pouding soufflé praliné

**Method**

Prepare, cook and serve as for Vanilla soufflé pudding (1271), adding 1 oz (30 g) of praline (1167) to the base mixture before the whipped whites.

## 1277 Cherry soufflé pudding
Pouding soufflé aux cerises
Pouding soufflé Montmorency

**Method**

Prepare, cook and serve as for Vanilla soufflé pudding (1271). Add 2 oz (60 g) of washed, dried, chopped glacé cherries to the base mixture before the whipped whites. Serve with Almond sauce (1176).

## 1278 Tapioca soufflé pudding
Pouding soufflé au tapioca

| 8 portions | Ingredients | 10 couverts |
|---|---|---|
| 1¼ pints | milk | 875 ml |
| 5 oz | seed tapioca | 175 g |
| 4 oz | butter | 140 g |
| 4 oz | sugar | 140 g |
| 4 drops | vanilla essence | 5 drops |
| 4 | yolks of egg | 5 |
| 4 | whites of egg | 5 |

**Method**

1. Boil the milk in a saucepan, rain in the seed tapioca, whisk continuously until reboiling, then simmer for 10 minutes, stirring occasionally.

2. Remove from the stove and whisk in the sugar, vanilla and butter. Add the yolks of egg one at a time.

3. Stiffly whip the whites of egg, then fold them into the base mixture with a wooden spoon.

4. With a small ladle, three-quarters fill 8 or 10 greased and sugared 5 fl. oz (140 ml) individual moulds.

5. Cook and serve as for Vanilla soufflé pudding (1271) with same sauces.

*Note.* Semolina or sago may be prepared in the same manner by using the same quantities of ingredients and changing the cereal.

## 1279
Pouding soufflé samaritaine

**Method**

1. Prepare a mixture as for Tapioca pudding soufflé (1278), using semolina in place of tapioca.

2. Line the base of the moulds with caramel as for Caramel cream (1239).

3. When the caramel is set, three-quarters fill the moulds with the semolina base mixture.

4. Cook and serve as for Tapioca pudding soufflé (1278).

## 1280
Zéphyr viennoise

| 8 portions | Ingredients | 10 couverts |
|---|---|---|
| 6 oz | butter | 210 g |
| 4 oz | caster sugar | 140 g |
| 4 oz | fresh crumbs of brown bread | 140 g |
| ½ oz | cocoa powder | 20 g |
| ½ oz | chopped almonds | 20 g |
| 2 oz | sultanas | 70 g |
| 2 oz | currants | 70 g |
| ½ oz | mixed peel | 20 g |
| ½ lemon | grated lemon rind | ½ |
| 1 | egg | 2 small |
| 5 | yolks of egg | 6 |
| 5 | whites of egg | 6 |
| 4 drops | vanilla essence | 5 drops |
| ¾ pint | red jam sauce (1182) | 525 ml |

**Method**

1. Cream the butter, sugar and vanilla essence in a basin until of a very light texture.

2. Add the whole egg(s) and cream them into the mixture; add the yolks one at a time, creaming between each one.

3. Add the crumbs and cocoa powder mixed together; then add the chopped almonds, lemon rind and cleaned fruit.

4. Stiffly whip the egg whites and fold them into the base mixture.

5. Three-quarters fill into greased and sugared individual moulds. Cook and serve as for Vanilla pudding soufflé (1271).

Serve with a red jam sauce flavoured with a little kirsch.

# 1281 PUFF PASTRY PRODUCTS

## 1282 Puff pastry cases
Bouchée, vol-au-vent

Although the term bouchée is generally associated with round puff pastry cases, the shape may also be oval, oblong, square or diamond. Bouchées vary in size, depending on the way in which they are used, from 40–75 mm in diameter when they are cut in circles. Vol-au-vent are cut larger for one or more portions and vary from 95–200 mm in diameter when they are cut in circles. Both should always be prepared from virgin paste. A 1 lb flour mix (i.e. 1 lb flour, 1 lb butter, etc.) will yield the following quantities when cut 5 mm thick. Production figures for 500 g flour mix are given in brackets.

Cut round, 40 × 5 mm thick, 42–45 pieces (50)
Cut round, 50 × 5 mm thick, 25 pieces (28)
Cut round, 60 × 5 mm thick, 18 pieces (20)
Cut round, 95 × 5 mm thick, 10 pieces (12)

### Method

1. Using a little flour, roll the paste in both directions to an oblong shape, bearing in mind the cutter size to be used, until 5 mm thick. Brush off any excess flour.
2. With the required size cutter dipped in flour, cut out the paste economically. Place the trimmings on top of each other, knock down with the rolling pin, cover and use for other purposes.
3. Turn the cut circles of paste over, place them on a damp baking sheet and brush off any excess flour. Allow them to rest for 30–60 minutes in a cool place.
4. Brush over with beaten egg (egg-wash). Using a smaller size plain round cutter, cut through the paste to two-thirds the depth. The edge of the cut to the outer edge should vary from 5–10 mm, according to the total size of the case.
5. Bake at the top of an oven at 190–200°C (375–400°F) for 16–22 minutes, according to size. The paste should have risen, be set quite firm at the sides, golden brown in colour and the edges will not depress.
6. Remove from the oven, cool slightly, with a small knife remove the uncooked paste from the centre, retaining the top of the centre (cap).

*Note.* In the smaller sizes, according to use, a thinner paste may be required.

## 1283 Puff pastry patties        Petits pâtés

### Method

1. Roll out the puff paste with a little flour until 3 mm thick. For the base, paste left over from bouchées may be used. Cut out with a 60 mm fluted cutter, invert and place on a damp baking sheet.
2. Brush the outer 10 mm edge of the paste with egg-wash.
3. Place the required filling in a dome shape in the centre.
4. Roll out virgin puff paste until 3 mm thick and cut it out with a 75 mm-diameter fluted cutter. Invert the paste, cover the filling and press all around the edges to seal. Let the patties stand for 30–60 minutes in a cool place.
6. Brush over with egg-wash and make a 10 mm incision in the centre, to allow steam from the filling to escape.

7. Bake at the top of an oven at 190–200°C (375–400°F) for 15 minutes, until the paste has risen, set and coloured, then move to a lower part to finish cooking. The total cooking time is 20–25 minutes, according to the filling.
7. Serve the patties hot, warm or cold on a flat dish with dish paper and garnish between them with sprigs of parsley if they are savoury.

## 1284 Jam turnovers        Chausson à la confiture

### Method

1. Roll out the puff paste to 3 mm thick, using the minimum of flour. Cut into circles 125–150 mm in diameter. Brush off any excess flour and insert the paste.
2. Egg-wash the edges and place a dessertspoon of jam in the centre. Fold the paste in half to the opposite edge and press the edges firmly together with the thumb to seal them.
3. Brush the surface with egg white, dip in granulated sugar and place the turnovers on a damp baking sheet. Allow to rest for 30–60 minutes in a cool place.
4. Bake at the top of an oven at 190–200°C (375–400°F) for 18–20 minutes until risen, set and golden brown, then place them on a wire grill to cool. Serve on a flat dish with dish paper. (Served hot as a sweet dish.)

## 1285 Apple turnovers        Chausson aux pommes

### Method

Prepare, cook and serve as for Chausson à la confiture (1284), replacing the jam with apple filling. Serve Custard sauce (1174), Anglaise (1173) or Almond (1176) separately.

### Filling for apple turnovers

| 8 portions | Ingredients | 10 couverts |
|---|---|---|
| 1½ lb | cooking apples | 750 g |
| 1 oz | butter | 30 g |
| 3 oz | brown sugar | 95 g |
| ¼ level teaspoon | cinnamon | 2 g |
| ½ | lemon | ½ |

### Method

1. Peel, quarter and core the apples. Slice them thinly, and place them into a pan greased with the butter.
2. Add the grated rind and strained juice of the lemon, sprinkle with the cinnamon and add 1½–2 tablespoons of water.
3. Cover the pan then cook on the stove for approximately 10–15 minutes, turning occasionally until the apples are soft. Add the sugar and dissolve it. Allow to cool.
4. If desired, an ordinary apple purée may be used.

## 1286 Eccles cakes
**Produces 24—25 pieces**

| | Ingredients | |
|---|---|---|
| 1 lb flour mix | puff pastry | 450 g flour mix |
| 4 oz | butter or margarine | 110 g |
| 4 oz | caster sugar | 110 g |
| 8 oz | currants | 225 g |
| 4 oz | chopped mixed peel | 110 g |
| ¼ level teaspoon | mixed spice | 2 g |
| | Coating | |
| 1 | egg white | 1 |
| 6 oz | granulated sugar | 170 g |

### Method

1. Using a little flour, roll out the paste until 1·5 mm thick then cut it into circles 110 mm in diameter. Egg-wash the edges.

2. Cream the butter and sugar together, then add the cleaned currants, mixed peel, lemon rind and mixed spice. Mix them thoroughly.

3. Place a tablespoon of the mixture in the centre of the paste. Draw the edges of the paste upwards to the centre and twist slightly to seal.

4. Turn the paste over and lightly roll the surface to keep the cakes 75 mm in diameter.

5. Brush the surface with loosened egg white and dip it in the granulated sugar. Place the cakes on a damp baking sheet, sugar side up.

6. With a knife point, make 3 incisions, 10 mm apart across the cakes to within 10 mm of the edge.

7. Bake in the top of an oven at 190°C (375°F) for 18–20 minutes until golden brown on top and underneath. Cool on a wire grill.

## 1287 Cream horns      Cornets à la crème
**Produces 30 pieces**

| | Ingredients | |
|---|---|---|
| 1 lb flour mix | puff pastry | 450 g flour mix |
| 6 oz | jam | 170 g |
| 4 oz | icing sugar | 110 g |
| 6 oz | caster sugar | 170 g |
| 1 | egg | 1 |
| 4 drops | vanilla essence | 4 drops |
| 2 pints | fresh cream | 1·1 litres |

### Method

1. Using a little flour, roll the paste into a rectangle 300 mm long and 1·5 mm thick.

2. Place the rolling pin on the paste and cut straight strips of paste 20 mm wide down the 300 mm length.

3. Egg-wash the surface. Take the horn mould in the left hand, raise one end of the paste on to the tapered end, with the dry side of the paste to the mould.

4. Wind the paste carefully around the mould, overlapping each edge of the paste by 5 mm. Finish off by smoothing the paste level at the top edge of the mould.

5. Dip the egg-washed paste into the caster sugar, on the reverse side to the finished edge.

6. Place on a damp baking sheet, the sugared side up, and rest them for 30–60 minutes in a cool place.

7. Bake in the centre to top of an oven at 190°C (375°F) for 20–22 minutes. When coloured a light golden brown, move to a lower position in the oven.

8. Remove from the oven, carefully remove the moulds and cool the horns on a wire grill.

9. Pipe a little of the jam in the bottom of each horn.

10. Make a Crème Chantilly (1151) with the cream, icing sugar and vanilla.

11. Using a piping bag and a 10 mm star tube, fill the horns with the cream, finishing with a rosette at the top. Serve on a flat dish on a doily.

## 1288                                Mille-feuilles

## 1289                Gâteau mille-feuilles

Allow 8 oz flour mix (225 g) of puff pastry for each gâteau. 1 lb (450 g) flour mix for strips or slices, trimmings from previous use, are good for this preparation.

### Method

1. For the strips, line 3 baking sheets, approximately 500 × 325 mm, with puff paste rolled out 3 mm thick, then dock (prick) it well with a fork or docker. For round (gâteau) Mille-feuilles, roll out the puff paste 5 mm thick, cut out circles of paste 250 mm in diameter, allowing 3 circles for each gâteau, then place them on a clean baking sheet and dock them well.

2. Allow the paste to rest for 1 hour and bake off at 200°C (400°F) for 15 minutes, then turn the paste over and cook it for a further 5–10 minutes until it is crisp. Remove it from the oven and allow it to cool.

3. Cover one layer of pastry with lemon curd or jam, place on top another layer of pastry, spread 5 mm thick with cold Crème pâtissière (1150), then cover this with the third sheet of pastry; press slightly with a baking sheet.

4. Brush over the pastry with boiling apricot glaze.

5. Prepare some water icing by sieving the icing sugar and

carefully adding sufficient warm water to form a consistency that will just spread evenly.

6. Prepare 4 greaseproof paper bags and fill them with:
 (i) thick apricot glaze (iii) coffee fondant
 (ii) thick red apricot glaze (iv) chocolate fondant
 Keep these bags warm on the hot plate.

7. With a palette knife, coat the Mille-feuilles quickly with the water icing, pipe evenly spaced lines across the surface, using the four bags in turn, then very quickly mark them with lines 25 mm apart from top to bottom with the point of a small knife, then in the reverse direction between these lines. Allow to set for 15 minutes.

8. Trim the edges of paste with a wet knife and cut the large sheet into 3 strips 100 mm wide.

9. Serve the gâteau on a round flat salver on a doily, the strips on an oval flat dish or planche on doilys.

*Note.* If desired, white fondant may be used in place of water icing.

## 1290 Gâteau Pithiviers

| 8 portions | Ingredients | 10 couverts |
| --- | --- | --- |
| 8 oz flour mix | puff pastry | 280 flour mix |
| 2 oz butter mix | frangipane (1155) | 70 g butter mix |
| 2 oz | raspberry jam | 70 g |
| 1 | egg wash | 1 |
| for dusting | icing sugar | for dusting |

### Method

1. Divide the paste into two-fifths and three-fifths. Roll the smaller piece in a round shape 3 mm thick and cut out a 250 mm circle (275 mm for 10 portions). Brush off any excess flour, invert and place it on a damp baking sheet. Roll out the larger piece for the cover 5 mm thick and cut it 10 mm larger than the base circle.

2. Egg-wash the edge of the base and spread the centre evenly with the jam.

3. Using a piping bag and a 10 mm plain tube, pipe a single layer of the frangipane from the centre, spiral fashion, to within 20 mm of the outer edge.

4. Carefully cover with the larger circle of paste, press the edges firmly with the thumb to seal, notch up the edge with the back of a knife point.

5. With the point of a small knife, make 2 mm-deep incisions running in circles from in the centre to within 25 mm of the outer edge; the incisions at the outer edge should be approximately 25 mm apart. Allow to rest for 30–60 minutes in a cool place.

6. Egg-wash, then bake at 190°C (375°F) at the centre to top of the oven for 12–15 minutes until it has risen and set. Place lower in the oven, reduce to 150°C (300°F) and bake for a further 30 minutes

7. Dust liberally with icing sugar. Return to the top of the oven at 190°C (375°F) to glaze the sugar golden brown. Cool on a wire grill.

8. Serve on a round flat salver with doilys.

## 1291 Dartois

### Method

1. Use the same ingredients as for Gâteau Pithiviers (1290).

2. Divide the paste into two-fifths and three-fifths. Roll the smaller amount to an oblong 375 long by 100 mm wide and 3 mm thick; trim it to size. Carefully place it on a damp baking sheet.

3. Evenly spread the centre of the paste with jam, and egg-wash the edges. Using a piping bag and a 10 mm plain tube, pipe four strips of the frangipane in one layer the length of the paste to within 10 mm of all edges.

4. Roll out the larger piece of paste 5 mm thick and 110 mm wide. Carefully place this on top, press the edges to seal and notch them with the back of a knife point. Allow to rest for 30–60 minutes in a cool place.

5. Egg-wash, mark with back of knife into 8 or 10 equal size pieces and mark each portion with a simple design.

6. Bake, glaze and serve as for Gâteau Pithiviers from 6 in method.

## 1292 Jalousie

### Method

1. Prepare, cook and serve as for Dartois (1291).

2. When the top cover of paste is rolled and trimmed, fold across the width, then cut through the paste at 5 mm intervals to within 10 mm of the two edges. Then unfold the paste, roll it up, place one end of it over the end of the base and unwind; seal the edges.

## 1293 Mince pies

| 8 portions | Ingredients | 10 couverts |
| --- | --- | --- |
| 8 oz (flour mix) | puff pastry | 280 g (flour mix) |
| 8 oz | mincemeat | 280 g |

### Method

1. Prepare as for Puff pastry patties (1283), using the mincemeat as the filling. Generally the circles of paste are cut 50 mm for the base and 60 mm for the top.

325

AN APPROACH TO PROFESSIONAL COOKERY

2. When cooked, dust the pies liberally with icing sugar, using a dredger. Return to the oven to glaze the sugar golden brown.

3. Serve hot on a flat dish on a doily.

## 1294 Mincemeat

| 8 portions | Ingredients | 10 couverts |
|---|---|---|
| 4½ oz | stoned raisins | 160 g |
| 3 oz | sultanas | 100 g |
| 3 oz | currants | 100 g |
| 2½ oz | Barbados sugar | 85 g |
| 4½ oz | prepared beef suet | 160 g |
| 4½ oz | peeled apple | 160 g |
| 1 oz | cut mixed peel | 35 g |
| ¼ | grated rind and juice of lemon | ⅓ |
| ¼ | grated rind and juice of orange | ⅓ |
| ¼ level teaspoon | mixed spice | 1 g |
| tablespoon | rum | 25 ml |
| tablespoon | brandy | 25 ml |

### Method

1. Wash and dry all the fruit.

2. Finely chop the suet with a little sugar, cut the peel and chop the apple.

3. Mix the ingredients together with the orange and lemon juice and, lastly, the spirits.

4. Place the mixture in air-tight containers and keep them in a dry cool store until required.

*Note.* Mincemeat should be kept for approximately one month before use. The quantity given is when it is used for Mincemeat tart (1321); the quantity varies for mince pies according to their size.

## 1295 Apple slice    Bande aux pommes

| 8 portions | Ingredients | 10 couverts |
|---|---|---|
| 8 oz flour mix | puff pastry | 280 g flour mix |
| 1½ lb | cooking apples | 840 g |
| 3 oz | sugar | 100 g |
| ¼ pint | apricot glaze (1180) | 175 ml |

### Method

1. Roll out the puff paste approximately 350 mm long to a thickness of 5 mm. (Roll out to 450 mm long for 10 portions.) Cut two 25 mm wide strips the length of the paste and place these aside.

2. Resume rolling the paste to approximately 140 mm wide and 3 mm thick. Roll it on to the rolling pin, then unroll it on to a damp baking sheet. Trim to 125 mm wide to the required length of 350 mm (450 mm for 10 portions).

3. Egg-wash 25 mm along each side, carefully place the 25 mm strips on top and press them firmly in position;

notch the edges with the back of a knife. Well prick the centre of the paste between the strips.

4. Prepare three-quarters of the apples into a purée (1306, 3), sweeten with the sugar and allow to go cold.

5. Spread the apple purée evenly along the paste inside the outer strips.

6. Peel, quarter and core the remaining apples. Cut them into thin slices and three-quarters overlap them across the bande.

7. Cook in the centre to top of an oven at 190–220°C (375–400°F) for 10–12 minutes to rise and set the edges. Finish cooking on a lower shelf for a further 15 minutes.

8. Cool slightly, then, using a tablespoon, carefully mask across the fruit with boiling apricot glaze; allow it to set.

9. Trim the edges. Serve on a flat dish on doilys or on a planche.

*Note.* When designated Chantilly, pipe Crème Chantilly (1151), along each edge with a 10 mm star tube, or in a rosette on each portion.

## 1296 Fruit slice    Bande aux fruits

### Method

1. Prepare the pastry as for Bande aux pommes (1295). After allowing it to rest, bake it blind, i.e. with no filling.

2. When cool, spread the centre with ¾ pint (½ litre) of hot pastry cream (1150) and allow it to set.

3. Cover the pastry cream with fruit. The fruit may be poached, canned or fresh. Cherries must be stoned, bananas in slices sprinkled with lemon juice. Pineapple in half slices or sections, rhubarb as for compote, and other fruits, e.g. peach, pear, etc. may be left in halves or cut in segments.

4. Carefully glaze the fruit with boiling apricot glaze (1180). Use a red glaze for red fruits, i.e. raspberries, cherries, etc.

5. If desired, a variety of fruits may be used, in which case they are arranged the length of, not across, the slice as in other fruits.

6. Trim the edges and ends when set. Serve on a flat dish on doilys or on a planche.

*Note.* When designated Chantilly, decorate with Crème Chantilly (1151).

## 1297 Pigs ears    Palmiers

### Method

1. Puff paste trimmings are ideal for the making of these.

Sprinkle the slab or table with caster sugar when rolling the paste. Turn the paste, so that it rolls in plenty of sugar, to a thickness of 1·5 mm; keep the paste approximately 300 mm wide.

2. Fold the 300 mm width three times from each edge to the centre, then fold one side on to the other, making six layers joined on one side.

3. Cut this into 5 mm-wide strips, place the strips on a damp baking sheet, with the layers showing, leaving space of 40 mm between them so allowing them to spread.

4. Bake in a hot oven 220°C (425°F) for 12–15 minutes, turning the palmiers over with a palette knife to caramelise the sugar on both sides. Remove and cool them on a wire grill.

5. Serve on a flat dish on a doily.

6. When served as a pastry, they may be served plain or joined together with Crème Chantilly (1151).

## 1298                             Palmiers au parmesan

**Method**

1. Prepare and cook as for Palmiers (1297), using Parmesan cheese in place of caster sugar when rolling.

2. Served in place of cheese straws with soups, and served at cocktail receptions.

## 1299 Cheese straws               Paillettes au fromage

**Method**

1. Roll out puff pastry trimmings with Parmesan cheese previously mixed with a little cayenne pepper. Turn the paste during rolling to absorb the cheese. Finish by rolling it to an oblong 250 mm wide and 3 mm thick.

2. Using a rolling pin as a straight edge, cut the paste into 5 mm-wide strips down the 250 mm width of paste.

3. Twist the paste by holding it at each end and turning.

Place on to a baking sheet 10 mm apart; press the ends to the baking sheet to hold the straws in position.

4. Bake till golden brown in the top of an oven at 200°C (400°F) for approximately 8–10 minutes. Remove from the oven, trim both ends straight and cut them across into 3 lots to give a length of approximately 75 mm.

## 1300 Sausage rolls

**Method**

1. These are made in various sizes, according to use. For buffet receptions, the size is often only 60–75 mm in length, with a pork sausage meat (263) filling of approximately 10–15 mm in diameter. For this size, an 8 oz (or 250 g) flour mix of puff pastry and 1 lb (or 500 g) of sausage meat will produce 16–20 pieces. Larger sizes require the paste and filling in proportion.

2. Roll out the paste with a minimum of flour to an oblong shape 3 mm thick and trim the edges straight.

3. Roll the sausage meat to the required thickness using a little flour. Place along the paste to within 25 mm of the edge. Egg-wash the paste on the other side of the filling.

4. Roll the paste over so that it covers the filling, and beyond it for about 10 mm. Press the filling to level out the overlapping edge of paste. Cut the paste where the double layer of paste finishes.

5. Cut the sausage rolls into the required lengths, place them on a damp baking sheet and egg-wash the surface. With a knife point, make 3 evenly spaced small incisions in the paste. Mark the flat 10 mm edge with the back of a fork. Allow to rest for 30–60 minutes.

6. Bake at the centre to top of an oven at 190°C (375°F) for 15 minutes, then lower in the oven for a further 8–10 minutes until golden brown and cooked.

7. Serve the rolls hot or warm on a flat dish with a doily and garnish between them with sprigs of parsley.

---

## 1301 FRUIT PIES, TARTS, VARIOUS FLANS, BAKED ROLLS, DUMPLINGS, STRUDEL

### 1302 Fruit pies

| 8 portions | Ingredients | 10 couverts |
|---|---|---|
| 8 oz flour mix | sweet short paste (1139) | 280 g flour mix |
| 2 lb | named fruit | 1·125 kg |
| 6–8 oz | sugar | 210–280 g |
| 5–8 fl. oz | water | 175–280 ml |
| 1 | egg (egg-wash) | 1 |

**Method**

1. Prepare the paste and allow it to rest in a cool place.

2. Prepare the fruit, washing it if necessary and drain it. (See preparation notes against types below.)

3. Place the fruit into a 2¾ pint (2 litre) pie dish. Smaller pie dishes may be used if desired.

4. Sprinkle the fruit with the sugar and add the water and any other ingredients, i.e. cloves, etc.

5. Using a little flour, roll out the paste to an oval shape approximately 40 mm larger than the top edge of the pie dish. For large pies, the paste is rolled to 5 mm thick, for small pies to 3 mm thick.

6. Place a reversed pie dish on the paste and cut 25 mm larger than the dish. Cut a 10 mm band from the trimmings.

7. Brush the edge of the pie dish with water and press the 10 mm band of paste firmly on it. Egg-wash the paste.

8. Invert the paste covering and place it over the fruit. Press it lightly towards the centre to allow the paste to cover the fruit without stretching.

9. Press down the edge of the paste on the band with the thumbs. Cut off any excess paste at a 45° angle. Thumb the edge smooth then make notches with the back of a knife 5 mm apart. Allow it to rest 15–30 minutes.

10. Brush over with egg-wash, dredge with caster sugar and place the pie on a baking sheet.

11. Bake in the centre to top of an oven at 200°C (400°F) for approximately 15 minutes until set and lightly coloured. Reduce the temperature to 175–180°C (350–360°F) and continue to cook for a further 15–20 minutes until the fruit is cooked. Test by cutting under the edge of the paste and lifting it at one end: the fruit should be soft but not broken.

12. Place the pie on a flat dish with dish paper with a pie frill around the dish. In a sauceboat on an underflat with a doily, serve Custard sauce (1174) or Sauce anglaise (1173).

*Note.* If individual pies are made, the pie dishes are placed together and the rolled paste is placed over the top then trimmed around the pie dishes.

### Preparation notes

**Apple pie**: Peel, quarter and core the apples, then cut them into sections 5 mm thick at the outer edge. Add 2 cloves and use 8 oz (280 g) of caster sugar. No cloves should be used when other fruits are mixed with the apples.

**Cherry pie**: Remove the stalks and wash the cherries. Use 6 oz (210 g) caster sugar.

**Blackberry and apple pie**: Use 25 per cent washed blackberries in place of apple.

**Cranberry and apple pie**: Use 25 per cent washed cranberries in place of apple.

**Damson pie**: Remove the stalks then wash the damsons. Use 8 oz (280 g) of caster sugar.

**Gooseberry pie**: Remove the stalks and tails then wash the gooseberries. Use 8 oz (280 g) of caster sugar.

**Greengage or plum pie**: Remove the stalks, wash the greengages, cut them in half and remove the stones. Use 8 oz (280 g) brown sugar.

**Loganberry or mulberry and apple pie**: Use 25 per cent washed loganberries or mulberries in place of apple.

**Raspberry and redcurrant pie**: Use 50 per cent of each picked and washed fruit with 8 oz (280 g) of caster sugar.

**Rhubarb pie**: Trim away the ends, remove the outer skin if stringy and cut the rhubarb into 40 mm lengths. Use 8 oz (280 g) of brown sugar.

**Rhubarb and apple pie**: Use 25 per cent rhubarb in place of apple. Use brown sugar.

## 1303 Dutch apple tart

| 8 portions | Ingredients | 10 couverts |
|---|---|---|
| 10 oz flour mix | sweet short paste (1139) | 350 g flour mix |
| 1¼ lb | cooking apples | 700 g |
| 2 oz | sultanas | 70 g |
| 3 oz | caster sugar | 100 g |
| ½ level teaspoon | mixed spice | 2 g |
| ½ | lemon | ½ |

### Method

1. Prepare a sweet short paste, adding ¼ level teaspoon (1 g for 10) of baking powder to the flour. Allow the paste to rest.

2. Peel, quarter, core and slice the apples into a basin. Add the cleaned sultanas, sugar, the grated rind and strained juice of the lemon. Sprinkle with the mixed spice and mix them together.

3. Roll three-quarters of the paste into a ball and, with a little flour, roll it out until 5 mm thick. Line a greased 200 mm (225 mm for 10 portions) flan ring with the paste on a greased baking sheet. When it is lined, remove the excess paste by rolling the pin across the top. Egg-wash the edge.

4. Fill the case with the apple mixture. Mould the quarter of the paste and trimmings into a ball and roll it out 5 mm thick, large enough for the cover.

5. Cover the apple with the paste and press the edges firmly together. Remove any excess paste from the edge.

6. With the back of a knife, mark lightly into 8 or 10 portions. Let it rest for 30 minutes.

7. Egg-wash the surface and dredge it lightly with caster sugar. Make a small incision in the centre to allow the excess steam in cooking to escape.

8. Bake in the centre to top of an oven at 200°C (400°F) for 12–15 minutes until set and lightly coloured. Reduce the heat to 175°C (350°F) and bake it for approximately 30–35 minutes in all.

9. Serve on a hot round salver. In a sauceboat on an under-flat with a doily, serve Custard sauce (1174) or Sauce anglaise (1173).

### 1304 Treacle tart

| 8 portions | Ingredients | 10 couverts |
|---|---|---|
| 8 oz flour mix | sweet short paste (1139) or | |
| | sugar paste (1140) | 280 g flour mix |
| 12 fl. oz | golden syrup | 420 ml |
| 5 oz | white breadcrumbs | 175 g |
| ½ | grated lemon rind | ½ |

### Method

1. Prepare the paste and let it rest for 15 minutes.

2. Line with the paste a 200 mm (225 mm for 10 portions) greased flan ring on a greased baking sheet. (See recipe 1303, 3 in method, for lining.) Cut off the excess paste.

3. Mix the syrup, crumbs, and lemon rind together and pour it into the paste lining. Damp the edge of the paste with egg-wash.

4. Roll out the trimmings to an oblong 225–250 mm in length and 3 mm thick. Cut it into 5 mm-wide strips.

5. Place the strips 25 mm apart across the filling, pressing at each edge to remove any excess paste. Alternate the direction of each strip so that they form a trellis pattern.

6. Bake in the centre to top of an oven at 200°C (400°F) for 15 minutes, then reduce the temperature to 190°C (375°F) for a further 20 minutes to complete baking.

7. Serve the tart on a hot round dish. If desired, a Custard sauce (1174) or Sauce anglaise (1173) may be served separately.

### 1305 LINING OF FLANS

It is imperative that all flans are correctly lined, or the finished flan, after it has been cooked, may (a) be shrunk, because the paste has been stretched, (b) leak, because the paste is uneven in thickness, or (c) be cracked.

Flans should be lined as follows:

1. Roll the paste lightly with the hand into a ball, then flatten it slightly with the palm of the hand. Use 8 oz (250 g) flour mix of sugar paste.

2. Using enough flour to prevent the paste sticking, roll the paste in all directions until it is 40 mm larger all round than the flan ring and 4–6 mm thick. Use a 200 mm ring for 8 portions and a 225 mm ring for 10 portions.

3. Lightly dust the slab or table with flour and place the greased clean flan ring into position. Fold the paste in half so that it can be easily moved and place it across the ring. Loosely unfold the paste.

4. Support the edge of the paste with one hand. With the fingers of the other hand, gently ease the paste down until it is square with the slab and the side of the flan ring. Lightly press the paste into position with the thumb. A rounded bottom edge will shrink when cooked.

5. Lightly press the paste to the side of the ring to prevent air pockets or cracks.

6. Lightly ease the top edge of the paste slightly inwards. Remove the excess paste by rolling a rolling pin across the top of the ring.

7. With a little flour on the finger and thumb, raise the edge 5 mm above the flan ring; at the same time, finish with the edge sloped at a 45° angle towards the inner side.

8. Crimp the edge with a pair of tweezers dipped in flour. When doing this, support the inside of the paste with one finger.

9. Finally, pass the edge of the thumb around the flan ring edge to make sure no paste is over-hanging the side, so that the ring can be easily removed from the flan when cooked. Unless it is to be filled with a liquid, dock (prick) the bottom of the paste.

### 1306 Apple flan          Flan aux pommes

| 8 portions | Ingredients | 10 couverts |
|---|---|---|
| 8 oz flour mix | sugar paste (1140) | 280 g flour mix |
| 2 lb | cooking apples | 1·125 kg |
| 4 oz | sugar | 140 g |
| 6 oz | apricot glaze (1180) | 210 g |

### Method

1. Make the paste and allow it to rest for 10–15 minutes.

2. Place aside one-quarter of the smaller apples for the decoration of the flan.

3. Wash and quarter the remainder of the apples and remove the core. Place them in a fairly shallow pan, then add the sugar and 5–10 mm of water. Cover, bring to the boil, toss over and cook for 8–12 minutes until soft. Drain on a sieve and pour off any syrup. Rub the apple through the sieve on to a wide tray. Allow the purée to cool completely.

4. Line the flan (1305) and put it on a greased baking sheet. Three-quarters fill the flan with the cold purée.

5. Peel and quarter the remainder of the apples and remove the core. Thinly slice the apples and neatly arrange them around the outer edge of the top of the purée, so that each slice three-quarters overlaps the next. Continue to cover, slightly overlapping each circle of slices, until all the purée is covered.

6. Place the flan in the centre to top of an oven at 200°C (400°F) for approximately 10 minutes until the paste is set. Reduce the temperature to 160°C (325°F) and bake for a further 20–25 minutes.

7. When cooked, carefully remove the ring and return the flan to the oven for 3–4 minutes to dry out the edge of the paste. At this stage, if desired, the edge of the flan may be egg-washed to give a glazed finish to the paste.

8. When cool, mask the fruit in the direction of the flow of the slices with boiling apricot glaze and allow it to set.

9. Serve the flan on a flat round salver on a doily. If served hot, Custard sauce (1174) is served separately.

*Note.* When designated Chantilly, the flan is finished with rosettes of Crème Chantilly (1151).

### 1307 Soft fruit flans

**Method**

1. Line the flan (1305) with sugar paste (1140), prick the bottom and let it rest for 15–30 minutes.

2. Cut a circle of greaseproof paper and line the flan with it so that it comes 20 mm above the paste. Fill the lining with haricot beans.

3. Place the flan to bake in the centre to top of an oven at 200°C (400°F) for approximately 8–10 minutes to just set the paste. Remove the beans and paper, place the flan lower in the oven, reduce the temperature to 190°C (375°F) and bake for a further 10–15 minutes until the paste is a light biscuit colour and just firm. When cooked with no filling, the term 'cooked blind' is used.

4. Three-quarters fill the flan with $\frac{3}{4}$ pint (525 ml) of pastry cream (1150) and allow it to cool and set.

5. Neatly cover the surface with the prepared fruit, according to the recipe, and mask it with boiling apricot glaze. Use a red glaze for red fruits.

6. Clean the base edge if necessary and place the flan on a round salver on a doily.

*Note.* Decorate the flan with rosettes of Crème Chantilly (1151) when so designated, e.g. Flan aux pêches Chantilly.

### 1308 Banana flan      Flan aux bananes

**Method**

1. Prepare the flan (1305), cook it 'blind' then fill it with pastry cream (1150).

2. Peel 3 bananas, cut them into slices 3 mm thick, slightly on the slant, and place them on to a plate with the juice of a lemon to retain the colour.

3. Arrange them neatly, half overlapping in circles, to cover the pastry cream.

5. Finish as from 5 in method of 1307.

### 1309 Pineapple flan      Flan aux ananas

**Method**

1. Prepare the flan (1305), cook it 'blind' then fill it with pastry cream (1150).

2. Cut the slices of canned pineapple in halves, then cut these in half to give 4 half slices per ring.

3. Arrange the slices half overlapping round the flan with the pointed ends towards the centre, if necessary complete the covering with quarter slices.

4. Finish as from 5 in method of 1307.

### 1310 Apricot flan      Flan aux abricots

**Method**

1. Prepare the flan (1305), cook it 'blind' then fill it with pastry cream (1150).

2. Cut the halves of poached or canned apricots in half. Arrange the sections neatly on end touching each other in circles so that they completely cover the pastry cream.

3. Finish as from 5 in method of 1307.

### 1311 Peach flan      Flan aux pêches

### 1312 Pear flan      Flan aux poires

**Method**

1. Prepare the flan (1305), cook it 'blind' then fill it with pastry cream (1150).

2. Lay the flat side of the half peaches or pears (poached or canned) on a board. Cut them into wedge-shaped sections 5 mm wide on the outer edge and tapering to the centre.

3. Arrange the sections neatly touching each other in circles around the flan so that they cover the pastry cream.

4. Finish as from 5 in method of 1307.

## 1313 Cherry flan — Flan aux cerises

**Method**

1. Prepare the flan (1305), cook it 'blind' then fill it with pastry cream (1150). Alternatively, spread the lined flan with a little raspberry jam, pipe a 10 mm layer of frangipane (1155) from the centre to the edge, bake it for 30 minutes until light golden brown, then let it cool.
2. Drain the stoned poached or canned cherries well. Arrange them neatly touching each other to completely cover the filling. The stalk end from where the stone is removed is placed underneath.
3. Finish as from 5 in method of 1307 using a red glaze.

## 1314 Strawberry flan — Flan aux fraises

**Method**

1. Prepare as for Flan aux cerises (1313).
2. Select, if possible, small to medium sized strawberries. Remove the stalk, wash the strawberries, then thoroughly drain them on a cloth. If larger fruit are used, cut them in halves and place the cut side down.

## 1315 Gooseberry flan — Flan aux groseilles

**Method**

1. Line the flan (1305), cook it 'blind' then fill it with pastry cream (1150).
2. Prepare the gooseberries as for compote (1364) and well drain them. Arrange them neatly touching each other in circles so that the circles completely cover the pastry cream.
3. Finish as from 5 in method of 1307.

**Alternative method**

1. Line the flan (1305). Top and tail dessert-type gooseberries, then wash and drain them.
2. Arrange them neatly to well fill the flan. Sprinkle with caster sugar.
3. Bake the flan, first at the top of the oven at 200°C (400°F) for 10 minutes to set the paste, then place it lower in the oven at 175° (350°F) for a further 20–25 minutes until the paste and fruit are cooked. Allow it to cool.
4. Finish as from 5 in method of 1307.

## 1316 Rhubarb flan — Flan au rhubarbe

**Method**

1. Line the flan (1305). Cut off the ends of the rhubarb, removing the skin if necessary, then wash and drain it.
2. Cut it into 40 mm lengths and arrange them in lines to well fill the flan. Sprinkle with brown sugar. Cook as in alternative method of Gooseberry flan (1315) and finish with extra-sweet red glaze.

## 1317 Raspberry flan — Flan aux framboises

**Method**

1. Prepare as for Flan aux cerises (1313).
2. Pick the raspberries, removing any stalks or mildewed fruit. Only wash and thoroughly drain if any grit is apparent.

## 1318 Bakewell tart

| 8 Portions | Ingredients | 10 couverts |
|---|---|---|
| 8 oz flour mix | sugar paste (1140) | 280 g flour mix |
| 4 oz butter mix | frangipane (1155) | 140 g butter mix |
| 2 oz | raspberry jam | 70 g |

**Method**

1. Line the flan with the paste (1305), prick the bottom and spread it with the jam.
2. Using a piping bag and a 15 mm plain tube, pipe the frangipane from the centre, spiral fashion, to the outer edge of the paste, using all the mixture.
3. Roll the trimmings 225–250 mm long and 3 mm thick and cut them into 5 mm-wide strips. Arrange the strips on top in opposite directions to form a 25 mm spaced trellis pattern. Press the strips well on to the edges of the lined ring.
4. Bake at the centre of an oven at 200°C (400°F) for 10 minutes to set the paste, then reduce the temperature to 160°C (325°F). When lightly coloured, move lower in the oven. Bake for 35–40 minutes in all. The centre should be springy to the touch.
5. When cooked, brush over with 3 oz (100 g) of icing sugar prepared into water icing (1171).
6. Serve warm on a flat salver on a doily. If desired, a Custard sauce (1174) may be served separately.

## 1319 Almond flan — Flan amandine

**Method**

1. Prepare, cook and glaze as for Bakewell tart (1318).
2. After piping the frangipane, sprinkle with 1 oz (35 g for 10) of filleted or flaked almonds. No strips of pastry are used.

## 1320 Flan normande

| 8 portions | Ingredients | 10 couverts |
| --- | --- | --- |
| 8 oz flour mix | sugar paste (1140) | 280 g flour mix |
| 1 lb | cooking apples | 560 g |
| 2 oz | caster sugar | 70 g |
| 12 fl. oz | milk | 420 ml |
| 2 | eggs | 3 small |
| 4 drops | vanilla essence | 5 drops |
| few grains | nutmeg | few grains |

### Method

1. Line the flan with the paste (1305).
2. Peel and quarter the apples and remove the core. Cut them into sections 5 mm thick at the outer edge, tapering to the centre.
3. Do not prick the base of the flan. Arrange the sections of apple touching each other in a circle to cover the base of the flan.
4. Bake at the top of an oven at 200°C (400°F) for approximately 10 minutes to set the paste.
5. Heat the milk and sugar to blood heat, whisk it on to the beaten eggs and vanilla, then strain the liquid. Slowly fill it into the flan and lightly sprinkle the surface with a few grains of nutmeg.
6. Reduce the temperature of the oven to 150°C (300°F). When the custard is set and lightly coloured, move the flan to the bottom of the oven to finish cooking. The overall cooking time is approximately 35–40 minutes.
7. Remove the ring. Serve the flan on a hot round salver.

### 1321 Mincemeat tart

| 8 portions | Ingredients | 10 couverts |
| --- | --- | --- |
| 8 oz flour mix | sweet short paste (1139) or sugar paste (1140) | 280 g flour mix |
| 8 portions | mincemeat (1294) | 10 portions |

### Method

1. Prepare, cook and serve as for Dutch apple tart (1303), using either paste.
2. Replace the apple mixture with the mincemeat.

### 1322 Apple meringue flan        Flan aux pommes meringué

### Method

1. Prepare an apple flan (1306) without the apple slices on top. When cooked, allow the flan to cool.
2. Prepare an ordinary meringue (1165), using 3 whites of egg for 8 portions, 4 for 10 and 5 oz (175 g) of caster sugar.

3. Using a piping bag and a 10 mm star tube, pipe 20–25 mm-high rosettes of the meringue, touching each other to cover the apple completely.
4. Decorate the meringue with quarters of glacé cherries and small diamonds of angelica.
5. Dredge the surface of the meringue with caster sugar. Glaze light golden brown in the top of an oven at 190–200°C (375–400°F).
6. Serve warm or cold on a round salver.

### 1323 Apricot meringue flan        Flan aux abricots meringué

### Method

1. Prepare, cook and finish as for Flan aux pommes meringuées (1322).
2. After lining the flan, three-quarters fill it with apricot pulp in place of apple purée.

### 1324 Lemon meringue flan        Flan au citron meringué

### Method

1. Prepare the flan (1305) and bake it 'blind' (see 2 and 3 in method of 1307).
2. When cooked, fill the flan with a lemon curd filling for flans (1158).
3. Finish as for Flan aux pommes meringué (1322) from 2 in method).
4. The flan may be served warm or cold.

### 1325 Flan aux poires Bourdaloue

### 1326 Flan aux pêches Bourdaloue

### Method

1. Prepare the flan (1305) and bake it 'blind' (see 2 and 3 in method of 1307).
2. When cooked, half fill the flan with pastry cream (1150) and cover the cream with halves, quarters or sections of poached or canned pears or peaches.
3. Mask the fruit with the remainder of the boiling pastry cream; use a 1 pint or 700 ml milk mix for 8–10 portions.
4. Cover the surface with flaked almonds and dredge it with icing sugar. Glaze a light golden brown under a very moderate salamander.
5. Serve on a round salver with a doily.

## 1327 Baked jam roll

| 8 portions | Ingredients | 10 couverts |
|---|---|---|
| 1 lb flour mix | sweet short paste (1139) | 500 g flour mix |
| 6 oz | jam | 185 g |
| 1 | egg (egg-wash) | 1 |

### Method

1. When preparing the sweet short paste, sieve ½ oz (20 g) of baking powder with the flour.

2. Using a little flour, roll the paste to an oblong shape 350 × 250 mm × 3 mm thick. Brush the edges with egg-wash.

3. Spread the jam evenly to within 20 mm of the edges. Roll the 250 mm width to form a roll 350 mm long and approximately 55 mm wide. For 10 portions, increase the length to 450 mm.

4. Place the roll on a greased baking sheet with the seam underneath. Brush completely over with egg-wash.

5. Mark the paste with the back of a fork, slightly on the slant, across the width.

6. Bake in the centre to top of the oven at 190°C (375°F) for approximately 15 minutes, then reduce the temperature to 150°C (300°F) and bake for a further 25 minutes. Should the roll become coloured before cooking is complete, move it to a lower part of the oven.

7. Lightly trim off both ends and cut the roll into portions on the slant. Serve on a hot flat dish. In a sauceboat on an underflat with a doily, serve Custard sauce (1174), Jam sauce (1182), or Almond sauce (1176).

## 1328 Baked apple dumplings — Rabottes de pommes

| 8 portions | Ingredients | 10 couverts |
|---|---|---|
| 1 lb flour mix | sweet short paste (1139) | 500 g flour mix |
| 8 × 5 oz | cooking apples | 10 × 140 g |
| 4 oz | caster sugar | 125 g |
| 8 | cloves | 10 |
| 1 | egg (egg-wash) | 1 |

### Method

1. Using a little flour, roll out the paste 3 mm thick. Cut it into squares approximately 150 mm long and egg-wash the edges.

2. Peel, core and wash the apples. Place one apple in the centre of each piece of paste, fill the centres with the sugar and place 1 clove in each.

3. Bring the paste up the sides of the apples to the top, to completely envelope them; seal the top ends tightly. Invert and place them on a greased baking sheet, 25 mm apart. Egg-wash all over.

4. Roll out the trimmings of paste and make a 25 mm fluted circle of paste for each apple; place these on top of the apple and egg-wash them. Allow to rest for 20–30 minutes.

5. Bake in the centre of an oven at 200°C (400°F) for 15 minutes to set; reduce the temperature to 160°C (325°F) and bake for a further 25 minutes. Test the apples by piercing them with a knife point; it should penetrate to the centre without undue pressure.

6. Dredge very lightly with icing sugar. Serve on a hot flat dish. Serve Custard sauce (1174) or Sauce anglaise (1173) in a sauceboat on an underflat with a doily.

## 1329 Baked date and apple slice

| 8 portions | Ingredients | 10 couverts |
|---|---|---|
| 12 oz flour mix | sweet short paste (1139) or sugar paste (1140) | 420 flour mix |
| 1½ lb | cooking apples | 850 g |
| 4 oz | dates | 140 g |
| 4 oz | brown sugar | 140 g |
| ½ level teaspoon | cinnamon | 2 g |
| 1 | egg (egg-wash) | 1 |

### Method

1. Using a little flour, roll the paste to an oblong shape approximately 350 mm long × 210–225 mm wide and 3 mm thick (425 mm long for 10 portions).

2. Cut a base strip 350 × 100 mm wide and place it on a greased baking sheet. Egg-wash the edges.

3. Peel, quarter and core the apples. Cut them in thin slices, add the chopped and stoned dates and the sugar and sprinkle with the cinnamon. Place the mixture on the paste to within 10 mm of the edge.

4. Cut the covering strip of paste 110–125 mm wide, place it over the apple mixture and seal the edges all round by pressing with the thumb. Finish by notching the edge of the paste with the back of a knife.

5. Egg-wash the surface. Mark across into 8 or 10 portions and scroll across with the back of a fork.

6. Bake as for apple dumplings (1328, 5 in method).

7. Trim off the ends, cut the slice in portions and dust them lightly with icing sugar. Serve on a hot flat dish with Custard sauce (1174), or Sauce anglaise (1173) in sauceboats.

## 1330 Baked raisin and apple slice

### Method

1. Prepare, cook and serve as for Baked date and apple slice (1329). Replace the dates with cleaned raisins.

## 1331 Apple strudel — Apfel-strudel

| 8 portions | Ingredients | 10 couverts |
|---|---|---|
| 12 oz | strong flour ⎫ | 420 g |
| 1 oz | butter ⎪ paste | 35 g |
| ½ level teaspoon | salt ⎬ | 2 g |
| 10 fl. oz | tepid water ⎭ | 350 ml |
| 3 lb | russet-type apples | 1·7 kg |
| 6 oz | sultanas | 210 g |
| 4 oz | white breadcrumbs | 140 g |
| 6 oz | caster sugar | 210 g |
| 5 oz | butter | 175 g |
| 2 oz | ground almonds | 70 g |
| ½ level teaspoon | cinnamon | 2 g |
| 1 | lemon (zest and juice) | 1 |

### Method

1. Sieve the flour and salt into a basin and make a bay in the centre. Melt the 1 oz (35 g) of butter, add the water and pour it into the bay.

2. Absorb the flour and work it to a very smooth dough. Place it on a floured cloth, cover with a basin and keep it in a warm place for 30 minutes.

3. Peel and core the apples, then thinly slice them into a basin. Sprinkle with the cinnamon, grated lemon zest and strained lemon juice. If desired, sprinkle with a little brandy.

4. Fry the breadcrumbs a very light golden brown in half of the second amount of butter. Melt the other half of the butter.

5. Place the dough on an evenly floured large cloth and, with a rolling pin, roll it to an oblong shape approximately 350 × 250 mm, then place the back of the hands under the paste and gradually stretch it from each corner and sides until it is very thin.

6. Sprinkle the dough with the melted butter, then the crumbs, apples, sugar, almonds and cleaned sultanas.

7. Take hold of one side of the cloth with both hands and roll the paste and filling into a roll approximately 375 mm long × 75–85 mm in diameter.

8. Seal the ends by twisting them tight; remove any excess paste. Place the hand and arm under the roll and carefully place it on a greased baking sheet. Brush over with melted butter and let it rest for 15–20 minutes.

9. Bake in the centre to top of an oven at 200°C (400°F) for approximately 35–45 minutes. Trim off each end, dust with icing sugar and serve it on a hot flat dish. Serve Sauce anglaise (1173) separately.

## 1332 Black cherry strudel — Kirschen-strudel

### Method

1. Prepare, cook and serve as for Apple strudel (1331). Replace 75 per cent of the apples with stoned black cherries (fresh or canned). Before rolling, sprinkle with kirsch.

---

# 1333 JELLIES, BAVAROIS, MOUSSE, COLD CHARLOTTES

## 1334 Plain lemon jelly — Gelée au citron

| 8 portions | Ingredients | 10 couverts |
|---|---|---|
| 2 pints | water | 1·4 litres |
| 8 oz | granulated sugar | 280 g |
| 2 oz | gelatine | 70 g |
| 2 | whites of egg | 3 |
| 1 small | bayleaf | 1 |
| 6 | coriander seeds | 10 |
| 50 mm piece | cinnamon stick | 50 mm piece |
| 2 | lemons | 3 |

### Method

1. Soak the leaf gelatine for 3–4 minutes in cold water then squeeze it dry.

2. Remove the zest of the lemons with a peeler, place it in a clean saucepan and add the juice. Add all the other ingredients.

3. Whisk frequently until boiling; remove the whisk. Move the pan from the heat to the side of stove, cover and allow to stand for 15 minutes.

4. When the jelly is clear, pass it through a jelly bag which has previously been well washed and rinsed in cold water. Care should be taken to avoid breaking the clarification when ladling the jelly. If the first ladle or two of the jelly is not clear, return it through the bag until it runs clear and shiny.

5. Plain lemon jelly is generally used for various types of jellies as a base.

6. It may be set in a mould or moulds in a refrigerator and unmoulded by dipping the moulds in hot water for 1 second, then turning the jelly out on to a cold flat dish.

7. If desired, decorate up the sides with Crème Chantilly with a piping bag and a 10 mm star tube.

## 1335 Mixed fruit jelly — Gelée aux fruits

| 8 portions | Ingredients | 10 couverts |
|---|---|---|
| 8 portions | plain lemon jelly (1334) | 10 portions |
| 8 oz | drained mixed fruits | 280 g |

## Method

1. Prepare the jelly and allow it to cool. Place 10 mm of jelly in a clean mould or moulds and place the moulds in a tray of ice and water to set the jelly.

2. Prepare the fruits; blanch, skin and remove the seeds from grapes; stone cherries; cut peaches, apricots, pine apples and pears into segments; cut away all skin and pith from oranges and cut out the fruit from between the skin; skin and cut bananas as required into 5 mm-thick slices.

3. Place the fruit in a decorative manner on the set jelly. Add a little more jelly and let it set. Repeat the operation of adding fruit and jelly until the mould or moulds are full. Finish setting in a refrigerator. The jelly may be coloured if desired.

4. Unmould and finish as for Gelée au citron (1334).

### 1336 Vanilla Bavarian cream — Bavarois vanille

| 8 portions | Ingredients | 10 couverts |
|---|---|---|
| 1 pint | milk | 700 ml |
| 4 oz | caster sugar | 140 g |
| 1 oz | gelatine | 35 g |
| 4 | yolks of egg | 5 |
| 4 | whites of egg | 5 |
| 4 drops | vanilla essence | 5 drops |
| ¼ pint + ¼ pint (decoration) | cream | 175 ml + 175 ml (decoration) |

### Method

1. Place the leaf gelatine to soak in cold water. If ground gelatine is used, place it in a small mould, cover with a tablespoon of water and place it in a bain-marie until dissolved.

2. Mix in a china basin the yolks, sugar and vanilla essence.

3. Boil the milk, whisk half of it on to the yolks and sugar and whisk it back into the remainder of the milk.

4. Place the pan on the heat and bring the mixture almost to boiling point, but do not boil. Using a wooden spatule, stir until the mixture thickens.

5. Remove the pan from the fire, stir in the well squeezed-out leaf gelatine or liquid ground gelatine and strain the mixture into a basin to cool.

6. Stir the mixture in ice water until on the point of setting, then fold in the loosely whipped cream, then the stiffly whipped whites of eggs.

7. Pour into moulds very lightly greased with sweet almond oil or rinsed in cold water (a 2 pint mould for 8, 1·5 litre mould for 10; smaller size moulds are also used).

8. Place to set in refrigerator.

9. Serve on a cold round flat dish. Turn the cream out of the moulds by dipping them in hot water for 1–2 seconds, then releasing the edge of the cream with the fingers. Decorate up the sides with sweetened whipped cream with rosettes on top, using a piping bag with a 10 mm star tube.

### 1337 Coffee bavarois — Bavarois Moka

#### Method

1. Prepare and serve as for Bavarois vanille (1336); add sufficient coffee extract or essence (approximately 1 dessertspoon) to flavour and give a light coffee colour when the mixture is strained.

### 1338 Chocolate bavarois — Bavarois au chocolat

#### Method

Dissolve 1 oz (35 g) of chocolate or cocoa powder in a quarter of the milk and bring it to the boil; whisk to dissolve the chocolate. Add the remainder of the milk, then prepare and serve as for Bavarois vanille (1336).

### 1339 Strawberry bavarois — Bavarois aux fraises

#### Method

1. Reduce the quantity of milk used by 25 per cent. When the mixture is prepared and cooling, add ¼ pint (175 ml) of prepared strawberry pulp and a few drops of cochineal.

2. Finish and serve as for Bavarois vanille (1336). Place fresh strawberries on the rosettes of whipped cream around the base.

### 1340 Raspberry bavarois — Bavarois aux framboises

#### Method

Prepare and serve as for Bavarois aux fraises (1339). Replace the strawberry pulp with raspberry pulp and use fresh raspberries around the base.

### 1341 Praline bavarois — Bavarois praliné

#### Method

Prepare and serve as for Bavarois vanille (1336). Add 1½ oz (50 g) of praline (1167) to the mixture when it is at setting point.

### 1342 Ribbon bavarois — Bavarois rubané

#### Method

1. This is usually made with 3 or 4 different coloured and flavoured bavarois.

2. One-third or one-quarter fill the moulds with vanilla bavarois (1336) and set it in the refrigerator.

3. Finish and add a similar amount of raspberry or strawberry bavarois (1339, 1340) and allow it to set.

4. Finish with one or two more layers of chocolate and/or coffee bavarois (1338, 1337), setting each flavour before adding the next.

5. Serve as for Bavarois vanille (1336).

### 1343 Banana bavarois      Bavarois aux bananes

**Method**

1. Set 5 mm of lemon jelly in the bottom of the mould. When it is set, cover it with 3 mm-thick slices of peeled banana, the slices half overlapping each other and arranged in circles to the centre. Cover with 5 mm of jelly and set.

2. Fill the mould with Bavarois vanille (1336), adding 4 oz (140 g) of 5 mm diced banana just as it reaches setting point. Set and serve as in 1336.

### 1344 Orange bavarois      Bavarois à l'orange

**Method**

1. Set 5 mm of orange jelly in the bottom of the mould. When it is set, arrange a star pattern of orange segments (free of skin and pith) then cover them with 5 mm of jelly and set.

2. Prepare a Bavarois vanille (1336), adding the zest of 2–3 oranges to the milk. Colour the base orange with a few drops of yellow and red colour. Fill into the moulds just as it reaches setting point. Place in refrigeration.

3. Unmould on to a round flat dish and decorate with rosettes of cream on top and around the base. Place orange segments free of skin and pith on the rosettes.

### 1345 Peach bavarois      Bavarois aux pêches

**Method**

1. Set a star of segments of peach in lemon or peach jelly in the base of the mould. (See 1344.)

2. When set, fill with Bavarois vanille (1336), adding 4 oz (140 g) of 5 mm dice of peach to the mixture at setting point.

3. Serve as for Bavarois vanille.

### 1346 Mousse      Mousse

**Method**

1. The basic mixture is prepared in the same manner as for the various flavoured bavarois with the following adjustments.

2. The milk content is reduced by 25 per cent when making the base.

3. The amount of cream incorporated into the base is doubled in quantity. The cream shown for decorative purposes remains the same.

4. The prepared mixture, when it is at setting point, is poured into (a) individual serving cups, i.e. coupes, (b) individual moulds, or (c) larger moulds if desired. Place to set in a refrigerator.

5. When set, dip the moulds in hot water for 1 second and turn out the mousse on to a flat dish. Decorate the sides of the mousse with sweetened whipped cream.

6. In all cases, decorate on top with rosettes of sweetened whipped cream. Decorate the rosettes with violet or rose petals, chocolate nibs or pieces of fruit, according to the designation of the mousse. Always serve mousse chilled.

7. If in coupes, place the coupe on a flat dish with dish paper or a doily.

### 1347      Riz à l'impératrice

| 8 portions | Ingredients | 10 couverts |
|---|---|---|
| ½ pint milk mix | vanilla bavarois base (1336) | 350 ml milk mix |
| ½ pint | milk | 350 ml |
| 1½ oz | carolina rice | 50 g |
| 1 oz | caster sugar | 35 g |
| 1 oz | diced glacé fruits | 35 g |
| ¼ pint | raspberry jelly | 175 ml |
| ¼ pint | thin sauce Melba (1189) | 175 ml |
| 1 | lemon (in zest) | 1 |

**Method**

1. Line the bottom of a clean charlotte mould with liquid raspberry jelly, 5 mm in depth, and allow it to set.

2. Boil the milk, add the washed rice, reboil, then add the sugar.

3. Add the bouquet of zest of lemon and allow the rice to simmer gently for 30 minutes.

4. Prepare a vanilla bavarois, strain it and place it to cool.

5. Turn out the rice and place it to cool; remove the lemon zest.

6. Mix a little of the bavarois mixture with the cold rice then fold in the remainder, at the same time sprinkling in the diced glacé fruits.

7. Fill the moulds and allow to set.

8. Dip the mould in hot water and turn it out on to a silver salver. Cover the surrounding base of the dish with a thin Melba sauce (1189).

9. Decorate with whipped cream if desired.

336

*Note.* If desired, jelly may be set on a serving dish to replace the Melba sauce.

## 1348 Russian charlotte — Charlotte à la russe

| 8 portions | Ingredients | 10 couverts |
|---|---|---|
| 3 egg mix | sponge fingers (1381) | 4 egg mix |
| ¾ pint milk mix | vanilla bavarois base (1336) | 525 ml milk mix |
| ¼ pint | cream for decoration | 175 ml |

### Method

1. Line the base and the sides of a 2 pint (1·5 litre) charlotte mould with trimmed sponge fingers. They must fit very tightly with no gaps between.

2. Fill the mould with the vanilla bavarois at setting point. If the mixture is not at setting point, the sponge fingers will become soaked and soft. Set in a refrigerator.

3. To serve, trim the top edge of the biscuits level with the mould and turn the mould out on to a round flat dish. Decorate between the crevices of the sponge fingers on the sides with sweetened whipped cream, then pipe rosettes of cream around the base and top edge and place small pieces of crystallized violets on the rosettes. Use a 10 mm star tube for piping.

## 1349 — Charlotte moscovite

### Method

1. Line the bottom of the charlotte moulds with 10 mm of raspberry jelly and let it set firm.

2. Line the sides of the mould with trimmed sponge fingers and fill the mould with vanilla bavarois mixture at setting point. Place to set in refrigerator.

3. Dip the mould in hot water for 1 second to release the jelly and finish as for Charlotte russe (1348).

## 1350 — Charlotte royale

### Method

1. Prepare a 3 egg Swiss roll (1380), using raspberry jam. When cold, cut it into 5 mm-thick slices and completely line a charlotte mould.

2. Finish the preparation and serve as from 2 in method of Charlotte russe (1348).

## 1351 — Charlotte Montreuil

### Method

1. Line the base of the charlotte mould with 5 mm of lemon or peach jelly and let it set. Arrange a star pattern of peach segments on the jelly, add more jelly to cover the peaches and let it set.

2. Line the sides of the mould with thin slices of Swiss roll (1380) filled with apricot jam.

3. Fill with Vanilla bavarois (1336) at setting point.

4. When set, dip the mould in hot water for 1 second and unmould on to a round flat dish. Decorate the sides with sweetened whipped cream and rosettes of cream around the base.

---

# 1352 FRUIT CONDÉS, CRÉOLES, TRIFLES, COMPOTES, FRESH FRUIT SALADS, FOOLS

## 1353 Apple Condé — Pommes Condé

| 8 portions | Ingredients | 10 couverts |
|---|---|---|
| 4 × 5 oz | cooking apples | 5 × 140–150 g |
| 1 pint | stock syrup (1170) | 700 ml |
| ¼ | lemon (in zest) | ¼ |
| 10 mm | cinnamon stick | 10 mm |
| 8 portions | prepared rice for Condé (1228) | 10 portions |
| ¾ pint | apricot glaze (1180) | 525 ml |
| 1 oz | angelica | 35 g |
| ½ oz | currants | 20 g |
| ¼ pint | cream (for decoration) | 175 ml |

### Method

1. Prepare and cook the rice for Condé, cover it with a buttered paper and allow it to go cold.

2. Peel and core the apples, cut them in halves and poach them in the stock syrup with the cinnamon and lemon. Turn the apples during cooking. Allow to cool in the syrup.

3. If the consistency of the rice permits, add a little sweetened whipped cream.

4. Place the rice mixture inside a flan ring on a round salver large enough to allow 25–50 mm all around the ring. Alternatively, dress the rice in cups (coupes) or in small individual dishes for individual service.

5. Well drain the fruit on a wire grill. Mix a few drops of yellow colour and cochineal on a plate and, using a brush, very lightly colour the centre of the apple with it to give the natural-coloured bloom.

6. Equally space the fruit on the rice. Place a small stalk of angelica in the top of the apple to represent the stalk and a washed currant at the base.

7. Glaze the fruit, rice, then the base of the dish with the boiling apricot glaze.

8. When set, decorate around the edge, between the fruit, and also in the centre, with rosettes of sweetened cream using a 10 mm star tube. For individual service, pipe a small rosette or 4 stars on each side.

### 1354 Pear condé                          Poire Condé

**Method**

Prepare, finish and serve as for Pommes Condé (1353), using half pears in place of half apples.

### 1355 Apricot condé                       Abricot Condé

### 1356 Peach condé                         Pêche Condé

### 1357 Pineapple condé                     Ananas Condé

**Method**

1. Prepare, finish and serve as for Pommes Condé (1353). No colouring is used on the fruit.
2. Allow 3–4 halves of apricots and half a peach per portion.
3. Pineapple slices are cut in halves, then across to make 4 pieces. Arrange the slices half overlapping with the pointed ends to the centre.

### 1358 Pineapple créole                    Ananas créole

| 8 portions | Ingredients | 10 couverts |
|---|---|---|
| 8 portions | prepared rice for Condé (1228) | 10 portions |
| 6–8 | slices of pineapple | 8–10 |
| 1½ oz | angelica | 50 g |
| 1 oz | currants | 35 g |
| 1 pint | apricot glaze (1180) | 700 ml |

**Method**

1. Prepare and cook the rice as for condé, cover it with a buttered paper and allow it to go cold.
2. Cut the pineapple rings in halves, then across to produce 4 pieces from each slice. Allow 3 pieces per portion.
3. Dress the rice in a dome shape in the centre of an oval dish, allowing 50 mm on either side of the rice. Smooth the surface of the rice with a palette knife, keeping it dome-shaped to represent a half pineapple.
4. Dip the palette knife in hot water and mark a 25 mm trellis pattern across the rice. Place a washed currant in each section.
5. Cut the angelica in long stalks and place in one end of the rice to represent the top of the pineapple. Arrange the pineapple overlapping around the rice.

6. Mask the rice, pineapple and the base of the dish with the boiling glaze and let it set.

*Note.* If desired, decorate around the base with rosettes of sweetened whipped cream.

### 1359 Banana créole                       Banane à la créole

**Method**

1. Use the ingredients as for Ananas créole (1358), replacing the currants with glacé cherries and the pineapple with 1 banana per portion.
2. Prepare and cook the rice as for condé, cover it with a buttered paper and allow it to go cold.
3. Boil 1 pint (700 ml) of stock syrup (1170) in a shallow pan. Peel the bananas, split them in halves lengthways and place them in the syrup. Move the syrup from the stove and allow the bananas to poach in the latent heat for 2 minutes. Drain on a wire grill or cloth.
4. Dress the rice flat, 25 mm deep, in a suitable dish (entrée type). Arrange the half bananas on top, mask the fruit and rice with boiling apricot glaze and let it set.
5. Decorate around the edges with rosettes of sweetened whipped cream. Place a quarter glacé cherry and a small diamond of angelica on each rosette.

### 1360 Sherry trifle

| 8 portions | Ingredients | 10 couverts |
|---|---|---|
| 8 oz | sponge cake (1377) | 280 g |
| 1 pint | milk | 700 ml |
| 2 oz | granulated sugar | 70 g |
| 1½ oz | custard powder | 50 g |
| 4 drops | vanilla essence | 5 drops |
| ½ pint | jelly | 350 ml |
| 2 fl. oz | sherry | 70 ml |
| ¼ pint | cream | 175 ml |
| 2 oz | jam | 70 g |
| 1 oz | roasted flaked almonds | 35 g |
| 1 oz | angelica | 35 g |
| 1 oz | glacé cherries | 35 g |

**Method**

1. Split the sponge cake through the centre with a knife and spread it with the jam.
2. Reform the sponge, and place it into a 50–75 mm-deep glass bowl. Soak the sponge with the jelly; if desired, stock or fruit syrup may be used. Sprinkle with the sherry and place it to set in a refrigerator.
3. Boil the milk, sugar and vanilla, thicken with the diluted custard powder, whisk until reboiling, then allow the mixture to cool. Pass it through a fine conical strainer over the soaked sponge and place it to set.

4. Decorate the surface with rosettes of sweetened whipped cream. Sprinkle all over with the roasted flaked almonds and place quarters of glacé cherries and small diamonds of angelica on the rosettes. Use a 10 mm star tube for piping.

5. Serve chilled on a round salver with a doily.

## 1361 Fruit trifle (except banana)

### Method

1. Using the same ingredients, prepare as for Sherry trifle (1360, to include 3 in method).

2. Arrange the fruit attractively on top. Peaches and pears are cut in segments which are arranged in a star pattern. Allow 6 oz (210 g) of fruit for 8 or 10 portions.

3. Mask the fruit with boiling apricot glaze and allow it to set.

4. Decorate around the edge of the dish with rosettes of sweetened cream. Sprinkle the almonds around the edge but not on the fruit. Place quarters of glacé cherries and small diamonds of angelica on the rosettes.

5. Serve chilled on a round salver with a doily.

## 1362 Banana trifle

### Method

1. Prepare and serve as for Fruit trifle (1361) with these exceptions: place the split and jammed sponge or sponge fingers in a shallow entrée-type dish, soak and cover in the same manner as 1361.

2. Poach ½ a banana per portion (see 3 in method 1359) and finish in the same manner as for 1361.

## 1363 Individual trifles

### Method 1 (using shallow dishes)

1. Use the same ingredients as for large trifles.

2. Split the sponge, spread it with jam and cut to a diamond shape 50 × 40 mm on the sides.

3. Place one piece in each shallow dish, soak it with jelly, syrup and sherry as required by its designation.

4. Mask with cool custard, allow it to set, then place it in a refrigerator.

5. Decorate with fruit at each corner if for fruit trifle.

6. Finish by decorating with rosettes of whipped cream, glacé cherries, angelica and roasted flaked almonds. Serve chilled on an underflat with a doily.

### Method 2 (using glass coupes)

1. Use the same ingredients as for large trifles.

2. Split the sponge, spread it with jam, then cut it into 10 mm dice.

3. Half fill glass coupes with the diced sponge, then proceed as for Method 1.

4. Serve chilled on an underflat with a doily.

## 1364 Stewed fruits — Compote de fruits

| 8 portions | Ingredients | 10 couverts |
|---|---|---|
| 2 lb | fruit | 1·125 kg |
| 1½ pints | water | 1 litre |
| 12 oz | sugar | 420 g |
| ½ | lemon (zest and juice) | ½ |

Dried fruits, if used, should be washed, soaked in cold water for several hours and rewashed before cooking. Prunes and figs are cooked as for hard fruits, but simmered in a covered pan on the stove with a small stick of cinnamon added.

### Method

1. Make a stock syrup with the water, sugar, lemon zest and juice.

2. Place the prepared fruits in a suitable shallow container and cover it with the boiling stock syrup. Hard fruit are covered with a sheet of greaseproof paper and poached in a medium oven until just cooked, then allowed to cool in the syrup. Medium hard fruits are reboiled and allowed to cool. Soft fruits are allowed to cool in the boiling syrup.

3. **Hard fruit**

**Apples:** peel, cut them in halves, core and shape, then cook them in the oven with 1 clove added.

**Pears:** peel, cut them in halves, core and cook them in the oven.

**Pineapple:** peel, cut them in rings or sections, core and cook them in the oven.

**Apricots:** pierce all over with a needle and cook them in the oven.

**Plums:** as for apricots.

**Peaches:** blanch and skin them, cut them in half, remove the stone and cook them in the oven.

**Rhubarb:** wash, remove leaves and skin if necessary, cut them into equal lengths and cook them in the oven.

### 4. Medium-hard fruit

**Cherries**: pick and wash the fruit, cover with boiling syrup, reboil, then cool.

**Blackcurrants**: pick and wash the fruit, cover with boiling syrup, reboil, then cool.

**Gooseberries**: pick and wash the fruit, cover with boiling syrup, reboil, then cool.

### 5. Soft fruit

**Redcurrants**: pick and wash the fruit, place in a china basin, cover with boiling syrup and cool.

**Whitecurrants**: pick and wash the fruit, place in a china basin, cover with boiling syrup and cool.

**Strawberries**: pick and wash the fruit, place in a china basin, cover with boiling syrup and cool.

**Raspberries**: pick and wash the fruit, place in a china basin, cover with boiling syrup and cool.

**Blackberries**: pick, and wash the fruit, place in a china basin, cover with boiling syrup and cool.

**Pears**: peel, cut in half, remove the core and cut into segments.

**Cherries**: pick and remove the stones.

**Grapes** (white): skin and remove the pips.

**Grapes** (black): cut in halves and remove the pips.

**Peaches**: blanch, cut in halves, remove the stones and cut in segments.

**Pineapple**: peel with a knife, remove the eyes, cut in half, remove the core and cut into 10 mm dice or ¼ segments.

**Banana**: skin and cut into 3 mm-thick slices.

2. Allow the fruit to macerate in the refrigerator then arrange it in glass bowls or timbales and decorate it by arranging some of the different fruits neatly on top.

3. Serve the fruit chilled. Place the dish on a round salver with a doily and, in a sauceboat on an underflat with a doily, serve 1 pint (700 ml) of fresh cream.

*Note.* If the fruits listed are not all in season increase the quantities of those available accordingly, bearing in mind their colours and flavours. If desired, the fruit salad may be sprinkled with kirsch.

## 1365  Fresh fruit salad — Salade de fruits — Macédoine de fruits

| 8 portions | Ingredients | 10 couverts |
|---|---|---|
| 2 | oranges | 3 |
| 2 × 4 oz | apples (sweet) | 3 × 100 g |
| 1 | pears | 2 |
| 8 oz | cherries | 280 g |
| 4 oz | grapes, black | 140 g |
| 4 oz | grapes, white | 140 g |
| 8 oz | bananas | 280 g |
| 2 | peaches | 3 |
| 1 small or ½ medium | pineapple | 1 small or ½ medium |
| 4 oz | sugar | 140 g |
| 1 | lemon | 1 |
| ¼ pint | water | 175 ml |

### Method

1. Have ready a suitable basin containing the water, sugar and lemon juice. To this, add the fruit immediately after it has been prepared, shaking the basin to mix them together. The bananas are added last of all.

### Preparation

**Oranges**: peel with a knife and cut out each section; remove the skin and seeds.

**Apples**: peel, cut in half, remove the core and cut into segments.

## 1366  Fruit fools

This is a light cream fruit purée which can be piped into silver or glass coupes for service; a piece of the particular fruit used is normally placed on top. The fools may also be served in larger services in bowls.

| 8 portions | Ingredients | 10 couverts |
|---|---|---|
| 1½ lb | fresh fruit | 840 g |
| ½ pint | cream | 350 ml |
| 4 oz | caster sugar and | 140 g |
| 12 oz | granulated sugar ⎫ syrup | 420 ml |
| 1 pint | water ⎭ | 700 ml |

### Method

1. Prepare the fruit and cook it as for compote (1364). When strawberries, loganberries or raspberries are used, retain a few in the raw state for decoration.

2. Thoroughly drain the fruit on a hair or fine sieve; place the liquid aside for other uses.

3. Place aside sufficient of the cooked fruit for decoration: 1 or 2 of each small fruits such as gooseberries and a small 5 mm-thick section of apple. Rub the remainder of the fruit through the sieve; it should give 1 pint (or 700 ml) of dry purée.

4. If fresh cream is used, mix the cream and fruit purée together in a basin and add the sugar. Place the basin on crushed ice and whisk until the mixture will stand lightly on the whisk.

5. If synthetic cream is used, whisk the cream in a basin until it stands, then fold in the fruit purée and sugar.

6. Pipe the mixture into the coupe glasses or bowl with a 20 mm star tube. Decorate with a piece or pieces of the fruit used. If desired, a rosette of whipped cream may be piped on each portion and the fruit placed on the cream.

*Note.* When banana is used, it is not cooked.

### 1367 Junket (plain)

| 8 portions | Ingredients | 10 couverts |
|---|---|---|
| 2 pints | fresh milk | 1·4 litres |

| 4 oz | caster sugar | 140 g |
| 4 drops | vanilla essence | 5 drops |
| ½ fl. oz (4 teaspoons) | rennet essence | 20 ml |

### Method

1. Place the sugar, milk and vanilla essence into a clean pan and warm it to 40°C (105°F), just above blood temperature Do not overheat or the junket will not set.

2. Stir in quickly the rennet essence, mixing well, then immediately pour into a glass bowl or 8 or 10 individual coupe glasses. Sprinkle lightly with finely grated nutmeg.

3. When cold and set, place to chill in refrigerator.

4. Serve on round flat dish on a doily.

*Note.* If a flavoured junket is required, i.e. raspberry, strawberry, etc., the flavouring and colouring is added before the rennet essence.

---

## CHOUX PASTE PRODUCTS

**Basic mixture**

### 1368 Choux paste — Pâte à choux

| | Ingredients | |
|---|---|---|
| 1 pint | water | 1 litre |
| 10 oz | cake flour | 500 g |
| 8 oz | butter or margarine | 400 g |
| 2 level teaspoons | salt | 10 g |
| 1 level teaspoon | caster sugar | 5 g |
| 8-9 | eggs | 14-16 |

### Method

1. Place the water, butter, salt and sugar to boil in a saucepan.

2. Move the pan from the heat and add the sieved flour, mixing with a wooden spatula.

3. Replace the pan over the heat and stir continuously until the mixture (panade) leaves the sides of the pan clean.

4. Remove the pan from the heat and place it on a triangle to cool slightly.

5. Add the eggs one at a time, thoroughly mixing evenly. For smaller quantities, beat the eggs and add a little at time.

6. When the paste is ready, the mixture should just drop from the spatula.

*Note.* For some uses in the kitchen, the mixture may be adjusted to include more flour.

### 1369 Chocolate éclairs — Éclairs au chocolat
Produces 20 pieces.

| | Ingredients | |
|---|---|---|
| ½ pint water mix | choux paste (1368) | 280ml water mix |
| ¾ pint | fresh cream | 420 ml |
| 2 oz | icing sugar | 55 g |
| 2-3 drops | vanilla essence | 2-3 drops |
| 12 oz | fondant | 350 g |
| 1½ oz | covering chocolate or cocoa powder | 45 g |

### Method

1. Prepare the choux paste (1368) and place it into a piping bag with a 10 mm plain tube.

2. Pipe into 75 mm lengths on to a lightly greased baking sheet. Egg-wash and mark the surface lightly with the back of a fork.

3. Bake at the top of an oven at 200°C (400°F) for 30–35 minutes until the sides of the paste are firm and crisp; if necessary, move to a lower position when coloured. Remove and allow to cool.

4. Cut along one side of the length with a pair of scissors or sharp knife.

5. Whip the well chilled cream in a bowl, add the sieved icing sugar, and vanilla and mix them thoroughly. The cream should just hold to the whisk when removed.

6. Using a piping bag and 5 mm plain tube, fill the cases.

7. Carefully warm the shredded chocolate to blood temperature, the fondant likewise, and combine them. When

cocoa powder is used, warm it with a tablespoon of stock syrup.

8. Glaze the cases by dipping the top surface into the fondant; hold the case on end and wipe away the excess fondant with the fingers, commencing half way along the surface. Allow the fondant to set.

9. Place into éclair paper cases and serve them on a flat dish with a doily.

*Note.* If desired, the cases may be filled with Pastry cream (1150).

### 1370  Coffee éclairs                              Éclairs au café
**Method**

Prepare, cook and serve as for Éclairs au chocolat (1369). When preparing the fondant, add enough coffee extract or essence to give a light coffee colour and flavour in place of chocolate.

### 1371                                         Rognons à la crème
**Method**

1. Prepare, cook and finish as for Éclairs au chocolat (1369). Pipe the choux paste into a kidney shape.
2. When glazed, over-pipe with a thin line of fondant, the shape of the case, down the centre. Rognons may be finished with chocolate or coffee fondant.

### 1372  Cream buns                            Choux à la crème
**Method**

1. Use the same ingredients as for Éclairs au chocolat (1369).
2. With a piping bag and a 10 mm plain tube, pipe the paste into mounds 45 mm in diameter × 20 mm high in the centre (the mixture should produce 22–24 pieces), egg-wash the surface and flatten the point. When not required glazed with fondant, sprinkle the buns with chopped almonds.
3. Bake, cool and finish as for Éclairs au chocolat. May also be finished with coffee fondant or pink fondant and decorated with a ½ glacé cherry on each.

### 1373                                          Cygnes en surprise
**Produces 15–16 swans.**
**Method**

1. Prepare ½ pint (280 ml) water mix of choux paste (1368).
2. Using a greaseproof paper bag and a 3 mm tube, pipe out 20 swans necks, approximately 75 mm long, on to a greased baking sheet. Over-pipe the top ends to form the head.

3. Place the remainder of the paste into a bag with a 10 mm plain tube, and scroll a pipe-shaped oval approximately 60 mm long × 40 mm wide; taper the finish to a point to give a 75 mm length.
4. Egg-wash both and bake them in the centre to top of an oven: the necks for 5–7 minutes, the bodies for approximately 30–35 minutes at 200°C (400°F) until crisp and firm. Allow to cool.
5. Cover the base of a large oval dish with a green coloured fruit jelly to a depth of 5 mm and let it set in a refrigerator
6. Prepare a fruit salad (1365), cutting the large fruits in 10 mm dice. Drain the fruit well and bind it with a double-thick, well reduced Sauce Melba (1189) flavoured with a little kirsch.
7. With a sharp knife, cut the choux paste bodies to divide them in two. Divide the top scrolled half in two, lengthways, for the two wings and dust them with icing sugar.
8. Fill the base piece with the fruit salad in a dome shape. Prepare ½ pint of Crème Chantilly (1151) and pipe two scrolls with a 5 mm star tube the length of the fruit, leaving a gap in the centre of 20 mm.
9. Place the two wings in position at the centre, so that they rest on the cream. Pipe a scroll of cream down the back.
10. Place a small dot of stiff water icing (1171) in the eye position on the head and insert a currant for the eye. Place the necks in position.
11. Set neatly on the firm jelly.

### 1374                                 Cygnes glacés, Sauce Suchard
**Method**

1. Prepare, cook and finish the choux paste swans as for Cygnets en surprise (1373).
2. When required, fill the body with a scoop of vanilla ice cream, pipe a scroll with cream and place the wings and neck in position.
3. Serve on a cold flat dish on a doily, in a sauceboat on an underflat with a doily, serve hot Sauce Suchard (1188).

### 1375                                    Profiteroles au chocolat
½ pint water mix of choux paste (1368), will produce 48 pieces – 12 portions.

**Method**

1. Using a bag with a 10 mm plain tube, pipe out the paste in a dome shape 25 mm in diameter × 10 mm high in the

centre on to a greased baking sheet. Egg-wash, then flatten any points left in piping.

2. Bake in the top of an oven at 220°C (425°F) for 16–18 minutes until very crisp. Allow to cool.

3. With a bag and a 5 mm plain tube, fill through the base with Crème Chantilly (1151), cold pastry cream (1150) or cold chocolate flavoured pastry cream. For the latter, add 1 oz (35 g) of cocoa powder to the flour per pint (litre).

4. Finish in any of the three following ways: (i) place the profiteroles in a 25 mm deep dish, mask over with 1 pint (700 ml) for each 8 or 10 portions of cold strained Chocolate sauce (1187) and finish with grated chocolate on top; (ii) glaze them with chocolate fondant and set them in a pyramid on a round flat dish surrounded with cold, strained thin chocolate sauce; (iii) dust them with icing sugar, serve them in a pyramid on a flat dish with a doily, and serve cold strained Sauce Suchard (1188) separately in a sauceboat.

---

## 1376 SPONGES, GÂTEAUX, SPONGE FINGERS, SWISS ROLLS, BAKED SPONGE PUDDINGS

### 1377 Genoese sponge (8–10 portions)　　　　　　　　　Génoise

| | Ingredients | |
|---|---|---|
| 4 oz | cake flour | 110 g |
| 4 oz | caster sugar | 110 g |
| 2 oz | butter | 55 g |
| 4 | eggs | 4 |
| 4 drops | vanilla essence | 4 drops |

#### Method

1. Using a brush, well grease a 200 mm in diameter × 50 mm deep sponge tin with clarified fat. Flour the tin, knock out the surplus and place the tin on a baking sheet.

2. Beat the eggs, sugar and vanilla in a basin (not aluminium) over a pot of hot water. Whisk continuously at blood temperature until the mixture thickens and will form a ribbon.

3. Remove from the heat and whisk it until cold. With a wooden spoon, gradually fold in the sieved flour, then the melted butter. Clear all flour spots without over-mixing.

4. Pour the mixture into the prepared mould. Bake in the centre of an oven at 180°C (350°F) for approximately 30 minutes. If cooked, the centre should be firm and springy to the touch.

5. Turn out on to a wire grill to cool and use as required.

*Note.* For a three egg mixture, use a tin 175 mm in diameter.

### 1378 Coffee Genoese sponge

#### Method

Prepare as for Genoese sponge (1377), adding 1 dessertspoon of coffee extract or essence to the eggs and sugar before folding in the flour.

### 1379 Chocolate Genoese sponge

#### Method

Prepare as for Genoese sponge (1377), replacing ½ oz (15 g) of the flour with cocoa powder. Sieve the flour and cocoa together 3–4 times to mix them thoroughly.

### 1380 Swiss roll

#### Method

1. Grease a 375 × 300 × 10 mm deep edged baking sheet or Swiss roll tin with clarified fat, line it with greaseproof paper, then grease the paper.

2. Prepare a Genoese sponge (1377), omitting the melted butter, up to and including 3 in method.

3. With a palette knife, spread the mixture with long strokes 5 mm deep.

4. Bake at the top of an oven at 200–220°C (400–425°F) for 7–8 minutes till a light golden brown.

5. Turn out on to a caster-sugar-dredged piece of greaseproof paper. Remove the cooking paper.

6. Using a palette knife, spread the sponge evenly and quickly with warmed apricot or raspberry jam (use only smooth-type jams).

7. Press the edge over to give a firm centre, then, holding the paper, roll the sponge up quickly while it is hot. Undo the paper, re-roll the sponge tightly and stand it on a wire grill, with the end seam underneath, to cool.

*Note.* When the roll is required for cream or butter cream filling, roll the sponge without any jam and allow it to go cold. Unroll, spread with the whipped or butter cream, then re-roll the sponge.

For chocolate roll, use the same proportions of flour and cocoa powder as for Chocolate Genoese sponge (1379).

## 1381 Sponge fingers      Biscuits à la cuillère
**Produces 32 fingers**

| | Ingredients | |
|---|---|---|
| 4 oz | cake flour | 110 g |
| 4 oz | caster sugar | 110 g |
| 4 | yolks of egg | 4 |
| 4 | whites of egg | 4 |
| 4 drops | vanilla essence | 4 drops |

**Method**

1. Mix the yolks of eggs, sugar and vanilla in a china basin with a wooden spatule to a light froth.
2. Fold in the stiffly whipped whites of egg, then gradually fold in the flour. Do not overmix.
3. Line a baking sheet with greaseproof paper, then, using a 10 mm plain tube and bag, pipe it out into 75 mm lengths, 25 mm apart.
4. Dust the fingers with icing sugar and bake at 190°C (375°F) for 12–15 minutes until golden brown and set, then remove them from the oven.
5. Release the fingers from the paper by passing a palette knife underneath them.

## 1382 Victoria sponge sandwich

| | Ingredients | |
|---|---|---|
| 5 oz | cake flour | 140 g |
| 4 oz | caster sugar | 110 g |
| 4 oz | butter or best margarine | 110 g |
| 1 level teaspoon | baking powder | 1·5 g |
| 2 | eggs | 2 |
| 4 drops | vanilla essence | 4 drops |

**Method**

1. Cream the fat, sugar and vanilla essence in a basin until a very light texture.
2. Gradually add the beaten eggs. Lightly mix in the sieved, well mixed flour and baking powder.
3. Equally divide the mixture into two previously greased and floured shallow sponge tins (175 mm in diameter).
4. Place them on a baking sheet and bake at the top of an oven at 180°C (350°F) for 13–15 minutes until the sponge is golden brown and firm but springy in the centre.
5. Unmould on to a wire grill to cool.
6. Spread one half with jam and place the other half on top. The pan bottoms should both be at the centre. Dredge the top with icing sugar.
7. Serve on a round salver with a doily.

## 1383 Coffee gâteau      Gâteau Moka
**Method**

1. Prepare a Coffee Genoese sponge (1378). Prepare a 6 oz (170 g) butter mix of butter cream (1154); add enough coffee extract or essence to flavour and lightly colour it.
2. With a sharp knife, carefully cut across the depth of the sponge to divide it in 3 layers. Turn the sponge when cutting to prevent a ragged edge.
3. Spread the sponge with the coffee butter cream and re-form it to its original shape.
4. Spread the top surface and sides with the butter cream. Coat the sides with roasted flaked almonds.
5. Using a piping bag and a 5 mm star tube, pipe a scrolled or rosette border around the outer top edge. With a small greaseproof bag filled with butter cream, write or print the word 'Moka' in the centre.
6. Serve on a round salver with a doily.

## 1384 Chocolate gâteau      Gâteau au chocolat
**Method**

1. Prepare a Chocolate Genoese sponge (1379).
2. Then finish as for Coffee gâteau (1383), using chocolate butter cream, adding 1 oz (30 g) of cool dissolved block chocolate to the basic butter cream in place of coffee.
3. Coat the edges of the gâteau with chocolate nibs or chocolate vermicelli in place of almonds.
4. Write or print 'Chocolat' in the centre.

## 1385 Praline gâteau      Gâteau praliné
**Method**

1. Prepare a Genoese sponge (1377).
2. Then finish as for Coffee gâteau (1383), adding 1 oz (30 g) of praline (1167), to the butter cream in place of coffee.
3. Write or print 'Praliné' in the centre and evenly space a few hazel nuts on the rosettes or scrolled edge.

## 1386      Gâteau ratafia
**Method**

1. Prepare a Genoese sponge (1377). Prepare a praline butter cream (see 2 in method of 1385).
2. Split the sponge across into 3 layers, spread with butter cream and reform to its original shape.
3. Spread the top and sides liberally with the praline butter cream.

4. Cover the top and side surfaces with ratafia (small button macaroons, 1442) and dredge the top lightly with icing sugar.

5. Serve on a salver with a doily.

## 1387 Orange gâteau — Gâteau à l'orange

### Method

1. Prepare a Genoese sponge (1377). Add to a 6 oz (170 g) mix of butter cream (1154) the finely grated rind of 1 orange and one or two drops of yellow and red colour to give an orange tint.

2. Prepare 2 oranges in segments free of all skin and pitch, as for orange cocktail.

3. Carefully split the sponge through in 3 layers, spread with butter cream and reform it to its original shape.

4. Spread the top and side with butter cream and coat the sides with roasted flaked almonds.

5. Pipe rosettes of butter cream around the edge with a 5 mm star tube.

6. Arrange a star of the orange segments in the centre and place the remainder, evenly spaced, across each alternate rosette with the pointed end to the centre. Brush the centre orange with apricot glaze (1180).

7. Serve on a flat salver with a doily.

## 1388 Peach gâteau — Gâteau aux pêches

### Method

1. Prepare and finish as for Orange gâteau (1387), omitting the orange rind from the butter cream, which is coloured pale pink.

2. Use segments of canned peach in place of orange segments.

## 1389 Pineapple gâteau — Gâteau aux ananas

### Method

1. Prepare a Genoese sponge (1377). Prepare a 6 oz (170 g) mix of butter cream (1154) and colour it a light pink tint.

2. Carefully split the sponge in 3 layers, spread with butter cream and reform it to its original shape. Spread the top and sides with butter cream and coat the sides with roasted flaked almonds.

3. Cut 3–4 slices of pineapple in halves and cut them in half again. Arrange the slices half overlapping on the top with the pointed ends to the centre.

4. Brush the pineapple with boiling apricot glaze (1180).

When cold, decorate around the outside edge of the sponge with rosettes of the butter cream with a 5 mm star tube.

## 1390 — Gâteau printanier

### Method

1. Prepare a Genoese sponge (1377). Prepare an 8 oz (225 g) mix of butter cream (1154).

2. Split, spread and coat the sponge as in 2 of 1389.

3. Divide the remaining butter cream into 4 parts and colour them natural, pale pink, pale green and chocolate.

4. Mark the top surface with a palette knife into 8 equal sections.

5. Using a bag and a small star tube, pipe stars of the various butter cream to completely cover the surface. Decorate 2 opposite sections at a time, out of the 8, and use a different colour on each, i.e. natural, then chocolate, green, and finally pink.

6. Serve the gâteau on a salver with a doily.

## 1391 Baked jam sponge pudding

| 8 portions | Ingredients | 10 couverts |
|---|---|---|
| 7½ oz | cake flour | 250 g |
| 6 oz | caster sugar | 200 g |
| 6 oz | butter or best margarine | 200 g |
| 1½ level teaspoons | baking powder | 5 g |
| 3 | eggs | 4 |
| 4 drops | vanilla essence | 5 drops |
| 6 oz | jam | 200 g |

### Method

1. Grease and sugar a 2¾ pint (2 litre) pie dish, or, if required, use smaller pie dishes, and spread the jam in the bottom.

2. From the other ingredients prepare a batter sponge mix as for Victoria sponge sandwich (1382).

3. Place the mixture in the pie dish and level it with a palette knife. Clean the edge of the pie dish and place it on a baking sheet.

4. Bake in the centre of an oven at 180°C (350°F) for approximately 25–30 minutes (slightly less for smaller pie dishes). When cooked, the sponge should be firm but springy in the centre.

5. Lightly dredge the top with icing sugar and wipe the pie dish. Place a pie frill around the dish and serve it on an underflat with dish paper.

If desired, the sponge may be served with a separate Custard (1174), Vanilla 1175, or Almond sauce (1176).

*Note.* For variety, the sponge may be prepared with golden syrup instead of jam.

## 1392 Baked sultana sponge pudding

**Method**

Prepare, bake and serve as for Baked jam sponge pudding (1391), omitting the jam. Add 3 oz (100 g) of cleaned sultanas to the prepared sponge when mixed. Serve any of the sauces listed in 1391.

---

## 1393 PANCAKES—CRÊPES

### 1394 Basic mixture and preparation

| 1 pint | Ingredients | ½ litre |
|---|---|---|
| 1 pint | milk | 500 ml |
| 7 oz | cake flour | 175 g |
| 1 oz | butter (melted) | 25 g |
| ½ level teaspoon | salt | 1 g |
| 1 level teaspoon | caster sugar | 2 g |
| 2 oz | clarified margarine or lard | 50 g |
| 2 | eggs | 2 |

**Method**

1. Sieve the flour, salt and sugar into a basin and make a bay in the centre.
2. Beat the eggs, place them in the bay and gradually whisk the milk into the eggs, at the same time absorbing the flour. When all the flour is worked in, whisk well, then add the melted butter and strain the mixture.
3. Warm a clean pancake pan over a fire, run in a little clarified butter, run out the surplus then add sufficient pancake batter to just cover the bottom of the pan. Tilt the pan while pouring in the batter to allow it to run easily.
4. Fry until the edges of the pancake just begin to colour golden brown, then toss it over or turn it with a palette knife. Moisten around the edge of pan with clarified butter, finish cooking then stack the cooked pancakes on top of each other between plates to keep hot.

*Note.* The basic 1 pint mixture will make 36 pieces and the ½ litre mixture, 30 pieces; allow 3 pieces per portion.

### 1395 Lemon pancakes            Crêpes au citron

**Method**

1. Prepare as in basic preparation (1394), adding the finely grated rind of a lemon to the mixture after it has been strained.
2. To serve, dip the pancakes in caster sugar and fold them into four. Serve 3 pancakes per portion, slightly overlapping each other, on a hot oval dish, with a section of lemon on the side for each portion.

### 1396 Orange pancakes            Crêpes à l'orange

**Method**

1. Prepare and serve as for Lemon pancakes (1395).

2. Replace grated orange rind for lemon in the mixture.
3. When serving, spread the pancake with orange butter, fold it in four, place the pancakes on a dish, overlapping each other, and dust them with icing sugar. Place sections of orange on the side of the plate.
4. For the orange butter, cream together 4 oz (100 g) of butter with 6 oz (150 g) of sieved icing sugar and add the grated and strained juice of 1 large or 2 medium oranges. Set it in the refrigerator.

### 1397 Jam pancakes            Crêpes à la confiture

**Method**

1. Prepare as in basic preparation (1394).
2. To serve, spread the pancake with warm jam and either fold it in four or roll it. If rolled, trim the ends.
3. Serve very hot on a lightly buttered hot flat oval dish. Dredge with caster sugar.

### 1398            Crêpes couvent

**Method**

1. Prepare as in basic preparation (1394).
2. Prepare 1 pint (½ litre) of pastry cream (1150).
3. Mix a half of the pastry cream with 6 oz (150 g) of cooked or canned pear cut into 3 mm dice and spread the mixture on the pancakes.
4. Roll the pancakes and place them in a buttered oval shallow earthenware dish.
5. Add sufficient boiling milk to the remaining pastry cream to thin it to a sauce of masking consistency. Mask this sauce over the pancakes.
6. Sprinkle the surface with crushed ratafia (1442) and gratinate under a salamander or colour lightly in the top of an oven at 220–230°C (425–450°F) for 2–3 minutes.

### 1399            Crêpes Georgette

**Method**

Prepare, finish and serve as for Crêpes couvent (1398). Replace the pear with diced pineapple macerated in a little kirsch.

## 1400 Apple pancakes   Crêpes normande

**Method**

1. Prepare as in basic preparation (1394).
2. For 8 or 10 portions, peel, quarter, core and slice 1½ lb (840 g) of apples. Melt 2 oz (70 g) of butter, add the apples and ¼ level teaspoon of cinnamon. Cover the pan, cook the apples on the side of the stove until they are soft then add 3 oz (100 g) of caster sugar and stir the mixture to a purée. Alternatively, prepare the apples as in Apple flan (1306, 3 in method).
4. Spread the pancakes with the purée, roll, trim the ends and place them on a hot dish. Place in hot oven for 1 minute then dredge them with caster sugar.

---

## 1401 FRITTERS—BEIGNETS

For those fritters that are coated with batter, it is best to use a yeast batter (677) with a little extra sugar added when mixing it.

## 1402 Apple fritters   Beignets de pommes

| 8 portions | Ingredients | 10 couverts |
|---|---|---|
| 8 oz flour mix | yeast frying batter | 280 g flour mix |
| 4 × 5 oz | cooking apples | 5 × 140 g. |
| 1 oz | caster sugar | 35 g |
| ¼ level teaspoon | cinnamon | 1 g |

**Method**

1. Wash, core, and peel the apples when required and cut them into 5 mm-thick slices.
2. Sprinkle them with the sugar mixed with the ground cinnamon.
3. Check that the Pâte à frire is the right consistency, then pass the slices of apple through the batter, taking the excess batter off on the side of the basin, and drop them into deep, smoking fat at 180°C (360°F). Allow to fry until golden brown, turn over and when the other side is coloured, remove the fritters from the fat with a spider and drain them on a pastry grid.
4. Place the fritters on a tray, dust them well with icing sugar and glaze them golden brown under a salamander or at the top of a very hot oven at 260°C (500°F).
5. Serve 2 pieces per portion on a hot oval flat dish with a doily, with sauce served separately.
6. The fritters can be served dusted with icing sugar instead of glazing.

   Suitable sauces for fritters are: Anglaise (1173), Custard (1174), Vanilla (1175), Almond (1176), Apricot (1181).

## 1403 Banana fritters   Beignets de bananes

**Method**

1. Allow 1 medium banana per portion. Peel it and cut it into 3 equal sized pieces, on the slant, to give a length of approximately 60 mm.
2. Finish and serve as for Apple fritters (1402) from 2 in method). Serve the same sauces as in the previous recipe.

## 1404 Pineapple fritters   Beignets d'ananas

**Method**

1. Cut large slices of pineapple into 3 sections and small slices in halves. In both cases, allow 3 pieces per portion. Drain the slices well on a wire grill.
2. Finish and serve as for Apple fritters (1402, from 2 in method) and serve the same sauces.

*Note.* If desired, the drained pineapple may be coated with boiling pastry cream (1150) and allowed to set cold before passing through the batter.

## 1405   Beignets soufflés

**Method**

1. Using a bag and a 10 mm star tube, pipe out choux paste (1368) on to lightly oiled greaseproof paper in rings 40 mm in diameter
2. Holding the edge of the paper, pass the rings into 160°C (320°F) hot deep fat and remove the paper. Shake the pan carefully to help the beignets to soufflé, or keep them moving with a spider, and, when golden brown after 5–6 minutes, remove them and drain them on a pastry grid.
3. Split the beignets on one side with a sharp knife, and, with a paper bag, pipe a little jam in each. They may also be filled with pastry cream.
4. Serve the beignets very hot – 3 pieces per portion – dust them with icing sugar and place them on an oval flat dish on a doily. Serve in a sauceboat, on an underflat with a doily, any of the sauces in 1402.

## 1406   Beignets soufflés Porto Rosa

**Method**

1. Prepare as for Beignets soufflés (1405). When cooked, allow them to cool.

347

2. Brush the beignets with strained raspberry jam and dip them in grated chocolate.

3. Fill with Crème Chantilly (1151) flavoured with a little raspberry pulp.

4. Serve cold on a round salver on a doily.

---

## 1407 SWEET SOUFFLÉS

### 1408 Vanilla soufflé     Soufflé à la vanille

| 8 portions | Ingredients | 10 couverts |
|---|---|---|
| 12 fl. oz | milk | 420 ml |
| 3 oz + 1½ oz | caster sugar | 100 g + 50 g |
| 1½ oz | cake flour | 50 g |
| 1 | whole eggs | 2 small |
| 3 | yolks of egg | 4 |
| 6 | whites of egg | 8 |
| 4 drops | vanilla essence | 5 drops |

**Method**

1. Place the milk and vanilla essence to boil.

2. Mix in a basin the whole egg, yolks and sugar. Whisk the mixture, then mix in the sieved flour until it is smooth.

3. Pour on the milk, replace in pan, whisk until reboiling and smooth, then cool slightly, stirring occasionally.

4. Whip up the whites of egg until they are stiff and standng, then whisk in 1½ oz (50 g) of caster sugar.

5. Fold the whites into the cooled base and lightly mix it until no white streaks can be seen.

6. Fill 2, 3 or 4 greased and sugared soufflé cases or timbales with the mixture and level it with a knife. The 8 portions can easily be set in 2 × 1 pint or 4 × ½ pint cases and the ten in 2 × 700 ml or 4 × 350 ml cases.

7. Place the cases on a baking sheet and bake them in the centre of an oven at 190°C (375°F) for the larger size and 200°C (400°F) for the smaller size. The cooking time is 30–35 minutes for the 1 pint (or 700 ml) cases and 20 minutes for the ½ pint (or 350 ml).

8. Lightly dredge the surface with icing sugar and serve immediately on a round or oval flat dish on a doily.

### 1409 Lemon soufflé     Soufflé au citron

**Method**

1. Prepare, cook and serve as for Vanilla soufflé (1408).

2. Add the finely grated rind of 1 lemon to the milk and add the strained juice to the basic mixture when removed from the stove.

### 1410 Orange soufflé     Soufflé à l'orange

**Method**

1. Prepare, cook and serve as for Vanilla soufflé (1408).

Add the grated rind of 1 orange to the milk and 2–3 drops of yellow and red colour to give an orange tint.

2. Remove all skin and pith from the segments of two oranges.

3. After levelling the mixture in the cases, place the orange segments attractively on top.

### 1411 Chocolate soufflé     Soufflé au chocolat

**Method**

1. Prepare, cook and serve as for Vanilla soufflé (1408).

2. Dissolve 1 oz (35 g) of grated block chocolate in the milk. Alternatively, replace ½ oz (20 g) of the flour with cocoa powder. The alternative is the better method.

### 1412 Praline soufflé     Soufflé praliné

**Method**

Prepare, cook and serve as for Vanilla soufflé (1408). Add 1 oz (35 g) of praline (1167) to the mixture before the whites.

### 1413 Cherry soufflé     Soufflé Montmorency

**Method**

Prepare, cook and serve as for Vanilla soufflé (1408). Add 2 oz (70 g) of quartered glacé cherries, macerated in a dessertspoon of kirsch, to the mixture before the whites.

### 1414     Soufflé Rothschild

**Method**

1. Prepare, cook and serve as for Soufflé Montmorency. Replace the cherries with mixed candied fruits cut in 3 mm dice and macerated in the kirsch.

2. Before baking, decorate the top surface with halves of glacé cherries and 20 × 10 mm diamonds of angelica.

### 1415     Soufflé sicilienne

**Method**

Prepare, cook and serve as for Soufflé à l'orange (1410). Add 1 oz (35 g) of praline (1167) to the mixture before the whites.

## 1417 Baked apples

| 8 portions | Ingredients | 10 couverts |
|---|---|---|
| 8 × 7 oz | cooking apples | 10 × 200 g |
| 4 oz | brown sugar | 140 g |
| 4 oz | butter | 140 g |
| 8 | cloves | 10 |

### Method

1. Wash and core the apples and make an incision 3 mm deep around the centre.

2. Place the apples in a 50 mm-deep tray, fill the centre with the sugar, add 1 clove per apple, then push the butter into the cavity.

3. Add water to come 10 mm up the apples. Bake in the centre to lower part of an oven at 190–200°C (375–400°F) for approximately 35–40 minutes. Test the centre with the point of a knife: it should penetrate easily.

4. Serve the apples on a hot flat dish and mask them with a little of the syrup. Serve Custard sauce (1174) in a sauceboat on an underflat with a doily.

## 1418                                 Pommes bonne femme

### Method

1. Prepare, cook and serve as for Baked apples (1417), omitting the cloves.

2. Mix the butter and sugar with 4 oz (140 g) of cleaned sultanas and ½ a level teaspoon (2 g) of cinnamon and place the mixture in the cavity.

## 1419 Apple charlotte             Charlotte de pommes

| 8 portions | Ingredients | 10 couverts |
|---|---|---|
| 2½ lb | apples (dry russet type) | 1·4 kg |
| 4 oz | brown sugar | 140 g |
| 4 + 4 oz | butter | 140 + 140 g |
| 8 oz | bread | 280 g |
| ½ level teaspoon | ground cinnamon | 2 g |
| 1 | lemon | 1 |
| 4 drops | vanilla essence | 5 drops |

### Method

1. Peel, core and cut the apples into 8 pieces.

2. Melt half the butter in a shallow pan (sauté), stir in the sugar and continue to stir until it begins to caramelise.

3. Add the apples, cinnamon, vanilla, grated lemon rind and strained juice and cook until the apples are tender.

4. If the mixture is a little soft, add some cake or breadcrumbs.

5. Prepare the moulds by lining them with thinly cut slices of bread (in 25 mm strips) dipped in melted butter.

6. Fill the lined moulds with the mixture and cover it with crusts of bread to protect it while cooking.

7. Bake in an oven at 200°C (400°F), until the bread is crisp and golden brown (approximately 1 hour).

8. Allow to rest and cool a little before turning out the charlotte on to a hot round flat dish.

9. Serve hot Apricot sauce (1181) in a sauceboat on an underflat with a doily.

## 1420                                     Crème frite

| 8 portions | Ingredients | 10 couverts |
|---|---|---|
| 1½ pints | milk | 1 litre |
| 8 oz | caster sugar | 280 g |
| 4 oz | cake flour | 140 g |
| 2 | whole eggs | 3 |
| 6 | yolks of egg | 7 |
| 4 drops | vanilla essence | 5 drops |

### Method

1. Prepare the ingredients as for Pastry cream (1150).

2. Run it into a buttered and sugared tray to a depth of 20 mm, level the surface, cover with a buttered paper and allow it to set cold.

3. Cut into 16 or 20 square or oblong pieces and pass each piece through beaten egg and fresh white breadcrumbs.

4. Deep fry 8 or 10 pieces at a time at 180°C (360°F) for 2–3 minutes until golden brown, then drain.

5. Serve on a hot flat dish on a doily with Apricot sauce (1181) in a sauceboat.

## 1421                                   Crème américaine

| 8 portions | Ingredients | 10 couverts |
|---|---|---|
| 1½ pints | milk | 1 litre |
| 6 oz | caster sugar | 210 g |
| 1 oz | cornflour | 35 g |
| 8 | yolks of egg | 10 |
| 4 drops | vanilla essence | 5 drops |

### Method

1. Dilute the cornflour with a little of the milk. Boil the remainder then whisk the diluted cornflour into it and reboil.

2. Mix in a basin the yolks, sugar and vanilla. Whisk the thickened milk into it and replace in the pan. Stir over the heat to thicken; do not allow to boil. Allow to cool slightly.

3. Pour 5 mm of the cream into a 30 mm-deep entrée-type dish and dredge it well with caster sugar. Caramelise the

surface with a hot iron and repeat the process until all the cream is used.

4. Serve the cream warm or cold on an underdish with dish paper.

## 1422 Rice croquettes      Croquettes de riz

| 8 portions | Ingredients | 10 couverts |
|---|---|---|
| 8 portions | rice for Condé (1228) | 10 portions |
| 2 oz | glacé fruits | 70 g |
| 2 | eggs | 2 |
| 8 oz | white breadcrumbs | 280 g |

### Method

1. Increase the quantity of the rice by one-third to give a stiff mixture. Allow it to cool in a shallow tray covered with a buttered paper.
2. When cold, add the glacé fruits, cut in 3 mm dice, and mix thoroughly.
3. Mould the rice into 24 or 30 small croquettes and pass each one through the beaten egg and crumbs.
4. Deep fry 8 to 10 portions at a time at 180°C (360°F) to a light golden brown, then drain.
5. Serve on a hot flat dish with a dish paper with hot Apricot sauce (1181) in a sauceboat on an underflat with a doily.

## 1423 Pear Colbert      Poire Colbert

## 1424 Apricot Colbert      Abricot Colbert

| 8 portions | Ingredients | 10 couverts |
|---|---|---|
| 8 portions | rice for Condé (1228) | 10 portions |
| 16 | halves of poached pears or | 20 |
| 24 | halves of poached apricots | 30 |
| 1 oz | angelica | 35 g |
| 2 | eggs | 2 |
| 8 oz | white breadcrumbs | 280 g |

### Method

1. Increase the quantity of the rice by one-third. Allow it to cool in a shallow tray covered with a buttered paper.
2. Well drain the fruit on a cloth or wire grill. Mould sufficient of the rice to the fruit to reform the fruit to its full size. Allow 1 large or 2 small pears and 3 apricots per portion.
3. Pass through the beaten egg and breadcrumbs then deep fry 8 to 10 pieces at a time at 180°C (360°F) until golden brown; drain.
4. Serve the Colbert on a hot flat dish with dish paper and place a small stalk of angelica in the top of each piece. Serve Apricot sauce (1181) separate.

## 1425 MISCELLANEOUS COLD SWEETS

### 1426      Oeuf à la neige

| 8 portions | Ingredients | 10 couverts |
|---|---|---|
| 1 pint | sauce anglaise (1773) | 700 ml |
| 4 egg white mix | ordinary meringue (1165) | 5 egg white mix |

### Method

1. Prepare the sauce, allow it to go cold, then strain it into 1 or 2 glass bowls or timbales.
2. Boil 50 mm of water in a shallow pan then move it to the side of the stove. Mould the meringue up the side of the basin with a tablespoon and, with a second spoon dipped in water, cut out the meringue in an egg shape and carefully drop the pieces into the hot water. Allow 3 pieces per portion.
3. Poach the meringue over a low heat for 1–2 minutes, turning the pieces with a wooden spoon. Do not boil the water, or the meringue will blow.
4. Lift from the water with a perforated spoon, drain the excess water on a cloth, then float the 'eggs' in the sauce. Serve the bowls on an underflat with a doily.

### 1427      Pommes meringuées

| 8 portions | Ingredients | 10 couverts |
|---|---|---|
| 3 egg mix | génoise (1377) | 4 egg mix |
| 8 ×4 oz | cooking apples | 10 × 110 g |
| 4 oz | jam | 140 g |
| 1 oz | glacé cherries | 35 g |
| 1 oz | angelica | 35 g |
| 5 whites of egg mix | ordinary meringue or Italian meringue | 6–7 whites of egg mix |

### Method

1. Prepare the sponge and level it to just over 12 mm to give 20 mm when cooked. Cook in a shallow tray lined with greased paper.
2. Peel, core and wash the apples. Place them in a shallow tray with 10 mm of stock syrup (1170) and cook them in the centre of an oven at 190–200°C (375–400°F) for approximately 30 minutes, turning them over in the syrup during cooking until soft in the centre. Allow them to cool.
3. Split the sponge into two halves 10 mm thick and cut each half into circles 75 mm in diameter with a plain cutter. Place these on clean baking sheet 40 mm apart.

4. Well drain the apples and place one on each piece of sponge. Fill the centre of the apple with jam, then, with a bag and a 10 mm star tube, cover the apples with the meringue, starting to pipe from the sponge upwards to the top.

5. Sprinkle well with caster sugar and decorate on top with a half glacé cherry and 2 diamonds of angelica.
6. Colour golden brown in an oven at 190°C (375°F).
7. Serve cold on a round flat with a thin jam (1182) or red apricot sauce (1181) to cover the base of the dish.

## 1428 TARTLETS, BARQUETTES, CAKES

### 1429 Fruit tartlets — Tartelettes aux fruits
Produces 16–20 pieces.

| | Ingredients | |
|---|---|---|
| 8 oz flour mix | sugar paste for tartlets (1140) | 250 g flour mix |
| 1 lb | fruit | 500 g |
| 6 oz | red or apricot jam | 190 g |
| | apricot glaze (1180) | |

### Method

1. Using a little flour, roll out the paste 3 mm thick and cut it with a 60–75 mm fluted cutter.
2. Line the greased tartlet moulds, thumb the paste to 5 mm over the edge of the mould and turn the top edge slightly inwards. Prick the bottom of the paste with a fork. Place the moulds on a baking sheet.
3. If required to be cooked 'blind', place a paper tartlet case inside each pastry case and fill it with beans.
4. Bake in the centre of an oven at 190°C (375°F) for approximately 12–14 minutes, removing the beans after 5 minutes.
5. Finish the tartlets, according to the type, as follows:

**Apple tartlets**: line the tartlet tins with 3 mm-thick circles of paste cut with a fluted cutter and prick the bottoms. Three-quarters fill the cases with a cold apple purée. Neatly arrange thin slices of raw apple on the top and bake at 190°C (375°F) for approximately 15 minutes. Remove the tartlets from the tins and cool them on a wire rack. Carefully glaze the tops with boiling apricot jam, which has been melted, strained and reduced to a masking consistency, or apricot glaze (1180).

**Plum, gooseberry, fresh apricot**: line the tartlet tins as above, prick the bottoms and one-quarter fill them with frangipane (1155). Arrange the prepared fruit neatly on top (plums and apricots are stoned in halves or quarters) and bake at 175°C (350°F) for approximately 15–18 minutes. Cool, then glaze with the appropriate jam. For gooseberries, the apricot jam may be tinged green.

**Cherries, peaches, pears**: line the tartlet tins as above, prick

the bottoms and bake 'blind' at 190°C (375°F) for approximately 12–14 minutes till set and lightly coloured. When cool, half fill with boiling pastry cream. Arrange neatly on top of the tartlets the fruit which has been cooked compote fashion, drained, cooled and cut if necessary (cherries are stoned). Glaze the surface with the appropriate boiling jam.

**Soft fruit, strawberries, raspberries, blackberries, bananas**: prepare and cook the tartlets 'blind', as above. Half fill with boiling pastry cream, allow it to cool, then arrange the raw, prepared fruit neatly on top. Glaze the surface with the appropriate boiling jam. (Bananas are cut into 3 mm-thick slices.)

### 1430 Jam or lemon curd tartlets
### Method

1. Line the tartlet moulds as for Fruit tartlets (1429) and prick the bottoms.
2. One-third fill with jam or lemon curd for tartlets (1157).
3. Bake in the centre to top of an oven at 190°C (375°F) for approximately 15 minutes, then remove from the oven.
4. While still hot, fill two-thirds of the depth with hot jam or curd.

### 1431 Richmond maids of honour
Produces 30 tartlets.

| | Ingredients | |
|---|---|---|
| 1 lb flour mix | sugar paste for tartlets (1140) | 500 g flour mix |
| 8 oz | butter | 250 g |
| 8 oz | caster sugar | 250 g |
| 4 oz | desiccated coconut | 125 g |
| 4 oz | sago | 125 g |
| 4 | eggs | 4 |
| 1 | lemon (grated rind) | 1 |
| 1 pint | milk | 625 ml |
| 3–4 drops | vanilla essence | 3–4 drops |

### Method

1. Line 30 tartlet moulds as in 1 and 2 of method of Fruit tartlets (1429) and place them on a baking sheet.
2. Boil the milk, rain in the sago, whisk until reboiling,

351

cover the pan and simmer for 10 minutes, stirring during cooking. Tip out on to a shallow tray and cover with a buttered paper.

3. Cream the butter and sugar to a very light texture, then add the vanilla and grated lemon rind. Add the eggs 1 at a time, creaming the mixture between each one.

4. Mix in the cold cooked sago and coconut and mix thoroughly.

5. With a piping bag and a 20 mm plain tube, three-quarters fill the lined tartlets.

6. Bake in the centre to top of an oven at 190°C (375°F) for approximately 25–30 minutes until golden brown.

7. Allow to cool, then lightly dredge with icing sugar. Serve on a flat dish with a doily.

*Note.* Richmond maids of honour can be served as pastries, or, when they are made smaller, they can be served as a garnish to certain cold iced sweet dishes.

## 1432        Tartelettes lampion

Produces 30 tartlets.

### Ingredients

| | | |
|---|---|---|
| 1 lb flour mix | sugar paste for tartlets (1140) | 500 g flour mix |
| 6 oz butter mix | frangipane (1155) | 190 g butter mix |
| 4 oz butter mix | butter cream (1154) | 125 g butter mix |
| 4 oz | raspberry jam | 125 g |

### Method

1. Line 30 tartlet moulds as in 1 and 2 of method for Fruit tartlets (1429) and place them on a baking sheet.

2. Using a greaseproof paper bag, pipe a little jam in the bottom of each tartlet.

3. With a piping bag and a 10 mm plain tube, three-quarters fill each case with frangipane.

4. Bake in the centre to top of an oven at 190°C (375°F) for approximately 22–25 minutes until the paste is cooked.

5. Remove from the oven, turn the moulds over on to a tray to level the surface, remove the moulds and allow to cool.

6. Using a plain cutter 20 mm in diameter, cut through and remove the centre of the filling. Dip one side of these pieces in boiling red apricot glaze or strained red jam and set them aside.

7. Colour the butter cream pale pink with a little cochineal and, with a piping bag and a 5 mm star tube, pipe a small rosette of butter cream in the cavity.

8. Lightly dredge the surface with icing sugar and place the glazed centre on top of the butter cream.

9. Serve as a pastry on a flat dish with a doily.

## 1433   Fruit barquettes      Barquettes de fruits

### Method

1. Use the same ingredients as for Fruit tartlets (1429). This recipe is generally suitable only for soft fruits.

2. Place 30 barquette moulds close together, then roll out the paste to 3 mm thick and place it over the top of them. Using a small piece of the paste dipped in flour, press the paste into the moulds. Cut away the excess paste by rolling the pin across the top edges.

3. Prick the bottoms, bake 'blind' and finish as for soft fruit tartlets.

## 1434   Madeira cake

### Ingredients

| | | |
|---|---|---|
| 1 lb | butter or best margarine | 450 g |
| 1 lb | caster sugar | 450 g |
| 1¼ lb | cake flour | 560 g |
| 3 oz | cornflour | 85 g |
| 10 | eggs | 10 |
| 1 level teaspoon | baking powder | 3 g |
| 5–6 drops | vanilla essence | 5–6 drops |

### Method

1. Prepare the cooking tin or tins by lining them with thin cardboard then greased greaseproof paper.

2. Thoroughly mix the flour, cornflour and baking powder, sieving them together 3–4 times.

3. Cream the fat and sugar in a basin until very light in texture, then add the vanilla, then the eggs 1 at a time, creaming the mixture well between each egg.

4. Add the sieved flour gradually until it is all absorbed and the batter is clear of flour spots.

5. Fill the prepared moulds with the mixture to a depth of 50 mm, level the surface and dredge it lightly with caster sugar.

6. Place on a baking sheet and bake in the centre of an oven at 175°C (350°F) for 30 minutes, then reduce to 160°C (325°F). The baking time varies according to the size of tin used, but it is approximately 1¼–1½ hours. Test when the cake is ready by running a thin needle or knife blade into the centre: it should come away clean.

## 1435   Cherry cake

### Method

Prepare and cook as for Madeira cake (1434), adding 12 oz (340 g) of quartered glacé cherries to the batter, when the flour is cleared. Before cutting the cherries, wash them in warm water to clear the syrup and dry them thoroughly in a cloth.

## 1436  Dundee cake

### Method

1. Prepare a batter as for Madeira cake (1434), omitting the cornflour and baking powder. Add 1 level teaspoon (3 g) of mixed spice to the flour.
2. When the flour is absorbed, add 12 oz (340 g) each of cleaned sultanas and currants mixed with 6 oz (170 g) of chopped mixed peel.
3. After moulding the mixture into the tins, cover the surface fairly liberally with whole blanched and skinned almonds.
4. Bake in the centre of an oven at 160°C (325°F) for approximately 2 hours. When the almonds are golden brown, cover them with a piece of paper, if necessary, to prevent them burning.

## 1437  Rich fruit cake

| | Ingredients | |
|---|---|---|
| 1 lb | butter | 450 g |
| 1 lb | Barbados sugar | 450 g |
| 1¼ lb | cake flour | 560 g |
| 4 oz | ground almonds | 110 g |
| 1 lb | sultanas | 450 g |
| 1 lb | currants | 450 g |
| 4 oz | chopped mixed peel | 110 g |
| 4 oz | glacé cherries | 110 g |
| 2 level teaspoons | mixed spice | 6 g |
| 10 | eggs | 10 |
| 5–6 drops | vanilla essence | 5–6 drops |

*Note*: Treble fruit weight for wedding or Xmas cake.

### Method

1. Line the cooking tins, allowing for a depth of 60–75 mm, with cardboard and greased greaseproof paper.
2. Sieve the flour and spice. Clean the fruit, washing and drying the cherries before cutting them in quarters, and add the grated lemon rind to it.
3. Cream the butter and sugar in a basin to a light texture, then add the vanilla and a few drops of gravy browning to give a good colour.
4. Add the eggs 1 at a time, creaming the mixture between each one. If desired, 1 fl. oz (30 ml) of rum may be added at this stage.
5. Gradually absorb the flour and spice and mix until clear. Add the prepared fruit and thoroughly mix until it is evenly distributed throughout.
6. Place the mixture in the prepared tins to a depth of 60 mm and place them on a baking sheet. Bake in the centre of an oven at 160°C (325°F) for approximately 2–3 hours. Test when they are cooked by inserting a needle or a thin knife in the centre; it should come away clean.

## BISCUITS (garnish for ice sweets and petits fours)

### 1438  Piped shortbreads                    Sablés à poche

| | Ingredients | |
|---|---|---|
| 6 oz | butter or best margarine | 170 g |
| 4 oz | caster sugar | 110 g |
| 8 oz | cake flour | 225 g |
| 1 medium | egg | 1 medium |
| 2–3 drops | vanilla essence | 2–3 drops |

### Method

1. Cream the butter and sugar together in a basin until very light in texture.
2. Work in the beaten egg and vanilla.
3. Add the sieved flour and mix until the paste is smooth.
4. With a bag and a 10 mm star tube, pipe out the paste in various small shapes on to a greased and floured baking sheet.
5. Decorate the biscuits with glacé cherries, angelica, nuts, etc.
6. Bake at 200°C (400°F) for 12–15 minutes, according to size.

*Note.* The paste may be piped very small for petits fours.

### 1439  Scotch shortbread

| | Ingredients | |
|---|---|---|
| 10 oz | butter | 280 g |
| 6 oz | caster sugar | 170 g |
| 1 lb | cake flour | 450 g |
| 3 fl. oz | egg | 85 ml |
| 2–3 drops | vanilla essence | 2–3 drops |

### Method

1. Sieve the flour and make a bay in the centre.
2. Cream the sugar and eggs in the centre, add the butter and cream together, add the vanilla, then work the mixture into the flour.
3. Scrape the paste down 2 or 3 times with a palette knife until it is clear. The paste becomes oily if cleared by hand because of the heat.

4. Place in a refrigerator to set, then roll it out 5 mm thick. Cut the paste into fancy shapes, brush them with egg wash, dredge with caster sugar and decorate with glacé cherries and angelica.

5. Bake at 190°C (375°F) for 15–20 minutes, according to size.

*Note.* The times given are for individual biscuits and large-section rounds.

### 1440 Almond petits fours     Pâtés d'amandes gommés
**Method**

1. Place 1 lb (450 g) of ground almonds in a mortar or basin, gradually work in 7 fl. oz (200 ml) of white of egg and work them hard together to draw the oil from the almonds.

2. Gradually work in 1 lb (450 g) of caster sugar to give a smooth mixture.

3. Using a piping bag and a 5 mm star tube, pipe the mixture on to wax or rice paper on a baking sheet. Pipe various small designs approximately 30 mm long.

4. Decorate the top with small pieces of glacé fruits, almonds, etc. Allow to dry for at least 2–3 hours to form a crust then bake in the centre of an oven at 165–170°C (330–340°F) for 12–15 minutes till a light golden brown.

5. Remove from the oven and brush immediately with gum arabic or a heavy sugar syrup to give a nice shine. (Gum arabic is crushed, covered with twice the quantity of water, and allowed to stand for a few hours to dissolve.)

*Note.* When wax paper is used, place it on a hot wet baking sheet to free the biscuits.

### 1441 Macaroons     Macarons
**Method**

1. Place 8 oz (225 g) of ground almonds in a basin and gradually work in 5½ fl. oz (150 ml) of whites of egg with a spoon.

2. Gradually work in 1 lb (450 g) of caster sugar until the mixture becomes very smooth.

3. Using a bag and a 10 mm plain tube, pipe out shapes, 40 mm in diameter at least 25 mm apart, on to rice paper on a baking sheet.

4. Fold a damp cloth in 4, lengthways and dab it across the top of the macaroons to give an even crack when they are cooked.

5. Bake in the centre of an oven at 165–170°C (330–340°F)

for 16–18 minutes. If desired, a half of blanched and skinned almond may be placed in the centre before baking.

### 1442 Button macaroons     Ratafia
**Method**

Prepare as for Macaroons (1441). Pipe the mixture 10 mm in diameter. Bake them for approximately 10 minutes till a golden brown colour.

### 1443 Cornets and cigarette biscuits
**Method**

1. Cream together in a basin 4 oz (110 g) of butter with 5 oz (140 g) of caster sugar until very light in texture.

2. Gradually add 3 whites of egg a little at a time, creaming the mixture between each one, then work in 4 oz (110 g) of sieved cake flour until it becomes very smooth.

3. Well grease 3 large baking sheets. With a piping bag and a 5 mm plain tube, pipe the mixture 75 mm long for cigarette or in round mounds 30 mm in diameter for cornets. Leave a 40 mm space between when piping.

4. Knock the tray hard on a cloth on a table to flatten the mixture.

5. Bake in the top of an oven at 220°C (425°F) for 7–8 minutes until the edges are golden brown. Open the oven and remove the biscuits one at a time. For cigarette biscuits, roll each one around a pencil; for cornets, roll around the end of a cornet mould.

### 1444     Tuiles
Produces 32–35 pieces.

| | Ingredients | |
|---|---|---|
| 8 oz | butter | 225 g |
| 8 oz | caster sugar | 225 g |
| 8 oz | chopped or flaked almonds | 225 g |
| 1 oz | flour | 30 g |

**Method**

1. Cream the butter and sugar to a very light texture. Combine with the almonds and flour and mix them well.

2. Grease and flour 2–3 large baking sheets.

3. Place a dessertspoon of the mixture on the sheet for each biscuit, 40 mm apart, and flatten with the back of a fork.

4. Bake in the top of an oven at 170–180°C (340–350°F) for 7–8 minutes.

5. Raise the biscuits from the baking sheet with a palette knife and place them on a rolling pin to set them curved.

6. Serve on a flat dish with a doily.

## 1445 Cats' tongues          Langues de chat

| | Ingredients | |
|---|---|---|
| 4 oz | butter | 110 g |
| 4 oz | caster sugar | 110 g |
| 5 oz | flour | 140 g |
| 3 | whites of egg | 3 |

### Method

1. Cream the sugar and butter in a basin to a light texture, then add a little of the whites of egg at a time, creaming the mixture between.
2. Add the vanilla, then absorb the flour. Mix until smooth.
3. Using a bag and a 5 mm plain tube, pipe the mixture into 60–75 mm lengths, 30 mm apart, on to a greased baking sheet.
4. Bake at the top of an oven at 200°C (400°F) for 7–8 minutes until the edges are golden brown.
5. Remove them with a palette knife and put them on to a wire grill to cool. Serve on a flat dish with a doily.

## 1446 Brandy snaps

| | Ingredients | |
|---|---|---|
| 6 oz | butter | 170 g |
| 12 oz | caster sugar | 340 g |
| 8 oz | golden syrup | 225 g |
| 8 oz | flour | 225 g |
| ¼ oz | ground ginger | 7 g |

### Method

1. Cream the butter and sugar in a basin until very light. Absorb the sieved flour and ginger.
2. Mix in the slightly warmed syrup until very smooth in texture.
3. With a bag and a 10 mm plain tube, pipe the mixture 30 mm in diameter on to a well greased baking sheet; knock the baking sheet to flatten the mixture.
4. Bake in the top of an oven at 200°C (400°F) for approximately 8–10 minutes.
5. With a palette knife, take 1 snap at a time off the baking sheet, roll it around a piece of wood or metal 10–20 mm in diameter and let it set. Serve the snaps on a flat dish with a doily.

## 1447 Snow balls          Boules de neige

### Method

1. Mix together in a basin 8 oz (225 g) of ground almonds and 12 oz (340 g) of caster sugar. Gradually add enough whites of egg to make a stiff mouldable mixture.
2. Take small pieces of the mixture, place a half glacé cherry in the centre and mould each piece into 20 mm balls.
3. Moisten the hands with white of egg, roll them around the balls and drop the balls into icing sugar to give them a thick coating.
4. Place on a clean baking sheet and bake in the centre of an oven at 135–150°C (275–300°F) for 20–25 minutes until the balls just crack. Remove them and allow them to cool. Snow balls are served amongst a variety of petits fours.

---

## 1448 VARIOUS ICE PREPARATIONS

### General notes on ice mixtures

There are several methods of making various types of ice cream, but a successful recipe must be balanced in such a way that the ice cream will set correctly, being neither too hard nor too soft. The setting quality depends on the sugar content. If too much sugar is used, the ice cream will not set, and if too little is used, it will be too hard. A well made ice cream should mould easily and smoothly at the time of service and be the texture of firm butter.

Ice creams can be roughly divided into two types: (i) those in which the mixture is churned while at freezing point (custard-based ice cream and water ices), and (ii) those which are placed into moulds and then frozen (biscuit glacé, parfaits, soufflé glacé, mousse glacée, etc.).

It is possible for ice creams and moulded ices to be made from specified amounts of ingredients. Water ices and sorbets, for instance, are made from fruit syrups to which are added fruit pulps, wines and liqueurs, and it is therefore necessary to check the density of the prepared mixtures by using a sacrometer (Baumé or Pessesyrop sacrometers).

### Vanilla ice cream

Vanilla ice cream is made from a custard (true or synthetic) which is churned while at freezing point. Additional flavours – essence of coffee, chocolate, strawberry pulp, crushed pistachio nuts, praline, etc. – may be added to this basic mixture.

355

## Water ices

Water ices are made from sugar syrup with lemon juice and the juiced pulp of the desired fruit (18° of sugar) added to it.

## Sorbet, punch, spoom

These are made like water ices, but any wine or liqueur is also added to the mixture.

## Bombes

Bombes are bomb-shaped moulds which are generally lined (chemisée) with 10–20 mm of a custard-based or water ice. The centre is then generally filled with a different flavoured 'biscuit' ice mixture or, sometimes, with fruits in a thick syrup.

## Parfait

Parfaits are various fancy-shaped moulds filled with a parfait ice mixture then frozen.

## Soufflé glacé

Soufflés glacés are made from biscuit glacé mixture poured into prepared soufflée cases with greased paper bands extending one-third above the height of the case. The mixture is then frozen, the band removed and the top decorated and garnished according to recipe.

## Plombières and iced pudding

Plombières are custard-based ice creams with the addition of appropriate flavourings and garnishes poured into fancy moulds then frozen.

### 1449 Vanilla ice cream — Glace à la vanille

| 1 quart | Ingredients | 1 litre |
|---|---|---|
| 2 pints | milk | 1 litre |
| 8 oz | caster sugar | 200 g |
| 6–8 | yolks of egg | 5–7 |
| 8–10 drops | vanilla essence | 7–8 |
| 1 | or pod | 1 |

#### Method

1. Boil the milk and vanilla in a saucepan.
2. Mix the yolks and sugar in a basin to a light consistency then pour half the milk on to it, mixing well, and return all the mixture to the pan. Stir over the heat to thicken. Do not allow to boil, or the mixture will curdle.
3. Cool in a wide receptacle until cold, then strain. Churn the ice cream at freezing point until it reaches the consistency of firm butter.

*Note.* Where a freezing tub is used, the sleeve is packed with 5 parts crushed ice to 1 part freezing salt.

Various other recipes are used to produce a cheaper mix. If desired, the milk content may be reduced by one-eighth or one-tenth and, when freezing, the same amount of cream may be added.

### 1450 Coffee ice cream — Glace moka

#### Method

Prepare as for Vanilla ice cream (1449), adding sufficient coffee extract or essence to flavour and give a light coffee colour

### 1451 Chocolate ice cream — Glace au chocolat

#### Method

Prepare as for Vanilla ice cream (1449). When boiling the milk, add 1 oz (25 g) chocolate or cocoa powder or 2 oz (50 g) of block chocolate.

### 1452 Strawberry ice cream — Glace aux fraises

#### Method

Prepare as for Vanilla ice cream (1449); reduce the milk content by 25 per cent. When the mixture is cold, add ½ pint (250 ml) of strawberry pulp. If necessary, add 1–2 drops of cochineal to colour.

### 1453 Praline ice cream — Glace pralinée

#### Method

Prepare as for Vanilla ice cream (1449); when half frozen, add 2 oz (50 g) of praline (1167).

### 1454 Lemon water ice (18° density) — Glace au citron

| 1 quart | Ingredients | 1 litre |
|---|---|---|
| 12 oz | caster sugar | 300 g |
| 4 | lemons | 3 |
| 2 | whites of egg | 1½ |
| 2 pints | water* | 1 litre |

#### Method

1. Wash the lemons, remove the zest with a peeler, place it in a basin and add the sugar.
2. Squeeze the lemons and measure the juice: it has to be allowed for in the measured liquid.*
3. Heat the water until it is warm, pour it over the lemon zest and sugar ank let it stand until cold. Add the lemon juice, strain the liquid the whites of egg.
4. Churn freeze until it becomes smooth and set.

## 1455 Orange water ice — Glace à l'orange

### Method

Prepare as for Lemon water ice (1454); use 1 lemon and 4 oranges and add a few drops of yellow and red colour to give an orange tint.

*Note.* For tangerine or mandarin ice, use these fruits in place of oranges.

## 1456 Strawberry water ice — Glace aux fraises

## 1457 Raspberry water ice — Glace aux framboises

### Method

Prepare as for Lemon water ice (1454). Reduce the lemon by a half and reduce the amount of water by $\frac{1}{2}$ pint (250 ml); replace this amount with strawberry or raspberry pulp. Add a few drops of cochineal to colour.

### Strawberry or raspberry pulp

Wash the fruit, place it in a pan and add the same amount of caster sugar. Stir over the heat to extract the juice, cooking for a few minutes until the fruit is soft. Ensure the sugar does not burn. Rub the mixture through a hair or nylon sieve, cool and use as required.

## 1458 Chart of approximate syrup density from ingredients when a sacrometer is not available

1. 2 lb (1 kg) sugar and 1 pint (625 ml) water    30°    1 quart (1300 ml) bulk
2. 2 lb (1 kg) sugar and 1½ pints (935 ml) water    25°    2½ pints (1610 ml) bulk
3. 2 lb (1 kg) sugar and 2 pints (1250 ml) water    22½°    3 pints (1925 ml) bulk
4. 2 lb (1 kg) sugar and 2½ pints (1560 ml) water    20°    3½ pints (2235 ml) bulk
5. 2 lb (1 kg) sugar and 3 pints (1875 ml) water    18°    4 pints (2550 ml) bulk
6. 2 lb (1 kg) sugar and 3½ pints (2185 ml) water    16½°    4½ pints (2865 ml) bulk
7. 2 lb (1 kg) sugar and 4 pints (2500 ml) water    15¼°    5 pints (3175 ml) bulk

## 1459 Sorbet — Sorbet

### Method

1. Prepare as for Lemon water ice (1454); adjust the syrup density to 16°.

2. Where wines, liqueurs etc. are added, allowance must be made for the extra liquid when the basic syrup is prepared. Sorbets are churned at freezing point.

3. Serve the sorbet loosely in Paris goblets on an underflat with a doily or, alternatively, mould it in frozen fruit cases as designated by its name, e.g. Cassolette givrée normande: an apple and calvados-flavoured sorbet, served in a frozen apple case with a cap and pulled sugar or marzipan leaves.

## 1460 — Punch romain

| 1 quart | Ingredients | 1 litre |
|---|---|---|
| 6 oz | caster sugar | 150 g |
| 1 | lemon | 1 medium |
| 1 | orange | 1 medium |
| 3 fl. oz | cold tea | 75 ml |
| 4 oz sugar mix | Italian meringue | 100 g sugar mix |
| 2 pints | water* | 1 litre |
| 1½ fl. oz | rum or | 35 ml |
| 2½ fl. oz | champagne | 60 ml |

### Method

1. Wash the fruit and remove the zest with a peeler. Place the zest in a basin with the sugar and prepared tea.

2. Squeeze the juice from the fruit and add the water, rum or champagne to make up to the liquid content*.

3. Test the mixture with a sacrometer until it reads 16½° syrup density. Place into the churn to freeze and, when the mixture is beginning to set, add the prepared meringue.

4. Continue to churn until the mixture is frozen and light. With a bag and a 20 mm plain tube, pipe into Paris goblets until they are three-quarters full; pull away the tube to form a point.

5. Immediately place the glasses in a refrigerator cabinet or ice cave at a low enough temperature to hold the mixture at freezing point.

## 1461 — Spoom granité

### Method

Prepare as for Sorbet (1459), using a 14° density syrup.

## 1462 Basic mixture — Biscuit glacé

When $75 \times 250$ mm frames are used, the mixture will produce 24–30 portions, according to the size of the portions.

| | Ingredients | |
|---|---|---|
| 12 oz | caster sugar | 340 g |
| 8 | yolks of egg | 8 |
| 8 | whites of egg | 8 |
| ¾ pint | cream | 425 ml |
| ½ pint | water | 285 ml |
| 4–5 drops | vanilla essence | 4–5 drops |

357

**Method**

1. Mix the yolks, sugar, water and vanilla in a well-tinned pot (do not use aluminium as it will discolour).
2. Cook in a bain-marie over the gas, stirring occasionally to keep the sides clean, until the mixture thickens to the consistency of scrambled egg.
3. Place the mixture in the machine bowl and allow it to beat until it has gone cold and has doubled in volume.
4. Fold in the softly whipped cream (just thickened) then the whipped whites of egg (not over stiff).
5. Line 75 × 250 mm biscuit moulds with greaseproof paper. Fill the moulds to the top with the mixture, smooth it with a palette knife, then cover the top with another greaseproof paper and lid.
6. Place in a deep freeze cabinet for 6–8 hours, or overnight, to set.
7. Serve out of the frames on a base of wafer biscuits. Decorate with a scroll or rosettes of Crème Chantilly(1151) and decorate the top of the cream with rose or violet petals, quarters of glacé cherries, diamonds of angelica, etc.

*Note.* Liqueur and/or garnish when used, is mixed in before the whites of eggs. Fruit pulp is added before the cream with any colouring required. For a chocolate flavour, 1 oz (30 g) cocoa powder is added to the mixture when it is poached.

**1463**               **Biscuit glacé arlequin**

**Method**

Mould with 2 layers of chocolate mixture with vanilla mixture between them.

**1464**               **Biscuit glacé praliné**

**Method**

Add 3 oz (85 g) of praline (1167) to the mixture after the cream.

**1465**               **Biscuit glacé marquise**

**Method**

Mould two alternating layers each of vanilla and strawberry mixtures.

**1466**               **Biscuit glacé napolitaine**

**Method**

Mould with one alternating layer each of vanilla, strawberry and pistachio mixtures.

**1467**               **Biscuit glacé Rothschild**

**Method**

Add 3 oz (85 g) of chopped glacé fruits, macerated in kirsch, after the cream and 2 oz (55 g) of 5 mm diced sponge after the egg whites to a vanilla mixture before moulding.

**1468**               **Biscuit glacé tutti-frutti**

Add 4 oz (110 g) of chopped glacé fruits, macerated in kirsch and Grand Marnier, to a vanilla mixture.

**1469**               **Bombe Alhambra**

**Method**

1. Line the mould with vanilla ice and fill the centre with strawberry flavoured biscuit glacé mixture (1462).
2. Set for 6–8 hours, or overnight, in a deep freeze cabinet.
3. Unmould by running under hot water for 1–2 seconds. Set the bombe on a base of wafers and decorate up the sides with Crème Chantilly (1151), with a bag and a 10 mm star tube. Pipe a rosette on top. Cut some wafer biscuits across from corner to corner and insert them in the cream as fins of the bombe.
4. For this bombe, place strawberries in between the cream around the base.

**1470**               **Bombe Archiduc**

**Method**

The mould is lined with strawberry ice and the centre filled with praline biscuit mixture (1464). Serve as in 3 of method (1469).

**1471**               **Bombe Cyrano**

**Method**

Line the mould with praline ice and fill the centre with poached cherries in a thick Sauce Melba (1189) flavoured with kirsch. Serve as in 3 of method 1469.

**1472**               **Bombe Frou-Frou**

**Method**

Line the mould with vanilla ice, and fill the centre with Biscuit glacé tutti-frutti (1468), using rum in place of the liqueur.

## 1473 Basic mixture of parfait — Parfait

| 1 quart | Ingredients | 1 litre |
|---|---|---|
| 2 pints | milk | 1 litre |
| ½ oz | cornflour | 15 g |
| 1 lb | caster sugar | 400 g |
| 4–5 drops | vanilla essence | 4–5 drops |
| 16 | yolks of egg | 14 |
| 16 | whites of egg | 14 |
| 1 pint | cream | 500 ml |

### Method

1. Dilute the cornflour with a little of the milk. Boil the remainder of the milk, whisk in the diluted cornflour and reboil.

2. Mix the yolks, sugar and vanilla in a basin, add the thickened milk, return the mixture to the pan and poach it without boiling to thicken. Allow to go cold, then strain the liquid.

3. When cold, add liqueur or flavouring, then the whipped cream, and then the stiffly beaten whites of egg.

4. Fill parfait moulds with the mixture and place them in deep freeze for 6–8 hours or overnight.

5. Serve as for Biscuit glacé (1462) from 7 in method.

## 1474 Iced puddings — Plombières

### Method

Plombières, or iced puddings (the outer coating for bombes), are custard-based ice creams of the desired flavour to which has been added an extra ¼ or ½ pint (125–250 ml) of cream with 1 or 2 oz (25–50 g) of sugar per quart (litre) of basic custard. The cream and sugar are lightly whisked and added to the ice cream in the freezer at the stage when it is beginning to set.

## 1475 Various ice cups — Coupes

### General notes

1. An average portion of 2 oz (55 g) of fruit is served in a fruit ice cup and, unless they are small enough to be served whole, i.e. cherries, grapes etc., the fruits are cut into 10 mm macédoine.

2. When finished according to the recipe, the coupes are served on a flat dish with dish paper or a doily. Wafers (gaufrettes) or specific biscuits, such as Langues de chat, are served separately on a flat dish with a doily.

## 1476 — Coupe Alexandra

### Method

This is a macédoine of fruit (1365) served with strawberry ice with a rosette of Crème Chantilly on top (1151) and a violet petal on the rosette.

## 1477 — Coupe brésilienne

### Method

Macerate 10 mm diced pineapple with maraschino, and serve it with lemon water ice with a rosette of cream decorated with quarters of glacé cherry and diamonds of angelico.

## 1478 — Coupe Clo-Clo

### Method

Place a tablespoon of purée de marron in the base of the coupe with vanilla ice cream. Set pieces of marron glacé on top and decorate around them with 4 stars or rosettes of whipped cream flavoured with strawberry pulp.

## 1479 — Coupe Edna May

### Method

This coupe consists of poached stoned cherries served with vanilla ice cream and masked with Sauce Chantilly (1186) coloured pink with raspberry purée with a rosette of whipped cream on top.

## 1480 — Coupe Jacques

### Method

Coupe Jacques is a macédoine of fruit (1365) served with ½ lemon and ½ strawberry water ice decorated by a rosette of whipped cream with a grape on the rosette.

*Note.* Vanilla and strawberry cream ices are served in some establishments.

## 1481 — Coupe Jamaïque

### Method

Macerate 10 mm dice of pineapple in rum and serve it with coffee ice. Decorate with a rosette of whipped cream and place a violet petal on the cream.

## 1482 — Coupe Madeleine

### Method

Serve a 10 mm diced pineapple with vanilla ice cream and mask them with cold Apricot sauce (1181) flavoured with maraschino. Place a rosette of whipped cream, with a violet petal on it, on the top.

**1483**                    **Coupe Malmaison**

**Method**

Peel and stone grapes and serve them with vanilla ice cream with a rosette of whipped cream on top. Cover with a dome-shaped veil of spun sugar.

**1484**                      **Coupe midinette**

**Method**

Place vanilla ice cream in the base of the coupe with a half peach slightly to one side of it. Mask the peach with Sauce Melba (1189). Place a meringue shell on the other side, and decorate the top with a rosette of whipped cream with a violet petal in the centre.

**1485**                      **Coupe Mont Blanc**

**Method**

Place a tablespoon of purée de marron in the base of the coupe and put vanilla ice cream and roughly broken pieces of meringue shell on top; decorate around the top with four stars or rosettes of whipped cream.

**1486**                   **Coupe Montmorency**

**Method**

As for Coupe Edna May (1479), using Sauce Melba (1189) instead of Sauce Chantilly.

**1487**                      **Coupe Thaïs**

**Method**

Place carefully selected, washed and drained strawberries, macerated in sugar and curacao, in the base of the coupe and add ½ vanilla and ½ strawberry ice; decorate the top with a rosette of cream and put a strawberry on the rosette.

**1488**                      **Coupe Vénus**

**Method**

Place sliced peaches in the coupe with vanilla ice on top and mask them with Sauce Chantilly (1186) flavoured with curaçao. Decorate the top with a rosette of whipped cream and put a strawberry on it. Cover with a dome-shaped veil of spun sugar.

**1489 Iced fruit sweets**

For iced fruit sweets, scoops of ice are placed in a silver timbale or glass dish and fruit placed on top. They are then masked with the sauce, according to the recipe, and decorated with rosettes of Crème Chantilly (1151). If desired, the fruit and ice may be placed in separate dishes. Serve the dishes on an underflat with a doily.

**1490 Peach Melba**               **Pêches Melba**

**1491 Strawberry Melba**         **Fraises Melba**

**Method**

Serve vanilla ice cream with peaches or strawberries on top masked with Sauce Melba (1189). Decorate with rosettes of cream with violet petals on the cream.

**1492**                      **Pêche cardinal**

**1493**                      **Fraises cardinal**

**Method**

As for Pêche or Fraises Melba (1490/1), with strawberry ice cream in place of vanilla. Sprinkle filleted almonds on the surface after masking with the sauce.

**1494**                   **Poire Belle-Hélène**

**Method**

1. Serve small whole (4 oz or 110 g) poached pears around scoops of vanilla ice cream and decorate with rosettes of whipped cream.
2. Serve hot Sauce Suchard (1188) separately in a sauce-boat on an underflat with a doily.

---

## 1495 PASTRY PREPARATIONS FOR THE KITCHEN

**1496 Raised pies**

**Method**

1. With a brush, well grease the moulds to be used and place them on a greased baking sheet.
2. With a little flour, roll three-quarters of the patty paste (1145) into a pocket shape (for round, oval or oblong moulds) until it is 5 mm thick.
3. Carefully place the paste inside the moulds without stretching it. With a piece of paste dipped in flour in the hand, press the paste into position at the base, then the sides. Allow the top edge to overlap the mould slightly.

4. Egg-wash the top edge. Fill the case according to recipe.

5. Roll out the remainder of the paste for the cover till 5 mm thick. Place this on top, press it with the hands to the centre, then firmly on to the side edges. Cut off any excess paste.

6. Press the edges firmly, then finish with pastry tweezers, or crimp with the fingers, and egg-wash.

7. Decorate on top with paste leaves and roses, as desired. Allow the pie to rest for at least 1 hour.

8. Egg-wash. Bake in the centre of an oven at 200°C (400°F) for the first 12–15 minutes to set the paste, then reduce the temperature to 140°C (280°F) to cook the contents. The baking time varies according to the size: large pies with raw ingredients will require 2–2½ hours.

*Note.* For hand raised pies, use hot water paste (1144). Mould the paste by pressing the clenched hand into the centre of the ball of paste, then gradually raise the sides to the desired height and thickness. Alternatively, place the paste over a suitably sized mould, press it to the desired size, invert and remove the mould. Finish as from 6 in method.

**1497** Baked hams and ham paupiettes for Sous la cendre: see 863 and 864.

**1498** Barquettes, short paste: see 1433; use short paste in place of tartlet paste.

**1499** Bouchées and vol-au-vent: see 1282.

**1500** Bread rolls: see 1192.

**1501** Bridge rolls: see 1193.

**1502** Canneloni: see 610.

**1503** Capelletti: see 611.

**1504** Chausson (savoury types for hot hors d'oeuvre): see 111; use a 50 mm fluted cutter and savoury fillings.

**1505** Cheese palmiers: see 1298.

**1506** Cheese straws: see 1299.

**1507** Choux paste: see 343 or 1368.

**1508** Cornish pasties: see 774.

**1509** Dartois d'anchois: see 111, hot hors d'oeuvre.

**1510** Flans, savoury: see 1305; use short paste or puff paste trimmings for lining the flans, 1522–24 for fillings.

**1511** Fleurons: roll out the puff paste 3 mm thick and cut it out into crescent-shaped pieces with a 50 mm fluted cutter. Invert the pieces and place them on a baking sheet. Let them stand for 30 minutes then egg-wash and bake at the top of an oven at 200°C (400°F) for 8–10 minutes until crisp.

**1512** Nouilles: see 604; Nouilles vertes: see 606.

**1513** Pancakes: see 1394.

**1514** Patties: see 1283. For Pâte à bortsch, use a 30 mm fluted cutter and duck and pork forcemeat.

**1515** Pies, covering of hot meat, poultry and game pies: see Steak pie (777).

**1516** Puddings, lining and covering with suet paste: see Steak and kidney pudding (780).

**1517** Profiteroles for soup garnish: pipe out choux paste (343) the size of a pea with a 3 mm plain tube. Bake at the top of an oven at 200°C (400°F) for 6–7 minutes.

**1518** Ramequins: line the tartlet moulds with short paste (see 1429), fill them with Cheese soufflé mixture (1540), level it with a palette knife and bake them in the top of the oven at 190°C (380°F) for 10–12 minutes.

**1519** Ravioli: for paste, see 607; for preparation of, see 608.

**1520** Tartlets, preparation and cooking of: see 1429; use short paste or puff paste trimmings.

*Note.* Other preparations include Coulibiac, Cournick, Rastagaïs, etc.

# Savoury flans and tartlets - Savouries

# Savoury flans and tartlets - Savouries

## 1521 SAVOURY FLANS

### 1522  Cheese and bacon flan                 Quiche lorraine

| 8 portions | Ingredients | 10 couverts |
|---|---|---|
| 8 oz flour mix | short paste (1138) | 280 g flour mix |
| 4 oz | streaky bacon | 140 g |
| 4 oz | Gruyère or Cheddar cheese | 140 g |
| 2 | eggs | 3 |
| 12 fl. oz | milk | 420 ml |
| 1 level teaspoon | salt | 4 g |
| ¼ level teaspoon | ground white pepper | 1 g |
| few grains | nutmeg | few grains |

### Method

1. Using a little flour, roll the paste 5 mm thick. Line a 200 or 225 mm flan case for 8 or 10 portions with the paste (see 1305) and place it on a greased baking sheet. Do not prick the bottom. Let it stand for 30 minutes.

2. Cut the skinned bacon into lardons 25 × 5 × 5 mm, blanch, then lightly fry them and place them to cool.

3. Cut the cheese into 5 mm dice and sprinkle it into the flan with the bacon.

4. Beat the eggs, salt and pepper. Add the milk then strain the liquid.

5. Carefully fill the eggs and milk into the flan case to within 5 mm of the top edge. Lightly sprinkle the surface with a little nutmeg.

6. Bake the flan in the centre of an oven for 30–35 minutes, at 180°C (350°F) for the first ten minutes and at 160°C (325°F) for the rest of the time. The paste should be cooked and the filling set with a golden surface.

7. Serve the flan on a hot round salver.

### 1523  Mushroom flan                 Flan forestière
### Method

Prepare, cook and serve as for Quiche lorraine (1522). Replace the cheese and bacon with 8 oz (280 g) of washed and sliced closed mushrooms lightly fried in 1 oz (35 g) of butter; do not allow them to go crisp.

### 1524                 Flan suisse
### Method

1. Prepare, cook and serve as for Quiche lorraine (1522), omitting the cheese and bacon.

2. Line the base of the flan with slices of boiled potatoes, 30 mm in diameter, 5 mm thick (12 oz or 420 g). Sprinkle them with 4 oz (140 g) of grated Gruyère cheese, then add the custard.

## TARTLETS

### 1525                 Tartelettes lorraine
### Method

1. Use the ingredients of Quiche lorraine (1522).

2. Line 16 or 20 deep, 50 mm-diameter tartlet moulds with the paste. Shred the bacon and grate the cheese.

3. Finish as for Quiche lorraine (1522); bake for 15–16 minutes. Serve on a hot flat dish on a dish paper and garnish between the tartlets with sprigs of parsley.

### 1526                 Tartelettes forestière
### Method

Prepare the ingredients of Flan forestière (1523) in tartlets (2 and 3 in method of 1525).

### 1527                 Tartelettes suisse
### Method

Prepare the ingredients of Flan suisse (1524) in tartlets (2 and 3 in method of 1525).

## SAVOURIES

### 1528  Preparation notes

Savouries must be served immediately after they have been cooked so that they do not go dry. Toast must be freshly cooked with the crusts and corners removed after toasting. It is assumed that the following dishes will be served on half slices of trimmed buttered toast, with the exception of Buck rabbit which is generally served on a three-quarter trimmed slice

Except where otherwise mentioned, savouries are served on a hot flat dish with dish paper or a doily and garnished on each side with sprigs of washed parsley.

The quantities given in imperial measurements are for 8

portions and those in metric measurements are for 10 portions.

#### 1529 Angels on horseback — Anges à cheval

**Method**

Place 24–30 oysters in a sauteuse, cover them with cold water, poach for 1–2 minutes then refresh. Wrap each in one-third of a thin slice of streaky bacon. Place 4 or 5 to a skewer, season them with cayenne pepper and grill under a salamander on each side till light golden brown. Place on half slices of buttered toast. Serve 3 pieces per portion.

#### 1530 Asparagus tips on toast — Pointes d'asperges sur croûte

**Method**

Allow 3–4 tips – cut 45 mm long from the head – per portion and place the remainder underneath the tips on each half of trimmed buttered toast. Season with salt and ground white pepper, sprinkle with Parmesan cheese and melted butter, heat in the oven and colour the cheese lightly under the salamander.

#### 1531 — Beignets au fromage

**Method**

1. Prepare ¼ pint (175 ml) water mix of choux paste, reducing the fat content by a half.
2. Add 2 oz (70 g) of grated Parmesan cheese.
3. Using a 10 mm star tube, pipe 24 or 30, 40 mm-diameter rings of the paste on to greased paper.
4. Deep fry them at 170°C (340°F) by dipping the paper in the fat then pulling it away. Keep the fritters on the move during frying for approximately 5–6 minutes until they become crisp.
5. Drain and serve on a hot flat dish on a doily; garnish with fried parsley.

#### 1532 — Bouchée Ivanhoë

**Method**

1. Boil ¼ pint (175 ml) of béchamel with 3 fl. oz (100 ml) of cream or milk. Add 12 oz (420 g) of flaked cooked smoked haddock, free of skin and bone.
2. Season with cayenne papper and bring back to the boil. Fill 16 or 20 small 40 mm bouchées with the haddock filling. Place a teaspoon of cooked tomato concassé on top and a half slice of pickled walnut on the tomato. Place the pastry caps on at an angle.

3. Place on a hot flat dish on a dish paper and garnish between them with sprigs of parsley.

#### 1533 Buck rabbit

**Method**

1. Prepare and serve as for Welsh rabbit (1554).
2. Finish on trimmed three-quarter slices of buttered toast with a poached egg on top of each.

#### 1534 — Canapé baron

**Method**

1. Prepare and grill 8 oz (280 g) of open mushrooms, 8 or 10 slices of streaky bacon and 16 or 20 slices of bone marrow.
2. Serve on trimmed and buttered toast cut either in half slices or in 50 mm-diameter rounds, the slices of bacon cut in halves and placed across, the mushrooms on top of the bacon, dark side up, with the marrow on top.

#### 1535 Anchovies on toast — Canapé d'anchois

**Method**

On each half slice of trimmed and buttered toast place 3–4 anchovy fillets across the length, or 3 knots of anchovy in line. Season with cayenne pepper, brush with oil and pass through an oven to heat. Brush with melted butter and serve.

#### 1536 — Canapé Diane

**Method**

1. Season with salt and milled pepper 24 or 30 halved pieces of chicken livers and lightly fry them in a little fat. Cook them underdone.
2. Prepare and serve as for Anges à cheval (1529), replacing the oysters with the chicken livers.

#### 1537 — Canapé Fédora

**Method**

Prepare and serve as for Canapé baron (1534), omitting the bone marrow. Place 1 or 2 stuffed olives on top of the mushrooms and bacon.

#### 1538 — Canapé Ivanhoë

**Method**

1. Prepare the smoked haddock as for Bouchée Ivanhoë (1532).

2. Serve in a dome shape on half slices of trimmed and buttered toast. Place a hot buttered slice of tomato on top of each and a slice of pickled walnut on the tomato.

## 1539 Champignons sous cloche

**Method**

1. Wash and peel 1 lb (560 g) of mushrooms.
2. Divide them equally into 8 or 10 buttered special glass fireproof dishes and season them with salt and milled pepper.
3. Cover with cream, place the covers on the dishes, bring to the boil and simmer gently on the side of the stove for 8–10 minutes.
4. Serve the dishes on an underflat with a doily.

## 1540 Cheese soufflé          Soufflé au parmesan

| 8 portions | Ingredients | 10 couverts |
|---|---|---|
| ¾ pint | milk | 525 ml |
| 3 oz | butter | 100 g |
| 3 oz | flour | 100 g |
| 6 oz | grated Parmesan cheese | 210 g |
| ¼ level teaspoon | salt | 2 g |
| few grains | cayenne pepper | few grains |
| few grains | grated nutmeg | few grains |
| 8 | yolks of egg | 10 |
| 8 | whites of egg | 10 |

**Method**

1. Lightly grease the soufflé dishes with a brush, line them with a little of the grated Parmesan cheese and shake out any surplus. Place the dishes on a small baking tray.
2. Mix the butter and sieved flour together to a smooth paste (Beurre manié).
3. Boil the milk, salt, cayenne pepper and nutmeg in a saucepan. Remove from the heat, add the Beurre manié and thoroughly dissolve it with a small wooden spatula.
4. Replace the pan over the heat, stir continually until re-boiling and smooth in texture. Remove from the heat and allow to cool for 1 minute.
5. Well mix in the yolks of egg one at a time then incorporate the grated cheese, retaining a very small amount to sprinkle on top of the finished mixture.
6. Whip the whites of egg until they will stand on the whisk, then fold them into the mixture.
7. Pour the mixture into the prepared soufflé dishes to a depth of 40 mm before it is cooked and level the surface. Sprinkle with cheese.
8. Place the soufflé on a baking tray in the centre of an oven at 200°C (400°F) and bake for 20 minutes.

9. Place the dish on round silver under flat with a doily; serve immediately.

## 1541 Curried prawns or shrimps on toast

**Method**

1. Boil ½ pint (350 ml) of curry sauce (413), and add 12 oz (420 g) of washed picked prawns or shrimps.
2. Bring to boiling point then serve in a dome shape on half slices of buttered and trimmed toast.

## 1542 Croûte Derby

**Method**

1. Boil ¼ pint (175 ml) of béchamel with 3 fl. oz (100 ml) of cream or milk then add 8 oz (280 g) of 5 mm-diced cooked ham.
2. Season with cayenne pepper and bring to the boil. Serve in a dome shape on half slices of buttered and trimmed toast. Place a slice of pickled walnut on top of each.

## 1543 Croûte Mont d'Or

**Method**

1. Prepare 6 eggs (7 eggs for 10) of scrambled egg (540).
2. Serve in a dome shape on half slices of trimmed and buttered toast. Place on top a dessertspoonful of Welsh rabbit mixture (1554) and quickly colour it golden brown under the salamander.

## 1544 Curried ham on toast          Croûte Radjah

**Method**

1. Prepare as for Curried prawns on toast (1541), replacing the prawns with 8 oz (280 g) of 5 mm-diced cooked ham.
2. Place a small piece of chutney mango on top of each.

## 1545 Croûte Windsor

**Method**

Prepare and serve as for Croûte Derby (1542). Place 1 or 2 small open grilled mushrooms on top in place of the pickled walnut.

## 1546 Croûte yorkaise

**Method**

1. Prepare as for Croûte Derby (1542), omitting the walnut. When boiling, remove the mixture from the heat, add 2 yolks of egg and mix them well in.

2. Place in a dome shape on half slices of trimmed and buttered toast. Glaze golden brown under a salamander.

### 1547 Kipper on toast

**Method**

1. Fillet and skin 4 or 5 kippers and cut each fillet into 3 pieces on the slant.

2. Place these on an oiled tray, brush them with oil and season with cayenne pepper. Lightly grill on each side under a salamander for 2–3 minutes.

3. Serve 3 pieces overlapping on each half slice of trimmed and buttered toast and brush them with melted butter.

### 1548                    Moelle sur croûte

**Method**

1. Cut 3–4 10 mm-thick slices of bone marrow on the slant for each portion.

2. Season them with salt and milled pepper and place them on a tray.

3. Grill for 1–2 minutes on each side and serve them on half slices of trimmed and buttered toast.

### 1549 Mushrooms on toast          Champignons sur croûte

**Method**

1. Wash, peel and grill 1 lb (560 g) of open mushrooms (977 g).

2. Serve 3 pieces overlapping, dark sides up, on each half slice of trimmed and buttered toast and brush them with melted butter.

### 1550                    Oeufs farcis Mornay

**Method**

1. Allow 2 halves of hard boiled egg per portion.

2. Prepare as for Oeufs Chimay (589). This recipe may also be prepared without duxelle.

### 1551 Sardines on toast

**Method**

1. Allow 2 large or 3 small sardines per portion.

2. Remove the skin, place them on an oiled tray, brush them with oil and season them with cayenne pepper.

3. Lightly grill on each side under a salamander.

4. Brush them over with melted butter and serve them on half slices of trimmed and buttered toast.

### 1552 Scotch woodcock

**Method**

1. Prepare Scrambled egg (540) with 6 eggs (7 for 10).

2. Serve in a dome shape on half slices of trimmed and buttered toast.

3. Place 2 thin strips of anchovy across the toast from corner to corner. Place a caper in each space.

### 1553 Soft roes on toast          Laitances sur croûte

**Method**

1. Allow 2 large or 3 small soft roes per portion. Remove the silver thread, wash the roes and dry them on a cloth.

2. Pass them through flour, place them on an oiled tray, brush them with oil and season with salt and cayenne pepper.

3. Sprinkle lightly with white breadcrumbs.

4. Grill for 3–4 minutes under a salamander then neatly arrange the roes on half slices of trimmed and buttered toast. Brush the roes with melted butter.

### 1554 Welsh rabbit

**Method**

1. Boil $\frac{1}{4}$ pint (175 ml) of béchamel, add 8 oz (280 g) of grated Cheddar cheese and stir until it has dissolved.

2. Remove from the heat, stir in 2 yolks of egg, mix well, then add 1 teaspoon of Worcester sauce and 1 teaspoon of prepared English mustard.

3. Mould the mixture to a slightly dome shape on half slices of trimmed and buttered toast and place them on a tray.

4. Colour golden brown under a moderate salamander.

*Note.* When prepared from a beer base, reduce $\frac{1}{2}$ pint (350 ml) of old ale to $\frac{1}{8}$ pint (90 ml) and add it to half the quantity of béchamel. Finish as above.

# Commodities - Price charts for food costing

# Commodities – Price charts for food costing

In all spheres of catering, it is necessary to maintain up-to-date prices of food commodities for costing purposes.

Space has been left in the unit columns for inserting tin sizes, etc.

With the introduction of decimal currency it will be found easy, for food costing, to link prices in decimal currency to metric quantities given in recipes.

| Item | Unit | Price | Item | Unit | Price |
|---|---|---|---|---|---|
| Anchovies | tin | ......... | tinned | tin | ......... |
| Anchovy essence | bot | ......... | Chocolate block | lb | ......... |
| Angelica | lb | ......... | Chutney | jar | ......... |
| Almonds, | | | Cinnamon, | | |
| flaked | lb | ......... | ground | lb | ......... |
| ground | lb | ......... | whole | lb | ......... |
| nibs | lb | ......... | Cloves | tin | ......... |
| split | lb | ......... | Cocoa | lb | ......... |
| whole | lb | ......... | Coconut | lb | ......... |
| Apricots, | | | Colourings, | | |
| dried | lb | ......... | green | bot | ......... |
| tinned | tin | ......... | red | bot | ......... |
| Arrowroot | lb | ......... | violet | bot | ......... |
| Artichoke bottoms | tin | ......... | yellow | bot | ......... |
| Asparagus | tin | ......... | Cornflour | lb | ......... |
| | | | Crab meat | tin | ......... |
| Baking powder | lb | ......... | Crystalised violets | lb | ......... |
| Barley | lb | ......... | Currants | lb | ......... |
| Beetroot | tin | ......... | Curry powder | lb | ......... |
| Bombay duck | pkt | ......... | | | |
| Butter | lb | ......... | Dates | lb | ......... |
| | | | | | |
| Candied peel | lb | ......... | Eggs, | | |
| Capers | ½ gal | ......... | dried | lb | ......... |
| Caviar | jar | ......... | fresh | doz | ......... |
| Celery hearts | tin | ......... | Essences, | | |
| Cheese, | | | almond | bot | ......... |
| Cheddar | lb | ......... | lemon | bot | ......... |
| Danish blue | lb | ......... | raspberry | bot | ......... |
| Dutch | lb | ......... | rum | bot | ......... |
| Gruyère | lb | ......... | strawberry | bot | ......... |
| Parmesan | lb | ......... | vanilla | bot | ......... |
| Cherries, | | | | | |
| cocktail | jar | ......... | Fécule | lb | ......... |
| glacées | lb | ......... | Figs | lb | ......... |

| | Unit | Price | | Unit | Price |
|---|---|---|---|---|---|
| Flour, | | | Mixed spice | lb | ......... |
|   cake | lb | ......... | Mustard, | | |
|   strong | lb | ......... |   English | tin | ......... |
| Fondant | lb | ......... |   French | jar | ......... |
| | | | | | |
| Gelatine, | | | Nutmeg, | | |
|   leaf | lb | ......... |   ground | lb | ......... |
|   powder | lb | ......... |   whole | lb | ......... |
| Gherkins | jar | ......... | | | |
| Ginger | | | Oil, | | |
|   ground | lb | ......... |   corn | tin | ......... |
|   root | jar | ......... |   nut | tin | ......... |
| Glucose | lb | ......... |   olive | tin | ......... |
| Golden syrup | lb | ......... | Olives, | | |
| Grapes | tin | ......... |   Manzanilla | jar | ......... |
| Gravy browning | bot | ......... |   Spanish | jar | ......... |
| | | | | | |
| Ham, Parma | tin | ......... | Paper, greaseproof | lb | ......... |
| Haricot beans | lb | ......... | Pâté de foie | tin | ......... |
| Hazelnuts | lb | ......... | Peaches | tin | ......... |
| Herrings, rollmop | jar | ......... | Pears | tin | ......... |
| Honey | jar | ......... | Peas, | | |
| Horseradish | jar | ......... |   green, split | lb | ......... |
| | | |     whole | lb | ......... |
| Jams, | | |   yellow, split | lb | ......... |
|   apricot | tin | ......... | Pepper, | | |
|   marmalade | tin | ......... |   cayenne | lb | ......... |
|   raspberry | tin | ......... |   ground | lb | ......... |
|   red currant | tin | ......... |   paprika | lb | ......... |
| | | |   whole | lb | ......... |
| Lard | lb | ......... | Pimentoes | tin | ......... |
| Lentils | lb | ......... | Pistachio nuts | lb | ......... |
| | | | Papadums | pkt | ......... |
| Macaroni | lb | ......... | Prunes | lb | ......... |
| Mace | lb | ......... | | | |
| Margarine, | | | Raisins | lb | ......... |
|   cooking | lb | ......... | Rennet | bot | ......... |
|   pastry | lb | ......... | Rice, | | |
|   table | lb | ......... |   Carolina | lb | ......... |
| Marrons, | | |   ground | lb | ......... |
|   glacés | tin | ......... |   Italian | lb | |
|   purée | tin | ......... |   patna | lb | ......... |
| Marzipan | lb | ......... | Rosemary | lb | ......... |
| Milk, | | | | | |
|   evaporated | tin | ......... | Salt, | | |
|   dried | lb | ......... |   celery | tin | ......... |
| Mint sauce | jar | ......... |   table | lb | ......... |

| | Unit | Price |
|---|---|---|
| Sauerkraut | tin | ......... |
| Semolina | lb | ......... |
| Shrimps | tin | ......... |
| Snails | tin | ......... |
| Sugar, | | |
|     Barbados | lb | ......... |
|     caster | lb | ......... |
|     Demerera | lb | ......... |
|     granulated | lb | ......... |
|     icing | lb | ......... |
|     loaf | lb | ......... |
| Sultanas | lb | ......... |
| Sweetcorn, | | |
|     creamed | tin | ......... |
|     large | tin | ......... |
|     small | tin | ......... |
| | | |
| Tapioca | lb | ......... |
| Tarragon | jar | ......... |
| Thyme | lb | ......... |
| Tongue | tin | ......... |
| Tomato, | | |
|     ketchup | bot | ......... |
|     juice | tin | ......... |
|     purée | tin | ......... |
| Treacle | lb | ......... |
| Truffles | tin | ......... |
| Turtle, | | |
|     herbs | pkt | ......... |
|     meat | lb | ......... |
|     soup | jar | ......... |
| | | |
| Vanilla pods | lb | ......... |
| Vermicelli | lb | ......... |
| Vinegar, | | |
|     brown | jar | ......... |
|     white | jar | ......... |
| | | |
| Walnuts, shelled | lb | ......... |
| Worcester sauce | bot | ......... |

## CONVENIENCE COMMODITIES

| Commodity | Unit | Price |
|---|---|---|
| | *Tins or packets as per wholesale list* | |
| **Soups, powdered** | | |
| Asparagus | ......... | ......... |
| Celery | ......... | ......... |
| Chicken | ......... | ......... |
| French onion | ......... | ......... |
| Green pea | ......... | ......... |
| Ham and pea | ......... | ......... |
| Kidney | ......... | ......... |
| Minestrone | ......... | ......... |
| Mock turtle | ......... | ......... |
| Mushroom | ......... | ......... |
| Onion white | ......... | ......... |
| Oxtail | ......... | ......... |
| Scotch broth | ......... | ......... |
| Spring vegetable | ......... | ......... |
| Tomato | ......... | ......... |
| | | |
| **Vegetables, dried** | | |
| Cabbage | ......... | ......... |
| Carrot, diced | ......... | ......... |
|     sliced | ......... | ......... |
| French beans | ......... | ......... |
| Garden peas | ......... | ......... |
| Onion slices | ......... | ......... |
| Parsnip dice | ......... | ......... |
| Potato | ......... | ......... |
| | | |
| **Pastry mixes** | | |
| Batter, all purpose | ......... | ......... |
| Caramel mix | ......... | ......... |
| Lemon pie filling | ......... | ......... |
| Puff pastry, dry | ......... | ......... |
|     frozen | ......... | ......... |
| Scone mix | ......... | ......... |
| Short pastry | ......... | ......... |
| Sponge mix | ......... | ......... |
| Yorkshire pudding | ......... | ......... |

## MEATS, FRESH

| Beef | Unit | Price Home | Price Import |
|---|---|---|---|
| Aitchbone | per lb | ......... | ......... |
| Brisket | per lb | ......... | ......... |
| Chuck steak | per lb | ......... | ......... |
| Clod | per lb | ......... | ......... |
| Fillet | per lb | ......... | ......... |
| Forequarter | per lb | ......... | ......... |
| Fore rib | per lb | ......... | ......... |
| Hindquarter | per lb | ......... | ......... |
| Middle rib | per lb | ......... | ......... |
| Oxtail | per lb | ......... | ......... |
| Plate | per lb | ......... | ......... |
| Rump | per lb | ......... | ......... |
| Shank | per lb | ......... | ......... |
| Shin | per lb | ......... | ......... |
| Silverside | per lb | ......... | ......... |
| Sirloin | per lb | ......... | ......... |
| Sticking piece | per lb | ......... | ......... |
| Suet | per lb | ......... | ......... |
| Thick flank | per lb | ......... | ......... |
| Thin flank | per lb | ......... | ......... |
| Topside | per lb | ......... | ......... |
| Wing rib | per lb | ......... | ......... |

## Lamb

| | Unit | Price Home | Price Import |
|---|---|---|---|
| Best end | per lb | ......... | ......... |
| Breast | per lb | ......... | ......... |
| Carcass | per lb | ......... | ......... |
| Leg | per lb | ......... | ......... |
| Loin | per lb | ......... | ......... |
| Middle neck | per lb | ......... | ......... |
| Saddle | per lb | ......... | ......... |

## Offal

| | Unit | Price Home | Price Import |
|---|---|---|---|
| Heart, ox | per lb | ......... | ......... |
| remainder | each | ......... | ......... |
| Kidneys, calves | per lb | ......... | ......... |
| lambs | per lb | ......... | ......... |
| ox | per lb | ......... | ......... |
| Liver, calves | per lb | ......... | ......... |
| lambs | per lb | ......... | ......... |
| ox | per lb | ......... | ......... |
| pigs | per lb | ......... | ......... |
| sheeps | per lb | ......... | ......... |

| | Unit | Price Home | Price Import |
|---|---|---|---|
| Sweetbreads, lamb | per lb | ......... | ......... |
| ox | per lb | ......... | ......... |
| veal | per lb | ......... | ......... |
| Tongue, calves | per lb | ......... | ......... |
| ox | per lb | ......... | ......... |

## Pork

| | Unit | Price Home | Price Import |
|---|---|---|---|
| Carcass, headless | per lb | ......... | ......... |
| whole | per lb | ......... | ......... |
| Hand and spring | per lb | ......... | ......... |
| Leg | per lb | ......... | ......... |
| Loin | per lb | ......... | ......... |
| Spare rib | per lb | ......... | ......... |
| Trotter | each | ......... | ......... |

## Veal

| | Unit | Price Home | Price Import |
|---|---|---|---|
| Best end | per lb | ......... | ......... |
| Breast | per lb | ......... | ......... |
| Middle neck | per lb | ......... | ......... |
| Leg | per lb | ......... | ......... |
| Loin | per lb | ......... | ......... |
| Scrag | per lb | ......... | ......... |
| Shoulder | per lb | ......... | ......... |

## MEATS, FROZEN

| | Unit | Price |
|---|---|---|
| Beef and onion steaklets | 24 × 3 oz | ......... |
| Beef cutlets | 24 × 4 oz | ......... |
| Braising chops | 24 × 4½ oz | ......... |
| Breaded veal | 24 × 3 oz | ......... |
| Club steak | 12 × 8 oz | ......... |
| | 12 × 10 oz | ......... |
| Hamburgers | 48 × 2 oz | ......... |
| Minute steaks | 12 × 3 oz | ......... |
| | 12 × 4 oz | ......... |
| Pork chops | 24 × 4½ oz | ......... |
| Rump steaks | 12 × 4 oz | ......... |
| | 12 × 5 oz | ......... |
| | 12 × 6 oz | ......... |
| | 12 × 8 oz | ......... |
| Sirloin steaks | 12 × 4 oz | ......... |
| | 12 × 5 oz | ......... |
| | 12 × 6 oz | ......... |
| | 12 × 8 oz | ......... |

| | Unit | Price | | Unit | Price |
|---|---|---|---|---|---|
| Sliced liver | 12 × 3 oz | ......... | Cod, fillet | per lb | ......... |
| Strip steaks | 12 × 4 oz | ......... |   whole | per lb | ......... |
| | 12 × 5 oz | ......... | Conger eel | per lb | ......... |
| | 12 × 6 oz | ......... | Dab | per lb | ......... |
| | 12 × 8 oz | ......... | Dover sole | per lb | ......... |
| T-bone steaks | 12 × 8 oz | ......... | Eel | per lb | ......... |
| | 12 × 10 oz | ......... | Flounder | per lb | ......... |
| Veal escalope | 20 × 4 oz | ......... | Grey mullet | per lb | ......... |
| | 20 × 6 oz | ......... | Haddock, fillet | per lb | ......... |
| | | |   whole | per lb | ......... |
| | | | Hake | per lb | ......... |

## POULTRY AND GAME, FRESH

| | Unit | Price | | Unit | Price |
|---|---|---|---|---|---|
| | | | Herring | per lb | ......... |
| Capon | per lb | ......... | John Dory | per lb | ......... |
| Duck | per lb | ......... | Lemon sole | per lb | ......... |
| Grouse | each | ......... | Mackerel | per lb | ......... |
| Hare | per lb | ......... | Perch | per lb | ......... |
| Partridge | each | ......... | Pike | per lb | ......... |
| Pheasant | each | ......... | Plaice | per lb | ......... |
| Plover | each | ......... | Red mullet | per lb | ......... |
| Poularde | per lb | ......... | Rock salmon | per lb | ......... |
| Poulet de grain | per lb | ......... | Salmon | per lb | ......... |
| Poulette reine | per lb | ......... | Salmon trout | per lb | ......... |
| Poussin, double | per lb | ......... | Skate | per lb | ......... |
| Snipe | each | ......... | Trout | per lb | ......... |
| Teal | each | ......... | Turbot | per lb | ......... |
| Turkey | per lb | ......... | Whitebait | per lb | ......... |
| Wild duck | each | ......... | Whiting | per lb | ......... |
| Woodcock | each | ......... | | | |

## POULTRY, FROZEN

## FISH, FROZEN     packs

**Fillets**

| | Unit | Price | | packs | Price |
|---|---|---|---|---|---|
| Chicken roll | 12 × 2½ lb | ......... | Cod | 2/7 lb | ......... |
| Ducklings | 4 × 4 lb | ......... | Haddock | 7/14 lb | ......... |
| Half chicken | 15 oz | ......... | Hake | 5 lb | ......... |
| Quarter chicken | 24 × 7½ oz | ......... | Lemon sole | 7 lb | ......... |
| | 24 × 6½ oz | ......... | Plaice | 7 lb | ......... |
| Roasting chicken | per lb | ......... | | | |
| | per lb | ......... | **Whole** | Unit | Price |
| | per lb | ......... | Dover sole | per lb | ......... |
| Turkey | per lb | ......... | Halibut | per lb | ......... |
| Turkey roll | 8 lb | ......... | Salmon | per lb | ......... |
| | | | Trout | 10 lb × 7/9 oz | ......... |

## FISH, FRESH

**Portions**

| | Unit | Price | | | Price |
|---|---|---|---|---|---|
| Bream | per lb | ......... | Cod | 72 × 3 oz | ......... |
| Brill | per lb | ......... | Fish fingers | 100s | ......... |
| Carp | per lb | ......... | Haddock | 24 lb × 4/5 oz | ......... |

| | | | | | |
|---|---|---|---|---|---|
| Hake | 72 × 3 oz | ......... | Egg plant | lb | ......... |
| Halibut steaks | 10 lb × 7/8 oz | ......... | Leek | lb | ......... |
| Plaice | 24 × 4 oz | . ...... | Lettuce | piece | ......... |
| | | | Mint | bunch | ......... |
| | | | Mushroom, button | lb | ......... |

## CRUSTACEA, FRESH

| | Unit | Price | | | |
|---|---|---|---|---|---|
| | | | grilling | lb | ......... |
| | | | Onion | lb | ......... |
| Crab | per lb | ......... | button | lb | ......... |
| Crawfish | per lb | ......... | spring | bunch | ......... |
| Crayfish | each | ......... | Parsley | bunch | ......... |
| Lobster | per lb | ......... | Parsnip | lb | ......... |
| Prawns | per lb/pt | ......... | Peas | lb | ......... |
| Shrimps | per lb/pt | ......... | Potato | lb | ......... |
| | | | Radish | bunch | ......... |
| **Frozen** | | | Salsify | lb | ......... |
| Crab | per lb | ......... | Seakale | lb | ......... |
| Prawns | per lb | ......... | Shallot | lb | ......... |
| Scampi | per lb | ......... | Sorrel | lb | ......... |
| | | | Spinach | lb | ......... |
| **Molluscs, fresh** | | | Swede | lb | ......... |
| Mussels | per gal | ......... | Sweetcorn | piece | ......... |
| Oysters | per 100 | ......... | Tomato | lb | ......... |
| Scallop | each | ......... | Turnip | lb | ......... |
| Snail | each | ......... | tops | lb | ......... |
| | | | Vegetable marrow | piece | ......... |
| | | | Watercress | bunch | ......... |

## VEGETABLES, FRESH

| | | | |
|---|---|---|---|
| Artichokes, globe | piece | ......... | |
| Jerusalem | lb | ......... | |
| Asparagus | bundle | ......... | |

## VEGETABLES, FROZEN

| | | | | | |
|---|---|---|---|---|---|
| Beans, broad | lb | ......... | Asparagus | 2½ lb | ......... |
| French | lb | ......... | Beans, sliced | 3/5 lb | ......... |
| runner | lb | ......... | whole | 3 lb | ......... |
| Beetroot | lb | ......... | Broccoli spears | 2/5 lb | ......... |
| Broccoli | lb | ......... | Brussel sprouts | 3 lb | ......... |
| Brussel sprouts | lb | ......... | button | 3 lb | ......... |
| Cabbage | lb | ......... | Corn on the cob | 4 lb | ......... |
| Cabbage, savoy | lb | ......... | Peas | 3/7 lb | ......... |
| red | lb | ......... | Potato chips | 6½ lb | ......... |
| Cardon | lb | ......... | croquettes | 5 lb | ......... |
| Carrot | lb | ......... | Mixed vegetables | 2 lb | ......... |
| Cauliflower | piece | ......... | Spinach, leaf | 2 lb | ......... |
| Celeriac | lb | ......... | purée | 2 lb | ......... |
| Celery | head | ......... | | | |
| Chestnuts | lb | ......... | | | |

## FRUITS, FRESH

| | | | | | |
|---|---|---|---|---|---|
| Chicory | lb | ......... | Apple, cooking | lb | ......... |
| Cucumber | piece | ......... | dessert | lb | ......... |
| Curly kale | lb | ......... | Apricot | lb | ......... |

| | Unit | Price |
|---|---|---|
| Banana | lb | ......... |
| Blackberry | lb | ......... |
| Cherry | lb | ......... |
| Coconut | piece | ......... |
| Cranberry | lb | ......... |
| Currants, black | lb | ......... |
| red | lb | ......... |
| white | lb | ......... |
| Damson | lb | ......... |
| Gooseberry, large | lb | ......... |
| dessert | lb | ......... |
| Grapefruit | piece | ...... |
| Green fig | piece | ......... |
| Greengage | lb | ......... |
| Lemon | piece | ......... |
| Lime | piece | ......... |
| Medlar | lb | ......... |
| Melons, | | |
| cantaloupe | piece | ......... |
| charentais | piece | ......... |
| honeydew | piece | ......... |
| ogen | piece | ......... |
| tiger | piece | ......... |
| water | piece | ......... |
| Nectarine | piece | ......... |
| Orange | piece | ......... |
| Peach | piece | ......... |
| Pear | lb | ......... |
| Pineapple | piece | ......... |
| Plum | lb | ......... |
| Pumpkin | piece | ......... |
| Quince | piece | ......... |
| Raspberry | lb | ......... |
| Rhubarb | lb | ......... |
| Strawberry | lb | ......... |

## FRUITS, FROZEN

| | | |
|---|---|---|
| Apples, sliced | 5 lb | ......... |
| Blackberries | 2/5 lb | ......... |
| Blackcurrants | 2/5 lb | ......... |
| Cranberries | 2/5 lb | ......... |
| Raspberries | 3 lb | ......... |
| Strawberries | 3 lb | ......... |

## DAIRY PRODUCE

| | Unit | Price |
|---|---|---|
| Milk | per pint | ......... |
| Cream, double | per pint | ......... |
| single | per pint | ......... |
| Ice Cream | | |
| chocolate | per gal | ......... |
| coffee | per gal | ......... |
| raspberry | per gal | ......... |
| strawberry | per gal | ......... |
| vanilla | per gal | ......... |

## CANNED GOODS

### Sizes

| Code | Fl. oz | G | Principal commodities |
|---|---|---|---|
| — | 4 | 113·3 | Cream |
| — | 4½ | 127 | Strained fruits, fish, vegetables |
| — | 5 | 141 | Baked beans, peas |
| — | 6 | 170 | Evaporated milk, milk puddings, beer, soft drinks |
| — | 8 | 226 | Meat puddings, meat, baked beans, spaghetti, vegetables, fruit, fish roe, meat and fruit pies (uncooked) |
| A.1 | 10 | 283 | Baked beans, soups, vegetables, meat, fish |
| | 11 | 311 | Milk products (full cream, condensed, sweet and unsweetened) |
| E.1 | 14 | 396 | Fruits, meats, vegetables, fish |
| | 14½ | 411 | Evaporated milk (tall tins) |
| Tall | 15/15½ | 439 | Evaporated milk, milk puddings, animal foods |
| Tall | 1 lb | 453 | Beer, soft drinks, evaporated milk |
| Flat | 1 lb | 453 | Meat and fruit pies, tongues, meats, sweet puddings |
| A.2 | 1¼ lb | 566 | Fruit, vegetables |
| A.2½ | 1¾ lb | 793 | Fruit, vegetables |
| | | **Kg** | |
| | 6 lb | 2·7 | Fruit, vegetables, meats (catering packs) |
| A.10 | 6¾ lb | 3 | Fruit, vegetables, meats (catering packs |